PEOPLE AND POLITICS IN FRANCE,
1848–1870

This book is about politicisation and political choice in the aftermath of the February Revolution of 1848, and the emergence of democracy in France.

The introduction of male suffrage both encouraged expectations of social transformation and aroused intense fear. In these circumstances the election of a 'saviour' as President of the Republic, in the person of Louis-Napoleon Bonaparte, and his subsequent *coup d'état* were the essential features of a counter-revolutionary process which involved the creation of a system of directed democracy as the basis of regime legitimacy and as a prelude to greater liberalisation once social order had been restored. The State positively encouraged the act of voting.

But what did it mean? How did people perceive politics? Although denied the vote, what roles did women play? How were political ideas diffused and how were they received? What forms of political organisation can be identified? How did communities and groups participate in political activity? These and many other questions concern the relationships between local issues and personalities, and the national political culture, all of which increasingly impinged on communities as a result of substantial social and political change.

ROGER PRICE is Professor of History, University of Wales, Aberystwyth. His many publications include *A Concise History of France* (1993) and *The French Second Empire: An Anatomy of Political Power* (2001), both published by Cambridge University Press.

NEW STUDIES IN EUROPEAN HISTORY

Edited by
PETER BALDWIN, University of California, Los Angeles
CHRISTOPHER CLARK, University of Cambridge
JAMES B. COLLINS, Georgetown University
MÍA RODRÍGUEZ–SALGADO, London School of Economics and
Political Science
LYNDAL ROPER, University of Oxford

The aim of this series in early modern and modern European history is to publish outstanding works of research, addressed to important themes across a wide geographical range, from southern and central Europe, to Scandinavia and Russia, and from the time of the Renaissance to the Second World War. As it develops the series will comprise focused works of wide contextual range and intellectual ambition.

For a full list of titles published in the series, please see the end of the book.

PEOPLE AND POLITICS
IN FRANCE,
1848–1870

ROGER PRICE

CAMBRIDGE
UNIVERSITY PRESS

CAMBRIDGE UNIVERSITY PRESS
Cambridge, New York, Melbourne, Madrid, Cape Town, Singapore, São Paulo, Delhi

Cambridge University Press
The Edinburgh Building, Cambridge CB2 8RU, UK

Published in the United States of America by Cambridge University Press, New York

www.cambridge.org
Information on this title: www.cambridge.org/9780521837064

© Roger Price 2004

First published 2004
Reprinted 2006
This digitally printed version 2008

A catalogue record for this publication is available from the British Library

Library of Congress Cataloguing in Publication data
Price, Roger, 1944 Jan. 7–
People and politics in France, 1848–1870 / Roger Price.
p.   cm. – (New studies in European history)
Includes bibliographical references and index.
ISBN 0 521 83706 5
1. France – History – Second Republic, 1848–1852.   2. France – History – Second Empire,
1852–1870.   3. France – Politics and government – 1848–1870.   I. Title.   II. Series.
DC272.5.P75   2004   2003065206

ISBN 978-0-521-83706-4 hardback
ISBN 978-0-521-10013-7 paperback

For Heather

Contents

Acknowledgements

I started work on this book a long time ago but in the intervening period failed to avoid the temptation to head off along a number of tangents. Even a planned chapter on the Bonapartist state turned into a separate book. Although the British research assessment system discourages the investment of time in such long-term research projects, nevertheless it has to be worth resisting the pressure to publish prematurely. I owe a great deal, therefore, to the support and patience of family, friends, and colleagues. Certainly, little could have been achieved without the assistance of the archivists and librarians of the Archives nationales; Service historique de l'Armée de Terre; Bibliothèque nationale; Centre de Documentation of the Société nationale des chemins de fer français; University of East Anglia; University of Wales, Aberystwyth; University of Wales, Bangor; and the National Library of Wales. Research leave and funding were generously provided both in Norwich and more recently at Aberystwyth and further indispensable financial assistance obtained from the British Academy, Leverhulme Trust, and Wolfson Foundation. The timely provision of additional leave by the Arts and Humanities Research Board greatly assisted the task of finally completing the book.

I am extremely grateful to William Doyle, Richard Evans, Douglas Johnson, Gwynne Lewis, and the greatly missed Vincent Wright for supporting various grant applications, and to fellow members of the history research seminars at the University of East Anglia and at Aber, as well as to generations of students, for creating intellectually stimulating environments. I owe a particular debt to William Davies of Cambridge University Press for the encouragement and support he has provided for this and other projects, to Jean Field who so efficiently copy-edited the text, to Colin Heywood, Christopher Johnson, and Heather Price for offering valuable and constructive criticism of earlier drafts of the manuscript, and to the Frugère family who provided a home-from-home at Bois Colombes on numerous occasions.

Above all I have to thank Richard and Luisa, Siân, Andy and Molly, Emily, Hannah, and my dearest Heather for all their encouragement and love.

Abbreviations

AHG	Archives historiques du Ministère de la Guerre
AN	Archives nationales
APP	Archives de la Préfecture de Police
BN	Bibliothèque nationale
DM	Division militaire
(G)OC	(General) Officer Commanding
jp	juge de paix
MI	Minister of the Interior
MJ	Minister of Justice
PG	procureur général
PI	procureur impérial
PR	Procureur de la république

Introduction

From 1845 until the end of 1851 France experienced a prolonged and intense crisis. It began with poor harvests in 1845 and 1846 which brought on a collapse in consumer and investor confidence. Economic difficulties were intensified by an international financial crisis and industrial over-production. Misery, insecurity, and widespread disorder brought into question the legitimacy of the July Monarchy, created by revolution in 1830. In February 1848 the Government was overwhelmed suddenly by the development of a revolutionary situation in its capital city. Ineffective crisis management resulted in the establishment of a republican Provisional Government, which in the absence of alternative centres of resistance was able to impose its authority on the country. Popular sovereignty was recognised through the introduction of 'universal' male suffrage, enlarging the electorate from the 250,000 previously enfranchised by a tax qualification to over 9 million. This created an immense sense of expectancy amongst the supporters of political and social change and equally intense social fear amongst conservatives.

In the months that followed, those politicians who had unexpectedly gained power struggled to impose their authority on a country beset by a renewed crisis of confidence and mass unemployment. Disagreeing on objectives themselves, they sought to restore order amongst competing socio-economic interest groups, communities, and political groups determined to affirm the primacy of their particular interests. The population rapidly underwent an 'apprenticeship in politics' as newspapers, political clubs, and mass meetings flourished in the new era of 'liberty'. The first elections in April returned a Constituent Assembly dominated by socially conservative republicans. Instead of the social reform expected by the Parisian *classes populaires* most of the newly elected deputies demanded financial retrenchment and social order. The decision in June to close the National Workshops which had provided work relief to the unemployed, and which many had taken to be the first step in the creation of a new society founded on co-operative association and freedom from capitalist exploitation, pro-voked a renewal of conflict in the capital – the June insurrection, a struggle, on the one hand for 'social justice' and on the other for 'social order'. The rising was crushed brutally by the well-prepared military forces mobilised by the republican government.

In December 1848 the second manifestation of 'universal suffrage' resulted in the election, with a massive majority, of a Prince-President. Louis-Napoleon Bonaparte, nephew of the great Emperor, secured substan-tial support from every social group, due to the potency of a Napoleonic myth which promised 'all things to all men'. Subsequently the Bonapartist pretender used his executive authority to challenge the power of the Legisla-tive Assembly elected in May 1849 and gradually to secure the appointment of men dependent on himself to key positions in government, the bureau-cracy, and the army. At the same time, and in spite of the intensification of police and judicial repression, left-wing agitation continued through the *démocrate-socialiste* movement. On the basis of 'socialist' electoral successes and exaggerated reports of secret society organisation, the government and the conservative press were able to arouse an often hysterical fear of social revolution within the social elites, the Catholic clergy, and the much wider groups with negative memories of revolution and its aftermath in 1789 and 1848. In order, he claimed, to restore political stability and spread reassur-ance, Bonaparte launched a campaign for constitutional revision, which would have allowed him to seek election to the presidency for a second term. When this was blocked by the *démocrate-socialiste* minority in the Assembly he launched a carefully prepared *coup d'état* on 2 December 1851. Although directed against both his republican and monarchist opponents, the fact that serious resistance came only from the left ensured that repub-licans bore the brunt of police and military repression. The short-lived risings in Paris and rural areas of south-east and central France were used to justify both the Prince-President's actions and a reign of terror involving over 26,000 arrests, as part of a 'final' settling of accounts with the left. The *coup* was legitimised by a popular plebiscite. A year later another well-prepared and brilliantly successful plebiscite sanctioned the restoration of the hereditary empire.

The Bonapartist regime would be characterised by repression – aimed especially at an irreconcilable republican opposition, by a system of directed democracy, and by social engineering, involving both the construction of a clerical educational system and efforts to enhance national prosperity through economic modernisation. The regime's claim to legitimacy was based on the popular vote and it could hardly afford to risk electoral defeat.

Every election turned into a plebiscite on its future. Unlike its predecessors, however, and in contrast with twentieth-century regimes similarly based on systems of controlled democracy, this would be a regime which sought to make the hazardous transition from its authoritarian origins towards liberal democracy. The re-establishment of social order and the prosperity for which it claimed credit and actively stimulated by means of massive infrastructure investment, urban renewal, and trade treaties, together with political liberalisation, provided the means by which it aspired to widen, deepen, and ensure the permanence of mass support. Liberalisation was bound to be difficult. It made it possible for those with grievances and with visions of alternative political and social systems to express their demands with increasing facility. Previous allies were turned into critics by a foreign policy which appeared to challenge the interests of the Papacy and Universal Church, and by a commitment to 'free-trade' which threatened the security and prosperity of important vested interests. It would take the renewal of 'social fear' to secure the re-establishment of an alliance committed to preserving social order and to supporting a 'liberal' empire which would be legitimised by a massive vote of approval in the plebiscite of May 1870.

Rather than taking an institutional or party political approach to political history, this book will consider how people experienced a quarter of a century of political change. In these complex circumstances, what motivated individual behaviour? How did people perceive politics? To what extent was protest institutionalised? Although denied the vote, what role did women play? Why were people sympathetic to one political option rather than another? What was the significance of tradition and 'myth', of the individual and collective 'memory', of the relationship between past and present? To what extent did political loyalties change? What were the means by which political ideas were spread and how were they received? What forms of political organisation, both formal and informal, can be identified? To what extent did the members of various communities and social groups participate in political activity? To what extent did voting represent the free expression of opinion or social and administrative pressure? What did participants hope to gain from voting or from the greater degree of engagement implied by militancy? Or, conversely, what were the reasons for apathy and indifference? These are questions about the relationships between local issues and personalities and the national political culture which increasingly impinged on communities as a result of substantial political and administrative and also socio-economic change. They are questions about the possession and use of power, and the means by which

Table 1. *Electoral participation*

Date of election	Turnout (% of registered voters)
April 1848	84.0
10 December 1848	75.1
29 February 1852	63.3
21 June 1857	64.5
31 May 1863	72.9
23 May 1869	78.1

Source: A. Lancelot, *L'Abstentionnisme électoral en France* (Paris 1968), p. 15; M. Crook, 'Electoral participation in France, 1789–1851' in M. Cornick and C. Crossley (eds.), *Problems in French History* (London 2000), pp. 55–6.

those with limited political power adapted to their situation and sought to gain access to influence.

The institutional structure of the political system itself helped determine the repertoire of possible action. The repression, which had commenced in 1848 during the conservative Republic, promoted a widespread de-mobilisation. Paradoxically, however, the retention of manhood suffrage allowed the political apprenticeship of the masses to continue. Moreover, the context would change dramatically again in the 1860s when, in spite of continued constraints, it became clear that political activity was less hazardous. It was possible to start re-constructing the political structures destroyed after 1848.

High participation rates, at least in general elections, throughout both the Second Republic and the Empire (see table 1) suggest that the electorate took politics seriously and, as Maurice Agulhon has pointed out, 'C'est en votant qu'on apprend à voter, c'est en campagnes (électorales) qu'on apprend *la politique*' although, he added, this was only a stage in a process of politicisation.[1]

Thus, a political imperative developed, characterised by a growing sense of citizenship, an acceptance of the duty to vote, and an appreciation of the potential benefits which might ensue. Engagement in politics, whether to assert claims or make judgements and to confirm or challenge authority, served to enhance personal status. Involvement in contention with fellow citizens and agents of the state established and gradually extended the repertoire of political action. Habitual, even if intermittent, participation in political processes built up confidence and commitment, contributed to

[1] M. Agulhon, 'Présentation' to M. Agulhon, *et al.*, *La politisation des campagnes au 19e siècle* (Rome 2000), pp. 5, 7.

a democratic socialisation, altered perceptions of the state, and stimulated the development of a mass political culture, characterised by its 'richness' and 'complexity' and by contributions from a range of political traditions – Bonapartist, Legitimist, Catholic, and Liberal, as well as Republican.[2]

Recently, historians have been undergoing a crisis of causality, as the state-centred and structural Marxist approaches dominant until the 1980s have been discredited. Analysis has adopted a 'cultural turn', based on the assumption that 'cultural systems define the goals of action, the expectations about other actors, and even what it means to be an 'actor' (i.e. whether the relevant actors in a system are individuals, groups, families, and so on) . . . '.[3] The obvious objection is expressed by Charles Tilly – 'culture and identity, . . . language and consciousness, as changing phenomena [themselves need] to be explained' rather than offering the 'ultimate explanation of all other social phenomena'.[4]

The essential problem, then, is where to start? Prioritising particular elements within an explanatory framework immediately suggests that they have greater weight. As a result, in the past, when explaining political behaviour, social historians have accorded too much importance to the explanatory significance of socio-economic structures. More recently, cultural historians have over-reacted by according some sort of autonomous power to ideas. Any attempt to reconcile these two approaches, furthermore, carries with it the danger of circularity, evident in the aspiration that, whilst accepting the importance of 'discourse and rhetoric in moulding class identity' the historian should not be led to ignore 'material interests'.[5] Nevertheless, whilst carefully considering the intellectual debates of the moment, the historian certainly should not be swayed too easily by fashion. Nothing will be gained from replacing a socio-economic reductionism with an intellectual one. It might also be hoped that historians will resist the populist temptation of returning to the 'old' political history with its exclusive focus on institutions, 'events', and 'great' men.

The problem remains that of identifying viable analytical categories and developing forms of discourse which do justice to the complexity of life and allow meaningful explanation. Considering the articulation of political

[2] S. Hazareesingh, *From Subject to Citizen. The Second Empire and the Emergence of Modern French Democracy* (Princeton, N.J. 1998), p. 11.
[3] G. Steinmetz, 'Introduction: culture and the state' to G. Steinmetz (ed.), *State/Culture. State Formation after the Cultural Turn* (London 1999), p. 27.
[4] 'Epilogue: now where?', in Steinmetz, *State/Culture*, p. 411.
[5] R. Magraw review of Aminzade in *Social History* 1995, p. 383.

ideas is just the beginning. More important still is the analysis of their diffusion and reception. Thus establishing the *context* for the development of political behaviour is of crucial importance. Certainly, the study of politics as a self-contained activity, ignoring its social, cultural, and historical context, has a very limited explanatory value. Explanation depends on relating political interests to other aspects of life, in a manner which avoids reductionism and which fully appreciates the complexity of human existence, the potential for individual self-contradiction, and the tensions which exist within any group of human beings. It needs to be borne in mind that 'the mental images of society that people carry around in their heads need have little connection to their day-to-day interactions'.[6] Although the primary focus of this book will be on politics, if this is viewed as a form of social activity its manifestations will need to be set within social and institutional contexts characterised by rapid change and shifting expectations, by both expanding opportunities and heightened insecurity and a widespread search for alternative life strategies.

The question of relationships between local communities and the central state as well as those between one social group and another will also need to be addressed. Inevitably political roles developed in response to the constraints and possibilities of time and place. They also emerged from an existing political culture which was both traditional in that it was the product of history and social myth, and ever changing, in response to shifting socio-economic and political structures and perceptions. Individual predispositions also have to be taken into account and an effort made to keep in mind the simple fact that for most of the population, and for most of the time, politics is only one and generally not the most important determinant of behaviour. Social identities are formed by a 'multiplicity of systems of representation', in private as well as public contexts.[7]

This then will be a book about 'people' and 'politics' within varied and changing socio-economic, cultural, and political contexts. Political roles were partly the product of socialisation processes within discrete families and communities identified by their particular cultures – the customs, language, and belief systems which gave their inhabitants a sense of identity – and also by their location within the broader structures of the nation. A sense of place is surely vital given that 'individuals are embedded within a given context that structures their social interactions, constrains information

[6] D. Knoke, *Political Networks. The Structural Perspective* (London 1990), p. 16.
[7] A. Corbin, 'Du Limousin aux cultures sensibles' in J.-P. Rioux and F. Sirinelli (eds.), *Pour une histoire culturelle* (Paris 1998), p. 107.

exchanges and determines their political responses'.[8] Yet extrapolations based on micro-studies are best avoided. The structure and dynamics of social systems differ between places and over time. A sense of the shifting balance between continuity and change is essential. In the light of this, one question historians constantly need to ask themselves is what is an acceptable level of generalisation?

The essential methodological problem involves identification of the basis for political choice. To what extent do autonomous individuals take decisions concerning politics, and to what extent are these subject to collective influences? Methodological individualism, based on the assumption of rational-critical decision-making by self-conscious individuals, offers little help in explaining social interaction, or, indeed, individual behaviour within a social context. Theories of 'rational choice', focusing on the 'rational subject', offer little guidance to the real world. Furthermore, the context for individual decision-making is determined, largely, although not exclusively, by socialisation. Understanding political behaviour requires identification of groups of people whose action/inaction and patterns of behaviour can be subjected to analysis and explanation.

People are 'formed' by their association with others and through processes of social interaction, which produce shared and competing understandings and representations defined, self-evidently, through discourse. Identity takes shape and is internalised as part of the experience of a particular *espace vécu*, within a family and community and a daily, lived, social hierarchy.[9] Cutting across this vertical articulation there were undoubtedly horizontal divisions based, for example, on membership of voluntary associations and neighbourhood social networks. That the boundaries between groups were often fluid underlines the crucial importance of cultural intermediaries, frequently coming from outside the particular group they sought to influence. Thus association with members of other social groups, as well as the tensions between groups, contributed to the definition of identity. So too did the language of political debate and the experience of contacts with government officials and those representing other social institutions, and most notably religious associations. Both habitual social intercourse and interventionist institutions acted to encourage and sometimes restrain commitment to political activity.

It follows that, in everyday life, each individual habitually performed a variety of roles establishing 'multiple dimensions of identity' and complex

---

[8] Knoke, *Political Networks*, p. 46
[9] See e.g. W. Kashuba, 'Culture populaire et culture ouvrière, catégories symboliques' in A. Lüdtke (ed.), *Histoire du quotidien* (Paris 1994), p. 177.

patterns of motivation,[10] with individuals tending to accord precedence sometimes to one role, sometimes to another. Their identities were defined by upbringing within the family, within peer groups defined by age and gender, by association with neighbourhood, socio-professional, confessional, leisure, and 'party' political groups within the community, and also by their place within a wider social system made up of identifiable and distinctive social networks, including those associated with that problematic entity 'class'.

Whilst appreciating the complex nature of human society and of individual identity, just like the contemporary observer, the historian is forced to categorise in order to identify the historical actors and achieve some understanding of how they perceived the world in which they lived. This book is envisaged as a contribution to the 'new' political history by a social historian interested in employing the analysis of political culture(s) to bridge the gap between political and social history by means of the consideration of 'mentalities and collective attitudes', but without ignoring the broader context of work and community within which attitudes are formulated.[11] Although imposed from the present onto the past, the analytical framework employed would probably have been intelligible to people in the past. It should not simply be an abstract, an artificial construction, but should relate closely to the language and content of the sources. The historian must make every effort to avoid both anachronism and over-simplification. The dangers of 'reification' and of 'reductionism' need to be borne in mind. The process of establishing categories can easily result in over-simplification, in the prioritisation of particular social relationships, and in the tendency to concentrate either on inequality and conflict or else solidarity and alliance as the characteristic social relationships.

Any form of social classification does less than justice to the complexities of human existence. Clearly, every individual has a multifaceted identity – as member of a family, gender, and age group, of a community, professional or confessional association and, potentially at least, of a 'class'. For this reason alone, taken in isolation, 'class' fails to offer an explanation of political choice. It will be argued, however, that the category which does the least damage to our understanding of human relationships in France, in the period with which we are concerned, is *class*. Would the employment of such alternatives as 'community, culture, and tradition' result in

---

[10] R. Gould, *Insurgent Identities. Class, Community, and Protest in Paris from 1848 to the Commune* (London 1995), p. 26.
[11] See also A. Prost, 'What happened to French social history?', *Historical Journal* 1992, p. 677.

a more revealing analysis?[12] Would their use be any less likely to provoke accusations of 'reductionism'? The concept of class has meaning, even if disputed, for historians, and would have been comprehensible to many of the historical actors. Contemporaries thought in terms of and were in part motivated by concepts of class. Both political sloganising and the discourse of learned journals and pamphlets or mass circulation newspapers revealed a commitment to the language of class as a means of thinking about society. Historical concepts of class, those possessed by the historical actors, were closely related to everyday social interaction and representation and frequently emerged from social or political conflict. The social enquiries so common in the 1840s further contributed to making 'classes' more 'visible'.[13]

However, if it is accepted that *class* retains considerable value as an explanatory concept, this can be the case only if it is used flexibly. It has to be recognised that class membership is only one of the factors influencing behaviour and that individuals have diverse, often shifting, and frequently conflicting objectives and loyalties. Class then becomes 'a process and a performance' rather than a pre-determined category.[14] A class-based sense of identity is created 'only through the articulation of experience by means of discourse'.[15] 'Class' is thus a social construct and culture, in the widest sense, and including politics, creates 'webs of significance', integrating visions of the past and the future, and mediating between the individual and his/her experience.[16]

In the light of what has been said above, the chapters which follow will consider the political experience of the Second Empire in relation to 'class', on the grounds that this is likely to be the least 'deforming' approach to take and providing that it is borne in mind constantly that the initial identification of social 'groups' on the basis of profession and income only has limited explanatory value, as part of a multi-causal model of social change. It might be helpful to quote E. P. Thompson's definition of 'class' as

---

[12] A. Hemingway, 'Marxism and art history after the fall of communism' in A. Hemingway and W. Vaughan (eds.), *Art in Bourgeois Society 1790–1850* (Cambridge 1998), p. 12.

[13] See e.g. A. Desrosières, 'Comment faire des choses qui tiennent. Histoire sociale et statistiques' in C. Charle (ed.), *Histoire sociale, Histoire globale?* (Paris 1993), p. 34.

[14] C. Harrison, *The Bourgeois Citizen in 19th Century France. Gender, Sociability and the Uses of Emulation* (Oxford 1999), p. 8.

[15] M. Cabrera, 'Linguistic approach or return to subjectivism? In search of an alternative to social history', *Social History* 1999, p. 86.

[16] See G. Stedman-Jones, *Languages of Class* (London 1983), pp. 7–8; E. Accampo, 'Class and gender' in M. Crook (ed.), *Revolutionary France* (Oxford 2002), p. 95.

a social and cultural formation (often finding institutional expression) which cannot be defined abstractly, or in isolation, but only in terms of relationships with other classes; and ultimately, the definition can only be made in the medium of *time* – i.e. action and reaction, change and conflict. When we speak of *a* class we are thus thinking of a very loosely-defined body of people who share the same congeries of interests, social experiences, traditions, and value-systems, and who have at least a *disposition* to *behave* as a class, to define themselves in their actions and in their consciousness in relation to other groups of people in class ways.[17]

This is at least an approach which avoids the reductionism of some forms of Marxist class analysis whilst preserving something of value. One might go further and affirm that class membership is only one of a number of factors influencing behaviour and not always the most significant. Rather than employing *class* as a privileged explanatory factor it is reduced to a convenient but also meaningful means of entry into an historical society.

Membership of a particular social class can be related to such factors as wealth, income, education, access to information, lifestyle, religion, mutual recognition, and integration into particular social networks, and to such polarities as security/insecurity and power/dependence – a complex of material and non-material factors, all contributing to the production of 'systems of representation' and to the formation of social consciousness.[18] As will become evident rapidly, class identity was far from uniform. Social status, especially for non-elites, was largely defined in relation to local socio-economic structures and traditions, and face-to-face relationships. Internal differences reflected individual personality, community structures, and the particular interests of discrete sub-groups, as well as differing regional, generational, and gender experiences. Although gendered behaviour tended to be overwhelmingly class specific, the role played by women in the formation of social identity and thus, indirectly, in the development of political discourse should not be underestimated.

The possession of wealth and ability to control access to scarce resources largely determined the share of social and, indirectly, of political power an individual might expect. The question of who possesses power and how it might be exercised is thus central to our concerns. It requires consideration of the unequal distribution of resources and its effects on relationships between the dominant (the State and social elites) and the dominated (middle classes, peasants, and workers). Additional requirements

---

[17] 'The peculiarities of the English', *Social Register* 1965, p. 357.

[18] See e.g. A. Prost, 'Sociale et culturelle indissociablement' in Rioux and Sirinelli, *Pour une histoire culturelle*, p. 141; M. Savage, 'Space, networks and class formation' in N. Kirk (ed.), *Social Class and Marxism* (London 1996), p. 68.

include identification of the economic, social, institutional, and ideological bases of dominance, and consideration of contemporary definitions of rights, duties, obligations, and expectations, as well as the coercive and non-coercive means of securing compliance to an established moral and social order. Obviously the State has a key role in defining the limits of acceptable behaviour through its judicial and policing systems. In addition, those who control state agencies are able to exercise considerable influence, and to enjoy a degree of autonomy. Thus we need 'to look at power structures in society and how they are constructed, and investigate both the origins and forms of class domination as well as the reaction of the dominated'.[19]

Domination it must be remembered does not mean 'total control' but the 'ability to set the terms under which other groups and classes must operate'.[20] Those with power were able to define the political 'opportunity structure',[21] that is, the degree to which, at any one time, dissent might be tolerated, the extent to which political organisation building was possible, as well as the intensity of the more informal politicisation of day-to-day social interaction. Even in its bureaucratic-authoritarian phase the Second Empire combined a disjunctive democracy with recognition of the rule of law. Although grossly biased towards the interests of the wealthy the legal system offered at least some protection to the entire population, including social and political nonconformists. Conversely, a key feature of the subsequent transition towards liberal democracy involved an effort by the authorities to control the parameters of the new regime.

In addition to defining State–Society interaction, the chapters which follow will attempt to identify distinctive social groups and dissect them, in an effort to understand their internal dynamics and divisions, by considering the language, images, day-to-day intercourse and symbolic action, the social perceptions, fears, and aspirations which contributed to the creation of a sense of identity. The analytical difficulties are evident from the first two chapters, dealing with a *social elite* composed of nobles and non-nobles (*haut bourgeois*), landowners, financiers, and industrialists with often sharply differing family traditions and political allegiances but a shared interest in protecting private property – the primary source of social status and influence – as well as in securing privileged links with the State. It was from this *relatively* cohesive group that the vast majority of ministers, senior civil servants, judges, and military commanders were drawn. Shared social origins and membership of the same or contiguous social networks furthermore

---

[19] S. Berger, 'The rise and fall of 'critical' historiography', *European Review of History* 1996, p. 227.
[20] G. W. Domhoff, *Who Rules America Now?* (Englewood Cliffs, N.J. 1983), p. 2.
[21] Knoke, *Political Networks*, p. 77.

ensured that a small minority of citizens enjoyed superior access to senior state officials, and that they were able to develop key roles as power brokers between the State and local communities. These are all considerations which relate to such fundamental questions as: who rules and how? How are elites reproduced?[22]

The potentially threatening effects of cultural and political fragmentation on this social elite were offset by habitual patterns of socialisation and shared understandings of social relationships. The sense of common interest was reinforced by prevalent perceptions of external threats and a determination to control the presentation of information to subordinate groups through the schools, churches, and the media. In the last resort the State served to guarantee the existing social order by recourse to repression. The challenge to the established social and political order in 1848, and again in the late 1860s, was a powerful reminder of the need, in moments of crisis, to subordinate internal differences and to uphold the executive power which protected social order. It must also be borne in mind, however, that the rise of opposition to the authoritarian regime was also, to a substantial degree, elite led. Furthermore, and due to the existence of manhood suffrage, a challenge to the regime from part of the social elite required efforts to mobilise mass support.

The chapters dealing with the social elites will be followed by one on the middle classes. Both in the past and present the use of the terms *bourgeoisie* or middle classes has been problematic. There was a considerable gulf between, say, the successful businessman (merchant, factory owner, etc.) or professional, located just outside the social elite, and the small shop or workshop proprietor. Social status also varied between urban and rural localities with very different socio-professional structures, levels of wealth, cultures, and lifestyles. These were, on the one hand, people who largely shared with the social elite a commitment to social order and the safeguarding of the private property which appeared to hold out the prospect of upward social mobility. On the other hand, they might also be alienated from the established order by unequal access to power and the belief that their vital interests were being neglected. In a conflictual situation, members of these intermediate classes, and especially those belonging to the liberal professions, were able to mobilise considerable organisational and financial resources and to influence the diffusion of information, although on the

---

[22] See also C. Charle, 'Légitimités en péril. Eléments pour une histoire comparée des élites et de l'Etat en France et en Europe occidentale (19e–20e siècles)', *Actes de recherche en sciences sociales*, 1997, pp. 39–40.

basis of local or regional rather than national social networks. Individuals would have to choose between exercising conservative or democratic patronage towards less politically active members of the middle classes, as well as the peasants and workers whose political response had been rendered so crucially important by the democratisation of 1848.

The fourth and fifth chapters will consider peasants and politics. The American historian Gordon Wright warned that 'rural France is almost infinitely diverse, and almost any generalisation about the peasantry becomes partially false as soon as it is formulated'.[23] Understanding peasants requires consideration of regional social structures based on landownership, employment, community, and kinship, as well as the geography of links with external social networks. The obvious consequence of the introduction of manhood suffrage was to increase the importance of the peasants' political role as well as to establish conditions more favourable to the creation of a sense of identity.[24] Economic and demographic change during the Second Empire would do much to reinforce these processes. Nevertheless, limited incomes, leisure, and education ensured that peasant participation in politics would be reserved largely to subordinate roles and that a long-term commitment was difficult to sustain.

The same was true of the working classes. French writers began to refer to a working class around 1830/2 in relation to the social conflict which followed the 1830 Revolution. Post-modernist historians have described the notion as a fictional construct produced by discourses written about workers by *bourgeois* intellectuals. The work of economic historians in charting the slow, uneven, and fragmentary nature of industrialisation and the multiplicity of experience and identity this produced has contributed to this scepticism. Alternatively, a sense of identity particular to a 'working class' might be seen as emerging from conflict with employers and the state, from a shared insecurity, and as being reinforced substantially by the hopes of social reform, raised and then dashed during the Second Republic and the Second Empire.

Doubtless there were varying degrees of class-consciousness and, as in the case of every other social group, a multiplicity of internal divisions can be identified, associated with such factors as differing levels of training, skill, and thereby ambition, negotiating strength in the labour market, earning capacity, lifestyle, and culture. In these respects, how significant

---

[23] *Rural Revolution in France. The Peasantry in the 20th Century* (London 1964), p. v.
[24] See also J.-L. Mayaud, 'Ruralité et politique dans la France du 19e siècle', *Histoire et sociétés rurales* (1999), p. 135.

was competition and conflict between workers? Did workers identify primarily with workplace, trade, neighbourhood, or class? How important was politics amongst all their other concerns? Clearly, although it might be possible to identify a social group in terms of shared lifestyle this has only a limited value in relation to the explanation of political behaviour. Certainly it seems evident that 'the actions of the poor can be fully understood only in the context of the larger structures that limit their choices and constrain their options'.[25]

In general, 'No social group has ever been autonomous enough to possess a culture of its own.'[26] The hierarchical and class-based representations of society favoured by historians need to be adapted to take account of all manner of interaction between groups, constructed on the basis of patron–client relationships, those of landlord and tenant, employer and employee, on paternalism as well as exploitation, and on the sense of community and of nationality represented by a rich assortment of festivals and celebrations. Members of the same social group might both share and dispute values. Less obvious, perhaps, was the manner in which one social group might serve as a reference group to another, influencing its manners, lifestyle and aspirations. Through its legal, police, and educational systems the State also defined behavioural norms, encouraged conformity, and punished deviation, with its agents called upon on occasion to engage in the crucially important task of crisis management. The Roman Catholic Church was its only real competitor. It is worth stressing the importance of religion in many an individual's sense of identity and the significance of the Church as an institution enjoying cross-class support – as well as generating widespread cross-class anti-clericalism.

If socio-economic and institutional structures imposed a sort of regulatory framework on political behaviour, so too did memories of the past, constructed both from direct personal and familial experience and the traditions transmitted between generations. These, constantly re-interpreted, provided a prism through which contemporary events might be viewed. 'Thought about the past is an important element in social creativity because it is part of the information which people use in making decisions which affect the future' – but 'what past?' 'Memory' can create a shared sense of community but is always selective.[27] In political terms language and

[25] T. Sugrue, *The Origins of the Urban Crisis. Race and Inequality in Postwar Detroit* (Princeton, N.J. 1996), p. 14.

[26] G. Stedman-Jones quoted by K. Boyd and R. McWilliam, 'Historical perspectives on class and culture', *Social History* 1995, p. 94.

[27] J. Davis, 'History and the people without Europe' in K. Hastrup, *Other Histories* (London 1995), pp. 25–6.

symbols might have a resonance and a mobilising impact, serving to reinforce the identity of particular social and political groupings, partly by means of identifying the other side in a situation with potential for conflict. Tradition and ideology, past and present, interacted and, in spite of the growing influence of the printed word, oral traditions served as the principle forms of cultural acquisition and communication for most of the population.

In the context of mid-nineteenth-century France the impact of the 1789 Revolution on processes of political acculturation is clear. The first revolution provided a *mythe fondateur*[28] justifying a range of political options and stimulating fierce debates. The impact of events between 1789 and 1815, of internal upheaval and incessant war, had been both inspirational and traumatising. Conflicting images, complex 'memories', would to a large degree determine subsequent political allegiances. These would vary between regions as well as the individuals, families, neighbourhoods, and communities within them, as a result of different experiences and explanations of the past. The significance of 'generation', of a shared set of formative experiences, providing a link between the individual and group – a shared vision, evident in vocabulary, symbols and songs – should also be noted.

The traditions emerging from this complex, and violent, period provided a reservoir of ideas, ranging from those favourable to absolute monarchy, to constitutional monarchy, conservative republicanism, radical Jacobinism, *sans-culotte* egalitarianism, and Bonapartism. Evocation of the past thus represented a choice amongst political images. Republicans aspired to the eventual 'completion' of the Revolution through realisation of the principles enshrined in the Declaration of the Rights of Man and the Citizen, reinterpreted by some, by the 1840s, to include democracy, education, and even the right to work. In contrast, conservatives engaged in a search for stability, made all the more desperate by the powerful re-emergence of the revolutionary menace in 1848. They were determined to defend private property, social hierarchy, religion, and monarchy as the bases of a Christian civilisation threatened by 'barbarism'.

Each generation and each social group thus sought appropriate models for understanding their present and in so doing reconstructed their past. Tradition and innovation effectively coalesced. The final, revolutionary overthrow of the Bourbons in 1830 was followed by another period

---

[28] C. Mazauric, 'France révolutionnaire, France révolutionnée, France en révolution: pour une clarification des rythmes et des concepts', *Annales historiques de la Révolution française* 1988, p. 137.

of agitation in favour of democracy and social reform, before social fear amongst the property-owning classes encouraged a return to governmental repression. The limited widening of the franchise for national elections had been accompanied, however, by the creation of far more substantial, if still restricted, electorates for municipal elections and the selection of National Guard officers. It seems evident that non-inclusion was already coming to be seen as humiliating. Local democracy, at least, was on the move, and well before 1848.[29]

The advent of the Second Republic in 1848 encouraged a re-affirmation of the various political traditions – of a radicalism prepared to contemplate insurrection as the means of challenging the established socio-political order, as well as of a moderate republicanism committed both to parliamentary democracy and the protection of social order; of a liberal constitutional monarchism and a reactionary, clerical monarchism; and of an authoritarian Bonapartism as the ultimate solution to political instability and guarantor of prosperity. Latent political sympathies re-emerged, and were revised. Established values might well be questioned. In a situation of crisis, where expectations and fears had been aroused, even those previously indifferent to politics, or excluded by a restricted franchise, were drawn in by manhood suffrage.

Political 'parties' existed, not as permanent organisations, but in the form of *partis d'opinion*[30] where informal groupings of like-minded individuals were able to appeal to issues which concerned wider sections of the population. Whatever the circumstances, relatively small minorities of political activists continued to diffuse ideas through the press and by word-of-mouth, and to influence political aspirations. Of course, to insist upon their importance is not to claim that they created a politics out of thin air, but to recognise their role in 'the processes whereby meanings are constituted'.[31] To a substantial degree they controlled the flow of information through their efforts to create a political rhetoric, which would help to sustain the commitment of those with other, more pressing demands on their time and energy. Moreover, the efforts of these militants were generally directed beyond, as well as towards, their 'class of origin'. Their ideas were quite as likely to meet with rejection, out of either indifference or hostility, as with sympathetic acceptance. These various responses, silence, as well as approbation or condemnation, all require consideration.

---

[29] See e.g. C. Guionnet, *L'apprentissage de la politique moderne* (Paris 1998), *passim*.
[30] R. Huard, 'Aux origines d'une structure nouvelle, le parti vers 1830–vers 1880' in S. Berstein and M. Winock (eds.), *L'invention de la démocratie, 1789–1914* (Paris 2002), pp. 185–6.
[31] P. Joyce, (ed.), *The Historical Meanings of Work* (Cambridge 1987), p. 15.

The sources for this study are many and varied: each has value and short-comings as a form of historical documentation. Particularly characteristic of France are the official reporting systems created during the Revolutionary-Imperial period in the form of the hierarchical, bureaucratic structures of the Ministries of the Interior, Justice, and War. These, mutually supportive and also competing, hierarchies exemplified the central government's need for information and its determination to diversify the sources. Inevitably, of course, the numerous, and frequently voluminous, reports from prefects, state prosecutors (procureurs généraux), generals, police officials, schools inspectors, and academic rectors, together with the results of public and private social enquiries, tell the historian more about the preoccupations of their authors, and of the social elite from which they were recruited, than about the non-elite groups they were supposed also to be observing. Officials wrote about what they, rather than their subjects, assumed was important. Moreover, as career bureaucrats, they were usually concerned to tell their superiors what it was assumed they would want to hear. Montal-ivet, former prefect, and Minister of the Interior during the First Empire, had concluded reluctantly that, as a result, 'we know nothing of what's happening'.[32]

This is too pessimistic. Used critically – subject to close textual analysis, and 'decoded' – and in conjunction with the widest possible range of alternative sources of information, such reports remain valuable. However, it is essential to locate their perceptions within the discourses shared by senior officials and the social elites to which they belonged. Making sense of reports, from whatever source, dealing with other social groups is, of course, more problematical. Reliance on police/judicial archives, for example, can most certainly produce a dark picture of social relations.[33] Any kind of dialogue between unequals is obfuscated by social distance, mutual suspicion, linguistic differences, and assigned 'codes' and 'roles'.[34] 'Resis-tance' on the part of the 'popular' classes was only too likely to be dismissed as 'pathological'.[35] Official reports and social enquiries, and any course of action they recommend, need to be closely related to frequently stereotyped perceptions of the 'other'. The 'procédures d'élaboration de ce savoir' and

---

[32] J.-L. Pinol, 'L'héritage d'une tradition politique' in Y. Lequin (ed.), *Histoire des français 19e–20e siècles*, III: *Les citoyens et la démocratie* (Paris 1984), p. 32.

[33] See e.g. S. Patural, 'Elites et archives judiciaires: notables lyonnais en conflit (1848–60)', *Cahiers d'histoire* 2000, p. 773.

[34] F. Chauvaud, 'La parole captive. L'interrogatoire judiciaire au 19e siècle', *Histoire et archives* 1997, *passim*.

[35] N. Dirks, G. Eley, and S. Ortner (eds.), *Culture/Power/History* (Princeton, N.J. 1994), pp. 19–20.

its internal logic will need repeatedly to be defined in the course of this book.[36]

The central problem we face then is to overcome the silence of the masses. The vast majority of citizens never proclaimed their opinions. Alain Corbin 'sur les traces d'un inconnu' – the sabot maker and peasant Louis-François Pinagot – asked whether 'we are able to understand the ways in which he conceived of authority and the relationships which he was able to establish with those who possessed power? What was the nature of his political imagination?' Was Pinagot ever interested in debates which 'transcended the community in which he lived'?[37] Clearly, those few peasants or workers who left memoirs were unusual, however grateful we may be for their efforts. Much can nevertheless be gleaned from a range of sometimes unlikely sources, including economic and social enquiries, although again their content was largely determined by the concerns of the politicians and officials who asked the questions. Even the apparent certainty of statistical information is destroyed by the realisation that the statisticians' definition of categories was far from 'objective'. Similarly, too much can too easily be read into election results. Every form of information thus represents a particular view of 'reality'. Every document has to be related to the context in which it originated, and regarded 'not as a reflection of some external reality, but as an integral part of that reality'.[38] Every effort has to be made to appreciate the importance of 'contextualisation, complexity, nuance', and to explore 'linkages'.[39] Where does that leave us? In all honesty, attempting to see old sources anew, trying – without a master-plan – to fit together the pieces of a very large and complicated jigsaw, some of which are misshapen and others lacking their piece of the picture, in order eventually to arrive at an impression of France during the Second Empire.

[36] A. Corbin, *Le monde retrouvé de Louis-François Pinagot. Sur les traces d'un inconnu 1798–1876* (Paris 1998), p. 249.

[37] Ibid. p. 247.

[38] J. Scott, 'Statistical representations of work: the politics of the Chamber of Commerce's, *Statistique de l'Industrie à Paris, 1847–48*' in S. Kaplan and C.-J. Koepp (eds.), *Work in France. Representations, Meaning, Organization and Practice* (London 1986), p. 363.

[39] N. Kirk, 'Class and the *linguistic turn*', in N. Kirk (ed.), *Social Class and Marxism* (London 1996), p. 125.

CHAPTER I

Dominant classes: the social elites

INTRODUCTION

A social elite might be defined as an aristocracy of birth, wealth and of influence, the latter made up of the key decision makers in both the public and private sectors of society.[1] Traditionally 'notables' had been landowners and land remained a privileged form of investment. A process of inter-penetration of 'traditional', partly noble, and 'modern' elites had long been under way, however. Economic and social change and the growing wealth and complexity of capitalist society facilitated an expansion of the elite to absorb increased numbers of businessmen, bureaucrats, and professionals. Thus, opportunities for upward mobility led to a partial renewal of the social elites, although its scale remained limited by the importance of inheritance as the main source of wealth and status. Moreover, although the ultimate symbol of success was no longer entry into the nobility, and economic achievement counted for more, cultural values derived from the 'ancient' landowning class continued to define social *mores*. The renewed experience of revolution in 1848 and the intense 'social fear' it revived also served to encourage the development of 'class' consciousness and a greater sense of solidarity.

Elite membership thus depended on the mutually reinforcing combination of economic, social, and political power, which gave its members both status and authority. It was made possible by the possession of wealth, which financed a particular lifestyle and culture. It was signified by acceptance within supportive family and social networks. Whatever their differences, the members of this social elite had vital interests in common, most notably possession of property and a determination to safeguard their place in society. More than any other social group the elite, noble and non-noble, in

[1] See e.g. W. Serman, 'Les élites militaires françaises et la politique, 1871–1914' in R. Hudemann and G.-H. Soutou (eds.), *Elites in Deutschland und Frankreich im 19. und 20. Jahrhundert* (Munich 1994), p. 211.

spite of its inner divisions, had values and a lifestyle in common, as well as a strong sense of identity. As a result it existed as something akin to a national class with less substantial local and regional differences than those found amongst peasants and workers. Members of the social elite also enjoyed the self-confidence and sense of superiority revealed in a contemporary definition of the *classes dirigeantes* by Comte Albert de Mun, as 'those on whom the advantages of education, knowledge, and wealth . . . confer, *vis-à-vis* those who lack these gifts, an authority, an influence, in a word, the means of moral and material action, the precise use of which constitutes social leadership'.[2]

Within the elite, it might be useful to distinguish those individuals who made up the *state elite*, the ministers, deputies and senior civil servants, and military commanders who to a large degree determined how the authority and the power of the state should be exercised. Its members exercised authority through the administrative and legal systems and normally possessed a monopoly of armed force. Thus, a small number of individuals took crucially important and often controversial decisions concerning internal and international affairs, which, as in the case of a declaration of war, might have implications for the very existence of the regime they served.

Nevertheless, the wider social elite from which the state elite was recruited inevitably gained privileged access to its power. A superior capacity for organisation, access to information, and a share in the power of the state, ensured that, in spite of internal rivalries, its members were at least capable of achieving operational unity against external threats. They were additionally able to exercise informal authority derived from the control of scarce resources and access to valued information. In spite of the existence of manhood suffrage, and the mounting challenge from the middle and working classes so evident in 1848, elites were able to retain considerable influence. Explaining this will involve moving beyond a focus on the state and the formal apparatus of authority to an analysis of 'how power is acquired and transmitted in society as a whole,'[3] and to the study of politics as part of everyday social practices. This will require consideration not only of divisions within elites, and the complex character of their relationships with the state, but also interaction with 'subordinate' and 'dependent' social groups.

A considerable degree of caution will be required. 'Because a man emanates from a specific type of class background, it does not inevitably follow that he will later adopt policies which are designed to promote class

---

[2] Quoted S. Kale, *Legitimism and the Reconstruction of French Society, 1852–83* (London 1992), p. 13.
[3] J. Gledhill, *Power and its Disguises. Anthropological Perspectives in Politics* (London 1994), p. 22.

Table 2. *Occupations of deputies elected in 1852 and 1869*

	1852		1869	
	Number of deputies	%	Number of deputies	%
Landowners, without other profession	97	37	85	30
Former civil servants	29	11	53	18
Businessmen	57	20	65	22
Lawyers	30	12	44	15
Other professionals	25	10	28	10
Former military	22	8	13	5

Source: E. Anceau, *Les députés du Second Empire* (Paris 2000), p. 62.

interests corresponding to that background.'[4] Moreover, political commitment varied in intensity over time and between people, and frequently ringing statements of political principle doubtless concealed far more mundane personal ambitions or local rivalries. Certainly, significant 'caste' divisions, as well as political differences, were evident. These reflected varied economic and regional interests and also different social origins, family and confessional allegiances. Whilst inter-marriage was symptomatic of fusion, marital endogamy, especially amongst nobles, signified resistance. The fragmentation of the elites in the recent past had proved and would prove again to be a source of considerable political instability.

ELITE STRUCTURES: STABILITY AND RENEWAL

The difficulties inherent in social classification are all too evident. Even where probate archives provide useful information, for example, analysis of socio-professional structures is complicated by individual engagement in multiple occupations. The information provided by memoirs and administrative reports similarly needs to be handled with critical care. At least in the case of elites the authors of official documents were drawn from a similar social milieu to those on whom they were reporting and a reasonable degree of accuracy and understanding might be expected. Certainly, official reports were obsessed with the behaviour of members of this narrow social milieu – 'la seule qui pense et qui parle'.[5]

Eric Anceau has provided invaluable information on the social origins of deputies elected to the imperial Corps législatif (see table 2). Ministers and

[4] A. Giddens quoted in H. Newby, C. Bell, D. Rose, and P. Saunders, *Property, Paternalism and Power. Class and Control in Rural England* (London 1978), p. 228.
[5] PG Limoges, 15 July 1867, AN BB30/378.

senior civil servants were recruited from the same narrow circles. Very few deputies were professional politicians. Generally, they were men of maturity, mostly drawn from landowning families with traditions of service to the State and, as time passed, they included a growing number of men experienced in the professions, as well as representatives of big business. Many had multiple occupations. Most were inspired by a sense of responsibility to their families, social peers, communities, and religious faiths, as well as by personal ambition. Their socialisation had led them to expect to enter public life, and provided the context for most of their formative experiences, amongst which 1848 loomed large. Furthermore, the relative longevity of the upper classes weakened generational differences, and reinforced conservative influences. Nominally, at least, a large majority would remain loyal to the imperial regime until its final collapse.[6]

A useful distinction might be made between membership of national and of regional elites, with members of the first group enjoying access to central government and the latter more restricted in their social and political ambitions. A study of the local elites represented in the departmental conseils généraux in 1870 reveals that 33.6 per cent registered themselves as landowners; 30 per cent belonged to the liberal professions; 21 per cent were officials; and 15.5 per cent were primarily businessmen.[7] Although this is not an entirely satisfactory proxy for elite membership, it is probably as close as we can get. It has been calculated that in Bourgogne in eastern France, membership of the national social elite – people with influence in Paris – would have been restricted to only about 0.3 per cent, some 3,000 people belonging to 600 to 700 families, whilst the departmental councils would have been elected from amongst a well-off group making up around 3 per cent of the population.[8]

Geographically wealth was distributed unevenly, with substantial concentrations in Paris and the surrounding area and in five other departments – the industrialising Nord, Seine-Inférieure, and Rhône and the rural (and residential) Seine-et-Oise and Marne.[9] The Paris basin and Normandy and areas of plain and river valley more generally, were dominated by rich landowners. In comparison, in less well-endowed regions, especially the uplands and including much of central and southern France, where

[6] E. Anceau, *Les députés du Second Empire* (Paris 2000), pp. 295–307, 110–11, 523–5.

[7] L. Girard, A. Prost, and R. Gossez, *Les conseillers généraux en 1870* (Paris 1967), pp. 45–6.

[8] P. Lévêque, 'La Bourgogne de la Monarchie de Juillet au Second Empire', Doc. d'Etat, Univ. de Paris I, 1976, p. 406; 5 per cent in Calvados according to G. Désert, *Une société rurale au 19e siècle. Les paysans du Calvados, 1815–95* (Lille 1975), I, p. 261.

[9] A. Daumard, 'Wealth and affluence in France since the beginning of the 19th century' in W. Rubinstein (ed.), *Wealth and the Wealthy in the Modern World* (London 1980), pp. 100–1.

investment in the land was less attractive, business and professional men resident in towns like Dijon, Aix-en-Provence, and Toulouse came to the fore. Within a single department, like the Calvados in Normandy, there were marked differences between the cereal-growing plains where 41 per cent of the wealth was concentrated in the hands of 1 per cent of the population, predominantly nobles; the pastoral areas of the Bessin and Pays d'Auge, where a much less well-endowed rural *bourgeoisie* was dominant; and the isolated and economically backward *bocage*, with its relatively impoverished and more democratic rural community.[10] In northern France where textiles and coalfield development had – from at least the 1820s – rapidly enriched part of the *bourgeoisie* in cities like Lille, these developments had little effect on the socio-professional structures of marketing and administrative centres like Arras or Saint-Omer.[11]

During the Second Empire the only significant sociological change in the membership of the conseils généraux appears to have been within the business category, where industrialists tended to replace merchants and bankers.[12] Stability was, thus, the primary characteristic and landowner-ship, regardless of profession, continued to be the dominant trait. For traditionalists, land remained the key element in a family's patrimony, to be passed on intact to the next generation. Its possession provided a reasonable income, and enhanced social status, partly as a result of the responsibilities entered into on behalf of dependents like domestics and tenants, as well as the wider community. Although anxious to reinforce their social status, others, who saw land primarily as an investment, had a weaker sense of obligation towards rural communities. Increasingly too landowners sought to enhance their incomes through urban/industrial investment and professional employment. Whilst social attitudes changed less rapidly than economic structures, the balance of economic power was certainly shifting in the direction of the financiers and industrialists, towards the very rich who enjoyed superior access to information and investment opportunities.

WEALTH AND PROFESSION

Although social and political influence, often deeply rooted in local communities and maintained through social networks, cannot simply be equated

---

[10] Désert, *Calvados*, I, pp. 261–5.
[11] Y.-M. Hilaire, 'La vie religieuse des populations du diocèse d'Arras, 1840–1914', Doc. d'Etat, Univ. de Paris IV, 1976, III, p. 971.
[12] Girard, Prost, and Gossez, *Conseillers généraux*, pp. 51–2.

to wealth, a high income was necessary to enjoy the lifestyle, which denoted and allowed continuing elite membership. The Second Empire was a time of difficulty for some groups, but for most represented a period of substantial wealth creation.[13] Although most wealth was inherited, economic expansion provided opportunities for enrichment and continued to alter the distribution of wealth. The exercise of influence and political activity was, of course, focused on the capital city in which aspiring members of the national elite resided for at least part of the year. Perhaps as many as 10,000 people were involved.[14] Participation in Parisian high society is estimated to have required an annual income of at least 50,000f. As well as the costs of entertaining, a fashionable town house, furnished in the style of the eighteenth century, with much added 'Victorian' clutter, was essential, together with servants and carriages, and in addition a substantial place in the country. In provincial cities the cost might be reduced to as little as 20,000f.[15] Family reputation or function might compensate for a lower income but appearances could not be preserved indefinitely.

Within this changing economy the possession of 'real' property in buildings and land remained important as a source of both income and status. Nobles and the traditional *haute bourgeoisie* largely retained customary investment practices, which, at least until the mid-1870s, offered good returns. The attractiveness of landownership was confirmed, as the value of arable and pasture increased by 33 per cent and vineyards by 43 per cent between mid-century and the 1880s, at the same time as rental income, which had already increased by 52 per cent between 1821 and 1851, rose by a further 42 per cent by 1881.[16] The provision of capital for agricultural improvement was frequently restricted by the social pressure for expenditure on sumptuous new or 'modernised' residences, which immobilised large sums of money.[17] However, high rural population densities still ensured a plentiful supply of tenants and labour and kept rents high and wages relatively low. Rising urban demand for food contributed to making this something of a golden age for landowners. Lending money, through notaries, and at high rates of interest to peasants anxious to purchase land also remained a lucrative activity.[18]

[13] E. Anceau, *Les députés*, pp. 480–1, compares the wealth of deputies and conseillers généraux in 1852 and 1870.

[14] L. Girard, *Nouvelle histoire de Paris. La Deuxième République et le Second Empire* (Paris 1981), p. 308.

[15] Girard, Prost, and Gossez, *Conseillers généraux*, p. 60.

[16] Y. Lequin, 'Les citadins, les classes et les luttes sociales' in M. Agulhon (ed.), *Histoire de la France urbaine*, IV: *La ville de l'âge industriel* (Paris 1983), p. 477.

[17] See e.g. P. Grandcoing, *Les demeures de distinction. Châteaux et châtelains au 19e siècle en Haute-Vienne* (Limoges 1999), pp. 14, 371.

[18] G. Postel-Vinay, *La terre et l'argent. L'agriculture et le crédit en France du 18e au début du 20e siècle* (Paris 1998), pp. 207f.

Nevertheless, it was evident that the *relative* importance of the land as a source of wealth was declining. Also attitudes were changing. It was increasingly accepted that 'stocks and shares are more attractive than land . . . they are exempt from tax, and provide more substantial incomes, whilst the increase in their value is dazzling; people are carried away in spite of the uncertainty'.[19] It was the *grande bourgeoisie* in Paris and the more dynamic industrial and commercial centres which enjoyed particularly rapid enrichment. Thus stocks and shares already made up 17.3 per cent of the wealth of the Parisian *haute bourgeoisie* in 1847 compared with 8.3 per cent for nobles. The latter were also far more likely to invest in state bonds for a secure income than in the more speculative shares.[20]

Although a stigma was still firmly attached to 'speculation' and any kind of 'money-grubbing' activity, this could not detract from the growing economic pre-eminence of the entrepreneur, of an increasingly assertive *aristocratie d'affaires*. In Paris wealthy bankers like Rothschild and Pereire competed for influence with the older, noble, and service elites, playing a key role in the development of the most dynamic sectors of the modern economy – in railways, ports, coalmining, and metallurgy, as well as in urban renewal.[21] Business boomed and was increasingly concentrated in textile and engineering centres like Lyon, Lille, Rouen, and Mulhouse; in modern metallurgical and mining complexes like Le Creusot and Saint-Etienne; and the growing ports of Marseille and Bordeaux, in all of which competition for power was evident between established and rising elites. Eugène Schneider, ironmaster, mine-owner, 'master' of Le Creusot, and president of the Corps législatif in the 1860s, symbolised this new industrial wealth.[22] Resource endowment, access to modern communications, and the ability to increase productivity distinguished dynamic from declining economic sectors like the charcoal iron industry of the Ardennes and Jura.[23]

The various forms of professional employment also enjoyed growing esteem, not only in relation to the income they afforded, but also according to the degree of independence and the opportunities for leisure they offered. Service to the State was honoured above private enterprise. A career in the upper echelons of the civil service or the officer corps, that is, membership of the state elite, was an occupation fit for a gentleman and many

[19] PG Nancy, ? Feb. 1856, AN BB30/381.
[20] A. Plessis, 'La Banque de France sous le Second Empire', Doc. d'Etat, Univ. de Paris I, 1980, 1, p. 292.
[21] N. Stoskopf, *Les patrons du Second Empire. Banquiers et financiers parisiens* (Paris 2000), pp. 37, 328–30.
[22] *Les Schneider, Le Creusot. Une famille, une entreprise, une ville (1836–1960)* (Paris 1995), *passim*.
[23] Girard, Prost, and Gossez, *Conseillers généraux*, pp. 107–15.

families had long-established traditions of service.[24] More generally, participation in public affairs – as a deputy or more commonly a member of a departmental or arrondissement council or of the administrative committee of a charitable bureau de bienfaisance or hospital – was the distinguishing feature of a member of the local social elite. A similar traditional status hierarchy continued to exist in relation to the economic professions. The ironmaster, the traditional provider of the weapons of war, stood above the textile entrepreneur; the industrialist, as creator of wealth, above the trader or even the banker – who might earn respect and invitations to mix in high society due to his wealth but was invariably suspect as a speculator. The respect offered to individuals thus reflected a complex of traditional concepts of honour, virtue, and value to society.

FAMILY AND SOCIETY

Wealth, and most notably inherited wealth, provided access to social networks based upon a shared lifestyle and core ideological and political interests. The relatively small minority of representatives of 'new' wealth desperately sought to secure acceptance by adhering to established patterns of behaviour.[25] Individuals were known through the reputation of their families. Personnel dossiers full of letters of recommendation certainly suggest that promotion within the army or administration depended at least as much on family origin and connections as on ability. In these circumstances the choice of a marriage partner was an important means of consolidating success, a matter of concern to the entire family, a question of 'duty or reason' rather than inclination.[26] Relatively large families and the importance attached to kinship facilitated the widening of social networks. Weddings and funerals were occasions for reinforcing links. Such opportunities for social theatre were celebrated with great pomp and ceremony. Aristocratic models of public behaviour and culture won widespread acceptance.[27]

Sociability reinforced cohesion and in this women were expected to play a central role. The ideal wife belonged to an established and influential family, was financially well endowed and cultured, capable of entertaining and being received into society. Although the primary roles of women were as mistresses of households and mothers, the women of the Schneider family,

---

[24] See e.g. C. Charle, 'Les spécificités de la magistrature française en Europe', *Crises* 1994, p. 68.

[25] See e.g. C. Pellissier, 'Les sociabilités patriciennes à Lyon du milieu du 19e siècle à 1914', Doc. de l'Univ. de Lyon II, 1993, I, pp. 105, 155.

[26] Anceau, *Les députés*, p. 201.　　　[27] See e.g. Pellissier, 'Les sociabilités', III, p. 1063.

like many others, also reinforced the social and political authority of their husbands by supervising the distribution of charity to the 'deserving' poor.[28] The informal influence of women on the conduct of business and politics was clearly evident but difficult to chart. Although young women were poorly prepared for the rigours of sex and childbirth, and as a result were frequently physically and emotionally exhausted, they tended to outlive husbands, who were generally significantly older. In Lyon in 1851 34 per cent of upper-class women aged over fifty were widows and thus had recovered their autonomy.[29]

Membership of a variety of voluntary associations was another vital means of being seen and of asserting personal worth. These might include gentlemen's clubs, the most prestigious of which maintained their exclusivity through high subscriptions and careful co-option. Members of the Corps législatif, whilst in Paris, favoured the Cercle Impérial, the Union and the Cercle agricole – Bonapartist, Legitimist, and Orleanist in their sympathies – as well as the Jockey Club, popular with sportsmen regardless of political affiliation, and the Cercle des chemins de fer which attracted financiers.[30] In Lyon, businessmen gathered in the Cercle de Commerce, sportsmen at the Jockey Club, the local aristocracy in the Cercle du Divan, and devout Catholics at the Cercle de Lyon. Less formally, regular gatherings occurred at prestigious cafés.[31] Learned societies, charitable and religious bodies, most notably the congregations of the Société de Saint Vincent de Paul, as well as political committees or economic pressure groups representing the interests of specific industries – or in the case of agricultural committees and chambers of commerce, particular localities – all provided additional reasons for meeting.

Membership of these bodies was regarded as an obligation and represented a means both of securing and affirming status. Sociability was thus a means of acquiring social capital. In addition, charity was regarded as a moral obligation, and the display of compassion it involved was an undoubted source of influence and status. In addition to performing 'good' works, members of charitable associations were able to enjoy the company of their peers and such manifestations of upper-class good taste as the 'charity' ball. Furthermore, according to the Catholic Church, it was a means of securing Eternal Salvation and, more prosaically, a means of

---

[28] M. Offerlé, 'Les Schneider en politique' in *Les Schneider*, p. 298; see also J. Lalouette, 'Actes, regards et images des femmes') in A. Corbin, J. Lalouette, and M. Riot-Sarcey (eds.), *Femmes dans la cité* (Paris 1997), pp. 22–7.
[29] Pellissier, *Les sociabilités*, II, p. 763.   [30] Anceau, *Les députés*, pp. 426–31.
[31] Pellissier, 'Les sociabilités', II, p. 566.

gaining the gratitude of recipients, of encouraging orderly behaviour and, in times of crisis, of preventing disorder. Paternalistic concern for dependents, and paupers more generally, was a feature of the idealised traditional rural community, frequently taken up by large industrial employers like the Schneiders or the Protestant entrepreneurs of Mulhouse.

Thus, networking in its various forms enabled individuals to make use of accumulated social and symbolic capital. It reinforced the internal stability and confirmed the essential unity of social elites. More mundanely, it offered a useful means of acquiring economic as well as social and political information. In the absence of organised political parties the various forms of sociability also provided the structures and occasions for political organisation. Although only the very rich could participate fully in 'high society' and enjoy the Paris season, there were opportunities for those with similar pretensions but less wealth, as well as for the less spendthrift or well connected, to enjoy a similar calendar of events in Lyon, Aix, Dijon, Le Mans, and a host of provincial cities. Outside Paris, even in the largest cities, where the local elite rarely included more than a few hundred people, it was possible to know everyone who mattered. In such small groups the pressure to conform was of course intense. Being seen in the right places, a mark of distinction, was essential to social success. Invitations to events given or attended by particularly eminent families or such worthies as the bishop, prefect, or military commander counted for a great deal. The reward for conformity was a share in the group's collective power.

The château, newly constructed or 'restored', provided an additional setting for the affirmation of status and of family and regional solidarities. It facilitated the construction of networks of alliance between members of the national elite and those with only local influence.[32] Autumn was spent on country estates. Shooting was especially popular, and hunting with hounds enjoyed a revival. The 'season', beginning in Paris in November, with its balls, dinners, and exchanges of visits provided further occasions for reinforcing old friendships and making new acquaintances, and for introducing the young into society. Following an interruption for Lent, receptions and balls continued until May when, at the first sign of summer heat, there was another exodus to country houses, spas, and the coast. These varied social gatherings thus provided a basis for cohesion in spite of the geographical dispersal of regional elites.

---

[32] C.-I. Brelot, 'Itinérances nobles: la noblesse et la maîtrise de l'espace, entre ville et château, au 19e siècle' in Brelot, *Noblesse et villes* (Tours 1995), *passim*.

A powerful sense of *noblesse oblige* was reinforced by the desire to secure gainful and respectable employment, as well as access to patronage. Administrative and political authority were manifestations of economic and social power, but also means of reinforcing them. Thus, and in spite of distaste for the need to appeal to a mass electorate, elected office came rapidly to be accepted as a means of serving the community and State and legitimising social superiority. Wealth, status, and culture were the essential qualifications for participation in public life, which was not, however, without its costs. Thus substantial funds were necessary to contest elections and, in spite of the payments made to deputies, to cover the additional expenses of representation. The deputy or conseiller would be expected to pay frequent visits to ministers and officials, to attend receptions at the prefecture and bishop's palace, be seen at agricultural shows, and subsidise local good causes. For the electorate, wealth legitimised authority. It offered a guarantee that an aspiring deputy or public figure was a member of the privileged social circle which controlled the state, and that he possessed the appropriate social and political contacts to secure the share of public patronage, jobs, and funds, which his constituents expected.

From Metz, F. de Carcy observed that 'one finds in every gathering of high society, the prefect, the military, judicial, financial and even the religious authorities . . . all in close contact, and able to take decisions immediately on matters of public concern',[33] whilst the liberal politician Buffet maintained it was essential for anyone with political ambitions to use such occasions to cultivate his neighbours.[34] At such public displays of status 'correct' behaviour was essential. Fashionable dress, polished manners, a sense of personal dignity, and the ability to engage in 'polite' conversation were necessary. According to one observer, 'real' aristocrats, even married couples, would never use the personal *tu* form of address when a third person was present. This was a mistake only the *nouveaux riches* were likely to make.[35] For women, the couturier Worth became from 1858 the supreme arbiter of taste, with the crinoline, costing between 700 and 1200 francs without expensive accessories, as perhaps the perfect symbol of elite display. Unfortunately, it occupied so much space that hosts were forced to invite fewer guests to receptions.[36]

---

[33] F. de Carcy, *Mémoires* (Metz 1979), p. 50.

[34] Nassau William Senior papers, Journal entry 2 May 1857, University of Wales, Bangor. Bangor MS 24644. On Tocqueville's high opinion of Senior's accounts of conversations see S. L. Levy, *Nassau William Senior 1790–1864. Critical Essayist, Classical Economist and Advisor of Governments* (Newton Abbot 1970). Levy (p. 161) describes Senior as 'the prince of interviewers' with an 'unique memory and keen understanding'.

[35] Ibid. 1 May 1857.   [36] Girard, *Nouvelle histoire*, p. 311.

Snobisme required newcomers to adopt norms of behaviour largely derived from aristocratic practice. They had a particular need to be seen, and were obliged to engage in the demanding process of securing recognition of the social status to which they laid claim. Achille Fould, scion of a Jewish banking family, was described as 'a witty man of the world . . . , lover of the fine arts, who even knows a little about finance, which he has picked up from his brother Benoît, the eminent banker'.[37] In other words, he was a 'good chap', and potentially a very useful contact because of his acquaintances amongst the members of such august bodies as the Jockey Club. Membership of the elite also depended upon an ability to speak its language and share its assumptions, and on a general culture based on the rhetorical traditions provided by a classical schooling, followed by instruction in the law. A legal training was always useful for a landowner or for those careers in the administration, which provided an invaluable supplement to the incomes of a younger generation, which had not yet come into its inheritance. Even successful businessmen, like the Mulhouse textile *patriciat*, found it necessary to secure a classical rather than a technical education for their offspring.[38] Attendance at the appropriate private school, like the Catholic college at Marc-en-Baroeil, favoured by the wealthiest business families in the Nord, additionally established a network of contacts for a young man, and with the 'right' sort of people.[39]

In spite of diverse origins, differing self-perceptions, and tensions over political and religious questions, there were powerful pressures for conformity within the elite. Thus, whilst each retained its *caste* pretensions, there was a growing fusion between nobles and *grands bourgeois*, a shared sense of belonging to the ruling class and of the need to defend this social superiority. Intensified by the experience of 1848, social fear would reinforce awareness of the need for collaboration. Nevertheless, internal stresses require consideration.

Nobility

Historians have disagreed over the significance to be attached to the nobility, and especially over whether it should be regarded as part of the wider social elite, of the class of *grands notables* identified by A.-J. Tudesq,[40] or

---

[37] By E. Ollivier, quoted F. Barbier, *Finance et politique. La dynastie des Fould* (Paris 1991), p. 159.

[38] A. Prost, *L'enseignement en France, 1800–1967* (Paris 1968), pp. 59–60.

[39] F. Barbier, *Le patronat du Nord sous le Second Empire: une approche de prosopographique* (Geneva 1989), p. 29.

[40] A.-J. Tudesq, *Les grands notables en France (1840–49): Etude historique d'une psychologie sociale*, 2 vols. (Paris 1964).

as a distinct social group. A process of fusion was certainly well under way, but it is hardly possible to deny that the nobility retained a separate sense of identity. Although less pronounced than under previous regimes, tensions survived between the noble and non-noble components of the ruling elite. Contemporaries were well aware of these. Nobles themselves continued to assume that they belonged to a world apart and were determined to distinguish themselves socially, by the use of a title or at least the *particule* (*de*), and a characteristic lifestyle and ideology. In many cases, possession of a château symbolised an attachment to family and the land. Many noble families attempted to mix socially only with their own kind. Although noblemen might marry the daughters of wealthy *bourgeois*, as they always had, the reverse was extremely rare.[41] Nobles remained determined to preserve their autonomy, particularly in those areas in the west, Midi, and centre where they still controlled large estates and claimed political power and where memories and myths of the Revolution reinforced their hostility towards *bourgeois* elites.[42] Few areas were entirely devoid of such tensions.

Identifying nobles is not always easy, due to the frequent adoption by ambitious families of the *particule* and of a noble lifestyle and pretensions. Usurpation of titles had ceased to be an offence in 1832, and although legal protection was restored in 1858 along with a Conseil du Sceau du Titre to protect genuine nobility and rally nobles to the regime, the law remained a dead letter.[43] In terms of behaviour there was certainly little to distinguish the 'true' noble with a legally authenticated title, from the 'false' noble. In fact the renewal of the ranks of nobility, a group otherwise doomed to demographic decline, largely depended on such recruits.[44] Even then it is evident that the nobility were too few in number to dominate an expanding elite.

This was a group in which, more than any other, birth, as well as money, continued to influence social stratification. In terms of their wealth, nobles enjoyed the considerable advantage of having inherited assets over centuries. The Revolution had left these intact, to a substantial degree. The abolition of primogeniture, together with those provisions of the civil code which required more or less equal division of inheritances amongst heirs,

---

[41] See e.g. A. Daumard, 'Noblesse et aristocratie en France au 19e siècle' in G. Delille (ed.), *Les noblesses européennes au 19e siècle* (Rome 1988), p. 102.

[42] See e.g. Tudesq, *Notables*, 1, pp. 8–9.

[43] C. Marcilhacy, *Le diocèse d'Orléans sous l'épiscopat de Mgr Dupanloup 1849–79* (Paris 1962), p. 392.

[44] A.-J. Tudesq, 'L'élargissement de la noblesse en France dans la première moitié du 19e siècle' in Delille, *Les noblesses*, p. 124.

appears to have been accepted generally by the nobility in spite of considerable concern that repeated division of the patrimony would lead to its eventual destruction. Improved management of their affairs, efforts to ensure 'good' marriages, to secure the inheritance of relatives without issue, as well as increasing professional employment, were the means of avoiding such an outcome and of ensuring a family's ability to *tenir son rang* although, as in every generation, individual families suffered the consequences of extravagance and the subdivision of property through dowries and inheritance.[45]

Overall, nevertheless, there is evidence to suggest that at least those nobles serving as elected departmental councillors enjoyed relative enrichment during the Second Empire in comparison with their non-noble colleagues. Over 50 per cent of them had incomes of over 30,000f. in comparison with only 28 per cent of non-nobles.[46] This reflected both an ability to secure increased income from the land, through better farming and improved market access, and the willingness of the wealthiest and best informed to participate, alongside the *haute bourgeoisie*, in new ventures. Not surprisingly, it was those landowners with the most capital, willing and able to take risks, who were the most adaptable, and willing to risk alienating local opinion through the pursuit of profit and the amalgamation of farms into larger units better suited to drainage, to complex crop rotations, and specialisation. In this respect nobles resident in and around Paris were the best placed. In a rich agricultural region like the Beauce 332 families controlled at least 150,000 hectares.[47] The Seine-et-Marne also attracted the wealthy, so that old-established aristocratic families like the Haussonville near Provins, the Choiseul at Vaux-le-Vicomte, the Lafayette at La Grange rubbed shoulders with ennobled financiers like Baron Hottinguer at Guermantes and the Rothschilds with their vast neo-Renaissance château at Ferrières.[48]

However, whilst landlords with an interest in agronomy were encouraged to create larger farms and search out tenants with the capital to exploit them, it was still far more common to rent out land in small plots, partly because estates themselves rarely formed a concentrated bloc, but mainly as a means of maximising income and the size of the dependent clientele. In the Franche-Comté at Deschaux, for example, 93 tenants farmed 193 hectares of land belonging to the Vaulchier family in the 1870s. Most of them were renting land to supplement their own small farms. Rather than

[45] G. Postel-Vinay, 'Les domaines nobles et le recours au crédit' in Delille (ed.), *Les noblesses*, p. 213.
[46] Girard, Prost, and Gossez, *Conseillers généraux*, p. 80.
[47] J.-C. Farcy, *Les paysans beaucerons au 19e siècle* (Chartres 1989), I, p. 274.
[48] P. Bernard, *Economie et sociologie de la Seine-et-Marne, 1850–1950* (Paris 1953), p. 170.

competing with the small landowner, in this situation the large landowner provided the peasants with the means of economic survival.[49]

In comparison with other notables, nobles continued to hold a higher proportion of their wealth in land and were committed to landownership in particular *locales* for social as well as economic reasons. The preference given to fellow nobles in land sales illustrates their determination to preserve a rural power base.[50] Nevertheless, the situation was changing rapidly, partly due to the rising tide of migration to the cities, which reduced population densities and the competition to rent farms and obtain work, and partly to the creation of more competitive markets. The ability to make speculative profits from short-term fluctuations in grain prices largely disappeared from the 1850s, as did much of the profit from the forests, the essential source of fuel and building materials in a pre-industrial society. Metallurgy and mining were traditional areas of aristocratic endeavour, adjuncts to landownership, means of fully exploiting the resources of the *domaine*, and as such perfectly respectable forms of business activity, not leading to *dérogeance* or loss of noble status. Nobles had thus been involved, usually as lessees, in the exploitation of innumerable mines, quarries, and watermills, and in the process of rural proto-industrialisation, which, during the Second Empire, was rapidly being displaced by competition from more modern enterprises. The *crise d'adaptation* caused by the transport revolution and the growing use of coal and iron would reduce abruptly the incomes derived from the wood and water resources of landed estates, and with these the ability to combine the exploitation of farms, forests, ponds, and mills in an almost feudal fashion.[51]

Nobles adapted to changing circumstances by investing growing proportions of any surplus income in stocks and shares, taking advantage in particular of the security offered by the state and railway companies. The tradition of lending to farmers through notaries declined sharply. There was a growing determination to keep careful account of expenditure and to increase incomes and, if possible, set aside contingency funds. Noble indebtedness appears to have been far less of a burden than under the *ancien régime*, although over-enthusiasm for agricultural improvement remained dangerous. For the great majority, however, the commitment to capitalism remained a passive one, that of the rentier. Although, in 1851, 70 of the 166 private owners of shares in the Bank of France had pretensions to nobility, and this had risen to 81 of 180 in 1870, almost all owed their wealth to past

---

[49] C.-I. Brelot, *La noblesse réinventée. Nobles de Franche-Comté de 1814 à 1870* (Paris 1992), I, pp. 325–8.
[50] Ibid. pp. 269–74.
[51] See e.g. J.-L. Mayaud, *Les secondes républiques du Doubs* (Paris 1986), pp. 68–72.

generations rather than their own efforts.[52] Others assumed largely orna-
mental directorships of major enterprises, particularly banks and insurance
companies, although a small minority undoubtedly became active businessmen, including Denis Benoist d'Azy in mining and metallurgy and the
Duc de Galliera, a director of the Crédit mobilier and the Est and Nord
railway companies.[53]

Although increasingly nobles were committed to the efficient employment of their wealth and the sources of their income were becoming more
varied, more modern, and more *bourgeois*, the objective remained that of
preserving an essentially noble lifestyle. They continued to conceive of
property as part of the family patrimony, held in trust for future generations, rather than as a simple economic asset. Their perspective was the long
term and they tended to view the speculation associated with figures close
to the imperial regime like Morny or Mirès, with disgust. Furthermore,
Eugène de Mirecourt's influential works on the stock exchange adopted
a violently anti-Semitic discourse, blaming 'Jewish finance' for the moral
decay, which threatened the social hierarchy.[54] The attitudes nobles adopted
towards capitalism were also revealed by their own choice of occupations.
Generally this reflected family influence and was subordinated to family
interests. The prefectoral and diplomatic corps and the magistrature were
areas of activity legitimised by inherited *noblesse de robe* traditions. Certainly a business career was regarded as less honourable than the public
service.[55] Salaried employment also meant loss of independence, although
earnings might well be higher.

Whatever their feelings about the regime of the *coup d'état*, the young,
particularly those belonging to less well-endowed families, could not afford
the luxury of standing on principle and refusing to serve indefinitely. Frequently, the alternative appeared to be a dangerous idleness. For Gustave
de Beaumont, considering his son's future, 'this is how the question posed
itself: to become an officer or to do nothing except fish for trout and chase
hares'.[56] Service in the army, maintaining the traditions of the *noblesse
d'épée*, was a respectable position to take up whilst waiting for marriage or
an inheritance. It conformed to aristocratic ideals of service to the state and

[52] Plessis, 'Banque de France', i, pp. 230–41.
[53] Ibid. ii, p. 628; R. Locke, 'A method for identifying French corporate businessmen', *French Historical Studies* 1977–8, p. 291.
[54] V. Thompson, *The Virtuous Marketplace. Women and Men, Money and Politics in Paris, 1830–70* (London 2000), pp. 160–1.
[55] See letters between Alexis de Tocqueville and Gustave de Beaumont 8 and 15 April 1852 in Tocqueville, *Oeuvres complètes*, XIII, 2 (Paris 1978), pp. 110, 106.
[56] Letter to de Tocqueville, 5 Nov. 1857, *Oeuvres complètes*, III, p. 509.

a strong sense of *noblesse oblige* created by both family tradition and religious conviction. Service legitimised the privileges acquired with wealth. For officers, time with the regiment was anyway interspersed with frequent home leave, making it easier to maintain social contacts. For those who chose to remain longer and make a military career, generally the support of a powerful patron was required to secure promotion. The development of more meritocratic criteria for selection was becoming apparent, with a decent education becoming a prerequisite for admission to the Saint-Cyr military academy or the Ecole Polytechnique, which trained military engineers. Nevertheless, the culture of aristocratic amateurism continued to flourish. Co-option and nepotism – favouritism – remained the key modes of recruitment throughout the public service. At the end of the Empire almost 35 per cent of generals were nobles.[57]

What was distinctive about the lifestyle which nobles were so determined to perpetuate? In the first place, whether based on town house or provincial château, noble sociability involved a public statement of pride in a name and ancestry, and a commitment to 'honourable' behaviour and to an encompassing set of social ideals. It reflected, furthermore, a determination to appear *comme il faut*, and to accept responsibilities to family, friends, and dependants. This provided the grounding for a very definite feeling of superiority, for a sense of caste, and a desire to maintain social distance. As the gendarmerie commander in the Breton department of Côtes-du-Nord observed, the result was that 'the nobility, the bourgeoisie, and the people . . . live very different lives; there's no real disagreement between them, but rather a coldness born of differences in status, which ensures that they avoid each other'.[58]

Even deprived of its seigneurial associations, the château, together with its surrounding park, retained considerable symbolic importance. Substantial resources were likely to be devoted to its embellishment and furnishing, often in a neo-Gothic or neo-Renaissance style, and particularly by the wealthiest nobles who were establishing a model for others to emulate. This was a place for receptions and balls and a base for hunting, with numerous servants, and the carriages and horses in the stables, which were essential for constant coming and going. In Franche-Comté an income of at least 25,000f. to 30,000f. was judged to be necessary to maintain this sort of elegant aristocratic lifestyle.[59] Otherwise compromises would have to be made, and probably were by the majority. A town house might be

[57] Tudesq, 'L'élargissement de la noblesse', p. 131.
[58] 31 July 1869, AHG G8/166.   [59] Brelot, *Noblesse*, I, p. 434.

maintained in a provincial city rather than in Paris, or worse still only a single residence; an 'old-fashioned' château might be repaired rather than reconstructed; fewer servants might be employed and a more frugal style of life endured. Nevertheless, it was essential to preserve appearances sufficiently at least to ensure the proper entry into society of the younger *male* generation in the hope that its members would acquire the contacts necessary to secure the family's position. Impoverishment brought the risk of growing social isolation, difficulty in establishing sons in careers and in finding dowries for daughters, and eventual *déclassement*.[60]

To avoid such shame, it was essential to acquire social and cultural capital and support from social networks. Individual social intercourse was controlled carefully. If possible, non-nobles were excluded. Especially close links were maintained with relatives; even distant kin often providing vital links to more diffuse networks. As a result the nobility remained the most closely integrated of social groups. With the memories of 1789, and especially 1793, reinforced by the renewed loss of privilege in 1830 and the intense social fear re-awakened in 1848, the experience of revolution did much to reinforce this solidarity and at the same time to obstruct the process of fusion through which a more homogeneous elite made up simply of the wealthy, was being created. Exclusivity was, thus, a source of both strength and weakness. Whilst it created strong bonds of mutual support between nobles and, in the absence of modern party organisation, would provide an informal organisational structure for Legitimist politics, it also threatened to isolate nobles from other socially conservative groups. More than this, the code of conduct, a refined politeness, and apparent self-confidence and arrogance, helped to preserve a deep and widespread hatred for the nobility, especially in areas previously torn apart by the Revolution.

This was not entirely typical, however. Although new wealth challenged aristocratic pretensions to social leadership, social and political isolation might be avoided as a result of 'the consideration, which easily attaches itself to an old name, to great wealth, and to habits of benevolence and charity'.[61] Amongst a traditional landowning and office-holding bourgeoisie, which in a previous century would have aspired to nobility, nobles continued to win respect and to serve as a social model. Furthermore, patronage might be employed to build up a clientele, although this would require a compromise between the objective of maximising income and that of securing influence.

---

[60] See e.g. N. Claret-Ploquin, 'Noblesses en déclassement, noblesses en souffrance', *Cahiers d'histoire* 2000, pp. 757–67.

[61] PG Nancy, 3 April 1857, AN BB30/381 re nobles in Meurthe.

In a rather blatant effort to win election as a deputy in Loir-et-Cher in 1867 the Duc de la Rochefoucault-Doudeauville organised a fête at his château de la Gondinière. According to an official report: 'he wrote a circular letter to the mayors in his canton, engaging them to convoke the notables of their communes for 11 September . . . adding that he was anxious to discuss with them the measures which needed to be taken for the distribution of charity and in order to obtain a new railway line for the locality'.[62]

It was important to secure allies. In this respect the clergy were the obvious partners for a nobility drawn increasingly towards religion since the Revolution with growing sincerity and commitment. This was true particularly of the younger generations educated at religious colleges like Stanislas or Vaugirard in Paris or the Jesuit establishments at Brugelette in Belgium, Chambéry in Savoy, and Fribourg in Switzerland, and anxious to find reassurance in a sea of change. They tended to perceive God's Holy Order, in other words, traditional society, with its hierarchical structures, and the Roman Catholic Church as being threatened with destruction by Revolution, and the less dramatic progress of materialism and secularisation.[63]

The grande bourgeoisie

'New' wealth was represented by a *grande bourgeoisie*, which had, since 1830, achieved dominance not only in commerce, industry, and the professions but also in government. In comparison with the relative cohesion of the nobility, this was a more diverse group in terms of origins, profession, the structure of its wealth and political affiliations. Its socio-professional structures varied with local economic conditions. Clearly some regions were more congenial to economic activity than others. However, improved communications facilitated the growing concentration of this elite in Paris – the political and financial decision-making centre. Even there the very wealthy had diverse and complex economic interests. Thus the regents of the Bank of France, drawn predominantly from the city's traditional banking circles, retained one-fifth to one-tenth of their wealth in property with two-thirds of this in the capital itself, mostly accounted for by their own luxury accommodation. The rest of their wealth was made up of capital invested in their own businesses as well as in a range of profitable enterprises as they took advantage of superior access to economic information.[64]

[62] PG Orléans, 8 Oct. 1867, AN BB30/382.
[63] See e.g. M. Launay *et al.*, *La noblesse nantaise au 19e siècle* (Nantes 2000), pp. 13–14.
[64] Plessis, 'Banque de France', I, p. 236.

This *grande bourgeoisie* could be distinguished from the remainder of the bourgeoisie by the great wealth, which provided its members with the means to enjoy a distinctive lifestyle and acquire political influence. It was composed of 'traditional' elements, including the most eminent civil servants and professionals invariably blessed with substantial private incomes, together with large landowners, many of whom had retired from public life or business. To these might be added the most successful businessmen amongst for example the textile *patronat* of Lille or Mulhouse, or men like the metallurgical and engineering entrepreneurs Eugène Schneider and Jean-François Cail – the latter one of the very few examples of a career from rags to riches[65] – the financiers Pereire and Mirès (before his fall), and Henri Germain who inherited capital made in the Lyon silk industry and went on to found the Crédit lyonnais bank. Parallel hierarchies existed within each of these groups as well as passages between them.

To be socially acceptable required more than wealth – a necessary but not a sufficient qualification. There needed to be a surplus sufficient to fund, as well as a willingness to enjoy, gracious living. Certainly, one's life should not be absorbed by business activity. In Rouen 2 per cent to 3 per cent of families qualified, a minority amongst them headed by self-made men like the textile entrepreneur Pouyer-Quertier, most, like the Waddington family, having inherited and accumulated wealth in a process of social promotion spread over two or three generations. In Normandy success in business continued to be celebrated by the adoption of the lifestyle of the country gentleman and the provision of a classical education for children, indicative perhaps of an initial sense of social inferiority,[66] whilst – although the contrast should not be exaggerated – in the Nord and Alsace, if a country house was likely to be purchased, successive generations tended to retain a greater commitment to a patriarchical, family-centred mode of life and to industrial enterprise and technological innovation, viewing business as an exciting and creative end in itself, rather than simply a means of achieving upward mobility.[67] The award of the Legion of Honour to the Roubaix textile magnate Motte-Bossut in 1863 celebrated twenty years of effort and the opening of his third mill, one of the largest in France, its structure, symbolically, inspired by that of the medieval castle.[68]

---

[65] On Cail see Barbier, *Patronat du Nord*, pp. 104–10; on Schneider, P. Jobert, *Les patrons du Second Empire*, II, *Bourgogne* (Paris 1991), pp. 191–7.

[66] J.-P. Chaline, 'La bourgeoisie rouennaise au 19e siècle', Doc. d'Etat, Univ. de Paris IV 1979, p. 199.

[67] PG Colmar, 20 Jan. 1863, AN BB30/376.

[68] J. Lambert-Dansette, *La vie des chefs d'entreprise 1830–80* (Paris 1992), p. 53.

The Revolution and economic expansion had increased opportunities. The lucky few had enriched themselves through property speculation, in textiles and to a lesser extent metallurgy. Now they could choose from amongst a growing range of 'traditional' and 'modern' investments. These included land, which offered a regular income as well as providing collateral and increasing credit-worthiness; state bonds – a secure investment favoured by rentiers and the retired; and shares, particularly those in major utilities like the railway companies. Diversification further enhanced security. Social contacts provided access to information concerning investment opportunities; whilst political power was employed to ensure that the income derived was virtually tax free. However, as technology became more expensive the larger amounts of capital required for entry into the business elite had increasingly restricted entry. A period of social openness was followed by one of closure. Inherited position became more significant, with most businesses growing by means of the re-investment of profits, and even large enterprises seeking to reduce borrowing and maintain their independence.[69]

For businessmen a secure investment environment was of crucial importance. This depended on social order and political stability and additionally, for many, on a protected internal market together with low wages costs. The Second Empire was a time of renewed opportunity, with rail construction, industrial re-structuring, urban renewal, and growing commercial activity as well as increased government borrowing. Close links were maintained between ministers and the directors of the major financial houses, which floated state loans. This *haute banque* enjoyed considerable profitability. Flexible family-based structures made it relatively easy for its members to adapt to changing circumstances. There was, however, bitter rivalry to secure potentially lucrative investment opportunities, most notably between the Pereire and their associates in the Crédit mobilier and financiers linked to the Rothschilds and Talabots. Rail concessions, the reconstruction of the port of Marseille, 'gateway to the east', and control of the iron mines at Mokta-el-Hadid in Algeria were all hotly disputed.[70]

Represented, along with leading industrialists, on the Council of Regents of the Bank of France, these financiers were supremely well informed, and through interlocking directorates were involved in most modern joint-stock enterprises, particularly in insurance and transport. The capital of the companies in which they were involved is calculated to have risen from

---

[69] See e.g. D. Gordon, *Merchants and Capitalists. Industrialization and Provincial Politics in mid-nineteenth-century France* (London 1985), p. 181.

[70] Stoskopf, *Banquiers*, pp. 52–3.

100 million francs in 1851 to 2.5 milliard by 1870.[71] Immensely creative as such figures were, the public associated them frequently with 'illicit' speculative activity. Together with their ostentation, this inevitably provoked considerable hostility. Significantly too, if by 1870 the capital of the largest of the merchant banks, that of the Rothschilds, had risen to 40/50 million francs, this was already much inferior to that of the leading joint-stock banks – the Société générale (170 million) and Crédit lyonnais (95 million).[72] Together with the rise of major industrial companies this development was indicative of a shift within capitalism away from its commercial origins.

An *aristocratie bourgeoise* was nevertheless being established, increasingly caste-like in terms of its recruitment. It certainly included the small group of around 200 regents of the Bank of France who frequently shared business information and collaborated in floating government loans or shares in the major companies of which they were directors. These business links were often reinforced by inter-marriage between, for example, members of the Pillet-Will and Hottinguer families and the Delesserts. A shared Catholicism might be another binding force, as was the Protestantism of the Mallets and Lefebvres. The journalist Capefigue transmuted these representatives of the *haute banque* into a single *haute famille*.[73] Such close links, and the apparent freedom to manipulate financial markets which it made possible, increasingly offered justification for an intellectual and journalistic assault on the *deux cents familles* who supposedly controlled the economy.[74] Another important sub-group was made up of the richest members of the textile *patronats* of the Nord and Alsace, the latter made up of some dozen families (Dollfus, Mieg, Schlumberger, Koechlin, etc.).[75] Unlike most bourgeois groups, which had accepted birth control as a means of preventing the dispersal of capital, the *patronat* of the Nord and Alsace had large families. This increased the likelihood that each generation would include dedicated and carefully educated entrepreneurs. These were groups with a strong sense of common interest. Their capacity for action was reinforced by informal sociability, balls, dinners, membership of *cercles*, as well as by inter-marriage.[76]

The choice of marriage partner was certainly too important to be left entirely to the young people concerned, although generally they were

---

[71] C. Charle, *Histoire sociale de la France au 19e siècle* (Paris 1991), p. 105.

[72] Plessis, 'Banque de France', II, p. 499.   [73] Ibid. p. 508.

[74] G. Duchêne, *L'empire industriel. Histoire critique des concessions financières et industrielles du Second Empire* (Paris 1869).

[75] M. Hau, *L'industrialisation de l'Alsace (1803–1939)* (Strasbourg 1987), p. 399.

[76] E.g. Barbier, *Patronat du Nord*, pp. 20–2.

well known to each other and frequently were cousins, something which prevented loss of capital by the extended family. Solidarity and the re-investment of profits were the secrets of continuing success within an economic structure which remained dominated by family enterprise. Marriage symbolised an alliance between families, with potential implications for each in terms of access to capital and markets. If sufficiently able, and willing to commit themselves to business rather than adopt a preference for leisure or public life, the male children would provide the next generation of business leaders. On marriage they gained substantial settlements and full entry into the social elite. Eugène Schneider, for example, settled one and a half million francs on each of his sons and daughters. Félicie married her cousin Alfred Deseilligny who would be a key figure in the subsequent development of the mining/metallurgical complex at Le Creusot.[77] Similarly the three children of the banker Alexis Pillet-Will were each provided with 1 million francs to establish themselves, although 80,000f. – 400,000f. appears to have been more usual.[78]

Schneider, the ironmaster, able to double his wealth every 6 to 10 years,[79] was a potent symbol of the *fête impériale*. According to the correspondent of *L'Indépendance belge* (5 March 1865):

the dinner given last evening by M. Schneider [in his Paris mansion in the rue Boudreau] was really splendid. A grand gallery, constructed in the garden, filled with fresh flowers, and decorated with mirrors, had been added to the princely rooms of this beautiful and elegant mansion. A buffet was also installed there in a very serviceable fashion. Rarely have I encountered such a gathering of elegant people. We danced until three, and the dinner itself, as magnificent as it was, proved to be insufficient to silence the orchestra conducted by Strauss. Most of the members of the Senate, the Chamber, and the Conseil d'Etat were present at this wonderful occasion

along with leading financiers and industrialists. This was a world in which to receive and be received represented acceptance, in which a house was part of a social theatre.

The wealthiest financiers and industrialists also seemed to be developing a marriage strategy which extended family links beyond business circles into the world of the old nobility and high political circles, providing of course that a 'name' was backed by the requisite levels of wealth. Members of the '200 families' frequently lived in the fashionable faubourg Saint-Germain in Paris, although progressively they moved out of the crowded

---

[77] Lambert-Dansette, *La vie des chefs d'entreprise*, p. 38.
[78] Plessis, 'Banque de France', I, p. 306; II, p. 710.   [79] Ibid. II, p. 646.

city centre towards the west and newly developed and increasingly prestigious *quartiers* which offered more comfortable dwellings around the Parc Monceau and Avenue de l'Impératrice. The banker Louis Fould instructed the architect Henri Labrouste, responsible for his new mansion near the Bois de Boulogne, to 'build me a mansion appropriate to my status and tastes'. This required a monumental facade and space for receptions and to display his art collection. The private rooms were to be furnished in the Louis XIII style.[80] A mansion in the countryside was also indispensable. The machine builder J.-F. Cail purchased a house on the rue de Rivoli in Paris and 1,000 hectares of land in Anjou on which he constructed his château.[81] These moves made possible both closer integration into the social elite and, through greater spatial segregation, a distancing from the potentially revolutionary and undoubtedly disease-ridden poorer classes.

However, few successful industrialists or indeed their wives, who played such a crucial role in entertaining, initially possessed the culture and confidence necessary to mix in Parisian high society. Amongst the textile *patronat* the selection of marriage partners from within a narrow social group and geographical area nevertheless reinforced their ability to dominate local economic and political life. By the 1860s these business elites were also coming to share the taste for luxury of the older-established elements of the social elite. Previous generations had single-mindedly and often puritanically devoted themselves to business success. The inheritors adopted aristocratic *mores*, engaged in conspicuous consumption, developed polished manners, took an interest in high culture, and constructed ever more elegant residences. This *bourgeois patriciat* needed to distinguish itself from the great mass of middle-class families.

The political elite of the July Monarchy had been composed of *grands notables* – landowners, financiers, professional men, and civil servants, together with some liberal nobles. Its collective consciousness had developed both in opposition to the reactionary claims of the Restoration nobility and, increasingly, in defence of social order against 'socialism' and 'communism'. A shared sense of social superiority had matured as part of a search for the ethical foundations of the existing social order, which it was generally agreed rested on *la religion, la famille et la propriété*. In a society created and blessed by God, and by the Church, which represented His Divine presence, the authoritarian, paternalistic family provided a model for social relations, with peasants or workers taking the place of children and

---

[80] Barbier, *Finance*, pp. 250–1.   [81] Lambert-Dansette, *La vie des chefs d'entreprise*, pp. 53–4.

accepting their subordination to their God/father/master. Property was a reward for virtue and provided a patrimony, which linked the generations. This was a social vision which nobles and haut bourgeois could share. These overwhelmingly conservative ideals were largely taken for granted by their proponents and widely diffused through family socialisation, the churches, schools, and media so as to serve as 'core' beliefs for society as a whole, providing a means of identifying the interests of 'society' with those of the social elites and justifying rejection of criticism as well as repressive action against critics, on essentially moral grounds. The experience of 1848 and the Second Republic had been traumatic. Debate on the meaning of revolution and on the means of avoiding a repetition was inevitably intense.

SOCIAL POWER

Its moral basis

Although the objective of creating a society integrated around the values of dominant elites was never entirely achieved, their members nevertheless possessed multifaceted means of exercising influence. In spite of disagreements, they enjoyed a *relatively* high degree of unity as a result of intensive face-to-face interaction or at least the mutual awareness through reputation made possible by their small number. Family socialisation and formal education ensured that individuals were mostly confident of their right and duty to exercise dominant social roles. Furthermore, their possession of political power reflected the ability of a small part of the population to influence the behaviour of the vast majority and to secure the implicit consent, or at least coerced acceptance, of their subordination by most of the population, for most of the time.

Of course, self-consciousness was also defined in relation to those social groups which did not possess the attributes on which elites prided themselves – wealth, education, independence, and leisure. Wealth was perceived to be the reward for ability and hard work, for the creative role played by the landowner or entrepreneur, from which everyone benefited – 'it is he who invents, who directs, who engages in business and procures employment for workers, which they would lack if it were not for his activity, his intelligence, his reputation, and the confidence he inspires'.[82] That wealth was largely inherited could be justified in terms of the accumulative effort of the family over generations. This sense of family, of patrimony, and

[82] *Moniteur industriel*, 16 April 1848.

commitment to private property, was shared by the diverse groups which constituted the social elite. Furthermore, it provided a means of celebrating the common interests of the wealthy and the mass of small property owners, artisans, and peasants. The prospect of possessing property encouraged self-improvement and the adoption of elite values. It was seen as a vital element in the preservation of social order. This amounted to more than simple ideological 'manipulation'.

Convinced as they were of the eternal validity of the existing social system, members of the elite refused to believe that discontent was justified. The events of 1848 had nevertheless revealed the precarious state of the existing social order and the very real threat of a 'social war'.[83] In a letter to the English political economist Nassau William Senior, Alexis de Tocqueville, however, claimed that the 1848 Revolution had not been caused by misery, but resulted from the ignorance of the laws of political economy which had rendered the masses susceptible to the influence of unprincipled agitators and to 'the social power of chimerical ideas on the relative condition of the worker and of capital'.[84] The traumatic experience of social conflict had made it all the more important to deny the realities of class, even if the very act of denial itself constituted an affirmation of 'class' consciousness.

Social commentators tended to express respect for the 'deserving' poor that at least worked hard, enjoyed a respectable family life and respected their 'betters',[85] although even they were often equated with children. According to one clerical 'expert', the Abbé Mullois, 'the French worker is not really malicious . . . Left to himself, he is sensible, affectionate, on occasion admirable; his undoing is his weakness and frivolity; this is taken to excess as a result of wine, orgies and contact with degraded beings.'[86] Those who had misled the masses, the 'reds', the secret society organisers, the bar-room plotters, *déclassé* elements and embittered failures, *l'écume de la société*, together with class traitors, posed the real threat. A secondary threat was posed by urbanisation and the creation of the criminalised *classes dangereuses* revealed by the social enquiries of the 1840s. It was claimed that these, the corrupted elements amongst the poor, entirely lacked self-control and were motivated solely by greed and envy.[87]

This social fear was reinforced by everyday encounters on the streets which increased the contempt which the well-off, increasingly refined and

[83] See e.g. Alfred Motte letter to parents, 26 June 1848, quoted J. Lambert, *Le Patron* (Paris 1969), p. 83.
[84] 10 April 1848, *Oeuvres complètes*, VI (Paris 1991), p. 101.
[85] Distinction used by employers at Chalons – Prefect Saône-et-Loire, 23 June 1868, AN F12/4652.
[86] *Le Messager de la Charité* 12 March 1854, AN AD XIX 688.
[87] A. Gueslin, *Gens pauvres, pauvres gens dans la France du 19e siècle* (Paris 1998), pp. 104–7.

'sensitive', felt for the poor, as well as their determination to distance themselves from those who performed hard physical labour, dressed shabbily,
smelled disgustingly, and who, in this age of cholera, might be seen as car-
riers of disease.[88] Society had to be protected from these people through
the development of more effective forms of domination. Better policing
and particularly improved socialisation and moral instruction were necessary.[89] Church and school were to serve as 'elite dominated institutions of
socialisation and social control'.[90] Many observers claimed that already the
events of 1848 had promoted a return to religion amongst the *haute bourgeoisie*, similar to that which had inspired the nobility after 1789.[91] Religion
provided an ideological bastion. The grain merchant and miller Darblay,
whose social status can be estimated from his position as President of the
Comice agricole of the Seine-et-Oise, insisted that 'only the Christian religion ... can provide the moral foundation which will allow us to ward off a
total upheaval and save the world from the confusion which threatens it'.[92]
There were few discordant voices. *Régénération morale et religieuse* appeared
to be the only alternative to the class struggle.[93]

Religion offered both a justification for poverty – providential – and
encouraged resignation to their lot on the part of the poor. It enjoined
obedience to the representatives of the state and to social superiors. Even
where members of the political elite remained indifferent to the day-to-day
activities of the Church it was possible to share Voltaire's conviction that
un Dieu pour le peuple was essential. The problem was how to win back
the poor to religion.[94] Thus, in town and country, substantial sums were
provided by the elites and state for the construction and renovation of
churches and schools and the payment of priests and teachers. Although
notables remained ambivalent about wider literacy, it was generally assumed
that primary instruction could be used to develop religious faith and self-
discipline. It was certainly not intended to promote social mobility. Fleury,
the mayor of Rouen, in a speech at the laying of the foundation stone for
the church of Saint-Sever, for the construction of which the town council
had recently voted a subsidy of 600,000f., reminded his audience that,

[88] See e.g. A. Corbin, *Le miasme et le jonquille* (Paris 1982), p. 168.
[89] See e.g. A. Audiganne, *Revue des Deux Mondes*, Sept. 1851, p. 895.
[90] R. Aminzade, 'Class Struggles and Social Change: Toulouse, France 1830–72', PhD, Univ. of
Michigan 1978, p. 249.
[91] See e.g. J. Maurain, *La politique ecclésiastique du Second Empire de 1852 à 1869* (Paris 1930), pp. 322–3.
[92] Quoted A. Melucci, 'Idéologies et pratiques patronales pendant l'industrialisation capitaliste: le cas
de la France, 1830–1914', Doc. d'Etat, Ecole pratique des hautes études, n.d., p. 108, note 112.
[93] J.-O. Boudon, *Paris, capitale religieuse sous le Second Empire* (Paris 2001), p. 202.
[94] See Abbé Mullois, editorial in *Le Messager de la charité*, 12 March 1854, AN AB xix 688.

'at this very moment, Messieurs, we can see rising, close to each other, two edifices created with the same objective, that of the moralisation of mankind; not far from here the prison in which criminals will atone for their breaches of trust against the social order, and on this spot, the church, a pious sanctuary, existing to protect men from sin'. [95]

Paternalism and self-justification

A paternalistic approach to social relations was a vital component of elite self-identification and self-justification. *Bienfaisance* was a primary characteristic of the public man. It combined pity with a sense of responsibility. Frequently, religious faith provided inspiration. Social fear was another factor, and although the sincerity of many of those engaged in charitable giving should be stressed, the instrumental objective of social control cannot be ignored. Briefly serving as Interior Minister following the *coup*, the Comte de Morny made this clear in two circulars sent to prefects on 8 January 1852 in which he identified the criteria for selecting official electoral candidates. They were instructed to identify 'men enjoying public esteem . . . sympathetic towards the labouring classes, and who, through the beneficent use of their wealth, have acquired a well-merited reputation and influence'.[96] A voluntary act of generosity was thus both a means of gaining prestige and, in an age of manhood suffrage, a useful means of building a dependent clientele.

Officials praised the sense of responsibility displayed by paternalistic employers and longed for the spread of relationships which reinforce 'the dependence of the worker, moralise him, and release him from the passions which engender disorderly habits'.[97] There was, however, occasional dissent. The state prosecutor at Colmar described supporters of liberal opposition amongst the *hauts barons* of the Alsatian textile industry as 'reigning despotically over their workshops'. They were 'as liberal in theory as they are absolute in their industrial management'. Of the Protestant philanthropists of Mulhouse he observed that 'when one considers that the efforts of their philanthropy tend, for the most part, only to compensate for the wrongs caused by their industry, and barely diminish their immense wealth, it is permissible to adopt a certain degree of scepticism towards their self-congratulatory applause'.[98]

---

[95] Quoted Chaline, 'La bourgeoisie rouennaise', p. 963.   [96] *Moniteur universel*, 20 Jan. 1852.
[97] PG Limoges, 12 Jan. 1855, AN BB30/378.   [98] 24 April 1866, 17 April 1867, AN BB30/376.

A substantial part of the social elite and particularly their womenfolk nevertheless regularly practised the Christian virtues of Church attendance and charitable activity. They shared in an increasingly intense piety, rigorously observing their religious obligations – daily mass, regular prayer, frequent consultation of their spiritual advisors. Moreover, a pronounced sense of *noblesse oblige* had the great advantage of emphasising the subordinate situation of the recipient. Additionally, assisting the poor was a means of satisfying popular conceptions of social justice embedded in the traditional 'moral economy' which required assistance by the 'rich' in moments of personal or communal crisis. Failure to conform to such expectations would threaten the social status of the offender, putting at risk 'the consideration which so easily attaches itself to a family name and to great wealth'.[99]

Charitable activity was thus a vital element of the management of social relations. In March 1854 landowners in the Paris region were congratulated for the 'spontaneous enthusiasm with which [they] accepted the need to make sacrifices in order to assist the poor classes, substituting their beneficent influence for the shameful influence that troublemakers would otherwise inevitably have attempted to exercise by abusing the misery of the poor'.[100] Reserving assistance for the 'deserving' poor made it an effective means of ensuring compliance. Whilst congratulating himself on the superior food he provided for his agricultural labourers, the Vicomte de Sesmaisons, a landowner in the Manche, added that 'although these people are content and happy, they also realise that they face dismissal not only as a result of bad behaviour, but due to repeated minor mistakes'.[101] Notables prided themselves on the face-to-face relationships they maintained with 'their' peasants and at the same time maintained a definite air of superiority.

Typically, a special commission established by the departmental council of the Manche to consider the problem of poverty insisted that assistance to the poor was an urgent need. It firmly rejected the 'utopian' suggestions put forward by 'communists' in favour of what it described as the Christian solution. This was based on the assumption that there would always be rich and poor, and indeed that this was *Providential* in that 'it offers to men the means and merit for establishing closer relationships through the act of generosity on the one hand, and of gratitude on the other'. Charity 'is one of the duties of the rich'. It 'is not, however, something to which the poor

---

[99] PG Nancy, 3 April 1857, AN BB30/381.   [100] PG Paris, 4 March 1854, AN BB30/432.
[101] Quoted A. Guillemin, 'Le pouvoir de l'innovation. Les notables de la Manche et le développement de l'agriculture', Doc. de 3e cycle, EHESS, 1980, p. 260.

have any right'. Thus, in order to encourage close relationships between rich and poor, charity should result from private initiatives, with state intervention kept to an absolute minimum and reserved for exceptional, and temporary, circumstances. The English Poor Law was firmly rejected as a model.[102]

The landowner should be concerned to emphasise the solidarity which prevailed within the rural community. He was the *pater familias*, dispensing practical advice and defending the community's interests. Possibly occupying administrative office himself, and with a reputation for having friends in high places, he possessed the ability to win subsidies for roads and railway lines, schools and churches. Even absentee landowners might use such promises to preserve their influence. A distinction might thus be made between notables who brought their local influence to bear on the central administration and those who employed their influence from within the central government to consolidate their local influence. The château might be seen as the physical symbol of this commitment to the community. More than this, 'its buildings reinterpret the past and provide a programme for the present'.[103] Its domestic staff, luxurious furnishings, and reconstruction, so common in this period, not only added to the status of the landowning family, it ensured their residence for substantial parts of the year. During the autumn months in particular there would be opportunities for visiting villages and indulging the ideal of harmonious social relationships. In the interests of harmony it might also seem wise to avoid competing with peasants for the purchase of small plots of land, to tolerate rent arrears and avoid recourse to the law, and to favour successive generations as tenants.[104]

Speeches at agricultural shows exemplified the traditional rural notables' appreciation of their responsibilities and their totalitarian objectives. Speaking at a reception for the new prefect in April 1857 the president of the Gers Agricultural Society, M. d'Abbadie, asserted that 'we, landowners, have accepted immense obligations towards the numerous people that Providence has placed under our wings... We exercise a real mission... offering guidance, advice, and good example.' At a *fête agricole* at Mirande the following September, Henri de Rivière stressed that 'the landowners' task would be incomplete if they contented themselves with increasing the produce of the land; they are also responsible for instructing their dependents, for broadening their practical knowledge, and saving them, through sound

---

[102] Report from Commission départementale de la Manche to Commission d'assistance publique dans les campagnes 1872, AN C3081.

[103] Grandcoing, *Les demeures de la distinction*, p. 14.   [104] See e.g. Brelot, *Noblesse*, 1, pp. 290, 328f.

advice, from being carried away by fanciful ideas'.[105] These were clearly occasions on which a public demonstration of social superiority was possible, at which a department's most eminent landowners, gathered together on a platform, affirmed their leading roles as agricultural innovators and distributed prizes to faithful tenants and labourers.[106]

The Comte Albert de Saint-Léger, a substantial landowner in the Yonne, saw his labourers as 'deprived of the moral qualities which might assure their independence'. They needed support, including the right to graze their goats in Saint-Léger's woods, and to glean in his fields following the harvest. His too were the funds which paid for three *soeurs de Saint-Joseph* to instruct their children. The approval of Le Play, Polytechnic-trained engineer and traditionalist Catholic, and future imperial senator, who would come to be regarded as one of the founding fathers of sociology, is evident in his observation that 'the author of these subventions preserves . . . for the community the traditional virtues of protection and assistance. This regime imposes a burden on the proprietor for which . . . he receives no material compensation. However, he is assured of the moral rewards which are so esteemed by those of a generous nature.'[107] Sharecropping in central France and the south-west, although frequently condemned for promoting technical backwardness, attracted praise for encouraging just such face-to-face interaction. This was contrasted with the relationships based on a cash nexus, so characteristic of the factory but also increasingly of 'modern' farming. In this respect, capitalism threatened to bring social disorder and to encourage the diffusion of 'the barbaric ideas and vicious habits promoted by a sensual and sceptical civilisation'.[108] Whatever its economic failings, sharecropping remained a potent means of reinforcing social influence.

Perceptions of danger

Yet, and in spite of these efforts and expectations, frequently, just below the surface there must have existed tensions caused by competition for resources, sometimes generating real hostility between peasant communities and landowners, lasting for generations. Frequently, too, notable power was limited by strained resources or by peasant landownership which

---

[105] Quoted P. Feral, *La Société d'agriculture du Gers sous le Second Empire* (Auch 1973), p. 20.
[106] See G. Flaubert, *Madame Bovary*, ch. 8.
[107] Quoted M. Vigreux, *Paysans et notables du Morvan au 19e siècle* (Château-Chinon 1987), p. 414.
[108] Comice agricole de Laval 1870 quoted Denis, 'Reconquête ou défensive' in S. Köpeczi and E. Balász (eds.), *Noblesse française. Noblesse hongroise* (Budapest 1981), p. 132.

underpinned a degree of independence. In impoverished parts of the Limousin, which had proved unattractive to either noble or urban bourgeois investment, the result was a virtual absence of notable patronage and influence.[109] More generally, the landowners who responded to the 1866 Agricultural Enquiry were almost unanimous in expressing concern about growing migration from the land, rising agricultural wages and the changing quality of social relationships in the countryside.[110]

In this case, there is clearly a need to allow for a considerable amount of exaggeration. Nevertheless, population statistics which reveal that 2,123,000 people left rural areas between 1851 and 1871,[111] together with an increase of some 30 to 40 per cent in agricultural labourers' wages, combine to suggest the end of an era in the countryside in which 'overpopulation' had placed those with control over scarce resources in a position of considerable strength. As the incomes of peasant farmers and labourers rose they became less dependent on landowners and were better able to purchase small farms in the active land market created by the transfer of landlord capital into more lucrative investments.[112] The increase in the number of peasant-proprietors, together with migration, ensured that there were fewer potential tenants and labourers competing for land and work. It was becoming easier for the rural poor to resist, or through migration to escape from, relationships of dependence. Rising absenteeism further reduced landlord influence.[113]

Complaints about absenteeism had long been common, particularly from the Paris region where large tenants replaced their landlords as the group with the most influence. Two-thirds of landowners in the fertile grain-producing plains of the Beauce were estimated to spend little time on their estates.[114] As a result, 'living far from their estates, having relationships with their tenants only through intermediaries, most of the large landowners see their estates simply as a source of income, and a place of occasional residence.'[115] Furthermore, the development of commercial farming practices, designed to increase their incomes, ran contrary to the landlords' other traditional objective of closely controlling social relationships.

[109] A. Corbin, *Archaïsme et modernité en Limousin au 19e siècle* (Paris 1975), I, p. 261.
[110] R. Price, 'The onset of labour shortage in French agriculture in the 19th century', *Economic History Review* 1975, *passim*.
[111] F. Caron, *An Economic History of Modern France* (London 1979), p. 112.
[112] See e.g. PG Nancy, 2 Feb. 1856, AN BB30/381.
[113] See e.g. G. Désert, 'St-Pierre-sur-Dives et le pays d'Auge, 1813–1910' in M. Lévy-Leboyer (ed.), *Le revenu agricole et la rente foncière en Basse-Normandie. Etude de croissance régionale* (Paris 1972), p. 89.
[114] Farcy, *Paysans*, I, pp. 269–70.
[115] 1866 Enquête quoted J.-C. Farcy, 'Agriculture et société rurale en Beauce pendant la première moitié du 19e siècle', Doc. de 3e cycle, Univ. de Paris X, n.d., p. 156.

These changes were rapid in some areas, gradual in others, particularly in the west and uplands. In the single department of the Nord, notables retained substantial influence in the northern areas where they owned considerable amounts of land and shared in an intense religious life, but much less in southern parts where peasant landownership was more substantial and their competition for land with both secular and religious landlords centuries old. Nevertheless, the expression of discontent generally remained timid.[116] In the southern department of Hérault, as landlords moved into Béziers and Montpellier and rising wine prices increased their economic independence, the younger generation of peasant farmers felt able to abandon the Legitimist politics of their forefathers.[117] Even in the west the triumphant popular reception given to the imperial couple as they toured Brittany in 1857 aroused considerable concern amongst the overwhelmingly Legitimist rural elites.[118] The widespread rumour in 1856 that the nobility and clergy were cornering food supplies as part of a plot to destabilise the regime was a sign of the times.[119] Bonapartism, and a regime which increasingly claimed credit for prosperity, was a potentially unsettling factor in social relationships. Writing to his friend Alexis de Tocqueville in January 1858, Gustave de Beaumont was alarmed that 'this despotism only wounds the sensibilities of the enlightened classes, whilst it gratifies the passions of the masses'. Certainly, they could take peasant support for granted no longer.[120]

In these circumstances, if not demoralised, rural elites were certainly alarmed by what they perceived to be the sudden rejection by *their* peasants of relationships of dependence into which it had been assumed the poor had entered freely. A respondent to the 1870 Enquiry from the Deux-Sèvres complained, with an air of astonishment, that 'the rural worker has come to regard himself as the equal of other men'.[121] Even more anguished were the tones of a letter from a member of the prestigious Société des agriculteurs de France residing in the Isère and according to whom

the rural worker has become grumpy, insolent, sour, envious; he distrusts his employer and rarely asks for advice, being, on the contrary, disposed to listen to and follow the bad advice of those who buy him a drink in the *cabaret*. Universal suffrage, politics and socialism, which little by little penetrates everywhere, are

[116] B. Ménager, 'La vie politique dans le département du Nord de 1851 à 1877', Doc. d'Etat, Univ. de Paris IV 1979, III, p. 1250.
[117] G. Cholvy, *Religion et société au 19e siècle. Le diocèse de Montpellier* (Lille 1973), II, p. 1033.
[118] See e.g. PG Rennes, 12 Oct. 1858, AN BB30/386.   [119] PG Angers, 8 Jan. 1854, AN BB30/371.
[120] Quoted A. Jardin, *Histoire du libéralisme politique* (Paris 1985), p. 394.
[121] Chambre consultative d'agriculture canton St-Mairent (Deux-Sèvres), AN C1160.

the cause of these changes. One finds only jealousy, an obsession with status and becoming something in the community. More than ever this is a struggle of *ignorance* against *learning*, of *la veste contre l'habit*, and all this resulting from the illusion of instruction which has given birth to a class of *déclassés*.[122]

Their fears might have been grossly exaggerated, but certainly many representatives of the rural elite believed that their world was threatened by the various manifestations of modernity – education, manhood suffrage, urbanisation, and the growing ambitions of the lower classes. On rare occasions landlords might seem willing to accept a portion of the blame for this deteriorating situation. In a study of Breton agriculture, published in 1867, R. de la Pervanchère criticised 'the indifference with which most landowners abandon rural concerns for the distractions of the town'.[123] More generally, however, there was a tendency to blame peasant 'greed' and 'immorality' for the deterioration in relationships. A gross materialism, which was associated with alcoholism, the growing taste for 'luxuries' and insubordination, appeared to be threatening hallowed Christian principles. Invariably landlords blamed the corrupting influence of the towns for this growing 'demoralisation' of the rural population.

Urban-industrial relationships

It seemed self-evident that it would be even more difficult for notables to exercise influence in large cities with their mobile populations. Moreover, in a pastoral letter in November 1868, Mgr le Courtier, Bishop of Montpellier, recognised that rising wages meant that workers were less dependent on upper-class charity and were developing a new sense of pride and dignity.[124] There was still hope, however, that paternalistic links of dependence might be re-created. The ideal was to establish in an urban setting the close social links, which, in spite of growing difficulties, it was still believed characterised the countryside. J. A. de Lerue expressed the widely held belief that, in spite of misgivings concerning 'indiscriminate' giving which served to encourage idleness,

philanthropic acts, even when incomplete or unproductive, retain their moral value . . . They accustom men to the practice of good, revive noble sentiments in their hearts, and successfully combat the bad instincts, in bringing together individuals who would otherwise be isolated by birth, wealth and education. They

[122] AN C1156.
[123] *L'agriculture en Bretagne* (1867), pp. 68–9, quoted M. Launay, *Le diocèse de Nantes sous le Second Empire* (Nantes 1983), II, p. 838.
[124] Cholvy, *Diocèse de Montpellier*, II, pp. 1326–7.

impose on the most passionate soul that romantic poetry, born of religion and grief, which is so full of charm for elevated spirits.[125]

Furthermore, charitable giving was preferable to holding the working class down by force.[126]

Writing in the *Journal des Economistes*, A. E. Cherbuliez insisted that charity

must, in order to be in harmony both with the religious principles which inspire it, and with those of economic science, endeavour to restore the morality of those living in misery, and to combat the discouragement, lack of foresight, and the vicious inclinations which might otherwise develop, by applying to such good works the direct and personal influence of one man on another.[127]

Thus, he succeeded in marrying liberal economic theory to Christian faith. Public assistance – along the lines of the National Workshops of 1848 – which liberals claimed had, in authoritarian fashion, attempted to re-distribute wealth, was an offence against the universal truths of economic science and a first step down the road to socialism. It would do nothing to solve the causes of poverty. On the contrary by interfering with market mechanisms it would inevitably increase unemployment and misery.[128] These were the views expressed by Adolphe Thiers in an influential report to the National Assembly in 1850.[129]

However, the exercise of urban patronage depended on the commitment of substantial financial resources as well as the continued willingness of potential recipients of assistance to accept their subordinate status. This was easier to achieve in medium-sized towns with traditions of popular Legitimism such as Avignon, Nîmes, or Toulouse where, in 1858, around 2,000 workers were organised in the Saint François Xavier friendly society,[130] than in Paris, Lyon, or Marseille where rapid population growth had overwhelmed the available resources, leaving most of the population outside lay and clerical patronage networks. Already, revolution had made a substantial contribution to the weakening of traditional social hierarchy. Now industrialisation was creating a society which was far more difficult to control.

---

[125] *De la bienfaisance publique et privée dans le département de la Seine-Inférieure* (Rouen 1852), p. XI, quoted Y. Marec, *Pauvres et philanthropes à Rouen au 19e siècle* (Rouen 1981), p. 39.
[126] E.g. PG Limoges, 12 Jan. 1855, AN BB30/378.   [127] Vol. 28, 1851, p. 217.
[128] See also Y. Charbit, *Du Malthusianisme au populationnisme. Les économistes français et la population, 1840–70* (Paris 1981), p. 67.
[129] *Discours parlementaires de M. Thiers*, vol. VIII (Paris 1880), p. 449.
[130] Aminzade, 'Class Struggles', p. 218.

In general, employers rejected any blame for the existence of poverty. It was simply assumed that the market set wage levels,[131] and that it was the responsibility of the worker himself, through hard work, thrift, and self-improvement to better his family's situation.[132] Failure was due to laziness and moral and intellectual inferiority. The sheer improvidence of the poor was only too evident from the size of their families.[133] At least poverty provided a useful and necessary sanction without which there would be little incentive to labour. As the economist Charles Dunoyer pointed out, 'in the best of social organisations, misery as well as inequality are to a certain degree, inevitable . . . It is good that there are these inferior places in society into which those families which behave badly are likely to fall, and from which they will be able to raise themselves only by dint of good behaviour; destitution is this fearful Hell!'[134]

The growing industrial *patronat* adopted extremely authoritarian attitudes towards its labour force. Employers expected passive obedience and firmly rejected any challenge to their own authority or that of the managers or foremen who were their representatives. The unrestricted right to hire and fire and reduce wages at will was highly prized. Officials, perhaps unsympathetic towards business values, frequently insisted that most employers were exclusively concerned with profit and, because they could rely on the state to repress strikes, adopted a severe attitude towards their workers.[135] Certainly, discipline in the workplace was usually harsh. Factory regulations sought to impose new behavioural norms and to limit poor time-keeping, absenteeism, negligence, and insubordination. This was especially the case in 'modern' large-scale enterprises, where workers were required to keep pace with the movements of machinery, or work as a member of an *équipe*. Fines or the threat of instant dismissal were the norm. The frequent use of military language in the literature on labour relations is further evidence of a determination to impose order. The message was clearly voiced by A. Gratiot, an employer at Essonnes near Paris, in a school prize-giving speech: 'In the workshop I am your chief, you are my soldiers. I command, you must obey me.'[136]

Nevertheless, many employers drew inspiration from traditional Christian teaching, which assumed that the 'master' had paternal responsibilities

---

[131] See e.g. Kolb-Bernard, report to Lille Chamber of Commerce, 22 Sept. 1848, quoted P. Pierrard, *La vie ouvrière à Lille sous le Second Empire* (Paris 1965), p. 188.

[132] 'Du développement du travail par les machines', *Moniteur industriel*, 18 May 1856.

[133] L. Reybaud in *Revue des Deux Mondes*, April 1846, p. 54.

[134] C. Dunoyer, *De la liberté du travail* (Paris 1845) quoted Tudesq, *Notables*, p. 569.

[135] See e.g. PG Rouen, 5 July 1853, AN BB30/387.   [136] Quoted Melucci, *Idéologies*, p. 192, note 46.

towards his labour force. In a typically condescending speech, in 1865, Albert de Broglie a director of the Saint Gobain glassworks insisted on the shared interests of 'master' and 'man', describing the enterprise as

a large family, which includes the shareholders, the directors, the management, the foremen, and the workers, and unites them in the same feelings of affection . . . In a family, the youngest and weakest is always the one who is preferred; the youngest and weakest . . . , those who suffer, those who struggle against destitution, the orphans . . . the aged . . . , the infirm, the sick. And our workers!

He expected respect and obedience.[137]

In some large textile mills, in the coalfields of the north, in modern ironworks, as well as in state arsenals and on the railways, discipline was reinforced by a range of paternalistic measures. The mining-metallurgical complex at Le Creusot and the Compagnie des mines de la Loire around Saint-Etienne, together with the Japy watch manufactury at Beaucourt and the Seydoux textile mill at Le Cateau, probably offered the most developed examples, providing compensation in case of injury, free medical assistance, subsidised housing, provision of wood or coal for domestic heating, allotments in which to cultivate the household's vegetables, education and professional training for the young, and eventually pensions for the worker (at 55/60 after 25/30 years service), and sometimes for widows and dependants.[138]

At Marquette, in the suburbs of Lille, Scribe frères constructed 'salubrious' housing for their 350 employees and even provided a bar, open between 5 and 10 p.m. and instruments for the works band. Gardens were another means of diverting workers from excessive drinking.[139] At La Ciotat near Marseille the Messageries impériales created a *cité ouvrière* for around 800 people in 1858 offering a kitchen and three rooms for a low annual rent of 60f.[140] By 1867 the Protestant entrepreneurs Dollfuss and Koechlin in Mulhouse had constructed 800 model homes for 6,000 people.[141] It was expected that tenants would live an ordered 'moral' life. The construction of somewhat larger houses for foremen and engineers

---

[137] *Discours prononcé à St Gobain le 22 oct. 1865* (Paris 1865).

[138] M. Hanagan, *Nascent Proletarians. Class Formation in Post-revolutionary France* (Oxford 1989), pp. 116–17; B. Martin, *La fin des mauvais pauvres. De l'assistance à l'assurance* (Seyssel 1983), pp. 38–9; S. Vaillant-Gabet, 'La gestion de la main-d'oeuvre chez les Seydoux au Cateau-Cambrésis (1830–1914)', *Revue du Nord* 2002, pp. 731–42.

[139] L. Murard and P. Zylberman, *Le petit travailleur infatigable ou le prolétaire régénéré. Villes-usines, habitat et intimités au 19e siècle* (Fontenay-sous-Bois 1976), p. 114.

[140] L. Gaillard, 'Le logement et les cités ouvrières dans la région marseillaise sous le Second Empire', *Actes du 90e CNSS Nice 1965*, III (Paris 1966), p. 353.

[141] PG Colmar, 5 April 1859, AN BB30/376.

provided constant visual evidence of subordination, even as the *patronat* itself moved away from houses close to their premises in search of more salubrious settings.[142]

The provision of model accommodation certainly met with official approval and was encouraged by subsidies, such as the 10 million francs provided by decree in March 1852 for the improvement of housing in manufacturing towns.[143] Cheap loans provided by employers for house purchase reflected the belief that ownership of property, together with family commitments, were strong 'moralising' forces. Subject to fewer restraints, bachelors were always regarded with suspicion.[144] The truck system was another means of ensuring that indebtedness to the employer was a powerful restraint on the worker's independence. The company shop also offered opportunities for simple financial exploitation, particularly in the more isolated textile villages in the Vosges or Flanders and mining communities along the edge of the Massif Central.[145]

At its most extreme, paternalism created the silk factories of the southeast where young girls – an estimated 40,000 – worked for several years on the basis of contracts signed by their parents, in workshops decorated with images of the Virgin Mary, lodged in factory dormitories, and were supervised, at work and leisure, by nuns.[146] Mgr Plantier, Bishop of Nîmes, expressed the Church's appreciation of 'companies inspired ... by a genuine Christian spirit ... From the moment when they lay the foundations ... of a factory, they build at the same time a church, they call for a priest, they establish schools entrusted to the religious congregations ... God was the sovereign master of the entire project.'[147] Parish priests could be expected to reinforce the employer's authority. In some communities only those they recommended would be able to obtain work.[148]

Mutual aid societies might also be established, funded by employer and worker contributions (perhaps 2 per cent of earnings) and sometimes the income from fines. These societies were central features in developing systems of authoritarian control even if, in some cases, selected workers

[142] E.g. Ministre de l'Intérieur to Ministre de l'agriculture, du commerce et des travaux publics, 16 July 1853, AN 12/2370-4 re cotton manufacturers of Bar-le-Duc.

[143] L. Gaillard, 'Le logement', p. 350.

[144] E.g. Murard and Zylberman, *Le petit travailleur*, pp. 24, 203.

[145] M. Perrot, *Les ouvriers en grève. France 1871–90* (Paris 1974), I, pp. 281–2; H. Carel, 'Le département de la Haute-Saône de 1850 à 1914', Doc. ès Lettres, Univ. de Paris-Sorbonne, 1970, pp. 264–5.

[146] V. Turgan, *Les grandes usines*, VII (Paris 1867), p. 220, provides a description of the most famous of these *manufactures-internats* at Jujurieux.

[147] Quoted R. Huard, 'La préhistoire des partis. Le parti républicain et l'opinion républicaine dans le Gard de 1848 à 1888', Doc. d'Etat, Univ. de Paris IV 1977, p. 722.

[148] E.g. J.-P. Burdy, *Le soleil noir. Un quartier de St-Etienne, 1840–1940* (Lyon 1989), pp. 146–7.

were given access to their accounts and involved in the administration.[149] Altruism combined with economic calculation. These inducements offered means of solving labour shortages and retaining skilled workers, and of encouraging self-discipline. The employer's behaviour was frequently informed by a sense of Christian responsibility, which conveniently mixed traditional conceptions of social hierarchy with 'modern' concepts of labour relations. Social Catholics, like the engineer Frédéric Le Play, appointed to the Conseil d'Etat in 1855 and the imperial senate in 1867, advocated what was almost a form of semi-feudalism.[150]

The pride taken in his reputation as a 'just and benevolent' employer by the Legitimist Benoist d'Azy, proprietor of forges at Alais, Anzin, and Fourchambault, might be seen as concealing a form of assertive self-interestedness.[151] Whilst it was accepted widely that charitable assistance ought to be provided to workers during crises, this represented nothing more than a gracious concession to workers by their *patron*. It was not theirs by right. The Marquis de Vogüe in a letter to his wife during the 1854 subsistence crisis, wrote that the provision of cheap bread for his glass-workers 'conserves to my gift the characteristics of charity and liberty which the increase, pure and simple, of wages would not'.[152] The railway companies were similarly willing to subsidise bread prices and offer a temporary *indemnité de charité*, because such measures had the advantage of being far easier to reverse than wage increases.[153] As the former Interior Minister Léon Faucher recognised, they were a sign that 'our chiefs of industry understand, like the English aristocracy, that it is essential to anticipate the threat from socialism'.[154]

In some of the mushrooming new industrial centres, the absence of a large and influential middle class made moralising intervention by the entrepreneur all the more urgent.[155] As the scale of the enterprise grew, the idealised face-to-face relationship between 'master' and 'man' was replaced by more authoritarian relationships, with managers and foremen serving as intermediaries. A. P. Deseilligny, Schneider's son-in-law, nevertheless optimistically concluded, after rehearsing the social dangers posed by the new industrial agglomerations, that 'modern industry . . . carries with it the moral remedy, in the institutions of patronage and providence it has

---

[149] See e.g. Société de secours contre la maladie entre les ouvriers de l'étab. François Keittinger et fils, described in Marec, *Pauvres et philanthropes*, p. 41.

[150] E.g. J.-P. Burdy, 'Paternalismes industriels. Les rapports sociaux dans le bassin de la Loire au 19e siècle' in S. Michaud (ed.), *L'Edification. Morales et cultures au 19e siècle* (Paris 1993), pp. 35–6.

[151] Kale, *Legitimism*, p. 187. [152] Quoted Melucci, *Idéologies*, p. 76.

[153] PG Colmar, 21 July 1870, AN BB30/390. [154] *Revue des Deux Mondes*, Feb. 1860, p. 951.

[155] P. Leroy-Beaulieu, 'La question ouvrière', ibid. March 1870, p. 100.

developed and by its efforts in favour of education'.[156] Instruction improved the quality of the labour force and provided specific technical skills. Above all, though, industrialists viewed it as the primary means of socialisation, of moralisation, and of subordination in a mass society.[157]

Workers should also be subject to the decisions taken by such employer-dominated local organisations as municipal councils and the charitable bureaux de bienfaisance, as well as by voluntary associations like the Société de Saint Vincent de Paul through which the clergy and local notables selectively distributed public and private assistance.[158] Emile Cheysson, another director of the Le Creusot company, described a system in which 'assistance is given in the light of information provided by workers' delegates, acting in groups of three, in each of the six *quartiers* of the commune. Information is also provided on the past history and the moral standards, as well as the level of misery of the applicants.'[159] Workers were thus themselves recruited for the purpose of social control, identifying the 'deserving' poor in compliance with the behavioural norms established by their employers and clergy. Moreover, in return for the provision of work and assistance, the ironmaster and deputy Eugène Schneider assumed that he had the right to offer political guidance to his workers. Dissent was blamed on a small minority of 'bad' workers, usually outsiders, who had led astray the otherwise fundamentally 'good' workers. The employer's duty was to protect the 'good' by means of the selective dismissal of 'troublemakers', in this case those who had challenged his authority by voting against his interests.[160] The management at the Le Creusot ironworks was so determined to maintain its own forms of *discipline paternelle* that it was even accused of excluding the state's police and justice from the community it dominated.[161] The state prosecutor at Douai similarly complained that in the mining centres of the north even 'the subordinate agents of justice are at the discretion of company directors'.[162] Generally, however, the authorities were anxious to accommodate employer interests.

Charitable giving helped to justify wealth and inequality and, hopefully, to safeguard social order. As the director of the Rouen Société maternelle wrote in 1854, it helped 'to establish between rich and poor those moral

---

[156] J.-P. Deseilligny, *L'influence de l'éducation sur la moralité et le bien-être des classes laborieuses* (Paris 1868).

[157] See e.g. C. Robert, *La suppression des grèves par l'association aux bénéfices* (Paris 1870), p. 120.

[158] E.g. Prefect Moselle, 20 Aug. 1853, AN F8/210.

[159] E. Cheysson, *Le Creusot, conditions matérielles, intellectuelles et morales de la population, institutions et relations sociales* (Paris 1869).

[160] Offerlé, 'Les Schneider,' pp. 295–6.   [161] PG Dijon, 7 March 1858, AN BB30/420.

[162] AN BB30/377.

bonds which will prevent the latter from giving themselves up . . . to despair and especially to those evil instincts which give rise to envy, and in consequence lead them to consider the prosperity of those most favoured by fortune as a benefit for themselves'.[163] The benevolence of the *maître* would assure him the respect of *ses gens*. Charity, freely given, thus remained fundamental to perceptions of social relationships, and those employers who failed to live up to these ideals – including the textile entrepreneurs of Roubaix in the north and of Lodève and Bédarieux in southern France – were likely to be criticised severely, especially by the Legitimist and clerical proponents of an organic Christian society.[164]

However, only a minority of large, highly capitalised enterprises could afford to engage in a fully fledged industrial paternalism. Increasingly too, competitive pressures ensured that businessmen were more frugal with their resources. Instead of developing a strategy at the level of the enterprise they might join other well-off urban residents in distributing assistance within the community, as members of the committee of the local bureaux de bienfaisance, which in some one-third of communes distributed the aid provided by private charity and state subsidy, or else the *conférence* of the Société de Saint Vincent de Paul. Their wives, *dames de charité*, visited the sick and the infirm, and other 'deserving' poor, particularly families with small children, and distributed clothing, food, and fuel. The lists of subscribers to various charities publicised their generosity.[165]

Increasingly, too, local elites had supported government efforts to estab-lish and supervise the network of primary schools. This was not without a certain ambivalence. The Lille textile patron Auguste Mimerel observed that 'sedition has almost always been fomented by the better paid. They are motivated much less by misery than by economic ideas and proposals for social reform which they would have been much happier to have known nothing about.' He added hastily: 'not that we want to impose limits on the instruction of the people, but we would prefer whatever restores to the individual a sense of contentment with his position in society and encour-ages him to improve it by means of orderliness and work, rather than ideas which lead him to ruin himself in pointless complaints and in unrealistic projects'.[166] Thus, it was generally accepted that teaching should be heavily impregnated with a religious, moralising message designed to encourage

[163] Quoted Charbit, *Du Malthusianisme*, p. 111.
[164] See e.g. Ménager, 'Vie politique', III, pp. 1224–5; Cholvy, *Diocèse de Montpellier*, II, p. 819.
[165] See e.g. sous-préfet Béziers, Nov. 1854, AN F1 CIII Hérault 15; H. Maneglier, *Paris impérial. La vie quotidienne sous le Second Empire* (Paris 1990), pp. 60–1.
[166] *Du paupérisme dans ses rapports avec l'industrie* (Lille n.d. 1850s?), pp. 11–12.

the poor to accept the place in society which God had ordained for them, and to obey their social superiors. Instruction would serve as a powerful tool of socialisation, conditioning the ways in which the masses received and used information.

CONCLUSION

After 1848, the social discourse of the upper classes was informed increasingly by fear of revolution and the construction of a counter-revolutionary culture. Further industrialisation and the concentration of more and more impoverished people in the cities – the barbarians within the gates – intensified social fear. There were, it appears, two very different perceptions of the development of social relationships. The first essentially traditional and 'ruralist', the second reflecting a commitment to economic and social modernisation. For adherents of the former the rural population offered a base upon which social order might be restored. 'The countryman is not the rioter. Greatest in number, he is also in terms of morality.'[167] Ruralists perceived a threat to traditional values from urbanisation and closer contacts between town and country. Jules Brame, deputy for the Nord, condemned conscription and urban reconstruction for dragging peasants from their villages.[168] There was an urgent need to preserve the rural population from 'the barbaric doctrines and vicious habits produced by a sensual and sceptical civilisation',[169] and above all, from the influence of Paris, the centre of disorder and revolution, the supreme symbol of the urban menace.

This attack on industrialisation and urbanisation and on economic liberalism was based on an idealised and essentially paternalistic conception of social relationships. Certainly the rural elites had a high opinion of their own mission. There were, however, few signs of the emergence of a coherent understanding of social change. Landowners singularly failed to recognise that by seeking to increase their own revenues and investing spare cash in stocks and shares they were contributing to the processes of social change they condemned so vigorously.

The modernisers, represented by such journals as the *Moniteur industriel* and *Journal des Economistes*, adopted a more optimistic perspective. Agreeing with some of the regime's leading apologists they insisted on

---

[167] Speech by President, Société d'agriculture du Gers, at *fête agricole* de Lectoure Aug. 1856 quoted Feral, *La société d'agriculture*, p. 18.

[168] *De l'émigration des campagnes* (Lille 1859), pp. 80–1, 100–1.

[169] Comice agricole de Laval, *Compte-Rendu des séances des 18–21 mai 1870* quoted M. Denis, 'Les royalistes de la Mayenne et le monde moderne', Doc. d'Etat, Univ. de Paris-Sorbonne, pp. 632–3.

the pressing need to develop communications and encourage the mechanisation of industry. Social order was conceived as both a precondition
for growth and a consequence of greater prosperity. Together with education, prosperity offered a solution to the problems caused by poverty
and ignorance.[170] This perspective also influenced the debate on free trade.
Michel Chevalier was convinced that tariff protection, by restraining economic growth, threatened social order.[171] The journalist Henri Baudrillart
observed that 'the improvement in living standards is the body snatched
from misery, the soul rescued from crime and vice; for the State it represents the assurance offered by a more advanced civilization, a greater
degree of security, more active charity, a generalised sense of responsibility,
a greater degree of equality'.[172] J.-J. Rapet took up the same theme. With
improved housing the worker 'will spend more time with his family, concern himself more with his children, bring them up with greater care, and
prepare for the future a more moral generation, better able itself to practise the virtues of family life which provides the basis for the well-being of
States'.[173]

The moderate republican Jules Simon agreed with clericals and notables of every political persuasion that the fundamental reason for misery
and disorder was the absence of a 'decent' family life – on the bourgeois
model – and that its restoration was the essential means of securing discipline in the factory and throughout society. Considerable emphasis was also
increasingly placed on the responsibilities of the wife and mother, caring
for her children, and providing comfort for her husband which would
counter the corrupting attractions of the bar.[174] This of course ignored
both the absolute need for many working-class women to find employment as well as the employer's own desire for docile and cheap labour.
In this modernising perspective migration from the countryside was seen
to be the means of easing population pressure on the land and providing a much-needed labour force for industrialisation. In marked contrast
with the ruralist approach, the industrialist A.-P. Deseilligny condemned
conditions in the countryside as 'coarse and brutal'.[175]

Ruralists and modernisers could agree at least on the validity of the principle of individual responsibility. Thus liberals assumed that as a result of

---

[170] See e.g. M. Chevalier, *Journal des Economistes* 22, 1849, p. 354.
[171] *Examen du système commercial connu sous le nom de régime protecteur* (Paris 1852), p. 93.
[172] 'Du progrès économique, ses conditions, son état présent', *Journal des Economistes* 20, 1848, p. 374.
[173] 'Du bien-être pour les classes laborieuses', *Journal des Economistes* 28, 1851, p. 372.
[174] 'Du travail des filles dans les manufactures', *Moniteur industriel*, 13 Sept. 1857.
[175] Deseilligny, *De l'influence de l'éducation*, p. 177.

the abolition of 'feudal' privilege in 1789, equality of opportunity already existed. It was entirely possible for the able and energetic to accumulate wealth and gain social status. According to Michel Chevalier, 'the equality of rights and the unity of the laws are the common conquest of the Third Estate, bourgeoisie and workers. There are no new principles worth seriously considering.'[176] However, the optimism of the modernisers was frequently tinged with anxiety. Thus the influential journalist Lavollée would react with horror to the language employed in the report of the worker delegates sent by the government to the 1862 London Exposition: 'They've raised the question of the tyranny of capitalism, of the scourge of competition, the greed of the employers, the exploitation of man by man. They've taken us back to 1848, with all its ideas and slogans.'[177] The strike waves of the 1860s, a sign of the deteriorating social climate, reinforced these concerns.[178]

Chevalier himself pointed out in the report of the international jury on the 1867 Paris Exposition that 'it is manifest that the working populations are no longer content with their situation . . . It would be irresponsible not to take this into account . . . They are convinced that capitalism is their implacable enemy.'[179] Alarmed by the well-organised character of the strikes, the editor of the *Moniteur industriel* (7 April 1867) saw them as evidence of a vast conspiracy. Election results also appeared to suggest that there were substantial numbers of people who remained dissatisfied with their material conditions, social status, and share in political power and who might be prepared to support a renewed effort to 'complete' the Revolution. The gendarmerie commander in the Department of Seine-et-Marne warned in April 1870 that 'the social question thrusts itself forward. The different classes of society are equal before the law, but they have never been so divided; war is forever declared between those who have and those who have not.'[180]

Established social relationships were being challenged due to the impact of industrialisation, urbanisation, the commercialisation of farming, migration from the countryside, and politicisation. Responding to these changes represented a major challenge for elites. The threat to social order had to be contained. Thus the economically and socially dominant groups made

---

[176] *Revue des Deux Mondes*, April 1850, p. 137; see also J. Sempé, *Grèves et grévistes* (1870), p. 60 – one of the numerous pamphlets making this point.
[177] *Revue des Deux Mondes* 1864, p. 864.
[178] See e.g. P. Leroy-Beaulieu, 'Les coalitions ouvrières en France', *Moniteur industriel*, 14 May 1865.
[179] *Exposition universelle de 1867 à Paris. Rapports du Jury international*, 1 (1868), p. cdliv.
[180] Monthly report in AHG G8/176.

more deliberate efforts to impose their own values, beliefs, and perceptions of the world. As fear of revolution increased in the late 1860s, most members of the social elite would again subordinate their particular interests to the perceived need to re-impose social order. Although they might disagree about politics and engage in often bitter debate over social policy and particularly the role of the Church, they were united in their determination to defend their own privileged position. Sharing a 'coherent repertoire of justificatory ideologies',[181] elites were able to call for support from the State when their vital interests appeared to be under threat, and support the brutal employment of armed force to crush dissent. Whatever the political complexion of the State it exercised a preservative role, affording protection against the demands of the poorer classes. This fundamental unity needs to be borne in mind when considering the range of political options favoured by the wealthy. That such varied options existed also, however, revealed potentially dangerous fissures.

[181] Newby, Bell, Rose, and Saunders, *Property, paternalism*, p. 344.

CHAPTER 2

Coming to terms with 'democracy'

THE CHALLENGE

The granting of voting rights to all adult males in 1848 and the subsequent *descente de la politique vers les masses* (Agulhon) aroused great alarm. It appeared to threaten to replace elite dominance with that of 'passionate, ignorant and unstable majorities'.[1] It was still assumed widely within the social elite that only a small minority possessed the ability and knowledge necessary to take important political decisions. Thus, according to the Breton Legitimist Henri de la Broise: 'Every citizen is equal, but it does not follow from this that every opinion has the same value. We cannot accept that the vote of an honest labourer might have the same authority as that of M. Thiers.'[2] Indeed, writing to the liberal politician, his close friend the historian Mignet warned that manhood suffrage would serve 'in turn and at rapid intervals, [as] an instrument of anarchy and an instrument of servitude'.[3] A senior education official, sharing his concern, admitted that 'universal suffrage frightens me, as it frightens every honest man. It carries in itself the seeds of catastrophe, of a social revolution which will break out one day if we persist with it . . . No one should ignore the dangerous instincts and the burning passions of the lower classes.'[4]

THE EXERCISE OF INFLUENCE

In practice, however, democracy did not have the disastrous consequences so many notables had anticipated. Election results during the Second Republic had been better than anticipated. For one thing, candidates were

---

[1] A. Bailleux de Marisy in *Revue des Deux Mondes* 1867, quoted Daumard, *Les bourgeois et la bourgeoisie en France* (Paris 1981), p. 131.
[2] *Le vrai et le faux libéralisme* (1866), quoted M. Denis, 'Reconquête ou défensive', in Köpeczi and Balász, *Noblesse française. Noblesse hongroise*, p. 135.
[3] 7 March 1852, BN naf 20618.   [4] Academic rector Aix, report on Aug. 1858, AN F17/2649.

overwhelmingly drawn from the ranks of notables possessing what were assumed to be the necessary cultural qualifications and influence. The vast majority of citizens were excluded, or excluded themselves.[5] In many areas democracy appeared to reinforce the influence of local elites who were able to exert considerable direct influence on the electorate through the exercise of their roles as bureaucrats, landowners, businessmen, and practitioners of the liberal professions or as dispensers of charitable assistance. Supported by the clergy, landowners were particularly well placed to make use of traditional networks of influence. Local social power and the creation of a 'system of dependence'[6] was closely linked to the national power exercised through wider social networks and the contacts developed through political and administrative activity.

Analysis of the political exercise of social authority needs to bear in mind that 'most power interactions occur in complex situations'.[7] To a substantial degree efforts by members of the social elite to secure control were unplanned and uncoordinated and depended on the more or less willing cooperation of subordinate groups. There was a widespread belief that landlords and employers were the natural representatives of their fellow citizens.[8] Judging whether peasants or workers had genuinely internalised respect for their 'betters' or were simply making the best of inherently unequal situations is, however, extremely difficult. They might resent their subordination bitterly. 'Subordinate' groups were able to reinterpret ideas and to resist, or at least displace, efforts to control their behaviour and in this sense a process of 'dynamic interaction between elite and mass political cultures' was constantly under way.[9] There must often have been a marked contrast between public appearance and private attitudes – on both sides of the divide. Rich and poor doubtless developed stereotypes of each other based upon a mixture of myth and personal experience. Insubordination, malicious gossip, and even anonymous destruction of property were probably common, but only occasionally revealed to the historian.[10] Nevertheless, normally the poor assumed that they had little choice but to behave in a manner which would not cause offence to those who controlled their access

[5] See also B. Lacroix, 'Retour sur 1848', *Actes de la recherche en sciences sociales*, 140, 2001, p. 45.

[6] E. Phélippeau, *L'invention de l'homme politique moderne. Mackau, l'Orne et la République* (Paris 2002), p. 79.

[7] Knoke, *Political networks*, p. 12.

[8] See e.g. P. Hamman, 'La notabilité dans tous ses états? Alexandre de Geiger à Sarreguemines, un patron en politique sous le Second Empire', *Revue Historique* 2002, p. 320.

[9] L. Diamond, *Political Culture and Democracy in Developing Countries* (London 1994), p. 151.

[10] See e.g. F. Ploux, *Guerres paysannes en Quercy. Violences, conciliations et répression pénale dans les campagnes du Lot (1810–60)* (Paris 2002).

to land, work, credit, and charity. High levels of total or functional illiteracy reinforced cultural subordination. Feeling powerless, peasants and workers must frequently have assumed that there was no alternative but to accept rules of conduct laid down by those with social and/or political authority. Resistance to elite dominance was restrained by this sense of powerlessness. Dependency turned into deference when the poor were persuaded that their situation was natural and proper.

In the light of this, election campaigns might be seen as manifestations of social power, an assertion of status, the expression of a strong sense of *noblesse oblige*, and often as part of a competitive process amongst local elites. Louis Girard has revealed that most of the candidates for the 1869 elections were notables dependent on their local influence, with a secure electoral base in the particular locale in which their land, château, or factory was located. Success depended upon the geographical extension of this influence by means of the support of other notables.[11] Nevertheless, elites felt obliged to adapt to 'democracy'. Voters needed to be mobilised on a much larger scale than during the previous period of restricted suffrage. However distasteful the experience might be, committees had to be established, agents appointed, posters and ballot papers printed, constituencies had to be visited, meetings addressed, and voters 'treated'. Electoral 'capital' had to be accumulated and a repertoire of actions designed which combined traditional forms of domination with an appeal to democracy.[12]

The financial cost of such activities could easily mount up, imposing a particular burden on candidates deprived of official support. Full use, therefore, needed to be made of mutual support within elites as well as of the vertical links of (inter-)dependence with other social groups. In the absence of formal party organisation notables established electoral committees and mobilised their clienteles. Membership of agricultural and learned societies, of chambers of commerce, municipal councils, of the committees administering local hospitals, schools, and the bureaux de bienfaisance responsible for the distribution of public assistance, as well as voluntary associations like the Société de Saint Vincent de Paul were useful positions from which to exercise influence.

Informal means of communication were increasingly combined with the facilities offered by the press. Through their ownership and control of the major Parisian newspapers, wealthy notables were also able to exert a considerable degree of control over the flow of information and to satisfy a

---

[11] L. Girard (ed.), *Les élections de 1869* (Paris 1960), pp. v–vi.
[12] See e.g. Phélippeau, *L'invention de l'homme politique moderne*, pp. 175–93.

variety of objectives including the generation of profits, financial speculation, and the extension of political influence.[13] Although access to information remained a luxury, its cost was falling rapidly with the appearance of
the first mass circulation newspapers like Millaud's *Le Petit Journal* in 1863,
printed on cheap paper by steam-driven rotary presses. By concentrating
on sensationalist stories like the Troppman murders, adopting a simple
style, and remaining determinedly apolitical, circulation was pushed up to
593,000 by 1869.[14] This new mass media offered escapism and encouraged
apathy. In addition, however, the press allowed the elites to establish, to
a large degree, the themes for political debate – taken up by provincial
newspapers – and to present a range of options to the electorate.

POLITICAL OPTIONS

In his recent study of Second Empire deputies, Eric Anceau identified five
familles politiques – Legitimists, Orleanists, Bonapartists, independents,
and republicans – and pointed out that an individual could belong succes-
sively to two, even three, of these tendencies.[15] Previously, Louis Girard had
defined four political attitudes amongst the departmental councillors holding office in 1870. In the first place, there were the apolitical who, if they had
political preferences, were willing to cooperate with any regime committed
to the defence of social order. Secondly, there were the committed Bonapartists. Thirdly, those who had rallied to the imperial regime whilst retaining a sentimental attachment to previous regimes. Finally, the representatives of opposition, clearly under-represented in these quasi-governmental
bodies.[16] These political identities represented the political traditions and
family loyalties established during a turbulent recent past, and adapted to
changing local and national circumstances with the passing of the generations. In the absence of modern political parties, loyalties could be defined
in terms of membership of particular social networks and voluntary and
religious associations, and subscriptions to journals and newspapers, which
similarly represented adherence to a particular political culture.

The membership of each of these political groups changed over time, due
to a large extent to mortality; all of them were subject to internal division.
Each was composed of men who shared certain basic assumptions and an

---

[13] M. Martin, 'Presse, publicité et grands affaires sous le Second Empire', *Revue historique* 1976,
pp. 377–8.
[14] F. Caron, *La France des patriotes de 1851 à 1918* (Paris 1985), pp. 158–9.
[15] Anceau, *Les députés*, p. 64.
[16] Girard, *Les élections*, pp. 132–4. Similar categorisation by PG Douai, 2 April 1866, AN BB30/377.

often sentimental attachment to regimes they had served previously. They were divided by memories, personal hostilities, and genuine differences of principle. The changing political and institutional context also influenced behaviour. As fear of revolution declined, and the regime engaged in a difficult process of liberalisation, the expression of divergent views became all the more likely. Regime liberalisation also offered a greater share of power to the elites.

Bonapartists

Initially, in the aftermath of the mid-century crisis, the regime had benefited from a strong groundswell of support from the propertied classes, whatever their political sympathies. The *coup d'état* was the culminating event in a counter-revolutionary offensive, which had commenced in April/June 1848. There was a widespread belief that it had saved France from anarchy, and sympathy for the values associated with the Bonapartist tradition, namely national honour, economic prosperity, social order, the protection of religion, and respect for the constitution of 1789, even if the last ensured that non-nobles were more likely to welcome an imperial restoration than were nobles.[17] In this situation the state prosecutor at Aix optimistically concluded that the regime could expect 'for a long time . . . the serious and deliberate support of most of those who had supported the old parties'.[18]

In spite of the regime's recognition of 'universal' suffrage, political repression lifted the menace of social revolution. Substantial expectations were stimulated. Achille Fould's friend, François Ragelle, receveur des finances at Bagnères-sur-Bigorre, was a fervent partisan of the regime, pointing out that 'God had given to the Emperor the most immense, the finest and the most difficult of missions, the re-establishment of social order and the preservation of peace.'[19] Concern that Louis-Napoleon, like his uncle, would be tempted by military adventures had been tempered by the pledge made in his speech at Bordeaux on 9 October 1852 that *L'Empire, c'est la paix.*[20] The re-establishment of empire, with its court and respect for tradition and hierarchy did much to reconcile the upper classes. Amongst the courtiers were the more committed supporters of the regime, the old-established Bonapartist families like the Murat, Ney, and Cambacérès, who

---

[17] See PG Riom, 8 Oct. 1862, AN BB30/386.   [18] 12 May 1852, AN BB30/370.
[19] Letter of 11 Feb. 1859 in Barbier, *Finance*, p. 278.
[20] See e.g. PG Nancy, 2 Nov. 1852, AN BB30/381.

combined personal devotion to the Emperor with support for strong government and firm security policies. More generally, in families whose members had served in the administration or army, there existed 'a profound sentiment of hierarchy, a strong sense of deference towards power and authority'.[21]

In many respects, the Bonapartist restoration also represented that of the elites, after the terrifying experience of 1848. In spite of the state centralisation which Bonapartism implied, and which was symbolised by the system of official candidature, the appointment of officials and selection of electoral candidates ensured that key political institutions remained firmly in upper-class hands. Although committed Bonapartists like Persigny might favour new men, entirely dependent on the regime, the simple truth was that there were relatively few individuals with the social and cultural qualifications believed to be necessary for the purposes of public representation. Ruefully, Persigny would admit to the Vicomte de Falloux that 'we have given the legislature to the upper classes. We have openly chosen and supported our candidates, but from the highest ranks of society, from the great landowners, wealthy mayors and so on.'[22] The social origins of its leading supporters thus ensured that the regime was firmly orientated towards the right.

Representatives of the regime would constantly feel obliged to compromise with these notables who, whilst recognising their indebtedness to Louis-Napoleon, frequently possessed political principles which ensured that their support was less than whole-hearted and would remain conditional. According to the procureur général at Montpellier, the upper classes wanted strong government but supported the imperial regime without enthusiasm, regarding it as an 'expedient' and hoping that it would serve as a transition to something better. To illustrate the point he reported that when he had refused to promote a young judicial official because of his lack of devotion to the Emperor he had been told that 'after so many revolutions, so many governments overthrown and when nothing can guarantee that this one will be more durable than the others, how can you expect anyone to irrevocably commit themselves to it?' This, he concluded, was an attitude widespread amongst the upper classes. Moreover, 'if this is the belief of those who owe everything to the Emperor, what must be the dispositions of those who claim that he has done no more for their property and personal security than, by other means, would the leaders of the old

---

[21] Comte de Franqueville, *Souvenirs intimes de la vie de mon père* (Paris 1878), p. 504 – describing the attitudes of the former director of the Corps des ponts et chaussées.
[22] Quoted T. Zeldin, *The Political System of Napoleon III* (Oxford 1958), p. 11.

parties!'[23] Thus the oath of loyalty to the regime appears to have been taken with reservations by many senior army officers in spite of the conspicuous favour shown towards individuals of aristocratic origin like Castellane or MacMahon.[24] It was perceived to represent 'an engagement simply to serve their country, or perhaps their country and the Emperor, but certainly not the Napoleonic dynasty'.[25]

Although this situation prevailed throughout the first decade, nevertheless government officials appear to have been increasingly confident that, as the state prosecutor at Riom would report in October 1859, 'we are moving closer and closer towards the strengthening of the Empire and the complete appeasement of the parties . . . The Head of State is popular. The Nation will follow him. The various parties are reduced to silence. There is a profound sense of calm.'[26] The apparent durability of the regime, particularly following the birth of an heir in 1856, made continued hostility appear futile.[27] Growing prosperity reinforced its credibility.[28]

In these circumstances, it was hardly surprising that the Emperor's apparent change of course, with the liberalisation of the 1860s, caused considerable surprise and substantial discomfort for the first two groups identified by Girard – the authoritarian Bonapartists and *ralliés*.[29] The changes in the political and institutional context which ensued clearly had a substantial impact on their perceptions of the regime. It would be pointed out that 'the circumstances in which the reforms were announced, their unexpectedness, and the contradictions which they appeared to impose so suddenly on the accepted organs and defenders of the Government, were disconcerting for its most loyal supporters'.[30] Thus, prior to the 1869 elections, government supporters in the Pyrenean region were described, as 'irresolute, divided, profoundly alarmed', in contrast with 'its enemies [who] who have never been so confident of success in the very near future'.[31]

The liberal politicians and journalists frequently quoted by historians were not entirely representative of the *classes aisées*, amongst whom many remained concerned that the threat of a democratic revolution would be renewed if universal suffrage ceased to be subject to governmental direction.[32] They complained that the pace of change was too rapid,[33]

---

[23] 30 June 1852, AN BB30/380.
[24] W. Serman, 'Le corps des officiers français sous la Deuxième République et le Second Empire', Doc. d'Etat, Univ. de Paris-Sorbonne 1976, III, pp. 1309–11.
[25] Prefect, 14 April 1856, AN F1 CIII Gers 8.   [26] 7 Oct. 1859, AN BB30/386.
[27] Prefect, 10 July 1856, AN F1 CIII Ariège 7.   [28] Mayor Pont-Evêque (Isère), AN C.1156.
[29] See e.g. PG Pau, 15 April 1861, AN BB30/384.   [30] PG Rennes, 23 April 1867, AN BB30/386.
[31] PG Toulouse, 8 Jan. 1869, AN BB30/389.   [32] See e.g. PG Rouen, 12 April 1862, AN BB30/387.
[33] PG Orléans, 1 Jan. 1864, AN BB30/382.

and that the re-education of the masses had not made sufficient progress.[34] There was disagreement about liberalisation. 'Part of the upper classes are frightened and blame the Emperor for leading the masses towards socialism . . . Others, however, notably those associated with the Orleanist party, welcome these measures, in a hostile spirit.'[35] Was a return to a parliamentary system a prerequisite for stability as liberals insisted? The fate of those monarchies which had resisted the extension of public liberties suggested that this might be the case.[36] Or did the return to apparently incessant debate in the Corps législatif and press present a renewed threat to political stability? Typically Napoleon appears to have tried to conciliate all sides of the political debate and only succeeded in delivering a confused message to the public.

Emile Ollivier criticised the Emperor for engaging in a 'nerve-wracking semi-liberalism, which frightens some, without satisfying the others'.[37] Businessmen complained about a widespread loss of confidence and its impact on economic activity.[38] The ferociously reactionary General Ducrot insisted in February 1868 that 'Our Emperor took a wrong turning the day on which he ceased to support himself squarely on the army, which had given proof of its solid devotion, in order to search for a new basis of support amongst what is pompously referred to as public opinion, and which, in reality, represents only the opinions of some wretched individuals, insatiable Jews, chattering lawyers, insufferable teachers, shady businessmen, cowardly and vain bourgeois.'[39] Authoritarian Bonapartists led by Baron Jérôme David, grandson of the painter and godson of Jérôme Bonaparte, together with Adolphe de Granier de Cassagnac, organised opposition to reform at the Club de la rue de l'Arcade. However, in spite of his opposition, in 1869 David was appointed to the Conseil privé by the Emperor, joining such devoted servants of the regime as Rouher and Persigny, as well as subsequently to the vice-presidency of the Corps législatif, adding to the confusion.[40]

As the pace of change accelerated, and their anxiety grew more intense, the authoritarian Bonapartists would have welcomed another *coup d'état*. This would, as *Un peureux* – the anonymous author of a pamphlet entitled

---

[34] PG Douai, 8 April 1865, AN BB30/377.
[35] Prefect, 27 May 1867, AN F1 CIII Saône-et-Loire 13.
[36] See e.g. PG Rouen, 20 Jan 1861, AN BB30/387.   [37] *L'Empire libéral*, x (Paris 1905), p. 414.
[38] E.g. PG Aix, 26 June 1869, AN BB18/1785.
[39] Quoted Serman, *Le corps des officiers*, III, p. 1330.
[40] J. Tulard (ed.), *Dictionnaire du Second Empire* (Paris 1995), p. 343, re Conseil privé and pp. 406–7 on David.

De la nécessité d'un nouveau coup d'état avant le couronnement de l'édifice[41] –
put it, prevent 'a renewed outburst by those men against whom society has
always to hold itself on its guard'. More realistically, Bonapartist journalists,
representing twenty-one newspapers, met in October 1869 to organise a
systematic press campaign in support of a return to strong government and
the system of official candidature.[42] Apparently deserted by a government
intent on liberalisation, these Bonapartists, the regime's most whole-hearted
supporters within the elite, would remain irresolute in spite of their growing
social fear.[43]

The expression of dissent

The upper classes were overwhelmingly monarchist, believing that monar-
chical institutions, whether Bonapartist, Bourbon, or Orleanist, were the
necessary basis for an ordered, hierarchical society, and associating the
Republic with the Terror of 1793 and the chaos of 1848. However critical of
the Bonapartist regime some of them might be, monarchist politicians were
rarely seen as posing a threat to its survival and met with far less intense
repression than republicans. Fear of revolution, together with repression,
had promoted the dissolution of opposition initially. However, a more critical stance towards the regime would develop gradually amongst liberal
Bonapartists as well as more obvious opponents.

Upper-class critics possessed substantial political resources. Informal
social networks and newspapers facilitated debate. The arenas chosen during the authoritarian empire were private rather than public, the gentlemen's club, dinner party, or *salon* – such as that presided over by Mme
d'Haussonville in the Orleanist interest or that of Mme Hérold favoured
by rising republican stars like Ollivier and Picard – rather than the press and
parliament.[44] According to the procureur général at Nîmes, 'a mis-placed
vanity prevents many of those who have played a more or less important
role in the ranks of the old parties, from openly rallying to a government
whose creation they had ardently opposed'. Typically, families associated
with the Bourbon or July monarchies refused to attend receptions at the
prefecture or to illuminate their dwellings to celebrate public anniversaries

---

[41] (Paris 1869).
[42] Resolutions of Réunion des journalistes conservateurs des départements held 7–11 Oct. 1869 at Hôtel
   du Louvre in Paris (Paris 1869).
[43] See e.g. OC 1re Légion gendarmerie, 31 May 1869, AHG G8/177.
[44] Anceau, *Les députés*, p. 420; J. Prévotat, 'La culture politique traditionaliste' in S. Berstein (ed.),
   Les cultures politiques en France (Paris 1999), p. 79.

or military victories.[45] Semi-public gestures of hostility were also frequent. In the middle of the *Te Deum* sung in the cathedral at Poitiers to give thanks for the Emperor's deliverance from Orsini's assassination attempt in 1858, Mme de Rohan-Chabot and her companions walked out ostentatiously.[46] In order to 'secretly undermine the Regime',[47] the upper classes engaged in 'a conspiracy of lies and slander', in the clever epigrams which characterised this *opposition des salons*.[48] In the security of family gatherings they could safely poke fun at the bad taste of the imperial court.

These activities did not represent an immediate threat to the regime because their participants were unwilling or unable to organise a mass movement. Nevertheless, they were potentially dangerous. Those who took part in them voiced constant criticism of the leading personalities and acts of the government. At private social gatherings, they engaged in *dénigrement incessant*.[49] It appeared that 'to the license of the press has succeeded the license of private conversations and secret confidences, less rapidly corrupting . . . but more perfidious, as a result of the air of secrecy they attempt to maintain, and from which they acquire an illusory strength'. The effect was to 'devalue insensibly men and institutions'.[50]

Constantly, official reports warned about the strength of this 'latent' opposition.[51] They complained about a widespread unwillingness to accept the authoritarian empire – 'a dictatorship . . . an arbitrary regime' – as anything more than a temporary solution to the problem of disorder.[52] In December 1860, the Interior Minister, Persigny, complained about the continued failure of efforts to reconcile 'distinguished adherents' of previous regimes.[53] The situation was rendered all the more dangerous because amongst the irreconcilable were many of the Empire's own officials. As time passed, the public expression of opposition also became more common. The wealthy classes had wanted to be saved from revolution by strong government but with the red menace apparently smashed they now regretted their 'exclusion' from power and were reported to be simply waiting a suitable occasion to 'take up their flag'.[54] The early death of the Emperor or military defeat and the collapse of the regime were certainly the great hopes of the more extreme Legitimists.[55]

[45] 9 April 1859, AN BB30/382.   [46] PG Poitiers, 19 July 1858, AN BB30/385.
[47] PG Montpellier, 30 June 1853, AN BB30/380.   [48] PG Orléans, 25 July 1853, AN BB30/382.
[49] PG Nancy, 5 Jan. 1863, AN BB30/381.   [50] PG Montpellier, 30 June 1853, AN BB30/380.
[51] PG Metz, 7 March 1852, AN BB30/380.
[52] Report of secret agent 'P.P.' to Interior Minister, 9 Feb. 1852, AN 116 AP 1.
[53] Circular to prefects, 5 Dec. 1860, AN 45 AP 11.
[54] Prefect, 15 July 1855, AN F1 CIII Morbihan 13.
[55] See e.g. PG Lyon, 6 Feb. 1854, AN BB30/379.

A sense of grievance was always likely to develop within the social elites as a result of the restrictions imposed by the regime on their political freedom. Dissent would be reinforced by reactions to specific government policies and the frustration induced by a political system which made it difficult to exercise effective influence over policy formulation. In contrast with the stormy years of the Second Republic the press was comparatively silent. Censorship and fines, together with widespread apathy reduced readership and financial support. Orleanists were unable to maintain a newspaper even in an important city like Lille.[56] In Moulins the *Ami de la Patrie* folded in 1856 after twenty-five years.[57] The disappearance of a newspaper deprived its readers of an organisational base and source of cohesion. It followed that 'freedom of the press is close to the hearts of the upper classes who associate it with their means of exercising influence and control'.[58]

During the 1850s, the moderate expression of dissent was nevertheless tolerated by the regime, probably as a safety valve. In addition to official tolerance the surviving newspapers depended on the willingness of wealthy shareholders to offer financial resources to match those provided to the pro-regime press by government subsidy and payment for the publication of official notices. The three Parisian newspapers with the largest numbers of provincial subscribers – the *Journal des Débats*, *La Presse*, and *Le Siècle* – helped to keep the spirit of opposition alive amongst the well-off and well-educated. The moderate republican, and very profitable, *Siècle* whose shareholders included Bonapartists and Orleanists like Morny and de Tocqueville,[59] was to be found in many cafés, and was probably the most widely read. Its circulation was 21,325 in April 1853 and peaked at 52,300 in August 1861, before declining to around 35,500 by early 1870 as liberalisation stimulated competition.[60] Its influence was increased further by the regional newspapers, which frequently reprinted its articles.[61] Censorship ensured that the contributors to these liberal newspapers were cautious in their criticism of the regime, resorting to descriptions of analogous situations of dictatorship in the ancient world or praise for the institutions of Britain, Belgium, and the United States. During the first decade, *Le Siècle* avoided direct attacks on the government but spoke for the principles of 1789, attacked aristocratic pretensions and financial 'feudalism' and was viciously anti-clerical.

[56] PG Douai, 29 July 1856, AN BB30/377.　　[57] PG Riom, 19 July 1856, AN BB30/386.
[58] PG Besançon, 13 April 1865, AN BB30/373.
[59] Nassau William Senior, Journal, 9 May 1857, report on conversation with M. Rivet, Bangor MS 24644; Tulard, *Dictionnaire*, p. 628.
[60] Tulard, *Dictionnaire*, p. 629.
[61] See e.g. PG Nancy, 3 April 1857, AN BB30/381 re *L'Impartial* of the Meurthe.

In the 1860s, the easing of administrative controls, as well as the reawakening interest in politics, combined to increase newspaper readership and encourage the establishment of new papers. As fear of revolution receded it was probably inevitable that members of the social elite should come to demand the more complete restoration of the influence over decision-making they had exercised during the July Monarchy.[62] Thus, in Grenoble, the *Impartial dauphinois* was established with the support of the Périer family as a means of furthering the political ambitions of Auguste-Casimir Périer.[63] Although they remained suspicious of the proclivities of manhood suffrage, many notables were ready to accept liberal democracy and to encourage popular political mobilisation in support of their own particular claims.

The system of government was to be increasingly subject to criticism. Official candidatures were condemned as exclusive and intimidatory and resulting in a falsification of the electoral process. The system meant that government policy was subject to control only by deputies it had itself selected, a case of 'the controllable choosing its own controllers'.[64] Local elites resented a system which threatened their independence and dignity, as well as their local power. The imposition of outsiders as official candidates by administrative *fiat* was especially resented.[65] Thus the election of the authoritarian Bonapartist Granier de Cassagnac in the Gers in 1869 was condemned because he owed his success to the peasant vote, and in spite of the almost universal opposition of his fellow notables.[66] Notables wanted to return to a situation where local oligarchies selected candidates for election themselves.[67] The number of new official nominations was limited to the positions vacant, of course, and ambitious younger men were especially likely to feel excluded. In Saint-Etienne the 1860s saw a challenge to the established elite of silk-ribbon manufacturers from ironmasters like Jules Holtzer and Frédéric Dorian aggrieved by their political exclusion, the failure of the government to place orders for their products and by the regional rail monopoly of the Paris-Lyon-Mediterranée Company.[68]

Exceptional measures and especially the *loi de sûreté générale* of 1858 – a panicky response to the Italian nationalist Orsini's attempt to assassinate the Emperor – provoked intense disquiet. The appointment of

---

[62] Point made by e.g. PG Montpellier, 22 Jan. 1870, AN BB30/390.

[63] F. Belle-Larant, 'La loi Guizot et la fondation de l'enseignement primaire public dans le département de l'Isère', *Actes du 77e CNSS Grenoble 1952* (Paris 1952), p. 166.

[64] PG Besançon, 17 April 1869, AN BB30/389.

[65] See e.g. PG Nancy, 12 April 1863, AN BB30/381.   [66] PG Agen, 4 April 1870, AN BB30/390.

[67] See e.g. PG Aix, 6 July 1869, AN BB30/389.   [68] Gordon, *Merchants*, pp. 78, 84–5.

Espinasse, a general with a reputation for brutality, to the Interior Ministry threatened military dictatorship at a time when even to most official observers the police state no longer appeared necessary.[69] This brief return to arbitrary government, together with some of the Emperor's other initiatives, stimulated growing criticism of personal rule and demands for a return to parliamentary government.[70] The experienced liberal politician Adolphe Thiers proved to be a particularly effective critic.[71] There were constant complaints concerning financial policy and especially the 'excessive' expenditure on public works, and most notably on the embellishment of Paris.[72]

In addition the Comte de Montalembert condemned the aesthetics of Haussmannisation, the 'profuse expenditure on . . . straight streets, extending for miles, dirty and dusty and windy, in which every house has the cachet of a Bonaparte taste: the vulgarest that ever deformed a great capital'.[73] Together with excessive military spending this could result only in higher taxation and bring forward the nightmare prospect of an income tax. Few things frightened the rich as much as the prospect of being obliged to share their wealth. New taxes, introduced in 1862, on carriages and luxury horses were very badly received.[74] The cost of bureaucracy, employing 'vast' numbers of 'blood suckers' was roundly condemned.[75] Condemnation of 'extravagance' and the demand for a 'balanced budget' were frequently repeated means of criticising government policy.[76] More technical criticism focused on the impact of 'excessive' government borrowing on interest rates and business activity.[77]

The objective was to impose closer parliamentary control over government expenditure, both as a means of preventing tax increases and a vital stage in the re-assertion of elite control.[78] As the state prosecutor at Lyon warned in December 1861, 'the war against the finances has become . . . an auxiliary in the War against the Institutions'.[79] All sections of the community could support the principle of tax reduction. Fould's open letter to the Emperor on the state of the finances in November 1861 was greeted with enthusiasm, although this rapidly diminished once it was realised that his

---

[69] See e.g. Prefect, 8 July 1858, AN F1 CIII Ariège 7.
[70] Criticisms summed up by E. Ordinaire, *Des candidatures officielles et de leurs conséquences* (Paris 1869), pp. 2–9.
[71] See e.g. PG Bordeaux, 13 July 1865, AN BB30/374.
[72] See e.g. PG Besançon, 15 July 1865, AN BB30/374.
[73] Conversation reported by N. W. Senior, Journal, 27 May 1860, Bangor MS 24649.
[74] PG Rouen, 10 July 1862, AN BB30/387.   [75] PG Besançon, 17 April 1869, AN BB30/389.
[76] See e.g. PG Nancy, 6 Oct. 1862, AN BB30/381.
[77] E.g. PG Rouen, 9 Jan. 1862, AN BB30/387.
[78] See e.g. PG Nancy, 10 Oct. 1861, AN BB30/381.   [79] 27 Dec. 1861, AN BB30/379.

major objective was to increase receipts through the taxation of salt and sugar rather than reduce expenditure. The government's frequent recourse to loans further discredited it by associating it with financial speculation.[80] The Legitimist deputy Berryer condemned the close links between some of the regime's leading figures and the Crédit mobilier investment bank, denouncing the latter as a 'a gambler who *voit les cartes*'.[81]

Alarm about the condition of the finances was also closely associated with criticism of foreign policy. The Crimean War appears to have been quite popular. A war against Russia, the great pillar of reaction and oppressor of the Poles, appealed to a broad left still inspired by Jacobin/imperial chauvinism, as well as to the right, Catholic and monarchist, anxious to secure protection of the Holy Places and inspired by the idea of a crusade against the heretical and barbaric eastern power.[82] War in 1859 against Austria, the other great Catholic and conservative power, and in support of Piedmont a state which posed a threat to the integrity of the Papal states, appealed to the left, but appalled the right, led by the clericals Falloux and Montalembert, for whom 'the Prince, champion of Order, is taking sides with the revolutionaries'.[83] They were convinced both that the security of the Papal States was a necessary safeguard for the spiritual independence of the Holy Father and that the Church was the 'the most secure rampart against demagogy'.[84]

On this occasion Catholics enjoyed the support of liberals like Thiers and Guizot for whom this was a war 'without motive and without pretext' and who refused to accept that vital French interests were at stake.[85] Indeed there was concern about the creation of a more substantial, unitary Italian state, which might one day rival France. Drouyn de Lhuys who would serve as Foreign Minister twice briefly (in 1852 and 1862) told Nassau William Senior (on 1 June 1860) that 'I do not think his [the Emperor's] mind perfectly sound', but added that his 'insanity is not folly'. According to Drouyn, Napoleon was pursuing the centuries-old objective of gaining France's natural frontiers. He would seek to achieve this 'stealthily', by 'fraud', 'slowly and tortuously'. Drouyn's fear was that the Emperor would underestimate the risks.[86]

---

[80] See e.g. PG Nancy, 5 Jan., 5 April 1862, and 15 Jan. 1865, AN BB30/381.
[81] Quoted by P.-M. Pietri, Paris Prefect of Police, 10 July 1856, AN 45 AP 7.
[82] R. Marlin, 'L'opinion franc-comtoise devant la guerre de Crimée', *Annales littéraires de l'Université de Besançon* (1957), p. 3; see also L. M. Case, *French Opinion on War and Diplomacy during the Second Empire* (Philadelphia 1954).
[83] PG Lyon, 10 July 1859, AN BB30/ 379.   [84] Ibid. 22 Dec. 1866.
[85] PG Lyon, 10 July 1859, AN BB30/379.
[86] Conversation with Senior, Journal, 1 June 1860, Bangor MS 24649.

From the south-west it was reported that 'the conservatives, and I apply that epithet to all the men of order, regardless of party, react with sorrow and terror to the overthrow, in a neighbouring country, of all the principles of justice and morality and, in their place the success of brute force, the boastful and brazen triumph of revolution'.[87] In contrast republicans and many liberals supported the government's policy. Victory at Solferino stimulated a sense of patriotic pride, as did the annexation, following a plebiscite, of Nice and Savoy.[88] Even Thiers was delighted by this outcome, telling Senior that 'the worst humiliation of 1815 has been wiped out, and one portion at least of our natural frontier has been restored to us'.[89] However, the truce signed hastily at Villafranca on 11 July 1859 which left Venetia in Austrian hands left liberals and republicans dissatisfied, whilst the Italian nationalist threat to Rome continued to alarm conservatives and required an expensive French military presence to protect the Eternal City.

Such unexpected consequences inevitably raised doubts about the Emperor's judgement. The 'Roman Question' was to be a constant subject for debate, at least amongst the 'political classes'.[90] A Norman landowner, the Baron de Janzé, complained that the social elites had 'allowed the imperial government to establish its dictatorship on condition that it provided them with an unalloyed security. Now, they say, this is lacking. The country seems always to be on the eve of some war from which it cannot hope to profit.'[91] The confidence of conservatives and clericals, who had been amongst the regime's strongest supporters, had been shattered by events in Italy. So too had that of liberals like Dr Véron, editor of *Le Constitutionnel*, who had wanted to believe Napoleon's promise, in his speech at Bordeaux in 1852, that the Empire meant peace.[92] The economist Hippolyte Passy found it intolerable that 'peace or war depends on the caprice of an individual'.[93]

The lengthy intervention in Mexico (1861–7) seemed to confirm their worst fears that involvement in costly and futile foreign adventures, simply at the Emperor's whim, was only too likely.[94] In Brittany, suspicions of the Emperor's intentions, which had first surfaced during the 1848 presidential elections, were revived. It was claimed by clericals that this closet

---

[87] PG Pau, 10 Oct. 1860, AN BB30/384.   [88] See e.g. Prefect, 10 July 1859, AN F1 CIII Loiret 12.
[89] Senior, Journal, 19 May 1860, Bangor MS 24649.
[90] See e.g. PG Douai, 3 April 1861, AN BB30/377.
[91] Conversation with Darimon 22 Oct. 1859, reported in Darimon, *Histoire d'un parti. Les cinq sous l'Empire (1857–60)* (Paris 1888), p. 294.
[92] Conversation with Darimon, 28 July 1859, reported ibid. pp. 282–3.
[93] Senior, Journal, 25 May 1860, Bangor MS 24649.
[94] See e.g. PG Lyon, 30 Dec. 1863, AN BB30/379.

'socialist' – 'is carried away . . . by his secret aspirations . . . towards the most dreadful ideas, such as the abandonment of the Papacy, the absolute separation of Church and State, compulsory education, and a ban on teaching by the clergy and the religious orders'.[95] The legalisation of strikes and toleration of workers' organisations only seemed to confirm such apocalyptic fears.[96]

The Prussian victory over Austria in 1866, which upset the entire European balance of power, seemed to many observers to presage a struggle for continental supremacy.[97] Napoleon's efforts to secure Luxembourg in 'compensation' for Prussian expansion were swept aside humiliatingly by Bismarck. The regime's subsequent efforts to ensure military readiness for any future conflict were opposed vigorously in the conservative press and in the Corps législatif. There might have been general agreement on the need for a strong army but there was widespread opposition to providing the men and money. Indeed, it was assumed widely that France already had the finest army in the world.[98] On this issue it was possible for critics to appeal beyond the elites to a wide section of the electorate, including the rural population, anxious about the possible extension of conscription and taxation.[99]

A general air of crisis developed with adverse consequences for both political relationships and business confidence. Pacific speeches by the Emperor and ministers could do little to calm the situation. An increasingly assertive and confident press fuelled constant criticism.[100] Thiers was especially effective in insisting, at every opportunity, that a parliamentary regime would have saved France from these disasters'.[101]

The commercial treaties, particularly that negotiated with Britain in 1860, were another cause of substantial disquiet. They resulted in a significant reduction in the tariff protection previously enjoyed by agriculture and industry. It has been assumed generally that prior to this threat businessmen were too absorbed by the opportunities presented by expansive economic conditions to take a sustained interest in politics.[102] However,

[95] PG Rennes, 15 July 1865, AN BB30/386.
[96] See Interior Ministry circular 31 March 1868, quoted by J. Rougerie, 'Le Second Empire' in G. Duby (ed.), *Histoire de la France III* (Paris 1972), p. 99.
[97] See e.g. PG Rennes, 23 April 1867, AN BB30/386.
[98] See e.g. PG Lyon, 22 Dec. 1866, AN BB30/379.
[99] See e.g. PG Rennes, 26 Jan. 1867, AN BB30/386.
[100] See e.g. OC gendarmerie de la Seine, 28 April 1869, AHG G8/165.
[101] PG Rouen, 12 Jan. 1867, AN BB30/387.
[102] See e.g. J. Lambert-Dansette, 'Le patronat du Nord. Sa période triomphante (1830–80)', *Bulletin de la société d'histoire moderne* 1971–2, p. 8.

business success reinforced self-confidence and a determination to condemn political decisions which appeared to pose a threat to vital interests. In general, businessmen were committed liberals, insisting that, whether through taxation or interference in the labour market, state intervention in the economy would threaten the viability of their enterprises, whilst at the same time demanding state intervention to protect them from foreign competition. The sudden weakening of this protection, without consultation, caused dismay.

According to a guest at a dinner attended by the republican deputy Darimon this substitution of one economic regime for another was an act of 'pure tyranny'.[103] Established expectations had been overturned. As well informed as anyone, the economist and political commentator Léonce de Lavergne was quite optimistic in his assessment of the competitiveness of large sections of French industry but, as he told Senior, 'our manufacturers are in an agony of terror; they are more frightened than your farmers were before 1846' (repeal of Corn Laws in Britain).[104] In the debate on the Address from the Throne in 1863 the coal and steel magnate, and stalwart of the regime, Eugène Schneider, expressed a widely held view in asserting that, 'I do not like the treaty, because I do not like revolution of any kind', and warning furthermore that 'the adverse consequences would only become evident over time'.[105]

Some businessmen, including Schneider, would soon come to realise that their modern, highly capitalised enterprises were competitive in international markets. Importers of raw materials, the producers of luxury goods like silk, clothing, paper, *articles de Paris*, and wine, together with merchants involved in international trade, all welcomed the prospect of easier access to external markets.[106] Protectionists were to be far more vocal, however. Even deputies previously praised for their unstinted support for the regime became extremely critical. The representatives of Haute-Saône – the Marquis d'Andelarre concerned about the impact of 'free trade' on cereal and wool prices, and the Marquis de Grammont alarmed by the declining value of his forests and charcoal forges – now successfully stood for election as opposition candidates.[107]

In the 1850s, the mere hint of reductions in tariffs had provoked outcry and warnings of catastrophe. In the following decade, the impact of

---

[103] Darimon, *Histoire d'un parti*, p. 319, entry of 3 Feb. 1860.
[104] Conversation with Senior recorded in Journal 8 May 1860, Bangor MS 24649.
[105] Quoted J. Vial, *L'industrialisation de la sidérurgie française, 1814–64* (Paris 1967), p. 433.
[106] See e.g. PG Aix, 6 Oct. 1860, AN BB30/370, re reactions at Marseille.
[107] PG Besançon, 13 July 1863, AN BB30/373; see also Carel, 'Le département de la Haute-Saône' vol. I, p. 404, vol. II, p. 877.

improved communications in intensifying competition, of the American Civil War on the textile trades, or of fluctuating domestic harvests on agricultural prices, all appear to have been discounted, and virtually every economic ill blamed on the commercial treaties by 'a population imbued with protectionist ideas'.[108] Criticism was voiced frequently by local chambers of commerce and emerging pressure groups like the Comité des Forges.[109] Fairly typically, at the beginning of 1868 a petition from the Tourcoing Chambre consultative des arts et manufactures insisted that its members were losing money still in spite of massive investment in new textile machinery. It concluded that only a complete ban on imports would improve the situation.[110]

The textile *patronat* in the Nord and Rouen areas frequently combined a heartfelt protectionism with devout Catholicism and demanded the establishment of parliamentary controls over this rogue Emperor, as the only means of safeguarding their material and spiritual interests. 'Freedom' again became an acceptable demand.[111] Léonce de Lavergne told Nassau William Senior that 'on the whole the treaty and the quarrel with the Pope have given Louis-Napoleon a great shake'. He added that 'they have shewn, however, the deep-seatedness of his power. Either of them would have overturned any other government.'[112]

Gradually conceded from 1860, initially by a regime at the height of its power, liberalisation was a means of conciliating the political elite. At the beginning it involved little more than a debate on the contents of the Emperor's annual speech from the throne, and an extension of budgetary controls. The *classes élevées* had already begun to forget 'past dangers', however;[113] therefore, the effect of the decree of 24 November 1860 was to 'provoke debates, reawaken hopes, rekindle fears which had been written off, and thus to create, in some respects, a new state of affairs'.[114] The imperial letter of 19 January 1867, which promised much greater freedom for the press and public meetings, would have an even more substantial impact.[115]

The critics of the regime within the elite welcomed these reforms but proved difficult to satisfy. Every concession seemed to encourage further

---

[108] Points made in internal memo Ministère de l'agriculture. Bureau des céréales. 20 Jan. 1866, AN 45 AP 23.

[109] Anceau, *Les députés*, pp. 321–2.   [110] 10 Jan. 1868, AN 45 AP 23.

[111] See e.g. Chambre consultative des arts et manufactures de Roubaix to Ministre de l'agriculture,? Dec. 1867; Prefect Seine-Inférieure to Minister, 27 Jan. 1868, AN 45 AP 23.

[112] Senior, Journal, 8 May 1860, Bangor MS 24649.

[113] PG Grenoble, 10 Dec. 1857, AN BB30/378.   [114] PG Rouen, 20 Jan. 1861, AN BB30/387.

[115] See e.g. PG Dijon, 9 July 1867, AN BB30/377.

demands from 'liberals' who were convinced that the regime had no choice but to conciliate those social groups from which it recruited its own person-nel.[116] Nevertheless, in demanding parliamentary government liberals were also desperate to satisfy the needs of social order. They conceived of 'liberty' in restricted terms, intended to meet the demands of their own kind, the wealthy, well-educated, property owners. There was a comforting assump-tion that workers and peasants were not really interested in questions of 'high politics'[117] but alongside this, as Lavergne told Senior, was always the nagging fear that 'a free press will give us socialism, plunder, insecurity, in short all the evils which accompany the rule of the uneducated part of the community'.[118] Liberals remained intensely suspicious of manhood suffrage even if they increasingly accepted, with more or less good grace, that it had become impossible to turn the clock back.[119]

It is evident that the causes and cadres existed for a renewal of political opposition within the elite. Generally, this was not organised but involved 'numerous scattered personalities'.[120] According to the procureur général at Douai, 'the industrialist, the merchant, the lawyer, the government offi-cial rub shoulders with the aristocracy and the bourgeoisie',[121] all of them determined to control the Emperor's initiatives. In these circumstances pressure for change from within the social elites posed a growing threat to the authoritarian–bureaucratic system constructed following the election of Bonaparte to the presidency in December 1848. The gradual emergence of political leaders like the independent liberal Adolphe Thiers, the Legit-imist barrister Berryer, or the moderate republican turned liberal Bona-partist, Emile Ollivier, would give this opposition added credibility and focus.[122] Increasingly, dissent turned into a more profound form of resis-tance. The renewal of parliamentary debate in the 1860s, and the growing newspaper publicity it received, revived old aspirations[123] and provided the opportunity for political activists to widen their influence within the social elites and throughout the electorate. Opposition would take varying forms – Legitimist, Orleanist/liberal, and republican – although it needs to be remembered that, regardless of their sentimental attachments to previous regimes and aspirations for the future, most of the regime's critics would

[116] See e.g. PG Aix, 11 April 1869, AN BB30/389.
[117] See e.g. PG Angers, 9 April 1862, AN BB30/371.
[118] Senior, Journal entry 8 May 1860, Bangor MS 24649.
[119] See e.g. PG Nancy, 20 Jan. 1870, AN BB30/390.
[120] OC gendarmerie, Cie de la Loire, 28 July 1868, AHG G8/152.
[121] 2 April 1866, AN BB30/377.   [122] See PG Rouen, 12 Oct. 1862, AN BB30/387.
[123] See e.g. PG Bordeaux, 20 Jan. 1864, AN BB30/374.

remain loyal to the Emperor, and that relatively few overt representatives of opposition parties would manage to secure election.[124]

Opposition – Legitimist and clerical

Legitimists represented an important part of the socio-political elite. Of 957 opposition departmental councillors in 1870, 415 have been identi-fied as Legitimists (14.8 per cent) or clericals (19.4 per cent). They were mainly landowners and retired army officers, and to a lesser extent bureau-crats and lawyers; 69.5 per cent of them were nobles compared with only 28 per cent of Orleanist councillors, 14 per cent of liberals and 3.7 per cent of republicans.[125] Certainly contemporaries identified Legitimism with the nobility, and nobles were more likely to be Legitimists than to adopt any other political affiliation. They gave the movement a certain 'tone'. More than any other group, save perhaps the clergy, they had lost, materially and socially, from the revolutions, which had 'afflicted' France since 1789. Their Legitimism was based upon a Manichean view of the world and idealised visions of the *ancien régime*. It was characterised by an obvious prefer-ence for rural society, for paternalistic social control, and for a Christian monarchy. Confident in their own superiority they affirmed their sense of responsibility towards those whose birth, lack of instruction, and poverty rendered them naturally inferior. Legitimists affected to despise such man-ifestations of the modern world as urbanisation, the greedy speculation they associated with economic modernisation and, using an increasingly vicious anti-Semitic discourse, with 'Jewish finance'.[126] They objected to the state centralisation, which deprived 'natural' elites of their proper influ-ence. A regime committed to 'modernisation' could only exacerbate such fears.[127]

Like other political groups the Legitimists represented an amalgam of opinions. The proponents of another Bourbon restoration reacted in four ways to the *coup d'état* and to the establishment of the Empire. They rallied, 'from hatred of demagogy',[128] or else they accepted a 'temporary' *rapprochement*, remained in opposition, or retired from politics. Few Legit-imists accepted the regime without reserve.[129] They resented the 'weakness, which forces them to recognise Napoleon III as sovereign'. However, 'His

---

[124] R. Price, *The French Second Empire. An Anatomy of Political Power* (Cambridge 2001), ch. 8.

[125] Girard, Prost, and Gossez, *Conseillers généraux*, p. 139.

[126] See e.g. Thompson, *The Virtuous Marketplace*, p. 160.

[127] See e.g. pamphlet signed B., *Notes et réflexions pour M. le Comte de Chambord* (1870).

[128] PG Riom, 14 April 1866, AN BB30/386.   [129] See e.g. PG Poitiers, 29 Jan. 1858, AN BB30/385.

Majesty is only in their eyes *un souverain de fait*. The comte de Chambord, on the contrary, is . . . not simply a pretender, he represents a principle.'[130] One day, God would restore the true king.[131] Ministers were advised that Legitimism should not be regarded simply as 'an interest, it is a tradition, a cult' and for many took on 'the dignity of a religious faith'.[132]

There were, however, bitter divisions amongst Legitimists, particularly over the policy of political non-engagement demanded by the Comte de Chambord, the 'legitimate' King Henri V. In the Frohsdorf Manifesto published in October 1852 Chambord called for electoral abstention and resignation from all official posts for which an oath of loyalty to the Emperor was required. Nevertheless, in excluding the army Chambord recognised the existence of powerful traditions of service to the State. The imperial regime would be able to appeal to these in its effort to rally the nobility. After all, many noble families had rallied to a previous Empire. The Corps législatif elected in 1852 would include 81 apparent nobles including 2 princes, 4 dukes, 15 counts, 5 viscounts, 5 marquis, and 7 barons.[133] Once again, and in spite of their frequently asserted veneration for 'their' king, most Legitimists were determined to avoid the inactivity and apathy which abstention implied.[134]

This was certainly the line adopted both by intransigent opponents of the Empire like the influential lawyer Berryer and politicians associated with the *Gazette de France*, as well as by more moderate figures like the Comte de Falloux and associates of *L'Union*. Relatively few politicians or civil servants followed Chambord's instructions to refuse the oath of allegiance and resign their functions. As a result, by offering influential Legitimists a role in local and central government the regime would do much to detach them from older loyalties. In the Gard this initial rapprochement led to the selection of three Legitimists as official candidates for the February 1852 elections – the Duc d'Uzès, the Marquis de Calvières, and the Nîmes businessman Léonce Curnier.[135] However, the conditional nature of this alliance could be seen in Calvières' warning to the Prefect of the Gard, that

we should not ask more from him than he can give, more than his honour and his conscience permit him to offer. Personal devotion should not be expected, but rather a prudent and sincere cooperation in all those acts necessary to re-establish religious ideas, respect for order, the family, property and authority. To this degree,

---

[130] PG Riom, 11 July 1859, AN BB30/368.   [131] PG Poitiers, 31 Jan. 1854, AN BB30/385.

[132] PG Caen, 13 April 1859, AN BB30/375.

[133] B. Ménager, *Les Napoléon du peuple* (Paris 1988), p. 203.

[134] See e.g. PG Rouen, 4 Aug. 1852, AN BB30/387.

[135] R. Huard, 'La préhistoire des partis', Doc. d'Etat, Univ. de Paris IV 1977, p. 617.

and whilst safeguarding their own principles, which might in a new crisis provide a haven for France, the Catholics of the Gard will be the firmest supporters of order and society.[136]

With 'red' revolution threatening, it was easy to support the extension of the authority of the Prince-President in December 1851, but more difficult to vote for the re-establishment of the Empire a year later. Indeed, the Marquis would resign in protest.[137]

The state prosecutor at Poitiers warned that

under the [conservative] republic, which they accepted as a transition from which they might profit, [the Legitimists] moved closer to the administration and even involved themselves in its actions, assuming positions from which they hoped one day to assume command. However, on 2 December, on the eve of the hereditary empire, the more exalted amongst them dramatically detached themselves; the moderates less ostentatiously established a distance between themselves and the administration; and the clever continued to occupy their places, in order to profit from the present, whilst reserving their position for the future, for they, nonetheless, remained Legitimists.[138]

Subsequently, as the imperial regime began to take on an air of permanence there appeared to be every likelihood, especially amongst the young and non-nobles, that Legitimist sympathisers would rally on a more permanent basis. The passing on of the faith between the generations was particularly problematic in regions where support was limited anyway.[139]

In most areas, the practice of universal suffrage reinforced a growing sense of weakness and isolation. The procureur général at Montpellier noted that 'if the leaders continue, stoically, to parade their loyalty, their bored subordinates rally, and the rabble scatters'.[140] The motives of such *ralliés* varied, as did their level of commitment. The primary attraction of the Bonapartist regime was the promise of strong government from a regime sympathetic to the elites. Personal career ambitions were also important. In most areas prefects were anxious to secure the services of influential members of the social elite as senators,[141] deputies, conseillers-généraux, mayors, and administrators of hospitals and bureaux de bienfaisance. Thus, many Legitimists were prepared to take the oath of loyalty as the price of protecting their local patronage. They realised that the widespread withdrawal from public life, which had followed the 1830 revolution, had resulted in a substantial loss

---

[136] Letter of 15 Jan. 1852, AN F1 CIII Gard 5.
[137] J. Maurain, *La politique ecclésiastique du Second Empire de 1852 à 1869* (Paris 1930), p. 301.
[138] 15 April 1859, AN BB30/385.   [139] See e.g. PG Paris, 10 Nov. 1868, AN BB30/389.
[140] 5 July 1858, AN BB30/380.
[141] 58 per cent of 169 senators were nobles – D. Higgs, *Ultraroyalism in Toulouse* (London 1973), p. 135.

of influence.[142] Moreover the Empire at least represented an improvement on both the republic and the regime of the 'usurper' Louis-Philippe.[143]

In practice, almost always, there were definite limits to Legitimist opposition. In the Nièvre, for example, the nobility 'does not appear disposed to rally . . . , but they are not interested in destroying the regime because, on the one hand, it provides security, and on the other, they are afraid that a new revolution will bring back socialism'.[144] It followed that 'those people who console themselves for the power they have lost with witticisms are not . . . in the mood to fight or plot to recover it'.[145] They retained their 'political sentiments as a sort of cult'.[146] Their opposition was reduced to a 'war conducted by women and the old'.[147] At its most extreme this might involve a pilgrimage to the Pretender and the distribution of commemorative medals and manifestoes. In Poitiers during the procession of the relics of Sainte-Rodegande through the streets in July 1854 the appearance of decorations in the shape of the fleur-de-lys caused concern.[148]

Of most Legitimists it might be said that 'they regret the past and await the future, without really taking into account the means of realising their dreams, dreading even anything which might weaken an order of things to which they are indebted for their personal security and the tranquil enjoyment of their wealth'.[149] Furthermore, as the Comte de Falloux insisted, whatever their personal political proclivities nobles had responsibilities towards the people and a duty to defend the interests of the Church.[150] The Marquis de la Rochejaquelain who had opposed the coup initially, subsequently rallied and in 1853 was appointed President of the departmental council of Vienne and an imperial senator. In these positions he would be prominent in efforts to persuade the government to pursue the policies favoured by Legitimists and the clergy.[151]

Many Legitimists rallied because the clergy were sympathetic towards a regime which accorded them so much material and moral support.[152] Falloux complained about this to the Bishop of Rennes.[153] However, as the secretary to the Bishop of Vannes told the Prefect of Morbihan in December 1858, many priests appear to have been happy to escape from their former

---

[142] PG Riom, 14 July 1862, AN BB30/386.　　[143] PG Caen, 13 April 1859, AN BB30/375.
[144] Prefect, quoted Vigreux, *Paysans et notables du Morvan*, p. 368.
[145] PG Poitiers, 25 July 1853, AN BB30/382.　　[146] PG Orléans, 1 July 1859, AN BB30/368.
[147] PG Montpellier, 8 July 1853, AN BB30/380.　　[148] PG Poitiers, 28 Jan. 1855, AN BB30/385.
[149] PG Caen, 13 April 1859, AN BB30/375.
[150] Comte de Falloux, *Memoirs*, ii (London 1888), p. 322.
[151] Maurain, *Politique ecclésiastique*, p. 242.
[152] Point made re Gard, Vaucluse and Ardèche by PG Nîmes, 9 April 1859, AN BB30/382.
[153] PG Rennes, 10 April 1859, AN BB30/386.

dependence on an 'arrogant' nobility.[154] Although personally an unbeliever, Napoleon convincingly posed as a defender of the faith, making major concessions to the Church over education, providing subsidies for church construction and restoration, and improving the stipends of the clergy. For as long as this alliance between Church and State survived Legitimists would be unable to count on the mass support for their cause which only the clergy could mobilise.

Nevertheless, potential opposition remained a cause of concern to the authorities, particularly in the presence of a wealthy Legitimist elite and an influential clergy. The two were bound together by a shared political ideology and by religious faith. By appealing to common traditions of resistance to revolution, and resentment of the 'new' *bourgeoisie*, they were able to mobilise mass support. This was especially the case in Brittany, where aristocratic landownership was associated with the creation of a dependent clientele, although the rural population appears to have been far less docile in the Breton-speaking areas of Finistère and Côtes-du-Nord, where the clergy and their flocks rallied to the Emperor, than in French-speaking areas. In the west the alliance between Legitimist landowners and the clergy was also strong in the *bocage* of Maine, Anjou, and the Vendée.[155] In the east and south of the Massif Central, the Rhône valley, and Languedoc, support was more urban than rural and less whole-hearted, except where, as in Gard and Hérault, confessional rivalries with Protestant communities remained intense. Similar, if less strong, support could be found in the Nord and Franche-Comté.[156]

In cities like Rennes, Poitiers, Lyon, Aix, Toulouse, and Marseille, centres of a vibrant religious life, the clergy were supported by nobles resident in their town houses as well as by a substantial minority of the middle-class inhabitants, drawn especially – in these commercial and administrative centres – from the ranks of landowners and lawyers rather than business-men. Le Provost de Launay, Prefect of the Loiret, reported the existence at Orléans of a 'compact and important core. Several hundred families, some of genuinely ancient nobility, most having usurped their titles or names . . . have formed themselves into a fasces on which is inscribed the emblem of Henri V.'[157] They added up to what the state prosecutor at Aix unkindly described as 'the debris of the aristocracy, clergy, and the

[154] Maurain, *Politique ecclésiastique*, p. 257.
[155] Ibid. p. 27; L. Le Gall, 'Le 2 décembre dans le Finistère, un *coup d'état* évanescent', *Revue d'histoire du 19e siècle* 2001/1, *passim*.
[156] Maurain, *Politique ecclésiastique*, pp. 293–4; Kale, *Legitimism*, pp. 43–71.
[157] 9 April 1859, AN F1 CIII Loiret 7.

traditional local bourgeoisie'.[158] 'In isolating themselves in their fidelity to the past, they believe they are preserving their social superiority.'[159]

Legitimism cannot, though, be equated simply with traditional sectors of society. Indeed, its traditionalist political ideas enjoyed substantial support from some of the wealthiest industrial innovators in centres like Lille and Tourcoing.[160] There were many influential non-nobles amongst Legitimist activists, men like Emmanuel Lucien-Brun in Lyon, Charles Kolb-Bernard in Lille, Ferdinard Béchard and Louis-Numa Baragnon in Nîmes, Maurice Auby and Jacques Hervé-Bazin in the Vosges, and Henri Carron in Rennes.[161] Often, Legitimism seemed to be a means of confirming an otherwise shaky social status, 'a matter of good taste, of vanity, paraded as if it was a title, flaunted like an old court of arms'.[162] In the Périgord, 'Allowing the public to believe that one is a Legitimist is a means of raising one's status; a noble, someone said, can only be a Legitimist, and from this belief to the reverse is only a short step.'[163]

However, the existence of a critical mass, providing mutual support and creating pressure for conformity was essential to the survival of Legitimism as a distinct political option. Without it, sympathisers were isolated, their political activity ineffective. Certainly, Legitimists were represented on every departmental council in 1870, with the exception of those in the Alps, the Charentes, Tarn-et-Garonne, and Bas-Rhin.[164] Nevertheless, wherever they lacked influence over the masses, as in the Paris region, Champagne, or Bourgogne, Legitimists were reduced to being generals without an army.[165] In such situations they were more likely to accept 'with the elegant courtesy which distinguishes them, all the relationships between themselves and the authorities which the occasion requires'.[166] As a result, in many cases Legitimist sentiments were in danger of becoming merely 'symbolic statements of social identity to be divorced from their apparent political meaning'.[167]

As time passed, official reports were increasingly optimistic, insisting on the growing weakness of commitment to the Legitimist cause.[168] However, from Poitiers, a residential centre for local landowners and hotbed of Legitimist agitation, Damay, the procureur général, complained that this had been achieved at the expense of concessions intended to encourage

[158] 6 Oct. 1863, AN BB30/370.   [159] PG Poitiers, 31 Jan. 1859, AN BB30/385.
[160] Ménager, 'Vie politique', II, p. 432.   [161] Kale, *Legitimism*, p. 23.
[162] PG Besançon, 15 July 1862, AN BB30/373.   [163] PG Bordeaux, 6 July 1859, AN BB30/374.
[164] Girard, Prost, and Gossez, *Conseillers généraux*, p. 140.
[165] See e.g. PG Caen, April 1859, AN BB30/375.   [166] PG Nancy, 7 August 1855, AN BB30/381.
[167] Higgs, *Ultraroyalism*, p. 148.   [168] E.g. PG Dijon, 8 Jan. 1863, AN BB30/377.

Legitimists to rally, but which only reinforced their potentially dangerous influence and gave them an exaggerated sense of their own importance.[169] The procureur général at Nancy suggested that prefects preferred dealing with men whose 'education and distinguished manner . . . ensure that both official and social relationships are as easy as they are agreeable'.[170] It was pointed out that, whilst in Paris, and in their dealings with ministers, Legitimists might appear to have rallied, in the bosom of their families and in provincial society they expressed themselves very differently.[171] The prefect of the Vienne, Rogniat, determined to adopt a less conciliatory approach but, not untypically, in 1857 his policy would be reversed by his successor Paulze d'Ivoy. Administering a department without the cooperation of a substantial part of the local elite had proved to be too difficult.[172]

Due to the tolerance shown by the administration towards conservative newspapers, a substantial Legitimist press had survived the *coup d'état* and subsequent repression. Certainly, their editors needed to be cautious. Legitimist newspapers frequently received warnings and on occasion prosecution followed. The most prominent journals were the three Parisian dailies – the intransigent and Gallican *Gazette de France*, and the more moderate but ultramontane *L'Union* and *L'Assemblée nationale*, which supported the cause of *fusion* between the Legitimist and Orleanist parties on the basis of recognition by the childless Comte de Chambord of an Orleanist prince as his legitimate heir. In addition, there was a sympathetic clerical press, including in Paris the liberal *Ami de la Religion* and Louis Veuillot's ultramontane *L'Univers*. These were supplemented in the provinces by such newspapers as the Besançon *Union Franc-comtoise*, the *Gazette de Languedoc* and the *Journal de Rennes* which frequently re-published articles from the Parisian newspapers – criticising the government, reminding readers of the great achievements of the Bourbon monarchs, describing the activities of the exiled Comte de Chambord, and developing social and political programmes. The enforced closure of a newspaper, such as the Orléans *Moniteur du Loiret*, was followed generally by the establishment of another with a different name or, as in this case, by the extension of the circulation of an existing newspaper – *La France centrale* published in Blois. Local landowners subscribed to a fund to attract a more experienced editor, Paul Beurtheret from the *Courrier de Lyon*, and promised to indemnify the printer if he faced prosecution.[173]

---

[169] 18 July 1859, AN BB30/275.   [170] 9 Feb. 1858, AN BB30/381.
[171] PG Angers, 6 Jan. 1859, AN BB30/371.   [172] Maurain, *Politique ecclésiastique*, pp. 242–4.
[173] PG Orléans, 2 Jan. 1860, 29 June 1861, AN BB30/382.

In the absence of modern political parties, the shareholders and the journalists producing these newspapers provided the Legitimist movement with its organisational base. They launched slogans and, in spite of their small circulations, stimulated debate. They received support from a network of voluntary associations – *cercles*, cultural groups like the Congrès breton meeting at Saint Brieuc in October 1856,[174] and especially charitable associations. Together with the informal gatherings of extended families and neighbours, these made up a diffuse network of associations involving national and local personalities, their associates and dependants. The commissaire de police of the canton of Barjols (Var) described the local Legitimists as represented 'by individuals of every condition, enjoying a certain affluence, devout rather than pious, with leaders whose personal merit is generally recognised, and who possess considerable wealth'.[175] The feast day of Saint Henri was always the occasion for celebratory dinners like the large gathering on the Princess Baciocchi's estate in Morbihan in 1858 where the celebrants hoisted the Bourbon white flag, fired guns, and set off fireworks.[176]

The Legitimist character of many of the local branches of the charitable Société de Saint Vincent de Paul and of the numerous confessional groups which associated middle-class clericals with nobles in regular gatherings, was a particular cause of official concern.[177] The Société grew rapidly from 500 *conférences* in 1852 to 1,000 by 1859 and 1,549 only two years later, when it claimed to have 100,000 members. In June 1854 Chevreau, prefect of Loire-Inférieure, appeared to confirm interior minister Persigny's worst fears in reporting that

the various *conférences de Saint-Vincent-de-Paul*, for which Legitimist propaganda is the real goal and charity the pretext, follow the lead of the clergy and are almost exclusively composed of partisans of the elder branch . . . They daily struggle against the local authorities, in an attempt to diminish their legitimate influence and take hold of a monopoly of public charity. The *conférences*, no doubt achieve much good. It is worth noting, however, that they limit themselves to assisting only a privileged, selected portion of the poor.[178]

As the number of *conférences* continued to grow, so did official alarm. Tension over the 'Roman Question' exacerbated the situation. Incidents

---

[174] PG Rennes, 12 Jan. 1857, AN BB30/386.
[175] Quoted E. Constant, 'Le département du Var sous le Second Empire et au début de la 3e République', Doc. ès Lettres, Univ. de Provence-Aix 1977, III, p. 888.
[176] OC gendarmerie Morbihan, report on July 1858, AN F7/4095.
[177] See e.g. PG Toulouse, 22 Aug. 1855, AN BB30/416.   [178] AN F1 CIII Loire-Inférieure 8.

like the distribution by a government official, the Garde-général des forêts Lamarque, at meetings of the Société at Saint-Jean-d'Anglély, of a brochure by Bishop Pie, violently critical of government policy, seemed intolerable.[179] There was widespread agreement amongst state prosecutors that the Société was abusing its privileged position. Some wondered how much harm these small gatherings could really do.[180] However, it was generally recognised that even if, formally, most *conférences* respected their regulations and avoided political debate, their members were mainly Legitimist sympathisers. The fact of membership thus increased the cohesion and social influence of groups whose loyalty to the regime was at least suspect.[181] Persigny, again Interior Minister in 1861, was concerned especially about the organisation's national and hierarchical structure, and decided on the dissolution of its Conseil supérieur in Paris and its provincial councils. This was followed by the closure of the 400 local *conférences* which, especially in the west, had refused to apply for official authorisation. It was also made clear to government officials that it would be prudent for them to distance themselves from the organisation.[182]

In spite of these blows, three developments were to lead to a revival and partial transformation of Legitimist activity. The regime's intervention in Italy in 1859 was perceived as both a revolutionary menace to the peace of Europe and as a sacrilegious assault on the temporal power, which alone safeguarded the independence of the Papacy.[183] The brochure by La Guéronnière – 'Le Pape et le congrès' – published in December 1859, which called on the Pope to abdicate his temporal power, was widely known to have been inspired by the Emperor.[184] Trust between the Emperor and influential Catholic clergy and laymen had been destroyed. For an utterly intransigent ultramontane like Louis Veuillot, editor of *L'Univers* – by far the most popular newspaper amongst the clergy and lay clericals – support for the Papacy and recognition of Papal infallibility were crucial to the defence of Christianity against the revolutionary menace.[185] In Legitimist newspapers like the *Journal de Rennes* or the influential *Espérance du peuple* published in Nantes, journalists identified the cause of the Papacy with that of the legitimate king who, alone, was capable of re-Christianising France.[186]

---

[179] PG Poitiers, 29 Jan. 1860, AN BB30/385.
[180] See e.g. PG Poitiers, 28 Oct. 1859, AN BB30/385.
[181] PG Angers, 7 Oct. 1858, AN BB30/371.   [182] Maurain, *Politique ecclésiastique*, pp. 555–65.
[183] See e.g. PG Orléans, 1 July 1859, AN BB30/382.
[184] PG Besançon, 21 May 1859, AN BB30/369.   [185] Girard, *Les élections de 1869*, p. 71.
[186] PG Rennes, 15 July 1865, AN BB30/386.

Education was another contentious issue. The loi Falloux of 1850 had been designed to increase the religious and moralising content of the school curriculum as well as the supervisory role of the clergy. Increasingly, however, government officials had registered alarm at the spread of clerical influence. Rouland, as responsible minister, had determined to protect lay teachers threatened with replacement by the teaching orders of the Church. A shift in policy was already under way before the Italian war, and would be reinforced by Duruy in the succeeding decade. This caused substantial resentment amongst those clericals who were determined to create a Catholic monopoly of education.[187] At the same time many Legitimists shared in the more general hostility towards the commercial treaties. Landowners were concerned about the threat to agriculture and to the value of their woodlands, as the traditional charcoal–metallurgical industry collapsed.[188] In Lille the militant Catholic businessman Kolb-Bernard turned against a regime which appeared to be attacking both his faith and enterprise.[189]

The development of a powerful liberal movement in the 1860s with which many Legitimists were to be associated, facilitated the expression of their grievances. Liberal Legitimists like Berryer, Falloux, and Montalembert clearly believed that the defence of Christian civilisation required active participation in public life, regardless of the injunctions of the Comte de Chambord. It had become a matter of some urgency to develop the constitutional means of controlling the Emperor.[190] Increasingly, the interests of the Church would come to matter more than loyalty to Chambord. A liberal like Falloux would feel obliged to criticise the Pretender himself, as well as the Bureaux des renseignements which represented him in Paris, for not consulting widely enough and for being out of touch with the rapidly changing situation in France.[191] Nevertheless, this renewal of the alliance with the clergy gave Legitimists new hope of extending their influence, offering a cultural substitute for their declining socio-economic power.

If Legitimism had become identified in many regions with the traditional landowning aristocracy, clericalism had a broader appeal, although still within strict social and geographical limits. Certainly, in the west and parts of the south and Flanders where the social influence of the clergy was

[187] Price, *Second Empire*, pp. 194–5.   [188] See e.g. PG Rennes, 7 April 1862, AN BB30/386.
[189] Barbier, *Patronat du Nord*, pp. 28–31.
[190] See e.g. speech by clerical deputy Keller 5 June 1861 quoted in A. Darimon, *L'opposition libérale sous l'Empire (1861–63)* (Paris 1886), p. 89.
[191] *Memoirs*, II, pp. 197, 327, 343f.

greatest they were drawn back into an alliance with the Legitimists. In consequence in Maine-et-Loire and Mayenne 'the Legitimists behave and speak with an audacity the like of which has not been seen for ten years. For them, and for the clergy, events in Italy provide a pretext for a more and more malevolent and unjust opposition.'[192]

Once again the pulpit offered a means of political agitation. The Papal encyclical of 19 January 1860 calling on bishops to mobilise the faithful in defence of the Holy See stimulated a vigorous response. Catholics were asked to contribute to the *denier de Saint Pierre* to finance the future defence of Rome and for volunteers to serve in the Pope's army. According to the state prosecutor at Rennes 'for the clergy and for the devout Catholics, so numerous in Brittany, the question of the Pope's temporal power merges with that of Religion itself'.[193] In an alarmist sermon the priest at Legé in the diocese of Nantes informed his congregation that 'the revolutionaries in Italy have not only dispossessed the Holy Father, but . . . they have pillaged and sacked the churches and monasteries' and warned them that within three months the churches would be closed in France. The vicar of nearby Vieillevigne in similarly apocalyptic tones threatened divine punishment for the Emperor and promised a return to the Terror – 'the priests will be torn from the altars and the churches burned to the ground'.[194] Much of this agitation would simply have gone unreported by clerical mayors.[195]

More than ever, Legitimists placed the Church at the centre of their public activity, using its festivals to display their political loyalty and religious and charitable associations as the motive for regular gatherings. The emotional impact on the Catholic elites of this trend within the Church towards a more sentimental, theatrical, and triumphalist ultramontane sensibility was certainly considerable. Its tone was markedly anti-Protestant and anti-Semitic and hostile to religious and political liberalism. It caused considerable offence amongst liberal and Gallican Catholics who believed that faith was a matter for the individual conscience, and who were critical of the excesses of Papal authoritarianism and of the drive for uniformity seen in the pressure to adopt the Roman liturgy.[196] However, Legitimists who had previously rallied to the Empire became increasingly critical. Although French military action to protect the remaining Papal territory would do

---

[192] PG Angers quoted Maurain, *Politique ecclésiastique*, p. 341.
[193] 19 Oct. 1859, AN BB30/386.   [194] Launay, *Diocèse de Nantes*, II, pp. 721–2.
[195] Concern of PG Riom, 5 July 1860, AN BB30/386.
[196] Pellissier, 'Les sociabilités', IV, pp. 985–1011; M. Sacquin, *Entre Bossuet et Maurras. L'antiprotestantisme en France de 1814 à 1870* (Paris 1998), pp. 89–108.

something to reassure clericals, relations with the regime would never be the same again. The procureur général at Orléans even considered that 'the Empire has forever alienated the Catholics'.[197] Other officials were confident that the situation could be retrieved. Themselves often fervent Catholics, they argued that, given the strength of Catholic sentiment amongst the elites, the government would have to adopt a conciliatory approach towards the Church.[198] The procureur général at Montpellier represented this clerical outlook perfectly in affirming that 'it is the Papacy that the Revolution attacks today, because it is the corner stone of the entire social edifice; once it has been overthrown, it will be easier to get the better of all the monarchies, of all the institutions, of all the consciences'.[199]

A decisive step was being taken in the renewal of the extreme right. Thus, and although Chambord continued to demand abstention, during the 1863 election campaign many Legitimists insisted that defence of the interests of the Church must assume priority over dynastic politics. Electoral candidates were judged by the clergy almost entirely according to their attitudes towards the Church. Clerical supporters of the regime like Chesnelong, deputy from the Basses-Pyrénées, found themselves on the same side as intransigent Catholic critics, like the Alsatian deputy Emile Keller. Those who failed to make an effusive public affirmation of support for the Papacy were likely to be condemned from the pulpit.[200] In return for support for the Holy Father the clergy were prepared to distribute leaflets and voting papers at the doors of their churches.[201] In 1863, Keller was denounced by Persigny as 'one of those blind people who, in attempting to encourage conflict between the Pope and the Emperor, are in reality enemies of religion and of their country and who ought to meet with the disapproval of all sensible people'. On this occasion, he failed to secure election following a vicious battle with the administration. He would be successful in 1869, however.[202]

Under pressure from many of its own supporters – and 93.6 per cent of deputies elected as official candidates considered themselves to be Catholics[203] – eventually, the regime would feel obliged to make concessions to the strength of feeling within the social elite. Liberalisation, together with the promise made by Rouher, carried away by his own eloquence, in December 1867, to provide, indefinitely, a military force to defend the Papacy, were part of the same effort to conciliate liberal and conservative

---

[197] 5 Jan. 1863, AN BB30/382.   [198] See e.g. PG Metz, 11 April 1861, AN BB30/380.
[199] 20 Oct. 1867, AN BB30/380.   [200] See e.g. Launay, *Diocèse de Nantes*, II, p. 776.
[201] See e.g. OC gendarmerie, 28 May 1869, AHG G8/165.   [202] Anceau, *Dictionnaire*, pp. 87, 327.
[203] Anceau, *Les députés*, p. 359.

opinion. The liberal Catholic Montalembert wrote a triumphalist letter to Thiers, a man without religious convictions, who believed nonetheless that the Church was the rampart of social order, to congratulate him on the speech which had led to this concession: 'Parliamentary government has been re-established thanks to you ... The Pope saved ... by you, and also by the power of free speech, of open debate ... which so many unreasoning Catholics had so cowardly repudiated since 1852.'[204] In the *Gazette de l'Ouest* Falloux called on the social elite to 'reconstitute the great party of order under the banner of Religion and Liberty'.[205]

In 1849 Catholics and liberals had combined to form the so-called 'Party of Order' and resist the revolutionary threat. Now they were coming together again, in support of political liberalisation and the restoration of their own authority at the expense of that of the Emperor. The abandonment by Napoleon of his anti-clerical education minister, Duruy, represented another major victory for clericals. The renewed fear of revolution as republican political activity and strikes intensified in 1869/70 would persuade clerico-Legitimists to turn once again to the regime for protection, however. A compromise was in order.[206] The Ollivier government formed on 2 January 1870 would include six, more or less liberal, clericals amongst its eight civilian ministers. Once again, Legitimists would be drawn into a political alliance in defence of social order and the Church, and at the expense of their allegiance to Henri V.

Opposition – Orleanists and liberals

As a set of ideas Liberalism was both libertarian, in favouring an extension of political freedom, and conservative in terms of the attitudes of its proponents towards social reform. Regardless of their 'party' affiliations, Bonapartists, Legitimists, Orleanists, and moderate republicans could all be liberals. Confusingly there were liberals in government and liberals in opposition. Indeed, according to one well-informed observer, by 1866, by which time liberalism had become fashionable, there were three kinds of liberals: '1. enlightened and serious men who believe this to be the best way to secure the dynasty; 2. opponents from right ... and left who are eager to popularise a weapon and a plan of attack; 3. mediocrities, initiated into politics neither by their studies nor education, but who always instinctively follow the most simple and fashionable trends'.[207]

---

[204] Quoted Maurain, *Politique ecclésiastique*, p. 830.
[205] 27 Oct. 1869, in Launay, *Diocèse de Nantes*, ii, p. 753.
[206] See e.g. PG Amiens, 6 April 1870, AN BB30/390.   [207] PG Douai, 2 April 1866, AN BB30/377.

The *coup d'état* had presented former supporters of the July Monarchy with a number of options, the most obvious being that of rallying to the new regime. The alternatives were to remain loyal to the Orléans family, to support a broader liberal opposition to the regime, or to move left towards its moderate republican critics. By 1870, of the 957 opposition-minded departmental councillors 157 retained Orleanist sympathies and a further 248 could be described as liberals. The former were committed to a particular form of monarchy, but in practice both groups were close in terms of their constitutional ambitions and eventually most of their adherents would be prepared to rally to a liberal empire.[208] The state prosecutor at Limoges described them as 'the wealthy or well-off bourgeoisie, which during the parliamentary regime was referred to as *le pays légal;* this sceptical and rebellious bourgeoisie regrets the importance and authority it once enjoyed, and which allowed it to ignore the interests of the people it exploited'.[209] Socially, they tended to be landowners, successful professionals and businessmen, former government officials, and politicians who had made a career during the July Monarchy. Only 14 per cent of these Orleanist and liberal councillors were nobles (compared with 69.5 per cent of Legitimist councillors).[210]

The Orleanists among them were to be found especially in the economically more prosperous regions and included such influential figures as the Duc de Broglie and Duc d'Audiffret-Pasquier and the textile magnate Pouyer-Quertier in Normandy, Chevandier de Valdrôme in Alsace,[211] the Perier family who had dominated the Isère between 1830 and 1848,[212] and the Rothschilds, resident at Ferrières, close to Paris.[213] In Rouen the proclamation of the Empire had been greeted with stony silence by the wealthy businessmen who made up the mounted National Guard. The wealthiest entrepreneurs in the neighbouring textile towns of Elbeuf and Louviers and the port of Le Havre were similarly suspicious of a regime which preferred universal suffrage to an electorate restricted to men of wealth and ability,[214] whilst the merchants of Marseille and Bordeaux were far from convinced that the Empire meant peace.[215] A significant proportion, especially in Alsace and the south, were Protestants, similarly regretting the influence they had enjoyed during the July Monarchy, and resenting

---

[208] Girard, Prost, and Gossez, *Conseillers généraux*, p. 146.   [209] 10 July 1853, AN BB30/378.
[210] Girard, Prost, and Gossez, *Conseillers généraux*, p. 139.
[211] Ibid. p. 148; Anceau, *Les députés*, p. 605.   [212] PG Grenoble, 12 Jan. 1859, AN BB30/378.
[213] PG Paris, 28 May 1861, AN BB30/384.   [214] PG Rouen, 7 Dec. 1852, AN BB30/387.
[215] PG Aix, 13 July 1852, AN BB30/370; PG Bordeaux, 20 Jan. 1864, AN BB30/374.

the favour shown by the imperial authorities towards the Catholic Church throughout the 1850s.[216]

At first, the expression of opposition was paralysed by social fear. Fear of revolution could persuade the most enthusiastic liberals to support authoritarian and repressive government. Thus, although he felt honour bound to re-affirm his loyalty to the Orléans dynasty, Louis-Philippe's former prime minister, Guizot, responding to an enquiry from Interior Minister Morny soon after the *coup*, declared that he intended to abstain from political activity, adding that

> I do not want to create any problems for a regime which is engaged in the struggle against anarchy . . . This is not the moment to hesitate. It is essential that dictatorship triumphs. We have not known how to sustain free government. Now we must know how to support the power necessary to engage in the work of flagellation, atonement and the repression of anarchy which none other could achieve.[217]

This expressed a preference for dictatorship in the classical sense of a temporary period of emergency rule, a concept made familiar to members of the elite by their immersion in Latin texts at school.

Mignet agreed with his friend Thiers that there was nothing that could be done in the circumstances. The upper and middle classes had welcomed the *coup*, and the *classes inférieures* were terrified. The army was disciplined to obedience. He concluded that 'in this situation . . . the best thing to do is to wait patiently. That's what you think and you are perfectly correct. We must abandon the government to the slippery slope, and do nothing to stop it. It should meet with no obstacles to its follies, so that France will suffer and grow weary of it.'[218] In the circumstances Tocqueville felt obliged to abandon public life.[219] Certainly he saw little point in standing for election to a departmental council deprived of real influence.[220] In private he condemned the 'terror', which had been part of the *coup d'état*, his own deportation without trial, as well as the use of 'the most odious procedures . . . to appease the resentment and especially to calm the fears of the conservative party'.[221]

Significantly, however, Léon Faucher, a former Interior Minister, another liberal, who in December 1851 had accepted the necessity of supporting Louis-Napoleon against *l'émeute*, insisted that in the longer term: 'I refuse

---

[216] See e.g. PG Colmar, 20 Nov. 1853, AN BB30/376; PG Grenoble, 9 April 1859, AN BB30/378.
[217] Guizot to Morny, 15 Dec. 1851, AN 116 AP 1.   [218] Letter of 20 June 1852, BN naf 20618.
[219] de Tocqueville to F. Lieber, 4 Aug. 1852, *Oeuvres complètes*, VII, p. 143.
[220] Letter to de la Rive, *Oeuvres completes*, VI(1) (Paris 1954), p. 351.   [221] Ibid. p. 132.

to [support] a government without principle, without scruples, lacking in intelligence and without morals.'[222] More generally there was regret at the passing of the Orleanist political system, for a parliamentary system based on a restricted electorate.[223] Such eminent politicians as Tocqueville, Rémusat, Broglie, and Thiers rejected the new regime on principle, partly because of its violent origins, partly because they found it difficult to renounce leading roles in political life, and were unwilling to accept a situation 'where parliamentary personalities are no longer able to negotiate on the basis of equality with government representatives'.[224] At the end of 1852 many Lyon businessmen were still described as Orleanist by the procureur-général although their loyalty 'takes less the form of a personal devotion to the princes of the House of Orléans, than regret for constitutionalism, for bourgeois government, for a situation in which personal relationships brought one close to the authorities, and one was able more easily to secure favours'.[225]

The worst fears of these liberals concerning Louis-Napoleon's 'socialistic' tendencies appeared to have been confirmed when a decree of 22 January 1852 confiscated the property of the Orléans family and diverted it to charitable purposes.[226] Morny, Rouher, Fould, and Magne, ministers with Orleanist backgrounds, had felt obliged to resign as a point of honour. Still in exile in Brussels, Duvergier de Hauranne asked Thiers to draw the attention of the British government to Bonaparte's plan to 'bring down the bourgeoisie'.[227] In general, however, commitment to the House of Orléans was less ideological and less whole-hearted than that to clerico-Legitimism.[228] The almost 'mystical'[229] sense of loyalty, which inspired many Legitimists, was entirely lacking. Instead, according to Charles de Rémusat, for Orleanists, and liberals in general, 'the legitimate king is he whose royalty is the most useful'.[230] The reserved attitude of the Orleanist princes towards French politics reinforced a tendency to almost forget their existence.[231] Orleanism was transformed easily into a liberalism devoid of dynastic loyalty.[232]

---

[222] Letter to M. Larive, *négociant*, 4 Dec. 1851, in L. Faucher, *Correspondance*, I (Paris 1867).
[223] E.g. PG Nancy, 3 April 1857, AN BB30/381.   [224] Ibid. 31 Dec. 1852, AN BB30/381.
[225] 11 Dec. 1852, AN BB30/379.
[226] Editorial, *L'Indépendance de la Moselle*, 7 March 1852, and report PG Metz, 7 March 1852, AN BB30/380.
[227] Letter of 25 Feb. 1852, BN naf 20618.   [228] PG Caen, 13 April 1859, AN BB30/375.
[229] Word used by PG Lyon, 11 Dec. 1852, AN BB30/379.   [230] *Mémoires*, v, p. 6.
[231] Point made by Jules Simon in conversation with Nassau William Senior reported in Journal, 30 May 1860, Bangor MS 24649.
[232] See e.g. PG Montpellier, 14 April 1867, AN BB30/380 re Narbonne, Béziers, and Montpellier.

Those who did rally, including such leading representatives of the imperial regime as Rouher, were motivated above all by a desire to maintain social order, recognising that 'hatred of revolution and fear of anarchy alone created the Orleanist party and that no government has more effectively imposed a barrier to the demagogic faction and established a more complete security for the future than that of the Emperor'.[233] This mattered far more than obligations to a deposed monarch. Moreover, encouraged by ambition, many former Orleanists would succumb to the regime's overtures. In the absence of a Bonapartist 'party' the government tended to prefer Orleanist/liberals as official electoral candidates.[234] In Brittany, for example, where the challenge came from the Legitimists, 'the old Orleanist party forms . . . the real political force, the most reliable support for the government of the Emperor'.[235]

The stick was probably less effective than the carrot. Nevertheless, leading liberals who had already been frightened by arrests and temporary exile in December 1851, remained concerned, throughout the succeeding decade, about the activities of a secret police, whose omnipotence they undoubtedly greatly exaggerated. Persigny, 'more imperialist than the Emperor', symbolised this imposition of a Bonapartism marked by the 'arbitrary harassment' of members of the 'defeated parties'.[236] Tocqueville warned his correspondents to express themselves with care because their letters were likely to be opened by the authorities.[237] Odilon Barrot, who had headed the Prince-President's first administration in 1849, recalled receiving a letter from Prefect of Police Pietri in February 1853, written as from one gentleman to another, which warned him that

I have, on several occasions, been informed that Mme Barrot in her salon not only encourages conversations extremely hostile to the government, but also allows the propagation of false news, of lying and slanderous rumours, that the most insulting comments are made about their majesties, and especially concerning the Empress, that malicious puns and inappropriate jokes are repeated in a fashion which is dishonourable and unworthy of polite society.

Pietri ended by demanding that Barrot set his house in order.[238] The moderate republican Jules Simon received a similar warning.[239] Whatever the reality, the rumoured activities of the secret police, amply confirmed by

---

[233] PG Grenoble, 10 Feb. 1854, AN BB30/378.
[234] See e.g. PG Metz, 10 March 1859, AN BB30/380.   [235] PG Rennes, 6 Jan. 1859, AN BB30/371.
[236] C. de Rémusat, *Mémoires de ma vie*, v (Paris 1962), pp. 151–2.
[237] E.g. letter to H. Reeve, 26 Nov. 1855, in *Oeuvres complètes*, vi(1), p. 135.
[238] Letter of 9 Feb. 1853, AN 271 AP 5.
[239] Senior, Journal, entry of 20 May 1855, Bangor MS 24637.

the preventative arrests which followed the Orsini affair, helped maintain both fear and bitter resentment. Tocqueville, although unequivocally condemning terrorism, complained that liberals had become isolated between 'despotism and a band of assassins'.[240]

Soon after the coup, Guizot had assumed optimistically that the restoration of the elite to political power was simply a matter of time, observing that, 'one can repress a riot with soldiers, one can win an election with peasants, but soldiers and peasants are not sufficient to govern with. The support of the upper classes that are by nature rulers is necessary. Now, they, for the most part, are hostile to the President.' He advocated non-cooperation in the meantime.[241] Yet, in 1857, after pointing to the widespread contempt for the regime within the 'enlightened classes', Tocqueville insisted that they were still too demoralised to actually oppose it. He claimed that 'they are so taken up with the hatreds of the past, and the fears of the future which occupy their imaginations, so demoralised by the disavowal of so many of the ideas and sentiments which motivated and guided them, so confused by their defeat, that they no longer know what to do, what to want.'[242]

Most liberals were unwilling to risk provoking unrest and anyway lacked the conviction and influence over the masses which the Legitimists, at least in some regions, possessed. An acquaintance of the British political economist Nassau William Senior complained that whilst irritated by the arbitrariness of the authorities and their interference with the proceedings of civil and criminal justice, and highly critical of the favouritism, corruption, and extravagance of ministers and courtiers, his neighbours near Toulouse were above all envious of those who enjoyed the regime's favours.[243] However, officials remained concerned that their political experience and membership of extensive social networks would give Orleanists and liberals considerable influence if a more broadly based revival of opposition were to occur.[244]

The liberalisation of the regime in the 1860s encouraged greater commitment. As fear of revolution receded, 'formerly demoralised and discouraged personalities have revealed a desire to take part in the political struggle once again'.[245] This re-awakening was not incompatible with loyalty to a regime which had proved its willingness to change and which continued to offer

[240] Letter to E. V. Childe, 23 Jan. 1858, ibid. VII, p. 223.
[241] Quoted L. Girard, *Problèmes politiques et constitutionnels du Second Empire* (Paris n.d.), p. 132.
[242] Letter to Reeve, 11 Feb. 1857, *Oeuvres completes*, VII, p. 212.
[243] Senior, conversation with Grimblot, reported in Journal, 20 May 1855, Bangor MS 24637.
[244] See e.g. PG Montpellier, 30 June 1853, AN BB30/380.
[245] PG Aix, 6 Jan. 1864, AN BB30/370.

guarantees of social order.[246] A shift in the balance between governmental and opposition liberals was nevertheless under way. In part it reflected the passing of the generations.[247] The system by which the government selected official candidates for election through its prefects was resented increasingly, especially by younger men attempting to break into politics.[248] There was also, as we have seen, considerable, and growing, disquiet within the elite concerning the Emperor's exercise of his personal power.

The various commercial treaties were introduced by decree in the certain knowledge that most deputies would have rejected them, if given the opportunity. This *coup d'état douanier* aroused widespread resentment. With the exception of industrialists or merchants engaged in the export trades or dependent on imported raw materials, most landowners and businessmen felt threatened. The first treaty, that negotiated with Britain in 1860, caused panic, particularly amongst those like the Norman textile entrepreneurs whose businesses were uncompetitive because of under-investment. At Rouen and Elbeuf, 'they spoke of nothing less than the absolute impossibility of meeting English competition . . . They prophesied the ruin of manufacturing industry, . . . the impoverishment of the employers and as a result the irreparable misery of the workers.' Widespread anger was expressed in numerous brochures and newspaper articles. 'Free trade' with such a powerful competitor seemed to the economist Charles Dupin to presage the reduction of France to a position of dependence similar to that of Portugal.[249]

In his role as a director of the Anzin mining company, Adolphe Thiers was an even fiercer critic. Senior recorded his complaint, over dinner, that the British had 'joined with our despot in a conspiracy to ruin the industry of France, by a fraudulent interpretation of the constitution'. He warned that liberals would see British ministers 'as the accomplices of a tyrant and a rogue'. The lesson drawn by Thiers was that nothing was safe 'under a despot, who is totally unrestrained by law or by principle, who has no settled rule of conduct, and changes the political, the territorial, the manufacturing and the commercial system of France according to the whim of the moment'.[250]

At the very least, businessmen suffered a serious loss of confidence, which led to short-term reductions in investment and employment and to a 'complete hostility towards the Government'.[251] Substantial investment

---

[246] See e.g. ibid. 2 July 1859.   [247] Point made by PG Nancy, 3 April 1857, AN BB30/381.
[248] See e.g. Gordon, *Merchants and Capitalists*, p. 142.
[249] Senior, *Journal*, entry of 25 April 1857, Bangor MS 24643.
[250] Ibid. 19 May 1860, Bangor MS 24649.   [251] PG Besançon, 19 Jan. 1861, AN BB30/373.

appeared to be a pre-requisite for competitiveness and this was often beyond the means of many small and under-capitalised enterprises.[252] Even those businessmen who had invested already in technical modernisation, and were competitive, complained that they were being denied the expected returns on their investments, that they had been given insufficient time to adapt, and that the investment in the transport infrastructure promised by the government was inadequate.[253] At Dunkirk ship owners and merchants who favoured trade liberalisation nonetheless voted for the opposition candidate Plichon because of the slowness with which port facilities were being improved.[254]

Even if allowance is made for the exaggerated nature of complaints from business interests it seems clear that, combined with cheaper transport, which facilitated import penetration, the treaties increased business uncertainty substantially. In the Nord the 1861 treaty with Belgium reinforced the alarm of textile and coal producers.[255] Even if the much-dreaded invasion of British goods did not occur on anything like the expected scale, and indeed the rate of growth of imports actually declined,[256] what mattered politically was that many businessmen *believed*, even after it had become clear that the prophets of doom had exaggerated, that government policy was contrary to their interests and that the regime was more attuned to the concerns of financial speculators and monopoly interests like the railway companies.[257] They were sufficiently confident in their authority to enrol their workers in the protectionist campaign and, more dangerously perhaps, in the condemnation of arbitrary government.[258] In December 1862, during the cotton crisis, when 118,498 people were judged to be in need of assistance in the Rouen area, Pouyer-Quertier, the president of the Comité central de bienfaisance, opposed state intervention which would have reduced the influence of a committee which was doing its utmost to make political capital out of the situation by blaming the workers' misery on the commercial treaty with Britain.[259] The declaration of solidarity between master and man by P. Warin, president of a workers' delegation,

---

[252] E.g. PG Dijon, 5 April 1860, AN BB30/377.

[253] Ménager, 'Vie politique', II, pp. 470–2.   [254] Ibid. III, p. 1217.

[255] See e.g. *Discours prononcés au meeting industriel de Lille le 8 nov. 1869 par MM. V. St. Léger, A. Delesalle, E. Agache. Delfosse, P. Warin et Leurent* (Lille 1869), p. 20.

[256] Tulard, *Dictionnaire*, pp. 102–3.

[257] See e.g. evidence of A. Pouyer-Quertier, filateur et tisseur de coton, peigneur de laine, Président de la Chambre de commerce de Rouen, *Enquête parlementaire sur le régime économique*, vol. I: *Industries textiles* (Paris 1870), p. 163.

[258] PG Douai, 9 April 1859, AN BB30/377; B. Ménager, 'La vie politique dans le département du Nord de 1851 à 1877', *Revue du Nord*, 1980, p. 718.

[259] M. Boivin, *Le mouvement ouvrier dans la région de Rouen, 1851–76* (Rouen 1989), I, pp. 138–9.

at a meeting attended by 2,000 people in Lille in November 1869, would be warmly applauded.[260] Brame and Plichon, deputies for Lille and Haze-brouck respectively, also tried hard to encourage opposition by persuading farmers that abolition of the sliding scale of tariff protection for cereals heralded the ruin of agriculture.[261]

Although the intensity of such criticism would vary with economic conditions the government would never succeed in restoring the confidence of important economic interest groups. The enquiries it set up to consider the impact of the treaties on the various sectors of the economy were dismissed as simply means of heading off criticism.[262] Only in the very different political circumstances of 1870 was the decision of the Ollivier administration to launch an enquiry taken to be the prelude to the restoration of tariff protection. In conciliatory mood, whilst recognising the significance of other factors affecting the economy, the textile entrepreneur and president of the Rouen Chamber of Commerce Pouyer-Quertier, still insisted that it was 'the treaty of commerce and the disastrous competition which followed [which] have been the principal cause of the ruins which cover our region'. Now, however, he claimed to believe that the fault was not the Emperor's. Instead he blamed 'his interpreters, MM. Rouher et Baroche', insisting that 'it is due to the imprudence of M. Rouher that the commercial regime has been imposed on the country'. It was Rouher who was responsible for the resulting 'harm and . . . catastrophes'.[263]

The commercial treaties had been followed by a series of liberalising measures, which maintained the attack on vested interests supposedly obstructing economic modernisation. Most threatening of all, from the business perspective, was the 1864 law legalising strikes.[264] This represented a major assault on the individualist conception of social relationships accepted by most liberals. Amongst the thirty-six deputies who voted against the legislation were leading industrialists like Seydoux, Kolb-Bernard, and Pouyer-Quertier.[265] Charles de Rémusat insisted that it was further proof of the Emperor's dangerous socialist tendencies.[266] A report from western France pointed out that such a radical measure was bound to cause disquiet 'amongst those likely to be frightened by every innovation and for whom order can be maintained only by the repressive use of force', and who

[260] *Discours prononcés au meeting industriel de Lille le 8 nov. 1869*, p. 28.
[261] PG Douai, 9 April 1859, AN BB30/377.
[262] E. Tallon, *Les intérêts des campagnes* (Paris 1869), p. 10.
[263] *Enquête parlementaire sur le régime économique*, I, pp. 156, 158.
[264] See e.g. Ministère de l'agriculture, du commerce et des travaux publics, *Enquête sur les résultats du traité de commerce de 1860* (Paris 1866), I, pp. 26–32.
[265] Ménager, 'Vie politique', II, p. 651.   [266] Rémusat, *Mémoires*, v, p. 241.

included most industrialists.[267] It was in this context that leading representatives of the metallurgical industry established the Comité des Forges as a pressure group to protect their interests.

It was hardly surprising that most economic protectionists were political liberals, their politics in large part a means of demanding closer control by parliamentary institutions over the regime's economic and social policy. In a meeting of businessmen at Lille in November 1869 the vice-president of the Tourcoing chambre consultative denounced the commercial treaties 'not only because of their results, but especially because of their origins'. Expanding on this point, he complained that 'the nation has not been consulted . . . it has not been involved in the negotiations; the Corps législatif has been pushed aside'. To enthusiastic applause he denounced Article 6 of the Constitution, which gave the Emperor authority to negotiate commercial treaties.[268]

However, liberal criticism of the Empire had become primarily an attack on the ways in which power was exercised rather than an assault on the existence of the regime.[269] It represented the determination of influential sections of the social elite to re-establish their right to participate in decision-making, and to impose restraints on the Emperor's personal power. It represented a desire to prevent 'excessive' government expenditure, which led to higher taxes, as well as foreign policy adventures, and to protect individual civil liberty. The budgetary issue was crucial. It was not simply a matter of preventing tax increases, as important as this was, but of imposing restraints on expenditure as a means of controlling policy decisions. It was assumed that the ability to determine the size of the military establishment would restrict the regime's capacity to wage war. *La paix et l'ordre financier* were linked intimately.[270]

The ultimate objectives were free elections and ministers responsible to parliament. During the 1860s Thiers, encouraged by such pillars of the regime as Morny and Walewski,[271] developed a programme of *libertés nécessaires*, which once secured would enable the country to 'regain control of its own destiny'. At least in private, as early as 1857, he had conceded that Napoleon III had 'shown, what is very rare, moderation in power. *Il sait reculer*, a knowledge not possessed by his uncle.'[272] In a letter to

---

[267] PG Angers, 8 July 1864, AN BB30/371.

[268] *Discours prononcé par M. Jules Leurent, vice-président de la Chambre consultative de Tourcoing, au meeting industriel de Lille du 8 nov. 1869, pour la défense du travail national et contre le libre échange* (Lille 1869).

[269] PG Riom, 6 April 1870, AN BB30/390.   [270] PG Besançon, 15 April 1865, AN BB30/373.

[271] Barbier, *Finance*, pp. 240–1.

[272] Conversation reported in Senior, Journal, 11 April 1857, Bangor MS 24643.

Louis-Philippe's son, the Duc d'Aumale, in January 1861, he noted of the Emperor, that 'his inclination has always been to believe . . . that repression was by its nature temporary. He told me himself that sooner or later it would be necessary to make concessions to the reawakening mood of independence.' Following the initial concessions made in the imperial decree of 24 November 1860, the objective would be to persuade Napoleon that further reform was necessary and that, in order to convince public opinion of his sincerity, changes in the personnel of government were also essential. Thiers hoped that eventually a compromise might be reached, concluding that if the Emperor 'is capable of yielding with dignity, he will be able to gain in longevity what he loses in absolute power, if not he'll face the threat of revolution'.[273]

Charles de Rémusat similarly accepted that Napoleon was not a reactionary afraid of change and that his constitutional knowledge was quite profound. However, he had less confidence in the Emperor's ability to develop a programme of reforms, criticising his 'practical incompetence' and insisting that 'the duplicity of his views and intentions, the mixture of calculated deceit with romantic dreams, and finally the force of habit, the influence of his entourage and officials, will invariably corrupt and cancel out all his plans for reform'.[274] A thoroughgoing purge of this entourage was something the Emperor seemed determined to avoid, however. Distrust survived.

Orleanist/liberals, moderate republicans, and some Legitimist/clericals shared a commitment both to social order and liberal reform. However, their ability to collaborate was quite limited. The failure of the monarchists to achieve 'fusion' following the death of Louis-Philippe in 1850 reflected fundamental differences of principle. In the early 1850s the question was frequently discussed in 'polite' society as a possible course of action in case of the Emperor's premature death. Until the birth of the Prince-Imperial, the Emperor's successor would have been his cousin the Prince Napoleon, a figure regarded with suspicion and contempt because of his lifestyle and supposed democratic leanings.[275] However, in 1857, following a visit to the Comte de Chambord in Austria, even the Duc de Nemours, previously its most forceful advocate within the Orléans family, accepted that fusion was dead. Nemours had presented Chambord with three pre-conditions for fusion – the establishment of constitutional government, the consent of the electorate, and acceptance of the tricolour flag which, according to

---

[273] 8 Jan. 1861, BN naf 20618.   [274] Rémusat, *Mémoires*, v, pp. 237–8.
[275] See e.g. Senior's record of conversation with Mme de Bury, 29 May 1855, Bangor MS 24637.

Nemours, 'today, in the eyes of France, is the symbol of the new social order and of the principles consecrated since 1789'. Chambord, whilst prepared to recognise substantial constitutional liberties, refused to concede them as of right, and had been unwilling to accept the banner of revolution.[276]

Legitimists mostly rejected the Revolution of 1789 in its entirety and looked forward to the re-creation of a hierarchical, organic society, and of a moral order based on the teachings of the Roman Catholic Church, and enforced by a Christian king. Orleanist liberals continued to resent the aristocratic pretensions they identified with Legitimism and were unable to accept 'divine right' conceptions of monarchy. Thus Léonce de Lavergne claimed to 'distrust a dynasty which claims the throne as a property, and considers the constitution as a favour which it granted and can therefore take back. I wish for a king by compact, not by right.' He would even have preferred a republic to Chambord.[277] Furthermore, liberals considered religion to be a matter for the individual conscience. They were critical of the intolerant excesses of ultramontane Catholicism and of the willingness of Legitimists to subordinate their political interests to those of the Church. It was hardly surprising that many members of both groups continued to prefer the Empire to a victory by the other.[278]

Liberals and moderate republicans remained divided over the suffrage question. Most liberals would have welcomed a return to the restricted electorate of the July Monarchy. They were not democrats. The year 1848 had confirmed their worst fears of manhood suffrage.[279] Their experience then had proved that political equality was a threat to moral and social order. It held out the prospect of 'socialism, plunder, and insecurity, in short of all the evils which accompany the rule of the uneducated part of the community'.[280] The Duc de Broglie was terrified by the prospect of the poor who, he believed, contributed little to the prosperity of the nation, being able to dispose of its vast wealth through taxation and the 'robbery' of the rich.[281] Thiers denounced a political system, which might 'sacrifice everybody and everything to the numerical majority'.[282]

---

[276] Copy of letter from Nemours to Duc de Broglie, 21 Jan. 1857, given to Nassau William Senior by Duvergier, Journal, 12 April 1857, Bangor MS 24643.

[277] Senior, Journal, 8 June 1855, Bangor MS 24637.

[278] See e.g. PG Aix, 27 Jan. 1854, AN BB30/370; L. Winnie, *Family, Dynasty, Revolutionary Society. The Cochins of Paris, 1750–1922* (London 2002), pp. 123–4.

[279] Conversation with Tocqueville, reported in Senior, Journal, 7 May 1857, Bangor MS 24644.

[280] Conversation with Léonce de Lavergne, Senior, Journal 8 May 1860, Bangor MS 24649. See also I. Boussard, 'Léonce de Lavergne, un libéral, un des pères de l'école d'économie rurale française (1809–90)', *Cahiers d'histoire* 2000.

[281] Conversation with Senior, reported Journal, 20 May 1860, Bangor MS 24649.

[282] Reported by Senior, Journal, 19 May 1860, ibid.

Liberals remained concerned that the republicans (or indeed the regime) might take advantage of the 'ignorant masses' to secure an electoral base hostile to the established elites. Indeed the journalist Prévost-Paradol equated the Empire with the worst kind of demagogic appeal to 'rural imbecility and provincial bestiality'.[283] Charles de Rémusat who initially assumed that manhood suffrage must 'share in the discredit of everything associated with 1848' did, however, claim to have revised his original judgement in the light of his own election in 1849. This successful outcome had cost only 12,000f. to 15,000f., three weeks' electioneering, and the use of his 'legitimate' influence. The cloud on the horizon, for Rémusat, remained the major cities, where 'the vanguard of the next revolution' seemed to be gathering strength. He was convinced that the impact of 'universal' suffrage needed to be restrained by means of a second chamber or strong monarchy, able to ensure that the State remained capable of satisfying its primary responsibility – the preservation of social order.[284]

Obviously, a divided opposition strengthened the regime's hold on power. Renewed efforts were made to cooperate. In May 1863 Nefftzer, editor of *Le Temps*, established a Comité de l'Union libérale which sought to attract all those, including Bonapartists, Legitimists, Orleanists, and moderate republicans, who might be prepared to compromise on the basis of a liberalised empire. Thiers and the eminent Legitimist lawyer Berryer agreed that this was the only means of effectively combating official electoral pressure. As a result, the 1863 electoral campaign was fought by an Orleanist-dominated Union libérale around forty of whose representatives were elected. These included official candidates like Jules Brame and Chevandier de Valdrôme, Catholics and protectionists like Kolb-Bernard and Plichon, and independents like Buffet and the former republican Ollivier. They could agree on short-term objectives and most notably on the need to impose greater control over the government machine. The divisive issue of a monarchist restoration was ignored.

The scale of support for the Union libérale varied. It was mainly an urban movement, strong where, as in the Nord, shared vital interests – the Church and local industry – seemed threatened.[285] Generally it was plagued by the heterogeneity of its component groups and their reluctance to subordinate their own particular interests. Thus, even where a local Union libérale had successfully been negotiated it was unlikely that clericals and republicans would vote for each other's candidates, a situation leading, for example,

---

[283] Tulard, *Dictionnaire*, p. 510.   [284] Rémusat, *Mémoires*, v, p. 48.
[285] Ménager, 'Vie politique', II, p. 792.

to the defeat of Thiers at Marseille in 1869.[286] Few Legitimists would have gone as far as Berryer, who supported the republican Grévy in an election in the Jura in August 1868. A year later, his death would considerably weaken the alliance, although Falloux continued to press for the cooperation of all those, save revolutionary republicans, who wished to limit the Emperor's personal authority.[287]

Following the elections a diverse group of some forty deputies began to meet regularly and constitute what became known in 1864/5 as the Tiers Parti – 'enemies of reaction as well as of revolution'.[288] Its leading members maintained close links with Thiers and his colleagues on the right as well as with the more moderate republicans.[289] Its twin objectives were liberal reform and social order. Many government loyalists sympathised.[290] The election address of Edouard Laboulaye, a candidate in Bas-Rhin in 1866, was fairly typical. He advised the Emperor that

> to reveal how we can make progress in a liberal direction, how we might improve the 1852 constitution, would at the same time be to serve the interests of the country and the government. Those who look to the future want to grasp liberty with both hands . . . Their great hope is to unite the prince and the country in a common effort.[291]

Increasingly effective collaboration was secured in the Corps législatif where the Tiers Parti appeared to be almost a reconstitution of the Party of Order of the Second Republic – conservative, clerical, and protectionist, as well as anxious to restore the powers of parliament. In March 1866 Buffet organised an amendment to the Address from the Throne which attracted sixty signatures, requesting the Emperor 'to develop fully the potential of the great act of 1860'.

Agreement on a whole range of issues remained difficult to secure, however. Thus whilst prominent liberals like Thiers and the Protestant Guizot were able to support Catholic demands for diplomatic and military action to protect the Papacy – in the interests of political and social conservatism rather than religious truth – and even moderate republicans like Favre and Picard were willing to leave religious issues in abeyance, many Orleanists and most republicans were indifferent or hostile.[292] In *Le Temps* (9 April 1863) Alphonse Peyrat questioned the value of an alliance between liberals

---

[286] Maurain, *Politique ecclésiastique*, pp. 935–6.
[287] In *Le Correspondant*, 25 Feb. and 25 March 1869 quoted ibid. p. 905.
[288] PG Riom, 14 April 1866, AN BB30/386.   [289] Tulard, *Dictionnaire*, p. 662.
[290] See e.g. PG Riom, 14 April 1866, AN BB30/386.
[291] Quoted F. Igersheim, *Politique et administration dans le Bas-Rhin 1848–70* (Strasbourg 1993), p. 586.
[292] Maurain, *Politique ecclésiastique*, pp. 360–1.

and democrats and those who favoured clerical absolutism and who condemned the basic principles of modern society. In 1864, publication of the Papal encyclical *Quanta cura*, accompanied by the Syllabus of Errors, which condemned the principles inherited from 1789, both confirmed the worst fears of Orleanist/liberals and gravely weakened liberal Catholicism.[293]

In these circumstances some liberals were to be increasingly attracted by the prospect of an alliance with moderate republicans. The procureur général at Rouen reported that as a means of 'repudiating the old conservative system' some liberals

display English and American theories on the unrestricted liberty of the citizen and adopt as their programme: the best of republics. Alongside the party's older figures, a new generation is establishing itself which has in its favour talent, boldness, energy and effective propaganda, and which in theory finds the two forms of parliamentary government – constitutional monarchy and the moderate republic – equally acceptable.[294]

This approach, in which both groups modified their programmes to stress their common commitment to parliamentarism, attracted support from amongst the educated professional and business classes. Most liberals, however, including Thiers and Rémusat, remained suspicious. Although obviously determined to oppose further revolutionary violence, even moderate republicans, like Jules Simon and Jules Ferry, appeared overly committed to democracy and social 'progress'.[295]

The limited concessions made by the regime during the 1860s had failed to satisfy most liberals. They appeared half-hearted, their impact reduced by 'the reluctance with which they were introduced'.[296] However, there were grounds for optimism. Disowned as an official candidate, the Comte de Flavigny stood as a liberal at Chinon in 1863, and in his manifesto insisted that 'France alone cannot remain behind, in the midst of the great liberal movement which is developing throughout the world.'[297] The failure of the regime's Mexican policy, together with the Emperor's indecision in the aftermath of the Prussian victory at Sadowa in 1866, further persuaded liberals, including those in government like Walewski or Chasseloup-Laubat, president of the Conseil d'Etat, of the urgent need to push for substantial constitutional change.[298] Considering the prospects for the 1869 elections, Rémusat concluded that even if the same people were elected

[293] See e.g. PG Rouen, 10 July 1862, AN BB30/387.   [294] 12 Jan. 1867, AN BB30/387.
[295] L. Girard, *Les libéraux français, 1814–75* (Paris 1985), p. 183.   [296] Rémusat, *Mémoires*, v, p. 237.
[297] Enclosed with report from PG Orléans, 7 April 1863, AN BB30/382.
[298] See e.g. letter from Mignet to Thiers, 29 July 1866, BN naf 20619; Faucher, *Correspondance*, I,
    p. 241.

they would be subject to intense, informal pressures from within their own *milieu d'origine*, from those 'absolutely disgusted by the worthlessness of their representatives'. The regime's obvious failings, the persistent rumours that major reforms were under consideration, together with their own desire to regain independence and self-respect, would ensure that these deputies exercised sustained pressure on the government.[299]

The Corps législatif elected in 1869 included 163 liberals (both governmental and opposition) alongside 80 authoritarian Bonapartists and 40 republicans. Of these, 116 deputies would be prepared to 'demand the right to question the government on the need to satisfy public opinion by associating it more effectively with the direction of policy'.[300] Ministers were informed by senior officials that this parliamentary action 'gives form and precise objectives' to the opinion of elites throughout the country.[301] A centre-left also emerged, with around forty members, clearly less committed to the Empire than to a liberal government. In spite of doubts and hesitations and frequent regret for the apparent security offered by the authoritarian regime, and although 'few people are capable of clearly defining the regime to which they are drawn by confused aspirations and contradictory ideas',[302] the current of support for liberal reform had gathered strength. Liberalism was *à la mode*,[303] as was constant gossip and criticism directed at the imperial family.[304] There was growing concern about the Emperor's obviously deteriorating health and the apparent 'senility' of the political leadership in general.[305] Liberals demanded that the regime accept that ministers should be responsible to the Corps législatif. This was an innovation finally conceded by an imperial letter published on 12 July 1869 and the *senatus-consulte* of 8 September.

In these changed circumstances Thiers and Rémusat agreed that finally the regime had accepted fundamental liberal principles, in advance even of the much vaunted constitutional *Charte* of 1830, and that liberals should cooperate with the government led by Ollivier and support it against left and right. Faced with the growing threat of revolution they should not seek to weaken further a regime which had engaged in firm repressive action against strikers and revolutionary republican demonstrators in Paris.

---

[299] Rémusat, *Mémoires*, v, pp. 235–7, 246.
[300] Quoted J. Rougerie, 'Le Second Empire', in G. Duby (ed.), *Histoire de la France*, iii (Paris 1972), p. 101.
[301] PG Nancy, 20 Jan. 1870, AN BB30/390; see also PG Paris, 20 May 1861, AN BB30/383.
[302] PG Riom, 11 Jan. 1870, AN BB30/390.   [303] PG Limoges, 6 April 1864, AN BB30/378.
[304] Rouher to Napoleon, 24 Nov. 1867, in A. Poulet-Malassis (ed.), *Papiers secrets et correspondance du Second Empire* (Paris 1873).
[305] Guizot quoted by E. Ollivier, *L'Empire libérale*, vol. ix (Paris 1895–1918), p. 204.

Instead they should accept the dynasty *en fait*, whilst refraining from proclaiming this until after the May 1870 plebiscite.[306] The appointment of a commission to discuss proposals for decentralisation was also welcomed. This, an idea that appealed especially to Legitimist opinion, had become more widely fashionable. The Duc de Broglie, for one, was an advocate of enhancing the powers of the departmental councils, elected bodies which seemed to be securely under the control of established elites and which might serve as an alternative to prefectoral despotism.[307]

The creation of the liberal Empire went a considerable way towards satisfying the political aspirations of liberal members of the social elite. The commission established to discuss reform of the administration of Paris in the wake of the dismissal of Haussmann – the symbol of authoritarian government – and that on the reform of higher education which seemed likely to free it from state control, as the Church had long desired, held out the promise of further change. However, in spite of a widespread sense of satisfaction liberals remained concerned about the Emperor's determination to retain substantial prerogative powers. These included the right to appeal to the nation by means of the plebiscite, as well as the reserved areas of defence and foreign policy. Ollivier's promise that for as long as he remained in office *réaction est impossible* did little to reassure them.[308]

Nevertheless, formerly irreconcilable liberals like Guizot and Barrot began to attend ministerial receptions. Louis-Philippe's former chief minister also agreed to chair the commission on the reform of higher education, and Barrot that on administrative decentralisation. As well as a return to political eminence, they also welcomed renewed access to the spoils of the patronage system. According to Rémusat, Guizot's support for Ollivier's candidature for membership of the Académie française, long a centre of polite opposition to the regime, was not unconnected with his determination to secure the appointment of his son Guillaume to head the division of the Ministère des Cultes responsible for Protestant affairs, although the younger Guizot's dissipated lifestyle might have appeared to disqualify him. After agreeing with Thiers that it might be politic to support Ollivier's ambition to secure election to this pantheon of the literary greats, Rémusat himself went on to canvass a judicial appointment.[309]

It was beginning to appear as if, as an editorial in the *Journal de Roubaix* proclaimed, 'The Empire of 2 December no longer exists.'[310] Liberals might

---

[306] Rémusat, *Mémoires*, vol. v, pp. 265–7.   [307] Girard, *Les libéraux*, pp. 191–2.
[308] Rémusat, *Mémoires*, vol. v, p. 264.
[309] Ibid. pp. 260–2; see also François Guizot, *Lettres à sa fille Henriette, 1836–74* (Paris 2002), p. 973.
[310] 4 Jan. 1870 quoted Ménager, 'Vie politique', vol. ii, p. 868.

continue to distrust the Emperor but as the *Echo du Nord* insisted, 'It would be wrong to sacrifice the interests of the nation because of the antipathy one might feel towards the Head of State. The presence of the Emperor on the throne should not be allowed to prevent those who have condemned the events of 1852 from righting the wrongs from which we have suffered.'[311] There was also the fact that, although they had enjoyed substantial success in mobilising support for their own political initiatives, by the late 1860s the elites were increasingly concerned about the re-emergence of an autonomous middle- and working-class political movement. The growing assertiveness of industrial workers, encouraged by the legalisation of strikes in 1864, had caused considerable disquiet. The repression, which followed the *coup d'état*, had postponed the re-appearance of a combative 'socialistic' challenge. Now reports from the major cities were again extremely alarming.[312]

In a circular to his workers, whose support he confidently took for granted, advising them on how to vote in the 1870 plebiscite, the sentiments expressed by the Saint-Etienne ironmaster Petin are revealing.

If you vote NO you can expect disorder, unemployment, civil war. Remember the misery and complete absence of work after the 1848 Revolution. If you vote YES, the government, its confidence restored by the support you have offered, will further develop those liberties to which you aspire, create more of those provident institutions which will guarantee the well-being of the worker in his old age, prepare all those laws necessary to improve the moral sense and material conditions of the worker, and lastly safeguard social order. Order, gentlemen, is work, employment for you and for us.[313]

Opposition – republicans

Within the elites there was relatively little support for republicanism. It was too closely associated with the Terror of 1793 and the chaos of 1848. Drawn mainly from the liberal professions and business circles, republicans made up fewer than 5 per cent of opposition conseillers généraux in 1870.[314] Official reports reveal considerable difficulty in understanding the allegiance of these 'class traitors'. They are portrayed frequently as men with a sense of grievance due to professional failure or personality problems.[315] The reality was more complicated, of course. Generally, republican notables

[311] 5 Jan. 1870 quoted ibid.   [312] See e.g. G. de Molinari in *Journal des Economistes*, June 1869.
[313] *Circulaire en faveur du plébiscite* (Rive-de-Gier 1870), in BN 4° Lb 56/2792.
[314] Girard, Prost, and Gossez, *Conseillers généraux*, pp. 143–5.
[315] See e.g. PG Aix, 2 July 1859, AN BB30/370.

were the product of family traditions reaching back to the First Republic. Whatever their motives, and regardless of their wealth, however, their politics ensured that they were largely pushed to the fringes of the elite and probably suffered from a sense of exclusion.

Following the demise of the conservative republic, many moderate republicans had been tempted to rally to an empire which promised order and national glory,[316] or else adopted a vague liberalism.[317] Sustaining the commitment of militants in the aftermath of revolution and civil war, and in the face of state repression was a major problem. Local political networks based on private gatherings in the homes of militants or political salons like that hosted by the Comtesse Marie d'Agoult (Daniel Stern) at her home in the Champs-Elysées, engaged in post-mortems and sought to keep the faith alive.[318] Clearly republican confidence in progress and eventual victory had been shaken. The closure of local newspapers had destroyed the organisational base for republican activity, and, together with repeated electoral failure, this caused further demoralisation. Coercion and disillusionment ensured that republican electoral candidates would be few and far between. Furthermore, the repression which had driven so many republicans into exile or inactivity once again allowed the moderates, who had presided over the Provisional Government of 1848, to eclipse the more radical *démocrate-socialistes*, dominant before the *coup d'état*. The respectable social position of such eminences as General Cavaignac, who had been responsible for the brutal repression of the June insurrection, limited the risks they took by becoming involved in political activity. They could not seriously be accused of plotting 'red' revolution and remained determined to reject all contacts with 'extremists'.[319]

Cavaignac, and Carnot, education minister in the Provisional Government, stood successfully for election in Paris in 1852 and along with Goudchaux, a banker and former republican finance minister, again in 1857. However, on principle, they refused to take the oath of loyalty to the Emperor and were unseated as a result. Otherwise, their republicanism was very moderate. They were distinguished from Orleanist liberals, whose social backgrounds and political ideas they shared, by their commitment to the parliamentary republic, and, if not always without misgivings, to manhood suffrage.[320] They were firmly opposed to violence. An eminent

[316] See e.g. PG Aix, 7 July 1860, AN BB30/370.   [317] PG Agen, 9 Sept. 1853, AN BB30/370.
[318] S. Hazareesingh, *Intellectual Founders of the Republic* (Oxford 2001), p. 1.
[319] See e.g. PG Montpellier, 8 Oct. 1862, AN BB30/380 re Garnier-Pagès' visit to the city.
[320] See e.g. A. Lecanu, *La Révolution par le suffrage universel* (Paris 1869), pp. 11f.

republican like Jules Simon could even earnestly hope that the sudden demise of the Emperor would not be followed by the advent of the republic. He was afraid that if republican militants managed to seize power in the capital, the government they established 'would not be the moderate republic of Cavaignac, but the republic of Ledru-Rollin, Louis Blanc and Caussidière', which would be smashed immediately and probably followed by an Orleanist restoration.[321]

Although equally moderate in their objectives Nefftzer and Havin, editors of the democratic newspapers *La Presse* and *Le Siècle*, were concerned increasingly that the refusal to take the oath of loyalty and exclusion from the Corps législatif would discourage potential supporters. The election committee they helped to establish in 1857, which included Cavaignac and Carnot, was divided on the issue. Nevertheless, both then and in by-elections the following year, the five republicans elected – the lawyers Ernest Picard, Emile Ollivier, and Jules Favre and the journalist Darimon in Paris, together with Dr Hénon in Lyon – were willing to take the oath of allegiance, with mental reservations, as the price of entering the Corps législatif. It was after all imposed on them by force and 'it cannot be your duty to God to keep a promise which it is your duty to your country to break'.[322] Their debating skills would add substantial weight to parliamentary opposition. In 1863 the Cinq were to be joined by a further twelve republican deputies whose commitment to a *révolution pacifique* increased their appeal to a broader liberal constituency.[323] Garnier-Pagès, another former Finance Minister in 1848, had organised a committee, again dominated by the men of 1848, whose members travelled by rail to over sixty towns in an attempt to persuade local republicans to present candidates.[324]

However, moderation carried its own risks. Once caught up in parliamentary processes, Ollivier and Darimon would be attracted increasingly by the prospect of a compromise with the regime. As a result, they faced growing suspicion from their erstwhile colleagues. During the debate on the legislation legalising strikes in 1864, which Ollivier had been asked to present on behalf of the government, Simon rejected collaboration and denounced what he saw as Ollivier's personal ambition.[325] The subsequent desertion of the republican movement by Ollivier and Darimon was taken to represent a warning about the danger of cooperating with the regime. Illustrating the unbridgeable gulf which had opened up, in December 1869

[321] Conversation with Nassau William Senior reported Journal, 10 June 1855, Bangor MS 24637.
[322] Senior, conversation with Rivet reported Journal, 9 May 1857, Bangor MS 24644.
[323] See e.g. PG Lyon, 1 April 1862, AN BB30/379.
[324] P. Pilbeam, *Republicanism in Nineteenth Century France, 1814–71* (London 1995), p. 249.
[325] See e.g. Rémusat, *Mémoires*, v, p. 242.

in a letter congratulating Ollivier on the forthcoming establishment of a liberal Empire, Darimon would condemn the blindness of their former colleagues. Whilst paying tribute to the achievements of the Cinq, the emphasis in his letter was on the success of 'a reign, which is transforming itself in order to oppose the threat of revolution'.[326]

The emergence of a more radical middle- and working-class movement in the later 1860s would represent a further challenge to the leadership offered by republican members of the socio-political elite. In Paris, during the 1869 election campaign, moderate republicans were subject to vicious attacks in the newly free press and at public meetings. They were condemned as too bourgeois and too conservative. In response, in a brochure on *La Révolution de 1869*, Arnaud de l'Ariège, another stalwart of 1848, expressed the hope that the Parisian population 'will not commit the immense mistake of inaugurating the period of radical change into which we are rapidly marching with demonstrations, the only effect of which will be to alarm the country and furnish new pretexts for the exercise of dictatorial power'.[327] Moderates were determined to disassociate themselves from the increasingly vocal revolutionaries and socialists, typically insisting that 'The left certainly wants to overthrow the empire; but it intends to accomplish this by legal means.'[328] They were anxious not to frighten the electorate.

Moderate republicans could promise 'progress without revolution' and present themselves as 'the real conservatives'.[329] Jules Favre was even prepared to compliment Adolphe Thiers, the brutal former Orleanist interior minister and hate figure for many republicans, for his services to the cause of liberty.[330] A militant in the Loiret since 1848, Louis-Adolphe Cochery stressed his support for peace, lower taxes and the *libertés nécessaires* in his election manifesto. He denied vehemently the charge made by his Bonapartist opponent that he was a supporter of revolutionary change, claiming that 'we have, in our ranks, the richest landowners in the area. For all of us, revolution would bring ruin. The value of our properties would collapse; the capital we have invested would be swallowed up in the tempests. No! Never a Revolution!'[331]

As in 1848/9, notables again ran the risk of losing control over the republican movement as part of a process of political and social polarisation. Nevertheless, within the republican movement, moderates were able to

---

[326] Darimon, *Les cent seize*, p. 221, entry of 29 Dec. 1869.
[327] F. Arnaud, *La Révolution de 1869* (Paris 1869), p. iv.
[328] Darimon, *Les cent seize*, p. 153, entry 31 Oct. 1869.
[329] *Independance du Midi*, 19 May 1869, quoted Huard, *Préhistoire*, p. 823.
[330] Letter 6 May 1864, BN naf 20619.
[331] *L'Independant de Montargis*, 29 May 1869, quoted by J. Goueffon, 'Le parti républicain dans le Loiret à la fin du Second Empire' in J. Viard (ed.), *L'esprit républicain* (Paris 1972), p. 291.

assume control over most newspapers as a result of their personal wealth.[332] Gastineau, editor of the Nantes *Phare de la Loire*, was dismissed because the *pseudo-démocrates* as he called them thought him too radical by far.[333] The social influence of republican members of the elite could also effectively be employed. In Saint-Etienne the ironmasters Dorian and Fourneyron benefited from their reputation as 'good' employers and their status as providers of work, to retain dominant roles in the republican opposition. Dorian easily defeated the socialist candidate Antide Martin.[334]

Partly, however, as a result of these inner divisions, partly due to the inability of even the moderates to escape entirely from association with the threat of 'red' revolution, and especially because of the positive appeal of the regime, only thirty republicans were to be elected in 1869. Failure could nevertheless still be blamed on government manipulation of voters and the 'immaturity' of the electorate, particularly in the countryside. Typically, Jules Ferry dismissed peasant voters as ignorant, superstitious, and naive.[335] Republicans could also insist that the rural vote counted for nothing alongside the enlightened urban response.[336] Thus it remained possible to conclude that 'the future is ours . . . as long as we refuse to compromise on our principles'.[337] The young Waldeck-Rousseau, for one, was scandalised by the wealth and intolerance of the clergy and by the renewal, in the late 1860s, of the alliance between Church and State.[338] The development of a secular educational system would one day provide the essential means of enlightening the rural population and of liberating it from the dead hand of clericalism.

At least republicans of all shades could agree to support a 'No' vote in the plebiscite of 1870. However, the campaign mounted by moderates was characterised still by its restraint. A *Manifeste de la Gauche* (20 April) signed by the republican deputies and the delegates of the *presse démocratique* pointed out that:

The 2 December submitted France to the power of a single man.
The new constitution will not establish government of the people by the people;
It is just pretence.
Personal rule has not been destroyed; its most important prerogatives have been preserved intact . . .

---

[332] See Anceau, *Les députés*, p. 511 on incomes of republican deputies.
[333] Launay, *Diocèse de Nantes*, II, p. 770.   [334] Gordon, *Merchants*, pp. 144–6, 151–3.
[335] P. Rosanvallon, *Le sacre du citoyen. Histoire du suffrage universel en France* (Paris 1992), p. 352.
[336] See e.g. J. Claretie, *La volonté du Peuple* (Paris 1869), pp. 27–8.
[337] H. Allain-Targé, *La République sous l'Empire. Lettres 1867–70* (Paris 1939), p. 30.
[338] P. Sorlin, *Waldeck-Rousseau* (Paris 1966), pp. 113f.

. . . Today, as then, a free hand is being demanded from you, the alienation of
your sovereignty, . . .
In the name of the sovereignty of the people and the dignity of the nation, in the
name of order and social peace, which can only be achieved through the conciliation
of interests and classes, within a free democracy . . .
Vote NO.[339]

The essential messages were irreconcilable opposition to the regime,
together with a renewed commitment to the preservation of social order.
Defeat would be followed by even more bitter denunciations of the peasant
voter, of this *être brut et grossier*.[340]

CONCLUSION

The 1870 plebiscite campaign revealed the growing intensity of social fear
amongst the social elites. This was the result of numerous press reports,
frequently subject to official manipulation, concerning violent strikes at
Decazeville, Aubin, and Le Creusot, and on the revolutionary speeches
made in numerous public meetings in Paris. An article in the Bonapartist
newspaper *La Patrie* (21 May 1870) illustrates the deliberate effort to intensify anxiety:

In the quartier Mouffetard the other evening a sinister-looking individual told
the concierge of a religious institution, as she was shutting the door: *You do well
to shut yourself in, you won't be able to stop them coming to cut off your head. In a
couple of weeks*, said another, *we'll be happy; no more work; no more taxes; no more
priests.*

Some of the children leaving school, who heard these demagogic vows told the
Sister who taught them, the following day: *Those horrible men want to kill the
priests. We hope that they'll wait for another week, so that we'll at least be able to take
our First Communion.*

Articles like this reinforced 'the fear and revulsion' which the 'proletariat'
inspired.[341] Memories of 1848 remained strong and anxiety about the future
became increasingly intense.[342] Some authoritarian Bonapartists believed
that this situation provided an opportunity to re-establish the regime
of the *coup d'état*. However, in a speech on 19 May 1870, the Emperor
assured liberals that no turning back was intended. Although Legitimist
and Orleanist/liberal leaders recommended abstention in the plebiscite,
once more most of their supporters would rally to the imperial regime.

---

[339] E. Arago *et al.*, *Manifeste de la Gauche* (Paris, 20 April 1870).
[340] Rosanvallon, *Le sacre*, p. 35.   [341] PG Dijon, 14 Jan. 1870, AN BB30/390.
[342] See e.g. PG Besançon, 14 Jan. 1870, ibid.

Already, in the 1869 election, those liberal candidates, including such eminences as Prévost-Paradol, Albert de Broglie, and Casimir Périer, who had
refused to rally to the liberalising empire, had been soundly defeated. For
most of the social elite, already sufficient liberalisation had been achieved.
Old doubts about universal suffrage had been re-awakened by disorder.
Liberals began to 'change their minds when faced with the consequences of
policies which would culminate in a social revolution'.[343] Clericals tended
to turn again towards the Bonapartist solution. A process of political polarisation between a Bonapartist/monarchist/liberal right and a republican left
was clearly under way.

The problem, according to the procureur général at Dijon, for both
the regime and its critics within the social elite was to reconcile 'the order
necessary for life in society with the full extension of liberty'. For the vast
majority of upper class voters

the nuances separating the old parties are fading . . . We can see re-appearing
ever more clearly, a situation similar to that of 1850. Aware of the demands of
universal suffrage, the men of order belonging to the different parties feel the
need to unite . . . They understand that due to the pressure of events there
are now only two parties, standing face to face, the friends of Monarchy and
those who proclaim themselves to be its adversaries. They realise that only the
Napoleonic Dynasty will be able to ensure that the banner of monarchy remains
unfurled.[344]

With official encouragement liberal, together with authoritarian Bonapartist politicians, organised pro-Yes committees. In the Nord these
included the leading figures in the protectionist and clerical campaigns
against the regime. The representatives of industrial interests, desperate
for security, centre-left deputies like Plichon and Brame, could hardly be
expected to support a 'No' campaign.[345] The ironmasters at Longwy in the
east similarly presented the choice as 'between order and disorder . . . To
support a *No* is to vote in favour of revolution, disorder, economic stagnation, the collapse of our power in the face of the foreigner.'[346] Furthermore,
liberal politicians welcomed the deployment of troops against strikers and
demonstrators on the streets of the capital. In his political bulletin the gendarmerie commander for the Paris region reported that 'many of those who
had appeared to distance themselves from the Government, are returning to it, and linking themselves more firmly to it, because it represents

[343] PG Nîmes, 18 Jan. 1869, AN BB30/389.   [344] PG Dijon, 14 Jan. 1870, AN BB30/390.
[345] Ménager, 'Vie politique', II, pp. 879–81.
[346] Quoted T. Lentz, 'Le plébiscite du 8 mai 1870 en Moselle', *Les cahiers lorrains* (1988), pp. 316–17.

order and security'.[347] By late April, the officer responsible for the city itself was convinced that the 'Yes' vote would be much larger than anyone had predicted.[348] As in December 1851 much of this renewed support was conditional and would no doubt weaken as social fear declined. In the meantime liberty with order was the essential theme. That, once again, the emphasis had shifted to the latter, however, marked a return to the position favoured by the social elites during the Second Republic. The success of the plebiscite would encourage a further rallying to the regime.[349]

The establishment of a stable liberal administration was never going to be easy. Although they had substantially restored their political power, members of the social elite remained divided by personal and generational rivalries, as well as ideological and tactical differences.[350] In the Corps législatif itself it was all too evident that the two most eminent liberals, Thiers and Ollivier, distrusted each other deeply. Certainly it is doubtful whether a ministry headed by Ollivier, an individual enjoying the support of the Emperor but otherwise isolated both at court and in government, could have survived for long.[351]

Ernest Picard, nevertheless, described the liberal empire as 'a sort of provisional government of the parliamentary regime'.[352] The eventual objective of liberal politicians should now be to secure dissolution of parliament and free elections to reinforce the liberal majority. In the meantime, however, the logic of the situation suggested that they should 'suspend all systematic and radical opposition'.[353] The reforms proposed by the *senatus-consulte* of 8 September 1869 thus secured the approbation of almost all liberal politicians, from the aged Guizot to Prévost-Paradol representing the younger generation. For protectionists the launching of an economic enquiry, together with the presence of Buffet in the new government, seemed to foreshadow the end of free trade; clericals were encouraged by the promise of greater freedom for the Church in higher education. Furthermore, again hostility to the regime was outweighed by fear of social revolution. Elites wanted strong government. The Party of Order was becoming more attractive than the Union libérale. Having revealed his willingness to adapt, and to liberalise his regime, Napoleon III appeared well placed to serve as a social and political arbitrator once more. For Darimon, the

[347] Ier Légion. Bulletin politique du Chef de Légion, 31 Jan. 1870, AHG G8/176.
[348] OC Cie. de la Seine, 28 April 1870, ibid.
[349] See e.g. PG Besançon, 8 July 1870, AN BB30/390; GOC Ier Légion gendarmerie, 31 May 1870, AHG G8/176.
[350] See e.g. PG Bordeaux, 12 April 1867, AN BB30/374; Igersheim, *Politique et administration*, p. 669.
[351] Point made by Persigny, 4 Jan. 1870, reported in Darimon, *Les cent seize*, p. 226.
[352] Ibid. entry of 2 March 1870.   [353] Ibid. p. 270.

former moderate republican, 'what has happened has no analogy in our history . . . This is a regime which has transformed itself in order to prevent a threatened revolution.'[354]

The liberal Empire appeared to have established a solid base of support within the social elite. Its adherents were convinced that they had recovered the political power they had possessed during the July Monarchy, whilst retaining the services of an Emperor who would guarantee their personal security and that of their possessions. It was almost the best of all possible worlds – 'the most effective means of reconciling order and liberty'.[355] Now Charles de Rémusat could accept that the nation possessed the *libertés nécessaires* and that, in this respect, the situation was even better than during the July Monarchy – 'We have everything the Charter contained and more again; there are no government officials in the elected chamber. The system is much more advanced than any we had proposed . . . It will come as a shock to the entire world to find that France enjoys more freedom than ever before.'[356]

[354] Ibid. p. 221, entry of 29 Dec. 1869.   [355] PG Besançon, 14 Jan. 1870, AN BB30/390.
[356] Quoted Girard, *Les libéraux*, p. 208.

CHAPTER 3

Aspiring social groups: the middle classes

INTRODUCTION: PROBLEMS OF DEFINITION

In spite of differences in lifestyle and political behaviour, the elites analysed in the previous two chapters were the most coherent of the social groups whose politics we are to consider. They were composed of relatively small numbers of people, adept at organisation and determined to protect their property, status, and influence. The 'middle classes' are far more difficult to define and their political behaviour is especially diverse. Moreover, whilst senior government officials – our privileged observers – were well informed about the activities and attitudes of elites to which they belonged themselves and, to a lesser extent, about the rural milieu in which they frequently resided, or even the workers who attracted attention because they were believed to pose a major threat to social order, they were less conversant with the middle classes.

However, contemporary observers certainly recognised their existence, employing terms such as *bourgeoisie, classes moyennes*, and *petite bourgeoisie* in more-or-less haphazard fashion. Used as an adjective the word *bourgeois* frequently had pejorative connotations – vulgarity, lack of taste, meanness, and timidity. This was certainly the case in Daumier's caricatures, and in the novelist Flaubert's contempt for philistinism. More positively, it might denote a commitment to work, thrift, property, order, liberty, and civil equality. According to the definition in the second edition of Pierre Larousse's *Grand Dictionnaire* published in 1867 the term *bourgeoisie* was applied to a member of the *classe moyenne*. The author observed that: 'In the eyes of the masses, whoever possesses a certain quantity of capital, whether that person exploits it directly or lives off the income he obtains' would have been included.[1] The socialist theoretician P.-J. Proudhon identified a 'landowning and capitalist aristocracy' which, confusingly, he described as

---

[1] See especially J.-P. Chaline, entry on bourgeoisie, in Tulard, *Dictionnaire*, pp. 205–6.

'the modern bourgeoisie', and which he believed was 'analogous, in terms of its numerical strength and the patronage it exercised to *l'ancienne noblesse*'. To this he opposed a *classe moyenne* which 'is made up of entrepreneurs, shopkeepers, manufacturers, farmers, intellectuals, artists, etc. living off their own efforts rather than that of their capital, privileges and properties, but distinguishing themselves from the proletariat because they work, as is commonly said, on their own account, are fully responsible for losses and have an exclusive right to the gains, whereas the worker labours in return for a wage'.[2]

Historians have sub-divided the *bourgeoisie* into *grande, moyenne*, and *petite* – upper, middle, and lower. Having placed the upper middle class in the social elite, our concern in this chapter then is essentially with the middle and lower middle classes, groups making up around 15 to 20 per cent of the total population.[3] In terms of income, this was a middle class in between the very rich (the social elite) and the masses. In terms of profession, J.-P. Chaline distinguishes a *bourgeoisie d'entreprise* engaged in industry and commerce including, at its base, a large mass of shopkeepers and master artisans and, at its summit, wholesale merchants, the proprietors of factories and luxury shops.[4] The 1851 census revealed the small scale of most of this business activity, estimating that nationally there were 124,000 employers in *grande industrie* employing 1,300,000 workers (a ratio of 1:11);[5] and 1,550,000 in *petite industrie* with 2,800,000 workers (1:2). The 1866 census makes it clear that subsequently concentration was slow. Chaline also identifies a *bourgeoisie de la rente* dependent on the interest from state loans, and revenue from rural and urban property, including, in predominantly working-class *quartiers*, the artisans and shopkeepers who enjoyed small rental incomes. His schema further includes a *bourgeoisie du savoir* including those who had secured diplomas through higher education and were employed in the liberal and cultural professions or state bureaucracy.

Income and the lifestyle it allowed were the major determinants of social status. At the top end of the middle-class hierarchy prosperous and successful landowners, professionals, and businessmen sought social acceptance, if not within the social elite, at least within an emerging caste of prosperous and 'respectable' local notables. Although the level of expenditure necessary to 'express a social position, to distinguish oneself from the masses', was very

---

[2] *La révolution sociale démontrée par le coup d'état* (Paris 1852), pp. 124–5.
[3] Daumard, *Les bourgeois*, p. 181.　　　[4] Chaline, entry on bourgeoisie in Tulard, *Dictionnaire*.
[5] Statistique générale de la France: Territoire et population, *Résultats généraux du denombrement de 1851* (Paris 1855); T.-J. Markovitch, 'L'industrie française de 1789 à 1964', *Cahiers de l'ISEA* (1967), p. 87 estimates 1:14.5.

much lower than that required by members of the social elite, it was still necessary to dress 'properly', live in decent, well-furnished accommodation, and employ domestic help. The young needed to be educated in the local *lycée* or college and taught the appropriate social skills. If they could afford the cost, members of the middle classes were likely to adopt some features of an idealised aristocratic lifestyle, spending their time taking care of their investments, socialising, engaging in intellectual pursuits and in local, voluntary, administrative activities.[6] These were activities which facilitated the emergence *within* the middle classes of coherent social networks whose members would play a leading role in local politics.

A family's position within the middle class, as well as the wider society, additionally depended on the status of the profession followed by its male head. Occupations were assessed in relation to the wealth they generated and, also, according to such factors as the degree of independence, leisure, and freedom from manual and 'money-grubbing' activity, they allowed. Landownership, possession of 'real' property, was more prestigious than investment in the 3 per cent state *rente* to which many families looked for a secure income. The liberal professions – particularly law and medicine, access to which depended on an expensive education – were more highly regarded than business and particularly 'trade', which required even a well-off shopkeeper to adopt a 'servile' attitude towards his clients.[7] Each profession also had its own hierarchy in large part determined by age, with wealth and status often increasing over time as a result of inheritance and successful professional activity. Furthermore, to an important degree, within their own callings, professional men and shopkeepers shared the status of their clients.

At the bottom end of the middle-class hierarchy, even its poorest members – the proliferating *petite bourgeoisie*, again a rather heterogeneous group of shopkeepers, master-artisans, and clerks[8] – were generally better off than the mass of peasants and workers. They possessed some property, some savings, and enjoyed a greater degree of security, even if they remained exposed to the vagaries of the economic cycle. Furthermore, although close to the masses in terms of origins and incomes the *petit bourgeois* 'distinguishes himself by a more independent situation, a slightly higher level of education' and especially because 'he is driven by a process of social emulation

---

[6] Chaline, 'La bourgeoisie rouennaise', p. 195.

[7] P. Harrigan, 'The social origins, ambitions, and occupations of secondary students in France during the Second Empire' in L. Stone (ed.), *Schooling and Society* (London 1976), p. 216.

[8] See e.g. G. Crossick and H.-G. Haupt, 'Shopkeepers, master artisans and the historian: the petite bourgeoisie in comparative focus' in Crossick and Haupt (eds.), *Shopkeepers and Artisans in 19th Century Europe* (London 1984), pp. 6–7.

which encourages him to copy, to the extent of his means, the *bourgeois* model, if only in terms of dress'.[9]

Thus the essential analytical problem is posed by the diversity of the middle classes, and the existence of internal divisions, which were often quite as profound as those separating the middle classes from other 'classes'. What did these diverse middle-class groups have in common? Other than convenience, is there any justification for considering them under a single classificatory heading? It might be argued that – together with members of the social elite and peasants – they shared a common interest in the ownership of property. In addition, they shared certain values, and especially a possessive individualism, a commitment to the family, and to hard work, and a willingness to accept personal responsibility. Individuals were generally obsessed by the need to improve or at least preserve their often hard-won social status. Thus to a large degree middle-class self-definition represented a negative response to anything that threatened this. The exclusiveness of the social elites and their enjoyment of the 'privileges' of wealth was frequently resented. In the early years of its constitution the modern capital market appeared particularly anarchic and subject to speculative excess. The activities of the 'finance aristocracy' – the bankers and the large-scale merchants who controlled interest rates, credit, and access to markets – were frequently perceived to be a major threat, and roundly condemned in both economic and moral terms.[10] Beneath them in the social hierarchy, the masses, tempted by the promise of revolution, appeared to pose a further menace.

SOCIAL GEOGRAPHY

Census returns and probate archives provide information on profession and wealth. Nevertheless, even counting the middle classes is rendered difficult by the divergent census categories employed and the fact that they undoubtedly lagged behind and distorted 'reality'. Also there were considerable geographical and chronological variations in socio-professional structures and in the determinants of status, making generalisations on the basis of micro-studies extremely hazardous. Moreover, the information provided offers only limited insights into social relationships, so that it is only by means of 'the global study of an urban society, and through the accumulated knowledge of a multiplicity of indicators that [the historian]

---

[9] Chaline, entry on bourgeoisie in Tulard, *Dictionnaire*, p. 206.

[10] See e.g. P. Verley, 'L'anticapitalisme quarante-huitard ou l'apprentissage des circuits de finance' in J.-M. Barrelet and P. Henry (eds.), *1848–1998. Neuchâtel, la Suisse, l'Europe* (Fribourg 2001), p. 103.

is able to define this social milieu and to understand in practical terms what it was to be *un bourgeois*'.[11]

Thus, in Lyon, the nation's second city, a group of wealthy *haut bourgeois* emerged from the rapidly growing silk, engineering, and chemicals industries. Beneath them in the hierarchy of wealth and status was a *moyenne bourgeoisie* leaving an inheritance worth anything between 50 and 250,000 francs and made up of *rentiers* living off the income from property, stocks, and shares; merchants; most members of the professions; together with the most successful shopkeepers and prosperous manufacturers (as opposed to industrialists). Below these came a much more numerous *petite bourgeoisie* made up of less-well-off *rentiers*, minor government officials and clerks in private enterprise, most of the small workshop owners, merchants, and shopkeepers, particularly those in food retailing.[12] The Crédit lyonnais, assessing the credit worthiness of enterprises in the Lyon silk industry in 1868 identified 20 large mechanised producers, a second group of 366 medium sized enterprises, then a mass of around 8,000 small, poorly equipped, essentially artisanal workshops, largely dependent on subcontracting for the larger firms.[13] Beneath them again was a world of poverty and insecurity into which small businessmen were constantly afraid of falling. Nevertheless, the Second Empire was a period of opportunity, during which substantial upward mobility seemed possible. In Lille in northern France, a major and rapidly developing textile, engineering, commercial, and administrative centre, the *haute bourgeoisie* has been estimated to have grown, during the Second Empire, from 1.5 to 6 per cent of the population, the middle and lower middle classes to have increased from 20.2 to 32.9 per cent.[14]

It is worth distinguishing between such major population centres and the numerous small provincial towns. In a country town in Normandy, like Bayeux, landowners were the wealthiest and most prestigious social group, followed by members of the liberal professions, merchants, and artisans. In the nearby port of Honfleur, merchants were the dominant group.[15] The many small towns and villages in the Paris region contained a rural bourgeoisie made up of wealthy farmers who no longer worked the land themselves and who dressed, lived, and educated and married their

---

[11] Chaline, entry in Tulard, *Dictionnaire*, p. 205.
[12] P. Léon, *Géographie de la fortune et structures sociales à Lyon au 19e siècle* (Lyon 1975), pp. 60, 150–1.
[13] P. Cayez, *Crises et croissance de l'industrie lyonnaise 1850–1900* (Paris 1980), p. 77.
[14] F.-P. Codaccioni, *De l'inégalité sociale dans une grande ville industrielle. Le drame de Lille de 1850 à 1914* (Lille 1976), pp. 64–5.
[15] G. Désert, 'Structures sociales dans les villes Bas-Normands au 19e siècle' in *Conjoncture économique, structures sociales. Hommage à Ernest Labrousse* (Paris 1974), p. 503.

children in a style which clearly distinguished them from the mass of peasant cultivators. The prefect of Seine-et-Marne considered that the 2,350 *grands fermiers* in the Brie 'form a caste which is perhaps unique'.[16] They had become the dominant influence in most rural communities, rather than the aristocrats whose land they rented. Socially they, or at least their better-educated children, tended to mix with *propriétaires-rentiers* living off rental income and the more successful merchants and professional men resident in the local market centres.[17] In economically less dynamic parts of central France like the Limousin, besides Limoges with its substantial industrial and commercial interests, some 10 per cent of the active population in little towns like Ussel were employed in the liberal professions or administration, whilst in towns lacking administrative functions the middle class was made up of landowners, merchants, and small manufacturers with a smaller proportion of professionals.[18] In numerous market towns and large villages (*bourgs*), millers and blacksmiths were also often men of some substance.[19]

The middle classes were then both urban and rural. Land remained a favoured investment, offering security and reasonable financial returns. Urban residents frequently possessed property in the countryside. Many of them had inherited wealth; others had retired from professional or business activity. An administrative and marketing centre like Angers, in 1856, sheltered 5,226 landowners out of a total population of 51,000, some no doubt living in quite straitened circumstances.[20] Even in a rapidly industrialising area like the Pas-de-Calais, whilst investing mainly in their own enterprises, and increasingly in railways or the local mining companies, businessmen continued to acquire land. Thus, whilst in 1851 60 per cent of merchants and manufacturers had either inherited or purchased land, by 1878 the proportion had risen to 76 per cent.[21] This preference for land was even more likely in upland areas and in the south and west, where business opportunities were more limited. Nevertheless, investment decisions were influenced increasingly by new opportunities. The purchase of stocks and shares, which appeared to offer a decent income for little effort, was becoming attractive.[22]

---

[16] 1859 quoted P. Bernard, *Economie et sociologie*, p. 173.   [17] See e.g. Farcy, *Paysans*, I, p. 400.

[18] Corbin, *Archaïsme*, I, pp. 19–20.   [19] Farcy, *Paysans*, II, p. 435.

[20] S. Chassagne, 'L'histoire des villes: une opération de rénovation historiographique?' in M. Garden (ed.), *Villes et campagnes, 15e–20e siècle* (Lyon 1977), p. 242.

[21] R. Hubscher, 'L'agriculture et la société rurale dans le Pas-de-Calais du milieu du 19e siècle à 1914', Doc. d'Etat, Univ. de Paris, 1978, III, p. 1584.

[22] E.g. PG Besançon, 3 July 1854, AN BB30/373.

Closely associated with landowners were members of the liberal professions, most of whom were only partially dependent on professional
earnings. Indeed, probate information revealed that in 1851 in the Pas-
de-Calais two-thirds of the wealth of this group was derived from property
ownership.[23] The law remained the most prestigious and exclusive of the
professions. In 1867 there were 4,895 law students[24] recruited mainly from
amongst the social elites and well-off bourgeois. Entry into the profession
frequently reflected family tradition, and membership of established social
networks provided a major means of advancement. Also it represented
the determination of up-and-coming landowners or businessmen to
enhance the reputation of their families by establishing their sons in
respectable professional careers. Solicitors (*avoués*) and notaries exerted
considerable local influence as a result of the building boom, the rising
price of land, and the growing demand for their services as financial intermediaries – providers of loans and mortgages. Barristers (*avocats*) worked
in a more crowded and competitive arena. Doctors were another group
whose status was rapidly improving, although a great disparity continued
to exist between the medical aristocracy made up of Parisian professors
and specialists and doctors dealing with the poor in town and country. In
1866 there were 16,822 qualified doctors, of whom 11,254 were practising,
together with 5,568 less-well-qualified health officers.[25]

Another feature of a modernising society was the growth of public and
private services. Whilst the key decision-making positions were occupied by
members of the social elite, individuals with a modicum of education were
offered employment with more limited responsibilities, but which nevertheless provided relatively secure remuneration and a pension – important
benefits in a pre-welfare society. Such highly trained groups as engineers,
especially those graduating from the *grandes écoles* – Polytechnique, Mines
and Pont et Chaussées – and typically employed by the government or railway companies, increasingly enjoyed considerable respect and substantial
rewards. Save in the most senior and prestigious posts, within the public sector salaries rarely exceeded 5,000f a year. This was the income a
lycée teacher in the provinces might expect as he approached retirement.
Secondary-school teachers, on the borderline between the *moyenne* and
petite bourgeoisie were recruited primarily from amongst the middle bourgeoisie, from the sons of the commercial and liberal professions, for many

[23] Hubscher, 'L'agriculture', III, p. 1592.
[24] R. Anderson, *Education in France, 1848–70* (Oxford 1975), p. 228.
[25] T. Zeldin, *France, 1840–1945* (Oxford 1972), I, p. 37; G. Weisz, 'The politics of medical profession-
alization in France, 1845–48', *Journal of Social History* 1978/9, p. 6.

of whom teaching must have represented downward or at best horizontal mobility. At least it preserved their bourgeois status. Moreover, each profession possessed its own internal hierarchy representing individual achievement and an earning potential which tended to reflect age and experience.

An industrial *patronat* was also rapidly emerging as part of this *moyenne bourgeoisie*. Whilst a small proportion of the most successful belonged to the social elite, most were part of an industrial bourgeoisie which controlled small or medium-sized enterprises. They generally belonged to families which had emerged in the late eighteenth and early nineteenth centuries, mainly from the commercial classes. During the 1840s and Second Empire the development of more integrated and competitive markets stimulated capital investment and the more rapid concentration of production, particularly in modernising sectors like mining, metallurgy and heavy engineering, and textiles. The cost of initial entry into these sectors became increasingly prohibitive; a small, mechanised weaving mill with 100 looms required an investment of 150,000 to 200,000 francs whilst previously handlooms had cost 40 to 50f. each.[26]

However, the pace of change should not be exaggerated. The scale of business activity varied considerably. Major sectors of the economy including building, foodstuffs, furniture, clothing, and luxury goods remained overwhelmingly small scale, responding to local consumer demand or rapidly changing fashions. In the 1860s, around 85 per cent of gross product was still accounted for by traditional industries.[27] Until quite recently, historians showed limited interest in socio-professional groups which, according to the Marxist schema, were doomed to disappear. Yet, in many respects, these were key intermediary groups. According to Ernest Labrousse, artisans 'were responsible for the bulk of production and distribution in the secondary and tertiary sectors. At the lowest levels and in the most basic forms, economically bordering on the wage-earners, they constituted a quasi-proletariat. At the highest levels . . . they bordered on the commercial petite bourgeoisie and represented a quasi-bourgeoisie, part of the world of the small businessman.'[28] By the early 1860s there were an estimated 1,420,000 employers, with 1,600,000 workers, engaged in handicraft production. Some 40 per cent of these were involved in the manufacture of shoes and clothing, 20 per cent in woodworking, 15 per cent in building, and 15 per cent in milling and baking.[29]

[26] J. Lambert-Dansette, *Genèse du patronat, 1780–1880* (Paris 1991), p. 172.
[27] J. Desmarest, *L'évolution de la France contemporaine. La France de 1870* (Paris 1970), p. 108.
[28] E. Labrousse (ed.), *Colloque d'histoire sur l'artisanat et l'apprentissage* (Aix 1965), p. 2.
[29] Markovitch, 'L'industrie française', p. 87; Desmarest, *L'évolution*, p. 164.

In Paris, according to the 1847/8 Chamber of Commerce enquiry, there were 64,816 *fabricants* employing 342,530 workers. Of these 32,583 worked alone or with a single worker, 25,116 employed 2 to 10 workers and 7,117 (i.e. 11 per cent of the total) more than 10. Using different criteria, the 1861 census estimated that there were 101,000 (including 18,000 in the annexed *banlieu*), employing on average 5.4 workers.[30] In spite of Haussmann's demolitions and rising rents, many small businessmen clung on in the old streets surviving behind the new boulevards. In trades as diverse as printing and precision engineering on the right bank of the Seine, and jewellery in the Marais, there was a practical need to remain close to the supply of skilled labour, markets, and suppliers. Aspiring small businessmen found new opportunities through subcontracting and the provision of specialised services. Building craftsmen, anxious to set up on their own, required very little capital.

In addition to urban, there were also substantial numbers of rural artisans, who formed an intermediary group, in terms of status, between the local bourgeoisie and the remainder of the population. Growing prosperity created new needs at the same time as the collapse of some forms of small-scale rural manufacture – metallurgy, textiles – promoted a process of ruralisation. In the cereal cultivating region of the Beauce (excluding Chartres) the *patrons* of shops and workshops made up 15 per cent of the male population in 1851 and their workers a further 8 per cent, that is, together around a quarter of the male inhabitants of this economically advanced rural area. Of the *patrons*, 15.1 per cent served agriculture as wheelwrights, blacksmiths, or coopers; 16 per cent were involved in the building trade as masons, carpenters, joiners, and roofers; 10 per cent were in clothing as tailors, weavers, and shoemakers. Taxation records for 1846 suggest that most of these artisans (79 per cent) had very modest incomes and in terms of living standards can have been very little better off than agricultural labourers. However, many rural artisans were able to supplement their incomes by cultivating small plots of land, and a minority were able to earn a decent living.[31]

Besides manufacturing, the statisticians responsible for the 1866 census estimated that nationally there were 700,000 individuals engaged in trade, including 220,000 retailing foodstuffs. The scale of their activities can be judged from the fact that they employed only 244,000 workers.[32] Most of these businesses were run by an individual and his or her family and served a local clientele. Nevertheless, a strict status hierarchy existed amongst

[30] Girard, *Nouvelle histoire*, p. 207.   [31] Farcy, *Paysans*, I, pp. 403, 409, 411–12.
[32] A. Plessis, *The Rise and Fall of the Second Empire* (Cambridge 1985), p. 95; Desmarest, *L'évolution*, p. 164.

tradesmen. Thus, whilst according to official figures there were in Paris, in 1856, 20,889 shops and market stalls selling food, around one-quarter of them cafés,[33] shopkeepers in such prosperous localities as the Chaussée d'Antin enjoyed much higher earnings and prestige than the mass of small traders in the popular *quartiers*. The latter, open all hours, forced by competition to extend credit to all comers, plagued by insecurity, constantly hovering above bankruptcy and proletarianisation, and frequently cheating on weights and measures in order to survive, were often despised by customers who, driven by their own insolvency, themselves frequently defaulted on debts.[34] At the bottom of the shopkeeping hierarchy were the numerous traders, who in Paris in 1865 paid 10 centimes for a place on the street and 25 to 40 centimes per square metre for a stall in one of the new covered markets.[35]

Ambition, nevertheless, set the *patron* apart.[36] Within an increasingly competitive environment, in which price levels tended to be set by the larger enterprises, the struggle to prosper or even survive was intense. Labour costs had to be kept to a minimum. Caution was of the essence and horizons often limited by unremitting hard work and a horror of disorderly habits. Even then, amongst a group of 1,147 artisans and shopkeepers active in the 4th arrondissement of Paris in the 1840s, 49.25 per cent are estimated to have experienced demotion and only 12.92 per cent promotion, although only 12.38 per cent of the sample actually suffered bankruptcy,[37] which, until 1867, carried with it the humiliating prospect of imprisonment for debt.

Although dramatic rags-to-riches stories existed to inspire the more ambitious, social mobility was generally a laborious step-by-step process, spread over generations. In terms of gaining entry into the middle classes, preserving an inherited situation, or upward mobility, success depended upon ability, hard work, thrift, inherited wealth and contacts, a 'successful' marriage which secured capital in the form of a dowry, as well as good luck and robust health. Within such diverse groups ambitions of course varied. For a former worker gaining the position of an 'independent' artisan or setting up shop was quite an achievement. For a family, status might be gained vicariously through the achievement of a child. A modicum of

[33] A. Husson, *Les consommations de Paris* (Paris 1856), pp. 65–6.

[34] A. Faure, 'L'épicerie parisienne au 19e siècle', *Le Mouvement social*, no. 108, 1979, p. 117.

[35] J. Gaillard, *Paris, la ville* (Paris 1977), II, p. 263.

[36] L. S. Weissbach, 'Artisanal responses to artistic decline: the cabinetmakers of Paris in the era of industrialization', *Proceedings of the 9th Annual Meeting of the Western Society for French History* (1982), p. 268; W. Sewell, 'Artisanal reponses to industrialization in nineteenth century France', ibid. p. 271.

[37] H.-G. Haupt, 'La petite bourgeoisie: une classe inconnue', *Le mouvement social*, no. 108, 1979, p. 14.

education opened up the possibilities of clerical, teaching, or bureaucratic careers. Only 5 to 6 per cent of the children of school age would receive a secondary education. It was expensive in terms of fees and earnings foregone. Nevertheless, some 27.7 per cent of these pupils came from the lower middle classes.[38] Even in the prestigious Parisian lycée Bonaparte a surprisingly high 30 per cent of the pupils were lower middle class in origin.[39] The proportions were higher in less prestigious provincial *collèges*, some of whose pupils would gain access to the professions eventually, but most of whom would leave school before securing the *baccalaureate* and pursue more limited ambitions.[40]

Many were attracted by the expanding state bureaucracy which, including the educational and postal services, employed 217,000 people by 1856. This was paralleled by the growing numbers of shop assistants and the technical and clerical workers required by private enterprise. The 1866 census suggested that some 116,000 people were employed in salaried positions in industry, many of them on the railways. Taking public and private employment together, there were 126,000 white-collar workers in Paris alone.[41]

For those with a lower-middle-class background, teaching in the *lycée* or *collège* promised social advancement and security. In contrast, primary-school teachers who would have earned only 700f after five years, no more than many workers, were recruited almost exclusively from the lower-middle, working, and peasant classes. For them there was little prospect of further social promotion, which must often have been the source of some frustration.[42] Nevertheless, along with clerical employees and assistants in the new department stores, teachers would have been distinguished from the 'lower classes' by their dress, manners, education and language, and by the sense of dignity derived from their modest achievements. However, the struggle to make ends meet and to preserve appearances was often a desperate one. The sharp rise in food prices following poor harvests certainly caused severe difficulty, particularly during the 1850s.[43] In the following decade serious problems were caused by price inflation and particularly rent increases in the cities.[44] In all these positions, job security

---

[38] P. Harrigan, *Mobility, Elites and Education in French Society of the Second Empire* (Waterloo, Ont. 1980), pp. 14–19.

[39] Harrigan, 'Social origins', p. 215.

[40] L. Berlanstein, *The Working People of Paris, 1871–1914* (London 1984), p. 148.

[41] P. Gerbod, *La condition universitaire en France au 19e siècle* (Paris 1965), pp. 110–11; Harrigan, *Mobility*, pp. 73–4.

[42] R. Price, *A Social History of 19th Century France* (London 1987), pp. 323–5.

[43] See e.g. Prefect Nord, report on March 1855, AN F7/4106.

[44] 1er Légion de gendarmerie. Bulletin politique du chef de Légion, 31 Jan. 1870, AHG G8/176.

and promotion depended on patronage, on earning and retaining the good will of hierarchical chiefs and influential local personages. This encouraged prudence and a sometimes humiliating subservience, which could provoke irritation, or else an almost instinctive conservatism.

Moreover, if, in terms of initial recruitment, secondary education was relatively democratic by European standards, the small numbers involved, and the even more restricted access to higher education, imposed severe limits on advancement. One study suggests that amongst the poorest 80 to 85 per cent of the population only 1.5 to 2 per cent might expect some social promotion,[45] whilst an analysis of a sample of 168 sons of *employés* living in the 13th and 18th arrondissements of Paris at the end of the Second Empire revealed that only 3 per cent had improved on the social position of their fathers, whilst 31 per cent had 'declined' into the ranks of manual labour.[46] However, the key question is how economic change and enhanced opportunities were *perceived* by contemporaries.

A CRISE D'ADAPTATION

Urbanisation and economic expansion enhanced the possibility of upward social mobility, but within a rapidly changing environment. Structural change in the economy, the commercial treaties, and, in particular, the transport revolution, created new business opportunities, but at the same time intensified competition. Areas which had previously been isolated from competition by the high cost of transport, as well as those that had enjoyed a *rente de situation* due to a privileged place within the pre-industrial transport system, now lost many of their competitive advantages. Regions like the Limousin, distant from the raw materials needed by the new industries, and which were late to be reached by the railways and even then provided with low-density networks with relatively high freight charges, were to be disadvantaged permanently.[47] There would be constant disputes between railway companies and local chambers of commerce, which complained about the negative impact of rail freight rate policies which favoured major urban centres and large-scale users.[48]

Most of those industries which used local raw materials – iron, wool, leather, and wood – to produce goods for regional and local markets, declined. The collapse of traditional charcoal- and water-powered

---

[45] Harrigan, *Mobility*, p. 62.   [46] Daumard, *Les bourgeois*, p. 181.
[47] See e.g. Corbin, *Archaïsme*, II, pp. 481–3.
[48] R. Price, *The Modernisation of Rural France: Communications Networks and Agricultural Market Structures in Nineteenth Century France* (London 1983), pp. 250–2.

metallurgy in upland zones of the Ardennes and Pyrenees was particularly dramatic.[49] Regions, towns, and industries experienced an on-going *crise d'adaptation* which, together with cyclical economic crises, guaranteed that a large part of the middle class was in an almost permanent state of insecurity. As a senior government engineer conceded, 'the continuous transformation of the means of communication, which is one of the major features of our epoch, has upset numerous interests, destroyed or compromised large numbers of established positions and fortunes'.[50]

New opportunities were especially evident in the service sector. Providing they were adaptable, merchants and retailers were able to take advantage of the more rapid circulation of stocks made possible by better communications, the electric telegraph, a more efficient postal service, and a growing and more prosperous population. A Bank of France report on trade in Toulouse is quite revealing:

Concentrated for many years in the hands of a small number of powerful houses, in shops which were like warehouses providing for all the needs of the city . . . and neighbouring departments, it has become extremely fragmented . . . Toulouse has become an immense bazaar in which the shopkeepers, as a result of easy and rapid communications are able to manage without intermediaries, and satisfy the demands of their customers by means of direct and increasingly regular supplies.[51]

Reports from other centres were less positive. The wholesale merchants in a riverside town like Orléans lost most of the intermediary entrepôt functions for the surrounding region as it became easier for retailers to deal directly with manufacturers.[52] A more clearly defined urban hierarchy developed. Increasingly, the wholesale grain, cattle, and wine trades were concentrated in the larger marketing centres. Small river- and sea-ports declined as centres with better facilities and rail links to their hinterlands captured their traffic. Gray (Haute-Saône), a river port, formerly a major centre of the grain trade in the Rhône-Saône corridor, thus lost out completely to Dijon, a major rail-hub, and to Marseille. Small flourmills faced growing competition from large industrial mills located in the major ports and rail centres.[53]

[49] E.g. Price, *An Economic History of Modern France, 1730–1914* (London 1981), pp. 109f.
[50] M. F. Vallès, *Des chemins de fer et des routes impériales au point de vue de l'importance de leurs transports respectifs* (Laon 1857), p. 3.
[51] 13 Aug. 1862, quoted A. Armengaud, *Les populations de l'est-Aquitain au début de l'époque contemporaine (vers 1845–vers 1871)* (Paris 1961), p. 251.
[52] Ministère de l'Agriculture et des Travaux Publics, internal memo. 22 Oct. 1850, AN F14/9555.
[53] Ibid. 29 Dec. 1858; Price, *Rural Modernisation*, pp. 325–6; P. Lévêque, *Une société en crise. La Bourgogne de la Monarchie de Juillet au Second Empire (1846–52)* (Paris 1983), I, p. 295.

Although changing economic conditions encouraged the creation of numerous small enterprises, inevitably many of them failed. In Paris, in 1857, those enterprises in difficulty appear to have been characterised by their small scale and the employment of artisanal techniques – in clothing, printing, metal-working, and the manufacture of straw hats and artificial flowers. Particularly exposed were newly established businesses with little capital, together with older establishments, which had over-extended and acquired unsustainable debts. Businesses with inferior equipment and consequently higher costs, or which suffered from a lack of liquid assets and working capital, were especially threatened by trade depression, in spite of often desperate efforts to save themselves by reducing stocks and cutting prices. Of course, this tactic reinforced the cut-throat character of the market place. The failure of under-capitalised local or regional banks was another major threat to business stability.[54]

Even in the expansive 1850s, manufacturers had to contend with the effects of a lengthy subsistence crisis (1853–6), the Crimean war, and such local difficulties as diseased silk worms.[55] In eastern France in 1857 drought reduced the waterpower available to factories and had disastrous consequences for enterprises which had failed to invest in a standby steam engine.[56] In 1860 the commercial treaty with Britain caused a furore. As we have noted, the effects of reductions in tariff protection were difficult to estimate. Pressure from more efficient internal producers, as a result of improved communications and market integration, was probably a more significant factor. Nevertheless, the treaty undoubtedly caused a substantial increase in uncertainty for businessmen.

The mere hint of a reduction in tariff protection was sufficient to cause panic. The initial response of manufacturers in Rouen, Louviers, and Yvetot to news of the withdrawal of prohibitions on imports in 1856 had been to frighten their employees with threats of wage cuts and unemployment – 'the odious spectacle of greed pretending to be compassionate in order to cheat ignorance', as the procureur général at Rouen described it.[57] Some manufacturers reduced wages and postponed investment decisions because of the uncertain future. Others did what the government had hoped, and increased capital investment in order to stimulate productivity and competitiveness.[58] In Normandy there was a marked contrast between the

---

[54] Lambert-Dansette, *La vie des chefs d'entreprise*, p. 168.
[55] See e.g. P. Léon, *La naissance de la grande industrie en Dauphiné (fin du 17e siècle–1869)* (Paris 1954), II, pp. 806–8.
[56] PG Besançon, 13 Jan. 1858, AN BB30/373.   [57] 8 Aug. 1856, AN BB30/387.
[58] See e.g. PG Paris, 4 Aug. 1865, AN BB30/383.

steam-powered mills in and around Rouen and the many small, water-powered rural mills established during the 1840s and 1850s when prices were high and protection seemed assured.[59] In the east, around Nancy, small-scale cotton weaving collapsed – 'these industrialists are not the men to transform their manufacturing by installing mechanical looms. They are comfortably off, and will wear out their old hand looms, until this old equipment is completely out of order, when they will give up business activity.' Their sons would be encouraged to enter the professions.[60]

The doubling of raw cotton prices as a result of the American Civil War would cause a further crisis. In Mulhouse it was claimed that the annual cost of provisioning a mill with 20,000 spindles, which had been 200,000f. formerly, rose to almost a million, an increase in costs which many of the smaller manufacturers could not absorb.[61] Even without a cotton famine many mills there, and in small southern towns like Lodève and Bédarieux, would have found competition with the larger-scale and more efficient manufacturers of the Nord and Alsace increasingly difficult.[62] In Normandy, by 1864/5 of thirty small water-powered textile mills in the Barantin and Pavilly valleys nine had ceased production and three had declared themselves bankrupt.[63] Reporting on the closure of small and medium-sized cotton mills, 'whose owners dispose of only a limited capital and credit', the procureur général at Rouen blamed

the constant fluctuations in the cost of raw materials, the extreme caution encouraged by the effects on the markets for finished products of the alternating rumours of peace or all-out war [in the United States], the divergent views on the yields of the cotton crops in India and the Mediterranean basin, the competition from textiles which cotton dominated in the past because of its cheapness, the speculative operations and panics which in every crisis precipitate or exaggerate rises and falls.

Such uncertainty was profoundly discouraging to entrepreneurs who, after investing in new equipment to meet British competition, were now obliged to leave much of this inactive.[64] The state prosecutor was also concerned that in response to the cotton famine the woollen producers of Elbeuf and Louviers had over-invested in new capacity and would themselves

[59] PG Caen, ? Jan. 1870, AN BB30/390.
[60] PG Nancy, 31 Dec. 1863 quoted O.Voillard, 'Recherches sur une bourgeoisie urbaine: Nancy au 19e siècle', Doc. d'Etat, Univ. des sciences humaines de Strasbourg 1976, I, p. 378.
[61] PG Colmar, 2 Feb. 1864, AN BB30/376.
[62] C. Johnson, *The Life and Death of Industrial Languedoc, 1700–1920. The Politics of Deindustrialization* (Oxford 1995); see also e.g. PG Colmar, 2 Feb. 1864, AN BB30/376.
[63] Lambert-Dansette, *Genèse*, pp. 298–9.   [64] 10 Jan. 1863, AN BB30/387.

face a severe over-production crisis when cotton production returned to normal.[65]

Similarly, the impact of changes in economic and social structures on the artisanal trades was complicated. High levels of demand, in more competitive markets, encouraged specialisation and innovation through a more developed division of labour as well as the introduction of new hand tools and machines, including small, and sometimes shared, steam engines, and sewing machines for the manufacture of shoes and ready-made clothing.[66] Subcontracting was a common cost-cutting expedient, especially in the building trades.[67] However, increasingly, the dominant figures in most small-scale trades were the merchants who provided the raw materials and distributed the finished product, whilst the master-artisan supported the initial set-up costs and most of the risks. The Lyon silk industry was dominated by 102 *fabricants*, wholesalers who by 1867 controlled 74 per cent of the output of the entire *fabrique*. This was produced in around 8,000 *ateliers*, small weaving shops employing some 30,000 *compagnons*.[68]

The vast majority of owners of silk-weaving workshops were highly skilled and capable of rapidly adapting to changes in fashion. They each possessed a small number of Jacquard looms and a limited capital derived from family, friends, savings, reinvested profits, and perhaps a dowry. However, for their working capital, they depended largely on advances from wholesalers. This lack of commercial independence and a frequent inability to keep proper accounts, ensured that these small master-craftsmen were constantly in an exposed situation. A failure to fully comprehend the workings of both financial and commodity markets, particularly acute in a transition economy, represented a further cause of instability. Moreover, workshops were constantly exposed to cancellation or the non-renewal of orders if demand declined. Increasingly too, the weaving of the less expensive cloths was transferred into the surrounding rural areas to take advantage of the supply of cheap and less assertive labour. Industrial growth in Lyon more and more depended on engineering and chemicals; businesses which were far less easy to enter because of the more complicated technology and higher

---

[65] 10 April 1865, AN BB30/387; see also P. Deyon, 'L'industrie amiénoise au 19e siècle et les séductions du protectionnisme', *Revue du Nord* 2000, p. 98.

[66] See e.g. C. Johnson, 'Economic changes and artisan discontent: the tailors' history (1800–48)' in R. Price (ed.), *Revolution and Reaction. 1848 and the Second French Republic* (London 1975), *passim*.

[67] Gaillard, *Paris, la ville*, III, pp. 430–55; P. Vigier, 'La petite bourgeoisie en Europe occidentale avant 1914', *Le Mouvement social*, no. 108, pp. 4–5.

[68] F. Bayard and P. Cayez, *Histoire de Lyon*, II (Le Coteau n.d.), p. 250; Lambert-Dansette, *Genèse*, p. 173.

start-up costs.[69] In nearby Saint-Etienne the workshop-based silk-ribbon and small-arms industries similarly declined in the face of growing competition, whilst capital-intensive coal mining and steel production expanded rapidly.[70]

In these circumstance the situation of workshop owners had become increasingly precarious. Tension was inevitable as a growing loss of independence and fear of proleterianisation spread through the artisanal trades. Even amongst the successful there was concern that today's prosperity might turn into tomorrow's misery. Often, intense effort was followed by a falling back into the ranks of the labouring classes.[71] The pace of change should not be exaggerated, however. If rapid modernisation occurred in some sectors of transport, metallurgy, or textiles, this co-existed with sectors and regions overwhelmingly dominated by small-scale family enterprise. The intensification of competition itself frequently encouraged a greater division of labour and an opportunity for individuals with limited capital to establish themselves.

The trade in foodstuffs is a good example. The number of shopkeepers increased substantially as general prosperity and consumer demand increased. The café owner became a key figure in the life of most communities. The southern town of Béziers, its prosperity based on the wine trade, was not untypical in seeing the number of licensed drinking establishments within its boundaries increase from 124 in 1855 to 229 in 1867, and this did not include an unknown number of clandestine establishments.[72] Nationally, by 1870 there were 364,875 registered *débits de boisson*.[73] Similarly, the number of bakers active within the newly enlarged boundaries of the capital rose from 920 in 1860 to 1,286 in 1869, and the number of butchers – 501 in 1850 not including 161 market stalls, rose to 1,574 by 1874.[74] Since time immemorial, official anxiety about food supply had ensured close surveillance of those involved in the grain trade, flour milling, and baking and to a lesser extent in wholesale and retail butchery. Thus, frequent reports and special enquiries offer insights into the opportunities they enjoyed and the problems they faced.

---

[69] Cayez, *Crises*, p. 77.

[70] D. Gordon, 'Industrialization and republican politics: the bourgeoisie of Reims and Saint-Etienne under the Second Empire' in J. Merriman (ed.), *French Cities in the Nineteenth Century* (London 1982), pp. 127–9.

[71] See e.g. Vigier, 'La petite bourgeoisie', p. 8; J. Jacquemet, 'Belleville au 19e siècle', Doc. d'Etat, Univ. de Paris IV, n.d., III, p. 1076.

[72] G. Cholvy, 'Biterrois et narbonnais. Mutations économes et évolution des mentalités à l'époque contemporaine', in Cholvy *et al.*, *Economie et société en Languedoc-Roussillon de 1789 à nos jours* (Montpellier 1978), p. 425.

[73] Charle, *Histoire sociale*, p. 182.   [74] Girard, *Nouvelle histoire*, p. 220.

In the 1850s, grain merchants were still harassed by officials because of the age-old suspicion that they were attempting to corner supplies to push up prices. Exemplary prosecutions were likely in an effort to reassure *les classes laborieuses*.[75] For similar reasons, until 1863 bakers were subject to municipal price controls. The authorities were anxious to prevent increases in the price of bread, which might cause popular unrest, and were only too likely to ignore bakers' complaints about the rising cost of the flour they purchased. If, in these circumstances, bakers sometimes refused to continue selling at a loss, coercion was likely to be employed. In Lille in March 1856, for example, fifteen bakers were prosecuted. To survive, bakers must frequently have had little choice but to cheat their customers through the use of false measures. Not surprisingly they were also repeatedly accused of cheating.[76] Already twice convicted for short measure, in March 1856 Pierre Dumortier, a baker in nearby Tourcoing, was sentenced to one month's imprisonment for re-offending.[77]

According to M. Decauville, an expert witness before the 1859 enquiry into the bakeries of Paris and the department of the Seine:

Baker and butcher are . . . the most unfortunate professions imaginable; it is almost impossible to exercise them honestly because of the constant vexations to which they are submitted, because of the incessant surveillance to which they are subjected by minor officials, due to the relationships they have with the owners and managers of establishments requiring payment and with the domestic servants responsible for provisioning their households who say: You can supply my house, but only if I benefit. It is impossible to be a baker or butcher without accepting these deplorable transactions.[78]

Following a poor harvest, as the price of bread and unemployment both rose, bakers who had extended too much credit in an attempt to attract customers, were all too likely to find themselves facing bankruptcy.[79] In the cities bakers increasingly purchased their flour from large-scale wholesale millers who themselves attempted to create a captive market through the extension of credit, leading to the sort of situation described by the Toulon Chamber of Commerce in explaining the closure of six bakeries between October 1866 and the following March – 'the worker pays cash at the café, he almost always makes his purchases on credit at the bakers, and often

---

[75] PG Paris, 26 July 1856, AN BB18/1553.
[76] See e.g. evidence of M. Doyère, membre du Conseil de surveillance de la boulangerie de Sébastopol, in Conseil d'Etat, *Enquête sur la boulangerie du département de la Seine* . . . (Paris 1859), p. 102.
[77] PG Douai, 8 March 1856, AN BB24/484–8.
[78] Conseil d'Etat, *Enquête sur la boulangerie*, p. 641.
[79] Ibid. p. 107, evidence of M. Berger, ancien syndic de la boulangerie de Paris.

moves home without paying his debts. The baker, in turn, is obliged to open an account with the grain merchant and the cost of interest, of discounting commercial bills, substantially increases his costs.'[80] In smaller towns and rural areas, bakers continued to rely on flour supplied by local water or wind mills whose owners were themselves forced into fraudulent expedients as improved communications intensified competitive pressure from the large steam-driven urban mills.[81]

Economic liberalisation and the ending of the restrictions on the bread trade in 1863 did not lead to the fall in the price of bread the authorities had anticipated. As a result bakers were accused of having colluded to prevent competition. In June 1865, at Le Mans, when the Widow Sauneau reduced her prices sharply in an attempt to increase market share, an alliance was formed by competitors, determined either to put her out of business or at least force her to sell bread at the 'normal' price.[82] Nevertheless, market integration, by means of rail and telegraph, did ensure that the subsistence crisis of 1853–6 would be the last of its kind, and far less severe than that of 1846/7.[83] Whilst consumers, and many small traders, benefited from greater price stability, it also sharply reduced the opportunities for speculative profits, which previously many landowners, merchants, millers, and some bakers had enjoyed.[84]

Conditions in most trades remained prosperous until at least 1866. Nevertheless, there is substantial evidence to suggest that, even if sharing in this prosperity, large sections of the middle classes, from factory owners to shopkeepers, were plagued by uncertainty. The small businessman with little capital, caught between pressure from his suppliers to pay for raw materials and the dilatoriness of his customers in paying their bills, was often at the mercy of the first economic crisis. In Paris in the 1860s and 1870s, 57 per cent of the builders and 60 per cent of the café owners who died left nothing to their descendants. Also the establishment in the capital and other major cities of *grands magasins* like Aristide Boucicaut's Bon Marché was beginning to cause concern amongst small shopkeepers.[85] The pace of change was too rapid. Furthermore, towards the end of the decade, a combination of poor harvests, a worldwide financial crisis, and, most

---

[80] Report 30 March 1867, quoted E. Constant, 'Var', vol. II, p. 400.
[81] See e.g. *Exposé fait au nom de l'administration municipale à la Commission des subsistances le 4 août 1854* (Nantes 1854), p. 4.
[82] J.-C. Devos, 'Les conséquences du décret du 22 juin 1863 sur la liberté du commerce de la boulangerie', *Actes du 93e CNSS 1968* (Paris 1971), pp. 352–3.
[83] Price, *Rural Modernisation*, ch. 6.
[84] Ministre de l'agriculture, du commence et des travaux publics to Justice, 16 June 1865, AN BB18/1715.
[85] F. Raison-Jourde, *La colonie auvergnate de Paris au 19e siècle* (Paris 1976), p. 175.

notably, the deteriorating international political situation again threatened business confidence. Typically, the state prosecutor at Besançon reported that 'transactions have ceased, commerce is inactive, credit is tightening', adding that, 'one would need to look back a long way to find examples of so much anxiety, and such business stagnation'.[86] The difficulties faced by the Crédit mobilier investment bank were a sure sign of widespread financial problems.[87] Once again politics had impinged upon economics, adding to the widespread sense of insecurity amongst the middle classes. Their perceptions of their plight, the explanations they offered for their predicament, together with growing social tension, would have significant political consequences.

AN EVOLVING 'CLASS' CONSCIOUSNESS

Middle-class self-definition in large part reflected shifting attitudes towards other social groups. These were always likely to be characterised by ambivalence. Thus, although often described as hostile to the social elites, members of the middle classes also frequently served as vital intermediaries between these elites and the masses. They were motivated by respect for their social 'superiors', by opportunities for advancement or profit, by shared religious faith or common political interests. The threat of revolution or the reduction of tariff protection caused widespread concern. Although the 'caste' pretensions of the very wealthy might be resented, their lifestyle was also likely to earn the admiration of a relatively prosperous *moyenne bourgeoisie*, the comfortably off landowners, businessmen, or professionals who aspired to upward mobility, if not directly for themselves then at least vicariously through the education of their sons or marriage of their daughters. Furthermore, many lawyers, artisans, or shopkeepers depended on elite patronage. In traditional city centres but also in newly developing *quartiers* like that around the Invalides in Paris, the rich were valued customers, their elegance and manners much admired.

   Indeed, admiration frequently took the form of an imitative lifestyle, although this too was not without ambivalence. As the novelist Emile Zola noted cynically – his fictional Plassans thinly disguising Aix-en-Provence:

the bourgeoisie, retired merchants, lawyers, notaries, the entire little world of well-off and ambitious people who inhabit the new part of the town do their best to give some life to Plassans . . . They make every effort to increase their popularity by referring to the worker as *mon brave*, talking to the peasant about the

---

[86] 12 Jan. 1867, AN BB30/373.   [87] PG Bordeaux, 10 Oct. 1867, AN BB30/374.

harvest, reading the newspapers, going for walks on Sunday with their women-folk . . . [However], even the most sceptical of them enjoys an intense sense of pleasure whenever a marquis or a count deigns to honour them with a slight mark of recognition. The dream of every bourgeois in the new town is to be invited to a salon in the quartier St-Marc. They fully understand that this is unrealisable, and this is what leads them to loudly declare themselves to be free thinkers, but free thinkers in word alone, strongly committed to order, who will throw themselves into the arms of whoever promises to be their saviour, following the least grumble from the people.[88]

Hostility towards the social elites was evident especially in economically depressed periods, when the very survival of businesses established during more prosperous years was under threat as the supply of credit dried up or became more expensive. The apparent indifference of the Bank of France, the citadel of high finance, to the fate of small businesses, as it increased its discount rate in order to limit demand for capital, exacerbated hostility towards the economic elite.[89] Indebtedness was a burning issue. Small businessmen seemed to be inescapably caught up in credit networks, both as lenders through the credit they extended to their customers, and as debtors, dependent on advances by wholesalers in order to purchase tools and raw materials. Typically, Parisian artisans sold goods on six months' credit and were paid by means of bills of exchange which could then be discounted (at a rate of at least 6 per cent for small businessmen) so that they could pay wages and purchase materials.[90] In 'normal' times credit circulated within trades between the wholesale merchant and the workshop owner, the retailer and the customer. When business was depressed, credit tended to dry up, and bankruptcies threatened this mechanism of mutual obligation.[91] In such circumstances, feeling threatened by the development of 'capitalism', small businessmen might share the age-old hostility of *les petits* against *les grands*. In Lyon, the silk merchants had long been resented for their harsh exploitation both of workshop owners and indirectly of the workers they employed. This hostility grew as they moved out of the city into country mansions, placing a growing social distance between themselves and the others.[92]

Attitudes towards the 'lower' classes were similarly often ambivalent. Although many *patrons* remained close to the workers they employed, and neighbourhood links were also significant, there were obvious differences of interest. The relations between *patron* and worker were frequently

[88] *La Fortune des Rougon* (Paris 1960), pp. 39–41. [89] See e.g. Gaillard, *Paris, la ville*, III, p. 388.
[90] Lambert-Dansette, *Genèse*, p. 29. [91] Gaillard, *Paris, la ville*, III, pp. 388–91.
[92] PG Lyon, 16 April 1869, AN BB30/389.

exploitative, as were those between shopkeepers who cheated on weight and quality and their customers, and those between landlord and tenant, moneylender and debtor. Sympathy for the poor was mixed with feelings of contempt and condescension towards those who appeared to lack the virtues associated by members of the middle classes with their own success and those who, as workers or domestics, were in a dependent position. Businessmen who had struggled to establish their own businesses or purchase property demanded respect and compliance. At a banquet to celebrate his appointment to the Legion of Honour, the Alsatian mill owner Antoine Herzog reminded his employees that 'I used to be a worker just like you; with God's help and hard work you can aspire, like me, to become an employer.'[93] There could be no excuse for failure.

Ownership of property, however small, combined with social aspirations, however limited, thus distinguished the lower middle classes from the workers. The 'class' consciousness of members of the middle classes was shaped by this sense of superiority over the property-less. Often, the gulf was not so much material as psychological, which explains the crucial importance of dress and appearance for the middle classes. Social distance had to be preserved. When faced with an apparent threat to their status from 'below', they were likely to turn towards the social elite for support. For many, including educated professionals like Ernest Renan, 1848 had been a considerable shock. He recalled how the threat of social revolution 'was for many energetic young spirits, just like the fall of the curtain which concealed the horizon'.[94] It had shattered his youthful idealism.

Amongst the comfortably off there was a strong feeling of distaste for 'lower' classes regarded as dirty and disease ridden as well as criminal and potentially revolutionary. The growing scale of enterprises and greater residential segregation ensured an increasing ignorance of working-class life and problems. Even where they lived and worked in close proximity, disputes over wages and working conditions caused frequent tensions in the relationships between small workshop proprietors, often former workers themselves, and their employees. Many successful small businessmen sought status and enhanced incomes from property ownership. They moved into 'better' neighbourhoods themselves and invested in housing to rent.

Disputes were frequent between small landlords, determined to maximise their incomes, and tenants, for whom finding the rent was a regular

---

[93] Lambert-Dansette, *Genèse*, p. 208.
[94] Quoted K. Swart, *The Sense of Decadence in Nineteenth Century France* (The Hague 1964), p. 94.

cause of anxiety.[95] In Paris, where pressure on accommodation was particularly intense, 74,062 people were reported to be living in rented rooms in 1856.[96] Landlords often adopted overbearing attitudes towards tenants as they sought to take advantage of rapid population growth to increase rents and neglect maintenance of their properties.[97] Hard times created considerable tension between demanding landlords and impoverished tenants.

Although in many cases religious faith and the charitable instincts it inspired, as well as the desire to enhance their social status, promoted efforts by members of the middle classes to offer assistance to the 'deserving' poor, officials frequently criticised the harshness shown towards the labouring classes.[98] The vast majority of medium or small manufacturers had neither the desire nor the resources with which to engage in philanthropic activity. In August 1853 Persigny, the Interior Minister, informed his colleagues indignantly that the cotton manufacturers of Bar-le-Duc made it a rule 'never to make the least sacrifice for their workers; in their eyes, the worker is a machine for making money, which they can leave inactive and not concern themselves with from the moment when there is no profit to be made from making it move'. In contacts with their employees, manufacturers were likely to affect 'an unbearable arrogance' which reinforced the workers' hatred of them as well as the attractiveness of revolutionary ideas.[99]

An official report on textile entrepreneurs in the Rouen area similarly insisted that their sole concern was to increase profits. The re-establishment of strong government following the *coup d'état* had encouraged them to treat their workers more harshly than ever – 'as they no longer fear riots, they return as far as possible to their old ways, their old exactions. The workers are unable to complain, because they would be dismissed by their master, denounced by him and unable to find work anywhere.'[100] Similarly, manufacturers in the southern mill towns of Lodève and Bédarieux appeared indifferent to the squalid living conditions endured by their workers.[101] The Prefect of the Tarn insisted in June 1856 that unregulated competition forced even the best-intentioned manufacturers in Mazamet and Castres to push down wages. His less compliant predecessor had condemned their 'immoderate desire for lucre'.[102]

---

[95] S. Magri, 'Les propriétaires, les locataires, la loi. Jalons pour une analyse sociologique des rapports de location, Paris 1850–1920', *Revue française de sociologie* 1996, pp. 400–2.

[96] Gaillard, *Paris, la ville*, ii, p. 213.   [97] Ibid. i, pp. 130–3.

[98] See e.g. Prefect, 15 Jan. 1855, AN F1 CIII Jura 14.

[99] Ministre de l'Intérieur to Ministre de l'agriculture . . . , 16 August 1853, AN F12/2370–2374.

[100] PG Rouen, 5 July 1853, AN BB30/387.

[101] Johnson, *Life and Death of Industrial Languedoc*, ch. 4.   [102] 11 June 1856, AN F12/2370.

In Limoges relationships between master and man in the porcelain industry were also claimed to be entirely devoid of paternalism, and characterised by 'relationships based on necessity, fear, mistrust, and envy'.[103] It was reported that there 'exists . . . between the employers, an informal convention according to which a worker leaving one factory cannot be employed in another without the approval of his former boss'.[104] Unique only in their scale were the efforts of the 600 employers in the Paris bronze industry in February–March 1867 to break the Société de Crédit mutuel des ouvriers en bronze organised amongst their 6,000 workers. Following a decision by the Société to employ the traditional artisanal tactic of isolating selected employers, the latter decided on a general lockout on 25 February and then on the following day proclaimed their determination to remain open and their willingness to reward those workers who turned up for work and who rejected union membership.[105]

In refusing to cooperate with official efforts to encourage the formation of mutual aid societies, J.-B. and F. Martin, manufacturers at Tarare near Lyon, reminded the authorities that previously these societies had provided a disguise for 'socialist' organisation and that 'this is an organisation directed against the employers, ready for every eventuality, and which is capable of secretly taking its own decisions, in spite of being apparently subject to supervision by the authorities'. The efforts of officially nominated presidents and honorary members like themselves to control the societies had met with resistance from secretive groups of workers. They warned that every mutual aid society would become, regardless of official intentions, 'an association of the proletarian against the bourgeoisie and of the worker against the *patron*'. The Martins furthermore insisted that these societies 'oppress those workers who do not support them and who are either ostracised or forced by the leaders to take part in action against their employers'.[106] In reality, in most industries a plentiful supply of cheap labour, dismissals, lockouts, and police support placed employers in a very strong position.[107]

Faced with seasonal and cyclical variations in demand for their products, employers were determined to insist on their absolute freedom to hire and fire workers. Even when recognising the misery of unemployed textile workers during the American Civil War they were all too likely to

[103] PG Limoges 1855 quoted Corbin, *Archaïsme*, I, p. 317.
[104] PG Limoges, 6 Oct. 1864, mis-filed in AN BB30/379.
[105] Paris Prefect of Police, 27 Feb., 13 March, and 4 April 1867, AN F12/4652.
[106] Undated letter, supported by PG Lyon, 8 Feb. 1857, AN BB30/379.
[107] See e.g. PG Rouen, 7 Jan. 1870, AN BB30/390.

conclude that charitable assistance only encouraged the workers' 'vicious habits'. Monetary assistance would be spent only on drink, and that in kind would be pawned for the same purpose.[108] The town council at Roubaix, where the woollen trades were rapidly expanding, encouraged the immigration of desperately poor Belgian workers as the 'indispensable' means of defeating the 'intolerable' demands of local workers.[109] A subsequent effort to reduce costs in 1867, which required that each worker operate two instead of one loom, caused substantial tension and a major strike. An official report claimed that the employers should have attempted to explain the 'necessities of commerce' to their workers but chose instead to assert their authority by imposing the change in an authoritarian manner and without explanation.[110]

Disputes over piece rates and working conditions were frequent. Employers insisted that they were always ready to discuss their terms of employment with individual workers. They condemned the regime's concession of the right to strike in 1864, and the growing toleration of workers' organisations, which followed, as a restraint on trade. They would be particularly horrified by the, greatly exaggerated, accounts of the development, in 1869/70, of branches of the Association Internationale des travailleurs in Paris, Rouen, and other industrial centres, seeing it as responsible for every strike, as well as the growing threat of social revolution.[111] Employers expected that their workers would be grateful for their jobs and on political issues should follow their 'masters'' lead.

Middle-class attitudes towards the rural population were as ambivalent as those they adopted towards workers. Increasingly, the very word 'peasant' took on pejorative overtones. Virtually at the bottom of the middle class hierarchy themselves, village schoolteachers could be especially brutal, perhaps from a sense of frustration, and a determination to differentiate themselves from their peasant neighbours. The authors of memoirs on the 'needs of primary education' requested by the education minister in 1860, described peasants in the Lyon region as 'only able to make vulgar comments, [as] dishonest, immoral . . . they practice disobedience, insubordination, rudeness, egotism, deceitfulness, indelicacy'; 'they are rude, uncivil, noisy, rowdy in gatherings, imbued with the most absurd prejudices, which

---

[108] Letter of 5 March 1863 in J.-P. Chaline (ed.), *Deux bourgeois en leur temps: documents sur la société rouennaise du 19e siècle* (Rouen 1977), p. 180.
[109] Letter to Prefect, 17 Jan. 1863, AN F1 CIII Seine-Inférieure 17.
[110] Prefect Nord, 26 and 28 Feb. 1867, AN F1 CIII Nord 16.
[111] See e.g. evidence of M. C. Delattre, fabricant des lainages purs, to *Enquête parlementaire sur le régime économique*, 1 (Paris 1870), p. 768.

transmit themselves from generation to generation'.[112] Critics of the regime frequently shared this view. Thus, following disappointing election results in 1869, the editors of the Toulouse republican newspaper *L'Emancipation* concluded that 'we need to turn towards the countryside still sunk deep in the intense darkness of ignorance'.[113] The ambivalence found in middle-class attitudes towards other social groups was also clearly reflected in their political views.

POLITICAL PARTICIPATION

The political positions adopted by members of the *classes moyennes* reflected their intermediate social position and particularly their contacts with the masses. Their potential influence was recognised by the official who referred to 'the middle classes, those who express and form public opinion'.[114] In so many places 'influence belongs to the middle class, which is to be found in the municipal administration, provides the *juge du paix*, and in commerce and industry'.[115] In a transition society, following the establishment of manhood suffrage, and in which so recently the authority of the social elites had been challenged, there were growing opportunities for middle-class groups to exercise influence. Professionals, especially lawyers and doctors, were particularly well placed, due to their functions and the status that went with education and property, to become the middle-class group most likely to engage in competitive political behaviour.[116] Landowners, themselves frequently educated in the law, even if not practising a legal profession, similarly possessed the social 'standing', rhetorical skills, leisure, and resources necessary for successful political activity. In many cases, activism itself was likely to further reinforce status.[117]

Whatever their sympathies, members of the middle classes possessed political experience, resources, and organisational skills. In every little town the informal sociability of the café – often taking on the political coloration of its clientele[118] – or of the more exclusive and private *cercle* – meeting in a room reserved in the better class of café or in a separate establishment – provided opportunities to read the newspapers, smoke and play cards, and

[112] Quoted P. Goujon, 'Associations et vie associative dans les campagnes au 19e siècle: le cas du vignoble de Saône-et-Loire', *Cahiers d'histoire* 1981, p. 136.

[113] Quoted S. Chassagne, 'L'histoire des villes' in Garden (ed.), *Villes et campagnes*, p. 241.

[114] PG Lyon, 4 June 1859, AN BB30/379.   [115] PG Grenoble, 9 July 1858, AN BB30/378.

[116] PG Paris, 4 Aug. 1865, AN BB30/384.

[117] See e.g. M. Offerlé, 'Professions et profession politique' in M. Offerlé (ed.) *La profession politique 19e–20e siècles* (Paris 1999), pp. 14–24.

[118] See e.g. J. Faury, *Cléricalisme et anticléricalisme dans le Tarn* (Toulouse 1980), p. 670.

discuss business or politics.[119] Such a gathering might even grace itself with the title Société litteraire.[120] Similarly, masonic lodges brought men together on a regular basis. Providing opportunities for conviviality, networking and enhancing social status, their members co-opted from the ranks of landowners, professionals and businessmen, largely educated in the same local secondary school, well-mannered, 'properly' dressed, and able to afford an annual subscription of 30 to 50f., they nevertheless contributed to the diffusion of an egalitarian discourse.[121]

These were all associations which occupied a social space quite distinct from that taken up by the elite *salon* on the one hand, or the *chambrées* and cafés frequented by tradesmen, artisans, workers, and peasants, on the other. At Mâcon the *cercle* was composed of '*des hommes d'affaires du pays* such as notaries, lawyers, . . . etc.' Senior government officials and members of wealthy landowning families maintained their distance by renting a room at the *café des mille colonnes*.[122] In the 1840s, Chalons had possessed three masonic lodges with members drawn from the liberal professions (about one-third), *négociants* (25 per cent), *commerçants* (17.3 per cent) and 'artisans' who were mainly successful *patrons* (15.6 per cent).[123] In Nantes in 1869 the three masonic lodges were overwhelmingly middle and lower middle class.[124] Thus, leisure activity was segregated according to social status and of course by gender.

Sociability, regular meetings in *cercles*, at cafés, dinners, and the theatre, made it relatively easy to develop contacts and ignore the legislation banning public meetings. The Second Republic had revealed the importance of informal social networks in the process of politicisation. During the 1850s political debate was, for some time, effectively stilled by fear. Meeting places were subject to close surveillance, especially in those areas in which the *démocrates-socialistes* had been active.[125] Afraid of losing their licences, café owners were themselves likely to restrict debate.[126] Masonic elders also made efforts, not always successful, to ban political discussion in order to protect their institutions.[127] Where this was not enough, and under pressure from the Interior Minister, the Grand Orient itself closed lodges,

[119] See e.g. PI Blois, ? April 1866, AN BB30/382.
[120] M. Agulhon, *Le cercle dans la France bourgeoise* (Paris 1977), pp. 17f; Ménager, 'Vie politique', II, p. 718 re regional differences in sociability.
[121] P. Goujon, 'Associations et vie associative', pp. 117–19.
[122] Prefect, 12 Jan. 1859, AN F1 CIII Saône-et-Loire 13.
[123] Lévêque, *Bourgogne*, II, pp. 700–3.   [124] Launay, *Diocèse de Nantes*, II, p. 905.
[125] E.g. PG Nancy, 12 April 1863, AN BB30/381.   [126] E.g. PG Lyon, 3 Feb. 1852, AN BB30/379.
[127] See e.g. C. Derobert-Ratel, *Les Arts et l'Amitié et le rayonnement maçonnique dans la société aixoise de 1848 à 1871* (Aix-en-Provence 1987), pp. 69–70.

as at Valence and Romans.[128] The only lodge surviving in Nancy, which had already been closed in 1852, was again under surveillance in 1857, because its forty active members were almost all known republicans.[129] The Cercle du commerce at Saint Pons was dissolved in 1856 as a result of its failure to join in a patriotic reception for the 35th infantry regiment on its return from the Crimea.[130] Moreover, censorship ensured that the press no longer provided controversial topics for daily discussion.

However, such heavy-handed action could lead 'respectable' middle-class citizens to express their resentment at being treated as potential subversives. In general, therefore, the authorities were much more tolerant of the solidly middle class *cercles* and masonic lodges than of the more popular cafés and *chambrées*.[131] In addition, certainly from 1856/7, it became increasingly evident that nothing could entirely prevent the reawakening of public debate, especially as new generations emerged which had not experienced the social fear of 1848 themselves and whose members were determined to assume a more active role in local affairs.[132] These *gens des villes* were seen increasingly as 'the only elements of what might be referred to as the political parties'.[133]

Together with growing discontent, regime liberalisation would result gradually in the (re)-politicisation of these organisations and, eventually, in the creation of more overtly political networks linked to newspapers, public meetings, and election committees and representing, in effect, the growing 'modernisation' of political activity. In these changing circumstances officials would be especially concerned to assess the extent to which the middle classes remained politically conservative, or were becoming proponents of innovation and change. These were key questions, given their central political role. Within shifting political contexts, generalisations about the political behaviour of such a heterogeneous entity were, and remain, hazardous. Whether as a voter or militant, the choice of which political 'party' to support was subject to a range of influences reflecting family and community tradition, perceived economic interest, confessional loyalties, and the impact of political ideology.

Most members of the liberal professions appear to have been conservative or liberal in their sympathies. They were, after all, property owners with an interest in social and political stability. Professional success was likely to reinforce conservative instincts, particularly in relation to those lower down the social hierarchy. Conversely, it was possible that disappointed expectations might stimulate dissatisfaction and resentment

[128] PG Grenoble, 12 Jan. 1856, AN BB30/378.   [129] PG Nancy, 3 April 1857, AN BB30/381.
[130] PG Montpellier, 16 July 1856, AN BB30/380.   [131] E.g. Constant, 'Var', II, pp. 603–5.
[132] See e.g. PG Paris, 25 May, 1866 re Reims, AN BB30/384.
[133] PG Aix, 28 Oct. 1867, AN BB30/370.

amongst these so-called *nouvelles couches*, and with it political dissent.[134] Competition between individuals, families, and factions for local influence were other potent factors, resulting in *querrelles de clocher* caused by 'rivalry for influence, jealousy over position, antagonism between cliques, individual rancours, disagreement over the appropriateness of police measures and administrative decisions'.[135] The adoption of a political label might also cloak personal ambition.

Thus the struggle for local influence frequently involved groups with indistinguishable social characteristics. The members of some professions – landowners and lawyers for example – were well represented amongst all political tendencies.[136] Certainly, if there was no monolithic middle class, there could be no monolithic middle-class politics. Individual members of the 'middle classes' accommodated themselves to a variety of political options. They might support *résistance* in defence of 'order' and 'property', or *mouvement* in protest against 'privilege'. In many localities middle-class opinion aligned itself with that of other social groups. In Gien 'the small tradesmen are generally afraid of losing their clients by expressing their political opinions and remain prudently silent'.[137] Election results suggest that most remained loyal to the imperial regime, but, at some stage, many would choose to support its Legitimist or liberal critics, or else become adherents of moderate, 'radical', or revolutionary republicanism. Political options could change over time. Paradoxically, information about middle-class support for the regime is more difficult to find than that on opposition. Official reports offer either the habitual, almost ritual, and generally uninformative, affirmations of public support or else focus on signs of dissent. The lack of precision in the language used to describe social groups compounds the difficulty.

Support for the regime

Initially, the imperial regime, widely seen as a simple continuation and reinforcement of the system inaugurated by the 1848 presidential election, attracted substantial middle-class support.[138] The desire for order, and the termination of the long mid-century crisis, as well as fear of 'socialism',

---

[134] On debate over this concept see F. Sawicki, 'Classer les hommes politiques. Les usages des indicateurs de position sociale pour le compréhension de la professionnalisation politique' in Offerlé, *La profession politique*, pp. 138–41.

[135] PG Rouen, 13 Oct. 1860, AN BB30/387.

[136] See e.g. P. Gonnet, 'La société dijonnaise au 19e siècle. Esquisse de l'évolution économique, sociale et politique d'un milieu urbain contemporain (1815–90)', Doc. d'Etat, Univ. de Paris-Sorbonne 1974, IV, p. 1009.

[137] PI Gien, April 1866, AN BB30/382.   [138] See e.g. PG Lyon, 6 May 1852, AN BB30/379.

proved to be strong motivators. In April 1852, in a tone almost of disbelief, Dr Hellis, head doctor at the Rouen general hospital, wrote to a friend in Paris that as a result of the *coup d'état,*

all those who used to protest are silent and humble; . . . instead of being pillaged, slaughtered and exiled, we live in tranquillity, and are able to attend to our little concerns . . . We choose clothes, go to the ball, swear the oath of allegiance for the tenth time, and are necessarily discreet, because it is said that even the walls have ears. What is there to say, in any case? The newspapers no longer influence opinion.[139]

In 1858, the schools inspector at Dijon pointed out that in the past the middle class had solidly supported republicanism as a means of opposing the pretensions of the nobility. However, the experience of 1848 and the radicalisation of part of the lower middle class as well as workers had stilled their agitation.[140] Greater prosperity, as well as repression, combined to encourage de-politicisation. There was much to celebrate during the *fête impérial.* So prominent in official propaganda, the themes of order and prosperity struck a real chord. Patriotic responses to military victories were encouraged. Houses and shops were decorated, parades and fireworks organised.

Nevertheless, levels of support would fluctuate over time. Immediately after the *coup d'état,* if the middle classes had appeared devoted to the Prince-President, it was frequently the case that 'fear mixes more than a little with enthusiasm'.[141] In the Allier, where peasants exhibited an unrestrained devotion to the regime, 'the middle class admires its tendencies, without feeling any great sense of devotion'.[142] Similarly, it was reported that, in Limoges, '*la classe moyenne* . . . is rather indifferent to the form and appearance' of the government and served it only 'out of egoism and by calculation'.[143] Criticism was common, at least in private. Often, however, it tended to be directed at ministers and officials, the agents of the regime, rather than at the Emperor himself.[144] There were also significant variations, both within and between localities. These often reflected long-established social and political rivalries and the ways in which imperial officials sought to take advantage of these. In the Seine-et-Marne, close to Paris, it was the middle class, along with the peasants, who were described as the most

[139] Letter to P. Floquet, 22 April 1852, in Chaline (ed.), *Deux bourgeois,* p. 162.
[140] Report of inspecteur d'académie, Côte d'Or, enclosed with Academic rector's report, 17 April 1858, AN F17/2649.
[141] Prefect, 24 June 1852, AN F1 CIII Isère 9.
[142] Academic Rector Clermont, 6 Jan. 1859, AN F17/2649.
[143] PG Limoges, 9 July 1858, AN BB30/378.   [144] See also ibid. 12 July 1856.

devoted supporters of the regime.[145] In contrast, the decision to buttress the influence of aristocratic landowners, in parts of the west and south for example, carried with it the risk of alienating the middle classes.[146]

The content and language of an electoral circular published in 1852 by a Dr Morin of Saint-Loup near Parthenay says a lot about wounded sensibilities:

You will be aware, that I was, but am no longer, the official candidate for the Corps législatif. Disloyal tactics, ignoble and treacherous intrigues, hatched as a result of old family friendships, have resulted in the candidate of the nobles of the arrondissement of Bressuire being given the support which was at first accorded to me; they have listened to the local gentry who were unhappy that I a simple bourgeois, had the insolence to marry a rich noblewoman . . .

I acquired my bourgeois status through the labour of my ancestors and by my own efforts; I am not willing to deny the noble profession to which I owe all that I am nor, like some people, to hide my origins under a borrowed name flanked by some stolen title.

He demanded to know whether 'I am being persecuted because I am a bourgeois?'[147]

In general, support for the regime declined with the growing economic and political uncertainty of its second decade, in reaction against fear of war, tax increases, and depression.[148] Substantial portions of the middle classes could, however, be expected to turn back towards the regime whenever social order appeared to be threatened, preferring a liberalising empire to the uncertainties of more radical change. In 1869/70 strike waves and violent demonstrations in the capital, luridly described in the conservative press, did much to reinforce support for the Emperor.[149] Publicists like Auguste Vitu wrote widely distributed pamphlets which warned about the re-appearance of the *insurgés de 1848*, the proponents of a *République démocratique et sociale*, and of *anarchie* – in short of all those 'savage appetites against time-honoured rights'. The abolition of property, the family, and religion was again in prospect.[150] Radical republican newspapers like the Parisian *Le Rappel* and *Le Peuple* of Marseille often frightened 'the bourgeoisie, the merchants, the industrialists [who] have reacted against the violent agitation which threatens the fundamental principle of order and that of the security of people and property'.[151]

---

[145] PG Paris, 28 May 1861, AN BB30/384.
[146] PG Rouen, 9 July 1864, AN BB30/387; PG Aix, 6 Oct. 1860, AN BB30/370.
[147] Enclosed with report from PG Poitiers, 9 March 1852, AN BB30/403.
[148] E.g. PG Toulouse, 8 Jan. 1869, AN BB30/389; Ménager, 'Vie politique', III, p. 252.
[149] See e.g. PG Besançon, 13 July 1869, AN BB30/389.
[150] A. Vitu, *Les réunions électorales à Paris* (Paris 1869), p. iv.
[151] PG Aix, 24 Jan. 1870, AN BB30/ 390.

The state prosecutor at Aix pointed out that 'unlike violent democrats, the middle class is not carried away by its appetites, nor by irreconcilable hatreds; it is in its interest to avoid the revolutions of which it will be the first victim'.[152] However, this distaste for the excesses of the opposition does not appear to have resulted in significant support for another authoritarian *coup d'état*. Liberty with order was the favoured combination.[153] M. Jumel, a merchant speaking at an election meeting in the Salle Molière in the rue Saint Martin in Paris in May 1869, wanted 'progress through order and without shocks, gradual progress'.[154] Emile Ollivier was applauded when he insisted, before a large audience in the Théâtre du Châtelet on 12 May, that *real* liberty depended on equality – 'Without equality, liberty is only the privilege of the few' – combined with order, without which equality would 'lead to the worst of despotisms'. It followed that liberty could be established only through constitutional, and not revolutionary, means – 'it is necessary to strive for the improvement of this government, not for its overthrow'.[155]

This was what large sections of the property-owning middle classes wanted. They would enthusiastically welcome the establishment of the liberal Empire. It was widely reported that the liberal reforms and the implicit promise of revision of the commercial treaties had satisfied many of the regime's critics.[156] Even life-long republicans, like Fulcran Suchet, writing in the *Progrès du Var* in May 1869, claimed to feel threatened from the left. He declared himself in favour of a constitution which 'promises sufficient liberty [and] assures serious control over the acts of the Government, and finally restores universal suffrage to mastery of itself'.[157] In Lyon shopkeepers rallied to the regime.[158] Paradoxically, there was great impatience with what were regarded as the sterile and time-wasting debates in the Corps législatif on the implementation of the reforms.[159] This shift in opinion was reflected in the *Bulletin politique* prepared by the Paris gendarmerie commander for January 1870. He concluded that the situation in the capital was far less alarming than might appear at first glance. Disorder would ensure that the middle classes rallied to the liberal regime.[160] Commerce had been frightened by the prospect of a return to the *mauvais jours de 1848*.[161]

---

[152] 4 Oct. 1868, AN BB30/389.   [153] PG Douai, 3 July 1869, AN BB30/389.
[154] A. Vitu, *Les réunions publiques à Paris, 1868–69* (Paris 1869), p. 45.
[155] Ibid. pp. 57, 59.   [156] See e.g. PG Rouen, 11 Jan. 1869, AN BB30/389.
[157] Constant, 'Var', v, pp. 1389–90.   [158] PG Lyon, 3 July 1864, AN BB30/379.
[159] E.g. PG Agen, 7 July 1870, AN BB30/390.
[160] Bulletin politique Ier Légion gendarmerie, 31 Jan. 1870, AHG G8/176.
[161] OC gendarmerie de la Seine, 26 Feb. 1870, AHG G8/176.

Whilst freedom of the press and public meetings might be welcomed in principle, respectable, and no doubt compassionate, professionals like Dr Hellis in Rouen were alarmed by the apparent preference of 'the masses who live in the workshops and in the cabarets' for a 'red' newspaper like *Le Progrès* rather than 'an honest newspaper'. He denounced 'universal suffrage' as 'a dangerous absurdity which will lead us to the abyss by placing power in the hands of ignorance, greed, and brutality'.[162] He insisted that equality before the law should never have been extended to politics.[163] M. Durand, the owner of a large industrial flour mill in Rennes, represented a widespread concern that relationships with workers were becoming increasingly difficult due to the efforts of *une certaine presse* which 'exaggerated workers' rights without telling them about their duties'.[164] The gulf which was perceived to exist between much, perhaps most, of the property-owning classes and those they viewed as 'inferior' is worth stressing. It remained the case, however, that even if most of the middle classes undoubtedly supported the regime, they remained relatively passive in comparison with the more active involvement of some of their social peers in opposition politics.[165]

Opposition: Legitimist, Orleanist, and liberal

Middle-class opposition to the regime was variable in strength – over time and between places. Throughout the first decade officials expressed frequent concern that as 'the memory of the danger grows fainter and more distant, . . . the security it enjoys will reawaken its independence and encourage a return to the short-sighted habits of a subversive and critical opposition'.[166] This would take various forms. In some areas, there was substantial support for an elite-dominated Legitimism. In the west, in Rennes and Nantes and many smaller centres, and in southern cities like Toulouse, although declining in significance, patron–client relationships, reinforced by clerical influences, continued to associate the producers and retailers of luxury goods as well as aspiring professionals, particularly lawyers, with aristocratic landowners.[167] In the Haute-Marne too the *petite bourgeoisie* was dependent on the local elite of rich landowners and ironmasters.[168]

---

[162] Letter 31 May 1869, in Chaline (ed.), *Deux bourgeois*, p. 190.
[163] Letter 22 July 1869, ibid. p. 192.   [164] AN C1159.
[165] Point made by PG Pau, 6 April 1859, re Landes, AN BB30/384.
[166] PG Dijon, 13 Jan. 1854, AN BB30/377.
[167] R. Aminzade, *Class, Politics and Early Industrial Capitalism. A Study of mid-19th Century Toulouse* (London 1981), pp. 221–5.
[168] Prefect, 13 April 1856, AN F1 C111 Haute-Marne 8.

There was also substantial support for a socially conservative liberalism which reflected disappointed expectations. Businessmen had generally assumed that the regime would provide tariff protection and low taxation, and that it could be depended upon to curb railway monopolies and to preserve public order. Only merchants involved in international trade and the manufacturers of luxury goods like silk, dependent on large export markets, had favoured trade liberalisation.[169] The small textile manufacturers of Les Andelys in Normandy claimed that the treaty with Britain had sacrificed French interests in return for support for imperial intervention in Italy. They had even 'solemnly considered if they should not replace a Sovereign who was doing so much damage to their business and, after modestly recognising that they had no-one to put in his place, they resigned themselves to attacking his popularity, taking care to spread the rumour . . . that a good industry was being sacrificed to a bad politics'.[170] It had also previously been assumed that officials would protect the 'free' market in labour by prosecuting striking workers. Many businessmen would thus find the regime's determination to reduce tariffs and legalise strikes utterly incomprehensible.[171] The defence of 'liberty' and of local industry and commerce against foreign competition and rail monopoly were two themes on which substantial portions of the social elites and middle classes could agree.[172]

Amongst the generally better-educated professionals it was the lost freedom of discussion in press and parliament which stimulated complaints. There was widespread agreement with liberal politicians that these had offered the most effective means of defending vital interests. At Nancy the notary Blaize and his brother-in-law, the eminent lawyer Volland, typically chose to support the liberal Orleanist option.[173] The audience at a public meeting at Tourcoing in 1869 was told that 'the 1860 Treaty was made without us, in spite of us, in contempt of the public principles which regulate the rights of the French nation'. These were based on 'the principles of 1789' which required 'the intervention of the nation in its own affairs'.[174]

The prospect of war also caused considerable disquiet which, following the Prussian victory over Austria in 1866, spread from 'the higher levels which habitually concern themselves with politics' into the middle classes,

---

[169] See e.g. Cayez, *Crises*, p. 18.

[170] PG Rouen, 12 April 1860, AN BB30/387. Similar reports from PG Amiens, 17 Jan. 1860, AN BB30/371 re Amiens, Abbeville, St Quentin, and Beauvais.

[171] See e.g. PG Bordeaux, 13 July 1865, AN BB30/374.

[172] E.g. Ménager, 'Vie politique', II, p. 725.   [173] PG Nancy, 3 April 1857, AN BB30/381.

[174] *Discours prononcé par M. Jules Leurent, vice-prés. de la Chambre consultative de Tourcoing, au meeting industriel de Lille du 8 nov. 1869 pour la défense du travail national et contre le libre échange* (Lille 1869).

engendering a widespread hostility, not towards the dynasty, but certainly against the Emperor's personal rule.[175] Excessive expenditure on Paris and Marseille and the speculative activities of close associates of the regime added to the sense of disquiet.[176] For workshop owners and shopkeepers, support for liberal politicians was additionally a means of distinguishing themselves from their employees and from working-class clients who frequently inspired them with 'fear' and revulsion and who were more likely to exhibit republican sympathies.[177] The overall, and for the regime alarming, result was that 'the different classes which make up society, without marching to the same step or obeying the same instincts, are nevertheless taking the same direction'.[178]

Republican opposition

The republican movement was a coalition of interest groups characterised by considerable social and ideological diversity. Official reports tended to emphasise its predominantly urban character, the importance of a rank-and-file made up of workers, artisans, and shopkeepers and the leadership role of professionals and businessmen.[179] It was this last feature which proved especially difficult for officials to understand and accept – 'by an inexplicable fecklessness, the bourgeoisie which would be the first victim of the revolutionary spirit, substantially contributes to its support'.[180] Of course, individual motivation is never easy to explain, but for the authorities such inconsequential behaviour could result only from moral flaws. Support for republicanism was likely to be seen as involving 'some young men without experience, whose opinions will change once they mix in society',[181] together with those who had failed in their professions, and the simply perverse or perverted.[182] According to the prefect of the Loiret, these were the men who had threatened social order in the rich agricultural Beauce during the Second Republic, and who 'continue to work in secret in the countryside because the sentiment which motivates them is greed'.[183]

In the aftermath of the *coup d'état*, however, the republican movement had been hopelessly fragmented by repression. Its local leaders had been intimidated and most of them would remain inactive for years afterwards. Prosper Rossi, a monumental sculptor in Toulon, remembered how close

---

[175] PG Aix, 4 Oct. 1868, AN BB30/389. [176] E.g. PG Lyon, 3 July 1864, AN BB30/379.
[177] PG Dijon, 14 Jan. 1870, AN BB30/ 390; see also Gaillard, *Paris, la ville*, pp. 138–9.
[178] PG Dijon, 13 Jan. 1869, AN BB30/389. [179] E.g. PG Caen, 17 April 1859, AN BB30/375.
[180] PG Dijon, 9 July 1855, AN BB30/377. [181] PG Nancy, 3 April 1857, AN BB30/381.
[182] See e.g. PG Caen, 13 April 1859, AN BB30/375. [183] 31 Oct. 1853, AN F1 CIII Loiret 7.

police surveillance and frequent denunciations had completely demoralised local republicans.[184] It no longer seemed safe to discuss politics over a convivial drink. Many disillusioned middle- and lower-middle-class activists withdrew from politics. Others found the prospect of secret society activity distasteful, and possible involvement in violent protest unacceptable. In these circumstances, artisans and workers were frequently left to their own devices.[185] According to the police commissaire at Blois in the Loire valley, the result was that 'in the demagogic party there are many soldiers but no chiefs, properly called'.[186]

One potentially influential group, the primary schoolteachers who had been encouraged by Carnot, the republican education minister, to declare their support for the Republic early in 1848, had subsequently been severely disciplined. The vast majority of teachers would remain politically demobilised, and exercise an essentially conservative influence. The departmental regulations introduced as a result of the Falloux Law of 1850 typically insisted that 'the principal duty of the teacher is to give children a religious education and to profoundly engrave on their souls the sentiment of their duty towards God, towards their parents, towards other people, and towards themselves'.[187] They were to lead by example and generally inspectors' reports registered official satisfaction with the schoolteachers' professional commitment and general behaviour.[188] However, the expectation that lay primary schoolteachers would cooperate with the clergy in the task of moralising the young did cause considerable tension between two groups so strongly imbued with a sense of mission. Thus, in response to an official enquiry the village schoolmaster at Cabrières (Hérault) warned that 'the schoolteacher is obsequious, he trembles in front of M. le curé, but he hates being coerced with all his might. The priest sees the teacher as the propagator of anarchy. The teacher only sees in the priest the old determination to dominate.'[189] Nevertheless, most teachers continued to recognise that the open expression of such grievances remained unwise.

The impact of repression was always uncertain. Every community was believed to be sheltering its group of irreconcilables, often individuals who

---

[184] Constant, 'Var', I, p. 24, note 140.
[185] See e.g. J.-F. Gilon, 'Surveillés et condamnés politiques à Bordeaux entre 1850 et 1860', *Revue historique de Bordeaux*, 1986–7, p. 57.
[186] 17 June 1853 quoted G. Dupeux, *Aspects de l'histoire sociale et politique du Loir-et-Cher* (Paris 1962), p. 438.
[187] Quoted A. Prost, *L'enseignement en France* (Paris 1968), p. 178.
[188] Ministère de l'Instruction publique, *État de l'instruction primaire en 1864 après les rapports des Inspecteurs d'Académie*, 2 vols. (Paris 1866), *passim*.
[189] AN F17/10782.

had briefly enjoyed office in 1848, and were determined to regain their influence.[190] Occasionally elections provided proof of their existence. These were men inspired by principles or ambition, and who had acquired a taste for politics, as well as organisational experience.[191] Certainly individuals whose abilities and social roles earned respect within communities retained an influence disproportionate to their number. According to the prefect of Saône-et-Loire it was 'undoubtedly the bourgeoisie and the small traders who are the least well disposed. It is amongst them that every government has encountered opposition.'[192] In central France, in the impoverished Aubusson area of the Creuse, in the absence of a class of *grands notables*, it was those landowners and lawyers described as *une bourgeoisie de début*, still close to the soil and proud of its antecedents, which 'holds the people in its hands . . . It conducts their business, lends them money, flatters them with the numerous kinship links which exist between them and it.'[193] This was the *nouvelle bourgeoisie* determined to challenge the authority of existing social elites in the little towns of the Limousin like Bourganeuf or Tulle and which helped keep democratic traditions alive by linking the day-to-day problems of the rural population to political themes.[194] They would present a growing challenge to established elites partly because of their ability to mobilise financial and cultural resources.

Professionals in particular possessed the time, resources, verbal facility, self-confidence, and range of contacts, which allowed them to influence shopkeepers, artisans, workers, and peasants. Thus the republican movement in the 1850s appears to have been made up of small groups of militants with, in most communities, a local leadership drawn predominantly from amongst the *bourgeoisie* – landowners, professionals, and businessmen, together with lower-middle-class artisans and small traders, including the café owners who, whether from political principle or hope of pecuniary gain, and once their fear of seeing their licences revoked had declined, provided meeting places.[195] This was evident in the working class *quartiers* of Paris, in industrial centres in the Nord where, in 1858, 14 per cent of those included on police lists of militants were *industriels, professionals, propriétaires,* or *rentiers*,[196] and in Côte-d'Or where the prefect claimed that there existed an army, of which 'the cadres have survived but which has no

[190] See e.g. PG Besançon, 3 July 1854, AN BB30/373.
[191] See e.g. the concern expressed by PG Lyon, 17 July 1856, AN BB30/379.
[192] 3 April 1852, AN F1 CIII Saône-et-Loire 13.
[193] Sous-préfet Aubusson to Prefect Creuse, 26 June 1853, AN F1 CIII Creuse 8.
[194] Corbin, *Archaïsme*, II, pp. 816–17, 844–6.
[195] See Constant, 'Var', III, p. 873; Faury, *Cléricalisme*, p. 392.
[196] Ménager, 'Vie politique', I, pp. 404–5.

soldiers'.[197] These frequently shared the vague philosophical republicanism and anticlericalism found, even in the 1850s, in such Parisian newspapers as *Le Siècle* and *La Presse* as well as in the provincial newspapers which reprinted their articles.[198]

The possibilities for action might be limited, but informal organisation remained feasible on the basis of existing social networks and associations. By allowing elections, the regime itself provided regular opportunities for opposition to manifest itself. During the authoritarian empire, local officials frequently complained about informal gatherings in cafés and private homes, during which efforts, sometimes successful, to contest municipal elections were organised. Though generally without much evidence, they frequently assumed that this diffuse activity represented a return to the secret societies so common before the *coup d'état*.[199] The widespread distribution of letters and pamphlets from abroad – some of them justifying tyrannicide – and written by such intransigents as Victor Hugo or Felix Pyat, added to their alarm.[200]

Some militants remained cautiously and continually active. Their numbers were reinforced by the return of exiles and political prisoners as the regime's various amnesties – culminating in that of 1859 – took effect. Paris remained the centre of constant agitation, however muted. Some of its professionals, journalists, and students formed a sort of *bohème politique*, meeting in the cafés of the *Quartier Latin* to read and discuss illicit publications, and engage in a verbal violence influenced by Blanqui's revolutionary *putchisme*. They were also in contact with the younger worker militants. In the 1860s the police identified around 1,000 agitators who required close surveillance. Student life played a formative part in many political careers.[201] However, if they ever returned to politics, most former republican militants remained quiescent until the liberalisation of the 1860s. Previously politics had often been viewed either as too dangerous or as pointless, given the authoritarian character of government, although the prefectoral administration's constant interference in local affairs could cause considerable friction.[202]

Much depended on the milieu and the character of dominant personalities willing and able to exercise 'democratic patronage'; to re-affirm

---

[197] 4 June 1853, AN F1 CIII Côte d'Or 9.
[198] E.g. PG Dijon, 9 Jan. 1855, AN BB30/377; PG Pau, 15 April 1865, AN BB30/384.
[199] See e.g. PG Rouen, 3 Feb. 1859, AN BB30/387.
[200] See e.g. PG Dijon, 8 Sept. 1852, AN BB30/377.
[201] R. Nord, *The Republican Movement. Struggle for Democracy in 19th Century France* (London 1995), p. 35.
[202] PG Montpellier, 29 Sept. 1859, AN BB30/422.

traditions forged around historical landmarks like 1792 or 1848; and to take advantage of local rivalries, and popular resentment of local elites and authoritarian government. In industrial centres as diverse as Saint-Etienne – with its artisanal silk ribbon and small-arms manufacture and modern mining and metallurgy – or the textile town of Reims, new wealth adopted the republican label as part of its challenge to the older, established business elites who retained local political power.[203] Political participation was less risky for such people than for workers and peasants. Their social backgrounds and contacts largely preserved them from harsh treatment by the police and courts.

To a greater or lesser extent, similar tensions existed in most urban centres and with significant political consequences. In the cutlery manufacturing centre of Thiers, the opposition was claimed to be exploiting 'the jealous hatred of the cutlery manufacturers towards the bourgeoisie, their determination to secure a more prominent position in public affairs, and the thousand other circumstances related especially to the rivalries between families and between individuals'. Business rivalry spilled over into struggles for positions on the municipal and departmental councils and the chamber of commerce. The Cercle de commerce established by Prost, a lawyer and mayor in 1848, brought together around 100 businessmen in what the authorities claimed was a disguised political club.[204] From Strasbourg it was reported that 'there will always be a *petit commerce*, jealous because of its inferiority in comparison with large-scale trade, and a working class population disposed to vote with the class which is immediately superior to it and which is closely related by affinity, bias and shared sentiments'.[205]

Economic expansion intensified struggles for primacy within professions. It led to criticism of those with established situations and easy access to capital, and of the bankers and 'plutocrats' who controlled credit and were closely allied to the regime. Georges Duchêne expressed this resentment in a widely circulated book published in 1869, entitled *L'Empire industriel. Histoire critique des concessions financières et industrielles du Second Empire.* He warned about the economic revolution already well under way and its growing impact on 'our social equilibrium'. He was concerned that the growth of monopoly in finance, transport, commerce, and industry would lead to the creation of an 'industrial feudalism' in which the financiers would dominate society. According to his calculations, 183 people had secured

---

[203] Gordon, *Merchants, passim.*
[204] PG Aix, 7 April 1862, 8 Jan. 1863, AN BB30/370; see also Prefect, 14 Aug. 1862, AN F1 CIII Puy-de-Dôme 10.
[205] PG Colmar, 24 April 1866, AN BB30/376.

control of all the major economic enterprises. They formed 'the dominant class, the most energetic, the most dangerous in consequence, and utterly devoid of political principle . . . having only one preoccupation: to ensure complete enjoyment of its privileges'. The future was bleak. In place of a system which had allowed 'the spontaneous distribution of wealth, subject to the laws of the market', monopoly would result in the 'absorption of small-scale industry by large-scale: the suppression of the middle class, which will enlarge the ranks of the proletariat: at the top a few hundred hardened offenders, wasting hundreds of millions, at the bottom an entire nation, exhausted with fatigue and misery, manoeuvring according to the will of its leaders, with the precision of a disciplined army'.[206] The call was not for class conflict but, in Jacobin terms, for an alliance of the *petits* against the *gros*.

Developing an effective challenge to established notables already endowed with considerable social capital and official support would, however, take some time, and considerable effort. In practice, this mounting middle-class republican opposition to the Empire was to be seriously weakened by personal rivalries and disagreements over tactics and objectives. The re-affirmation of claims to leadership by the generation of older militants who had made their reputations during the Second Republic frequently conflicted with the ambitions of younger, and more impatient men. In many localities, the continuing predominance of *quarante-huitards* within the republican leadership was clearly evident. In the Gard although, by 1869, they made up only 17 per cent of a list of 101 leading activists, they provided most of the candidates for local elections.[207] In Lille, in 1870, one-third of militants, including most notably, Alphonse Bianchi, were identified by the police as belonging to the 1848 generation. This could cause considerable frustration for younger activists although, as in the case of Achille Bianchi, cohesive family structures could also ease the passage of republican memories and an intransigent militancy from one generation to the next.[208]

If the formative influences on the various age groups varied, the proportion of the electorate which had experienced the fears, and hopes, of 1848 was obviously in constant decline. The authorities at Rouen pointed out that the electorate in 1865 included almost 22,000 voters who had been aged less than fifteen in 1848.[209] Introduced to republican ideas as students, and facing obstacles at the start of their careers, young professionals might well

---

[206] Duchêne, *L'empire industriel*, pp. 1, 12–13, 52, 72, 18, 236.   [207] Huard, 'Préhistoire', III, p. 848.
[208] Ménager, 'Vie politique', II, p. 758.   [209] PG Rouen, 14 Oct. 1865, AN BB30/387.

see politics as a means of enhancing their reputations. They were described by the police frequently as 'the most ardent', recognisable by 'the audacity and violence of their intentions'.[210] It was also generally assumed that in most cases their views would moderate with time, as they enjoyed professional success and were more fully integrated into the appropriate social networks.[211]

In Paris, and other major cities, tension between republicans would be heightened further by social as well as generational differences, and especially the growing re-assertion of bourgeois leadership. A republican historiographical tradition which tended to disregard social divisions should not lead us to ignore the differences emerging between the spokesmen of the moderates, generally older and drawn from the ranks of successful and wealthy professionals, and 'radicals', more likely to originate in the *classes moyennes*, less settled socially and more interested in mobilising the masses; as well as between these bourgeois and working class militants.

The triumphalist announcement in *Le Siècle* on 1 June 1863, that 'the resurrection of the middle class to political life is, currently, the great fact which dominates the elections', caused considerable resentment amongst those working class militants who had remained active throughout the dangerous 1850s. There were particularly sharp disagreements over social policy and the question of public order. The experience of 1848, which had gravely weakened the confidence of many bourgeois republicans in the masses, had also revealed often bitter divisions between socially conservative moderates and 'radicals' and 'socialists' more or less committed to social reform. According to the state prosecutor at Lyon, writing on April Fools Day 1862, the fundamental difference was that 'some are inspired by ideas coming from London and Brussels and prepare a bloody revolution. Some accept as their only leaders the *comité des cinq*, which is how they refer to the opposition deputies, and will only pursue a non-violent revolution.'[212]

There were other differences over tactics. The abandonment of the abstentionist electoral position favoured by such stalwarts of 1848 as Hippolyte Carnot, and the acceptance by the five republican deputies elected in 1857/8 – Favre, Ollivier, Darimon, Picard, and Hénon – of the need to take the oath of loyalty to the regime so as to avoid being unseated, certainly caused disquiet. Subsequently, this was reinforced by the concern that others amongst the growing number of republican deputies and local

---

[210] OC gendarmerie cie de la Seine, 28 Jan. 1870, AHG G8/176.
[211] E.g. PG Nancy, 3 April 1857, AN BB30/381. [212] 1 April 1862, AN BB30/379.

councillors would follow Ollivier and Darimon and become integrated into a liberal-imperial political system.[213]

Undoubtedly most republican militants were irreconcilable. They were alienated forever from the regime by its origins and convinced that only republican institutions were compatible with the *genuine* liberty to which they aspired. They continued to believe in the possibility of human enlightenment and the progressive achievement of the political and social objectives of 1789, and in the eventual collapse of the imperial regime.[214] Most middle-class activists probably favoured a peaceful transition to a republican regime, insisting that with universal suffrage there was no need for insurrection.[215] Nevertheless, the greater freedom of speech permitted by the regime in the late 1860s allowed the major differences of opinion between republicans to emerge more fully into the open.

In place of the 'socialism' of 1849/51, the dominant current within the republican movement was now liberalism, an attraction 'towards English and American doctrines; the unlimited liberty of the individual, the weakening of all authority, the repugnance for all regulation'.[216] The programme outlined in Jules Simon's *La politique radicale* in 1868, in spite of its title, barely paid lip-service to the ideals of social reform, concentrating instead on condemnation of the Bonapartist state and vague notions of *la moindre action* and *la liberté totale*. Speaking at a public meeting in Paris in 1869, the editor of the *Côtes-du-Nord*, M. Marsais, attacked the memory of the first Napoleon and by implication his nephew. To shouts of approbation from his audience, he claimed that 'the privileges abolished on 4 August, were restored by the great man! It was he who re-established the nobility and the clergy, forgetting that he was the son of a popular revolution.'[217] In another meeting Jules Ferry attacked centralisation and its agent, the prefect – *ce pacha de la France impériale*.[218]

Ever since the Second Republic moderate republicans had sought to eliminate any lingering association between republicanism and the politics of class. This was not only personally congenial but appeared necessary in order to attract wider middle-class and peasant support. Speaking to an election meeting in Paris on 8 May 1869 Jules Simon vehemently denied that he was a communist. He insisted that, 'Socialism is an ambiguous word, which I cannot accept.' The following day, rejecting claims

[213] Price, *Second Empire*, pp. 366–7.
[214] On republican idealism see e.g. G. Cholvy, 'L'opposition à l'Empire dans l'Hérault' in M. Cadé (ed.), *L'histoire à travers champs* (Perpignan 2002), pp. 274–6.
[215] See e.g. Vitu, *Réunions électorales*, p. 141.   [216] PG Rouen, 11 Jan. 1866, AN BB30/387.
[217] Vitu, *Réunions publiques*, pp. 42–3.   [218] 4 May 1869, Vitu, *Réunions électorales*, pp. 83–4.

that he was an Orleanist, he pointed to a record of support for the freedom to hold meetings, army reform and disestablishment of the Church, and to loud applause concluded: 'I am being called the man of the bourgeoisie. Yes, I am, and also that of the worker; or rather the man who believes that the bourgeoisie and the worker are the people, and I am the man of the people.' With the additional need for working-class support in mind, however, Simon did insist that 'I will always support those reforms which are possible and necessary to regenerate and to invigorate society.' These *grandes réformes* were to be achieved through 'liberty, association, education'.[219] Similarly, at a public meeting in the capital in April 1870, Jules Favre associated social harmony with education through 'the mixture of rich and poor on the benches of every school'.[220] This was a discourse that rejected strikes and an independent workers' movement and insisted upon the community of interest between classes. The attitudes that moderates adopted towards the masses were every bit as moralising and condescending as those favoured by members of the social elite.[221]

In much of south-eastern France, in departments like the Gard, and in the towns of the Rhône valley, where Legitimist traditions had survived, middle-class-dominated electoral committees, and the republican press, were more likely to appeal to a Jacobin and democratic tradition.[222] As in Paris, it was self-confident middle-class militants who assumed leading roles, rather than the workers and peasants who generally lacked the assurance necessary to speak at public meetings. Thus, amongst a group of 101 militants in the Gard, 35 per cent came from the liberal professions; 22 per cent were wholesale merchants, bankers, or brokers; 15 per cent *propriétaires*; 15 per cent artisans or traders; 4 per cent clerks and 4 per cent workers.[223] In the south-west the rural bourgeoisie employed an anti-noble discourse, first elaborated during the Revolution, which denounced the nobility for its greed and hunger for power. This allowed republican landowners to appeal for political support from peasants, whilst at the same time exploiting them through sharecropping and money lending.[224]

---

[219] Ibid. p. 132.
[220] A. Dalotel, A. Faure, and J.-C. Freiermuth, *Aux origines de la Commune. Le mouvement des réunions publiques à Paris, 1868–69* (Paris 1969), pp. 64–5.
[221] See e.g. J.-Y. Mollier, 'Noël Parfait (1813–96): une trajectoire républicaine au 19e siècle' in A. Faure, A. Plessis, and J.-C. Farcy (eds.), *La terre et la cité. Mélanges offerts à Philippe Vigier* (Paris 1994), p. 276.
[222] Huard, 'Préhistoire', II, p. 465.   [223] Ibid. III, p. 848.
[224] R. Gibson, 'Les notables et l'Église dans le diocèse de Périgueux', Doc. de 3e cycle, Univ. de Lyon III 1979, II, p. 446.

The appeal made to the rural population in 1869 was, however, less radical than it had been in 1849. The central promise of cheap credit to purchase land and escape from debt had disappeared. Anyway, the relative prosperity of agriculture during the Empire, together with the relaxation of population pressure through migration, had probably reduced its attraction. There was also a determination to counter accusations that republicans supported the so-called *partageux*, the communists planning to seize the land. Fear of revolution might otherwise drive the property-owning classes back towards the regime.[225]

In order to impose a semblance of unity on the republican movement, middle-class militants focused their attention upon their common enemy, the regime, criticising excessive state expenditure and the level of indirect taxation. Anti-clericalism was another potent rallying cry and, in order to appear sympathetic to the largely working-class electorate from which they drew support, they called for attention to be given to the 'social question'. However, their social programme remained extremely vague and avoided clear commitments.[226] Indeed, there remained considerable concern amongst republican leaders about the possibility of losing control over the mass movement to 'socialists' and 'communists' willing to loose the anarchic passions of the urban poor in another bloody revolution.

As opposition to the Empire grew stronger, especially in the major cities, it became all the more difficult to contain personal, social, and ideological differences. It was cause for concern that many of those who attended electoral meetings in May 1869 appeared unwilling to accept that there was a substantial difference between Ollivier, 'the man of the lie and hypocrisy',[227] and a moderate republican like Ernest Picard. The latter had achieved notoriety as the first deputy to denounce the *coup d'état* in the Corps législatif, in January 1864. On 14 May 1869, nevertheless, he was shouted down in a meeting in a hall on the Boulevard Magenta for asserting that 'socialism is an utopia'. Furthermore, he was accused of being a friend of Jules Favre, 'the strangler of the people in 1848'.[228] Another moderate republican, Bancel, a candidate in Paris, whilst taking part in stormy hustings, largely paraphrased the Declaration of the Rights of Man, insisting on the need to protect property as well as liberty. One of his supporters, a merchant called Thirat, responded to a shout that Bancel was a revolutionary by admitting that 'he wants revolution but by legal means'.[229]

---

[225] E.g. P. Goujon, *Le vigneron citoyen. Mâconnais et Châlonnais (1848–1914)* (Paris 1993), pp. 212–13.

[226] Huard, 'Préhistoire', III, p. 825.

[227] Lefrançais, speech of 14 May 1869, in Vitu, *Réunions électorales*, p. 72.

[228] Ibid. p. 73.   [229] Ibid. pp. 39–40.

During the 1869 electoral campaign, the gulf widened between the eminent moderate republican veterans of 1848 Carnot, Garnier-Pagès, and Jules Favre, and their critics, further to the left. In Paris, the old socialist Dr Raspail, whose views had certainly mellowed with age, nonetheless allowed himself to be presented as a symbolic candidate against Garnier-Pagès.[230] Through the pen of Dr Guépin, philanthropist and long-time political activist in Nantes, the 'radical' newspaper *L'Union démocratique* denounced Favre and the other supporters of a liberal alliance which included Legitimists and Orleanist/liberals. Guépin supported the intransigence represented by the self-proclaimed Jacobin, Delescluze, and demanded the extension of municipal liberty, the 'suppression' of the proletariat and the organisation of *mutualisme* and old-age pensions.[231] In reaction, the moderate republican – in spite of its title – *Radical de l'Ouest*, directed at a popular audience, denounced 'the egoism of some, the utopianism of others' and insisted that 'we will never distinguish between social and political concerns'.[232] In this case, however, as so often, the differences between moderates and 'radicals' could be seen as largely cosmetic.

The up-and-coming lawyer Gambetta, who had honed his oratorical skills and enhanced his political reputation in the courts, also adopted a 'radical' position, highly critical of members of the older generation. In 1869 he stood for election in Paris against Carnot, although there was relatively little to distinguish their programmes. As Gambetta told an electoral meeting: 'Like you, I believe that there is no other sovereign than the people, and that universal suffrage, the instrument of that sovereignty is valuable and imposes obligations . . . only if it is completely free.' It followed that 'the most urgent of all reforms must be to free it from all tutelage, from every restriction, from all pressure, from all corruption'. Once this had been achieved 'universal suffrage . . . would be sufficient to achieve all the destructions that your programme demands, and to establish all the liberties, all the institutions of which we will, together, ensure the birth'. From this he could conclude that 'a progressive series of social reforms absolutely depends on the system of government and on political reform'.[233] Clearly, the emphasis in this speech was on questions which would unite rather than divide republicans. Confident in the future, at least for the moment, he insisted to his friend Juliette Adam that the 'liberties will favour us, believe me, they will pour down and drown the Empire little by little. We republicans

---

[230] Dalotel, Faure and Freiermuth, *Aux origines*, pp. 286–7.
[231] 9 Nov. 1869, quoted Launay, *Diocèse de Nantes*, II, p. 754.
[232] 24 Oct. 1869, quoted ibid. p. 753.   [233] Vitu, *Réunions électorales*, pp. 10–11.

have no interest in seeing the Revolution triumph by means of an uprising which would have as its representatives Delescluze, Flourens . . .'.[234]

Continuing his balancing act, Gambetta, whilst speaking in Belleville in May 1870, insisted, again on this occasion to a largely working-class audience, that they should focus their attention on political reform which was the indispensable precondition for the social reform they desired. He promised that the social problems which beset them could be resolved easily once a republican regime had been established, at the same time insisting on the urgent need to free 'the bourgeoisie and the provinces from fear and uncertainty'. He claimed that it was the Empire which posed the greatest threat to business interests because of its economic and fiscal policies, its militarism and reckless foreign policy. Nevertheless, and in spite of his caution, more moderate republicans would find the violent tone of Gambetta's language distasteful, especially when he went on to promise the suppression of standing armies and the election of officials, and attacked the Catholic church as the root of 'ignorance, of reactionary and vicious attitudes, enemy of the Republic, slave of ultramontanism' (13 May 1869). Two days later, he called for female 'emancipation', and pointed out that the education of women by the religious orders turned them into 'either idiots devoted to the childish practices of the Church or into prostitutes'.[235]

Particularly alarming for 'respectable' middle-class republicans were the diatribes launched at the public meetings in Paris and other major cities. These were all too reminiscent of the clubs of 1848. Thus, and in spite of an obligatory police presence, speakers repeatedly launched violent attacks on a regime which owed its existence to *le crime de décembre*,[236] on the army and church which were its vital supports, and on a social system based on exploitation. They insisted that there was nothing to distinguish moderate republicans from monarchist liberals. At a meeting in the Avenue Montaigne a speaker called Millières condemned Thiers, the great hero of liberal opposition, who 'has always spoken [of liberty] when he was not in power, but when he was, became the assassin of this liberty'. Thiers had proved himself to be a 'traitor' in 1830 and 1848.[237] Moderate republicans were denounced for supporting a bourgeois social order, which allowed the 'people' to remain ignorant, exploited and miserable. According to Théodore

[234] Quoted Constant, 'Var', v, p. 1419.   [235] Vitu, *Réunions électorales*, pp. 14–15.
[236] E.g. Jules Allix, speech at Salle Molière Nov. 1869, quoted Dalotel, Faure and Freiermuth, *Aux origines*, p. 183.
[237] Vitu, *Réunions électorales*, p. 23.

Brisson at Belleville on 27 December 1869, 'they are dealing with a gangre-
nous social body and they claim to be able to cure it with lukewarm water'.[238]

Verbose tirades like that of M. Ducasse at the Vieux-Chêne in Paris on 26
January 1869 were greeted with thunderous applause by lower-middle- and
working-class audiences. He declared that 'we are the implacable enemies
of despotic principles. We are those who march enthusiastically towards
the enemy, guns blazing, but holding more than sharp swords and guns,
because we hold in one hand the Rights of Man, and in the other, the
glorious motto: *Liberté, Egalité, Fraternité*.'[239] And so it went on.

During the hearing of his appeal against a fifteen-month sentence for
secret society activity in May 1869 Eugène Protot, a lawyer influenced
by the old revolutionary Auguste Blanqui, declared in a much-publicised
statement, that

we want, by means of revolution to destroy every form of political, military, religious
and capitalist tyranny and to create, in the debris of those old iniquities, eternal
peace between nations, absolute liberty and the equal well-being of every citizen.
No more agricultural, industrial, commercial and financial feudalism. No more
idle and corrupt demi-gods, imposing burdens on the masses exhausted by work
and deprivation.

In spite of repeated warnings from the court president, he denounced the
servility of the press and parliament, and a suffrage system dependent on
hoodwinking 'the poor and uneducated voter'.[240]

There is no doubt that utterances of this kind proved extremely offensive
to the many middle-class republicans who were frightened by the prospect
of revolutionary violence. For the sincere Catholics who remained committed republicans such attacks must have made reconciling their two faiths difficult. On the other hand, Gambetta's anticlericalism could be very appealing, particularly in a town like Poitiers where nobles and clergy were said
to 'refuse to believe that this *infâme bourgeoisie* could share their own religious sentiments, and confuse it . . . with the socialists, labelling them both
rouges'.[241] Similarly, in the Tarn, in towns like Albi or Castres, professionals
or businessmen appear to have rejected vigorously the subordinate position
traditional social elites expected them to assume within society and the
Church.[242] This was evident in the overwhelmingly republican sentiments
developing within the ranks of the younger generations of freemasons.[243]

[238] Vitu, *Réunions publiques*, p. 55.　　[239] Ibid. pp. 43–4.
[240] Cour impériale de Paris, *Chambre des Appels correctionnels. Audience du 9 mai 1867* (Paris 1867).
[241] Academic Rector Poitiers (a priest), 10 May 1858, AN F17/2649.　　[242] Farcy, *Cléricalisme, passim*.
[243] S. Hazareesingh and V. Wright, *Francs-maçons sous le Second Empire* (Rennes 2001), pp. 99–101.

In large part anticlericalism was a response to the ultramontane and politically reactionary stance taken by the Church since 1848. Republicans had welcomed the regime's intervention in Italy in 1859 and the deterioration in its relations with the Papacy, which had followed. By the late 1860s, however, as fear of social revolution grew, the state–church alliance was being reconstructed. Moderate republicans often adopted an anticlericalism which presumed that religion was a private matter. They condemned the clerical assumption that religion should inform and dominate every aspect of life, and insisted that the Church should restrict itself to spiritual questions. However, these views might be reconciled with religious faith and occasional church attendance. Radicals, including the youthful Dr Clemenceau, went further and totally rejected the baneful influence of the clergy. They expressed contempt for the irrationality of religious teaching and belief in such miracles as the apparitions at Lourdes – an 'insult to the progress of Science and an outrage to human Reason', according to the *Journal de Rouen* (8–9 February 1862). The same newspaper denounced the Papal Syllabus of Errors as a 'challenge launched by the spirit of the Middle Ages to the spirit of modern society' (25 December 1864). Papal interference in French affairs and the influence exercised by priests over women through the confessional were also condemned vigorously.[244] In this case, two faiths were in combat, the one based on Divine Revelation, the other on Human Reason. Clericalism and anticlericalism flourished in the same regions, feeding off each other, and creating an atmosphere of mounting intolerance.

The debate on education was of central importance to republicans and offered another means of mobilising wider support. Generally they insisted on the need for secular and obligatory instruction based upon rational principles. Jean Macé, a teacher himself, created the Ligue de l'Enseignement in 1866, as an avowedly apolitical association, but one critical of many of the central tenets of clerical ideology and of government support for the Church. Republicans typically compared the 'obscurantism' of the clergy with the enlightened programme of Science. The Church was portrayed as a threat to modern society, to the Nation and to the happiness of the family. According to an editorial in the Nantes *Phare de la Loire*, the catechism, the basic statement of faith, was itself

a bad book because, wanting to establish belief in the existence of God, it adorns the Creator with all the imperfections of the creation. It is a bad book, because it offers on the creation of the world, the flood etc. . . . explanations completely

[244] Chassagne, 'L'histoire des villes', pp. 240–1.

destroyed by Science. It is a bad book, because it substitutes the authority of the priest for that of society, for that of the father of the family. It is a bad book, because it replaces the law court with the confessional, human justice with a justice which will be exercised only after death.[245]

With growing frequency, the republican press employed a language which Catholics were bound to find offensive. Thus the *Phare* condemned 'the childish and idolatrous practices of clericalism, all the Jesuitical and obscurantist ranting'.[246] In the Tarn, Protestants were certainly determined to oppose Catholic pretensions, remembering the White Terror in 1815, a key historical reference point for them.[247] Catholic intolerance similarly distressed members of the Jewish community.[248] As members of an organisation long suspected by the Church, Freemasons were alarmed by the threat to excommunicate them.[249] Amongst the lower middle class, shopkeepers who were criticised by the clergy for opening on Sundays, and particularly café owners, who endured constant attacks for supposedly encouraging immorality, were especially likely to be attracted by anticlericalism.[250]

In the provinces it was regional newspapers such as *L'Avenir, journal démocratique du Gers* edited by Lissagaray, the future chronicler of the Paris Commune, which presented a programme very similar to that of Gambetta.[251] With their networks of local correspondents and links to the Parisian press and politicians they formed increasingly the basis of a republican 'party', just as they had during the Second Republic, substantially reinforcing the informal social networks on which previously republicans had largely depended. Journalists were again playing a political role of crucial importance. In the Nord, republicans were dependent increasingly on the weekly *Progrès du Nord*, published in Lille, which found its prestige considerably increased when it was defended against prosecution in 1868 by such a star of the Parisian bar as Picard. Rising from 760 in 1867 to 1,060 in 1869, its circulation remained small, but it was read widely in cafés and workplaces.[252] In the Tarn, local professionals and tradesmen belonging to the Albi masonic lodge *La Parfaite Amitié*, founded *Le Patriote Albigeois* in October 1869.[253] Further north, in Grenoble, the editors of *L'Impartial dauphinois* borrowed articles written by kindred spirits on newspapers like the Nantes *Phare de la Loire* or the *Progrès de Lyon*. They

[245] Launay, *Diocèse de Nantes*, II, p. 903.   [246] 2 July 1868, quoted ibid.
[247] Faury, *Cléricalisme*, p. 358.   [248] Nord, *The Republican Movement*, pp. 64f.
[249] Derobert-Ratel, *Arts et l'Amitié*, pp. 72–6.   [250] Faury, *Cléricalisme*, pp. 392–5.
[251] PG Agen, 8 Jan. 1870, AN BB30/390; G. Palmade, 'Le département du Gers à la fin du Second Empire', *Bulletin de la Société archéologique, historique et scientifique du Gers* 1961, p. 203.
[252] Ménager, 'Vie politique', II, p. 739.   [253] Faury, *Cléricalisme*, p. 74.

encouraged correspondents throughout the region to write stories about titillating scandals in order to attract readers.[254] Together with growing numbers of newspapers, the presses churned out increasing volumes of circulars and political tracts in order to sustain political agitation, although in many localities the republican middle classes remained too few or timorous to provide the necessary funding.[255]

To the dismay of moderate and indeed of many 'radical' republicans the newspapers which attracted the greatest public interest in the late 1860s were notorious for their extreme views and violent tone. These included, most notably, Rochefort's *La Lanterne* and its successor *La Marseillaise* and such provincial imitators as Naquet's *Le Peuple* published in Marseille. The first issue of *La Lanterne* in May 1868 sold 125,000 copies and its circulation grew with its reputation for outrageous comments, sarcasm, and sense of the ridiculous. The following was fairly typical: 'As a Bonapartist, I prefer Napoléon II . . . [the son of Napoleon I who died prematurely in exile], What a reign my friends! No taxes, no useless wars . . . No civil list!'[256]

The combination of electoral success in 1869 with growing social tension in the cities and the publicity given to revolutionary speeches in the Parisian public meetings, as well as to the strike waves of 1869/70, must both have increased the optimism of middle-class republicans, and stimulated substantial anxiety amongst the more moderate. However, probably the great majority would have agreed with the sentiments expressed by the veteran 'radical' activist Dr Guépin, in an editorial written for the Nantes newspaper *Union démocratique* and calling for a negative vote in the 1870 plebiscite. Guépin insisted that

the plebiscite proposes to enlist us in a state of permanent subordination towards the Head of State and his family. It also proposes to give him, whenever he wishes, the right to cancel the actions of the deputies chosen by us to control him. It goes even further: he demands that we usurp the prerogatives of voters as yet unborn . . . In the face of such demands, profoundly wounding to our dignity, some of them contrary to morality, what else can we do but respond with the loudest possible No.[257]

The result would be a devastating blow for all middle-class republicans. It seemed to Gambetta that 'the Empire is stronger than ever'.[258]

---

[254] PG Grenoble, 31 Jan. 1865, AN BB30/378.   [255] Huard, 'Préhistoire', III, p. 806.
[256] Quoted G. Pradalié, *Le Second Empire* (Paris 1969), p. 45.
[257] Quoted Launay, *Diocèse de Nantes*, II, p. 871.
[258] Quoted C. Seignebos, *La Révolution de 1848. Le Second Empire* (Paris 1921), p. 94.

CONCLUSION

As property owners, the middle classes had habitually looked in two directions. Generally they were committed to the preservation of order, but frequently resented their subordinate place within the established social and political systems. Once the threat of revolution had declined and state repression eased in the 1860s the opportunity had again presented itself to express their grievances. Political activists seized the chance to influence the various social groups with which they came into contact habitually, taking advantage of the intermediary place within the social structure occupied by the middle classes, together with their education and access to financial and organisational resources. In a political system which recognised manhood suffrage they were able to look towards the masses – *les petits* – for support and enter into competition with the social elites – *les gros* – for political power and control of the State, as the means of ensuring the realisation of the libertarian, and to a lesser degree, egalitarian objectives, established in 1789. Securing these objectives depended upon the successful promotion of a shift from a politics based upon patronage/clientelism towards one based on militancy/professionalism. However, the concession of greater political liberty by the regime proved to be more than sufficient for many of their erstwhile supporters. A regime which promised liberty with order would gain widespread middle-class support in the May 1870 plebiscite.

CHAPTER 4

Peasants and rural society: a dominated class?

INTRODUCTION

The establishment of manhood suffrage in 1848 substantially enhanced the political importance of the rural population, which made up an estimated 74.5 per cent of the total in 1852.[1] Probably around three-quarters of these people were engaged in farming. The figures are not very accurate but the number of men recorded as employed in agriculture was around 7,305,000 in 1856, rising to 7,995,000 by 1876. Contemporaries would have described the vast majority of them, rather loosely, as 'peasants'. This would have included all those landowners who cultivated the soil with their own hands, tenant-farmers, sharecroppers, and agricultural labourers – most of whom aspired to own, and many of whom would succeed eventually in acquiring land through inheritance and/or purchase. Peasants could make or break a regime which sought legitimacy through the ballot box.

The basic methodological proposition which informs this study is that understanding political behaviour requires contextualisation. This demands a detailed analysis of peasant life. Historians and social anthropologists have frequently debated the value of the label 'peasant', however. The word is replete with notions of a cohesive, stable, and essentially autarkic community, subject to change only from external forces. The reductionism implicit in such binary configurations as commercial/subsistence, town/country, central power/local power is symptomatic.[2] There is a tendency to overlook the constant need for rural populations to adapt to the natural environment, to demographic change, as well as to commercial opportunities and pressures. There is also a danger of underplaying the existence of many different forms of production within rural communities, the presence within the community of non-peasants – landowners,

---

[1] Classified as living in communes with a population of fewer than 2,000.
[2] R. Hubscher, 'Syndicalisme agricole et politicisation paysanne' in M. Agulhon *et al.*, *Politisation*, p. 135.

professionals, artisans – and complex inter-relationships between the local community and the wider society represented by the State, Church, and market.

Nevertheless, and in spite of the analytical difficulties inevitably caused by attaching a label to such a diverse group, the concept of the 'peasant' cannot simply be abandoned. The label had meaning as part of the developing self-image of many of the inhabitants of the countryside, and in terms of how they were perceived. Participation in politics itself would substantially reinforce the sense of identity derived from a shared profession and culture.[3] What is necessary is to accept the limitations inherent in categorisation, and use the concept flexibly.

The varied geography of France is a pointer to the great diversity of the peasant experience. The concerns of farmers on the cereal-growing plains of the north were very different from those cultivating vines in Provence or engaged in pastoral farming in the uplands of the Massif Central or Alps. In the single department of Eure-et-Loir the rich cereal growing plains of the Beauce, centred on Chartres, with its open fields and large villages, could be contrasted with the Perche, cut by valleys, with poor soils, forest, and lakes and small, dispersed farms and hamlets. Furthermore, within each of these broad eco-types peasant-proprietors, tenants, sharecroppers, and agricultural labourers each had their different interests, and each of these sub-groups its own hierarchy.

Achieving an understanding of peasant political behaviour involves penetrating the rural community, and considering the factors influencing day-to-day relationships within hierarchically ordered social systems in which an individual's position was determined by wealth, education, family solidarities, and reputation.[4] The community served as an institution of social and political regulation, but within it a multiplicity of internal alliances and antagonisms might develop, particularly as a result of disputes over access to scarce resources. Ideally, one would want to understand the specific social order which informed individual political behaviour, taking into account not simply formal social relations or the diffusion of political ideology but 'the attitudes and meanings with which they were infused'.[5] This would

[3] See e.g. A. Bleton-Ruget, 'Aux sources de l'agrarisme républicain: la propagande démocrate-socialiste et les campagnes (1848–51)', *Cahiers d'histoire* 1998, p. 283.

[4] See e.g. R. Dupuy, 'Le comportement politique de la paysannerie française du 16e siècle à la fin des années 1950', *Histoire et sociétés rurales* 1995, p. 16; J.-P. Jessenne, 'Synergie nationale et dynamique communautaire dans l'évolution politique rurale par-delà la Révolution française' in Agulhon *et al.*, *Politisation*, pp. 63, 78.

[5] K. Wrightson, 'The social order of early modern England: three approaches' in L. Bonfield, R. Smith, and K. Wrightson (eds.), *The World We have Gained* (Cambridge 1986), p. 192.

require the identification of *leaders d'opinion*[6] within the peasant community but also the cultural, and thus political, intermediaries linking the rural with the external world.

Furthermore, perceptions of the present were informed by memories and expectations constructed on the basis of past experience. These provided the basis for group identity. The weight of the past in the collective memory was extremely variable, however, determined as it was by the oral traditions of both the family and the community, and increasingly by the institutional influences of state and church.[7] Moreover, current experience might radically alter perceptions of both past and present. Thus, during the Second Empire the socio-economic structures of the rural world underwent substantial change, whilst increasingly the state offered positive assistance to rural communities in addition to tapping their resources. Nevertheless, understanding the complex inter-relationships between past and present is clearly of central importance to an assessment of political behaviour.

SOURCES

To an even greater degree than in previous chapters the sources for this might be described as seriously deficient. Peasants rarely spoke or wrote about themselves. Thus, most of the 'evidence' used in this chapter was provided by outsiders, non-peasants informed by a range of perceptions constructed, at least in part, on the basis of prejudices and misconceptions. The senior administrators and legal officials, themselves mostly landowners and members of the social elite, who wrote so many weighty reports, just like historians, found it difficult in their accounts of life and events in the countryside to arrive at an acceptable level of generalisation. They tended to emphasise consensus within the rural community and play down the existence of conflict, whilst focusing closely on whichever 'exceptional' events attracted their notice. Silence, the 'normal', is rarely subject to close analysis. So many things, especially matters of everyday concern, were never written down.[8] So much was deliberately concealed as subordinates, particularly village mayors, anxiously sought to avoid external interference in

---

[6] J. Nicolas, 'Un chantier toujours neuf', in J. Nicolas (ed.), *Mouvements populaires et conscience sociale 16e–19e siècles* (Paris 1985), p. 17.

[7] C. Guionnet, 'La politique au village: une révolution silencieuse', *Revue d'histoire moderne et contemporaine* 1998, pp. 780–4; J.-P. Rioux, 'La mémoire collective' in J.-P. Rioux and J.-F. Sirinelli (eds.), *Pour une histoire culturelle* (Paris 1997), pp. 337–9.

[8] See e.g. P. Jones, 'Towards a village history of the French Revolution: some problems of method', *French History* 2000, pp. 76–7.

communal affairs.[9] Yet administrative reports moving up the parallel bureaucratic hierarchies of the ministries of the Interior, Justice, War, and Education remain irreplaceable sources of information, even if they are written in a tone reminiscent of colonial administrators with a condescending concern for those they administered.

Alternative official sources of information are equally partial. These included the reports produced by the elected departmental and arrondissement councils with their limited administrative and supervisory powers, as well as the nominated advisory bodies (chambres consultatives d'agriculture and comices agricoles cantonaux) through which local notables responded to government enquiries concerning agriculture and rural society.[10] Even the apparently 'hard' statistical information generated by the developing state bureaucracy needs to be 'deconstructed'. Thus the questions asked in the various censuses and enquiries, as well as the subsequent presentation of information, reflected particular official or elite perceptions and concerns and imposed a simplifying construction upon the countryside. The socio-professional categories adopted by the official censuses consistently understate the complexity of rural societies, making it difficult to identify the different existential meanings of apparently uniform categories and to define change over time. It is also clear that the statistics on rural population are not very reliable. The president of the Commission statistique of the canton of Valence d'Albigeois (Tarn) typically complained about the unwillingness of the mayors of rural communes to fill in the questionnaires he sent them. He assumed that this was either because they just could not be bothered to engage in the time-consuming process, or were unwilling to risk upsetting their neighbours, because 'our peasants fear, or claim to believe, whatever one tells them, that these documents will be used to change the basis of the land tax'.[11] Whole areas of peasant life, including gender relationships, were virtually ignored. However, this should not lead us to deny all value to official reporting. The government's determination to be well-informed ensured that a considerable effort went into the collection and analysis of information.

The mass of official and quasi-official reports can be supplemented with the correspondence and memoirs of members of the landowning elite. These, of course, suffer from similar shortcomings of perspective. Generally, their views of the peasantry are stereotyped and cliché ridden and

---

[9] Price, *Second Empire*, p. 139.
[10] S. Canal, 'Quelques aspects de l'économie agricole du Tarn-et-Garonne vers le milieu du 19e siècle (d'après l'enquête de 1866)', *Revue géographique des Pyrénées et du Sud-Ouest* 1934, pp. 62–3.
[11] 1 Sept. 1865, AN F11/2689.

reveal far more about their authors' concerns than about the rural population. The peasant occupied a central place in conservative discourse, as the bedrock of resistance to subversion.[12] In their search for stability in the aftermath of the 1848 Revolution notables transferred to the peasant the virtues they normally associated with their own class – economy, foresight, hard work. For most conservatives, the peasants' famed passion for the land, a source of vice for Balzac in his novel *Les Paysans*, was a source of virtue. They adopted a romanticised, idyllic view of the countryside and of the peasant as a small property owner animated by common sense and ready to accept the advice of his parish priest and social superiors. Paintings were an influential feature of this conservative discourse and were reproduced in popular engravings and illustrated newspapers. In their different ways, Millet's representation of the harshness of rural life in *Le Semeur* (1850) and *Les Glaneuses* (1857) and Jules Breton's depiction of *l'ordre éternel des champs*, represented patient peasants devoted to securing the productiveness of *la terre nourricière*.[13] Similarly, the numerous priests who wrote about parish life favoured an image of the peasant as an element in the eternal order of things and as a being close to God. This harmonious model of rural life was frequently contrasted with a starkly drawn picture of the threat to social order posed by a miserable, and potentially criminal and violent urban proletariat. It followed that every effort needed to be made to persuade the peasant to stay in his village and to protect him from corrupting urban influences.

Moreover, conservative perceptions tended to assume that peasants had freely entered into very unequal social relationships and that a sense of common interest prevailed between 'rich' and 'poor'. Notables appeared unwilling to accept that often subordination must have appeared inescapable to people dependent on the 'rich' for land to rent, for work and frequently charity and that social relationships might involve dissimulation, as a consequence. This creates a serious difficulty for the historian. Etienne Baudry, a municipal councillor at Rochement (Charente-Inférieure), offered a warning to those observers who prided themselves on their understanding of peasants: 'In whatever way he presents himself, speaks to you, greets you, or flatters you; take care in what you say, for he is always distrustful.' As a result, 'even if he is being asked about something which has nothing to

---

[12] Léonce de Lavergne, 'L'enquête agricole', *Revue des Deux Mondes* 1868, p. 407.
[13] R. Hubscher, 'La France paysanne: réalités et mythologies' in Lequin, *Histoire des français*, II: *La société* (Paris 1983), pp. 136f.; M. Juneja, *Peindre le paysan* (Paris 1998), pp. 53–83; A. Baker, *Fraternity among the French Peasantry. Sociability and Voluntary Associations in the Loire Valley, 1815–1914* (Cambridge 1999), pp. 11–15.

do with his land, he will invariably reply: We poor know nothing about that; it's something for you gentlemen. For those who understand him, this reply does not in the least signify that he does not know anything about what he has been asked.' The only certainty was that the peasant 'rich or poor' would complain, bitterly, about his situation.[14] Historians, as well as social anthropologists, would do well to heed the gleeful comments of Jean-Marie Déguignet, a Breton peasant who had served with the army in the Crimea. He remembered how 'the story tellers made fun of the scholars [folklorists] . . . and for a glass of brandy men and women would use their imaginations to invent legends'.[15]

There was also a more pessimistic literature, exhibiting the landowners' contempt for people often apparently regarded as little better than animals. Thus, writing in the *Bulletin de la Société d'agriculture de la Haute-Vienne* in 1862 a major landowner observed that 'the sharecropper is above all lazy; he is dirty, stupid, a creature of habit, obstinate, distrustful, a womaniser, and drunk at the fair. He is a brutal and brutalised being. Looking at him closely, it is obvious that his civilisation is only skin deep. The only virtue he possesses, is patience.'[16] This was clearly a being from a different mental universe, capable of insensate violence. The subsistence disorders of 1846/7, or even worse the 'red' peasant who, in December 1851, had emerged from his lair to resist the *coup d'état* had appeared to confirm this. Paradoxically, republican intellectuals like Allain-Targé adopted a similar perspective in order to explain repeated electoral failure in rural constituencies. In a letter to his mother in 1867 he insisted that a future republic must use education 'to raise the thirty-five million brutes who make up the Nation to the level of active citizens and enlightened patriots'.[17] In a pamphlet published in 1869 Felix Pyat would insist that 'the army is the peasant who kills, just as the Empire is the peasant who votes'.[18] From his standpoint only an irrational being could vote against the republic.

The 'peasantry' was a changing construct, its characteristics varying according to the concerns of the observer. To counter the inevitable bias of particular forms of information, the historian is required to employ the widest possible range of sources in order to compare and contrast, and 'deconstruct'. In spite of the obstacles, an effort will be made to construct a

---

[14] *Le paysan aux élections de 1869* (Paris 1869), pp. 9, 44.
[15] *Mémoires d'un paysan bas-breton* (Ar Releg-Kerhuon 1998), p. 14.
[16] Quoted Hubscher, 'La France paysanne', p. 128.
[17] Quoted P. Vigier, 'Le bonapartisme et le monde rural' in K. Hanmer and P. Hartmann (eds.), *Der Bonapartismus* (Munich 1977), p. 12.
[18] Quoted P. Darriulat, *Les patriotes. La gauche républicaine et la nation, 1830–70* (Paris 2001), p. 241.

view of social relationships, lifestyles, and culture in the French countryside in a period when the rural world was in flux.

LANDOWNERSHIP

In spite of their shortcomings, the statistics[19] suggest that only a minority of peasants were independent landowners, depending solely on family labour and hiring workers during peak periods of activity or particular moments in the family's life-cycle. Indeed, in order to make ends meet or achieve their dream of owning land – the essential source of social status and material security – peasants resorted to a multiplicity of means of enhancing their family incomes. Thus, many peasant landowners, or at least members of their families, hired out their labour at some stage in the farming year. It is easy to conceive of a single individual owning a small plot of land, renting more, hiring out his labour during such peak periods of demand as the harvest, whilst occasionally helping his wife at the loom and working for months, or even years at a time, on the building sites of a distant city, whilst his family cultivated the land.[20] As a result of considerable effort, many of those listed as landless would eventually inherit, purchase, or at least rent land (see table 3).

It seems clear that there were an almost infinite variety of situations to which the accompanying tables cannot do justice. These national statistics also ignore the fact that landholding structures varied considerably, in relation to physical relief, economic opportunity, demographic pressure, and social power. The proportions of landowning notables, peasant landowners, tenants, and labourers, differed from place to place, with each *pays* distinguished by its characteristic landholding and agrarian structures.

Broad regional differences might nevertheless be identified. Large estates were dominant in the north of the Paris basin, between the Seine and the Loire, in parts of Bourgogne and the south-west, and in the lower valley of the Rhône. In some of the areas of most advanced commercial farming, in the Paris basin – on the rich plateaux of the Soissonnais and Valois for example – and in the north where fertile soils combined with easy access to market, the dominant social group tended to be not the absentee landowners but large-scale tenant farmers. Generally, they owned some land of their own, but more significantly possessed the capital, usually

---

[19] Price, *Rural Modernisation*, p. 353. The category 'landowners' includes non-peasants.
[20] E.g. R. Hubscher, 'Réflexions sur l'identité paysanne au 19e siècle: identité réelle ou supposée', *Ruralia* 1997, pp. 66–72; R. Hubscher and J.-C. Farcy, 'Introduction' to *La moisson des autres. Les salariés agricoles aux 19e et 20e siècles* (Paris 1996), pp. 6–10.

Table 3. *Agricultural labour force by status*

	1862		1882		1882 as a percentage of 1862
	Number (1,000s)	percentage	Number (1,000s)	percentage	
Landowners	1,813	24.7	2,151	31.2	119
Landowners who also rented land	649	8.8	500	7.3	77
Landowners who were also sharecroppers	204	2.8	147	2.1	72
Landowners who were also labourers	1,134	15.4	727	10.5	64
Total landowners	3,800	51.7	3,525	51.1	93
Non-landowners: tenant farmers	387	5.3	468	6.8	121
Sharecroppers	202	2.7	194	2.8	96
Labourers and domestics	2,965	40.3	2,707	39.2	91
Total: non-landowners	3,554	48.3	3,369	48.8	95
Total employed in agriculture	7,354		6,894		94

accumulated over generations, to invest in improved farming. Some of them would have been regarded as members of the rural bourgeoisie. Others remained peasants because of their culture, dress, manners, and willingness to engage in physical labour.[21]

These were polarised societies with relatively few independent small peasant proprietors. Nowhere, however, was this process of social polarisation as pronounced as in southern England. Many agricultural labourers in the Beauce owned some land and had realistic aspirations to possess more. Indeed the Bishop of Chartres denounced their land hunger as a primary cause of religious indifference – 'they are not working towards salvation, all their affections are for the land'.[22] In these densely populated areas, although outward subservience frequently concealed considerable social tension,[23] competition amongst the poor for land, work, and charity helped preserve elite social power. Local officials were appointed on their recommendation.[24] This was also the situation in areas where agriculture was less

[21] J.-M. Moriceau and G. Postel-Vinay, *Ferme, entreprise, famille. Grande exploitation et changements agricoles, 17e–19e siècles* (Paris 1992).
[22] Quoted Farcy, *Paysans*, vol. II, p. 969. See also Emile Zola, *La Terre*, which is set in the Beauce.
[23] See e.g. PG Paris, ? Feb. 1857, AN BB30/383; P. Bernard, *Economie et sociologie*, p. 173.
[24] Ménager, 'Vie politique', III, pp. 1215–16.

commercialised, in the west, south-west, south-east, and central France, and where, although again large-scale landownership predominated, most of the land was rented out to a mass of small tenant farmers. In contrast, in much of the south, east, and centre, where land was less expensive to purchase, small-scale peasant cultivation was already overwhelmingly dominant, although relatively few peasant landowners possessed as much as the three hectares normally regarded as making economic independence possible.

THE BURDEN OF POVERTY

If one adopts a long-term perspective, the first part of the nineteenth century appears to have much in common with the previous century. In spite of rising agricultural productivity the balance between population and resources remained precarious, culminating in the subsistence crisis of 1845/7. In most rural areas population densities reached their historical maxima around mid-century with a national average of seventy-three per square kilometre and densities of over ninety typical of parts of the Breton west, the Nord, in Alsace-Lorraine, and in the departments of Rhône and Isère in the south-east.[25] For as long as population densities were high, land hunger remained intense. Peasants continued to seek security and status through the purchase of land. Thus the creation of a farm was often the work of generations, and involved the patient accumulation of small and dispersed plots, purchased as a result of intense physical effort, emotional commitment and family solidarity. Sub-division of the soil, the clearance of marginal land, and indebtedness, together with periods of exhausting labour without counting the cost, interspersed with frequent underemployment, were characteristics of this rural world.

Although inescapably dependent on the market to earn the wherewithal to acquire land, pay taxes, and purchase necessities, the motivation of the mass of peasant cultivators and their basic psychology was very different from that of the minority of capitalist, commercial farmers. Survival depended on a labour-intensive agriculture supplemented by a wide range of additional activities, on *pluriactivité* which involved in particular rural manufacture and temporary migration involving peasants walking often long distances from upland areas to help with the harvest in the plains

---

[25] Hubscher, 'La France paysanne', p. 15; A. Moulin, *Peasantry and Society in France since 1789* (Cambridge 1991), p. 62.

before returning home to bring in their own crops, or from areas peripheral to productive agricultural regions like the Paris basin, where the five central departments (Seine, Seine-et-Marne, Oise, Eure-et-Loir, Loiret) attracted around 110,000 harvesters in 1852.[26] Especially in Paris and Lyon, the building industry provided work for longer periods. In the 1850s an estimated 500,000 men each year, coming especially from the Massif Central, Alps, and Pyrenees, found work in other regions.[27] Migration provided remittances which might help families to make ends meet in a crisis or, with luck, be accumulated for the eventual purchase of land.

In spite of unremitting effort, around mid-century, descriptions of living conditions in the countryside remained almost uniformly grim. Housing was generally overcrowded, humid, sparsely furnished, and uncomfortable. Two rooms, earthen floors, inadequate heating and ventilation, and limited lighting were typical.[28] Personal hygiene was also generally neglected. According to a doctor from Argelès-Gazost in the Pyrenees, writing in 1856: 'Peasants are generally dirty, not taking any care over their *toilette*.'[29] Even close to Paris 'the population is not very demanding in this respect'.[30]

Diet remained impoverished, frugal, and monotonous even in the most prosperous regions, dominated by whatever could be produced locally and did not need to be sold. The main elements everywhere were bread or potatoes and a variety of vegetables.[31] In their responses to the 1848 Enquête the delegates of nine cantons from the most prosperous areas of the Saône-et-Loire declared themselves to be satisfied with peasant diet. However, twenty-six others affirmed that diet was unsatisfactory.[32] The situation was especially difficult in the uplands and where, as in Brittany, population densities were particularly high. The Directeur des Contributions directes for the Haute Loire, in 1851 estimated that 85 per cent of the population were close to *indigence* and explained that 'this poverty is linked to that of the soil, to the severity of the climate, to the extreme and growing subdivision of property, to the growth of population, to its reluctance to emigrate . . . From this results [an] unthinking indolence . . . which is the result of its parsimonious habits, of its resigned attitudes, and of its disposition to be content with little, infinitely little.' He concluded that

---

[26] A. Chatelain, *Les migrants temporaires en France de 1800 à 1914* (Lille 1977), I, p. 184.
[27] Ibid. I, p. 42.   [28] A. and H. Combes, *Les paysans français* (Paris 1855), p. 105.
[29] Quoted J.-F. Soulet, *Les Pyrénées au 19e siècle* (Paris 1987), II, p. 49.
[30] 1870 Enquête, response of A. Petit from Neufmoutiers near Meaux (Seine-et-Marne), AN C1156.
[31] Price, *Rural Modernisation*, pp. 100–4.   [32] 1848 Enquête, AN C964 II.

the outsider can have no idea of the way in which they live, of their black bread, of their deprivation of wine and meat, even of the pork which they save for the periods of most exhaustive work, of their tendency to deprive themselves of any kind of comfort, of their constant preoccupation with saving, centime by centime. Only by coming close to misery every day can they hope to escape from it.[33]

Poor hygiene, combined with undernourishment, and periods of intense hard work, whatever the weather, resulted in widespread rheumatism and premature ageing, and in generally poor health.[34]

Debt remained a major problem, particularly in areas of small-scale and predominantly subsistence farming. Peasants borrowed to purchase land. They borrowed to buy out co-heirs, pay rents or taxes, or purchase the essential seeds, livestock, and equipment. Families might borrow to tide themselves over bad times – a poor or over-abundant harvest, a personal crisis due to accident or illness – or to finance a wedding. In the absence of credit institutions individuals were forced to borrow from family or neighbours, normally on a reciprocal basis, or else from moneylenders offering unrecorded, and technically illegal, 'usurious' loans. Only peasants with some property to serve as security could expect to secure longer-term loans at more favourable rates of interest.[35]

Those in need might have little alternative but to go, cap-in-hand, to a landowner to ask for the deferment of rent payments or else to a local notary, merchant, or 'rich' peasant to request a loan. In these cases the interest rates were likely to be at least 12 per cent but could easily reach 25 to 30 per cent. The worker-peasant from the Limousin, Martin Nadaud, remembered how his father, already in debt, sought to borrow money for a dowry. The problem was

to whom could we address ourselves to obtain a new loan, when the bad state of our affairs was already known in the neighbourhood? My father said, *Come and see a man I know very well . . . and who has a very obliging character.* We met him in the cabaret. As we were drinking and talking my father made the object of our visit known. He immediately responded: *I have 400f. in my cupboard, but I am not able to freely dispose of it, I have to pay for a cow at the next fair in Bourganeuf.* Finally, he decided to lend us this money for four months. I signed the agreement, although I was only 17: but to our great surprise, instead of giving us 400f., our man only handed over 360

– a real rate of interest of 30 per cent.[36]

[33] Quoted J. Merley, *L'industrie en Haute-Loire de la fin de la Monarchie de Juillet aux débuts de la 3e République* (Lyon 1972), p. 236.
[34] See e.g. 1848 Enquête, response of Dr A. Depoux from canton Pionsat (Puy-de-Dôme), AN C962.
[35] See e.g. G. Postel-Vinay, *La terre et l'argent. L'agriculture et le crédit en France du 18e au début du 20e siècle* (Paris 1998), Part I.
[36] M. Nadaud, *Léonard, maçon de la Creuse* (Paris 1976), p. 74.

Failure to repay at least the interest meant being trapped in a cycle of rising debt, growing dependence on the creditor, and eventual expropriation, ruin, and shame. The general lack of book-keeping meant that it was easy to slip into an irretrievable position. According to the mayor of Hastingues (Landes): 'regular accounts are rarely kept in the countryside. Each family attempts to proportion its expenses to its income, and it is only with great difficulty that this equilibrium is achieved.'[37] It was common to enter into debt to purchase land that offered a return of no more than 2.5 per cent on the capital borrowed.[38] The possibility of subsequently losing land often acquired as a result of generations of intense effort must have been the cause of considerable psychological distress. Although expropriation might only have occurred in a small proportion of cases the possibility was sufficient to maintain a generalised anxiety.[39]

Lending was a means of making money and also of acquiring social power. This is clear from the evidence of a Pyrenean peasant driven to denounce his creditors:

We had to take him, regularly, three times a week, all manner of provisions such as eggs, butter, beans, potatoes, cabbages, without taking into account the fact that our poor mother was obliged, twice a week, on Monday and Thursday, to give him a hearty meal and drink [*ribotes*] worth 2f.50 to 3 francs. This little game went on for 5 years.[40]

In Alsace, where Jewish cattle merchants frequently made loans, the result was widespread anti-Semitism, shared by the government officials who denounced 'the spirit of intrigue and rapacity which distinguishes this sect', and which threatened to reduce peasants to a level of misery and demoralisation comparable to that *du paysan irlandais*.[41] Moneylenders willing to lend to peasants might well have performed a useful service, but they could hardly expect to be popular.

The efforts intermittently made by sympathetic officials to prosecute 'usurers' – defined in law as those charging interest above 5 per cent – were certainly well received.[42] Occasionally, high and much publicised fines were levied – a M. Durand for example was fined 10,000f. at Sens (Yonne) in 1854.[43] Notaries, so often the middlemen in these transactions, risked

---

[37] AN C3356.   [38] See e.g. Raison-Jourde, *La colonie auvergnate*, p. 182.
[39] PG Pau, 18 Jan. 1858, AN BB30/384.
[40] Quoted Soulet, *Pyrénées*, ii, p. 81. The translation of *ribotes* is based on the *Trésor de la langue française* – a reference I owe to my colleague Emyr Tudwal Jones.
[41] PG Colmar, 31 Dec. 1857, AN BB30/376.
[42] A. Gueslin, 'Usure et usuriers dans les campagnes françaises au 19e siècle' in *Receuil d'études offerts à Gabriel Désert* (Caen 1992), p. 139.
[43] PG Paris, 26 Nov. 1853, AN BB30/383.

loss of office.[44] However, the main result was to force creditors into even more ingenious ways of disguising the rates they charged. Levying *droits de commission* on transactions was a favourite ploy.[45] Moreover, securing evidence of usurious practices was always difficult – 'the victims never complain, from fear of depriving themselves in the future of a last resort on which they might again be forced to depend'.[46] Peasants themselves were rarely able to contemplate the cost of recourse to law, especially when this would involve confronting educated notables and their networks of friends. The Crédit foncier was established in 1852, to loud fanfares, as an alternative source of borrowing. However, it required too many guarantees and was only really interested in lending to large landowners.[47] The economist Wolowski had warned Persigny the Interior Minister that this was likely to be the case during discussion of proposed legislation on sociétés de crédit foncier in May 1852. He insisted that rather than submit himself to a cumbersome, 'costly', and semi-public bureaucratic organisation, the peasant would continue to prefer the less humiliating and more familiar recourse to the usurer.[48]

THE 'IMPROVEMENT' OF AGRICULTURE

From around mid-century change in the countryside accelerated and intensified. In some forty years between *c*. 1840 and *c*. 1880 the traditional equilibrium (never immobility) of numerous rural communities was to be upset by external forces – demographic change, market integration, and the growth of state activity – with complex effects for social relationships within communities and between them and the enveloping regional and national societies, as well as for the processes of opinion formation and of politicisation which are our primary concern.

The most important single stimulus to change was the progressive development of communications and particularly the construction of rail and electric telegraph networks and the improvement of rural roads. Transport costs for bulky agricultural commodities fell by something of the order of 50 to 75 per cent.[49] These developments had commenced under previous regimes. During the Second Empire, however, the pace of change accelerated. The main strategic rail routes were completed. Communities not

---

[44] Ibid. ? Feb. 1857 re case of M. Thièry, notary at Vienne-le-Château.
[45] 1848 Enquête AN C948 1; see also J.-F. Soulet, 'Usure et usuriers dans les Pyrénées au 19e siècle', *Annales du Midi* 1978, p. 445.
[46] PG Caen, 13 April 1859, AN BB30/375.   [47] E.g. PG Metz, 11 July 1859, AN BB30/380.
[48] Report dated 1 May 1852, AN 44 AP 1.   [49] Price, *Rural Modernisation*, pp. 269–71.

served by the railways would constantly press for branch lines or at least improved road links to the nearest railway station or marketing centre. The regime responded with subsidies to encourage road works, so that whilst in 1840 13,825 km of local roads (*chemins vicinaux*) had been maintained by the local authorities, by 1873 this had risen to 288,830 km.[50]

The extension and improvement of communications resulted in a substantial modification of economic conditions.[51] Whereas previous improvements in transport had integrated regional markets, now, for the first time, a national market was established. Although many areas still lacked rail links, road improvement had a considerable impact on previously isolated rural communities, reducing the time and money wasted and the wear and tear on carts and draught animals. As Louis d'Andelarre, a landowner at Treveray (Meuse) insisted: 'It is not enough to plough and manure the fields; it is important to be able to get to them easily.'[52] Reporting on the Bresse and Dombes areas of the department of the Ain in 1866, M. Baudart, a senior government engineer, claimed that previously,

it took a considerable amount of time and powerful teams of oxen, to take two or three sacks of wheat to market across the clayey soil of these two areas, and in wet weather, the roads became impracticable. In the mountains, the roads suffered from other shortcomings, dangerous storms, steep slopes etc. Today, almost all the roads are viable, every locality is served; the number of markets has considerably increased and the foodstuff merchants provision themselves at the farms.[53]

Not surprisingly, road works, the provision of railways, and subsequently the charges levied by the railway companies, were major issues in local political life. At times transport issues seemed to be matters of life or death.[54]

Improved communications would have a substantial impact on agriculture, on living conditions, and the outlook of the rural population. The incentive to produce for sale was reinforced substantially, as was the dependence on the market, to purchase the inputs – fertilisers, livestock, improved tools – necessary to increase production, and generate the incomes needed to satisfy the growing interest in consumer goods. Even in upland areas like the Pyrenees, which remained distant from the railways, the establishment of new markets and fairs was indicative of this growing commercialisation.[55] With food supplies secured, and the lifting of the age-old nightmare

---

[50] A. Armengaud, *Les populations de l'est-Aquitain*, p. 211; see also Conseil général du Nord, *Rapport sur les chemins vicinaux par M. le Comte Martin* (Lille 1862).

[51] Price, *Rural Modernisation*, Part III.   [52] AN C959 11.

[53] Ministère de l'Agriculture, du Commerce et des Travaux Publics, *Enquête agricole*, XXVII (Paris 1872), p. 239.

[54] See e.g. ibid. V: *Nord* (Paris 1867), p. 207.

[55] C. Thibon, *Pays de Sault. Les Pyrénées audoises au 19e siècle : les villages et l'Etat* (Paris 1988), p. 106.

of 'famine', it became safer to specialise in the cultivation of whatever grew best rather than aim for local self-subsistence.[56] According to Alain Corbin, 'le Second Empire marque . . . la fin d'un monde'.[57]

Access to urban markets was greatly improved although the farmers' ability to respond to new opportunities and competitive pressures varied. Each *pays* experienced its own 'agricultural revolution', reflecting differences in natural conditions, farm structures, and the density and cost of communications. In spite of the loss of the quasi-monopoly status previously conferred on them by geography, it was those areas already most heavily engaged in commercial farming which responded with greatest ease to new opportunities. Thus, from the Seine-et-Marne, close to Paris, it was reported that agriculture was prosperous not only due to increased production 'but even more because of the ability to sell easily at high price; [the department] is crossed by several railway lines which provide rapid links with Paris and, to these major lines of communication is linked a dense network of roads radiating outward towards every commune, towards each farm'.[58]

Lacking capital, and always cautious, peasants often took time to respond. The majority tended to follow the lead of the more prosperous farmers, the 'opinion leaders' who were better informed, and financially and psychologically better able to cope with change. Generally they selected one or more 'profitable' products from within their polycultural systems on which to focus their efforts.[59] Change was usually gradual. If peasants in general were increasingly dependent on commercial activity, it should be borne in mind that, particularly in those regions less completely integrated into the market, the majority remained heavily committed to family subsistence. Additionally, it was still frequently the case that 'the small farmer, anxious to pay for the purchase or the rental of the land, thinks less of improvements than of immediate results, in order to make his payments. All too often his land is overused and badly cultivated'.[60] Often, considerable pressure to conform to established farming practices was exerted within family and community. A rare peasant witness to an enquiry, a sharecropper from Castets in the Landes, insisted that he farmed 'in following my father's example and taking his advice. My children do the same thing.' Even if he had favoured change he would have been restricted

---

[56] See detailed analysis by PG Grenoble, 10 April 1866, AN BB30/378.
[57] Corbin, *Le monde retrouvé*, p. 244.   [58] PG Paris, 5 Aug. 1863, AN BB30/384.
[59] See e.g. Comice agricole Perreux (Loire), AN C1157.
[60] V. Guichard, 'Statistique du morcellement de la propriété dans le département de l'Yonne', *Bulletin de la Société des sciences historiques et naturelles de l'Yonne* (Paris 1862), p. 85.

by the conditions of his lease – 'as a sharecropper I commit myself to cultivating the land . . . according to local usages'.[61]

In all except extreme situations, however, a complex of inter-related innovations increased the productivity of both land and labour substantially. New ploughs allowed better preparation of the soil, whilst improved hand tools, including the replacement of the sickle by the scythe as the most common harvest tool, made work easier. Peasant farmers were likely to favour low-cost, technically simple innovations, suited to the field structures and animal power available, and which fitted most easily into existing rotation systems and work routines. Mechanisation proper – the use of a reaping machine capable of cutting five times as much as a man with a scythe – remained limited to a small number of large farms. Nevertheless, between 1852 and 1862 in the Loir-et-Cher, which included much of the Beauce, the number of threshing machines increased from 16 to 300, 6 of them steam powered. Although the flail remained the typical threshing tool on small farms,[62] the falling cost and growing reliability of machinery, together with the efforts of threshing contractors, allowed some peasant farmers to escape from the back-breaking effort required previously.[63]

M. Ferron, president of the Comice agricole at Gray (Haute-Saône) maintained that 'although the rotation system has not changed, and techniques have changed very little, as a result of the increased cultivation of fodder, more careful preparation of the soil, and more abundant manure, the yields of the various crops, particularly cereals, have notably increased'.[64] There was, typically, more to sell, and at higher prices. Although substantial continuities with the past were evident, contemporaries appear to have become increasingly aware of change, as new commercial opportunities, evolving land and labour markets, and migration, combined to improve the prospects for earning a living.

Whilst risk avoidance remained a first principle, it seems clear that when opportunities were perceived, change could be quite rapid, as the extension of vine cultivation in southern France revealed. This was a response to the provision of rail access to urban markets in the north.[65] The Comice agricole of the canton of Bourg-de-Visa (Tarn-et-Garonne) reported in 1866 that 'thirty years ago, there was no market. The landowner was forced to

---

[61] AN C3356.   [62] Dupeux, *Aspects*, p. 212.

[63] See the *cayers* [*sic*] left by J.-B. Guerret, farming at La Chapelle-St-Sauveur (Saône-et-Loire), edited by R. Michelin, *Les larmes d'or. La vie rurale en Bresse bourguignonne de Louis-Philippe à Napoléon III* (Paris 2002), pp. 116–17, 126.

[64] AN C1160.

[65] See G. Marqfoy, *De l'abaissement des tarifs des chemins de fer en France* (Paris 1863), p. 112.

consume his own wine or sell it to local innkeepers. Today, wine merchants come to the cellars to make their purchases, and send it to Bordeaux, Paris, etc.'[66] Production of wine rapidly increased due to the cultivation of higher-yield grapes and the spread of the vines from the hillsides onto the previously cereal-cultivating plains – 'cultivation of the vine . . . which was only of secondary importance in our agriculture has in the last fifteen or twenty years become our principal industry'.[67] Growing wheat imports from Russia further encouraged this transformation. According to the state prosecutor at Aix, farmers in Provence were unable to secure a remunerative price for their wheat. Increasingly they 'have restricted its cultivation within the limits set by their own consumption. They no longer produce for sale, but only to feed their own households.' Instead they concentrated on 'cultivating the vine, olives, almonds, mulberry trees, on producing madder and teasels'.[68] On peasant farms cultivation was improved primarily by yet more physical effort. If conditions were improving, life was never going to be easy.

EVIDENCE OF RISING PROSPERITY

In spite of the vagaries of the weather and severe crises affecting partic-ular farm products and regions, the Second Empire was overwhelmingly a period of growing prosperity in the countryside. This unprecedented well-being was due to a fortuitous cyclical, and international, upturn in the prices of most agricultural commodities, stimulated by growing pop-ulation and urbanisation, and generalised by improved communications and market integration, for which the regime claimed and received much of the credit. There were difficult years, but overall the value of agricul-tural production increased, according to one calculation, by some 44 per cent between 1852 and 1862, and by a far less dramatic, but still significant 25 per cent, from 1862 to 1882. The importance of rising prices to this growing prosperity is suggested by the estimate that between 1852 and 1882 the value of agricultural production rose by 80 per cent, whilst volume grew by only 25 per cent.[69] The figures might vary quite significantly from place to place, reflecting differences in socio-economic structures and var-ied responsiveness to market changes, but generally the overall conclusions

---

[66] AN C1157.

[67] Ministère de l'agriculture, du commerce et des travaux publics, *Enquête agricole*, xxii (Paris 1867), p. 44, response of Société agricole des Pyrénées-Orientales.

[68] 14 April 1866, AN BB30/370.

[69] M. Agulhon, G. Désert, and R. Specklin, *Histoire de la France rurale*, iii: *Apogée et crise de la civilisation paysanne 1789–1914* (Paris 1976), pp. 247, 250.

would be similar. Improved access to markets ensured profitable sales for most farmers, promoting an almost euphoric ambience.

Enquiries by the Administration des Contributions directes in the Loir-et-Cher, to the south of Paris, suggest a rise in the net income of landowners of the order of 58 per cent (*c.* 34 per cent in terms of real income) between 1851 and 1879. At the other end of the social hierarchy, labourers' wages increased by around two-thirds.[70] Throughout the Paris region prosperous farmers were judged to be well able to pay such increases, however much they complained.[71] Those who profited most in Loir-et-Cher were the tenant farmers with large farms, cultivating primarily cereals and employing hired labour. They enjoyed an increase in real incomes of at least 125 per cent, whilst farmers employing solely family labour gained around 82 per cent.[72] Although, in contrast with the large *fermiers* of the Paris basin, most tenant farmers – particularly the sharecroppers common in the centre, west, and south-west – barely scraped a living, it was widely accepted that, with rents rising less rapidly than profits, they too were in an 'unprecedented position'.[73]

In Bourgogne vine cultivators benefited from an increase of 90 per cent in the price of *vin fin* in the 1860s and of 78 per cent for *vins ordinaires.* In the Beaujolais the net incomes of *vignerons* increased by an estimated 160 per cent. This encouraged both an extension of the vineyards and cultivation of higher-yield plants.[74] Further south, in lower Languedoc, the good years commenced around 1854 as rail began to improve market access.[75] Small-scale peasant farmers rapidly became less dependent on supplementary activities, and on those who offered them, as their incomes from vines doubled or tripled.[76] In the Hérault wages rose by 60 to 90 per cent.[77] No longer exclusively dependent on local markets, the large number of producers of ordinary wines were able to sell even the abundant harvests of 1858, 1859, 1863–4, 1867, and 1869 at reasonably high prices, whereas in the past prices would have collapsed, in the absence of a national market.

If the period between 1847 and 1857 was difficult for many vine cultivators, the years that followed – between the crisis caused by oidium and the

---

[70] Dupeux, *Aspects*, pp. 246, 259, 265.   [71] E.g. PG Paris, 3 Feb. 1863, AN BB30/384.

[72] Dupeux, *Aspects*, p. 286; see also Farcy, *Paysans*, 1, p. 555.

[73] PG Angers, 11 July 1863, AN BB30/371.

[74] R. Laurent, *Les vignerons de la Côte-d'Or au 19e siècle* (Paris 1958), p. 522; G. Garrier, *Paysans du Beaujolais et du Lyonnais*, 1 (Grenoble 1973), p. 392.

[75] See e.g. Marqfoy, *De l'abaissement des tarifs des chemins de fer*, p. 112.

[76] PG Dijon, 14 Jan. 1865, AN BB30/377; Cholvy, *Le diocèse de Montpellier* (Lille 1973), III, p. 799.

[77] G. Cholvy, 'Histoire contemporaine en Pays d'Oc', *Annales E.S.C.* 1978, p. 870.

onset of phylloxera – were prosperous.[78] Although increased competition created difficulties for traditional producers in northern departments like the Marne or Côte d'Or,[79] these pressures were offset by the substantial growth in consumption from, nationally, 51 litres per head in 1848 to 77 by 1872.[80] The threat of overproduction would only become evident in the late 1860s. In the meantime, large landowners, peasant farmers, and labourers were all able to benefit from the spread of this labour-intensive production. Greater prosperity led to a marked reduction in social tension in vine-cultivating areas.[81]

In these circumstances, many peasant families were able to realise their dream of acquiring land, and with it greater security and enhanced status. Nationally, the information available suggests a decline in the number of large estates as their owners took advantage of high land prices and lucrative alternative investment opportunities, and a consequent increase in the number of small farms. Parcellation of the land continued, with the number of taxable units (*côtes foncières*) increasing by 15 per cent between 1851 and 1881.[82] At the same time, as a result both of the enhanced ability to purchase land and withdraw from the hired labour force, and of migration, the number of agricultural labourers declined.

Of course, this prosperity was not shared equally. Major geographical and social distinctions were evident. The cultivator's independence could only be relative and was often fragile. The *vigneron*, often taken to be the symbol of the autonomous peasant, usually depended on large landowners and wine merchants for access to a grape press or for the sale of whatever he was unable to stock.[83] More generally, who could tell when a personal or social crisis might not reduce a family to destitution? Moreover, although more peasants were able to purchase or rent plots as migration reduced pressure on resources and large landowners sold up, competition remained intense and rents and land values were high in relation to farm income. Complaints about short leases, which discouraged investment by tenants, were also common.[84] Furthermore, poor natural conditions remained an inescapable obstacle to prosperity. Nevertheless, for some time at least,

[78] See e.g. Laurent, *Vignerons*, pp. 292–3; P. Roudié, *Vignobles et vignerons du bordelais (1850–1980)* (Paris 1988), p. 116.
[79] E.g. Laurent, *Vignerons*, pp. 201–2.
[80] G. Galtier, *Le vignoble du Languedoc méditerranéen et du Roussillon* (Montpellier n.d.), p. 125.
[81] E.g. PG Aix, 7 April 1861, AN BB30/370.
[82] P. Goujon, 'Le temps des révolutions inachevées' in J.-P. Houssel (ed.), *Histoire des paysans français du 18e siècle à nos jours* (Roanne 1976), pp. 281–2.
[83] Laurent, *Vignerons*, p. 515.
[84] See e.g. 1870 Enquête, response of Société agricole des Pyrénées-Orientales, AN C1161; PG Paris, 30 July 1868, AN BB30/384.

improved communications facilitated a limited process of economic and social convergence. Market integration also brought to an end the subsistence crises which since time immemorial had followed a succession of poor harvests. Even in the mountains, and densely populated and impoverished parts of Brittany, the reduced intensity of cyclical and seasonal price movements ensured that life became less precarious. An age-old cause of misery, insecurity, social tension, and popular protest disappeared, to the disadvantage of only the minority who had previously been in a position to secure windfall profits from speculation.[85]

As well as the terrifying threat of dearth, the burden of debt was also considerably diminished due in part to the increased money supply but especially as a result of greater peasant participation in a booming commercial economy.[86] Typically, in the Dauphiné, usury ceased to be regarded as a major problem in the more prosperous lowlands of the Isère, although it remained a cause of great anxiety in the Hautes-Alpes, *pays pauvre*.[87] In the upland arrondissement of Brioude (Haute-Loire), recorded mortgage debt remained substantial but nevertheless fell from a high of 313.02f. per inhabitant in the 1840s to 247.72f. during the 1860s.[88] Former moneylenders themselves were attracted increasingly by the less demanding procedures and apparently more secure prospects of investment in stocks and shares.[89] Indebtedness, such a potent cause of social tension and political unrest during the Second Republic, declined substantially.[90]

Nevertheless, in 1862 one peasant family in two still possessed no land. At the very bottom of the rural status hierarchy, there were around 3 million agricultural labourers. Their situation was determined largely by population density and the labour market. The 1848 Enquiry had revealed, almost everywhere, an excess of labour and substantial underemployment. This was a situation which invariably reinforced landowner power. Competition for tenancies and work kept rents high and wages around subsistence level. In marked contrast, some fifteen years later the employers of agricultural labour were almost unanimous in their complaints about a growing shortage of labour. Whilst the procureur général at Paris warned that the

---

[85] See e.g. 1870 Enquête, response of M. Flaxland, *propriétaire* at Kientzheim (Haut-Rhin) and secretary of Comice agricole Ribeauvillé, AN C1156; Price, *Rural Modernisation*, ch. 6.

[86] See e.g. PG Montpellier, 14 April 1861, AN BB30/380.

[87] PG Grenoble, 20 July 1859, AN BB30/378; see also 1848 Enquête, canton Domène, AD Isère 162M 1–2.

[88] J. Merley, *La Haute-Loire de la fin de l'Ancien Régime aux débuts de la 3e République* (Le Puy 1975), p. 569.

[89] PG Riom, 30 July 1855, AN BB30/386.

[90] See e.g. response of Société d'agriculture, sciences et arts de Poligny (Jura), AN C1161; Société d'agriculture de Quimperlé (Finistère), AN C1158.

'information' they provided exaggerated their problems, as well as their 'generosity' towards the rural poor, it was generally accepted that substantial changes were under way.[91]

The easing of population pressure as a result of increased permanent migration initially represented a reaction to the misery caused by the mid-century crisis. Increasingly, however, it constituted a positive response to the expansion of urban employment opportunities, with the most pronounced movement taking place from those rural regions close to the growing towns and industrial centres. These were areas where commercially orientated farms employed large numbers of labourers who, without land of their own, were relatively mobile. Population pressure was thus first eased in relatively prosperous regions rather than in the most over-populated and impoverished areas of Brittany, the centre and south-west.[92]

The responses to the 1848 Enquiry into working conditions frequently provided good reasons for migration. The delegates of the canton of Saint-Fargeau (Yonne) resented the fact that 'the agricultural labourer, the worker in the fields, is regarded as occupying the lowliest place in the social hierarchy';[93] those from Mamers (Sarthe) pointed out that because 'the land is so subdivided, there are a large number of unoccupied arms in the countryside'. Moreover, 'work in the fields is more arduous and less well rewarded than that in the towns, the food is less good, the clothing less elegant, amusement less lively and less frequent. If one is ill it is more difficult to find a doctor, and if one falls into misery to find assistance.'[94] It was the young, the unmarried, those without commitments and with little hope of ever acquiring land who left.[95] Although there was nothing like a 'rural exodus' during the Second Empire, the number of agricultural labourers nevertheless precipitately declined, by as much as one-third in two decades, effecting a major transformation of the labour market and contributing to the development of employer–employee relationships in place of those between 'master' and 'man'.[96] Almost everywhere, employers were forced to accept grudgingly the need to pay higher wages and provide more work during the quiet season. Thus the Second Empire saw substantial increases in agricultural wages, of the order of at least 50 per cent and more commonly two-thirds to three-quarters.[97] This was in spite of efforts to

[91] PG Paris, 9 Nov. 1859, AN BB30/384.   [92] Price, 'Onset of labour shortage', p. 264.
[93] AN C969.   [94] AN 965.
[95] See e.g. 1870 Enquête, Société d'agriculture de l'arrondissement de St.-Lô (Manche), AN C1161.
[96] G. Désert, 'Les salariés agricoles en Basse-Normandie au 19e siècle' in Hubscher and Farcy, *La moisson*, pp. 121–2; Y. Crebouw, 'Droits et obligations des journaliers et des domestiques, droits et obligations des maîtres', ibid. pp. 182–3, 192, 198.
[97] Agulhon, Désert, and Specklin, *Apogée et crise*, p. 224.

resist the pressure by means of the introduction of labour-saving tools and some machinery into the peak periods of labour need.[98]

In addition to conceding wage increases, landowners were also obliged to tolerate less deferential behaviour. The response of M. Estival, a lawyer and landowner in the Aveyron to the 1866 Agricultural Enquiry was not untypical. He maintained that in the recent past agricultural labourers had 'loved their masters and been loved'. They had 'always been content'. In recent years, however, he had detected a 'profound change of mentality'. Even in his isolated department, 'a critical spirit has emerged which rejects the paternalism of rural society, because it is possible to escape from it by emigration'.[99] In such circumstances, migration might be described as 'a form of disguised strike'. At the same time, on the large farms (400 to 600 ha.) in the Paris region a growing social distance developed as better-educated farmers and their more 'refined' wives refused to feed labourers in their farmhouses.[100] Monetarisation of the economy promoted more cost-conscious attitudes. Payment in kind declined.[101] This was less likely where peasant farmers employed hired labour during those periods of the family life-cycle when children were small and their wives absorbed with household responsibilities.[102] Whatever the scale of the farm, however, labourers were certainly still expected to engage in hard physical labour throughout the daylight hours. Their social status to a large degree depended on assessments of their capacity for work.

Even if their situation was becoming less desperate, labourers also remained only too aware of their continued dependence on landowners and large farmers for work. Generally, relationships between employers and their workers were worked out at an individual rather than collective level, and within the bounds of established 'master–servant' relations. Each year at local agricultural shows exemplary labourers, *vieux serviteurs*, were rewarded for their devotion, docility, and submission. The passing of the generations was much lamented. On the northern plains in particular, tied cottages and allotments and the equipment to cultivate them were introduced in order to reinforce subordination. In small communities, in which information was easily passed between their employers, recalcitrant workers could easily find themselves blacklisted. Working in isolation, labourers

---

[98] See e.g. Farcy, *Paysans*, I, p. 498.

[99] Ministère de l'agriculture . . . *Enquête agricole*, XIX, p. 187.

[100] P. Brunet, *Structure agraire et économie rurale des plateaux tertiaires entre la Seine et l'Oise* (Caen 1960), pp. 375–6.

[101] See e.g. PG Rouen, 2 Oct. 1855, AN BB30/433.

[102] F. Langlois, *Les salariés agricoles en France* (Paris 1962), pp. 152–4.

might gather in the village inn, and complain amongst themselves about their conditions. However, any kind of workers' gathering was only too likely to be condemned as a *club permanente*.[103]

The changes under way were not always seen as entirely negative in their impact. Exceptionally, a landowner or farmer might accept that labourers were entitled to a share of their growing profits, whilst probably denouncing their *prétentions exagérées*.[104] The Haut Rhin Agricultural Society pointed out that better-nourished workers were more productive, although its members believed that this offered little compensation for a situation in which 'a latent and only too real antagonism tends, more and more, to replace the cordial familial relationships'.[105] The vast majority of respondents to agricultural enquiries seem to have been unwilling to accept that, as a result of widening landownership and due to the greater possibility of escape through migration, labourers were less willing to submit to the 'tyranny' of the past.[106] Instead they complained about 'indiscipline' and a lack of respect, and the growing taste for 'luxury' amongst the labouring classes. Memories of 1848 and the 'utopian' theories, which had spread from the towns, was claimed to be another factor encouraging 'a hatred for all hierarchy, envy of all superiority'.[107] Meanwhile, continued recourse to 'universal' suffrage 'at more or less regular intervals, places domestics and labourers on the same level as those who employ them'.[108] Landowners, in effect, whilst welcoming economic change and especially the growing impact of market forces, rejected repercussions which ran contrary to their idealised conceptions of a stable social hierarchy.

IMPROVED LIVING CONDITIONS

Within a generation living standards in most areas were to be substantially improved. In between the difficult years of the mid-century crisis and the onset in the 1870s of a 'great depression', the expansion of demand for agricultural produce and rising prices, together with increased productivity, established, in spite of some harsh years, the conditions for greater rural prosperity. At the very least it might be agreed that 'the peasants' living conditions, even that of labourers . . . leaves less to be desired than it used to'.[109] Growing prosperity manifested itself in the improvement of

---

[103] 1870 Enquête, response from canton Dolus (Ille-et-Vilaine), AN C1159.
[104] PG Paris, 3 May 1864, AN BB30/384.   [105] AN C1156.
[106] PG Douai, 9 April 1859, AN BB30/377.
[107] 1870 Enquête, response of Chambre d'agriculture, arrondissement Lapalisse (Allier), AN C1158.
[108] Comice agricole Paimpol (Côtes-du-Nord), AN C1158.
[109] PG Nancy, 24 Jan. 1867, AN BB30/381.

living conditions, although it was evident that housing and furnishing, and even food and clothing, remained lower on the peasants' list of priorities than acquiring land.[110] Moreover, every community still had its desperately poor families. In the Pas-de-Calais these made up around one-third of the population, burdened by low incomes, too many children, age, or infirmity. The terrible pressure of poverty was nevertheless being relieved.[111] Food security was increased for everyone by the disappearance of dearth. Diet slowly improved.

There was a growing preference for bakers' bread (not necessarily more nutritious) instead of the thick-crusted loaves baked at intervals of several months on the farm or in communal ovens.[112] The increased consumption of meat was another indicator of change and was widely held to have resulted in more robust younger generations.[113] As agricultural productivity grew, and with it the creation of a larger surplus of income after subsistence needs had been met, expenditure on household consumer goods also increased. The purchase by peasants of dishes, glasses, cooking utensils, and clothing, drew the inevitable criticism of *l'amour du luxe* from upper-class observers.[114] Even more disturbing, from their point of view, and constantly denounced, was what was perceived to be the growing 'demoralisation' of the rural population. This was associated with the rapidly increasing consumption of alcohol and the seemingly inexorable rise in the number of cafés. These were developments made possible by the rise in incomes and declining real cost of drink. They also represented a transformation of the forms of popular sociability and entertainment.

Complaining, from the perspective of the late 1860s, about the amount of time his son spent, every Sunday, drinking and playing billiards, one, evidently prosperous, peasant witness, however admitted that 'the times have changed; business is better; the wages of farm servants have doubled and redoubled; money circulates more. These are the reasons why we dress less badly and find ridiculous amusements that cost nothing . . . like the *veillées* or games of forfeit. The inn is becoming the obligatory setting for every pleasure.' Young women too were anxious to imitate urban fashions. His daughter, like the others, 'is determined to look elegant . . . We are

---

[110] See e.g. A. Schweitz, *La maison tourangelle au quotidien. Façons de bâtir, manières de vivre (1850–1930)* (Paris 1997), pp. 15–16.

[111] Hubscher, 'L'agriculture', p. 1605.

[112] See e.g. Conseil d'Etat, *Enquête sur la boulangerie*, p. 126, evidence of Ch. Donon, grain merchant at Pontoise (Seine-et-Oise); p. 466 evidence of M. Morel, deputy mayor of Vernon (Eure).

[113] G. Désert, 'La viande dans l'alimentation des Bas-Normands au 19e siècle', *Actes du 93e CNSS. Tours 1968* (Paris 1971), p. 150.

[114] E.g. PG Metz, 12 Jan. 1865, AN BB30/380.

already far from the simplicity of my youth. This is the age of lace bonnets, which cost a lot to buy and which are in constant need of ironing. The dresses too are increasingly complicated.'[115] It was difficult to keep clean on farms surrounded by mud and manure. People were sparing in their use of water, which still had to be carried from wells or streams. The bodies and clothing of those who rarely washed more than their hands and faces invariably stank of sweat. Nevertheless, the possession of a presentable Sunday best set of clothing was becoming important.[116] At work the blue *blouse* became the universal form of male dress. In all of this the better off gave the lead and the poor followed, as far as they were able.[117]

In spite of the relatively low priority accorded to accommodation by peasants, the most obvious physical sign of improvement was the (re-) construction of farm buildings. One report insisted that 'Everywhere our villages are being transformed; thatch is giving way to slate, walls are being raised, doors and windows are being enlarged, tiled floors are replacing mud.'[118] The use of stone and brick in place of wattle and daub and slates or tiles in place of thatch improved protection from the cold.[119] In the more prosperous areas improvement spread rapidly through processes of imitation.[120] Even in Brittany, as F. Vassilière the former director of the farm-school at Rennes observed, new rural housing was more salubrious, 'air and light penetrate . . . people live separately from their animals, the bed has replaced the *armoire à étages*, on each of which master and servants used to sleep in a heap'. Oil lamps replaced candles; stoves provided heat more effectively than open fires.[121]

In these altered circumstances, family limitation was an increasingly widespread practice, indicative of changing attitudes and relationships, and of a greater optimism about the future.[122] As living standards slowly improved parents, particularly those with property to protect against sub-division, began to develop new aspirations for their children if not for themselves.[123] A contrast could be drawn between 'peasants who own noth-ing, and who consider their large families as their real wealth and a source of

[115] E. Guillaumin, *La vie d'un simple. Mémoires d'un métayer* (Paris 1904), pp. 200, 204.
[116] Hubscher, 'La France paysanne', pp. 22–3.   [117] PG Paris, 5 May 1866, AN BB30/384.
[118] PG Bourges, 5 Oct. 1863, AN BB30/374.
[119] See e.g. 1870 Enquête, Chambre consultative d'agriculture du canton de Crémieu (Isère), AN C1159.
[120] G. Désert, 'Aperçus sur l'industrie française du bâtiment au 19e siècle' in J.-P. Bardet (ed.), *Le bâtiment* (The Hague 1971), pp. 50–8.
[121] AN C1158.
[122] See e.g. re contemporary awareness, A. de Saint Léger, landowner at St Léger (Nièvre), evidence to Conseil d'Etat, *Enquête sur la boulangerie*, pp. 676–7.
[123] Point made by Dr Cordouan, *Histoire de la commune de Lorgues* (1864), quoted Constant, 'Var', III, p. 423.

income; and those who on the contrary, have a small property, and are anxious to prevent its subdivision; they are determined to leave their children in a more prosperous situation and only have a few'.[124]

The Second Empire thus coincided with the apogee of traditional rural civilisation, a period of prosperity during which the countryside remained densely populated and the larger villages and market towns continued to sustain a host of artisans, merchants, professionals, and officials, in which peasant culture retained its vibrancy and its relative autonomy. Nevertheless, there were signs of the growing domination of urban *mores*. The progressive extension of a commercial, monetised economy, as well as the widespread purchase of land by peasants, contributed to the broadening of horizons and the modification of attitudes. They were becoming more aware of and involved in the wider world. The rural population was shifting, more rapidly than ever before, towards a greater outward orientation and away from an inwardly orientated dependence on semi-subsistence farming, on family and the community, and upon the patronage of local notables. Although these changes might have done little to reduce fundamental inequalities as the better-off further enriched themselves, nevertheless, as the sous-préfet at Béziers observed in 1865, 'this prosperous situation, in increasing the number of those with property, in spreading affluence and well-being, has exercised a very favourable influence on opinion and provided new guarantees for the preservation and respect of the principles of public order, so seriously threatened during periods of crisis'.[125]

A CRISE D'ADAPTATION

Prosperity was not without its strains, however. In spite of general improvement, some areas and individual farmers experienced difficulties brought on by the intensification of competition. Fully appreciating the significance of on-going changes in economic structures was not easy. Many farmers found it 'strange that following a bad local harvest, the price of wheat does not increase immediately'.[126] It took time to respond to new commercial opportunities or competitive pressures. Growing dependence on the market and its uncertain price movements engendered a lack of confidence in even the most prosperous areas, reflected in the *Journal de Chartres* in

---

[124] PG Agen, 5 April 1868, AN BB30/370.
[125] Quoted R. Laurent, 'Les quatre âges' in F. Braudel and E. Labrousse (eds.), *Histoire économique et sociale de la France*, III, 1976, p. 17.
[126] Ministère de l'Agriculture, du commerce et des travaux publics, *Enquête agricole*, IX (Paris 1867), p. 30 re Allier.

1856 – 'with steam and railways the links, not only between our departments, but between the countries of Europe and between the continents, are undergoing substantial modification. What was good, rational and productive yesterday, may well no longer be tomorrow.'[127]

High prices for cereals, meat, dairy produce, and wine certainly encouraged efforts to increase production. However, quite rapidly, this would lead to the oversupply of internal markets and a sharp fall in prices between 1863 and 1866, which caused particular difficulties in regions where the productivity of land and labour remained relatively low, and presaged the much more difficult conditions of the 1870s to 1890s. The producers of *vins ordinaires* in more northerly climes complained about competition from the south,[128] and cereal producers in the uplands and in the south about competition from the north and east and the price levelling effect of cheap bulk transport.[129] Upland areas experienced the greatest difficulties. High levels of functional illiteracy reduced awareness of opportunity.[130] Poor access to markets limited the incentives for change. The response to the 1866 Agricultural Enquiry from the Lozère pointed out that 'the establishment of railways in neighbouring departments . . . at a time when the Lozère has not been endowed with a single railway, has had the effect of depriving our products of the markets they have served for centuries . . . The products of our soil . . . have to be consumed within a narrow radius, and have lost most of their value.'[131] Even allowing for exaggeration on the part of the landowners who provided evidence, it seems clear that existing inequalities within the communications system were frequently confirmed by rail construction.[132]

In such situations, peasants often persisted with what outsiders denounced as 'primitive' farming, employing techniques which, however, in the circumstances, were rational means of coping with thin and stony soils, steep slopes, and a short growing season. They relied on terracing the hillsides, on hand tools and the traditional light and manoeuvrable *araire*, which ploughed a shallow furrow. Above all, cultivation required intensive and back-breaking physical effort.[133] A more prosperous future depended upon the production of marketable commodities, and in this respect, although piecemeal innovation was widespread, for example, through

[127] Quoted Farcy, *Paysans*, I, p. 487.
[128] See e.g. PG Nancy, 15 Jan. 1865, AN BB30/381; PG Paris, 17 Feb. 1865, AN BB30/384.
[129] E.g. *Enquête agricole*, XXIV (Paris 1867), pp. 22–4 re Basses-Alpes.
[130] Prefect, 21 Oct. 1859, AN F1 CIII Lozère 9.   [131] *Enquête agricole*, XX (Paris 1867), pp. 12–13.
[132] Price, *Rural Modernisation*, pp. 314–99.
[133] See e.g. 1848 *Enquête* Canton Ax-les-Thermes, AN C945; P. Cornu, *Une Economie rurale dans la débâcle. Cévennes vivaraise, 1852–92* (Paris 1993), pp. 35–7.

cattle rearing and cheese production in parts of the Franche-Comté,[134] there were certainly major obstacles.

PARTICULAR CRISES

There were also some bad years, due to the adverse weather conditions and disease which, of course, continued to affect agriculture. Nothing could be done to combat the sudden devastating hail, which could strip fruit trees bare in seconds. A storm in the lower Alps in 1854 caused 'incalculable disasters. In several localities, the hail and torrents of water have not left a single crop or fruit tree standing.'[135] There were also more general crises, the severity of which historians have perhaps underestimated. Thus, in some areas, poor cereal harvests in 1853/4 and 1856/7 appeared to threaten renewed dearth. To a greater extent than previously, however, yields were sufficiently high for a majority of peasant cultivators and not just the landlords and big farmers to profit from high prices. As always it was those with nothing to sell but their labour, particularly the residents of upland areas with under-developed rail links, who suffered most.[136] In the Limousin, drought affected the harvests of 1854 and 1855. This was partially compensated for by abundant chestnut and potato crops, at least in 1855, and by the remittances of migrant workers benefiting from the prosperity of the Paris building industry.[137]

During the regime's first decade, economic and social conditions were probably at their worst in the Pyrenean region. In the Ariège, in 1854, the impact of a cereal harvest only half that of a 'normal' year was intensified by the re-appearance of potato disease,[138] and the intense fear caused by cholera.[139] It was hardly surprising that migration out of the region increased rapidly.[140] Serious crises affected other crops. Silk cultivation, a major source of income in parts of the south, was devastated by disease amongst the silk worms from which it never recovered. In the Ardèche production fell from 3.5 million kilogrammes of cocoons in 1850 to 550,000 in 1857. The value of land planted with the mulberries on which the worms had been fed collapsed.[141] Throughout the 1850s oidium affected the vines, with

---

[134] PG Besançon, 29 June 1855, AN BB30/373 re Doubs.

[135] GOC 9e DM, 26–31 July 1854, AHG G8/18

[136] See e.g. Prefect Loir-et-Cher, 25 Sept. 1856, quoted Dupeux, *Aspects* p. 411.

[137] Corbin, *Archaïsme et modernité*, I, pp. 423, 490–1.   [138] Soulet, *Pyrénées*, II, p. 27.

[139] ? Oct. 1854, AN Fi CIII Ariège II; see also M. Chevalier, *La vie humaine dans les Pyrénées ariégeoises* (Paris 1956).

[140] See e.g. report of conseiller général Queszat (Ariège), AN C1158.

[141] Cornu, *Economie rurale*, pp. 69–71.

production nationally falling from a high of 45 million hectolitres in 1851 to 11 million and 15 million in 1854 and 1855.[142] There was little understanding of its causes. Some farmers believed that the potato disease and that affecting the vine were the same.[143] This promoted a sense of helplessness.[144] Its incidence, nevertheless, fell from the middle of the decade as a result of treatment with sulphur. However, the Ardèche, which had suffered the impoverishing impact of silk disease and oidium,[145] was also to be amongst the early victims of phylloxera, *la maladie noire*, which appeared first in the Gard (1865) and Hérault (1867).[146] However, spreading from east to west phylloxera allowed departments like Aude and Pyrénées-Orientales to profit from an increasing market share and rising prices, until they too were afflicted.[147]

In 1864/5, and again in the summer of 1870, drought was the problem, substantially reducing supplies of fodder and water, and forcing many farmers to sell livestock for whatever price they could get.[148] In 1867 the impact of poor cereals and potato crops was rendered all the more severe by the glut of wine and collapse in its price. Cattle disease was also widespread, further reducing the prospect of some sort of compensatory income.[149] Generalisations about rural prosperity during the Second Empire need to take all these general and regional fluctuations into account. Nevertheless, and even if much of the increased revenue was creamed off by a host of intermediaries, increased productivity, together with rising prices, resulted in widespread rural prosperity. The fundamental questions we need to pose concern perceptions of change, and the degree to which these established pressures to re-negotiate existing social relationships.

THE RURAL COMMUNITY

Social relationships in the countryside were built upon small *sociétés d'interconnaissance*, each with a minutely developed sense of internal hierarchy related to the property, wealth, and influence of particular families and to an individual's age, gender, marital status, and reputation. The distribution of property determined access to land, the vital scarce resource. Generalisations are difficult. However, at the summit of any rural social

---

[142] Rougerie, 'Second Empire', p. 80.   [143] See e.g. PG Pau, 18 July 1856, AN BB30/384.
[144] PG Aix, 6 Oct. 1860, AN BB30/370.
[145] P. Bozon, *La vie rurale en Vivarais* (Paris 1963), pp. 371–82.
[146] PG Nîmes, 27 April 1869, AN BB30/389.   [147] Laurent, 'Les quatre âges', p. 18.
[148] E.g. PG Bourges, 9 Oct. 1865, AN BB30/374; PG Dijon, 13 July 1870 and PG Nîmes 12 July 1870 – both in AN BB30/390.
[149] PG Besançon, 13 April 1867, AN BB30/373; Laurent, *Vignerons*, pp. 202–3.

hierarchy might be found a small group of wealthy landowners, notables – noble or non-noble, owning several hundred hectares, inhabiting a *château*, and enjoying a wide network of contacts. Immediately below them in the hierarchy were the *petits notables* owning several dozen hectares. They were often professional men, merchants, or retired army officers or civil servants. They were educated and well dressed and definitely *messieurs*, serving frequently as juges de paix and conseillers généraux. Every market centre also had its share of notaries, lawyers, doctors, *pharmaciens*, merchants, shopkeepers, and artisans, and virtually every village its priest and schoolteacher. At the other end of the social hierarchy were the landless labourers, living in permanent misery, and between these two groups a heterogeneous mass of peasant landowners and tenant farmers.

Large numbers of artisans provided for local needs – blacksmiths, masons, carpenters, coopers – and together with the growing numbers of small shopkeepers, enjoyed increasing prosperity. In many communes agriculture and industry were mixed inextricably with families depending on incomes from both. Many, including tailors and shoemakers, and the large numbers of weavers, lace-makers, and nail-makers, dependent on urban putting-out manufacture, were already amongst the most impoverished members of the rural community, and faced a rapid growth in competition from machine-made goods. In Calvados, employment in the textile and clothing trades declined from 75,000 to around 14,000 in the ten years after 1852, whilst the number of women making lace fell from around 50,000 to 15,000/20,000.[150] Fortunately, this de-industrialisation of the countryside was balanced by growing agricultural and urban-industrial labour needs.

In these different contexts, what did membership of a 'community' imply? Local particularism and a sense of mutual dependence established a certain level of cohesion, the sense of belonging to a moral community. Frequently, a community of outlook, based upon shared values, had developed over centuries. Solidarity was especially evident against 'outsiders'.[151] Internal self-regulation was preferred to official intervention and a range of sanctions deployed against those who transgressed collective norms. These included brutal beatings, as well as ridicule, ostracism, and the ritualised practice of the *charivari*, with its abusive songs and discordant banging of pots and pans.[152] Many peasants lived in communities of faith. Thus, in the countryside of the west, in Flanders and in Alsace, the clergy exercised a

[150] Désert, *Calvados*, pp. 707, 713.
[151] M. Jollivet and H. Mendras, *Les collectivités rurales françaises*, vol. 1 (Paris 1971), p. 24.
[152] See e.g. Ploux, *Guerres paysannes*, pp. 294–301.

leading role in public life. In relatively egalitarian upland communities, in the southern Massif Central, Alps, and Pyrenees, people welcomed the reassuring presence of a priest who remained close to them in terms of social origins and poverty. There was almost unanimous attendance at Sunday mass – the central act of regular religious practice. In Flanders almost every adult received communion at Easter.[153] In the Bourgogne the parishes of the southern Charollais and Brionnais were distinguished by 75 to 90 per cent participation in the late 1840s.[154] In the diocese of Nantes 82.9 per cent of those over fourteen were *pascalisants* in 1863.[155]

In these circumstances, only marginal individuals or isolated groups like woodcutters were able to escape from the intense social pressure, which ensured conformity and reinforced faith. André Siegfried's evocative description is worth quoting: 'The atmosphere of religious life is evident everywhere: the sound of the bells, regular services, the presence, more evident than elsewhere, of a numerous clergy, the respect accorded to everything connected with the Church, to the practices of religion which so intimately blend into daily life; all this combines to create a milieu with an atmosphere deeply penetrated by . . . clericalism.'[156] With the support of resident local landowners, and two or three religious sisters, parish priests exercised sufficient influence to enforce conformity.[157]

A whole host of factors affected social inter-action – socio-professional structures, the characteristics of land ownership and use, culture, communications, and habitat structures. Of course, the degree to which peasants and non-peasants were integrated into a single moral community varied between places and over time. It depended on the strength and mutual awareness of inter-dependence on the one hand and conflict over access to scarce resources on the other. The degree of autonomy peasants possessed was likely to be limited by the economic and cultural power of non-peasants, derived from the potent combination of control of resources and access to land and employment, and additionally over the distribution of charitable assistance. Cultural dominance further depended on the ability of elites to make use of educational and religious networks and more generally to influence the flow of information. In addition they were frequently able to employ the legal and administrative institutions of the state to reinforce

[153] Ménager, 'Vie politique,' III, p. 1217.   [154] Lévêque, *Bourgogne*, II, p. 725.
[155] Launay, *Diocèse de Nantes*, II, p. 884; F. Boulard (ed.), *Matériaux pour l'histoire religieuse du peuple français 19e–20e siècles*, I (Paris 1982), p. 388.
[156] Siegfried quoted Launay, *Diocèse de Nantes*, I, p. 159.
[157] See e.g. Prefect, 5 July 1858, AN F1 CIII Landes 7.

their social dominance. These were the multifaceted means of exercising power and influence, which might reduce peasants to an overwhelmingly subordinate position.

The authority of large landowners was greatest in the west due to the existence of a long-established network of *châteaux* owned by families committed to exercising their rights and responsibilities, and benefiting from the weakness – numerically and in terms of status – of potential middle-class competitors for power. Their economic power was reinforced by the spiritual influence of the clergy in an alliance of mutual interest, so that 'an agricultural labourer who failed to take part in a religious ceremony would find it difficult to obtain a place on a farm'.[158] Idealised by many conservative social commentators and landowners and common in the south-west and central France, sharecropping provided a model of social paternalism in which, closely supervising the farmer, the resident landowner played a crucial role, 'involving himself in the life and interests of localities; he was known to their populations; he loved them and was loved. He came to the assistance of the population in a thousand different ways.'[159] In return the tenants of the two or three or sometimes even thirty to forty *métairies* grouped around an aristocratic or bourgeois *château*, were expected to behave deferentially. To a substantial degree the behaviour, though not necessarily the attitudes, of many peasants – as a subordinate class – was thus determined by members of local elites.

Where peasants believed that notables were exercising 'legitimate' influence, they might express genuine gratitude for access to land and work and for assistance in time of need. According to A. de St Léger, a major landowner in the Nièvre, during the Second Republic sharecropping peasants in the uplands of the Morvan had supported the cause of social order loyally, in marked contrast with the more independent peasant-proprietors and cash tenants living on the plains. However, he insisted that the preservation of such good relationships between landowners and 'their' peasants depended on year-round residence in the countryside, and was concerned that landowners were increasingly content to enjoy their incomes in the cities, investing little time or capital in their estates.[160]

Substantial hostility might develop towards landowners with reputations for rapacity. In much of central France there was bitter resentment of

---

[158] Enquête parlementaire sur la situation des ouvriers de l'industrie et de l'agriculture 1882, response of Mayor St Servin (Finistère), AN C3331.
[159] Conseil d'Etat, *Enquête sur la boulangerie*, p. 679.   [160] Ibid.

a tenancy system which involved the close supervision of sharecroppers by intermediaries known as fermiers généraux.[161] Difficult or changing economic circumstances could easily inflame latent grievances, particularly where a smallholding peasantry felt that its property or access to vital collective resources on common land or in forests was under threat. The expulsion of livestock from forest pasture, in order to protect a valuable source of fuel and building materials and of income for the landowner, exemplified very different conceptions – moral and legal – of property.[162]

As a result, outward signs of respect might conceal considerable hostility. Thus sharecroppers who in general were materially and culturally impoverished with especially high illiteracy rates and little chance of improving their circumstances, frequently despised landlords who exacted not only a substantial share of their product but also demanded quasi-feudal labour services and constant, and degrading, marks of respect and subordination. Emile Guillaumin in his true-to-life novel *La vie d'un simple*[163] recalled a *maître* who delighted in speaking to his sharecroppers during his summer residence in the countryside: 'he employed the familiar form of address (*tutoyait*) to everybody and, because he had a poor memory for names, or deliberately perhaps, he invariably applied to his interlocutor the term *chose* [thingummy]'.

'Ah well, Thingummy are you happy with the weather?'

'Mother Thingummy, could we take two chickens out of the rent, right now?'

This particular landlord delighted in bringing visitors to look at his sharecroppers as though they were exotic animals, laughing at their apparent naïvety and grammatically incorrect French.

However, the open expression of grievances was generally too risky, the parameters for resistance being narrowly defined by local elites and the state. Any sign of dissent met with immediate ejection and the effective blacklisting of the tenant concerned throughout the locality. As a result, as Emile Baudry, a landowner at Rochemont (Charente-Inf.) warned, the peasant instinctively distrusted the 'bourgeois', and if addressed, responded with care and dissimulated.[164] However, a sense of grievance might be expressed anonymously in a variety of ways, ranging from *placards* or shouts

---

[161] See e.g. P. Goujon, 'Les révélations du suffrage *universel*: comportements électoraux et politisation des populations de Saône-et-Loire sous la Seconde République', *Cahiers d'histoire* 1998, p. 281.

[162] See e.g. M. Goldberg, deputy for Bas-Rhin, to Minister of Justice, 12 July 1849, AN BB18/1460.

[163] On its value as a source see e.g. G. Garrier, 'L'apport des récits de vie et des romans *paysans*' in Hubscher and Farcy, *La moisson des autres*, p. 18.

[164] *Le Paysan aux élections de 1869*, p. 9.

in the night, to arson or cattle maiming, as well as the ritualised reversals of status associated with Carnival, and the warnings delivered through the *charivari*.[165]

Peasants were themselves differentiated according to wealth, family and kinship relationships, and reputation – itself largely determined by the individual's capacity for hard physical labour and success as a farmer.[166] However, with the exception of the sort of social polarisation between rich tenant farmers and their labourers found in villages in the Paris region and Flanders, differences in wealth amongst peasants rarely eliminated the cultural homogeneity of those who cultivated the land and experienced the same rhythm of work, faced similar problems, and participated in shared forms of sociability. Gender and age-group solidarities were also evident in gatherings on the village square or market place, around the blacksmith's forge in winter, at the wash-place and fountain, in the café or in Provence the *chambrées* – the popular drinking associations. People gathered following religious services, as a result of attendance at the various 'rites of passage' and the village *fête*, and through the *veillée* which brought together neighbours – and exceptionally both men and women – to share the cost of light and heat and to sew, knit, repair tools, talk, play cards, and listen to stories. These gatherings offered relief from the monotony of daily life, and provided ideal opportunities for discussing matters of common concern. According to the village schoolteacher at St André-le-Désert (Saône-et-Loire), in the long winter *veillées* 'they talk about everything and everybody, and in what terms, My God! It is there that rumours are fabricated, which then spread from house to house and take on a regrettable consistency.'[167]

Even so, one should not be tempted into romanticising relationships which were always likely to be upset by competition for work, land or municipal office, by disputes over property boundaries, access to fields and water, by stray livestock, or from a failure to reciprocate in the exchange of services.[168] Exploitative relationships also frequently existed between the better-off and poor peasants. Moreover, the better-off peasants were determined to enjoy the status which went with their success. In the Haut-Gévaudan each would demand that in church 'one sits according to his rank'.[169] In response, the 'rich' could expect to be accused of pride and

---

[165] E.g. PG Amiens, 4 Aug. 1852, AN BB30/371.   [166] E.g. Lévêque, *Bourgogne*, I, p. 469.

[167] Quoted P. Goujon, 'Associations et vie associative dans les campagnes au 19e siècle', *Cahiers d'histoire* 1981, p. 136.

[168] M.-R. Santucci, *Délinquance et répression au 19e siècle. L'exemple de l'Hérault* (Paris 1986), pp. 197–8.

[169] Quoted E. Claverie, 'A propos de dossiers d'assises, oppressions et conflits dans une société d'interconnaissance. L'exemple du Haut-Gévaudan', Doc. de 3e cycle, Univ. de Paris IV, n.d., p. 23.

aggressive behaviour by the 'poor'. It was often assumed that those who had enriched themselves could have done so only at the expense of their neighbours. Although normally preserving a united front against these neighbours, families themselves might be bitterly divided over the division of work or inheritances.[170]

Hard physical labour, exhaustion, and compensatory heavy drinking, together with vindictive gossip and the strong language habitually used by people with a limited vocabulary, were likely to encourage susceptibility to the slightest accidental or imagined slight. Frequent police reports concerning brawls or malicious damage to crops or trees, of chickens blinded or dogs with their tails cut off, make this clear. There was an intense sensitivity to the innumerable nuances of social status. Anything which appeared to threaten an individual's reputation or the 'honour' of his family, might provoke violence. Jacques Fauré, a labourer at Montboissier (Eure-et-Loir), was accused of firing a gun through his neighbour's bedroom window. He explained to the local juge de paix that 'I was annoyed with him because he had taken at least 10 cm from my field . . . I was unhappy with all the disputes.' Both his property and his dignity were threatened.[171] More serious were disputes like that involving four shepherds at Porta in the Pyrenees where, as was common in this area, the disputants had recourse to knives. One died and the other three were seriously wounded.[172] At Lacalm (Aveyron) when M. Menesiloux tried to prevent his neighbours from grazing their sheep in his pasture, verbal abuse degenerated into stone throwing, which ended with a fatal blow to the head.[173] Arson was a common threat.[174]

The future minister Rouland, when State Prosecutor at Paris in the early 1850s, insisted that the tranquillity of the countryside was an illusion. Rural areas were under-policed and numerous incidents involving poaching, theft, and violence simply went unreported.[175] Disputes were settled within communities wherever possible, often with the mayor, priest, or teacher acting as an intermediary.[176] External authority became involved

---

[170] S. Lapalus, 'Pierre Rivière et les autres. De la violence familiale au crime . . .', *Revue d'histoire du 19e siècle* 2001/1, pp. 242–4.

[171] Farcy, *Paysans*, II, p. 1059.   [172] GOC 11e DM, report on 26–31 July 1853, AHG G8/9.

[173] GOC 10e DM, 20–25 March 1862, AHG G8/88.

[174] E.g. J.-C. Farcy, 'Les archives judiciaires et l'histoire rurale: l'exemple de la Beauce au 19e siècle', *Revue historique* 1977, p. 344.

[175] Gaillard, *Paris, la ville*, p. 195, note 32.

[176] On shortcomings of rural police see e.g. F. Gaveau, 'De la sûreté des campagnes. Police rurale et demandes d'ordre en France dans la première moitié du 19e siècle', *Crime, histoire et société* 2000, *passim*; F. Chauvaud, 'Les violences rurales et l'émiettement des objets au 19e siècle', *Cahiers d'histoire* 1997, p. 79.

only when matters seemed to be getting out of hand. The costs and complexity of recourse to law were powerful disincentives.[177] Local officials were often caught up in a network of social obligations, which appeared to be of far greater significance than more distant responsibilities to the gendarmerie, sous-préfet, or prefect.[178]

If a strong sense of community nevertheless survived, it was, in the various ways outlined above, increasingly being eroded by the monetisation and commercialisation of relationships, and by a growing individualism which reflected increasingly powerful external foci of attention and sources of status. This shift from an inward to an outward orientation could be seen in attendance at the increasing number of fairs and markets and the growing social distance between well-off and poor peasants.[179] The café owner was often held up as the symbol of this shifting orientation. According to one respondent to the 1866 agricultural enquiry, he belonged to 'the *nec plus ultra* of professions' in which 'one earns whilst not really working, and through talking politics is well-informed about every political group'.[180] With the experience of the Second Republic in mind the authorities were only too aware of his potential role in any renewal of political activity. M. Besse, justice of the peace at Carignan (Ardennes), complained that it was in the *cabarets* that 'our agricultural servants get excited and encourage each other to adopt those notions of independence and insubordination which make their relationships with their masters so difficult'. He favoured much closer police supervision.[181] Afraid of losing their licences, café owners were forced to be cautious; nevertheless, the number of cafés expanded rapidly. Officials, in spite of their misgivings, were instructed to respect 'commercial freedom' unless café gatherings posed a threat to social order.[182]

The intensity of social intercourse was a key determinant of the spread of gossip and of information, both commercial and political. To some degree the vitality of popular sociability was determined by rural habitat structures. Collective activity was most likely to develop in areas where large villages with perhaps 2,000 to 3,000 inhabitants had developed around a water source. In such marketing centres lived members of the middle classes, artisans, and peasants. Proximity eased the processes of cultural interaction. The state prosecutor at Rennes recognised that 'a certain level of agglomeration is necessary to give birth to what is conventionally called

---

[177] 1882 Enquête, evidence of a *rentier* in the Bresse Chalonnaise, AN C3368.
[178] Farcy, *Paysans*, II, p. 999, note 22.   [179] E.g. Hubscher, 'L'agriculture', III, pp. 1391–2.
[180] 1870 Enquête, response from Dolus (Indre-et-Loire), AN C1159.
[181] Letter to PG Metz, 11 Jan. 1860, AN BB30/380.
[182] Interior Minister to Justice, 16 Aug. 1864, AN BB30/380.

political life'. This was less likely where the population lived in scattered farms and hamlets.[183] Isolated and self sufficient, the population in areas of dispersed habitat – particularly in Brittany, the centre-west and south-west – also appear to have been less interested in education.[184] The lack of alternative sources of information was likely to reinforce dependence on the leadership of local landowning elites and the clergy.

A single department like the Saône-et-Loire was divided into two distinctive regions. In that of *bocage* and dispersed habitat in the Charollais and Autunois in the west and Bresse in the east, isolation limited sociability largely to the family, immediate neighbours and to the wider group gathering at the parish church. In areas of open field and grouped habitat around Châlons and Mâcon, ease of movement and proximity to urban models promoted a richer associative life. The larger rural settlements – in this case above 300 to 500 inhabitants – with their socially more mixed populations were better able to support commercial enterprises like cafés, and voluntary groups including mutual aid societies and also devotional associations dedicated to the Holy Sacrament or Holy Family,[185] which assumed growing importance in the diffusion of ideas, both democratic and conservative, through the countryside. Nevertheless, it would be a serious mistake to attempt to develop some sort of causal link between habitat structures and social and political relationships. This would ignore both the historical factors determining the precise character of intra-community relationships and the impact of an 'external' world made up of other rural communities and of urban centres, within developing marketing networks.

WIDENING HORIZONS

In his influential *Peasants into Frenchmen*, Eugen Weber adopted rather uncritically the model defined by Roger Thabault in his study of *Mon village* (1944). He identified a process linked to the development of communications, conscription, education, the market economy, and the mass media, which together propelled peasants into the dominant national culture. Migratory labour movements provided another source of links to the wider world. The correlations drawn are suggestive but over-simplified. The growing intensity of links with urban centres certainly promoted the diffusion of all manner of new products and ideas. The isochronic maps

---

[183] 15 Oct. 1869, AN BB30/389.   [184] F. Furet and J. Ozouf, *Lire et écrire* (Paris 1977), I, pp. 183–4.
[185] Goujon, 'Associations et vie associative', pp. 112–14; on significance of habitat see e.g. G. Désert, 'Les éléments structurants de l'espace bas-normand, 1re moitié du 19e siècle', in S. Courville and N. Séguin (eds.), *Espace et culture* (St-Foy, Québec 1995), p. 296.

drawn by geographers in order to measure accessibility, however, suggest that the degree of integration of rural communities into wider communication networks varied considerably. The impact of proximity, involvement in urban 'putting-out' activity, temporary migration, and attendance at markets and fairs, depended upon the peasant family's location within an 'urban–rural continuum' ranging from the town (within which, or on the outskirts of which, many farmers lived), to the *bourg* – the large village marketing centre, the village, hamlet, and isolated farm, and on the regularity and intensity of these links. This further depended on the density of the urban network and on the quality of road links. Physical relief was another significant factor; so too were the functions and socio-professional characteristics of local market centres.

Market towns and villages on or close to busy routes prospered, attracting merchants, professionals, and artisans as well as farmers to their markets and cafés. The market place had always provided a forum in which even the most isolated peasant gained access to gossip and rumour. However, if access to a rapidly developing wine-marketing centre like Béziers might enlarge the peasants' mental universe, attendance at a small and stagnant *bourg* in the western *bocage* would have little impact.[186] The occasional visit to a more important town, a *grande ville* like Paris or Nantes, must have represented a considerable adventure. It could also turn into a nightmare, as naïve and inexperienced peasants sought to deal with grain and cattle merchants or innkeepers, or with even less familiar figures like notaries or government officials. These were men who dressed correctly, spoke 'another' language, and were often openly contemptuous. Whilst the big farmers in the long-commercialised Beauce were frequent visitors to the markets at Chartres, Etampes, and even Paris, small peasant cultivators would rarely have made more than an annual visit.[187] In these circumstances, at least initially, improved communications might lead to an intensification of peasant hostility towards the towns, which sheltered those who appeared to be exploiting them.[188]

Rapidly, however, better communications, greater commercial activity, wider instruction and increased migration altered perceptions of time and distance and reinforced socio-cultural relations between town and country. The mental universe of the peasant was expanding. In the south-west, by

---

[186] E.g. J. Renard, *Les évolutions contemporaines de la vie rurale dans la région nantaise* (Les Sables d'Olonne 1975), pp. 179–80; J. Juillard, *Préface* to R. Schwab, *De la cellule rurale à la région. L'Alsace 1825–1960* (Paris 1980), p. 7; J. Thomas, *Le temps de foires. Foires et marchés dans le Midi toulousain de la fin de l'Ancien régime à 1914* (Toulouse 1993).

[187] Farcy, *Paysans*, II, p. 1062.   [188] E.g. PG Paris, 8 Dec. 1853, AN BB30/432.

the late 1860s the rural populations of the Garonne valley and Pyrenean foothills can rarely have been more than two hours' travelling time from an urban centre. This was generally judged to be the maximum time a farmer could spend travelling to market, although the excitement generated by the gathering of people from across a wide area, and the transformation of a town into a *grand bazar*[189] might encourage much longer journeys to transact what at first sight might appear to be insignificant transactions. In contrast, in the departments of Aveyron, Dordogne, Lot, Lot-et-Garonne, and Haute Garonne large areas continued to lack practical access to railway stations, whilst much of the Landes as well as upland areas of Tarn, the east and north of Aveyron, and neighbouring parts of Lot, Lot-et-Garonne, and Tarn-et-Garonne were virtually deprived of urban centres. Although an estimated 74.1 per cent of the rural population in Hérault had been integrated into urban networks, in Aveyron the proportion fell to 14.7 per cent, and this was typical of much of the Massif Central.[190] Further integration would require decades and considerable investment in local road and rail networks. These areas remained *relatively* impervious to new ideas.

However, as part of a broader communications revolution, the accelerating transition from a predominantly oral to a written culture would also have a substantial impact on rural society. Assessing the effects of increasing literacy on the peasant's social consciousness is problematical. Traditional and new forms of communication co-existed. Nevertheless, it might safely be asserted that although the traditional oral culture and its linguistic forms survived, especially amongst the older generations, greater literacy established a wider range of cultural references and an enhanced awareness of alternatives, which facilitated the development of a critical consciousness. It simplified the process of communication between social milieux. Moreover, education had become for the state the essential means of ideological penetration into the countryside. Both the Guizot law (1833) and the *loi Falloux* (1850) were designed to reinforce moral and religious instruction and to promote social order. These were objectives internalised by village schoolteachers themselves through their training and professional practice.[191]

Sobriety, economy, hard work, respect for their social superiors and the performance of their duties towards God and the Emperor were the lessons

---

[189] Soulet, *Pyrénées*, I, p. 247.
[190] J.-C. Claverie, 'Villes et régions dans le S-O français pré-industriel', Doc. de 3e cycle, Strasbourg 1972, pp. 105–7, 108–11.
[191] See e.g. Goujon, 'Associations et vie associative', p. 137.

inculcated by lay and religious teachers alike. According to the state prosecutor at Rennes the most important effect of educating peasants was that
'in enlarging their ideas a little, they are rendered more prudent, more
careful in calculating the consequences of their actions'.[192] His colleague at
Nancy recorded 'a genuine improvement in terms of morality, manners and
elementary knowledge', and the promotion of 'habits of discipline, obedience, respect and work'.[193] The gendarmarie commander in the 'backward'
Breton department of Côtes-du-Nord claimed that primary instruction
resulted in 'peasants becoming more intelligent and less superstitious, and
linking themselves more closely to the government, because they understand better what it does'.[194]

The statistics on school attendance provide an exaggerated impression of
progress. In practice peasants frequently preferred to retain their children
to work on the farm. Even very young children could perform such tasks as
caring for livestock. When they did send them to school it was often on an
irregular basis.[195] Nevertheless growing literacy gradually widened the horizons of the rural population, particularly those of the younger generations.
The proportion of illiterate conscripts fell from 38.9 per cent in 1841/5 to
26.2 per cent in 1861/5 and 20.8 per cent in 1866/8, although with considerable regional variation. Illiteracy was substantially greater amongst young
men from the impoverished Breton west, the centre-west, south-west and
uplands, and particularly those from areas which combined relative poverty
with dispersed habitat, in which communication between inhabitants and
'cultural contamination' was more difficult, and where education continued to appear to have little practical relevance.[196] In some areas, particularly those in which sharecropping predominated, close landlord control
and their desire for cheap labour militated against peasants educating their
children.[197]

Moreover, assessing the degree to which more or less regular school
attendance resulted in functional literacy as well as the practical use made
of these skills remains difficult. The official figures reveal a flagrant contra-
diction between the statistics on school attendance and those on literacy.
Thus the *Etat de l'instruction primaire en 1864* suggested that 900,000 out of
4 million children aged nine to thirteen failed to attend school. Amongst the

---

[192] 9 Jan. 1862, AN BB30/386.   [193] 11 July 1864, 26 April 1865, AN BB30/381.
[194] 29 May 1870, AHG G8/176.
[195] See e.g. commissaire de police de Meaux, 11 July 1866, AN F17/9146; C. Heywood, *Childhood in
Nineteenth Century France* (Cambridge 1988), ch. 2.
[196] M. Gontard, *Les écoles primaires de la France bourgeoise (1833–78)* (Toulouse n.d.), p. 169.
[197] See e.g. 1848 Enquête, response from La Trimouille (Vienne), AN C968 1.

remainder, 34 per cent attended for less than six months each year. Education Minister Duruy estimated that 19 per cent of school leavers soon forgot what little they had learned.[198] The difficulty of assessing the achievement of the schools was summed up by a schoolteacher from Maine-et-Loire who warned that 'the pupil who justly counted amongst the best in the school, is barely able to scrawl his name by the time he reaches twenty. Don't speak to him of calculation, he doesn't understand. He undoubtedly still knows how to read, but what is the point? He probably doesn't open a book twice a year.'[199]

The poor quality of instruction was a serious problem. The senior school inspector in the Hérault, reporting in July 1866, was anxious about the teaching of reading, particularly in church schools where the primers typically in use, such as the *Devoir du Chrétien*, were largely devoid of interest for young children. He recommended instead works which might both stimulate a taste for reading and achieve the moralising objectives of education, such as *Petit Pierre ou le bon cultivateur* or the *Histoire des trois pauvres enfants*.[200] Nevertheless, a definite improvement in teaching standards was under way which would be assisted by the spread of more positive attitudes towards education. The contrasts between generations, regions, and genders were being reduced. There was still much to do, but attitudes were changing as everywhere complete illiteracy became a minority phenomenon, something of which to be ashamed.

Greater prosperity and aspirations for self-improvement promoted more positive attitudes. The spread of standard French in place of *patois* and regional languages, or at least the establishment of an intermediary bilingual situation, were other features of a rapidly changing cultural context. An estimated one-fifth of the population remained unable to speak French in 1864,[201] with much higher proportions in some areas. In Haute-Loire, for example, 41 per cent of school-age children were recorded as unable to speak French and 26 per cent in the neighbouring department of Lozère.[202] According to a report from Lavedan in the Pyrenees in 1854 the result was that the peasant 'has not become French. He calls foreigner anyone who does not speak his dialect; . . . he looks at him with envy, takes advantage of him and exploits him.'[203] In some areas, reluctance to learn French

[198] Furet and Ozouf, *Lire et écrire*, i, pp. 175, 184.
[199] Quoted C. Robert, *De l'ignorance des populations ouvrières et rurales de la France et des causes qui tendent à la perpétuer* (Montbéliard 1862), p. 33.
[200] Académie de Montpellier. Inspection de l'Hérault 23 July 1866, AN F17/9146.
[201] E. Weber, *Peasants into Frenchmen* (London 1976), p. 310.
[202] P. Jones, 'An improbable democracy: 19th century elections in the Massif Central', *English History Review* 1982, p. 533.
[203] Soulet, *Pyrénées*, ii, p. 309.

was supported by the clergy. In the German-speaking arrondissement of Sarrebourg this was due to a determination to protect their flocks from 'contamination'.[204] However, the ability to speak French, or at least a pidgin French, offered easier access to commerce, the administration, to justice and politics. The status of the language within the public world helped ensure that its growing use was seen as a sign of progress. In comparison, the vocabulary of patois forms of French or even of Breton and langue d'oc were regarded as inadequate in the public sphere. They became increasingly degraded and used only in private situations and by the *classe inférieure.*[205]

Assessing the impact of greater literacy on the popular consciousness is fraught with difficulty. Certainly, education was designed to promote conservative ideals. Nevertheless, there was widespread concern amongst officials, notables, and the clergy about the untoward effects of wider literacy; especially that it might provide access to a 'subversive' or 'immoral' literature. However, it appears to have been accepted generally that most of the rural population lacked the leisure, skills, and instinct required for regular reading.[206] For most peasants, newspapers were an expensive, time-wasting, and 'useless' luxury, full of difficult words, unfamiliar ideas, and images, difficult even for the most literate to assimilate.[207] They frequently preferred the more traditional fare, distributed by pedlars, which included devotional works and the traditional tales of saints and heroes reproduced from the eighteenth-century *bibliothèque bleue.*

These delivered an essentially conservative or apolitical message. Also popular were the almanacs, which combined predictions and practical advice. Six and a half million of them were published in 1869 alone. Lithographs, which decorated the walls of many cottages, were even more common. Together with other printers in Epinal, the firm of J.-C. Pellerin produced over 17 million prints during the Second Empire.[208] They tended to represent the virtues of thrift, hard work, and resignation to one's lot and to provide lurid images of battles, catastrophes, and portraits of great heroes, especially of Napoleon I and his nephew, together with accounts of the victories of the First and Second Empires. The immensely popular patriotic songs of Béranger reinforced the growing sense of nationalism in even the most isolated communities.[209]

[204] PG Nancy, 21 May 1859, AN BB30/369.

[205] See e.g. J.-F. Chanet, 'Ecole et politisation dans les campagnes françaises au 19e siècle' in Agulhon *et al., Politisation*, p. 101.

[206] E.g. Prefect Var, 21 July 1866, AN F17/9146.

[207] E.g. Prefect, 29 July 1853, AN F1 CIII Loiret 7.   [208] Weber, *Peasants*, p. 457.

[209] On contents of the pedlar's pack see Prefect Gironde, 15 Dec. 1866; Prefect Marne, 20 Nov. 1866 and Commissaire de Police Lisieux (undated), AN F17/9146; J.-J. Darmon, *Le colportage en librairie en France sous le Second Empire* (Paris 1972), p. 295.

If it clearly retained a substantial presence, demand for this traditional literature appears to have been in decline, as a result of changes in the cultural context. The reduction of printing and distribution costs, together with rising real incomes also increased the accessibility of a more 'modern' literature. Alongside popular folk tales like *Geneviève de Brabant* or *Gilblas* or the adventures of Robinson Crusoe and *The Thousand and One Nights*, pedlars' packs were also increasingly likely to contain works by contemporaries like Kock, Dumas, Suë, Soulié, and Ponson du Terrail.[210] The procureur général at Nancy expressed anxiety about this diffusion by pedlars of serialised '*romans à 4 sous* in profusion throughout the countryside'.[211]

By the late 1860s, new mass-circulation media were also developing. The prefect of Loir-et-Cher reported in July 1866 that 'the books most commonly distributed in the countryside by pedlars are dictionaries, almanacs, fairy stories, collections of songs, large numbers . . . of little works of piety, and numerous insignificant brochures, usually containing extracts from newspapers with stories about voyages, accidents, acts of heroism'. He noted, however, the growing competition of 'the little illustrated newspapers, at 5 to 10 centimes'.[212] These illustrated newspapers and most notably the *Petit Journal* were cheap, written in a simple style, apolitical, and full of 'useful' information, human interest stories, and lurid accounts of crimes. They certainly attracted the interest of some of the better-off peasants in the more accessible and prosperous areas. The Second Empire in this respect as in so many others was a period of transition. Most of the 'traditional' and the 'modern' reading matter remained apolitical, however, and much of it moralising and implicitly conservative in intent.

By means of press censorship and efforts to control the circulation of reading materials in the countryside, the regime made a considerable effort to ensure that this remained the case. A circular of 28 July 1852 required that each item in a pedlar's pack must carry an official stamp of approval. A commission was appointed in September to examine the publications habitually distributed by pedlars. Its objectives were clearly defined in a confidential document: 'This commission is charged with responsibility for the press intended for the inferior classes, much more important, without doubt, than that destined for the superior classes. Peddling is the instrument with which one can corrupt or moralise the popular classes whose role vis-à-vis governments is so vital.'[213] According to its published instructions the

---

[210] See e.g. Prefect Hérault, 24 July 1866 AN F17/9146.   [211] ? Feb. 1856, AN BB30/381.
[212] 23 July 1866, AN F17/9146; see also ibid. Commissaire de police Falaise on sales in market places.
[213] 14 July 1853, quoted Darmon, *Colportage*, pp. 108–9.

Commission should not hesitate 'to reject from the catalogue of authorised books those works wounding for morality, injurious for religion . . . misleading about history'.[214]

A special commission reporting in June 1858 further defined the objective of censorship as being the replacement of the 'eight million immoral books distributed by a thousand hands in our villages' with 'eight million good books offering instruction to populations impatient with their ignorance, opening up to them, after the labours of the day, the domain of honest sentiments and sound ideas, inspiring in them the worship of God, love for the nation, gratitude towards its sovereign, and popularising in the smallest village the most glorious representatives of our national literature'.[215] Much of this was wishful thinking. However, from 1862 efforts were made to establish communal libraries containing approved books, offering practical advice and moral guidance as a contribution to this official drive to promote social and political conservatism.[216] The relaxation of press censorship from 1861 was followed in 1868, as anxiety about the political situation and the rural voter grew, by the partial re-imposition of controls over the diffusion of popular literature which contrasted markedly with the general liberalisation of the press regime.

The authorities believed that the problem was not 'the peasant . . . [who] doesn't read the serious articles in the newspapers, but the village leader who passes on the news and comments on it as he wishes'.[217] During election campaigns or periods of political crisis a small minority of active readers, often artisans and innkeepers in the small towns and villages,[218] were able to act as opinion leaders, passing on news and views through the distorting prism of oral debate. The custom of reading aloud widened the circle of those with some sort of awareness of current politics. However, as educational and living standards improved and the relative, *real* cost of newspapers declined, a growing proportion of the population was able both to afford to purchase and to 'understand' the content of the press.[219]

Official reports generally exaggerated the threat, but by the late 1860s newspapers were again a significant influence on opinion in the countryside.[220] As early as 1863, from the Yonne it was reported that 'the rural population is not as disinterested in political questions as it is in other places;

---

[214] *Moniteur universel*, 8 April 1853.   [215] Ibid., 14 June 1858.
[216] See 'Réponses à la circulaire du 27 juin 1866 – Choix des livres à placer dans les bibliothèques scolaires', AN F17/9146.
[217] PG Besançon, 19 Nov. 1860, AN BB30/373.   [218] PG Paris, 8 Feb. 1869, AN BB30/389.
[219] See e.g. Michelin, *Les larmes d'or*, pp. 347–50.
[220] E.g. PG Grenoble, 23 Jan. 1869, AN BB30/389.

they have in every commune their newspapers, selected from amongst those with the most advanced opinions, which pass from hand to hand, are commented on by a few agitators and help to maintain public interest'.[221] In the Gers, in the late 1850s, the only local newspaper was the Bonapartist *Courrier du Gers*. This had a comparatively healthy circulation of 2,000, although 500 subscriptions to Parisian newspapers were also taken out in the department. By 1866, as the political situation changed, the *Courrier's* circulation had fallen to 800. Liberalisation and renewed political debate encouraged the foundation of new newspapers and the revival of old. The republican socialist *L'Avenir*, edited by the future communard Lissagaray, made an effort to appeal to rural readers on the basis of issues which concerned them and in a language they might understand. Its circulation rapidly rose to 1,200 in January 1869, mainly as the result of collective subscriptions.[222]

Not enough is known about the 'opinion leaders'. These certainly included non-peasants, landowners, professionals, artisans, but also peasants who enjoyed social status – successful farmers, the better educated, individuals with experience of the world gained from military service or migration, or those who had already earned a reputation as political activists in 1848. As a schoolteacher from the Eure warned, 'every village has . . . two or three strong personalities', able to read the Parisian and regional newspapers to which cafés frequently subscribed, 'who take on the responsibility of enlightening their fellow citizens'.[223] The cultural context was becoming increasingly propitious for political debate.

---

[221] PG Paris, 3 Feb. 1863, AN BB30/384.
[222] Palmade, 'Le département du Gers', pp. 180–2.   [223] AN F17/10786.

CHAPTER 5

Peasants and politics

INTRODUCTION: POLITICISATION

The context having been established, this chapter will consider the process of 'politicisation', by identifying the factors which led peasants to take an interest in politics, before considering the practical impact, in terms of political behaviour. Politicisation can be taken to involve some concern, often episodic, with the distribution of decision-making power, and especially with the practical impact of public policy decisions. Thus 'politicisation' need not require a detailed knowledge of, or a sustained interest in, political programmes and ideology. Even participation in elections, normally held to denote 'the modernity of practices, does not necessarily imply the modernity of attitudes'.[1] The peasant *might* well be operating in a different 'conceptual universe' from that of the political militant or historian.[2]

Certainly, interest in politics varied over time and between places. Within communities, historical experience, 'cultural' values, the economic and social pressures of a given time and place, together with personal predispositions, combined to influence political choice. So too did the propagandising and organising activities of individuals or groups with links to the state bureaucracy, to 'parties', and to influential people outside the community. This 'leadership' was of vital importance for peasants who were, in general, ill-equipped in terms of education and culture, and too absorbed in their daily routines, to represent themselves directly within the formal, institutionalised political arena. The state prosecutor at Dijon typically stressed the role of *les notabilités agricoles* in the preparation of the 1866 Agricultural Enquiry and the contrasting indifference of *les petits cultivateurs*.[3] This dependence on representation by members of other social groups

---

[1] P. Jones, 'La République au village dans le sud du Massif Central' in Centre d'histoire moderne et contemporaine de l'Europe méditerranéenne, *De la révolution au coup d'état: les répercussions des événements parisiens entre Alpes et Pyrénées* (Montpellier 1999), p. 100.
[2] Corbin, *Le monde retrouvé*, p. 271.   [3] 10 Jan. 1867, AN BB30/377.

epitomised practical recognition of unequal social and political power. It could also be the product of a genuine consensus on issues, or conceal different aspirations and a grudging acceptance of subordination, which in some circumstances might be subject to challenge.

Much depended on (changing) local socio-economic conditions, on landholding and habitat structures. There are no straightforward correlations to be drawn. The attitudes of peasants towards their social 'superiors', largely depended upon whether the relationship concerned was perceived to be 'primarily collaborative and legitimate or as primarily exploitative'.[4] In the first case, typical perhaps of the *bocage* areas of the west where resident nobles were often deeply immersed in communal life and able to exert personal influence, dependants might exhibit a genuine sense of obligation and deference. In the second, in the Bourbonnais with its non-resident nobles, relying on their agents to maximise rent income, 'status gives way to *power* and deference to *submission*'.[5] The end-result in terms of voting behaviour might be the same, nevertheless. This was less likely where such social controls were deficient and alternative value systems existed. Widespread landownership might help to provide the sense of independence required for a republican politics, although a 'democratic' social structure might well be associated with a strong sense of community of interest with notables and conservative voting practices. In any case, social relationships were the product of 'on-going negotiation and re-interpretation'.[6]

Peasant politicisation was especially likely in areas in which peasants enjoyed relative independence as a result of land ownership. This was a situation conducive to the 'horizontal' transmission of ideas. Propitious circumstances might also be created by competition within elites or between members of traditional elites and the aspiring middle classes for state power, or else due to the absenteeism of landowners. Much depended on the ability of middle-class political activists in the larger villages and country towns, able (but not necessarily willing) to mobilise opposition to elite dominance and to organise and formulate political alternatives; and on the existence of 'alternative' social institutions (cafés, mutual aid societies, etc.) as channels for the 'vertical' diffusion of ideas; as well as upon the determination of peasant opinion leaders to assert themselves.

It might, in any case, be worth bearing in mind Guy Michaud's warning that 'real political life has only a distant relationship with political

---

[4] J. C. Scott, *The Moral Economy of the Peasants. Rebellion and Subsistence in South-East Asia* (London 1976), p. 170.
[5] Ibid. p.176.   [6] Newby, *Property, Paternalism and Power*, p. 283.

doctrines'.[7] To a large degree, political behaviour reflected personal relationships within small communities. Adopting a particular political label might represent deep-seated individual and familial commitment, particularly where, in the past, the experience of revolution had been intense. Otherwise, ideology, the formal language of political debate, might simply lend respectability to purely local, factional quarrels,[8] it might represent individual or inter-family rivalry, faction conflict within communities, disputes between communities, social antipathy or sectarian hatred, or protest against specific governmental policies or economic circumstances.[9]

According to the procureur général at Bordeaux, peasants 'have only one passion, the ownership and cultivation of the land' – the essential source of prosperity and social status.[10] This was probably the most important factor explaining peasant politics. However, depending on the circumstances, the hunger for land could result in very different forms of behaviour. Much would depend on the factors affecting access to and retention of property, including the general economic conditions, for which governments tend to take the blame or gain the credit. In the last resort political preferences would be determined by the struggle to 'identify causes and assess blame',[11] as well as by estimates of the likely benefits and costs of political action. Frequently this resulted in the carefully calculated conformity associated with 'working the system to their minimum disadvantage'.[12]

Past and present

Each of the revolutions in government – 1789, 1814/15, 1830, 1848 – had involved periods, however brief, of intense political activity, when national events had impinged on local communities. A crisis of political authority had broken established habits of obedience, politicised existing internal divisions, and created conditions in which efforts were made to make politics appear relevant to the rural population.[13] Successive crises had renewed previously interrupted processes of politicisation. Invariably, the rural

---

[7] Quoted P. Vigier, *Histoire générale politique et sociale* (Paris CDU 1979/80), p. 4.

[8] See e.g. J.-L. Mayaud, 'Pour une communalisation de l'histoire rurale' in Agulhon *et al.*, *La politisation des campagnes*, pp. 161–2; and on rural politics Y. Deloyé and O. Ihl, 'Le 19e siècle au miroir de la sociologie historique', *Revue d'histoire du 19e siècle* 1999, pp. 47–51; Guionnet, *L'apprentissage*, pp. 11–38.

[9] See e.g. PG Paris, ? Oct. 1869, AN BB30/389.   [10] 9 April 1861, AN BB30/374.

[11] J.-C. Scott, *Weapons of the Weak: Everyday Forms of Resistance* (New Haven 1985), p. xvii.

[12] E. Hobsbawm, 'Peasants and politics', *Journal of Peasant Studies* 1973, p. 7.

[13] See e.g. J.-C. Martin, 'Face à la Révolution, quelle politisation des communautés rurales?' in Agulhon *et al.*, *Politisation*, pp. 112–14.

population had attempted to make the best of these complex and diverse situations. It had 'grasped what the revolution offered and discreetly complained about what it did not'.[14] Political behaviour in the present was thus influenced by memories of the past, by a sense of history, derived from personal experience, that of the family and community, and marked by specific local events. However chaotic its chronology and spatially limited its vision, 'experience' and 'memory' established the basis for 'political' decision-making.

This was especially true in areas scarred by the events of the first revolution, particularly where, as in the Vendée and parts of Brittany, the Rhône valley, and Provence, a brutal civil war had left an enduring impression. Jean Fontanes, a Protestant agricultural labourer at Anduze (Gard), remembered how during the Second Republic 'if a majority of us were republican, it was in memory of our beautiful revolution of 1793, of which our fathers had inculcated the principles which still survive in our hearts'.[15] Writing about the Hérault, in her novel *Le Francimen* (1860), Mme Figuier described villages with 'two dance-halls, and a young girl would be very careful not to dance at a ball other than that of her party . . . (white or red). It goes without saying that her fiancé always belongs to the camp of his betrothed, and if two young people belonging to different parties fall in love, which is rare, the parents will normally oppose the marriage.'[16] Perceptions of the past – and particularly of the Revolutionary/Imperial decades of internal violence and war, and of the more recent mid-century crisis – helped determine attitudes towards other families, social groups, and the state. Thus, in practice, there was a complex interplay between the local and national, the 'traditional' and 'modern'.

The Revolution of 1830 had briefly renewed democratic aspirations and been followed by a municipal electoral law in 1831 which had enfranchised many of the better-off peasants. The introduction of 'universal' suffrage in 1848 profoundly modified political conditions. An unprecedented effort was made to organise and influence voters. Moreover, the elections which followed suggested that peasant support was not likely to be unconditional and that the peasant even if, generally, following the lead of 'the small number who create public opinion',[17] nevertheless was acting as an 'agent of history'.[18] Indeed, manhood suffrage made possible the 'peasant coup

[14] P. M. Jones, *The Peasantry in the French Revolution* (Cambridge 1988), p. 231.
[15] A. Detrez, 'Autour du *coup d'état*, *1848*, 1909/10, p. 166.
[16] Quoted Cholvy, *Diocèse de Montpellier* (Lille 1973), pp. 801–2.
[17] PG Paris, 4 March 1861, AN BB30/384.
[18] R. Evans and R. Lee (eds.), *The German Peasant* (London 1986), p. x.

d'état' (Marx) represented by the electoral victory of Prince Louis-Napoleon Bonaparte in December 1848. Certainly many of the respondents to the 1870 Agricultural Enquiry would claim that the Second Republic had had a permanent effect on social relations, encouraging peasants to adopt more assertive and questioning attitudes.[19] However, most peasants had probably tried to avoid the risk-taking involved in political commitment, and their engagement in politics had been brief.

Memories and myths had survived, nevertheless, each with its own discourse and slogans, which influenced the ways in which people thought about politics and which prolonged the gestures of the past. In some areas peasants remained afraid that the communists, the *partageux*, were plotting to seize their land. In others it was the possibility of a feudal reaction and the re-establishment of the tithe and seigneurial dues which aroused fear. In a memoir written in 1861 a village schoolteacher in the Nièvre could ask 'How many peasants threaten you still with the Convention? How many believe in the privileged and tremble at the mention of the tithe? Not having the least understanding of our social organisation, they believe it to be unjust.'[20] Even when most of the population had relapsed into apathy after 1848, it was clear that renewed revolution had re-vitalised rural republicanism and created a new generation of militants. At the same time it had heightened conservative social fear. Social and political reflexes had been (re)-established which would endure for decades.

During the authoritarian Empire politics was kept alive largely as a result of disputes within local elites, as part of which dependants might be mobilised from 'fear, respect [or] sympathy'.[21] Regular elections provided the means of competing for status and power, something often justified by appeals couched in a universalistic political language. The political role of non-peasants within the rural community was thus of crucial importance in the on-going process of peasant politicisation. Debates conducted essentially by local notables personalised and factionalised differences but additionally interpreted and translated national politics into terms which possessed local resonance. This was not a one-way process. Peasants were not puppets. As a result of manhood suffrage effective influence within a community increasingly required a sympathetic understanding of peasant aspirations and the ability, or at least pretence, of pursuing them.

---

[19] E.g. 1870 Enquête, response of Société départementale d'agriculture du Bouches-du-Rhône, AN C1159; and of Comice agricole canton Perreux (Loire), AN C1157.
[20] Quoted Robert, *De l'ignorance des populations ouvrières et rurales*, p. 10.
[21] E. Weber, 'Comment la politique vint aux paysans. A second look at peasant politicisation', *American Historical Review* 1982, p. 302.

Moreover, 'any transfer of ideas . . . from one group to another entails a shift in meaning'.[22] Invariably, there was a local reading of events and ideas, which reflected social and cultural divisions as well as past political experience. Nevertheless, peasants continued to prefer to be represented by non-peasants, ideally local or regional figures who were 'known' and accessible (if only indirectly). Men whose qualifications (social, political, and cultural) suggested that they would be able to exert influence in the external world. That peasants frequently suspected the motives of their elected representatives ensured a constant interaction between elite and popular politics. Moreover, at least at the level of the village council, peasants increasingly came to challenge notables for election.[23]

Localism

Poorly educated farmers, absorbed with the struggle to make ends meet, generally had little interest in the finer points of political discourse. Few were interested in or possessed the education necessary to understand abstract political principles or constitutional structures.[24] Emile Baudry, a municipal councillor at Rochement (Charente-Inférieure), pointed out to upper-class politicians that 'there are eight million men for whom your words are like Hebrew; not that they lack intelligence, but because your language is beyond their understanding'.[25] Official reports continued to insist that peasants normally had little interest in politics, especially when work on the farm demanded their time.[26] Etienne Bertin, in Guillaumin's novel, claimed that 'in the countryside people normally show little interest in the affairs of government. Whether Peter or Paul is at its head, they have got to get on with the same hard tasks.'[27]

The issues which stimulated passionate debate within the elites or educated middle classes were not necessarily those which aroused the concerns of the rural population. Even when they were interested in the same issues it was not necessarily for the same reasons. Politics mattered when it was perceived to affect the peasant's vital interests. According to the state prosecutor at Aix, 'the rural masses are made up of peaceful people, avid above all for calm, order, security, and more concerned to secure a reduction in taxes, and in the number of conscripts, together with improvement of the

[22] J. C. Scott, 'Protest and profanation: agrarian revolt and the little tradition', *Theory and Society* 1973, p. 5.
[23] E.g. Goujon, *Vigneron citoyen*, p. 136.   [24] Point made by PI Blois,? April 1866, AN BB30/382.
[25] *Le paysan aux élections de 1869*, p. 1.   [26] E.g. PG Bordeaux, 9 April 1861, AN BB30/374.
[27] P. 120.

roads, than any other sort of reform'.[28] The President of the Agricultural Committee at Sarliac-sur-l'Isle (Dordogne) insisted that

for whoever is in close contact with the rural voter it is clear that politics plays a very secondary role in elections. For the peasant the political horizon does not exceed the limits of his immediate personal interests. A matter of roads, of enclosure, of rights of way, of fairs and markets, these are the themes which determine how he is to vote.[29]

To which might be added good prices for their produce. In these circumstances, politicisation was an accumulative process promoted intermittently by political activity, as well as by longer-term cultural change. Nevertheless, politics increasingly penetrated the popular consciousness.

The roles of political and cultural intermediaries from outside the peasantry as well as of 'opinion leaders' from within have to be taken into account. Peasants were offered explanations of their situation, not only from within their own ranks, but also by government officials, notables, priests, artisans, and innkeepers – all influencing the flow of 'information' – as well as by more overtly political activists of varying shades of opinion. Most of the time, however, conversation in village cafés was reported to rarely rise above 'banalities, or the narrow limits of individual and local interest'.[30] The interests of the peasant were likely to be both localised and personalised, their actual political content easily becoming more apparent than real. The state prosecutor at Aix maintained that most peasants 'have in political matters only indecisive aspirations and vague sympathies' influenced by personal experience and 'very often by the stimulus of local rivalries and struggles'.[31] It was 'local disputes, personal questions between the current mayor and whoever wants to replace him, which focus their attention. These are for them practical questions, both because they are discussed within the parish, and because they will lead to immediate results, such as the construction of a road, or a change in the labour service for which they are liable.'[32]

Rival groups frequently competed in local elections. Municipal power both enhanced personal status and offered access to the growing funds available to subsidise public works. It was a definite advantage for those who wanted exemption from school fees, work, or charity to belong to the *parti du maire*. In the absence of a genuine secret ballot, voting the wrong way could conversely be disadvantageous, and as a result 'recriminations against the government almost always originate in a grievance against the

---

[28] 20 May 1859, AN BB30/369.   [29] AN C3344.   [30] PG Colmar, 5 April 1859, AN BB30/376.
[31] 2 July 1859, AN BB30/370.   [32] PG Douai, 5 Jan. 1865, AN BB30/377.

mayor or the commissaire de police'.[33] In 'these little societies . . . the personality is everything and principles nothing'. In spite of this it was often 'the same questions [which] are debated' as at national level, but 'in personalised, rudimentary, and crude form'. Political militants were able to take advantage of the 'deep-rooted hatreds and the thousand other ferments' which festered in every village.[34]

The politicisation of popular culture also helped to sustain an interest in politics. This might involve nothing more than drawing a fleur-de-lys or an eagle on a wall, or hoisting the white flag of the Bourbons, or the red of the *démocrate-socialistes* in a public place. The mayor of Mazères (Ariège) was only too aware of the significance of such emblems when, in March 1852, he forbade 'every citizen or inhabitant of this commune to fly any flag, even the national flag . . . except, as is customary, on public holidays'. The prefect, not fully aware of local tensions, complained that: 'I cannot believe that the national flag raised in a window is likely to cause trouble or disorder.'[35]

The banned revolutionary anthem, the *Marseillaise*, was another potent symbol. Songs provided a means of demonstrating loyalty and expressing contempt without taking much of a risk. *Placards* might express anger about high food prices, and associate the discourse of the 'moral economy' with social hatred and political discontent. At Orbais (Marne) a crudely drawn *placard* posted during the night of 11–12 October 1853 carried a drawing of a scaffold from which two figures were hanging, one in ecclesiastical costume, the other wearing formal dress and a hat. Below this scene was written, 'Death to the nobles and clergy . . . You are enriching those bastards. We do not want a bastard tyrant . . . People pull the cord. Hang these mad dogs who devour France.'[36]

The politicised *charivari*, a public expression of contempt involving the banging of pots and pans and blowing of horns together with obscene songs, raised the level of conflict. Municipal *arrêts* frequently banned 'all rowdy songs, all gatherings likely to trouble public order'.[37] They also attempted to secure the early closure of *cabarets* and cafés. Carnival with its traditional permissiveness, along with village fêtes and political anniversaries – 24 February, 15 August, or 29 September, the birthday of the Legitimist pretender the Comte de Chambord – were all potentially dangerous moments in the calendar.

---

[33] PG Aix, 24 Jan. 1870, AN BB30/390.   [34] PG Dijon, 9 July 1855, AN BB30/377.
[35] Quoted Soulet, *Pyrénées*, II, p. 230.   [36] PG Paris, 18 Oct. 1853, AN BB30/432.
[37] Tarascon 1850, quoted Soulet, *Pyrénées*, II, p. 238.

Short-term factors

An interest in politics was also promoted by short-term factors. The greater material prosperity enjoyed by most of the rural population, especially when compared with the years of the mid-century crisis, certainly encouraged acceptance of the imperial regime. In 1872, the sous-préfet at Falaise (Calvados) would point out that 'the countryside accepts . . . every *de facto* government, without great love and without great hatred. As long as the public peace is preserved and its produce sells well these sentiments will not change.'[38] The government, which took credit for prosperity, was also invariably blamed for adverse circumstances.

Thus consumers of foodstuffs complained in the mid-1850s about what were regarded as excessively high prices. A decade later cereals producers were expressing concern about unremunerative levels, blamed by opposition politicians on the imports made possible by the government's more liberal tariff policy.[39] The creation of more competitive markets, together with constant change in internal markets as the railway network was extended, increased uncertainty.[40] As a result, according to an alarmed official 'one feels that this, the most solid base of the imperial dynasty would be weakened if the economic revolution does not slow down and if, between each new modification and that which follows it, there is not an interval long enough to allow an assessment of the effects of the first and to accustom people to thinking of the second'.[41]

Far more significant were the debates on military reform in 1867/8, which provoked considerable, and overwhelmingly negative, interest. Whilst it was reported repeatedly that peasants had little, if any, interest in the debates on political liberalisation, the belief, magnified by rumour, that the system of drawing lots – with as little as one-tenth of the age group inducted in any year – would be replaced by universal military service, so ending the prospect of drawing a *bon numéro*, caused considerable disquiet in the countryside.[42] In 1859 officials had already warned that continued peasant support for the war in Italy depended on avoiding increases in conscription and taxation.[43] Now, there was a widespread conviction that reform must be intended as a prelude to war.[44] Ministers were reminded that: 'Never will a more delicate question have to be discussed.'[45] There appeared to

---

[38] Quoted Désert, *Calvados*, p. 481.   [39] See e.g. Enquête agricole 1866, VI, Seine-et-Marne.
[40] See e.g. PG Aix, 20 May 1859, AN BB30/369.   [41] PG Dijon, 14 Jan. 1865, AN BB30/377.
[42] See e.g. PG Besançon, 12 Jan. 1867, AN BB30/373.
[43] PG Paris, 9 Nov. 1859, AN BB30/384 re Yonne.   [44] PG Nîmes, 9 April 1868, AN BB30/382.
[45] PG Lyon, 28 Dec. 1867, AN BB30/379.

be a very real danger, and official reports from all over France concurred, that 'muttering, irritation, the regrets of many families, will translate themselves into hostile votes . . . and we will have lost our most dependable supporters'.[46] Opposition groups were only too ready to take advantage of the government's embarrassment.[47]

Similarly, the regime's taxation policy was a matter of almost obsessive concern, particularly in vine-cultivating areas, which were subject to indirect taxes on the movement and sale of wine and to the inquisitorial powers of the *administration des droits réunis*. Tax reductions, such as the 50 per cent cut in the *droit d'entrée* in 1852, were certainly well received.[48] In contrast, officials consistently warned ministers about the adverse effect of tax increases on attitudes towards the regime.[49] Peasants took all too seriously rumours about budget deficits and the waste of money on the embellishment of Paris and distant military campaigns.[50] Whilst the great majority, amongst *les classes agricoles*, remained sincerely devoted to the government of the Emperor, it needed to be borne in mind that 'for them politics comes down to questions of taxation. This is a truth, which cannot be repeated too often to statesmen who, carried away by the whirlwind of high politics fail to appreciate . . . the deplorable effect produced by even the smallest increase.'[51]

Such concern appears to have led to the withdrawal of a proposed surtax on salt in 1862. However, peasants apparently welcomed an increase in the tax on luxury carriages.[52] Municipal impositions to improve roads, build schools, or restore churches could also provoke bitter dissent.[53] The introduction of a toll on livestock entering the market at Tarbes in May 1859 led to a major riot involving peasants arriving for market and to the sacking of the gendarmerie barracks on the market square. Troops eventually opened fire killing seven presumed rioters.[54]

Although they would remain its most reliable supporters, the combined impact of these short-term factors promoted a gradual loss of peasant confidence in the regime. Paradoxically, whilst the regime had sought legitimacy through the ballot box, its representatives had hoped that peasants would remain indifferent to political debate. They had typically insisted that the rural populations 'need strong administrative supervision and direction; it

---

[46] PG Lyon, 10 Oct. 1866, AN BB30/379.
[47] See e.g. pamphlet by M. de Benoist, *Utopies d'un paysan* (Clermont-Ferrand 1867).
[48] Laurent, *Les vignerons*, pp. 205, 474.   [49] E.g. PG Metz, 11 July 1864, AN BB30/380.
[50] PG Besançon, 17 April; PG Colmar, 24 July 1869, AN BB30/389.
[51] PG Nancy, 14 April 1864, AN BB30/381.   [52] PG Montpellier, 8 July 1862, AN BB30/380.
[53] E.g. C. de Lacombe, *Les préfets et les maires* (Paris 1869), pp. 11–12.
[54] Prefect Hautes-Pyrénées, report on May 1859, AN F7/4129.

is essential that it is the authorities who guide them',[55] and that peasants 'believe that they have placed the exercise of national sovereignty in the prince's hands, so that every election appears to them to be a waste of time'.[56] In the countryside, unlike the towns, abstention had often represented a mark of confidence in the regime.

However, during the 1860s, government representatives began rapidly to lose confidence in their ability to deliver the rural vote. As conflict between notables and competition to win peasant votes intensified, so did the politicising impact of elections, leading the state prosecutor at Besançon to conclude that 'parliamentary ideas, once discredited, have regained favour . . . , the movement that began among the upper classes is affecting the masses: the practice of universal suffrage and the reading of newspapers have altered their frame of mind. They understand the power that elections give them and insist on using it as they please. Henceforth, we shall have to take this new tendency into account.'[57] The Mayor of Mery-sur-Cher (Cher) warned that 'the Deputies and Clubistes have told them so often that they are sovereign that they are beginning to believe it'.[58] As a result, 'les aspirations de clocher font place à des aspirations plus large'.[59] Previously reserved to the 'rich', acquiring the right to vote had offered the rural voter a means of self-affirmation.

The peasant's understanding of the political process was not likely to be as developed at that of the educated notable. His interest in politics might not be as sustained. However, official reports stressed increasingly that a positive desire to vote was developing.[60] Nationally, abstention in general elections fell from 36.7 per cent in 1852 to 21.9 per cent in 1869.[61] Moreover, peasants were becoming 'every day more impatient with the efforts made by the administration to manage the elections, often with insufficient tact'. They were increasingly determined to make judgements about the actions of municipal and departmental councillors and deputies and even to consider alternatives. Provincial officials insisted that there was a need to take account of these developing *sentiments d'indépendance*[62] and to counter opposition efforts to persuade peasants that a vote against the government was an *acte de virilité*.[63]

---

[55] PG Limoges, 6 April 1864, AN BB30/378.   [56] PG Dijon, 12 Jan. 1865, AN BB30/377.
[57] 12 Jan. 1869, AN BB30/389.   [58] AN C1157.
[59] OC gendarmerie cie du Rhône, 28 Jan. 1869, AHG G8/165.
[60] E.g. PG Agen, 5 July 1869, AN BB30/389.
[61] P. Goujon, 'Le temps des révolutions inachevées' in J.-P. Houssel (ed.), *Histoire des paysans français du 18e siècle a nos jours* (Roanne 1976), p. 293.
[62] PG Agen, 5 April 1868, AN BB30/370.   [63] PG Caen, 13 Jan. 1866, AN BB30/375.

In the Grenoble area it appeared that the rural population 'more and more appreciates the predominance which universal suffrage offers them, and reveals a disposition to attach conditions to its votes'. In spite of their 'devotion' to the Emperor, peasants were increasingly inclined to register dissent with government policy by voting for the opposition.[64] This was the case even in 'some mountainous areas in the Cantal and Haute Loire' where peasant 'ignorance is extreme'.[65] In response, candidates felt obliged to make a greater effort to present themselves to their voters, to justify their actions and to make commitments.[66]

Of course, all this is not to claim that peasants – or most other people for that matter – were constantly or consistently interested in politics, or that they necessarily discussed politics using the ideological and constitutional terminology favoured by the better educated. That would be to impose an intellectual's understanding of politics on people with very different and, generally, more basic and practical concerns, but to whose problems politics, on occasion, offered a potential solution. Even the intellectual's political commitment is shaped by a multiplicity of factors, including the formative experiences of family and group socialisation; personal self-interest and moral judgement; the unconscious and irrational as well as rational and philosophical discourse. Nevertheless, a series of events, including most obviously revolutions, and of processes, including the construction of improved transport and educational networks, had intruded, to a greater or lesser degree, on most rural communities. A growing portion of the community was coming to associate the satisfaction of some of its local, day-to-day concerns and the protection of its vital interests, with at least the intermittent engagement in political activity represented by electoral participation.

THE PROCESS OF POLITICAL CHOICE

A multiplicity of factors linked to evolving socio-economic structures, to the historical experience of particular communities, and government policies, thus affected perceptions of the regime. Peasant interest in politics obviously varied over time and between places. The period between 1848 and 1870, one of revolution, counter-revolution, and subsequent liberalisation, nevertheless, saw a substantial broadening and deepening of politicisation. This was the case particularly amongst the younger generations, who were

---

[64] PG Grenoble, 23 Jan. 1869, AN BB30/389.   [65] PG Riom, 11 Jan. 1870, AN BB30/390.
[66] PG Angers, 11 Jan. 1869, AN BB30/389.

more literate and aware of socio-economic change, and of growing prosperity, and perhaps more optimistic and determined to use the potential of politics. Politicisation, however, is one thing; explaining the various political options adopted by peasants is quite another. Perhaps, as Peter McPhee pointed out in his study of *The Politics of Rural Life* during the Second Republic, 'while habitat patterns, location, literacy, and ethnicity facilitated politicization (*prises de conscience*), it was history and the social relations of production which explained specific political choices (*prises de position*)'.[67] However, in the absence of obvious 'structural' correlations, it might be more illuminating to consider evolving peasant perceptions of politics.

Of course, the documentary sources tell us more about the attitudes and activities of the reporters, that is, of government officials, of notables, and urban political activists than those of peasants. Indeed, whatever their political sympathies, most commentators concluded that 'peasants', because of their ignorance or dependence, could hardly be considered to be free agents in politics. Explanations of peasant voting tended to assume that ideas were simply diffused from above. That this 'trickling down' occurred, and was of crucial and perhaps decisive influence, is undeniable. It reflected control of the resources necessary for political organisation and propaganda. Nevertheless, the relationships which ultimately developed should be seen as part of a more complex interactive process between notables and peasants and between urban and rural societies, as a result of which the relevance of efforts to influence the state through institutionalised political activity appears to have been increasingly appreciated.

Precisely what this meant from the peasant perspective has still to be explored, however. Somehow, the historian has to adopt the perspectives of the rural community. It is important to try to take account of the 'meanings' people themselves gave to their political acts, and to try to escape from the concerns and language of the dominant discourse which, whatever our misgivings, inescapably provides most of the evidence. To add to the difficulties, the potential of electoral sociology as a source of 'hard' information is of course sharply reduced by the system of official candidature, and although detailed local and regional studies offer valuable insights into political trends, they do not always avoid the anachronistic temptation to analyse early mass elections in the manner adopted for modern long-established democratic systems.

---

[67] P. McPhee, *The Politics of Rural Life, Political Mobilisation in the French Countryside* (Oxford, 1992), pp. 148–9.

A widespread conservatism

Historians have frequently confused politicisation with republicanisation, as though a conservative vote was invariably irrational or pre-political, and proof of passivity. Traditional social groups and the Church certainly played a major role in the politicisation process. Inevitably, an electorate still serving its democratic apprenticeship and subject to repression was to a large extent mobilised on the basis of existing social relationships. By and large peasants voted in both national and local elections for personalities identified by their wealth and influence as well as by the reputations of their families and 'friends'. These were assumed to possess the influence necessary to protect the interests of their constituents. The electorate 'values above all the community of origin, of interests, and of the future, between themselves and their representative'.[68] In many communities this resulted in quasi-unanimous collective voting.[69]

From the government's point of view the selection of candidates from outside the charmed circle of local and regional worthies was, in any case, to invite failure. It would have humiliated local elites and weakened their support.[70] Landowners, businessmen, and professionals occupied public functions as deputies, mayors, administrators of charitable bodies, and members of agricultural and learned societies, gained official honours and enjoyed the status that went with an ostentatious lifestyle. To be well connected was vital and notables enjoyed a virtual monopoly of communication with the external, and especially the official, world. Thus the Comte Perrault de Jotemps, candidate for the conseil général of Saône-et-Loire in July 1867 boasted in his manifesto of 'my connections in Paris, my relationship with the Président of the tribunal at Mâcon, my friendship with the Senator and the Prefect', all of which 'places me in a position to be helpful in all kinds of circumstances, and you will be aware that I will not spare either approaches or recommendations when I am asked to make them'.[71]

Political life was dominated by the struggle for office between members of these elites and subject to intervention by the clergy and government officials. Whilst, especially in small communities, following the creation of a substantial municipal electorate in 1831, the better-off peasant might have hoped to become a municipal councillor, otherwise peasants were practically excluded from political representation. To a large degree they

---

[68] PG Rouen, 12 April 1869, AN BB30/389.

[69] See e.g. C. Estève, *A l'ombre du pouvoir. Le Cantal du milieu du 19e siècle à 1914* (Clermont-Ferrand, 2002), p. 309.

[70] E.g. PG Besançon, 12 Oct. 1868, AN BB30/389.   [71] Quoted Goujon, *Vigneron citoyen*, p. 279.

excluded themselves from a lack of self-confidence and a definite sense of inferiority. They were deficient in the social and cultural qualifications generally thought to be necessary. Emile Baudry, the municipal councillor at Rochemont in Charente-Inférieure, claimed that one peasant would not vote for another because he considered that such a candidate would be 'someone just like himself, just a neighbour. Now, should he make this neighbour a deputy, that is a gentleman, to whom he would no longer be equal?. . . *Ah! mais non!* Better to vote for all the bourgeois in the world.'[72]

The 'necessary' qualifications were defined by established elites and the administration. The prefect of Saône-et-Loire in 1852 insisted on the resignation of the mayor of Lugny, Antoine Tête, propriétaire-cultivateur, because 'he fails to represent the administration in the appropriate manner' and replaced him with Joseph Meunier, a rich landowner. At the same time seven councillors, 'all farmers', were replaced with large landowners and professional men. At nearby Loché in 1862 local landowners petitioned for the replacement of their mayor, a tenant farmer, because 'our neighbours are making fun of us'.[73] The mayor of Cortevaix, a businessman, regretted that 'the municipal council is entirely made up of more-or-less well-off farmers, sensible men generally, but almost completely without education, and incapable of drafting a motion or the simplest report'.[74] The parish priest at Epuisay in the Vendômois (Eure-et-Loir) even complained that the local councillors were not only debtors but ate without forks.[75] Anyway, for extra-municipal elections, peasants lacked the leisure and organisational, financial, and ideological resources necessary to mount a challenge. Poorly educated and ill informed, they were afraid of the authorities and influenced by the experience of the Second Republic which appeared to prove that an alternative politics was likely to be dangerous and ineffective.

Most of the rural population, preoccupied with making ends meet, normally took little interest in politics. The procureur général at Aix described 'the rural masses composed of individuals isolated from each other by their work, suspicious and ignorant', and as 'scarcely concerned with anything besides municipal quarrels and almost entirely indifferent to the great questions which agitate public opinion'.[76] The peasant might well respond, when asked about politics, that 'we, poor men, know nothing about that; it's something for you gentlemen'.[77] Whether this represented an honest

[72] *Les paysans*, p. 13.   [73] Goujon, *Vigneron citoyen*, p. 135.
[74] Letter to prefect quoted ibid. p. 115, note 29.
[75] J. Vassort, *Une société provinciale face à son devenir. Le Vendômois aux 18e et 19e siècles* (Paris 1995), p. 488.
[76] 28 Oct. 1867, AN BB30/370.   [77] Baudry, *Les paysans*, p. 44.

response or dissimulation was impossible to tell, given that 'we know that the peasant only humbles himself before gentlemen with authority because he believes that their arms are long enough to bend the law'.[78] There were powerful pressures for 'routine compliance' with the interests of the rich and powerful.[79]

The contempt evident in the condescending familiarity with which peasants were treated by their social 'superiors' contributed to the interiorisation of a sense of inferiority when faced with landlords, officials, the better educated and better dressed. Although obsequiousness and even stupidity might have been a pose, a 'public routine'[80] concealing peasant anger and resentment, the need to appear submissive nevertheless informed behaviour. In situations in which the established order appeared to be inescapable, people were more likely to make the best of their situation than to struggle against it. There were potential advantages in conforming to the stereotype of the respectable poor. Moreover, family upbringing socialised individuals into accepting authoritarian relationships. The sense of dependence was reinforced by a widely shared sense of respect for those who possessed the esteemed virtues of wealth and culture.[81] The result could be the survival of a powerful sense of community unanimity, often represented in its political behaviour.

It was generally sufficient for the regime's candidates to present themselves at public ceremonies and agricultural shows as elections approached and to secure the distribution of electoral addresses and ballot papers by officials and their own dependants. These evoked past successes and promised future order and prosperity in the vaguest terms. Every effort was made to preserve social distance whilst evoking a concern for popular interests. The promise of rewards for the community no doubt encouraged compliance and official candidates were in the best position to secure subsidies for schools, churches, an improved water supply, roads, and railways.[82] In a contested election free drinks were another incentive.[83]

Certainly, the introduction of manhood suffrage had been disconcerting. The risk that political antagonism might spread was often reduced through paternalism. Notables like Alexis de Tocqueville were both conscious of their responsibilities towards the poor and aware of the political necessity of working to reinforce their own prestige. Even when Tocqueville was away

[78] Ibid. p. 151.   [79] Scott, *Weapons of the Weak*, p. 281.   [80] Ibid. p. 288.
[81] Farcy, *Paysans*, I, p. 455; F. Chauvaud, *De Pierre Rivière à Landru. La violence apprivoisée au 19e siècle* (Paris 1991), p. 102.
[82] J. Albiot, *Les campagnes électorales 1851–69* (Paris 1869), pp. 463–4.
[83] E.g. PG Poitiers, 24 Oct. 1867, AN BB30/385.

from his estate at Valognes in Normandy, his steward was expected to serve as the intermediary between the local population and its most substantial landowner. The ideal remained the establishment of relationships based on a sense of shared interests. More specifically, the particular interests of the wealthier members of rural society were presented as the general interest. This might require costly concessions on such matters as rent arrears, which obviously created a tension between the need to maximise revenue and recognise the social responsibilities of the landowner. This was, nevertheless, likely to be regarded as money well spent, providing that the poor continued to see themselves as beneficiaries of the established social order.[84]

The exercise of benevolence both justified and reinforced social power. In addition to the direct control exercised over servants, tenants, and hired labourers, wealth and influence could be used to develop clientelism amongst wider sections of the community. In spite of the donors' sincere protestations of disinterested liberality, it was fully understood that those who received assistance would be called upon to reciprocate. Elections provided one, easily monitored, opportunity for manifesting gratitude. At St-Marcouf, in the Manche, the Comte de Pontgibaud occupied the offices of mayor and conseiller général and was thus the essential intermediary between the community and an administration increasingly generous with its subsidies. He wrote letters of recommendation and supported candidates for minor administrative posts, for loans and charity. He was able to compensate in this way for the fact that only a small proportion of the local population were directly employed by the château or worked its farms.[85]

In a hierarchical society wealth and paternalistic behaviour earned respect. Widespread impoverishment and insecurity created a diffuse sense of dependence. The poor needed to be prudent, and conform to upper-class images of 'respectability'. Thus, in the west, aristocratic landowners were able to determine the votes of 'the peasants who farm their land, although left to themselves they would express other sentiments'. The peasant's primary aim was not to compromise himself.[86] During the last major subsistence crisis in the mid 1850s, officials in the Melun region of Seine-et-Marne were relieved to see *nombreux châtelains* offer charity to the poor, 'substituting . . . their beneficent influence for the shameful influence which troublemakers would inevitably seek to exercise over the poor classes by

[84] Tocqueville, *Souvenirs* (Paris 1964), pp. 107, 134–5; see also A. Guillemin, 'Le pouvoir et l'innovation. Les notables de la Manche et le développement de l'agriculture (1830–75)', Doc. de 3e cycle, EHESS, 1980, pp. 230–2.

[85] Guillemin, 'Le pouvoir', pp. 239–41.   [86] PG Poitiers, 29 Jan. 1858, AN BB30/385.

taking advantage of their misery'.[87] Religion was another major influence. Respect for the teachings of the Church and its insistence on obedience, humility, and patience contributed substantially to the reinforcement of social hierarchy. For this reason, the paternalistic ideal came closest to realisation in the west and parts of Flanders and the interior of Provence where even newcomers, *bourgeois* purchasers of land, seeking to adopt the lifestyle of the country gentleman, took on the role of protector of *leurs gens.*[88]

Questioning established relationships

The sincere gratitude of the rural poor for assistance and advice was, how-ever, often tempered by resentment of the wealthy and clergy and of their own subordination. A strong sense of moral order survived. There was a widespread conviction that the 'rich' had obligations towards the less well-endowed members of the community. Those notables who rejected customary practices and failed to honour 'norms of tenancy, generosity, charity and employment'[89] were likely to suffer a loss of status, and expose themselves to malicious gossip or occasional reprisals in the form of theft, poaching, arson, or, indeed, political opposition. The growing absenteeism of landowners was frequently castigated. The transfer of capital into alterna-tive forms of investment and the growing urbanisation of the elite invariably resulted in a loss of personal interest in, and knowledge of, a community and its inhabitants, and in an increasing loss of influence.

In Seine-et-Marne, 'with a small number of exceptions the owners of farms in the Brie live in Paris, spending their wealth there, and are barely known in their communes, in which they only appear during the hunting season, the rights to which they defend with a severity which does not endear them to the rural population'.[90] In proximity to towns the pur-chase of land by urban investors further contributed to this breakdown in face-to-face relationships. The sous-préfet at Autun criticised landowners who with 'honourable exceptions' lived in the towns and 'provide little employment for the population and absorb all the revenue. They bring to agriculture neither technical knowledge nor capital'.[91] The existence

---

[87] PG Paris, 4 March 1854, AN BB30/432.

[88] Vigier, *Histoire générale*, p. 9; see also W. Brustein, 'A political mode of production analysis of political behaviour: the case of western and Mediterranean France', *Politics and Society* 1981, pp. 371–2.

[89] Scott, *Weapons of the Weak*, p. 282.   [90] PG Paris, 10 Nov. 1868, AN BB30/389.

[91] Quoted P. Lévêque, 'Large landed property and its influence in 19th century Burgundy' in R. Gibson and M. Blinkhorn (eds.), *Landownership and Power in Modern Europe* (London 1991), p. 68.

of large estates managed on strictly commercial principles could provoke considerable social tension, with or without discernable political consequences.

Although rural elites retained their ability to influence peasant political behaviour, the effectiveness of their efforts was undermined by their own factional divisions and competition for power, as well as by the occasional determination of both government officials and middle-class groups to challenge their dominance. The state prosecutor at Grenoble denounced the situation in the Drôme where 'idleness and pride have long since divided the *haute bourgeoisie . . .* into factions whose leaders become the representatives of a political party in order to give themselves more importance'. In his rather jaundiced judgement 'convictions play only a secondary role in their choice' and were far less significant than 'personal animosities'.[92] The electoral agitation this stimulated would play an important part in the diffusion of competing ideologies, and made it easier for peasants to consider the alternative attractions of upper-class, 'democratic', or state patronage. As a result the weakening of elite political influence in the countryside began before its relative economic decline. The introduction of manhood suffrage in 1848, and the political agitation which followed, represented a significant stage in this process.

Similarly, the influence of the Church was likely to be contested. For centuries it had been relatively weak in the Paris basin, Aquitaine, and the Mediterranean south. In these areas, popular religiosity might be combined with indifference or even hostility towards the clergy. Whilst almost every parish contained a group of fervent believers, largely composed of women, church attendance was irregular throughout the Paris region. Most peasants remained ignorant of religious dogma. In the diocese of Orléans, notorious for the 'indifference' of its population, in 1850 only 3.8 per cent of men over twenty received Easter communion.[93] On other Sundays, especially during the harvest, churches were virtually deserted.[94] The sous-préfet at Pithiviers in the Beauce observed that peasants were solely concerned with material matters and 'devote themselves with determination to their work, refusing to interrupt it even during Sunday services'. He maintained that 'this indifference does not mean that the rural population fails to behave with deference and consideration towards those priests who have earned their respect; but they do consider that the time spent in church would represent a loss of work and money'.[95] A report on the departments of Charente and

[92] 9 Aug. 1865, AN BB18/1717.   [93] Marcilhacy, *Le diocèse d'Orléans*, p. ii.
[94] Prefect, 30 June 1858, AN F1 CIII Loiret 7.
[95] Report to Prefect Loiret, 30 June 1859, AN F1 CIII Loiret 12.

Charente-Inférieure by the Academic Rector at Poitiers, himself a priest, could observe, with only a modicum of exaggeration, that: 'the peasants regard the priest as useless. He bothers them and costs them money.'[96]

Whilst the Church continued to play a major role in the acculturation of the rural population, there were frequent occasions for conflict. A community might be divided over the cost of restoring its church and presbytery, symbols of the ambitious programme of Catholic re-conquest, or else by a priest's determination to protect his flock, and especially young girls, from such obvious manifestations of evil as dancing and the café, and by his excessive eagerness to denounce the moral transgressions of his parishioners.[97] The practice of birth control was further evidence of growing tension. Contraception spread in spite of the Church's insistence that it was an act contrary to the will of God, which the clergy sought to resist through outright condemnation, and, more subtly, through the glorification of motherhood. However, in a world of change the message of resignation to one's lot contained in so many sermons was becoming less acceptable. Many were impatient with being preached at. The Abbé Devoille's condemnation of emigration, in which he warned the *Habitants des campagnes* to 'remain at home; better to scratch the soil with your finger nails, better to suffer poverty, than to thrust yourself into a whirlwind in which you will lose everything: faith, morals, and especially eternity',[98] would have met with a mixed reception.

In the Limousin, social structures and shared 'memories' appear to have been particularly resistant to clerical pretensions. An often anti-clerical bourgeoisie, hostile to the close alliance between the Church and State, revived tales of greedy priests, and of the burden of the tithe. This ensured a fierce hostility towards interference by the clergy in local faction disputes and communal affairs.[99] In the Dordogne and throughout the south-west, in the Maconnais and Morvan in the centre-east, and in other parts of central France, nobles and the clergy were still suspected of planning to re-claim their *ancien régime* privileges.[100] There were disorders in the Charentes in May–June 1868, beginning at Chevanceaux when crowds tried to smash a newly erected stained glass window in the church because it bore the court of arms of the Marquis de Lestranges. It was said that this heralded the re-establishment of the *ancien régime* and the tithe. The 'news' spread

[96] Academic Rector Poitiers, 10 May 1858, AN F17/2649.
[97] E.g. Faury, *Cléricalisme et anticléricalisme*, pp. 405–6.
[98] Abbé Devoille, *La charrue et le comptoir ou la ville et la campagne* (1854) quoted Hubscher, 'La France paysanne', pp. 135–6.
[99] Corbin, *Archaïsme*, i, p. 648.   [100] Weber, *Peasants*, p. 249.

rapidly and windows and furnishings bearing the fleur de lys were smashed in other churches.[101] More widely, it was assumed that the clergy should restrain their activities to their own sphere, an attitude that sharply conflicted with the self-righteous authoritarianism and totalitarian conception of their responsibilities characteristic of many priests and especially younger men with ultramontane sympathies.

Conservative and clerical elites constantly complained about the threat to traditional values and relationships posed by the spread of urban influences, particularly as improved communications intensified urban–rural links. Closer to hand an educated and politicised rural and small-town *bourgeoisie*, together with successful peasant farmers, increasingly contested the predominance of established notables. Generally less wealthy than members of the landed elite, the representatives of the liberal professions, middle-class landowners, merchants, shopkeepers, artisans, and the better-off peasants, enjoyed a certain status, nevertheless. Far more numerous than their competitors, and in close daily contact with the population, they were well placed to exercise influence both for and against the regime and the established social order.

According to the sous-préfet at Aubusson (Creuse) this *bourgeoisie* 'holds the people in its hand. . . It does their business, lends them money, flatters them by innumerable family connections.'[102] It might, as in parts of the west, prosper as part of the clientele of Legitimist landowners. Alternatively, it might demand its own share of local influence, but with diverse effects on politics. Thus, in the Beauce, the absence of resident landowners encouraged prosperous tenant farmers to affirm their support for the regime. In the Périgord, and much of the Limousin, efforts were made to mobilise peasant support for the regime on the basis of an anti-noble, anti-Legitimist, and anticlerical appeal. Peasant hostility against those perceived to be exploiting them, which might otherwise have focused on the rural *bourgeoisie* itself, was thus successfully diverted.[103] In contrast, in parts of the Mediterranean south, middle-class influence facilitated the re-awakening of democratic sentiments.

Whatever their political allegiances, manhood suffrage allowed the middle classes to gradually extend their influence. Given the status, resources,

---

[101] PG Bordeaux, 9 July 1868, AN BB30/385; PG Bordeaux 27 July 1868, AN BB18/1767; A. Corbin, *Le village des cannibales* (Paris 1991), pp. 10–11; F. Ploux, *De bouche à oreille. Naissance et propagation des rumeurs dans la France du 19e siècle* (Paris 2003), pp. 206–11.

[102] Report to Prefect, 26 June 1853, AN F1 CIII Creuse 8.

[103] R. Gibson, 'The Périgord: landownership, power and illusion' in Gibson and Blinkhorn (eds.), *Landownership and Power*, p. 90.

and organisational skills possessed by the rural *bourgeoisie* and in spite of widespread conservatism, it seems safe to conclude that they provided much of the impetus for the development of a democratic opposition in the countryside. At the local level the republican militants of the Second Republic had continued to meet informally, and to contest municipal elections, whilst waiting for the moment when it would once again be safe to attempt to mobilise peasant support.[104] The emergence of these *nouvelles couches* into public life had been delayed by counter-revolution, but was clearly resumed in the later 1860s. Most official reports on the rise of republican opposition concentrate on their activities, as do historians influenced by Maurice Agulhon's concept of 'democratic patronage'. This makes it difficult to assess the response of those 'who never proclaimed their opinions'.[105] In his novel *La vie d'un simple*, set in the Allier, Emile Guillaumin describes the republican Dr. Fauconnet using sojourns in his favourite café, as well as his visits to patients, to voice his criticism of taxation, conscription, and the favouritism of the mayor and local councillors. The sharecropper Etienne Bertin, however, silently wonders how seriously he ought to take the radicalism of this 'great demolisher of the bourgeois, himself living as a bourgeois'.[106]

If in most areas peasants retained a sense of subordination to rural elites, there were widespread signs that *la fin des notables* was coming closer. Growing prosperity reduced dependency, and increased the self-confidence of many peasants, influencing social relationships in most areas, and transforming them in some.[107] Together with regime liberalisation and the establishment of a more relaxed political context in the 1860s, this would have a substantial impact on electoral behaviour. As one indicator of this, in Saône-et-Loire, whereas only 13 per cent of village mayors were peasants in 1848, during the Second Empire the proportion rose to 37 per cent, although this was mainly in the smaller, more exclusively rural communes.[108] As prefectoral controls were relaxed conflict was more likely to emerge. Thus at Bonney the mayor selected by the administration in 1864 was harassed by councillors whom he described, in his letter of resignation, as 'all envious, ignorant men, peasants hostile to anyone wearing a morning coat and belonging to the *bourgeoisie*'.[109] These developments can be considered in relation to the various political options – first support for the regime;

---

[104] E.g. Goujon, *Vigneron citoyen*, pp. 151–3.   [105] Corbin, *Pinagot*, p. 248.

[106] Pp. 182–3; on value of this particular source see A. Baker, *Fraternity among the French Peasantry. Sociability and Voluntary Associations in the Loire Valley, 1815–1914* (Cambridge 1999), p. 9.

[107] E.g. PG Paris, ? Feb 1857, AN BB30/383; Laurent, *Vignerons*, p. 524.

[108] Goujon, *Vigneron citoyen*, pp. 108, 112–13.   [109] Quoted ibid. p. 136.

secondly, for a monarchist and clerical politics; thirdly, for liberalism; and finally for republicanism.

POLITICAL OPTIONS

Support for the regime

There are no simple explanations of the strength of Bonapartist sentiment. Bonapartism appears to have been a characteristic of both areas of advanced and of backward farming, of zones of prosperity and of poverty, of those of large and of small-scale property ownership, of clerical and anti-clerical regions, of areas with high and those with low levels of literacy. Voting was based on perceptions produced by reference systems based upon historical myth as well as personal, familial, and community experience, and mediated by local social structures. As a result, there were significant regional variations in the scale and characteristics of peasant Bonapartism (which themselves conceal local differences), as well as changes over time. Furthermore, in some regions peasant support represented an effort on the part of its adherents to emancipate themselves from domination by social elites. In other areas it was based on a commitment, shared with these elites, to the defence of social order.

The 1852 plebiscite revealed that support for the re-establishment of the empire, substantial everywhere, was strongest in the north-eastern quarter of the country running from Picardy into the Dauphiné. By 1870 popular support remained firm in the north, Picardy, Champagne, northern Lorraine, lower Normandy, along the northern and western borders of the Massif Central, Aquitaine, and in upper Languedoc. These areas were extremely diverse in terms of their social structures, culture, and historical experience. It seems likely that the reasons for supporting the regime were also diverse. Comparison of the results of these plebiscites also reveals a *relative* decline in support in the Ile-de-France, the lower Seine valley, upper Normandy, the south-east of the Paris basin and the entire east – from Alsace through the Rhône valley and Alpine region into the Midi, evident particularly where urban–rural links were intense as well as in areas experiencing economic difficulty. To compensate for these losses, however, the regime could pride itself on gains in the west – and especially in Deux-Sèvres, Vienne, Ille-et-Vilaine, Maine-et-Loire, Morbihan, and Vendée, in the Auvergne and southern Massif.[110]

---

[110] See especially Ménager, *Les Napoléon du people*, pp. 222–57; F. Bluche, 'L'adhésion plébiscitaire' in Bluche, *Le prince, le peuple et le droit. Autour des plébiscites de 1851 et 1852* (Paris 2000).

Almost a month before the December 1848 presidential election, the sous-préfet at Mortagne in Normandy had predicted that overwhelming rural support would ensure Louis-Napoleon's victory. In typically pejorative terms he reported that

the peasants, completely ignorant, full of prejudices, and ridiculous illusions, will not vote for a man, but for a name, a memory. The fame of Napoleon is so widespread in the countryside, his popularity such, that his name is sufficient to carry along the ignorant masses, who attach to whoever carries the name, immense prestige and fabulous power . . . According to them, Napoleon will reduce taxes and restore credit; their horses and cows will sell at high prices.

He added that if 'some old peasants remember their sufferings under Napoleon, . . . they cannot compete with the eloquence and enthusiasm of the old soldiers who, in the cabaret, recount the exploits of the great man'.[111]

Haussmann, sous-préfet in the Gironde at the time, recalled questioning a peasant about his voting intentions. He was impressed by the man's utter determination to support Louis-Napoleon regardless of his landlord's objections. This had led him to advise the landowner: 'Since you claim to be his superior, listen to me, follow, this time, your peasant, in case he learns to march without you.'[112] Chapuys-de-Montlaville, prefect of the Isère, insisted on the historical import of the event, observing that 'this election . . . has been marked by a significant fact. On this occasion, for the first time, the rural population has taken part in politics with its own objective. . . A new power is being created.'[113] The situation disgusted Ernest Renan, as it did many intellectuals. He would tell his friends that 'I'd much prefer the peasants I can kick up the backside to the peasants like ours who have been turned into our masters by universal suffrage.'[114]

Republicans and liberals agreed that the behaviour of most peasant voters was either irrational, offering certain proof of *imbécillité rurale*, or represented a failure on their part to take into account their supposed 'real' interests. Electoral failure could thus be blamed on the immaturity of the rural population, its naïvety and incredulity.[115] To make matters worse, administrative pressure, and most notably the system of official candidature, obstructed the democratic education that was so urgently necessary.

---

[111] Quoted Corbin, *Pinagot*, pp. 280–1; on the election see also A.-J. Tudesq, *L'élection présidentielle de Louis-Napoléon Bonaparte, 10 décembre 1848* (Paris 1965), *passim*; R. Price, *The French Second Republic. A Social History* (London 1972), pp. 208–25.

[112] *Mémoires* I (Paris 1890), p. 279.   [113] Quoted Vigier, 'Le Bonapartisme', p. 14.

[114] Reported in E. and J. de Goncourt, *Journal*, II: *1864–78* (Paris 1956), p. 595.

[115] J. Ferry, *La lutte électorale en 1863* (Paris 1863), *passim*.

In a widely read pamphlet *Le suffrage universel et les paysans* (1865), the republican journalist Eugène Ténot distinguished between the enlightened populations of the towns and the backward inhabitants of the countryside:

in 1848 it was as if there were two peoples side by side in France. One, burning with a new spirit, the other a century behind. And it is on the latter that the law of numbers imposes the responsibility for establishing our liberty. Isolated in their ignorance, intellectually foreign to the rest of the nation, all the great and generous ideas of the century have passed them by.[116]

There is certainly plenty of evidence to support republican complaints about pressure imposed on the electorate by the regime's representatives and supporters. Officials at all levels were mobilised to distribute election manifestoes and ballot papers carrying the name of the candidate favoured by the government. Typically, for the 1852 plebiscite, the prefect of Saône-et-Loire instructed mayors that 'a ballot paper will be . . . attached to every polling card and distributed simultaneously'.[117] The act of distribution, probably by the garde champêtre – the village policeman – could easily be taken as an instruction on how to vote. In the aftermath of the coup, 'mayors obey and are obeyed'.[118] Professional bureaucrats knew that their careers depended on their commitment. In the absence of a secret ballot pressure could be exerted easily, especially where the mayor and his subordinates, making full use of their local knowledge and exerting all manner of pressure, displayed a modicum of zeal. The use of different-coloured ballot papers for the various candidates – with white reserved for the government's man – and sometimes of transparent paper, made supervision easier. Suspected opposition supporters might also be omitted from the electoral register.[119]

Well into the 1860s the threat of repression must have discouraged many potential nonconformists. Even as the pressure eased, peasants could ill afford to ignore the recommendations of those with political or social authority. As one republican activist pointed out – 'everybody knows what freedom to vote means in the countryside. The peasant is at the same time simple and distrustful. Anything to do with the authorities inspires him not with respect, but fear. The gendarmerie sergeant is greeted respectfully when he passes; he is the real master of the countryside.'[120] It does need to be borne in mind, however, that this was not a totalitarian regime on the twentieth-century model. Voters did not go in fear of their lives. Whilst often effective, pressure would become increasingly

[116] P. 13.   [117] Quoted P. Goujon, *Le vignoble de Saône-et-Loire au 19e siècle* (Lyon 1974), p. 352.
[118] Prefect, 24 March 1852, AN F1 CIII Bas-Rhin 15.   [119] Price, *Second Empire*, pp. 96–7.
[120] Albiot, *Les campagnes électorales*, p. 275.

counter-productive. The regime's electoral strength rested primarily on its inheritance – the Napoleonic myth, and its claims to have re-established social order and prosperity. This suggests that primarily peasant support for the Second Empire represented a rational response to their own perceived interests.

The peasant vote was clearly influenced by particular conceptions of the regime and what it represented. Expectations of the Republic had been bitterly disappointed. Throughout France the Prince-President had subsequently attracted support as the protector of peasant property against both the threat of 'communism' and the restoration of the *ancien régime*. Like his uncle he guaranteed the gains of the Revolution and prevented further revolution. This was a Bonapartism which was both popular and anti-republican. The prefect of Côte-d'Or passed on what he claimed were the views of the rural population in this eastern department in July 1851, that is, before the onset of prosperity: 'we want Napoléon, why bother to change him . . . ? If he has not done much good, that's not his fault; he has prevented things getting worse, and that's already something, and his uncle guaranteed possession of the biens nationaux, and defended us against the reds, and against the nobles.'[121]

In the north and much of the Paris basin peasant farmers joined social elites in a *de facto* conservative alliance of property owners. In the department of the Nord, where 77.8 per cent of registered voters voted 'Yes' in December 1851, the tensions evident in other regions as a result of peasant hatred of the *ancien régime* and its contemporary representatives were comparatively weak. Even before 1789, the burden imposed on peasants by the seigneurial system and tithe had been relatively light. Peasant landownership was substantial and the hostility towards the bourgeois possessors of former *biens nationaux*, so characteristic of parts of the west, was also lacking.[122]

A diffuse Bonapartist legend promised order, prosperity, and equality but its appeal to patriotic sentiments certainly should not be underestimated, based as it was on a myth popularised by the old soldiers, who because of their experiences retained considerable influence in many communities – a generation rapidly disappearing in the 1850/60s, however.[123] Martin Nadaud, the peasant from the Limousin, remembered listening to readings from carefully preserved copies of *Bulletins de la Grande Armée*, the favourite literature of his father and of an uncle who had been wounded at

---

[121] Quoted Lévêque, *Bourgogne*, IV, p. 1472.   [122] Ménager, 'Vie politique', III, p. 1214.
[123] E.g. A. Petetin (Prefect Haute-Savoie), *Discussion de politique démocratique et mélanges 1834–61* (Paris 1862), p. 50.

Waterloo, as well as to renderings of the patriotic songs of Béranger.[124] The 'history' of a 'golden age' had been widely diffused by popular almanacs, lithographs, and songs.[125] In December 1848 it had been given flesh by the great Emperor's nephew.

There thus existed a powerful substratum of support for a second empire. The regime would make a considerable effort to reinforce its appeal by claiming credit for prosperity and contrasting its achievements with the disorder and misery of the Second Republic. The Second Empire fortuitously coincided with the period between the ending of the mid-century crisis and the onset of the 'Great Depression' – two decades of prosperity in the countryside for which it took much and deserved some of the credit. The mid-century crisis had revealed that, in spite of increased productivity, most rural communities remained vulnerable to dearth. Whilst the subsistence crisis in 1846/7 had done much to discredit Louis-Philippe, Napoleon, in contrast, would be credited with efforts to assist the poor, thus conforming to the precepts of the 'moral economy'.

As a result of the improvement in communications, and the increased efficiency of international food markets, popular fear of 'famine' finally disappeared from around the mid 1850s, considerably reducing social tension. Between 1853 and 1856, Government officials, expecting a repetition of the disorders of the past, given the scale of the harvest deficit, were to be shocked by the change of mood.[126] The emotiveness, which had previously underlain price movements, was sharply reduced. Although petty theft and begging remained widespread, market-place disorders were only sporadic in comparison with 1846/7 and were largely restricted to isolated forest and upland areas south of the Loire where transport costs remained high.[127] Often, too, high food prices were blamed on the regime's opponents. In parts of the west, the nobility and clergy were even accused by popular opinion of trying to provoke unrest by hiding or destroying food stocks.[128] In 1853, in the northern department of the Aisne rumours spread that local nobles had plotted to starve the people by throwing grain into the lakes on their estates. Fortunately, it was claimed, the Emperor had uncovered their machinations and ordered their arrest. *Placards* calling for revenge ended with the popular slogan *Vive l'Empereur*.[129]

[124] *Mémoires de Léonard*, pp. 68–80.   [125] E.g. PG Agen, 21 July 1854, AN BB30/370.
[126] E.g. PG Angers, 8 Jan. 1854, AN BB30/371; Price, *Rural Modernisation*, ch. 6.
[127] 'Troubles à l'occasion de la cherté des subsistences 1853–4', AN BB30/432.
[128] E.g. PG Angers, 8 Jan. 1854, AN BB30/371; Price, *Rural Modernisation*, pp. 138–142; N. Bourguinat, *Les grains du désordre. L'Etat face aux violences frumentaires dans la première moitié du 19e siècle* (Paris 2002), pp. 415–16.
[129] PG Amiens, 6 Feb. 1854, AN BB30/432.

Some areas did experience a recrudescence of food riots in the spring and summer of 1868 but as the state prosecutor at Orléans pointed out 'the population is better informed than it used to be and realises that it cannot blame these problems on the government, and that the local administration and its wealthy fellow citizens are doing everything possible to ease the situation'.[130] His colleague at Limoges observed that 'amongst the masses, understanding of the economy has made notable progress: we no longer hear . . . those absurd accusations about speculation, which used to be so frequent'.[131] In most areas rising productivity additionally ensured that a larger proportion of the rural population was self-sufficient or even had a surplus to market, marginalising the labourers and small cultivators still obliged to enter the market to purchase necessities.[132] Furthermore, migration had reduced population pressure on resources.[133]

A new equilibrium between population and resources was developing rapidly. In the uplands, one effect of this was that the endemic and frequently violent resistance to official efforts to regulate exploitation of the forests also sharply declined. Indeed the administration itself appears to have adopted a less negative attitude towards the needs of traditional pastoral farming communities, partly as a means of disarming opposition to re-afforestation and environmental protection.[134] Panegyrics on the Emperor's interest in agriculture and his willingness to amnesty poor peasants convicted of offences against the forest laws, contributed to the image of a caring ruler. In 1862 the prefect of the Ain reported that it was his policy to 'publish, even in the most humble hamlets, everything His Majesty has done for the honour of the nation, the prosperity of our countryside, and the well-being of the working classes'.[135] Substantial improvements in living conditions in the countryside were evident which undoubtedly encouraged peasant approval of the Second Empire. As a result of heightened prosperity peasants enjoyed higher prices for their produce and rising wages. Periods of depression were less intense, and the prospect of purchasing land was enhanced. A farmer who sold his livestock at an unexpectedly high price at the Mauriac market in November 1852 could naïvely express his pleasure by shouting: 'We have never sold as well. . . . *Vive Napoléon, vive l'Empereur*', shouts apparently echoed throughout the marketplace.[136]

---

[130] 15 April 1868, AN BB30/385.   [131] 13 April 1867, AN BB30/378.
[132] E.g. PG Riom, 11 Jan. 1855, AN BB30/386; PG Poitiers, 30 July 1856, AN BB30/385.
[133] See e.g. PG Agen, 25 Jan. 1857, AN BB30/370.
[134] Report of M. Thiriat, forest inspector at Foix 1859, quoted Chevalier, *La vie humaine*, pp. 726–7.
[135] 18 July 1862, AN F1 CIII Ain 9.   [136] PG Riom, 9 Nov. 1852, AN BB30/386.

Prosperity was the theme constantly stressed in official reports. From the Beauce, the sous-préfet at Châteaudun could report in 1853 that 'this return to a long lost well-being strengthens in the population its feelings of gratitude and a profound attachment to the Emperor'.[137] A decade later the message from the mayor at Bessines (Haute-Vienne) to villagers was still: 'if we are happy with the Emperor who protects agriculture, who loves us all like his children, then we must vote for him and consequently for his candidate'.[138] From Brittany it was reported that better prices for grain and livestock made it easier for peasants to escape indebtedness and achieve their dream of purchasing land.[139] A *vigneron* from Aubière (Puy-de-Dôme), would explain his support for the Emperor in similar terms in 1870, pointing out that 'above all the peasant wants his work to provide a living for himself and his family. For this two things are necessary: calm . . . and the certainty of obtaining for his harvest a price sufficient to compensate him for his effort'. In comparison with the immediate past 'now we eat good wheat bread, meat almost every day . . . our fathers lived in hovels we wouldn't want our animals to live in' and, he added proudly, 'our children all go to school'.[140] A great deal had changed.

The development of communications, in the widest sense, had also increased the state's capacity for penetrating rural society. It reinforced the effectiveness of the politico-administrative apparatus and ensured the more intensive diffusion of a 'national' culture. Improved social discipline and the decline of traditional forms of protest offer evidence of this. The providential state was being constructed. Although considerable, and sometimes dangerous, resentment of external intervention in community life survived, directed especially at conscription, taxation, and policing, the populations of the countryside were becoming more aware of such positive features of government activity as better-organised public assistance, subsidies for rural roads, schools, and churches.[141]

Peasants were reminded frequently that the Second Empire was *their* regime. The mayor of Bessines insisted that 'it was the rural population . . . which restored the glorious empire which has given us every possible happiness, and it must not abandon its good work'. In restoring to the people the universal right to vote, it was the Emperor who had given them the opportunity to judge his government.[142] The provincial

---

[137] 25 Feb. 1853, AN F1 CIII Eure-et-Loir 7.   [138] 10 May 1863 quoted Corbin, *Archaïsme*, II, p. 883.

[139] PG Rennes, 14 Jan. 1858, AN BB30/386; OC gendarmerie cie Finistère, 29 Oct. 1869, AHG G8/166.

[140] Quoted F. Chalaron, 'Bonapartisme et paysannerie dans le Puy-de-Dôme', *Revue de l'Auvergne* 1985, p. 238.

[141] E.g. PG Pau, 2 Sept. 1856, AN BB30/384.   [142] Quoted Corbin, *Archaïsme*, II, p. 883.

tours, which were such a feature of the imperial regime, offered peasants an opportunity to greet their monarch. At Rennes and the great Breton pilgrimage centre of Ste-Anne d'Auray, in 1858, they arrived in their thousands wearing local costume and marching behind their priests and parish banners.[143] Official posters and the popular press provided detailed reports on such imperial progresses, often associated with the inauguration of new railway lines or, as in 1856, with the provision of assistance to the victims of the floods in the Rhône, Saône, and Loire valleys.

In their, generally vague, electoral programmes and speeches on such occasions as the *fête de l'Empereur* – the national holiday celebrated on 15 August by the ringing of bells, religious services, processions, balls, and fireworks and the distribution of the *médaille de Sainte-Hélène* to surviving veterans of the revolutionary-imperial wars[144] – or at agricultural shows, official candidates could point to their achievements in securing subsidies for the construction of railways and rural roads, for schools and churches, and for drainage and irrigation, to their efforts to mitigate the effects of poor harvests (1853–6) and harsh winters (1861–2), and to the government's determination to preserve social order. According to the prefect of Loiret, for the peasant, political economy meant 'roads, more roads, and yet more roads'.[145] This was a sentiment expressed throughout the countryside.[146] Prior to elections, pressure was even likely to be placed on railway companies to ensure the timely completion of branch lines.[147] Voting for an official candidate might thus represent both the expression of gratitude to the Emperor as well as a rational means of attempting to secure the conditions for continued prosperity.[148]

Gratitude for prosperity might lead to an almost uncritical peasant confidence in the Emperor, or else to a belief that, whatever its shortcomings, his regime was to be preferred to the alternatives. It was not parliamentary business that concerned most peasants but the effectiveness with which the government satisfied local, material interests. 'Always busy, always taken up with hard work in the fields, they spend little time in the political domain, and market prices are the only part of the newspapers which they deem worthy of interest.'[149] As late as April 1870 the state prosecutor at Aix could report, with rare exceptions, 'the lack of concern of the rural population . . .

---

[143] Academic Rector Rennes, 11 Sept. 1858, AN F17/2649.

[144] Estève, *A l'ombre du pouvoir*, pp. 261–3.   [145] 6 Sept. 1867, AN F1 CIII Loiret 7.

[146] E.g. PG Paris, 8 Feb. 1869; PG Grenoble, 13 April 1869, AN BB30/389.

[147] E.g. Prefect, 18 Sept. 1868, and Ministre de l'agriculture, du Commerce et des Travaux Publics, to Ministre de l'Intérieur, 28 Jan. 1867, AN F1 CIII Hautes-Alpes 5, re PLM and Avignon–Gap line.

[148] See e.g. PG Rennes, 14 Jan. 1858, AN BB30/386.

[149] Prefect Loir-et-Cher, quoted by Dupeux, *Aspects*, p. 429.

[with] public affairs, theories of government, and the current of modern ideas'. Prosperity together with 'the respect for rights, for the principle of equality before the law, satisfies every aspiration', although, he conceded, the failure to achieve these objectives might lead to the rise of opposition in the countryside.[150]

If the rural population was not politicised in the narrow sense of the word, it was certainly interested in politics. According to Alain Corbin the massive peasant support for the regime in the Limousin in 1870 was due to five factors: contempt for politicians; hostility towards the urban centres of political agitation and the townspeople who exploited the peasant; a genuine love of the Emperor; and gratitude for prosperity; together with hatred for the aristocracy and clergy who were identified with the *temps des rois*.[151] This was a peasant Bonapartism that rejected both reactionary and revolutionary politics. Fear of the latter can be seen in the hostility towards Paris generated in many rural areas following republican electoral successes or reports of agitation in the capital which revived fear of the 'communists', the *partageux*.[152] During the legislative elections of 1863 and 1869, and more widely during the plebiscite campaign in the following year, the revival of *bourgeois* opposition, whether liberal or republican, sometimes strengthened popular Bonapartism. Explaining the peasant vote in 1863 the procureur général at Dijon concluded that 'they have obeyed two instincts rather than reason: enthusiasm for the name of the Emperor and distrust for the *bourgeoisie*'.[153] Peasants resented an urban bourgeoisie, which competed to purchase land, as well as the merchants and lawyers who were also perceived to be exploiting the rural population.[154]

In the south-west, in the Gers and Charentes, in the south-east, in Basses-Alpes and Drôme, and in the Limousin in Creuse and Corrèze, departments in which landowning notables were relatively few in number and unable to exercise close control over the countryside, successive prefects chose to appeal to the peasant population over the heads of the local social elites. They presented the regime as the defender of the *petits* against the *gros* on such issues as access to forests and usury, and as a rampart against an aristocratic and clerical reaction, in areas in which the collective memory was impregnated with hatred of the *blancs*, of nobles believed to be plotting to recover the property they had lost after 1789, and priests anxious to restore the tithe. The Justice of the Peace of the canton of Thiviers in the Dordogne

---

[150] PG Aix, 19 April 1870; similarly PG Bordeaux, 8 April 1870, AN BB30/390.
[151] *Archaïsme*, ii, p. 904.
[152] E.g. PG Riom, 7 July 1870, AN BB30/390; Ménager, 'La vie politique', p. 718.
[153] 5 June 1863, AN BB30/429.   [154] See e.g. PG Limoges, 13 April 1867, AN BB30/378.

reported in July 1851 that 'our peasants detest those they call nobles . . . the caste which was proscribed under the first republic, which was denounced as accomplices of the foreign invasion in 1814, as enemy of the Emperor in 1815, and as working to re-establish the Ancien régime during the monarchies'.[155] During the Crimean war nobles were even rumoured to be amassing gold in order to bribe the Russian Tsar to restore the Bourbons.[156] In 1868, widespread disorders in the Dordogne, Charentes, and parts of Gironde, were caused by rumours of plots to overthrow Napoleon and re-establish the tithe. These again revealed a peasant determination to defend a regime which they assumed protected their own vital interests.[157]

These rumours of conflict between the Emperor and social elites conflicted sharply with reality. Although some prefects, like Pietri in the Ariège and subsequently the Haute-Garonne, attempted to create a Bonapartist 'party' independent of the notables, in general the government's representatives were themselves too committed to protecting the existing social order to conceive of a sustained challenge to its established hierarchy. Therefore, the regime remained dependent on the support of the elites who claimed to serve as intermediaries between the State and the rural population. The outcome of any manifestation of support by peasants for the heir to the great Napoleon, to whom the people 'believe it has returned . . . the full exercise of sovereignty',[158] was thus, paradoxically, the election of the upper-class official candidates selected by the regime.

The conditional character of support for the Emperor from both these notables and the clergy, together with the rise of opposition in the 1860s, inevitably aroused concern about peasant susceptibility to this mounting wave of criticism. Disaffection amongst these local elites, leading to 'this constant disparaging of our institutions',[159] posed a threat to the regime's position in the countryside. Growing alarm also manifested itself in reaction to signs of a renewal of republican agitation in rural areas.[160] Anything that weakened peasant support clearly threatened the regime's ability to win elections and thus its claims to legitimacy. Even when recording the continued electoral successes of the regime, the more perceptive official observers were aware increasingly that peasant endorsement was also becoming conditional to a greater degree, and that in some areas 'the government would be seriously mistaken if it took the election results as proof of universal approval'.[161]

---

[155] AN BB 30/374.   [156] PG Bordeaux, 24 July 1854, AN BB30/374.
[157] E.g. PG Poitiers, 5 Oct. 1868 AN BB24/721; Corbin, *Le village des cannibales*, pp. 27–30.
[158] PG Dijon, 8 Sept. 1852, AN BB30/377.   [159] PG Besançon, 12 Oct. 1868, AN BB30/389.
[160] E.g. PG Angers, 11 Jan. 1870, AN BB30/390.   [161] PG Lyon, 29 July 1855, AN BB30/379.

Consideration, by peasants, of alternatives to Bonapartism, did not necessarily involve politicisation in the sense of an intellectual appreciation of the virtues of a particular set of institutions and ideology. If they were generally not attracted by the prospect of constitutional change, critics of the regime nevertheless managed to arouse interest in such issues as 'excessive' taxation and increased conscription, which they claimed were the result of the government's extravagance and warlike intentions. Widespread popular concern with these matters was suggested by official reports during the 1863 election campaign, and the situation continued to deteriorate. The ritual stress on the rural population's continued devotion to *l'Empereur des paysans et des soldats*,[162] was increasingly combined with warnings about a change of mood in the countryside.

The state prosecutor at Dijon pointed out in January 1864, that 'people talk a lot about the peasant, his common sense, his devotion to the Empire. This is all true, but not without qualification. The peasant's common sense is combined with all manner of prejudices and susceptibilities. He can easily be led astray. His devotion is very calculating, and has only himself and his own interests as its object.'[163] His colleague at Nancy concluded that 'the political sentiments of the countryside can be summed up in three points: a genuine attachment to the Emperor, fear of war, and a horror of taxes'.[164] Following the Prussian victory over Austria in 1866, there was a risk, according to the procureur impériale at Brignoles (Var), that proposals for military reform would 'shatter the confidence of the rural populations'.[165] The conviction was spreading that the demand for more men and money must be the prelude to a general European war.[166] This *mauvaise humeur*[167] would be translated into a growing unwillingness to lend unquestioning support to the government's candidates. In the Paris area, if 'confidence in the imperial institutions has not been weakened; . . . the popular masses . . . no longer accept direction by the administration in the choice of deputies as submissively as before'.[168] The Emperor's response to these reports of massive peasant hostility towards increased taxation and conscription was to substantially weaken his plans for army reform, a sacrifice of military efficiency to the needs of electoral victory which would ultimately prove fatal to the regime.

A renewed effort was also made to persuade peasants that 'it is necessary to vote for the Emperor'. During the 1869 electoral and the 1870 plebiscite

[162] PG Grenoble, 8 Sept. 1867, AN BB30/378. [163] 3 Oct. 1863, AN BB30/377.
[164] 5 Jan. 1862, AN BB30/381. [165] Quoted Constant, 'Var', IV, p. 1224.
[166] E.g. PG Agen, 5 April 1868, AN BB30/370. [167] PG Rouen, 12 April 1869, AN BB30/389.
[168] PG Paris? October 1869, AN BB30/289; see also PG Lyon, 9 July 1869 AN BB30/379.

campaigns they were again reminded of the prosperity they enjoyed. By playing on memories of 1848, the regime also sought to revive fear of the revolution, which would destroy their dreams. In 1869 the Bonapartist newspaper the *Courrier du Gers* described the moderate republican candidates Jean David as *le Marat du Midi* and Jules Favre as 'the man of 48, of disorder, of the 45 centimes'. The following year, the clerical newspaper *Le Conservateur* insisted that 'those who want a strong and respected government' would vote 'yes' because a negative response would lead to

la République . . . disorder, insurrection and civil war . . . the re-establishment of the regime of the 45 centime tax . . . This would ruin the countryside to the profit of the towns, where the right to work acclaimed by the socialists would lead inevitably to the re-opening of the National Workshops. . . . It would halt the growth in consumption; our products would no longer find markets; this is, in a word, Revolution.[169]

All the old fears were being revived. More positively, a vote 'Yes' could also be represented as a decision in favour of parliamentary government and greater electoral freedom, which would lead to a reduction in the size of the army and of taxation.

The ambiguities of the plebiscite hardly need stressing. However, for most of the rural population it seems likely that political stability, the defence of social order, and of their property and prosperity were the primary motives for supporting the Emperor's proposals. Officials could take comfort from the belief that for the peasant, 'the word *liberté* is . . . deprived of the meaning we attach to it . . . He who has secured all the liberty he can use wants, above all, order and security.'[170] In a very real sense the Second Empire represented the apogée of traditional peasant society. It was hardly surprising that the population, to which the regime appealed as their primary benefactor and protector, would respond positively in successive elections and plebiscites. Such concessions as the withdrawal of military reform appear to have reinforced the belief of most peasants that their best interests would continue to be served by supporting the man who could still meaningfully present himself as *leur empereur*. Nevertheless the experience of voting ensured that even a decision to support the regime and its candidates gradually came to be based less on passive adherence and more on a reasoned assessment of its merits. A vote for an official election candidate in 1869 might well express very different sentiments from a vote

[169] Quoted Palmade, 'Le département du Gers', pp. 184–5, 195.
[170] PG Limoges, 13 April 1867, AN BB30/378.

for the same candidate in 1852. Additionally, of course, peasant support represented a rejection of alternatives.

The clerico-Legitimist option

During the authoritarian decade, Legitimism provided the backbone of conservative opposition to the regime. Its leading figures were mainly large landowners, often nobles or those with pretensions to nobility, who, with the support of the clergy, diffused an ideology, which might be described as authoritarian, paternalistic, and theocratic, and designed to reinforce their influence over the masses. Peasant Legitimism might be understood as a response to pressure from landowners or their agents. It might also be ascribed to an almost instinctive respect on the part of the poor and insecure for their social 'superiors', as well as to a shared clerico-religious worldview.

The situation was confused because before the Emperor's breach with the Papacy in 1859, and again as a result of the renewed fear of revolution in 1869/70, many Legitimist sympathisers were drawn into close collaboration with the regime. In other respects too, Legitimists would remain divided. Some maintained a discreet and prudent opposition; whilst others sought to impose on their dependants the Comte de Chambord's injunction to abstain from political activity.[171] Two *vignerons* told the gendarmerie at Bresse-sur-Grosne in 1852 that 'M. de Murard, their master, had made them, and all the others, go to his house on the eve of the elections, on the pretext of paying their rent, but he had said to them that he was not going to vote, and that they would be well-advised to do the same. Of fifty voters linked with his household forty-nine did not vote.'[172] Such practices as the distribution by the parish priest of Yvias (Côtes-du-Nord) of medals celebrating the life of the pretender, Henri V, were taken very seriously by the authorities and his bishop in this case, at the prefect's insistence, transferred the priest to a less congenial parish.[173] Efforts by Legitimist sympathisers to blame the Emperor for the effects of poor harvests were also quickly punished. Jules Clouard, drinking in a bar at Folligny (Manche), was arrested for claiming that 'the Emperor is amusing himself at balls every day, instead of being concerned about the poor', and adding that 'Henri V would have been much better, because he and the nobles would have given bread to the poor'.[174]

---

[171] See e.g. sous-préfet Autun, 26 Feb. 1853, AN Fɪ Cɪɪɪ Saône-et-Loire 8.
[172] Report of 28 Nov. 1852, quoted Lévêque, *Bourgogne*, ɪv, p. 1515.
[173] Prefect Côtes-du-Nord, report on Oct. 1857, AN F7/3975.
[174] PG Caen, 17 Dec. 1853, AN BB30/434.

Clerico-Legitimism was most significant in areas with high levels of religious practice in Flanders and the west, and where, as in parts of the Massif Central and Languedoc, tensions with Protestant minorities remained intense. In all these areas the murderous conflict, which had accompanied the Revolution, remained fresh in people's minds. Landowners and priests cooperated in an attempt to control the material and spiritual lives of the population. The former provided financial assistance to the church and its growing network of schools and in return exercised, thanks to the clergy, an influence far greater than their wealth and personal influence would have allowed. The Comte de Falloux welcomed the fact that in the Vendée, 'the clergy are constantly on the move, working the countryside, under the aegis of the *grands seigneurs* associated with the bishop'.[175]

Where Legitimist landowners were able to attract mass support, as in the Breton departments of Ille-et-Vilaine, Morbihan, or Côtes-du-Nord, generally the administration felt obliged to search for a compromise, often selecting supporters of the Bourbon pretender as its official electoral candidates.[176] In the Vendée the local administration was 'unable to avoid being enveloped' by Legitimist notables.[177] In those areas in which priestly influence over the masses was limited, in contrast, concessions appeared unnecessary and likely to alienate much of the electorate. Peasant sympathy for the regime might have the useful effect of severely restraining the ability of Legitimist landowners and priests to mount opposition.

Ominously, from the Legitimist point of view, the clergy had increasingly rallied to the regime during the 1850s. This reflected the success of deliberate efforts to detach them from their habitual Legitimist alliance by increasing their stipends and subsidising their activities. Without the support of the clergy Legitimism was gravely weakened as a popular movement. For the clergy the alliance with Legitimists had never been without its tensions. As the secretary to the Bishop of Vannes told the prefect of Morbihan:

the clergy has marched alongside the *châteaux* for such a long time only because that was where it found the support it needed, but it has been distressed by the subordinate position to which it has been reduced so that, now that it is certain of the benevolence of the government, it has seized with great eagerness the opportunity to escape from a tutelage which sacrificed its dignity; it now realises that its authority over the population did not come from the *château* but, on the contrary, it was its own presence at the *château* which preserved for the local nobility what little influence they had.[178]

---

[175] Quoted M. Faucheux, 'La Vendée' in L. Girard (ed.), *Les élections de 1869* (Paris 1960), p. 160.
[176] Maurain, *Politique ecclésiastique*, pp. 240–1.   [177] PG Poitiers, 9 June 1852, AN BB30/385.
[178] 4 Dec. 1858, quoted Maurain, *Politique ecclésiastique*, p. 257.

This threatened to have a substantial impact on the peasant vote. Certainly, the growing tension between State and Church over such issues as control over education, the Emperor's Italian policy, and the threat this posed to the Pope's temporal kingdom, reinvigorated the alliance between intransigent Legitimists and much of the clergy. However, the efforts made to enlist the support of the rural population in the Papal cause, particularly by some of the younger, more ultramontane, clergy, enjoyed little success. The practice of religion continued without hindrance, and most peasants failed to appreciate that the regime's Roman policy constituted a threat to their faith.[179] Popular sympathy for the clergy was not increased by their seemingly unjustified attacks on the Emperor's government. In the Vendée peasant support could only be mobilised by linking the war in Italy to fears concerning conscription, but the rapid end of the war calmed these anxieties.[180] Legitimist landowners increasingly realised that in order to retain their influence over peasants they needed to 'leave political questions aside and present themselves as defenders of order and religion'. Legitimist opposition to the established authorities continued to be muted therefore.[181]

Moreover, in the west, and especially the south, clerico-Legitimist influence was also declining as the result of growing prosperity, the spread of peasant landownership, and rising landlord absenteeism. Together with the possibility of migration, these developments increased the peasant's sense of independence. In the Gard where landlord paternalism and hostility towards Protestants had helped to preserve Legitimist and clerical influence, support clearly declined along with the ability and willingness of the rich to provide charity and in reaction against their repeated political voltes-faces since February 1848.[182] In some communities, by the late 1860s, peasant support even appeared to be passing directly from Legitimism to an extreme republicanism.[183]

The Orleanist/liberal option

With growing force from the 1863 electoral campaign, liberals offered a more diffuse criticism of the regime's institutions and attempted to link this to rural grievances. The liberal candidate at Château-Chinon in 1869, in a *profession de foi* directed specifically at the peasantry, insisted that they

---

[179] PG Poitiers, 18 July 1859, AN BB30/385.   [180] Ibid. 28 Oct. 1859.
[181] PG Angers, 12 Oct. 1867, AN BB30/371.
[182] Huard, 'Préhistoire', p. 8; see also G. Cholvy, 'L'opposition', p. 270.
[183] PG Aix, 6 July 1869, AN BB30/389.

were being exploited by the regime: 'You plough, you sow, you harrow, you harvest, but I take the grain! I take the wheat! Thresh! Winnow! Sieve! But make sure, you and your neighbours, that you give me at least 400 million each year . . . Give me the money so that I can spend it on splendour and magnificence.'[184] Imperial taxation, extravagance, conscription, and the commercial treaties were all targets.

The precise impact of these criticisms is difficult to estimate, however. In the south where cereal prices were falling as a result of market integration this could be blamed on 'free trade' allowing the import of Russian grain along the Rhône-Saône corridor into central France.[185] However, this was offset by the unprecedented prosperity of the vineyards. Elsewhere cereal prices largely remained remunerative. Some regions including Normandy and Brittany also benefited from improved access for their dairy products to the British market.[186] Taxation and conscription were more potent weapons. It was claimed that these proved the urgent need for parliamentary controls to restrain the Emperor's personal initiatives. Touring the Arles constituency, Eugène Pelletan made speeches, which claimed, moreover, that it was government intransigence and the unrest it provoked which posed the major threat to the 'principles of order, of property, of the family'.[187]

This kind of propaganda would cause growing concern amongst government officials who felt that it was having a significant impact on the younger generation of peasant voters, as well as on those living in or close to the numerous little market centres who tended to be better educated and more aware of the issues.[188] Explaining opposition successes in 1869 in six of the eight constituencies in his area of responsibility the state prosecutor at Besançon blamed 'the disintegrating effect of the press', adding that as a result of the electoral campaign, 'in a few days, and as if by a sleight of hand, the prestige of the authorities has been weakened . . . the favourable attitude of the masses has been destroyed'.[189] The state prosecutor at Grenoble concluded that the election results had revealed a substantial decline in support for the regime in 'almost all those villages which have a little importance and are not lost in the mountains'.[190]

Administrative reports repeatedly claimed that this growing disaffection manifested itself in the desire to exercise a vote free from administrative

---

[184] 1 May 1869 quoted Vigreux, *Paysans*, p. 444.
[185] E.g. 1866 *Enquête agricole*, XXII Bouches-du Rhône, p. 97.
[186] Price, *Rural Modernisation*, p. 376.
[187] PG Aix, 24 Jan. 1870, AN BB30/390.   [188] E.g. PG Riom, 11 Jan. 1870, AN BB30/390.
[189] 13 July 1869, AN BB30/389.   [190] 7 July 1869, AN BB30/389.

interference. The state prosecutor at Colmar was surprised that peasants favoured increasing the powers of parliament, given that 'the mechanism of parliamentary government is absolutely unknown to the rural population'. Previously, he had assumed that 'brought up under the patriarchal regime which governs the farm' they would prefer a 'sovereign who, having the mandate to do good, must necessarily . . . have the power to exercise it'. He could only explain their 'desertion' as the result of widespread criticism of the Mexican expedition and of expenditure on the embellishment of Paris.[191] This encouraged peasants to support a movement which was 'essentially bourgeois'.[192]

Liberal election candidates were drawn from the same social milieu and generally possessed advantages similar to those favoured by the government in terms of local influence and the resources necessary to offer voters favours. Only rarely, however, were they able to dominate more than one or two cantons. This placed them at a considerable disadvantage faced with official candidates enjoying administrative support. Nevertheless, it was clear that liberal criticism, whether voiced by opposition, or increasingly by official candidates, was proving attractive to voters. The sheer volume of reports to this effect and the assumption, shared by the Emperor and his close advisors, that they dare not risk alienating peasant support, was to be a key factor in the dismantling of the system of official candidature, one of the defining characteristics of the regime.[193] Peasants were also increasingly likely to support republican candidates.

Republican options

During the Second Republic the establishment of the *République démocratique et sociale* had been presented by republican militants as the means of creating a more egalitarian society in which cheap credit would allow peasants to purchase land and escape from the suffocating burden of debt, and in which their social status would be enhanced considerably. The new era would be inaugurated following victory in the general and presidential elections due in 1852. The *coup d'état* had shattered these dreams. The culminating event in a long period of intensifying repression intended to demobilise republican activists, it was followed by numerous denunciations and intimidatory arrests particularly in those areas in the south-east and centre in which resistance to the *coup* had occurred briefly.

---

[191] 24 July 1869, AN BB30/389.   [192] PG Paris, 5 May 1866, AN BB30/384.
[193] Price, *Second Empire*, pp. 122–6.

In this settling of accounts with the left, over 26,000 suspected republican militants were arrested. Official policy was to incarcerate supposed ringleaders, only a minority of whom were peasants. The overall impact was crushing nevertheless. An atmosphere of fear was created deliberately. The republican movement was decapitated, discredited, and abandoned by most of its militants – isolated and discouraged – as well as by its potential supporters. Without its newspapers and organisation republican propaganda virtually disappeared from the countryside. Political activity was curtailed substantially.[194]

The seizure of power was followed by the *années silencieuses*. Collaboration between government agents and conservative notables was effective particularly in small communities. Until well into the 1860s, in most areas, the political opportunity structure was very different from that of the Second Republic. In the Jura 'the time has disappeared . . . when one could read the newspapers out loud in the bars as if they were the catechism. People read little now.'[195] 'Demagogues' had to be prevented from contaminating the mass of 'honest' peasants. Those suspected of republican sympathies were made aware of continued police surveillance. M. Ravin, a landowner at Fleury (Yonne) accused of talking politics to peasants in local *cabarets*, thus received a sentence of six months' imprisonment with a 1,000f. fine in December 1855.[196]

Official reports revealed a growing belief that the republican threat in the countryside had been reduced to insignificance. In the Basses-Alpes and Var, 'in the rural communes everyone knows everyone else and they keep an eye on each other; fear of being denounced as a demagogue is sufficient to eliminate many hostile votes'.[197] The prefect of the Ariège could still proudly affirm in November 1860 that 'no one any longer dares to admit to republican opinions'.[198] Uncooperative village mayors were dismissed, councils dissolved, cafés closed. The political paralysis induced by fear and discouragement was broken only through discreet personal contacts. Where it survived, opposition was localised and isolated. In spite of this apparent success, however, officials frequently warned against complacency.[199]

The *coup d'état* had shattered dreams. However, republican opposition in the villages never disappeared entirely. The brutal repression, which officials

---

[194] V. Wright, 'The *coup d'état* of December 1851: repression and the limits to repression' in Price, *Revolution and Reaction, passim.*

[195] PG Besançon, 19 Nov. 1860, AN BB30/373.   [196] PG Paris, 1 Sept. 1856, AN BB30/383.

[197] PG Aix, 28 June 1857, AN BB30/370.   [198] 14 Nov. 1860, AN F1 CIII Ariège 7.

[199] E.g. PG Angers, 3 Jan. 1853, AN BB30/371.

believed to be an unavoidable necessity, resulted in an enduring bitterness amongst those it affected as well as their families and friends. The *juge de paix* at Luc (Var), where a number of arrests had been made in December 1851, noted that 'people are aware of who the informers are . . . and as a result those who were accused, when they return, retain an implacable hatred for these *bourgeois*, these conservatives . . . guilty of unpardonable wrong in the eyes of those who have been the victims'. In August 1853, Pierre Montagne, a local farm labourer, would be accused of claiming, whilst threshing, that 'in 1851 we should have killed all the rich. If we had killed them, we would have had their property and we would have been much better off. We were betrayed, but we will get our own back. Whatever is postponed is not lost.'[200]

Folkloric forms of protest like the *charivari* continued to be employed to express communal displeasure, often against those suspected of having provided the authorities with incriminating information.[201] Throwing stones or daubing doors with excrement might otherwise express contempt. In December 1853, the painting of a cross in blood on a landowner's door at Cuisers (Saône-et-Loire) certainly caused alarm.[202] Social tension remained only too evident in some communities. During carnival in 1852 at Bourg-de-Péage (Doubs), peasants dressed in black pulled a plough through the streets whilst the ploughman, shouting 'Walk on, walk on! Another furrow', pretended to whip them. They were assumed to be protesting about the 'enslavement' of the poor.[203]

For some, at least, the divide between republicanism and a supposedly egalitarian Bonapartism had widened beyond repair. They could express their resentment by means of a simple and often violent discourse. The authorities took careful note of the expressions employed. The occasional drunken outburst overheard by the police raised a curtain on a sub-culture which otherwise remained elusive and thus, inevitably, frightening. The authorities were certainly likely to be alarmed by a conversation like that involving L. Thermet, in a village near Corbeil (Seine-et-Oise). He was reported to have asserted 'that all the landowners were rogues, that he wanted to sharpen his axe to cut off their heads, that he would like to eat their hearts, that a Revolution was needed to cut off their rascally heads'. For

---

[200] JP, reports quoted Constant, 'Var', III, pp. 854–5; see also PG Paris, 3 Feb. 1863, AN BB30/384 re arrondissements of Auxerre and Joigny.
[201] E.g. PG Aix, 24 Sept. 1853, AN BB30/407.   [202] GOC 8e DM, 1–15 Dec. 1853, AHG G8/67.
[203] PG Grenoble, 8 March 1852, AN BB30/378.

this drunken outburst he was sentenced to six months' imprisonment.[204] M. Devaux, a farmer at la Tremblade (Charente-Inférieure) received fifteen days in prison for praising the activities of the republican secret society la Marianne and publicly maintaining that 'For as long as the Bonapartists are in power, everything will go wrong. It's time again for blood and for the tyrants' heads to pave the streets of Paris.'[205]

The authorities continued to be concerned about gatherings in village cafés and *chambrées* and at fairs and markets. Were these simply manifestations of popular sociability or disguised political meetings? Successive efforts to regulate the activities of the denizens of these places, such as the *arrêts* of the prefect of the Var banning political discussion and newspapers from the *chambrées*, were ignored. The departmental police commissaire shared this obsessive concern with moral corruption and political subversion. He complained on 25 October 1853 that 'the days on which agricultural fairs or local feasts are held are those on which the demagogues and those under police surveillance in the department choose to meet and exchange visits, because they hope, and can be almost certain, in the middle of large gatherings, of escaping the surveillance of which they are the object'.[206]

Officials were appalled by frequent *propos séditieux*, by *propos injurieux contre l'Empereur* and obscenities directed against the Empress. They expressed concern about republican songs, subversive *placards* with their promises of arson and crude depictions of knives and guillotines, and even the wearing of red clothing. The badly written message on a *placard* found at Buisse (Isère) just before the plebiscite on the re-establishment of the Empire in December 1852, expressed what were assumed to be sentiments common in the area: 'Republic, he who you raised has betrayed you, he has become a cowardly deserter of the people's cause, but the day will come when these butchers will fall victim to their own treachery.'[207] Was its author a poorly educated villager or a professional man trying to conceal his identity?

As a result of the slow dissemination of official information, and in the absence of a widely circulating newspaper press, rumours, spreading rapidly by word of mouth, increasingly distorted, and revealing widespread latent anxiety, were another problem for the administration.[208] During a cholera epidemic in November 1853, it was claimed at Châteaudouble (Var), that 'the government is paying men to poison the population . . . ; the rich do

[204] PG Paris, 29 Nov. 1858, AN BB30/385.   [205] PG Poitiers, 31 Jan. 1857, AN BB30/385.
[206] Quoted Constant, 'Var', III, p. 859.   [207] PG Grenoble, 15 Dec. 1852, AN BB30/378.
[208] See e.g. F. Ploux, 'L'imaginaire social et politique de la rumeur dans la France du 19e siècle', *Revue historique* 2000, pp. 409f.

not die, because they are in agreement with the government; it is always the poor who are the victims'. At Hauterives (Drôme) a pedlar was chased by a stone-throwing crowd of women claiming that the government had paid him to poison the wells. The repetition of this particular rumour throughout the arrondissements of Valence and Die was blamed by the local commissaire de police on one Sophie Gay who, returning from the market at Valence, told acquaintances that a servant drawing water from a well in the town had discovered a sausage 'full of arsenic'.[209]

Republican sentiments throughout the 1850s manifested themselves most commonly through complaints about high food prices and in traditional forms of popular protest. An innkeeper at Sissy (Aisne) told his clients that 'Napoleon, Emperor of the French, is an accomplice of the village rich in keeping the price of wheat high', and complained that the poor were being sent to die fighting the Russians.[210] Gueyrand, a farmer at Lus (Drôme), passed on the 'news' in August 1854 that the French army was trapped in the Crimea and that Ledru-Rollin would seize the opportunity to return on 15 August, the feast day of Saint-Napoleon, to reward those who had resisted the *coup d'état*.[211] Its very precision gave the story a certain credibility. Political loyalties predisposed individuals towards particular interpretations of crises. A 35-year-old farmer and former secret society member from Buigny (Somme) was arrested in September 1855 for saying in the street that 'the Emperor was a rogue; and was to blame for the high price of wheat; that it was a good idea to overthrow him; not like Ledru-Rollin who was an honest man, interested in the good of the peuple'.[212] M. Cottenceau, a native of the little village of Villebois (Eure-et-Loir) was sentenced to a year in prison for wishing that bread was twice as expensive in order to 'punish the people for voting for Napoleon' and adding that bread had been cheaper under the Republic.[213]

Even during the years of most intense repression it was still possible to organise a quasi-political demonstration. Republicans frequently used the funeral processions of former militants for a display of strength. Municipal elections were also occasionally contested, with activists taking advantage of local social networks to deliver oral propaganda and ballot papers. The state prosecutor at Paris claimed that renewed electoral agitation in and around Bléneau in the Loing valley was the result of an amnesty which 'in permitting the return of the most compromised and dangerous individuals,

---

[209] PG Aix, 7 Sept. 1854, AN BB30/370; PI Draguignan, 18 Nov. 1853, quoted Constant, 'Var', IV, p. 865.
[210] PG Amiens, 2 Aug. 1854, BB30/434.   [211] PG Grenoble, 28 Nov. 1854, AN BB30/378.
[212] PG Amiens, 12 Sept. 1855, AN BB30/433.   [213] PG Paris, 5 May 1855, AN BB30/435.

in frightening the men of order, has re-awakened all the boldness of their adversaries'.[214] The sous-préfet at Beaune reported in September 1852 that in his arrondissement, judged to be the 'reddest' in the Côte-d'Or, 22 of the newly elected councils were 'unacceptable' and would have to be replaced with nominated commissions, 24 others left much to desire, whilst the supporters of social order had triumphed in the remaining 155. In this, but certainly not in all vine-growing areas it was the *vignerons*, generally living in large villages and consistently interested in politics, if only because of the impact of the alcohol tax on their incomes, who were frequently accused of harbouring republican sympathies.[215] Whilst many would retain their left-wing sympathies, others would, however, be attracted to the regime by growing prosperity.[216]

Nevertheless, in most communities, there were individuals or groups who failed to share in the 'good times' and continued to blame the regime. In the Drôme in 1859 these included tenant farmers unable to afford the price of land because of the silk disease, which had destroyed a vital supplementary income. Their situation was contrasted with that of peasants in the neighbouring departments of Hautes-Alpes and Isère who were prospering, clearing their debts and purchasing land.[217] Impoverished vine and cereals cultivators in the Yonne were similarly missing out on prosperity and it was assumed by officials that 'hatred of the authorities and of the principles of social order propagate themselves easily amongst people who are so discontented and envious'.[218] The forest code, which restricted access to woodland pasture and to wood for construction and fuel, was another cause of grievance.[219]

Social tension also remained a potent source of republican sentiment, especially where unpopular landowners were closely identified with the regime. An agricultural labourer called Robin working on the Briare-Angers road at Saint-Michel (Indre-et-Loire) was sentenced to fifteen months' imprisonment for telling passers-by that 'if work was difficult to find and bread so expensive, it was because Napoleon was in partnership with the rich; that it was necessary to overthrow him and have a good republic, when all would be much better; that it was necessary just like in the time of Polignac, to strike some matches and burn down the châteaux and the railways'.[220] A *placard* found at Rouvray-Catillon (Seine-Inférieure) in October 1855 written, it affirmed, on behalf of 'two million, five thousand,

---

[214] 22 Feb. 1853, AN BB18/1517.　　[215] Lévêque, *Bourgogne*, IV, p. 1556.
[216] E.g. PG Orléans, 1 April 1859, AN BB30/382.　　[217] PG Grenoble, 18 April 1859, AN BB30/378.
[218] PG Paris, 18 Feb. 1854, AN BB30/383.　　[219] PG Pau, 6 April 1859, AN BB30/384.
[220] PG Orléans, 9 Nov. 1855, AN BB30/433.

one hundred and sixty five of my colleagues', expressed regret at having previously voted for Napoleon. The Emperor was now denounced as 'ungrateful because it is us workers (*houvriers*) who have raised him to the rank of Emperor and today he is not firm enough to push away this disgusting clergy (*clerger*), these nobles who control him, who will destroy him and us as well'. The author called on everyone to shout 'down with the Emperor, down with the clergy, and *vive la république*'.[221] In some areas, the support provided by the clergy for political reaction had reinforced anti-clerical sentiment substantially.

It was difficult for the authorities to determine how 'political' this outpouring of envy, resentment, and sheer frustration really was. Those rural republicans, a high proportion of them artisans and professionals, who were determined to remain active, certainly used their personal contacts to keep the flame of resistance alive. They were relatively few in number and were, initially, able to achieve relatively little. Nevertheless, as the procureur général at Aix warned in July 1853, it was only repression which prevented a renewal of agitation in those parts of the Basses-Alpes in which resistance to the *coup* had occurred. He pointed out that

the nature of the country, the habits of populations living in the few, small centres, where, however, the houses just about touch each other, easily explains why this re-organisation . . . would face so little difficulty. All the inhabitants know each other, all, or almost all, took secret society oaths; they no longer meet, at least in obvious fashion, to talk about politics; but between men united by so many shared interests, a single word would be sufficient to re-establish what barely a few months of sustained effort originally established in so powerful a fashion.[222]

Similarly in the Var, where the popular drinking club, the *chambrée*, provided frequent occasions for private gatherings: 'sentiments have not changed, and almost everyone, on occasions, speaks of vengeance and of the revenge they will take when the struggle recommences'. In the Bouches-du-Rhône it was hostility between republicans and Legitimists, dating from the 1790s and revived in 1848, which ensured that an opposition politics survived. Forced by circumstances to dissimulate their activities, however innocent, republicans always risked giving the impression of involvement in secret societies. The authorities, always anxious, were only too likely to lend credence to every rumour.[223]

The first signs of real concern, however, re-appeared in administrative reports during the 1857 electoral campaign. The diffuse nature of republican

---

[221] PG Rouen, 14 Oct. 1855, AN BB30/433 – original orthography retained.
[222] PG Aix, 19 July 1853, AN BB30/370.   [223] Ibid. 6 Aug. 1853.

electioneering and the absence of an organisation linking the provinces to Paris offered some reassurance. Nevertheless, there was growing evidence that republican cadres were being re-constituted and an expectation that in some future election republican militants might turn their attention more fully towards the countryside.[224] From the Yonne, particularly agitated before the *coup d'état*, it was reported that the democrats would instantly revive 'at the slightest disaster, at the least event which encouraged their hopes'. Rumours that Napoleon had been, or was about to be assassinated, caused considerable official concern.[225] The republican revival would nevertheless be slow and hesitant. It was interrupted by the renewed wave of repression generated by Orsini's attempted assassination of the Emperor in 1858. The prestige of the regime was also subsequently reinforced by the wave of patriotism provoked by the war against Austria in 1859. The growth of official anxiety about the rural population would become much more evident during the 1863 election campaign, as increased numbers of republican electoral candidates attracted growing, if still limited, rural support in both local and legislative elections.[226]

Republican sympathisers increasingly *refait surface* in the 1860s as repression eased. Following municipal elections, in October 1865, the procureur impérial at Draguignan reported that whereas in upland areas apparent dissent largely resulted from an apolitical rivalry between local personalities, 'on the plain they march to the ballot as a result of a mysterious call, restoring those defeated in 1851 to political life'.[227] In most areas peasant republicanism was particularly evident in the larger villages, where militants, described as including doctors, notaries, shopkeepers, and artisans as well as peasants, were beginning to establish informal committees and distribute newspapers in an effort to restore links with the masses.[228] By 1867, peasants living in the town of Draguignan, and especially members of its nineteen *chambrées*, were said to be increasingly subject to the influence of six republican activists – a socially diverse group made up of a rentier, two peasant farmers, a cooper, and two lawyers. This was fairly typical of areas of small-scale farming and manufacture, which had experienced considerable republican agitation during the Second Republic. It was further noted that support for the left in other little towns in the area, like Hyères, Lorgues, and Bandol, was spreading, largely at the expense of popular Legitimism.[229]

---

[224] See e.g. sous-préfet Le Vigan, 4 July 1858, AN F1 CIII Gard 7, PG Montpellier, 10 July 1857, AN BB30/380.

[225] E.g. PG Paris,? April 1859; PG Pau, 6 April 1859, re arrondissement Bagnères – both in AN BB30/384.

[226] E.g. PG Angers, 11 July 1863, AN BB30/371; PG Riom, 2 Oct. 1863, AN BB30/386.

[227] Quoted Constant, 'Var', IV, p. 1156.   [228] See e.g. Dupeux, *Aspects*, p. 402.

[229] Constant, 'Var', IV, p. 1217, V, p. 1417.

The regime's liberalising measures in 1868 transformed the situation. 'Freedom' of the press and of meetings allowed the *petits républicains de village* to re-appear and provided them with 'a powerful weapon'.[230] It injected a new dynamism into republican agitation. The local press took up the themes of the capital's newspapers. As 'the extreme revolutionary press spreads . . . without restriction through the countryside', once again officials complained that republican activists threatened to 'corrupt' the peasants.[231] In condemning *L'Indépendent de Pau*, the local prosecutor complained of 'a system based on slander, lies, electoral programmes subversive of order, abuse, and personal attacks against everyone who represents, to any degree, social hierarchy, stability, truth, the good and just; re-calling the worst days of the republic'.[232]

The revival of peasant interest in republican politics was associated by the authorities with wider processes of social change and especially migration and the growing 'indiscipline' of those who remained in the countryside. There was concern amongst conservative landowners about what was seen to be the growing 'absence of religious and moral principles'.[233] Not untypically, the Comice agricole at Varennes (Haute-Marne) pointed out that 'the standard of morality of workers in the countryside has fallen to a frightening extent, due to easier contact with the towns, reading newspapers which mainly address themselves to the uneducated, and initiate them into the most perverse theories . . . ; lastly due to the influence of secret societies which today have their representatives everywhere'. The result was that 'the fine slogan liberty, equality, fraternity, is supported by those who understand it and practice it the least' and for whom 'liberty is licence; equality a universal levelling down; and fraternity a brutal familiarity'. From this there followed what was perceived to be an inevitable deterioration in social relationships.[234]

The 1869 general election revealed substantial republican minorities in the east – in Côte-d'Or, the southern Doubs, northern Jura, and along the Rhône-Saône corridor, in the south in the coastal regions of Provence and Languedoc, and in the south-west in the Garonne valley. Substantial continuities were apparent with the results in 1849, with the revival of support from amongst the rural population in departments on the Mediterranean coast and south-east (Bouches-du-Rhône, Vaucluse, Var, Basses-Alpes, Drôme, Hérault, Pyrénées-Orientales). These were areas in which the experience of the Second Republic had served to consolidate or awaken

---

[230] Sous-préfet Semur quoted Vigreux, *Paysans et notables*, p. 434.
[231] PG Bourges, 8 July 1869, AN BB30/389.   [232] PG Pau, 22 Oct. 1869, AN BB30/389.
[233] Reponse of M. de Cosse, landowner at Courville (Eure-et-Loir), AN C1156.   [234] AN C1159.

republican sympathies. At his most optimistic, the republican journalist Eugène Ténot could claim that '1848 . . . did not happen in vain . . . in more than 50 departments there is not a village, or perhaps a hamlet, where peasants have not preserved a faithful and fervent memory of what they then learned to love'.[235] Although much weaker, there were also signs of support for the republic in economically more advanced rural areas of the north and in upper Normandy and the Paris basin.

There are no simple explanations, but at least four factors should be taken into account – long-established family and community loyalties promoting faction divisions; the nature of local social relationships; the general political context including the scale and character of official intervention; and the gradual development of republican agitation. The use by republicans of the threat of higher taxes and increased conscription, associated with the government's proposals for military reform, proved especially potent, increasing the movement's appeal even amongst *des campagnards honnêtes*.[236] A 'black legend' focusing on imperial extravagance, and the waste of men and money, was being (re)-constructed in an effort to demystify the state and destroy its inherited prestige. The Republic was presented as the solution to every ill. In the impoverished countryside of the central Morvan, M. Tenaille-Saligny presented himself in 1869 as the candidate of 'radical democracy' and defender of the peasants against the sitting official candidate Lepéletier d'Aunay, representative, he claimed, solely of the interests of the big landowners. Questions of national politics were combined with local issues. In this case republicanism was associated with an ongoing struggle with absentee aristocratic landowners and their agents over access to the forests, which offered invaluable pasture for impoverished peasant farmers. Isolation and loose administrative control proved to be a further advantage, with poor communications in an area of forest and dispersed hamlets effectively depriving conservative Bonapartists of administrative support.[237]

Pierre Lévêque has shown how stable minorities strongly committed to the République démocratique et sociale survived in rural areas of the Côte-d'Or and particularly amongst the vine cultivators in the area between Gevray and Nolay. Typically these militants were relatively well educated, resident in large market villages (*bourgs*), and small towns with distinctive patterns of sociability, and as a result were able to preserve a considerable

[235] *Le suffrage universel et les paysans*, p. 24.
[236] PI Draguignan, 17 June 1869, quoted Constant, 'Var', IV, p. 1321.
[237] M. Vigreux, 'Des paysans républicains à la fin du Second Empire: les élections de 1869 dans le Morvan nivernais', *Revue d'histoire moderne et contemporaine* 1972, p. 444.

degree of independence. Together with artisans and professionals they were able to influence the populations of the surrounding marketing-cultural zones.[238] A process of geographical diffusion of republican sentiments occurred which was described by many contemporary observers as involving the spread of ideas and organisation from the larger administrative and marketing centres towards the smaller, predominantly agrarian, communities and along the main route ways.[239] As the sous-préfet at Chalon had observed in 1850, in the aftermath of a major cholera epidemic, 'ideas, like epidemics, propagate themselves along the major valleys'.[240] Employing similar imagery the state prosecutor at Lyon observed that 'along the railway lines, along the banks of the Saône and Rhône, it is possible to follow, with the votes, the progress of this contagious disease'.[241]

On 1 May 1870 it was the railway which brought the Parisian lawyer Floquet to Béziers, another major centre of agitation during the Second Republic, to address a crowd of over 1,200 people, including the representatives of over thirty rural communities who would be expected to pass on the message in their own villages subsequently.[242] Although public meetings gave an air of modernity to political campaigning, the direct transmission of information between close acquaintances, *de bouche à oreille*, was probably more effective. In the north-east of Haute-Vienne and north-west of Creuse in 1869 republican candidates gained over 30 per cent of the vote in cantons enjoying close contact with Paris and Lyon through itinerant peasant-masons.[243] Complaints about the influence of peasant-workers with links to urban republicanism also came from the Nivernais, from which rafts of wood were floated down-river to Paris,[244] and from the Var, where workers producing corks were concentrated in the small workshops of towns like La Garde Freinet.[245]

Although the structure and efficiency of communications networks is relevant to a discussion of the diffusion of political ideas, simple correlations between the geography of communications and political attitudes are best avoided, however. The rural populations of an 'advanced' area like the Nord – urbanised and with relatively dense communications networks – long resisted republicanism, whilst peasants in some isolated, 'backward' regions of the central Massif adhered to the republic. The presence of influential personalities, local social relationships, and the intensity of faction

[238] P. Lévêque, 'Décembre 1851: faibles réactions en pays rouges. Le cas de la Saône-et-Loire', *Revue d'histoire du 19e siècle* 2001/1, pp. 65–8, 71–4.
[239] E.g. PG Grenoble, 7 July 1869, AN BB30/389.
[240] 27 March 1850 quoted Lévêque, *Bourgogne*, IV, p. 1362.   [241] 27 June 1863, AN BB30/379.
[242] GOC 10e DM, 6 May 1870, AHG G8/176.   [243] Corbin, *Archaïsme*, II, p. 900.
[244] Chatelain, *Migrants temporaires*, II, p. 1084.   [245] PG Aix, 24 Jan. 1870, AN BB30/390.

rivalry were also relevant, as was the varying appeal of a variety of competing political messages. Simple awareness of a political programme, whether
republican or Bonapartist, clearly did not ensure its acceptance.

Similarly, it is unsafe to establish correlations between literacy and politicisation, although Lévêque's point ought to be considered, that voting
remained 'more instinctive than reasoned' in relatively isolated areas of
Bourgogne with high levels of illiteracy and that this ensured that allegiances were comparatively fickle. He takes the example of the canton of
Mesvres in which 75 per cent of the voters supported an electoral list headed
by the radical republican Ledru-Rollin in April 1848; 93.5 per cent voted
for Louis-Napoleon in December (and only 0.2 per cent for Ledru); 71
per cent supported the *démocrate-socialistes* in May 1849, whilst 1,512 voters
legitimised the *coup d'état* on 20 December 1851 and only 10 condemned
the Prince-President's actions. Subsequently there would be almost unanimous, and indeed enthusiastic support for the Emperor, who brought
order and prosperity, in marked contrast to the misery associated with the
republic.[246]

Similar trends might be identified in a number of other departments in
the western Massif Central (Creuse, Corrèze, Dordogne, Haute-Vienne)
and further north (Allier, Cher, Nièvre, Saône-et-Loire) in all of which
commitment to the republican cause appears to have been sustained far less
strongly. In the Gers, and much of the Limousin, areas that had appeared
strongly republican in 1849 turned into strongholds of Bonapartism.[247]
Were these apparent shifts in opinion proof of ignorance and naïvety on
the part of peasant voters, or perfectly rational responses to changing circumstances based on an essential continuity of aims and objectives?

Exactly how peasants responded to local and national republican politicians is difficult to determine. In all likelihood there were substantial differences between their world-view and that of the essentially bourgeois
political leaders who claimed to represent their interests. The character of
Dr Fauconnet in Guillaumin's *La vie d'un simple* might be taken to represent the rural bourgeoisie – 'he was a republican and kept up a determined
opposition to the local *gros bourgeois* and to the government of Badinguet'.
Even when visiting the sick he would seize the opportunity to proclaim his
commitment to 'the tax on capital, the suppression of permanent armies
and labour service, and to free education', as well as his loyalty to the exiled
and irreconcilable Victor Hugo and all the victims of the *coup d'état*. This

[246] Lévêque, *Bourgogne*, vol. IV, pp. 1523–4.   [247] Palmade, 'Gers', p. 185.

went together with his contempt for the village mayor and its 'incompetent' municipal council. His peasant interlocutor, Tiennon, had his misgivings, however: 'Without doubt, he would have done more for the people by visiting the sick regularly and by charging them less for his visits, than by holding forth every day in the café.'

Social relations were influenced by everyday relationships, and the realities of economic dependence, as well as by the memories and myths of the *ancien régime* and Revolution. The primary focus was on concrete local grievances. Abstract terms like liberty were related to personal experience. Prosperity, freedom from debt, and the ability to purchase land were all vital objectives. In the peasants' ideal world communal autonomy would probably have been reinforced and taxation and conscription abolished. Private property was sacrosanct, although the 'rich' who seemed to possess property in excess and use it for speculative or exploitative purposes might be subject to moralising criticism. 'Universal' suffrage had come to be seen as a means by which these goals might be attained. For peasants, 'liberty is a means, not an end. If they want it, it is not for itself, but for the guarantees it appears to offer; notably to be able to make their needs known publicly and to defend their interests.'[248]

Republican politicians enjoyed success where they were able to establish links between peasant aspirations and their own political ideology, largely through the activities of local militants working to persuade peasants to consider 'the republic as the ideal of progress'.[249] In many areas the ground was prepared by successive local elections. In an effort to attract support during the conseil général election at Givry (Saône-et-Loire) in 1867, for example, the democratic candidate Meulien, a retired cloth merchant and landowner, became an honorary member of the local *vignerons'* and artisans' association and of the mutual aid society, presenting each with a gift of 50f. He established close links with republican militants in every village and organised frequent meetings in their cafés. The local police *commissaire* noted that 'M. Meulien makes his rounds every day, visiting the communes in his big carriage drawn by two horses.'[250]

From around 1867 the politicisation of leisure activities was again evident, as it had been during the Second Republic, and was combined frequently with the creation of informal local electoral organisations. In addition to the ubiquitous cafés, many areas, and especially the larger villages, saw an

[248] PG Paris, 9 May 1866, AN BB30/384. [249] PG Agen, 9 Jan. 1869, AN BB30/389.
[250] Goujon, *Vigneron citoyen*, p. 283.

increase in the number and range of voluntary groups including masonic lodges and especially *chambrées* and musical associations. In the Gard, for example, sixty *orphéons* were founded between 1859 and 1866, some of them offering a disguise for political debate and organisation.[251] This (re-) politicisation of the cafés and *chambrées* owed much to the press. Many café proprietors had subscribed to the very moderate republican newspaper *Le Siècle*, which had been tolerated by the government throughout the 1850s. In November 1860, a report from the Jura observed that newspapers were far less common than in 1848, 'but those which the people are especially likely to have to hand, and on which the village political leaders draw are *le Siècle, la Presse* or *l'Opinion nationale*', with the first by far the most influential. Generally peasants themselves read very little, but newspapers were read aloud and commented upon by 'the village leader'.[252] By the late 1860s, more radical regional newspapers like the *Rappel de la Provence* were often preferred. Alone amongst the republican newspapers in Provence the *Rappel* appears to have made a special effort to appeal to peasants. Its low cost (12 francs a year) encouraged many *chambrées* to take out a collective subscription.[253]

In general the republican programme for the countryside was less radical than that of the *démocrate-socialistes* in 1849/51. The promise of cheap credit to enable peasants to acquire land and escape from debt had largely disappeared. Moreover, both the authorities and many republicans were increasingly alarmed by the violence of the language employed by radical journalists whose main concern was to appeal to an urban audience. Moderate republicans committed to legalism were anxious to refute official claims that they were advocates of socialism and violence, and concerned that the threat of revolution might alienate rural voters.[254]

The response of the twenty-three delegates of the Draguignan *chambrées* to Emile Ollivier's accusation that they were planning violence is indicative not only of their determination to protect their reputation but of the robust character of political debate by 1869. Ollivier was informed that 'You have dared to tell a lie and to exude slander.' Furthermore, 'You have dared to say that on the day of triumph we will strike the rich: We protest against these words, which are a gross insult and a lie, all the more hideous because it is so self-interested. You are afraid that the new generation will demand vengeance . . . but then the crime of 2 December was so great!' However,

---

[251] Huard, 'Préhistoire', III, pp. 695–6.
[252] PG Besançon, 19 Nov. 1860, AN BB30/373; see also PG Pau, 15 April 1865, AN BB30/384.
[253] PG Aix, 24 Jan., 19 April 1870, AN BB30/390.
[254] E.g. PG Grenoble, 6 April 1870, AN BB30/390.

they freely admitted that, 'what we do say in our *chambrées*, is that we are determined to demand relentlessly the rights snatched from the nation by a detestable power. What we do say is that we want to conquer education, reduce taxation, reform conscription, destroy pluralism, abolish personal rule, and finally create the perfect government! *La République démocratique et sociale.*' This was published in *La Sentinelle* on 2 May 1870 and then taken up in Paris by *L'Avenir national* and in Marseille by *L'Egalité.* The prefect immediately closed eleven of the *chambrées* whose delegates had signed this missive.[255]

In the villages of the Haute-Saône *La Cloche* and *La Marseillaise* spread the message.[256] The ephemeral nature of many of these newspapers reflected both continuing harassment by the administration and the weakness of the republican movement, especially in rural areas. Nevertheless, their creation represented a vital stage in the development of a mass movement, establishing as it did – in the absence of modern party structures – a network of local correspondents/political militants and linking individual activists to the 'party'. Together with public meetings and less formal gatherings, the newspapers provided direct links between bourgeois political leaders and the masses. Even in areas like the Pays de Sault, isolated in the Pyrenees and with high levels of illiteracy, as a result of easier distribution by post and lower cost the left-wing press appears to have circulated far more widely in 1869 than it had in 1849.[257] A substantial body of rural support for the Republic was emerging.

The resurrection of republicanism was far from general, however. It would be neither as intensive nor as extensive as during the Second Republic. Peasants in some former areas of republican strength like the Limousin had succumbed to the attractions of Bonapartism. More generally, the interest of peasants in politics remained diffuse and intermittent. They continued to accept members of other social groups as their political representatives. Nevertheless, the practice of universal suffrage probably did something to enhance the peasant's self-image. There were signs that a more prosperous and better-educated population was less willing to accept authoritarian government passively. The procureur général at Besançon, for one, warned that voters were exasperated with official 'interference' in elections.[258] Peasants were increasingly determined to make use of the electoral process to express criticism of the regime and their social superiors by supporting opposition candidates.

---

[255] Constant, *Var*, v, p. 1382.   [256] PG Besançon, 12 April 1870, AN BB30/390.
[257] Thibon, *Pays de Sault*, p. 138.   [258] 13 July 1863, AN BB30/389.

CONCLUSION

The sometimes-heated debate amongst historians concerning the chronology and degree of peasant politicisation has been confused by different definitions of 'politicisation'. Terminological and geographical variations account for many of their differences. Thus, in his book *Peasants into Frenchmen*, Eugen Weber distinguished between a concern with local affairs and personalities and a 'modern' politics based upon ideology and national concerns. By definition, peasants become 'pre-political' or 'apolitical' when their behaviour is contrasted with an idealised conception of the informed, rational voter. However, one wonders to what extent, even in the twenty-first century, voters make an informed choice between alternative philosophies. Weber claimed that for peasants 'national politics became relevant when national affairs were seen to affect the persons and localities involved'. He then proceeded to claim that this did not occur 'in those parts of rural France that I have looked at' – essentially the west, centre, and Midi – until after the 1870s.[259] His second thoughts[260] significantly brought this forward into the 1860s. Nevertheless, it seems clear that, in most regions, many peasants became 'aware' of politics much earlier. Memories of the past, of the *ancien régime*, Revolution, and First Empire established sympathies and predispositions, stimulated aspirations and generated anxieties, which were modified by the further experience of revolution in 1830 and particularly 1848, and by a prolonged, even if constricted, 'apprenticeship in democracy' during the Second Empire.

As Weber suggests, politicisation can be related to wider processes of integration into the nation, which gradually reduced the autonomy of rural communities, including more uniform bureaucracy, commerce, migration, military service, and education. The establishment of manhood suffrage in 1848 was a vital part of this process of integration. The holding of regular elections established the habit of voting and the use of the vote as a means of judging governments and of expressing or withholding support. Even under the system of official candidature prevailing throughout the Second Empire it was clear that a regime which claimed to base its legitimacy on popular sovereignty felt bound to respond to the perceptions of public opinion produced by the official reporting system and found it increasingly hard to reject democratic aspirations.

It is difficult to establish what voting meant in rural communes. Simplifying urban/rural and archaic/modern contrasts are only too commonplace

---

[259] Weber, *Peasants*, pp. 241–2.   [260] 'Comment la politique vint aux paysans', p. 358.

in the observations of nineteenth-century observers and historians. They are implicit in the diffusionist model of politicisation, involving the 'descente de la politique vers les masses', associated with Maurice Agulhon's pathbreaking study of *La République au village*, in which he sought to identify the social structures which facilitated an 'interpenetration . . . between *bourgeoise* and popular culture'.[261] This chapter has attempted to define more complex processes involving the diffusion of conservative as well as democratic ideas. Thus the possession of power and authority by landowners, employers, and the clergy ensured that they were regarded with respect and deference and even fear by most of the rural population. The Catholic Church played a major part in securing adherence to notions of a God-ordained, hierarchical social order. Primary instruction further contributed to the development of an internalised sense of inferiority. Subordination, and additionally the reciprocal, inter-personal obligations created in response to material insecurity, frequently established an almost overpowering sense of community. These were all emotions which might have promoted submissive behaviour.

In 1848 the radical republican newspaper *La Réforme* (24 March 1848) had expressed its concerns about the newly enfranchised peasant electorate, in denigrating terms similar to those used by Marx in his explanation of peasant conservatism in 'The Eighteenth Brumaire of Louis-Napoleon Bonaparte': 'Vassals of misery, they are still tethered to the glebe of ignorance; prejudices and ancient superstitions envelop them.' Another republican newspaper, the *Commune de Paris* (24 March 1848), warned that

in so many places political life hardly exists, intellectual activity is virtually non-existent. No political newspapers penetrate into these backward villages, almost excluded from the world. Gothic prejudices are still powerful and the idioms of the past allow the moral night to survive. . . . The efforts of the primary school teachers, these martyrs of our epoch, do not win the sympathies of the impoverished countryman, entirely absorbed by the care of his field and of his dung heap.

Throughout the Second Empire republican politicians would continue to blame failure on both the corruption of the electoral process and the 'ignorance' of the rural population. They were at pains to deny the regime legitimacy precisely because of its dependence on the peasant vote. Jules Ferry in a pamphlet on *Les élections de 1863* castigated peasant stupidity and ignorance, accusing them of blindly following the government's instructions.[262] In 1865 the influential journalist Eugène Ténot, in *Le suffrage*

---

[261] M. Agulhon, *La République au village* (Paris 1970), p. 239.
[262] J. Ferry, *Discours et opinions*, 1 (Paris 1893), p. 50.

universel et les paysans, claimed that it was simply ignorance and not administrative pressure which rendered peasants unfit to 'exercise sovereign power'. He bemoaned the fact that 'most peasants do not know how to read; many did learn and have forgotten; and amongst those able to read, how many never bother? To this primordial ignorance, mother of all others, might be added the most profound and incredible ignorance of politics.'[263] In two memorable phrases, the liberal politician Prévost-Paradol would describe the regime itself as a *campagnocratie impériale*, dependent on *bestialité provinciale*.[264] Conservatives similarly viewed peasants with suspicion, as intellectual and moral inferiors, the potential foundation for a stable social order, but always in danger of being led astray.[265] The word *paysan* was fast becoming a term of abuse.[266]

The 1870 plebiscite would prove to be a massive shock to republicans. It seemed clear that if peasants were increasingly likely to support republican candidates in local and even general elections when particular interests were being considered, in contrast, in a plebiscite, when the future of the regime itself appeared to be in question, they were likely to turn back towards an emperor for whom considerable latent respect survived. The Prefect of the Creuse had already pointed out in 1853 that, 'demagogy is far from having been defeated in the Creuse; if it is a matter of electing deputies, and the population was left to itself, the result would be bad'. However, he added that 'if it was a question of again voting for the Emperor they would once more be carried away with enthusiasm' as in December 1848.[267]

Clearly historians need to consider exactly how ideas were received and the extent to which the 'instrumentalisation of the procedures of the national debate' occurred, 'as a means of achieving locally defined objectives'.[268] Thus a conservative or Bonapartist vote need not necessarily represent ignorance, apathy or fear. It might also result from judgements based upon a negative experience of revolutionary upheaval or the positive association of the imperial regime with order and prosperity. Conversely, whilst rejection of 'subordination' together with support for the republic might

---

[263] Pp. 24–5.
[264] Quoted P. Vigier, 'La République, l'Anjou, la France', *Annales de Bretagne* 1992, p. 560.
[265] PG Paris, 5 Aug. 1863, AN BB30/384.
[266] J. Dubois, *Le vocabulaire politique et social en France de 1869 à 1872* (Paris 1962), pp. 85–7.
[267] ? June 1853, AN F1 C111 Creuse 8.
[268] A. Corbin, 'La violence rurale dans la France du 19e siècle et son dépérissement: l'évolution de l'interprétation politique' in *La violence politique dans les démocraties européennes occidentales* (Paris 1993), p. 65.

be the consequence of a process of political liberalisation, of education, and greater individual autonomy, they might alternatively be the product of a folk memory of exploitation or oppression, resulting from conflict within a community, or simply a determination to vote against any government which proposed to extend conscription and increase taxation. It seems perverse to dismiss such judgements as somehow pre-political.

CHAPTER 6

The formation of a working class

INTRODUCTION

As historians have come to question the use of 'class' as an analytical category, and to stress the danger of simplification implicit in the 'reification' of any analytical category, a vigorous debate has occurred concerning the viability of the concept of a 'working class'. Jacques Rancière has gone so far as to suggest that the notion is simply a fictional construct created by romantically inclined and woolly minded intellectuals with a commitment to the under-privileged.[1] Was the 'working class' nothing more than an illusion? Current orthodoxy would probably insist that social identity, the sense of belonging to a particular group, is the creation of a constant inter-relationship between discourse – the linguistic, cultural, and symbolic associations which establish an individual's sense of place and status – and experience – that of the day-to-day, of longer-term social change, and of political 'events'. Discourse gives meaning to experience; experience constantly modifies discourse. Perceptions, rather than some objective reality, determine behaviour. As an alternative to class, historians have (re-)discovered the family and community – the basic units of socialisation, as well as a variety of cultural and political institutions, focusing on relationships which invariably cut across those of class. Gender and generation have additionally become topics of primary concern.

It might, nevertheless, be argued that family and community relationships and both gendered and generational experience were to a large degree class specific, and that class remains an analytical key vital to our understanding of social inequality and competition for power. The focus of this and the following chapter will be the existential experience of diverse groups of workers, rooted in the workplace and in the family's struggle to make ends meet, together with the impact on the workers' social

[1] J. Rancière, 'The myth of the artisan: critical reflections on a category of social history' in S. Kaplan and C. Koepp (eds.), *Work in France* (London 1986), pp. 317f.

consciousness of a range of competing discourses. Relationships between workers and other social groups were also crucial determinants of social consciousness. Those with employers, landlords, shopkeepers, innkeepers, officials, policemen, teachers, and priests, were particularly significant. These were people who offered work, charity, and advice and who, through day-to-day relationships, contributed to the workers' own definition of social order and construction of value systems. They assisted in the establishment of behavioural norms, which were internalised, resisted, or re-interpreted by workers themselves. Both conflict and cooperation with the members of other groups contributed to an emerging sense of identity, although it does need to be borne in mind that 'various collective identities may be relevant to individuals at different times and in different contexts'.[2]

The effectiveness of the regulatory authority of state and church also has to be assessed. The range of what was legally and practically possible varied over time, and so too did the popular awareness of and interest in whatever political drama was being played out – for much of the time mainly by members of other social groups. The socio-economic situation was also rapidly changing. From the 1840s workers were required to adapt to 'fundamental changes in the organisation of production, conditions of work, community organisation and politics'.[3] This suggests something of the difficulty of analysing a transition society, and hints at the shifting importance of a variety of causal factors over time.

SOURCES

As always the nature of the sources is of fundamental importance. Very few workers committed their thoughts to paper. Almost by definition the autobiographer was not the typical worker. He or she generally offers glimpses into the lives of a small minority of relatively well-educated and/or committed militants.[4] The contributors to the workers' newspaper *L'Atelier* in the 1840s[5] claimed to represent the *classe ouvrière* whilst writing about the world of the skilled artisan. Linguistically too, their efforts deform day-to-day practice. Generally the language used is more polished than

---

[2] Gould, *Insurgent Identities*, p. 14.
[3] I. Katznelson, 'Working-class formation: constructing cases and comparisons', in I. Katznelson and A. Zolberg (eds.), *Working-Class Formation. Nineteenth-century Patterns in Western Europe and the United States* (Princeton, N.J. 1986), p. 22.
[4] M. Traugott (ed.), *The French Worker. Autobiographies from the Early Industrial Era* (Berkeley, Calif. 1993), Introduction; M. J. Maynes, *Taking the Hard Road. Life Course in French and German Workers' Autobiographies in the Era of Industrialization* (London 1995), pp. 4–5.
[5] A. Cuvillier, *Un journal d'ouvriers: L'Atelier, 1840–50* (Paris 1954), *passim*.

the everyday discourse of the streets and workplaces, employing reasonably correct French rather than *argot* or local patois. The informal discourse of the home, workplace, or café thus remains largely inaccessible. In addition whole realms of everyday experience are rarely described.

Songs, pamphlets, newspapers, almanacs, speeches, even graffiti painstakingly copied from walls by the police, together with the less reliable accounts of conversations overheard in bars or on the streets, all appear to offer 'authentic' insights into a discourse that was both spontaneous and stereotyped. They record the often malicious, 'offstage comments'[6] which allow brief and limited insights into the worker's self-image and attitudes towards social superiors and government. The short periods of relative freedom afforded by revolution, strikes, and even election campaigns, are especially valuable for the relative abundance of documentary and iconographic material they throw up. This reveals the sense of emotional release, the shortlived atmosphere of *fête*, and sense of engagement in the crowd. But how representative are these fragments from the past?

Invariably, as a result of the paucity of information generated by workers themselves, the historian remains heavily dependent on 'external' sources and especially official reports and quasi-official enquiries, and on the generally condescending and frequently contemptuous views expressed in academic and journalistic reports. Whenever they were aware of the presence of such observers, however, workers were likely to feel inhibited. Daily insecurity bred caution and constant self-censorship. It is also vital to bear in mind the difficulty non-workers faced in understanding behaviour, language, and gestures foreign to their own experience.[7] It is difficult to penetrate beyond the mask of dissimulation, represented in enquiries which depended on the cooperation of the capitalist class and on that of selected workers, frequently deferential and anxious to conform to the image the powerful wanted to present of them.

There was a time when historians looked to statistical data for some precision. The establishment of the Statistique générale de la France in 1833 represented growing concern within the socio-political elite about the social consequences of economic change and rapid urbanisation. In practice the results of both population censuses and industrial enquiries were extremely imprecise. The census offers only a particular construction of 'reality'. Awareness of the assumptions of those who defined its objectives, of the construction of the categories employed, and the questions asked,

---

[6] Scott, *Weapons of the Weak*, p. 41.
[7] E.g. P. Ansart, 'Des identités de métier à l'identité de classe, un devenir paradoxal?', *L'Homme et la société* 1995, pp. 103, 107.

is crucially important.[8] Census categories changed, making comparisons over time particularly difficult. The statisticians ignored the frequency with which workers, in their struggle to make ends meet, were forced to change professions in order to secure work, as well as the ease with which, in the skilled trades, employers and employees might experience a temporary or even permanent change of status. Other major sources of information are similarly problematic. The first industrial enquiry conducted between 1839 and 1845 covered only *grande industrie*, and even this was never clearly defined. Typically there was widespread suspicion that the questions asked were linked to an official effort to increase tax revenue, something hardly calculated to promote honest responses.[9] The *Enquête industrielle* conducted between 1861 and 1865 would again meet considerable ill will especially from employers determined to protest against the introduction of 'free' trade in 1860.[10]

The enquiry conducted by the Paris Chamber of Commerce in 1847/8 (which determined the format of that of 1860) was similarly flawed. It only covered the city, as it was then defined, ignoring the suburbs annexed in 1860. Commerce was excluded. The numerous casual labourers at work in the city were largely ignored. The large numbers of impoverished and dissatisfied master-craftsmen were counted as *industriels*. This procedure had the advantage of diminishing the number of workers, and established an image of the 'worker' as a relatively well-off and literate artisan. It 'proved' that 'in normal times, the working population of Paris leads a satisfactory existence in all respects'.[11] This was a politically significant conclusion to reach in a year of revolution and justifies Joan Scott's assertion that 'statistical reports were weapons in the debate on the *social question*'.[12] The same might be said of the many enquiries and official reports on social conditions. One partial exception was the national enquiry into working conditions and workers' lives launched in the aftermath of the February Revolution.[13] Employers and workers' delegates in every canton in France were invited to respond to a vaguely worded questionnaire and in some

---

[8] See e.g. M. Perrot, *Les enquêtes sur la condition ouvrière en France au 19e siècle* (Paris 1972), p. 11; T. J. Markovitch, 'Statistiques industrielles et systèmes politiques' in *Pour une histoire de la statistique* (Paris 1977), p. 317; J.-M. Chanut, J. Heffer, J. Mairesse, and G. Postel-Vinay, *L'industrie française au milieu du 19e siècle. Les enquêtes de la Statistique générale de la France* (Paris 2000), pp. 6–7.

[9] Chanut *et al.*, *L'industrie française*, pp. 15–17.

[10] M. Boivin, *Le mouvement ouvrier dans la région de Rouen, 1851–76* (Rouen 1989), vol. I, p. 12.

[11] *Statistique de l'industrie à Paris, 1847–8* (Paris 1851), p. 61.

[12] J. Scott, 'Statistical representations of work: the politics of the Chamber of Commerce's Statistique de l'industrie à Paris, 1847–8' in Kaplan and Koepp, *Work in France*, p. 335; see also C. Lemercier, *Un si discret pouvoir. Aux origines de la chambre de commerce de Paris* (Paris 2003), pp. 242–62.

[13] Assemblée constituante, *Enquête sur le travail agriculturel et industriel, loi de 25 mai 1848* – AN C943.

instances workers' representatives seized the opportunity. However, the organising role given to the juges de paix helped ensure a conservative bias in the membership of local committees and in the presentation of their responses.[14]

The influx of population from the over-populated countryside into the towns, and the pathological conditions created by overcrowding, under-employment, and poverty, provoked a growing fear of crime and disorder, which prompted substantial investigations in the 1830/40s. Invariably, the authors of these reports sought to impose a 'scientific' discourse on the descriptive language of their reports. Subsequently, provided with quotable examples, and impressed by the detail provided by the likes of Louis Villermé in his *Tableau de l'état physique et moral des ouvriers employés dans les manufactures de coton, de laine, et de soie* (2 vols., Paris 1840), historians have themselves concentrated on the extremes of misery. Jules Michelet was scathing at the time. In *Le Peuple* (1846) he condemned 'Noble writers . . . who . . . have undertaken, with the best of intentions, to make the people fashionable', but who 'have described, under the name of the people, a very limited class, whose lives, full of accidents, violence, and aggression, offer them colourful scenes, and a literary success based on the terror these inspire.'[15]

The various enquiries tend to equate the poor in general with the 'under-class', the so-called *classes dangereuses*, Marx's lumpenproletariat, made up of recent migrants experiencing something akin to the desperate misery of third-world shanty towns. What was exceptional, extreme – the hideous slums of the rue d'Etaques in Lille, for example – tended to be represented as normal, and as epitomising the problems caused by the moral degradation of the labouring classes. A 'culture of poverty' was identified which, it was claimed, resulted from the moral inadequacy and the innate inferiority of the working masses, who were represented as congenitally unable to resist the temptations of alcohol and vice and unwilling to make the effort necessary to escape from their ignorance. The poor were blamed for their own misery.

However, more optimistic assessments of popular morality and living standards also began to emerge. At a time when social order and prosperity both appeared to have been restored after the mid-century crisis, and during the authoritarian empire, the rhetoric changed in tone, contrasting,

---

[14] E.g. C. Johnson, 'Afterword' to Kaplan and Koepp, *Work in France*, p. 560; J. Charon-Bordas, *Ouvriers et paysans au milieu du 19e siècle, l'enquête de 1848 sur la travail* (Paris 1994), Introduction.
[15] 1979 edn, p. 15.

instead of equating the *classes dangereuses* with the *classes laborieuses*.[16] The latter were identified, on the basis of middle-class norms of behaviour, by their work ethic and respectful attitude towards their 'superiors'. As early as 1850 the economist Adolphe Blanqui whose previous, extremely pessimistic, reports on social conditions had made a considerable impression, felt obliged to admit that he had exaggerated by ascribing to workers in general conditions which were experienced by only marginal elements.[17] It was accepted increasingly that economic development would result in the improvement of living standards and the progressive integration of the working class into the emerging capitalist society. More efficient policing would contain those perverse individuals who had already been tempted by revolution in 1848.[18] However, the deterioration of the social climate in the later 1860s, and the growing numbers of strikes would again arouse doubts, engendering the kind of social fear which would lead in 1871 to military repression even more bloody than that of June 1848.

The shortcomings of the routine administrative and police reports on which historians continue to depend have already been rehearsed in previous chapters. However, there are often no alternative sources of information, and at least the reporting systems in place during the Second Empire, especially those organised around the procureurs généraux, were of a *relatively* high quality in terms of the range of information provided and the effort to achieve some degree of 'objectivity'. Nevertheless, their focus was generally restricted, and concentrated, not surprisingly, on protest and political unrest and upon the search for illegal organisations. The level of surveillance also varied over time, becoming much more intense when the authorities were anxious about popular unrest. Thus, invariably, reporting was selective and heavily biased. There is also a risk that excessive reliance on administrative reporting promotes an unhealthy interest in conflict. Moreover, a mass of actions went unnoticed and unreported or else was regarded as unworthy of comment. Officials, like historians, were also too likely to ascribe a definite sense of purpose to workers' activities. The desire to understand easily leads to the imposition of neat explanatory patterns on confused situations. All the historian can do is avoid taking evidence simply at face value, and adopt a critical approach, which compares, contrasts, and contextualises. Reconstructing the 'mental universe of ordinary men and women

[16] E.g. H. Baudrillart, 'Du progrès économique, ses conditions, son état présent', *Journal des Economistes*, 20, 1858, p. 374.
[17] Debate at Académie des sciences morales et politiques reported ibid. 26, 1850, p. 62.
[18] E.g. A. Audiganne, *Revue des Deux Mondes*, Sept. 1851, p. 895.

in the past'[19] and explaining their behaviour thus requires a considerable effort.

THE SOCIAL CONTEXT

Although the emphasis on the primacy of economic structures favoured by Marx and such eminent historians as Braudel and Labrousse in the 1960s and 1970s is no longer in fashion, it remains essential to consider what workers did and where they did it. In this respect, it is important to stress immediately the heterogeneity of the working-class experience. It seems evident that a wide variety of technologies and forms of industrial organisation, and distinctive local patterns of industrial activity, offered employment to workers with very different levels of skill, rewarded them in different ways, and created patterns of social interaction – and of conflict – which were extremely varied.

The workplace

During the Second Empire the stimulus afforded by major infrastructural investment and booming international trade presented entrepreneurs with new opportunities but in more competitive markets. As a result, the centre of gravity of French industry shifted quite decisively in favour of large-scale enterprise, due to the introduction of new techniques and of new forms of work organisation and discipline. 'Modern' industrial France with its steam power, mechanisation, and the concentration of production, its textile mills, iron and engineering works, coal mines, and over-populated popular *quartiers* developed mainly to the east of a line Le Havre–Marseille in departments like the Nord where workers made up around 52 per cent of the population, Seine (50 per cent), Seine-Inférieure, Bas-Rhin, Ardennes, Somme, Aisne, Rhône, and Loire (over 40 per cent). According to an official enquiry by 1866 of 2,898,000 industrial workers 52 per cent were employed in textiles and clothing; 16.5 per cent in the building trades; 10.56 per cent in metal working; 8.5 per cent in wood working; 5.5 per cent in the preparation of food; 4 per cent in the extractive industries; 2 per cent in paper making; and 1 per cent in chemicals.[20]

In textiles, factory production was most highly developed in Alsace, where firms specialised in high-quality cotton printing, and to a lesser

[19] W. Sewell, *Work and Revolution in France. The Language of Labor from the Old Regime to 1848* (Cambridge 1980), p. 10.
[20] Tulard, *Dictionnaire*, p. 946.

degree in the Nord (Lille-Roubaix-Tourcoing) and in the Rouen area. Small and medium-sized enterprises using water power, as well as dispersed rural weaving, survived for as long as they were able to take advantage of inexpensive workers.[21] Nevertheless, they were becoming less competitive, both as a result of technical change and migration, which reduced the supply of cheap labour. Whereas in the first half of the century industrial buildings had multiplied along the water courses of some hundred industrial valleys, increased use of the steam engine led to the desertion of the river valleys for sites close to railway depots and coal supplies in the suburbs of centres like Mulhouse, Rouen, and Lille. In these cities substantial capital was invested in new steam engines and machinery – in self-acting mules to spin all except the finest quality yarns, and in power looms for weaving – as well as in the buildings to house them. Growing competitive pressure was placed on older, smaller, and under-capitalised enterprises, forcing them to reduce costs or go out of business. To get the most out of their machinery, employers were forced to introduce frequent modifications to secure its smoother and more rapid operation and to demand more assiduous and intensive effort on the part of their employees.[22] The effects of cyclical and exceptional crises intensified competitive pressures.

Similarly, in metallurgy, market integration led to the rapid concentration of production in large, integrated plants employing coke for smelting and the steam engine as the power source, and to the closure of small forges using local ore, charcoal, and water power. Iron and steel production and heavy engineering were transformed with the creation of major enterprises like the Le Creusot (Saône-et-Loire) complex of furnaces, forges, and coal mines, which produced about 10 per cent of French cast-iron output.[23] Around it grew the mushrooming company town *par excellence* with a population of 1,200 in 1833 growing to 24,000 in 1866. Other major complexes included the metallurgy and engineering centre at Fives-Lille, the Derosne and Cail plant in Paris, and the state arsenal at Toulon with 5,000 workers, which was re-equipped to serve a new steam-propelled and armour-plated navy.[24]

Improved coal supplies were essential to the industrialisation process. Domestic production rose from 5 to over 13 million tonnes and the number of miners from 33,600 in 1851 to 91,900 in 1872, as deeper shafts and

[21] E.g. M. Rochefort, *L'organisation urbaine de l'Alsace* (Gap 1960), p. 224.
[22] E.g. W. Reddy, *The Rise of Market Culture. The Textile Trade and French Society, 1750–1900* (Cambridge 1984), pp. 240–1.
[23] A. Plessis, *The rise and fall of the Second Empire* (Cambridge 1985), p. 90.
[24] Constant, 'Var', I, p. 89.

more capital-intensive techniques were introduced to meet an apparently insatiable demand, although France would remain heavily dependent on imports.[25] This was one factor stimulating port development. Maritime activity was concentrated increasingly on major ports like Le Havre and Marseille with efficient rail links to their hinterlands. They experienced the expansion of shipbuilding, sugar refining, soap and chemicals manufacture, and flour milling, and substantial re-development as new docks and warehouse facilities were constructed, again requiring the introduction of new labour practices.[26] Competitive pressures grew especially intense in their hinterlands, in industries like flour milling.[27]

There were also, however, substantial continuities with the past. A dual economy developed in which the more traditional sectors retained a preponderant place in terms of employment. Thus, although the contribution of handicraft to total industrial production is estimated to have declined from 68.5 per cent in 1835/44 to 58.9 per cent by 1855/64, probably 70 to 75 per cent of industrial workers continued to be employed in small-scale household or workshop manufacture.[28] Far from representing a mere pre-industrial residual, small-scale manufacturers, providing they were prepared to adapt to increasingly competitive markets, were well placed to take advantage of the comparative advantages they enjoyed – including skilled labour and a reputation for quality and style in the production of luxury goods. They also predominated in the supply, to local markets, of perishable and non-transportable consumer goods like foodstuffs and housing. Survival, nevertheless, involved a constant struggle. Substantial change was often necessary, involving a greater division of labour between, and within, workshops, and an intensification of work. In addition to the factory and the workshop, domestic 'sweated' labour was also common; especially in the clothing trades, which employed large numbers of extremely poorly paid women. Furthermore, the streets, building sites, and ports were the place of employment of swarms of carters, porters, labourers, and stevedores.

Paris was exceptional in the scale and diversity of its manufacturing and service activities. The capital remained the country's major industrial centre, producing just under a quarter of total industrial production (by value)[29] and employing 15 per cent of the industrial labour force. More than 450,000 workers were employed, which meant that with their families over a million inhabitants of the capital depended on industrial employment.

---

[25] R. Magraw, *A History of the French Working Class* (Oxford 1992), 1, p. 240.
[26] E.g. W. Sewell, *Structure and Mobility. The men and women of Marseille, 1820–70* (Cambridge 1985).
[27] Constant, 'Var', 1, p. 274.   [28] Markovitch, *L'industrie française*, p. 85.
[29] B. Ratcliffe, 'Manufacturing in the metropolis: the dynamism and dynamics of Parisian industry in the mid-nineteenth century', *Journal of European Economic History* 1994, p. 288.

According to the 1847/8 Chamber of Commerce Enquiry, there were 64,816 *fabricants* and 343,530 workers (some 206,000 men; 113,000 women; 24,000 children). Of these *fabricants* 32,583 worked alone or with one worker; 25,116 employed 2 to 10 workers, and only 7,117 enterprises (11 per cent of the total) had more than 10 workers. The building industry averaged one employer for every thirteen workers. Less than 1 per cent of the total number of enterprises, an estimated 424 establishments, employed more than 50 workers.[30] The *statistique industrielle* of 1872 confirmed that a gradual process of concentration was under way with an 8.5 per cent increase in the number of enterprises and an increase in the labour force of something like 17 to 18 per cent.[31]

The city seems to have been divided, very roughly, into three industrial zones by the end of the 1860s reflecting competing pressures for land use. The centre, with its *grands boulevards*, was home to an enormous range of administrative, commercial, and industrial activities. It was extraordinarily congested, sheltering a host of small artisanal workshops producing consumer and luxury goods and the range of *articles de Paris*. Indeed, in spite of Haussmann's demolitions, the dense network of small workshops in the city centre, in streets like the rue Saint-Martin or rue du Temple, had continued to proliferate because of the need to be close to clients and the division of labour between workshops, which encouraged clustering. Outside the centre was an intermediary zone producing consumer goods and industrial equipment, with activities linked to the administration and university on the left bank, including printing and precision engineering. Further out, especially in the north and east, and in the suburbs annexed in 1860, an anarchic profusion of residential and industrial buildings developed, attracted by the canal and port facilities, proximity to the Paris market, and the low cost of land and labour in comparison with more central districts, from which most of these businesses would anyway have been excluded by the noxious smells they produced.[32] These included such major producers of steam engines and machine tools as Gouin at Batignolles-Monceau employing 1,500 workers and Cavé at La Chapelle a further 800, and alongside them the more traditional, often highly specialised metalworking workshops which thrived in the 10th and 11th arrondissments around the rues Oberkampf and Saint-Maur.[33]

[30] M. Daumas, *Evolution de la géographie industrielle de Paris et sa proche banlieue au 19e siècle* (Paris 1976), pp. 83, 103, 116.

[31] Ibid. p. 213.   [32] Jacquemet, 'Belleville', IV, p. 1271.

[33] J. Gaillard, 'Les usines Cail et les ouvriers métallurgistes de Grenelle', *Le mouvement social*, 1961, p. 35; J.-F. Belhoste *et al.*, 'Paris, ville d'usines au 19e siècle' in K. Bowie (ed.), *La modernité avant Haussmann* (Paris 2001), pp. 345–52.

Throughout the country, the response of small-scale producers to increasingly competitive markets was frequently dynamic and resulted in the introduction of new products and in technical and organisational change. The city of Lyon, and especially the hillsides and plateau of la Croix-Rousse and the la Guillotière *quartier* remained the centre of silk production, an industry still based on a network of small workshops, usually with 2 to 4 looms. Often worked by members of the same family, these looms supplied high quality cloth to the wholesalers who dominated the industry. It was convenient for them to distribute the thread and collect the finished cloth within the city. The all-important control of quality was also easier. From the 1820s, the introduction of the Jacquard loom, its movements programmed through the use of perforated cardboard patterns, had revolutionised weaving and increased productivity.

Merchants placed orders with highly skilled specialists and were easily able to adapt to volatile markets, without having to risk their own capital in expensive mechanisation. The pressure they exerted created considerable tension, as well as exacerbating that between the masters and the journeymen they employed. As late as 1877, when there were around 35,000 looms in the city itself – concentrating on the high quality end of production – and another 85,000 dispersed throughout the region, only 10,000 of them were powered. In the city as a whole, occupational structures were slow to change, although increasingly work was provided by the development of ironworks and engineering in the la Guillotière district and of chemicals production. Continued dependence on exports of silk – for 78 per cent of the product in the late 1860s – nevertheless left Lyon especially susceptible to fluctuations in trade, particularly with the USA. Frequent layoffs were a fact of life.[34]

In nearby Saint-Etienne, at the same time as large-scale steel and coal production developed, around 9,000 workers continued to be employed in small workshops producing firearms and ironmongery and weaving silk ribbons.[35] Additionally in the neighbourhood there were 177 flourmills, 109 saw-mills, 180 textile mills, and 100 metallurgical establishments dispersed along the watercourses to employ hydraulic power.[36] The three main groups of workers – domestic, factory, and miners – were divided

[34] Y. Lequin, *La formation de la classe ouvrière régionale: les ouvriers de la région lyonnaise (1848–1914)* (Lyon 1977), I, pp. 15, 84, 170; Cayez, *Crises*; G. Sheridan, 'Household and craft in an industrializing economy: the case of the silk weavers of Lyons' in J. Merriman (ed.), *Consciousness and Class Experience in 19th Century France* (London 1979), pp. 110–11.

[35] Lequin, *La formation*, I, p. 23.

[36] J. Merley, 'Les élections de 1869 dans le département de la Loire', *Cahiers d'histoire* 1961, pp. 71–2.

by wage levels, working conditions, residential segregation, and different forms of organisation and informal sociability. Amongst the factory workers, further distinctions existed between the highly skilled and well-paid employees of the foundries and engineering shops and the textile workers. In addition every establishment had its own distinct hierarchy of skills and rewards.[37]

Work and its rewards

Georges Duveau long ago concluded that there were four basic types of worker, defined as much by settlement patterns and the milieu they inhabited as by their trades.[38] First, those resident in the industrial village, typical of domestic outworkers on the Picardy plains or Lyonnais, or miners in the Pas-de-Calais, of workers in the water-powered textile mills of lower Normandy or the Vosges. These communities were all more or less isolated in the countryside, their residents able to work the land as well as in industry, and sharing, to some degree, the lifestyle and mentalities of their peasant neighbours. Distinctive mining communities were emerging, however. In the Pas-de-Calais rapidly growing mining villages and towns like Béthune and Lens contrasted markedly with stagnating marketing and administrative centres like Arras and Saint Omer.

Duveau's second category was workers residing in medium-sized towns like Orléans, Angers, Dijon, or Béziers, essentially service and administrative centres for wide rural hinterlands with diverse industrial activities such as flour-milling, distilling, tanning, brick and tile-making, and a range of artisanal crafts, and an absence of large-scale concentrated enterprises. Thirdly there were those living in small towns dominated by a single enterprise – typically Le Creusot, the major mining-metallurgical centre, or the textile town of Le Cateau – or by the manufacture of a single product like the textile centres of Reims, Elbeuf, Troyes, and Lodève. There were in fact considerable differences within this category. A metallurgical/engineering centre employed far more skilled workers and far fewer women and children than a mining or textile town. In all of them class structures were, however, relatively polarised.[39] Duveau's final category was workers resident in large urban centres with multiple functions, especially Paris and Lyon,

---

[37] R. Aminzade, *Ballots and Barricades. Class Formation and Republican Politics in France, 1830–71* (London 1993), pp. 81–2.
[38] G. Duveau, *La vie ouvrière en France sous le Second Empire* (Paris 1946), pp. 225–8.
[39] E.g. J.-P. Frey, *La ville industrielle et ses urbanités. La distinction ouvriers/employés. Le Creusot 1870–1930* (Brussels 1987), p. 5.

but additionally major port-cities like Le Havre, Bordeaux, and Marseille and old-established administrative/industrial centres like Lille, Rouen, and Limoges. These were all characterised by extremely diverse employment and complex inter-class relationships. The range of alternative employment opportunities made it more difficult for employers to dominate their workers.

In these circumstances, earning power and living conditions were also extremely varied. The main factor determining the rewards for labour was the geographically extremely fragmented labour market. According to Duveau there were four groups of Parisian workers: the largest, *le groupe normal*, *c.* 132,000 of them in 1860 earned 3 to 5f. a day; *le groupe heureux* – *c.* 19,000 – made 5f. to 6f.50; and *le groupe privilégié* – *c.* 15,000 – over 6f. 50. In contrast, *c.* 64,000 – *le groupe malheureux* – earned less than 3f.[40] Overall, wages increased by just over 2 per cent per annum for men and 2.8 per cent for women between 1852 and 1882.[41] Rewards were especially low in areas like Brittany and the Massif Central as a result of over-population and under-development,[42] although specific skills shortages might alter the picture. In sectors like building, migration, which restrained the tendency for wages to increase in major cities like Paris, promoted slight increases in the migrants' areas of origin.[43] The overall result was a gradual decline in regional income disparities.

Wage differentials remained substantial, however. According to the Nantes republican Dr Guépin, writing in the 1840s, within any community, there were three groups: *les ouvriers aisés* – skilled, literate artisans earning over 600f. a year, well fed and distinguished by the correctness of their dress from *les ouvriers pauvres* – often factory workers, earning less than 500f.; at the bottom of the heap came *les ouvriers misérables*, mostly recent migrants who lacked marketable skills and suffered from chronic underemployment.[44] The State Prosecutor at Colmar estimated that 80 per cent of the employees of the typical large-scale spinning or weaving mill, like those of Dollfus Mieg at Mulhouse, belonged to the category *ouvriers flottants*, earning around 1f.50 a day – women, children, and general labourers – and likely to face dismissal during a trade depression. His second category represented a *classe moyenne* amongst workers. Typically these earned 2f.50 to 2f.75 per day and included artisans in some of the less well-rewarded trades as well as the more skilled and secure textile operatives. The third, and by

[40] Duveau, *Vie ouvrière*, p. 320.
[41] J. Singer-Kérel, *Le coût de la vie à Paris de 1840 à 1954* (Paris 1961), pp. 129, 132.
[42] E.g. PG Angers, 10 Jan. 1868, AN BB30/371 re Cholet area.
[43] Désert, 'Aperçus sur l'industrie française', pp. 90–4.   [44] Lequin, 'Les citadins', p. 512.

far the smallest, category included the most highly skilled engineering and printing workers, clerks, and foremen.[45]

The response to the 1848 enquiry into working conditions from Amiens[46] insisted that 'moral' factors were as important as skills in the labour market in determining workers' earnings. According to its authors, 'a small number are able to get close to the middle class as a result of good conduct and relatively high wages throughout the year . . . Their number could be as high as one-twentieth of the working class population.' The class of factory workers, in comparison, was 'the least happy, it is so badly paid and has such difficulty in supporting itself that it becomes discouraged and scarcely knows how to survive from day to day. The little that it earns is often dissipated in the *cabaret*. It depends on assistance when unemployed, on the hospital when sick. It is generally puny, small in stature and lacking in energy.'

Artisans

The best-rewarded workers normally possessed skills acquired through lengthy apprenticeships and which were in relatively short supply. They included men employed in modern machine shops as well as workers in the more traditional luxury trades like cabinet making, jewellery, and printing. The value of professional skills further depended on the workers' ability to protect themselves from the 'degradation' which resulted from mechanisation and/or the employment of less skilled labour. In this, the customs of the trade, its 'remembered economy',[47] the strength of the occupational and residential community, and its consciousness of shared interests and values were of crucial importance.

The delegates elected by the Parisian cabinetmakers (*ébénistes*) to represent them at the 1867 International Exposition took great pride in the quality of the furniture they produced, and 'in the possession of skills which come close to those of the artist'.[48] The *bronziers* responsible for sculpture and the decorative features of expensive furniture were similarly proud of their artistry. They had a well-organised mutual aid society and lived mainly in adjoining districts of the 3rd and 11th arrondissements, both working and socialising together.[49] The hat-makers, organised in the Société philanthropique des approprieurs chapeliers, continued to control recruitment, using the threat of an *interdit*, the blacklisting of employers

---

[45] 20 Jan. 1866, AN BB30/376.   [46] AN C966.
[47] Scott, *Weapons of the Weak*, p. 178.   [48] AN F12/3112.
[49] Gould, *Insurgent Identities*, pp. 109–10.

who took on 'unapproved' labour.[50] The city's printing workers had similar, long-established traditions, although this did not prevent the development of intra-trade rivalry between, for example, the *conducteur* – the typesetter and press operator – anxious to avoid sharing his professional expertise with his assistant, the *margeur*. The importance attached to seniority and the often harsh treatment meted out to the younger craftsmen also created considerable inter-generational rivalry.[51]

Efforts might be made to control the pace of work as well. In 1868 the representatives of the Paris Chamber of Commerce complained that 'the workers dominate the workplace; if one of them attracts attention because of his skill or by working too hard, he is reported to the committee as work-happy (*gâte-métier*), and clandestine pressure is exerted on him until he leaves or submits to the rules which are imposed on him. The workers claim to reign in the workshop, and lay down the law to the employer.'[52] However, many 'artisans' were far more exposed to the vagaries of the labour market.

Although not all trades were affected to the same degree, mechanisation created a general sense of insecurity. The engineering employer Denis Poulot described how he had introduced machines to mass-produce standardised bolts and rivets as well as to reduce his workers' negotiating power. Initially the machines had proved to be rather unreliable. Their successful operation had very much depended on the good-will and intelligence of skilled operators. Subsequently, with the development of less complicated machine tools to thread bolts, operators required only a few weeks' training on the job. Production norms were established in relation to the capacity of the machine rather than the aptitude of the worker.[53] At the same time, commercial capitalism tightened its grasp over the artisanal trades, reducing the autonomy on which both masters and men had traditionally prided themselves. The key figures in this process were the wholesale merchants, who ordered goods, provided credit to purchase raw materials, and then marketed the finished product.[54] In many trades workshop *patrons* were effectively reduced to subcontracting. There were frequent, bitter

[50] Berlanstein, *Working People*, pp. 79–80.
[51] C. Nolat, *Physiologie de l'imprimerie* (Paris 1856); M. Rebérioux, 'Les ouvriers du livre' in H.-J. Martin and R. Chartier (eds.), *Histoire de l'édition française*, vol. III (Paris 1985), pp. 98–100.
[52] To Ministre de l'Agriculture, du Commerce et des Travaux Publics, 12 March 1872, quoted A. Cottereau, 'Vie quotidienne et résistance ouvrière à Paris en 1870' in D. Poulot, *Le sublime ou le travailleur comme il est en 1870 et ce qu'il peut être* (Paris 1980 re-print), p. 80.
[53] Ibid. p. 48.
[54] See also Chambre de Commerce de Paris, *Statistique de l'industrie à Paris* (Paris 1847), II, pp. 761–2; ibid. (1860), pp. 880–4; and *Reports of Artisans Selected by a Committee Appointed by the Council of the Society of Arts to Visit the Paris Universal Exhibition of 1867* (London 1867), II.

complaints that relationships between the *patrons* and their craftsmen had been reduced to a 'cash nexus' as a result of these pressures.[55]

Contrasts were drawn repeatedly between the idealised solidarity and stability of a mythologised past and a more individualistic present.[56] Throughout the artisanal trades skilled craftsmen had traditionally aspired to 'independence', to eventually running their own small businesses. This required relatively little capital, especially in the luxury and building trades where reputation and skill mattered more. However, once established these new masters were likely to attempt to establish a social distance between themselves and their former workmates. The very fragility of their businesses discouraged close relationships. Even where producers' cooperatives were established, the workers initially involved were likely to distinguish themselves as *ouvriers intelligents*, the 'best', as the organisers of the Association des constructions métalliques put it in 1865, when rejecting the right of the workers they employed to strike.[57]

Employers were certainly under constant pressure and passed this on to their workers. In Paris and other large cities the scale of demand and the geographical concentration of production promoted the constant simplification of tasks, encouraging specialisation by workshops and a division of labour, which reduced costs substantially. More specialised hand tools, and small or shared steam engines, required only limited investment. As a result of this process, by 1860 the 5,971 workers producing high-quality jewellery, although relatively well placed to resist mechanisation, were divided into twenty-three specialities, and those working on costume jewellery into twenty-two.[58] The introduction of piece rates was another means of reducing costs. According to the delegates of the Parisian cabinetmakers it served to 'create and maintain a continuous rivalry, and to crush every germ of solidarity between workers'. The few, the more robust and adroit, might benefit from the new arrangements. The majority were forced to engage in more intense labour in order to maintain their earnings. The competition of outworkers, the influx of newcomers, and the collapse of traditional apprenticeship systems, which had previously controlled entry into the labour force, all worsened the situation.[59]

The delegates of the jewellery workers, not a particularly militant trade, complained that the capitalists 'enjoy every freedom to establish a sort of

[55] See *rapport* of delegates of *tourneurs sur bois*, AN F12/3120.
[56] *Reports of Artisans*, ii, p. 9 goldsmiths; iii, pp. 3–5 woodturners.
[57] Quoted J. Gaillard, 'Les associations de production et la pensée politique en France (1852–70)', *Le Mouvement social* 1965, pp. 82–3.
[58] J. Gaillard, *Paris, la ville*, p. 439.   [59] AN F12/3112.

legal oppression, controlling the worker and breaking down his labour into distinct operations, creating specialisms and almost suppressing *l'ouvrier* [i.e. the skilled craftsman]'. The inevitable result of this intensified *division du travail* would be to 'diminish the intrinsic value of the worker, . . . to destroy his skills . . . and suppress the good taste and the sense of harmony which characterises and ensures the superiority of the French worker'.[60]

Examples of such tension could be multiplied to take in the furniture makers of the faubourg Saint-Antoine[61] or the toy industry of the quartier du Temple where 'the body, the chest, the head, the arms, the teeth, the eyes, the hair, the dresses, the gloves, the shoes, the hats of the doll are made by artisans who have no contact with each other'.[62] Similarly in artificial flower making, another Parisian speciality, a network of workshops produced the different parts of the flowers.[63]

M. Denière, a manufacturer of artistic bronzes, had mixed feelings about these trends, observing that 'Previously, the bronze industry . . . was made up of workshops in which the whole process was completed, in which the moulding, casting, turning, mounting, chasing, and gilding was carried out; today, these large manufacturing centres have been broken up, and each of the constitutive elements of our industry is carried out separately.' He accepted that, in spite of initial resistance from the *fondeurs* and *doreurs*, workers had come to accept this 'inescapable' trend and been rewarded with higher wages for increased productivity. If the quality of the product had declined, specialisation had also had the positive effect of encouraging the creation of new workshops.[64]

The rise of *confection*, where mass production, particularly of ready-to-wear clothing, shoes, and furniture replaced the manufacture of a high-quality item made to order for an individual customer, was another significant trend. This threatened both the worker's sense of pride in crafts-manship and earnings. Increasingly leather might be cut in a central work-shop and then distributed to shoemakers to be stitched in a domestic workshop. From the late 1850s a machine was introduced to nail the sole to the upper part of the shoe and replace hand-stitching altogether.[65] The

---

[60] Report of delegates of *joailliers*, quoted Cottereau, 'Introduction' to Poulot, *Le sublime*, p. 64.

[61] D. Willbach, 'Work and its Satisfactions: Origins of the French Labor Movement, 1864–70', PhD, Univ. of Michigan 1977, pp. 165–7.

[62] A. Cochin, *Paris, sa population, son industrie* (Paris 1864).

[63] D. Harvey, *Consciousness and the Urban Experience* (London 1985), pp. 117–18.

[64] M. Denière, fabricant de bronzes d'art à Paris to Ministère de l'agriculture, du commerce, et des Travaux Publics. Conseil supérieur du commerce, de l'agriculture et des travaux publics, *Enquête. Traité de commerce avec l'Angleterre* (Paris 1860), II, p. 140, session of 8 June 1860.

[65] Willbach, *Work and its Satisfactions*, pp. 167–8.

clothing trades similarly expanded through the extension of putting-out and of 'sweating' even before the introduction, from 1854, of the sewing machine. Amongst Parisian tailors there was a clear distinction between the elite *coupeurs* working either alone or for master tailors, and the *pompiers* employed only for alterations, or the less skilled employees of the ready-to-wear *confectionneurs* sweatshops. At the bottom of the earnings league came the *apiéceurs* working at home on piece rates. In a trade depression the supply of raw materials to outworkers simply ceased.[66]

Building workers complained about *marchandage*, a process of sub-contracting which encouraged competitive bidding between small entrepreneurs and forced down wages. The brief abolition of this practice in March 1848 had been warmly welcomed but the decree introduced by the new republican regime had proved ineffective. As a result, according to a well-informed English observer, writing in 1867,

a set of sub-contractors, half-foremen half little-masters, have sprung up, who take the work at a price from the large masters in whose name it is carried on, and then make their own terms with the men . . . The one large master would be very easily reached, but in all references to him he excuses himself on the plea that wages are no affair of his; they are a matter strictly between the sub-contractor and the workmen.[67]

The growing numbers of building workers, competition for employment, and the collapse of traditional forms of organisation like *compagnonnage*, further reduced their ability to resist exploitation.

The autonomy of the work process and the satisfaction gained from the exercise of a skill appeared to many artisans to be threatened. With the prospect of de-skilling, an entire way of life seemed to be endangered. A profound sense of injustice inevitably prevailed which affected labour relations. However, not all was doom and gloom. Efforts continued to be made to negotiate informal local trade-wide agreements on wage rates and the pace of work. Charles Hooper, a London cabinetmaker, was certainly impressed by what he considered to be the relaxed and more egalitarian atmosphere he detected in Parisian workshops.[68] Whilst anxious to raise productivity, employers were also often concerned to preserve quality and retain highly skilled workers. Relationships between 'master' and 'man' might be close from a sense of common origins and interests. However, they might be tense and conflictual due to individual ambition and externally imposed pressure. Conflict and cooperation might well co-exist.

[66] Johnson, 'Economic change', pp. 87–114.
[67] *Reports of artisans*, I, p. 468.   [68] Ibid. p. 7.

Certainly artisans did not object to all forms of technical change. Historians have probably over-romanticised the life of the skilled craftsman. Claude Corban, a typographer, reminded his readers of 'the intense boredom of workers condemned by the length of the working day to disheartening labour'.[69] It was the immense saving of effort, of wear and tear on the human body, which inclined the delegates of the Parisian engineering trades to welcome the age of the machine.[70] In general artisans complained bitterly when mechanisation or the employment of men and sometimes women, from outside the profession, threatened to lead to deskilling.[71] They embraced innovations which eased their physical burden or helped them to 'perfect' their skills, and condemned those which threatened quality.[72]

Factory workers

In spite of these pressures, artisans employed in small workshops *tended* not only to be better rewarded but to inhabit a different cultural universe from the mass of semi-skilled workers employed in factories, mills, and mines and as general labourers on the streets, in warehouses, docks, and on building sites. However, the contrast can easily be over-simplified. For one thing, it would be incorrect to regard factory workers as a uniform social category. Skill, place in the labour market, organisational strength, age, and gender also mattered. Their experience of work was extremely varied.

From the 1820s, cotton mills in northern towns like Rouen, Lille, and Mulhouse had come to exemplify the association between mechanisation and hard, monotonous labour tied to the rhythm of the self-acting mule – which in replacing the mule-jenny had tended to double labour productivity.[73] However, innovation was often gradual and piecemeal. The introduction of power looms into the woollen mills at Roubaix and Reims, for example, had to await the excess profits made during the 1860s cotton crisis.[74] Traditional, pre-factory assessments of skill and job prestige continued to influence the organisation of factory labour. Many so-called 'factories', in engineering for example, were made up of a series of semi-autonomous workshops. Even in the highly mechanised Parisian works of Gouin at Batignolles, and of Cail on the quai de Grenelle, which

---

[69] Quoted J. Rancière, *La nuit des prolétaires* (Paris 1981), p. 77.

[70] Delegates elected by ouvriers mécaniciens du dépt. de la Seine, AN F12/3116.

[71] Exposition universel de 1867, *Rapports des délégations ouvriers* (Paris 1868), I, p. 21, typographers.

[72] Ibid. I, *Rapport des ouvriers chapeliers*.

[73] Conseil supérieur de l'agriculture, du commerce et de l'industrie, *Enquête sur le traité de commerce avec l'Angleterre, industrie textile, coton* (Paris 1870), déposition de Pouyer-Quertier, pp. 1–30.

[74] Reddy, *The Rise of Market Culture*, p. 241; Gordon, *Merchants*, pp. 57f.

produced a wide range of railway equipment and textile machinery, distinctions existed between workers using general machines for repetitive tasks; those who adapted more specialised machine tools like the turret lathes, in use from the 1860s, to particular tasks; and the skilled craftsmen responsible for constructing and maintaining increasingly complex machines.[75] Within each of these groups individual competence or 'loyalty' to the employer might be rewarded financially and through greater job security.

Skill remained a source of privilege. Skilled workers within the factory, or mine, possessed the sense of status and dignity of the traditional craftsman, and pride in the mastery of new techniques. They were able to preserve a certain degree of autonomy in the organisation of their work. In the larger urban centres craftsmen were able to move from factory to workshop and back again with relative ease.[76] Nevertheless, developing processes of mechanisation and concentration, and the integration of the various stages of production, often closely associated with the replacement of human or waterpower with steam, had a substantial impact on the organisation of work and relative negotiating strength. Turgan's monographs on *Les grandes usines* published from 1860 reveal growing efforts to rationalise both the use of space and labour. The standardisation of engineering products, for example, required the rationalisation of work through a more calculated division of labour and an enhancement of the roles of engineers and draftsmen.[77] The empirical knowledge of the puddlers and iron founders essential to achieving the correct 'mix' in the furnaces or judging when molten metal had reached the correct consistency for casting or hammering was similarly threatened by the development of chemical analysis.[78]

In coal mines a fundamental division existed between the surface and the underground workers who enjoyed much higher status and earnings. Amongst the latter a distinction existed between the hauliers and the coal-face workers who needed to be physically strong, and able to assess the potential of the seams they were working as well as the stress on pit props and the threat from rock falls and gas.[79] Physical strength was always a considerable asset but effort was further stimulated by piece rates and competition between *équipes*.[80] On the railways a strict hierarchy was imposed

---

[75] Berlanstein, *Working People*, pp. 92–3.   [76] Lequin, 'Citadins', pp. 507–11.

[77] R. Gould, 'Trade cohesion, class unity, and urban insurrection: artisanal activism in the Paris Commune', *American Journal of Sociology* 98, 1992/3, pp. 735–6.

[78] J. B. Silly, 'La concentration dans l'industrie sidérurgique sous le Second Empire', *Revue d'histoire de la sidérurgie* 1962, *passim*.

[79] R. Trempé, *Les mineurs de Carmaux, 1848–1914* (Paris 1971), I, pp. 108–15.

[80] Prefect Pas-de-Calais, 25 Feb., 12 March 1859, AN F12/4651.

which encouraged engine drivers to lord it over their firemen and to virtually ignore the shunters and coalmen who did some of the most dangerous, dirty, and poorly paid work and who significantly adopted the label *sauvages*[81] – a clear case of an individual's identity being shaped by the opinions of other people.

Employment in the 'factory' was a mixed blessing for most workers. Perceptions varied. The delegates of the Parisian cabinetmakers in 1867 claimed that a furniture factory in the suburbs 'is known as Cayenne because there the workers not only lose their liberty but also their physical and intellectual capabilities'.[82] Working conditions could be extremely unpleasant. Furnace workers in the iron industry endured excessive heat; coal mining and building represented myriad dangers; the textile mills were characterised by noise, humidity, and dust; and chemical works by toxic fumes.[83] Fatigue and attempts to grease or repair machinery in motion, in order to avoid loss of earnings, increased the risk of becoming entangled in the drive shafts, belts, or fly-wheels which encumbered even the most modern mill. Improvement was slow in spite of government efforts to encourage the introduction of protective casings and grills.[84] An exhausting working day lasting 10 to 12 hours was normal,[85] although this was often shorter than that endured by domestic workers struggling to compete with factory competition.

However, the factory environment was gradually improving due to a combination of technical change, official regulation, and employer self-interest. New buildings were often spacious and airy. An improved layout increased productivity and reduced the likelihood of time-wasting accidents. The human effort required might be substantially reduced by mechanisation.[86] Furthermore, poor conditions increasingly earned a bad reputation for a mill owner amongst workers, fellow employers, and in the wider community.[87] In the Saint-Etienne arms industry the move from workshop to factory production certainly involved closer supervision and a loss of autonomy, but also meant higher wages and more regular work and even, with the establishment of a state arsenal, exemption from

---

[81] M. Stein, *The Social Origins of a Labor Elite. French Engine Drivers, 1837–1917* (London 1987), p. 215.

[82] *Rapport des délégations ouvriers*, I, p. 33.

[83] Y. Lequin, 'Les villes et l'industrie: l'émergence d'une autre France' in Lequin, *L'histoire des français 19e–20e siècles*, II, pp. 415–16; Y. Charbit, *Du malthusianisme au populationnisme. Les économistes français et la population, 1840–70* (Paris 1981), pp. 108–10.

[84] Prefect Aisne, 20 April 1852, in response to ministerial circular of 9 Dec. 1851 requesting information on accidents in mechanised industrial establishments, AN F12/4617.

[85] See e.g. Lequin, *Formation*, II, pp. 57–8.   [86] Melucci, *Idéologies*, pp. 182–3.

[87] E.g. A. Fortin, 'Aspects de la vie sociale du Pas-de-Calais durant le Second Empire', *Revue du Nord* 1970, pp. 22–4.

conscription.[88] In the Rouen area, where domestic weavers had been forced to work ever longer hours for declining rewards as machine competition increased, those 'workers gathered together in factories earn more, firstly because they produce more, and then because their concentration itself defends them against excessive exploitation'.[89]

Norbert Truquin, who had worked in an Amiens spinning mill, maintained that

in spite of all the drawbacks, the situation of workers in the mills was much better than that of domestic workers. Nothing is more brutalising than working in a cramped space, although it might appear to offer greater freedom. The domestic worker breathes in, all day, the unhealthy and nauseating fumes of coal and oil . . . In the factories, in comparison, the workshops are heated, adequately ventilated and well lit; order and cleanliness reign; the worker has company . . . When the foremen are absent, people tell stories, act out little dramas; jokers improvise a pulpit and have fun preaching; the time passes merrily.[90]

Thus, on the positive side there was comradeship. Even the quarrels and fights helped foster a sense of workplace community.[91] Nevertheless, the sheer monotony of a long working day engaged in repetitive tasks could often become almost unbearable. Truquin had also worked as a wool carder, and remembered how, after 12/13 hours he would fall asleep on his feet, in spite of biting his hands and banging his head against the wall. As well as boredom and frequent risk of injury there was the prospect, after years of physical effort, of repetitive strain injuries and all manner of occupational illnesses frequently leading to premature ageing.

In addition to low and fluctuating wage levels, and the continued neglect of safety and hygiene, factory workers frequently seem to have resented the imposition of strict discipline. Employers were determined to assert their authority. This was conceived of in traditional terms as that of 'master' over 'man'. Discipline was judged to be essential to ensure regular attendance and hard work on the part of a labour force made up of a mixture of former artisans, domestic workers, and peasants, with experience of a variety of work rhythms. Regulations were posted and often brutally enforced as contractual obligations. Fines or dismissal sanctioned lateness, poor-quality work, insufficient care of machines, talking, singing, swearing, blasphemy, use of alcohol and especially insubordination. The individual was to be subordinated to the rhythm of the machine, which imposed its own harsh

---

[88] Aminzade, *Ballots and Barricades*, p. 79.   [89] PG Rouen, 2 Feb. 1857, AN BB30/387.
[90] N. Truquin, *Mémoires et aventures d'un prolétaire* (Paris 1977), p. 51.
[91] E.g. M. Pigenet, 'Aux fondements d'une identité. Retour sur deux siècles de travail ouvrier', *Historiens et géographes* 1995, p. 253.

discipline. Order was imposed by the foremen who played a key intermediary role in the production process in establishments like the textile mills in Rouen where, 'with a few exceptions, the employers . . . only communicate with their workers through foremen whose main preoccupation is to push themselves forward at the expense of the workers'.[92]

Regulations and fines were only some of the methods employed to control the labour force. The directors of large organisations like the railway companies which needed to recruit and train substantial numbers of employees and to ensure the punctuality and safety of their services, as well as to satisfy shareholders, imposed a particularly rigid quasi-military discipline. An extremely detailed rulebook and a complex system of wages, bonuses, fines, and promotions bound the engine driver.[93] Clearly, for any business, controlling wage costs was of crucial importance. Wage systems themselves could be used to maintain discipline and increase productivity. *Marchandage* in the building industry and the *équipe* in mining and metallurgy encouraged workers, organised in teams and driven on by an autocratic senior worker, to compete for work. Piece-rates became increasingly common as a means of stimulating individual effort and reducing the necessity of constant supervision.[94]

Workers themselves tended to prefer payment by the hour with the tariff stated in writing. This was simple and unambiguous and less likely to encourage divisive competition. Nevertheless, the more skilled, dexterous or robust might well favour the sort of piece-rate system introduced in the ironworks at Le Creusot in the 1850s which led to wage increases of as much as 50 to 60 per cent, whilst doubling productivity.[95] Such systems had the effect of increasing individual earnings but also helped to sustain a sense of autonomy and a pride in skill.[96] Even so the worker delegates to the 1873 Vienna Universal Exposition expressed their resentment at the unilateral establishment of piece rates by their employers, pointing out that an increase in productivity was generally followed by the reduction of piece rates in order to stimulate a further intensification in the pace of work, and limit the workers' share in the benefits.[97]

---

[92] PG Rouen, 15 July 1854, AN BB30/387; see also A. Cottereau, 'Les règlements d'atelier au cours de la révolution industrielle en France' in A. Biroleau (ed.), *Les règlements d'atelier 1798–1936* (Paris 1984), pp. 4–18.

[93] Stein, *French Engine Drivers*, pp. 85–9; F. Caron, 'Essai d'analyse historique d'une psychologie du travail. Les mécaniciens et chauffeurs de locomotion du réseau du Nord de 1850 à 1910', *Le mouvement social* 1965, *passim*.

[94] L. Reybaud, *Le fer et la houille* (Paris 1874), pp. 107–8; Duveau, *Vie ouvrière*, pp. 263–6.

[95] J. Euverte, 'De l'organisation de la main-d'oeuvre dans la grande industrie', *Journal des Economistes*, Sept. 1870, p. 369.

[96] See e.g. Reybaud, *Fer*, p. 50, on iron puddlers.   [97] Berlanstein, *Working People*, p. 80.

Organisational and technological changes were inevitably potent causes of tension.[98] The procureur général at Rouen in 1853 maintained that textile entrepreneurs, 'with too few exceptions, are uniquely concerned with increasing their profits'. Furthermore, 'since the government has recovered its authority and they no longer fear riots, they have returned, as far as they are able, to their old practices, their old exactions', so that 'if workers complain, they are dismissed and will be unable to find work anywhere'.[99] However, authoritarian management did not always produce the expected results. The efforts of employers to impose discipline and destroy 'unacceptable' labour practices were countered by the development of new 'customs' and by discreet efforts to control the application of work norms when open complaints would probably have resulted in dismissal. J.-P. Drevet, employed at the Cail engineering works in Paris, recalled that: 'if we do not produce as much as we could, if we do not take care of the raw materials and the machinery, as well as we might, it is because we have no interest in the prosperity of our master; he pays us as little as he can, we do as little work as we can'.[100]

Domestic work

In addition to the workshop and factory the home continued to serve as a place of work. These domestic workers are especially difficult to count and their numbers fluctuated constantly. The most notorious urban example was the hand-loom weavers of Lille, living and working in damp cellars, bent double over their looms from dawn to dusk, their health destroyed by an inadequate diet, poor living conditions, inhaling fibres, and the constant strain of work.[101] Women with very young children and unable to work in the mills often took up sewing. The availability of cheap sewing machines – 54,000 of which were sold in the Seine department in the 1860s – gave a new lease of life to this form of 'sweated' household activity.[102] At mid-century, each of the major textile centres had employed large numbers of workers in the surrounding countryside. In the case of the technically advanced Mulhouse industry, cotton spinning and printing were concentrated in the town, but 85 per cent of the weaving took place in rural areas of Alsace and the Vosges. Similarly, the woollen centre of Roubaix provided work in

---

[98] E.g. F. Démier, 'Les ouvriers de Rouen parlent à un économiste en juillet 1848', *Le mouvement social*, April 1982, *passim*.

[99] 5 July 1853, AN BB30/387.   [100] Quoted Cottereau, 'Vie quotidienne', p. 73.

[101] A. Lasserre, *La situation des ouvriers de l'industrie textile dans la région lilloise sous la Monarchie de Juillet* (Lausanne 1952), p. 133.

[102] L. Tilly, 'Three faces of capitalism: women and work in French cities' in J. Merriman (ed.), *French Cities in the Nineteenth Century* (London 1982), pp. 184–5.

hundreds of villages throughout Picardy and Normandy, as did the Troyes-based hosiery trade.[103]

Whilst on 'moral' grounds official reports tended to favour the familial structure of domestic manufacture, they could hardly ignore the widespread and growing misery associated with it.[104] The limited autonomy domestic outworkers enjoyed as subcontractors, or as 'dependent producers'[105] was being eroded rapidly by competitive pressures. Domestic weaving was already in crisis in the Rouen area by 1848. Subsequently the numbers employed fell from around 109,500 to 61,000 by 1869.[106] Rural manufacture would virtually disappear from Alsace and the Vosges in the 1860s.[107] Certainly, efforts were made to increase productivity. M. Bary, a manufacturer of linen at Le Mans, who provided work for 1,200 looms in the surrounding countryside, claimed that the addition of the flying shuttle over the previous fifteen years to looms probably a hundred years old, had almost doubled their production.[108] Conditions continued to deteriorate, however. Very few young people entered these trades.[109] They preferred to join the mass of general labourers on the streets and along the quays, in the warehouses and on building sites. These labourers attracted far less interest from contemporary observers or subsequently from historians. More than any other group of urban workers, however, they endured hard physical labour, frequently in inclement weather, suffered considerable insecurity, for very little reward.

Women's work

The social consequences of industrialisation were extremely varied, between industries and places, but also according to gender. Women made up around 30 per cent of the active industrial population in 1866. Whilst they were virtually absent from metallurgy and machine building, they provided 51 per cent of the work force in textiles and 87 per cent in the clothing trades.[110] In Paris in 1860 there were an estimated 105,087 female workers compared with 234,442 male workers. Although most female factory

---

[103] G. Noiriel, *Les ouvriers dans la société française* (Paris 1986), pp. 24, 33–4.

[104] E.g. PG Paris, ? Feb. 1857, AN BB30/383 re hosiery manufacture in arrondissement of Arcis-sur-Aube.

[105] T. Liu, *The Weavers' Knot. The Contradictions of Class Struggle and Family Solidarity in Western France, 1750–1914* (London 1994), p. 138.

[106] Aminzade, *Ballots and Barricades*, pp. 90–1.

[107] Carel, 'Le département de la Haute-Saône', p. 243.   [108] *Enquête. Traité de commerce*, v, p. 312.

[109] F. Dornic, 'L'arrêt des rouets et des métiers à bras' in M. Lévy-Leboyer (ed.), *Un siècle et demi d'économie sarthoise 1815–1966* (Rouen 1969), pp. 31–40.

[110] M. Perrot, *Les ouvriers en grève. France 1871–90* (Paris 1974), I, p. 318.

workers were relatively young, harsh reality ensured that many were forced to work even after the birth of children, although at this stage in their lives, domestic work often replaced outside employment.[111]

Our evidence on women's work is overwhelmingly the product of male discourse. Typical of *bourgeois* witnesses was the well-known political economist Alphonse Audiganne who, following a visit to Rouen, complained that 'factory work [is] diverting women from their natural mission as wives and mothers'. His anxiety reflected his belief in the family as the foundation not only of morality but of social order. Furthermore, according to his somewhat fevered imagination, irreligion and the temptations resulting from the mixing of the sexes in their workplaces and overcrowded lodgings encouraged promiscuity, incest, adultery, and rape.[112] Significantly, though, the delegates of the Paris *mécaniciens* adopted a similar refrain, in insisting that 'nothing is more regrettable than to see the wife . . . reduced to abandoning her home for the workplace. The conjugal link is weakened, family life is diminished, the cleanliness and comfort of the home, the family's food, the care and education of the children, abandoned to themselves outside school hours, all suffers.'[113] Masculinity was equated with skill and responsibility. Women were largely excluded from the better-paid jobs. They entered such trades as shoemaking and clothing in large numbers just as the spread of *confection* and mechanisation 'degraded' these trades and even then met with bitter hostility from male workers threatened with displacement. Whatever the trade, their earnings were widely perceived to be a means of supplementing those of the male 'bread winner' and were 'naturally' lower.[114]

Constantly subject to male chauvinism and frequent sexual improprieties,[115] it is hardly surprising that many women came to interiorise their own inferiority, and to share the male ideals of womanhood and family life. In the interests of the family, they accepted the need to combine factory or domestic wage earning with housework. Many experienced repeated pregnancies, and suffered from the gynaecological problems caused by childbirth itself or back-street abortions. Women also endured the accumulated stress of making ends meet. They needed to economise on the purchase and preparation of food and clothes. Where menfolk engaged in hard

[111] J. Gaillard, *Paris, la ville*, p. 406; Ratcliffe, 'Manufacturing in the metropolis', pp. 306–8.
[112] *Les populations ouvrières et les industries de la France dans le mouvement social du 19e siècle* (Paris 1854), I, pp. 68–9, 138.
[113] AN F12/3115.
[114] See e.g. G. Désert, *Les archives hospitalières. Source d'histoire économique et sociale* (Caen 1977), p. 235.
[115] E.g. PG Nîmes, 16 July 1861, AN BB30/382.

physical labour, 'it goes without saying that within the family distribution [of food] is done very unequally. Physical labour demands substantial nourishment; men must have meat and wine; women and children have only a reduced portion.'[116] This intense burden might be contrasted with the male chauvinism of popular songs which described women sitting idly at home, spending far too much time and money on coffee, gossiping so much that they forget to prepare the breadwinner's meals, constantly nagging and bearing far too many children.[117] Unable themselves to earn a living wage, women rarely had an alternative to marriage. With children to care for, they were trapped, whilst husbands frequently sought solace through heavy drinking. The domestic violence this caused must often have created almost intolerably tense relationships.[118]

The struggle to make ends meet

To a substantial degree, perceptions of the workplace were established in the constant struggle for a living wage. Living standards were determined by extremely diverse individual and collective factors, including the general economic situation, levels of (un)employment, skill, wages, the number of dependants, and the cost of living, as well as age, gender, health, and regional variations in all these things. Unfortunately, the sources of information on wages are diverse and very varied in quality. None of them really provides more than rough estimates, and all tend to conceal the complexity of wage systems and individual situations.[119] Calculation of the movement of real incomes, that is, taking account of the changing cost of living, is particularly complicated.[120] According to Labrousse's calculations, overall, during the Second Empire, incomes rose by 45 per cent and the cost of living by 25 per cent. Other indexes suggest similar trends.[121]

---

[116] Reybaud, *Fer*, p. 150.

[117] P. Pierrard, *Les chansons en patois de Lille sous le Second Empire* (Arras 1965); W. Reddy, 'The moral sense of farce: the patois literature of the Lille factory workers, 1848–70', in Kaplan and Koepp, *Work in France*, pp. 374–5.

[118] L. Strumingher, *Women and the Making of the Working Class: Lyon, 1830–70* (St Albans, Vt. 1979), pp. 47–8; C. Chatelard, *Crime et criminalité dans l'arrondissement de St. Etienne au 19e siècle* (Saint-Etienne 1981), pp. 87, 200.

[119] A great deal of piecemeal information can be found in AN F12/2370-74; see also P. Sicsic, 'Wage dispersion in France, 1850–1930' in P. Scholliers and V. Zamagni (eds.), *Labour's Reward. Real Wages and Economic Change in 19th and 20th Century Europe* (Aldershot 1995), pp. 169–77.

[120] E.g. J. Rougerie, 'Remarques sur l'histoire des salaires à Paris au 19e siècle', *Le mouvement social* 1968, pp. 81–3.

[121] E. Labrousse, 'Le mouvement du salaire en France, de 1815 à 1870', *Information historique* 1955, p. 80; cf. e.g. J. Luciani, 'Logiques du placement ouvrier au 19e siècle et construction du marché du travail', *Sociétés contemporaines* 1990, pp. 5–6.

Most workers were primarily aware of, concerned about, and motivated by, the movement of nominal wages, together with the cost of basic necessities. Nominal wages increased by something of the order of 30 to 45 per cent between 1851 and 1869, following a long period of stagnation, and as a result of increasing productivity and the growing demand for labour. This encouraged employers to make concessions,[122] although the existence of a large pool of underemployed rural labour and growing migration eased the pressure.[123] During the Second Empire, it further appears that most workers also enjoyed greater regularity of employment and thus significantly higher annual incomes. Certainly there were periods of relative hardship but nothing to compare with the misery of the mid-century depression. Undoubtedly the best years were those between 1858 and 1866, when rising wages coincided with falling food prices. Even in these years of relative abundance, however, the process of economic development was discontinuous over both time and space.

Although 'informed' contemporary observers generally agreed that the burden had declined,[124] official statistics make it clear that poverty remained a heavy encumbrance. Thus whilst the regime would claim credit for the virtual disappearance of the threat of dearth as improved communications transformed food distribution and counter-cyclical investment in public works provided jobs, there would still be difficult years. Poor harvests in 1853, 1855, and 1856 imposed considerable hardship on families still heavily dependent on bread for sustenance.[125] Unemployment spread through manufacturing industry to coincide with the spectacular rise in the cost of living and decline in purchasing power. Armand Husson, the well-informed chef de division at the Prefecture of the Seine estimated in 1856 that around two-fifths of the Paris population were in need of municipal or private assistance.[126] Circumstances certainly varied. Every urban centre had a small minority of relatively well-off workers and a majority who were seriously impoverished in the sense that they found it difficult, even at the best of times, to obtain basic necessities and respect minimal obligations to children, parents, kin, and neighbours. In Lille, Rouen, and Bordeaux

---

[122] G. Weill, 'Le rôle des facteurs structurales dans l'évolution des rémunérations salariales au 19e siècle', *Revue Economique* 1959, p. 238.

[123] E.g. Prefect Haut-Rhin to Ministre de l'agriculture . . . , 17 July 1856, AN F12/2370-4; evidence of T. Legrand, textile manufacturer at Fourmies (Nord), in *Enquête. Traité de commerce*, III, p. 592.

[124] E.g. M. Vée, *Considérations sur le décroissement graduel du paupérisme à Paris . . . et les causes des progrès moraux et économiques des classes ouvrières* (Paris 1862), p. 6.

[125] See e.g. Prefect Marne, report on July 1855, AN F7/4078 re Reims; see also e.g. S. Muckensturm, 'L'indigence révélatrice des faiblesses d'une société: l'exemple bas-rhinois au 19e siècle', *Revue d'Alsace* 1988, pp. 133–7.

[126] Husson, *Les consommations de Paris*, pp. 36–9.

76 per cent, 75 per cent, and 79 per cent respectively of the population had nothing to leave to their descendants when they died.[127]

Few workers, regardless of skills, can ever have entirely escaped from the tensions associated with insecurity. According to Gobelin, a textile printer at Darnétal near Rouen, their essential ambition was 'to be able to make ends meet'. The approach of winter, which meant seasonal unemployment and the additional cost of heating 'inspires terror among these poor men, who will not be able to afford even the most basic necessities'. Lack of work was particularly feared for its 'degrading' consequences.[128] Only fragmentary information on unemployment exists.[129] However, in a period of accelerating economic change the impact of cyclical variations in the demand for labour was exacerbated by technological/structural factors. Those most likely to be without employment were workers with redundant skills together with the unskilled and newcomers, many of whom would have been engaged in an almost perpetual search for work.

Technological unemployment was widespread. The traditional rural, charcoal-using, metallurgical industry, for example, rapidly collapsed.[130] River ports on the various affluents of the Seine in the departments of Yonne and Nièvre, which had traditionally supplied Paris with wood, were devastated by rail competition and the increased use of coal as fuel.[131] In Reims the introduction of mechanised wool combing in the 1850s destroyed the livelihoods of some 10,000 hand wool-combers, virtually overnight.[132]

Production was increasingly concentrated. In the Rouen area in the 1860s fifty-three small water-powered mills closed, whilst entrepreneurs determined to meet both internal and British competition opened nine large steam-powered mills. Unsurprisingly it was the smaller, undercapitalised enterprises and those facing liquidity problems which succumbed.[133] Most serious in terms of the numbers affected was the accelerated collapse of rural weaving.[134] Factory work, even with low wages, offered greater security in

[127] Lequin, 'Les citadins', p. 499.
[128] *La vérité sur la position actuelle des classes laborieuses et sur la principale cause de leur malaise*, par Gobelin, ouvrier imprimeur en indiennes, de Darnétal – pamphlet accompanying letter dated 22 Nov. 1852, AN F12/2370-4.
[129] See e.g. statistics accompanying report from Ministre de l'Intérieur to Ministre d'Etat, 3 Dec. 1863, AN 45 AP 7.
[130] See also Prefect Nièvre, report on Dec. 1856, AN F7/4102 re workers dismissed by ironworks at Fourchambault and Imphy; Armengaud, *Populations*, pp. 230–2 re Catalan forges in the Pyrenees.
[131] PG Paris, 4 March 1854, AN BB30/432.
[132] K. Honeyman and J. Goodman, *Technology and Enterprise. Isaac Holden and the Mechanisation of Woolcombing in France, 1848–1914* (Aldershot 1986), ch. 7.
[133] PG Rouen, 10 Jan. 1864, AN BB30/387.
[134] PG Rouen, 2 Oct. 1855, AN BB30/433 re arrondissement Yvetot and resumé of reports prepared for Emperor on second half of 1856, AN BB30/368.

these circumstances.[135] The steady employment offered by the railways and
state enterprises like the post office and arsenals must have been much
treasured.

Seasonal unemployment was another problem, with the luxury trades
especially susceptible as a result of changes in fashion.[136] The silk industry
in the Lyon and Saint-Etienne areas, which normally experienced an annual
slack period as designs were changed and the Jacquard looms were re-set, was
also seriously affected by rising raw material costs in the mid-1850s as disease
spread amongst the silk worms.[137] The building trades were particularly
hypersensitive due to long term fluctuations in demand as well as the
short-term impact of inclement winter weather.[138] Even in technologically
advanced industries like machine building, orders were irregular, so that
periods of intense activity with extended workdays were likely to be followed
by lay-offs and short-time working.[139]

Observers also realised increasingly that in the new economy subsistence
crises were rapidly giving way to industrial crises of overproduction/under
consumption, associated with stresses in the international financial system.[140] Together with the restrictive credit policy of the Bank of France
and local banking failures, in 1867/8 the falling demand for manufactured
goods contributed to a collapse in confidence and to a crisis which appears
to have been as severe as that of 1848 in some textile centres, at least in terms
of the number of bankruptcies. Inevitably this resulted in lay-offs and short-
time working.[141] Employers enjoyed all the advantages of a 'flexible' labour
market, hiring and firing almost at will. Many small businessmen with little
capital to spare were obliged to reduce wages rapidly and dismiss workers as
demand for their products declined. Entrepreneurial freedom was greatest
in the case of rural and domestic workers whose raw material supplies were
simply cut off.[142] Where fixed capital costs were high – in large steam-
powered factories – employers were reluctant to leave their machinery idle
and might seek to reduce wage costs but to dismiss workers only as a last
resort.[143] When dismissals did occur they were likely to be highly selective.
Those employees known for their *bonne volonté* were retained, whilst the

[135] E.g. Prefect, 2 June 1858, AN F1 C111 Oise 11.
[136] Cochin, *Paris*, quoted H. Maneglier, *Paris impérial. La vie quotidienne sous le Second Empire*
(Paris 1990), pp. 49–50.
[137] Prefect, 4 Nov. 1857, AN F1 C111 Isère 7.   [138] PG Paris, 4 March 1854, AN BB30/432.
[139] Noiriel, *Les ouvriers*, p. 45.   [140] Price, *Rural Modernisation*, pp. 97–100.
[141] C. Fohlen, 'Crise textile et troubles sociaux: le Nord à la fin du Second Empire', *Revue du Nord*
1953, pp. 111–17.
[142] E.g. Prefect, 1 July 1854, AN F1 C111 Seine-Inférieure 9; PG Amiens, 9 July 1867, AN BB30/371.
[143] E.g. PG Paris, 30 July 1868, AN BB30/384 re Reims.

less productive and those identified as potential troublemakers were the first to be dismissed.[144]

Unforeseen events were another cause of severe recession, and most notably the American Civil War (1861–5). Interrupted supplies resulted in substantial fluctuations in raw cotton prices, due both to shortages and speculation on futures, and greatly exacerbated the difficulties of an industry which had probably anyway over-expanded during the 1850s. The levels of unemployment caused by the crisis are impossible to determine accurately. In the winter of 1861/2 it was claimed that 150,000 to 200,000 were without work in the Seine-Inférieure but this figure was based on the exaggerated accounts of mayors anxious for government assistance and industrialists who continued to encourage their workers to lay the blame for their misery on the commercial treaty with Britain.[145] Certainly the intensity of the crisis varied. Thus in the arrondissement of Mulhouse in October 1862, one large spinning mill which previously had laid in large stocks of raw cotton was operating normally and extremely profitably; in contrast, two others had closed and eight had introduced short-time working. A gradual improvement in the situation of the cotton industry became evident from around the early summer of 1863, although cotton prices continued to fluctuate widely.[146]

In the meantime, the difficulties of the cotton industry had encouraged the expansion of woollen and linen production.[147] In the Cholet area in the west rural weavers were able to adapt their handlooms to weave linen instead of cotton, whereas the cost of adapting mechanised factory looms was often too high.[148] There was substantial potential for profit. Nevertheless, and although weavers earned only around 1f.50 a day, manufacturers complained about rising wages. Auguste Mimerel at Roubaix even encouraged Belgian immigration to push wages down.[149] In any case, prosperity was short lived. The restoration of cotton supplies would cause a crisis for the now over-extended woollen and linen sectors.[150] As a result in 1865, workers who had moved from Rouen to Elbeuf and Louviers from 1862, as employment in cotton declined and woollens expanded, started moving back again.[151]

---

[144] PG Rouen, 15 Oct. 1863, AN BB30/387.

[145] C. Fohlen, *L'industrie textile au temps du Second Empire* (Paris 1956), pp. 265–76.

[146] PG Colmar, 12 Oct. 1862, AN BB30/376.

[147] PG Rouen, 10 July 1862, AN BB30/387; PG Metz, 12 Jan. 1865, AN BB30/380 re Sedan.

[148] PG Angers, 10 Oct. 1863, AN BB30/371. On costs see e.g. PG Amiens, 8 July 1863, AN BB30/371.

[149] Town Council Roubaix to Prefect Nord, 17 Jan. 1863, presumably mis-filed and found in AN F1 CIII Seine-Inférieure 17.

[150] On linen e.g. *Journal-circulaire du marché linier de Lille*, 22 Jan. 1868, AN 45 AP 23.

[151] PG Rouen, 11 Jan. 1865, AN BB30/387.

The American Civil War also seriously reduced demand for *articles de Paris* and other luxury goods.[152] In Lyon during the winter of 1861/2 30,000 silk workers were in regular receipt of charity.[153] The war was followed by the introduction of protective tariffs by the American government, a move which had the added effect of diverting British goods from American to European markets.[154] In 1866/7 concerns about deteriorating relations with Prussia further dented business confidence. The renewed sense of insecurity resulted in a reduction of orders by wholesalers and widespread short-time working, at a time when food prices were rising. It was reported that even 'the most honest worker lives from day-to-day, and he is still constantly haunted by the fear of unemployment'.[155] The poor harvest of 1867 ensured that in Lyon and the textile towns in the north the harsh winter of 1867/8 was one of the most miserable of the Second Empire.[156] Even then, in the neighbouring department of the Loire, whilst the textiles trades were depressed, the modern metallurgical and mining industries were prosperous.[157] The likely political implications of economic depression are thus difficult to discern.

Subsistence

In assessing working-class living standards, the budget of the family, the 'unit of subsistence',[158] rather than individual income is the relevant factor. The number of breadwinners, as well as their earnings, the number of dependants too young, too sick, or too old to work, fluctuations in the cost of living, together with major changes associated with the life-cycle of each family add up to a complex, extremely varied, and ever-changing reality and lend weight to stress on the importance of family solidarity. The average male wage in most occupations would not have been adequate to support a family. To achieve a modicum of comfort, and respectability within the local community, it was generally necessary for women and children to seek work and secure additional resources. Success also depended on constant effort, and good luck – in avoiding accidents or ill health and finding regular employment. Whilst unmarried males were likely to provide for their needs with relative ease, wage discrimination against women rendered the

[152] H. Vanier, *La mode et ses métiers: frivolité et lutte des classes* (Paris 1960), p. 64.
[153] PG Lyon, 27 Dec. 1861, AN BB30/379; Lequin, *La Formation*, I, p. 71.
[154] PG Lyon, 28 June 1866, AN BB30/379.
[155] Gendarmerie impériale. OC Cie. du Rhône, 27 April 1868, AHG G8/151.
[156] Ménager, *Vie politique*, II, p. 689.
[157] Merley, 'Les élections', *Cahiers d'histoire* 1961, pp. 60–4.
[158] Reddy, *The Rise of Market Culture*, p. 168.

situation of single women, outside the family or some form of cohabitation, extremely precarious. High mortality furthermore ensured that there were many single-parent families.

Age was another vital factor. Physical capacity and earning power declined from around the age of forty-five, especially in industries like mining, and for manual labourers in general. Victor Heitzmann, a skilled and relatively well-paid ouvrier-mécanicien at Le Creusot complained that 'reaching the age of forty, after hard work over a long period, the worker becomes weaker and is employed at secondary tasks for which the wages are very low'.[159] In coal mining, disabling accidents and the effects of dust ensured that few men could continue working at the coal face beyond forty and that most would die from the effects of silicosis in their fifties or, at best, early sixties.[160] This was at the same time as children were beginning to establish households of their own.

The numerous contemporary examples of 'typical' family budgets reveal how difficult it was to make ends meet.[161] Income might be supplemented in a variety of ways. In the smaller industrial centres it was often possible to rent a field or at least a vegetable garden.[162] Taking in lodgers was common. Nevertheless, the responsibility for feeding their families and making do with as little as possible must have imposed considerable psychological pressure on women, caught up in the 'economy of makeshift' with its circulation of second-hand clothes, and constant prudence in the use of soap, heating fuel, lighting oil, and everything perceived to be non-essential.[163]

For the great majority of families there appears to have been no margin of security, nothing in reserve. In general workers spent their entire incomes – around 60 per cent on food alone – and were unable to save. In the major industrial centres, when they died, 90 per cent left behind nothing save kitchen utensils, some well-worn clothing and a few sticks of furniture.[164] In these circumstances, the prospect of rising prices, short-time working, unemployment, sickness, or old age must have conjured up nightmares, from which not even the best paid could escape. The Parisian roofers' delegate to the 1867 Exposition pointed out that even in the best of times

---

[159] Quoted J.-B. Martin, *La fin des mauvais pauvres* (Seyssel 1983), pp. 44–5.

[160] 1848 Enquête, response of Saint-Etienne miners, AN C956 III; see also D. Bertaux, *Destins personnels et structure de classe* (Paris 1977), pp. 211–12.

[161] Boivin, *Mouvement ouvrier*, II, p. 89 re Elbeuf 1868; Price, *Rural Modernisation*, pp. 104–14.

[162] E.g. PG Caen, 13 April 1859, AN BB30/375 re textile workers at Domfront (Orne).

[163] F. Gouda, *Poverty and Political Culture. The Rhetoric of Social Welfare in the Netherlands and France, 1815–54* (Lanham, Md. 1995), p. 66; see also memoirs of J.-B. Dumay in Traugott, *The French Worker*, p. 313.

[164] A. Daumard, 'Le peuple dans la société française à l'époque romantique', *Romantisme* 1975/6, pp. 24–6.

the working-class family had barely enough to eat so that 'as a result of the slightest setback which upsets this frail budget, this honest, hard-working family has to endure misery.'[165] All too often undernourished and unhealthy men and women worked until they dropped.[166] The depressing result, according to the words of a popular song was that 'To live, for a labourer, is not to die'.[167]

In these circumstances, debt was a constant feature of working-class life, whether incurred through borrowing from family and friends, from the municipal pawnshop, from loan sharks, or in the form of credit from neighbourhood shopkeepers or as a result of the delayed payment of rent.[168] Dependence on charity was also common. The mutual aid societies, to which the better-paid might be able to afford to subscribe, provided only minimal relief in case of illness and old age. They did not possess the means and were indeed forbidden by law to assist the unemployed in case this served to 'encourage idleness'.[169]

Whilst the situation of most working-class families thus remained extremely precarious, various indicators confirm that living conditions were improving. After a lengthy period of stagnation or even decline, an essentially quantitative amelioration of diet occurred, as a result of the more efficient working of the market and rising incomes. Although, in Paris in the late 1860s, typically male workers still ate around 500 grams of bread a day, dipping it into a variety of soups and stews, a better nutritional balance slowly developed as consumption of meat, vegetables, and dairy products, especially cheese, increased. Nevertheless, it was evident that many workers and their families remained poorly nourished, with damaging consequences for their health and capacity for work.[170] The lack of calcium and vitamins as well as the frequent adulteration, contamination, and poor preparation of food had particularly damaging effects on children, increasing their susceptibility to rickets and scrofula, as well as to gastroenteritis and infections of the throat and chest. Poor nutrition also frequently affected eyesight.[171] M. Randoing, a cloth manufacturer at Abbeville, insisted that the British competitive advantage was due not only to cheap coal but to

---

[165] E. Saveney, 'Les délégations ouvrières à l'Exposition universelle de 1867. L'opinion des ouvriers sur l'industrie et sur eux-mêmes', *Revue des Deux Mondes* 77, 1868, p. 607.

[166] E.g. 1848 Enquête, response from canton of Hondschoote (Nord), AN C960.

[167] Quoted Harvey, *Consciousness*, p. 122.   [168] E.g. Boivin, *Mouvement ouvrier*, I, p. 70.

[169] Ministerial circular, 29 May 1852, quoted L. Gaillard, 'La vie ouvrière et les mouvements ouvriers à Marseille de 1848 à 1879', Doc. d'Etat, Univ. d'Aix, 1972, II, p. 487.

[170] Désert, *Archives hospitalières*, p. 179; M. Lévy-Leboyer and F. Bourguignon, *L'économie française au 19e siècle. Analyse macro-économique* (Paris 1985), p. 24.

[171] Heywood, *Childhood*, p. 170.

the fact that 'English workers feed themselves better than our workers; consequently, they are stronger and better able to endure the fatigue of the workplace.'[172] Acting on this assumption, in 1868 the directors of Le Creusot were able to congratulate themselves on the improvements in productivity, which had resulted from higher wages and the better diet this made possible.[173]

Trends in the food economy might have helped to generate a greater optimism within working-class families. However, from the widespread tendency to complain about the inflationary rise in food prices, it seems more likely that perceptions of change were primarily negative. The removal of controls on the price of bread (in 1863), as part of the programme of economic liberalisation, helped create the impression that the government was 'uncaring'.[174] The widespread belief that living conditions were deteriorating caused widespread agitation,[175] and would have significant political consequences.

Housing

Housing was another key indicator of living conditions. The regime's efforts to establish Paris as *la plus belle ville du monde* provided work with, at the height of the boom, 20 per cent of the Paris labour force engaged in building. However, reconstruction also resulted in severe dislocation, as slums were cleared and new boulevards developed. Unable to afford rents on the smart new streets, many workers were forced to move out of the city centre, whilst others, obliged by the high cost of public transport to live close to their places of work, crowded into the older streets left behind the impressive façades of the new. The rapid influx of people – and the 1866 census revealed that 66 per cent of Parisians had been born elsewhere – combined with the displacement of perhaps 350,000 of the established population, substantially reinforced trends towards social segregation and modified patterns of social interaction.[176]

Marked contrasts developed between the overwhelmingly working-class districts to the north and east of the emerging commercial centre, and

---

[172] *Enquête. Traité de commerce*, II, p. 190.　　[173] Deseilligny, *De l'influence de l'éducation*, pp. 244–5.

[174] See Rouher to Emperor, 27 Sept. 1867, in Poulet-Malassis (ed.), *Papiers secrets et correspondance du Second Empire* (Paris 1873); report of police commissaire Marseille to Prefect Bouches-du-Rhône, in F. Charpin, *Pratique religieuse et formation d'une grande ville (Marseille 1806–1958)* (Paris 1964), p. 249.

[175] Memo. Ministère de l'Intérieur. Direction de la Presse to Ministre de l'agriculture . . . , 21 Nov. 1864, AN F12/4651.

[176] F. Bourillon, 'Rénovation *haussmannienne* et ségrégation urbaine' in A. Fourcaut (ed.), *La ville divisée. Les ségrégations urbaines en question. France 18e–20e siècle* (Grâne 1996), pp. 100–4.

the more prosperous arrondissements of the south and west favoured by the upper and middle classes. The centre of gravity of working-class Paris itself shifted from the faubourg St Martin and the Hôtel-de-Ville and Bastille districts eastwards towards Belleville and Montmartre. This has been described as the 'central feature of the experiences of the capital's working class' during the Second Empire.[177] In a *Rapport de la Chambre de Commerce et du Préfet de Police sur la question des salaires ouvriers* written in June 1855, it was pointed out that:

In the old days they used to live on the upper floors of buildings whose lower floors were occupied by the families of businessmen and other fairly well to do persons. A species of solidarity grew up among the tenants of a single building. Neighbours helped each other in small ways. When sick or unemployed, the workers might find a great deal of help, while on the other hand, a sort of human respect imbued working-class habits with a certain regularity. Having moved north of the Canal St Martin or even beyond the *barrières*, the workers now live where there are no bourgeois families and are thus deprived of their assistance at the same time as they are emancipated from the curb on them previously exercised by neighbours of this kind.[178]

Generally housing conditions were at their worst in the larger cities where, due to substantial in-migration and lack of investment in low-cost housing, supply failed to keep pace with demand. Thus the situation was more difficult in Lille than in neighbouring Roubaix or Tourcoing, in Rouen than in Elbeuf or Louviers.[179] Overcrowding was common. Furnishing was rudimentary. Comfort was minimal. Accommodation was generally poorly ventilated, badly illuminated, too hot in summer, freezing in winter, and frequently damp. Sanitary facilities were neglected. The absence of running water discouraged cleanliness. As a rule water was carried laboriously from public fountains and used sparingly. Parasites thrived on dirty bodies. Workers might often be distinguished from the better off by their physical appearance, by their short stature, bent posture, dirtiness, and skin diseases.[180] Middle-class observers frequently, and with disgust, described them as a race apart. The economist Blanqui recalled with horror a 'sickly, nauseating smell, the smell of filthy people' – the stench of poverty so characteristic of workers' lodgings.[181]

---

[177] Magraw, *French Working Class*, I, p. 221.

[178] Quoted L. Chevalier, *Labouring Classes and Dangerous Classes* (London 1973), pp. 198–9.

[179] Heywood, *Childhood*, p. 167.

[180] G. Soudjian, 'Quelques réflexions sur la stature des jeunes Parisiens sous le Second Empire', *Ethnologie française* 1979, pp. 69–84.

[181] P. Pierrard, 'Habitat ouvrier et démographie à Lille au 19e siècle', *Annales de démographie historique* 1975, pp. 41–2; on growing bourgeois sensitivity see A. Corbin, *Le miasme et la jonquille. L'odorat et l'imaginaire social, 18e–19e siècle* (Paris 1982), pp. 67–72.

To the smell of sweat was added the stench of overflowing cess pits, rotting debris, of cooking, lamp oil, and burning coal. In Lyon in the middle of the century 'most of the streets in which workers live . . . are narrow and muddy, the houses are dirty, cramped, damp; the lavatories, mostly located on the staircases, are badly cared for and revolting; the walls of the buildings and courtyards are, due to neglect by the landlords, coated with a thick layer of dust in which insects multiply without hindrance'. It followed that 'the dwellings correspond to the squalor of the buildings, the walls and floors are smoky, the cramped space forces the tenants to place their children's beds under the eaves where air is lacking and vermin swarm'.[182] And Lyon, as the prefect of the Rhône insisted, was no worse than other large cities.[183] Overcrowding also implied the constant noise of children playing, women shouting and gossiping, and drunks quarrelling. Shared misery might well have encouraged reciprocal assistance and solidarity. Additionally it resulted in frequent disputes and violence.[184]

Together with some new construction, the work of the commissions de salubrité established by the law of 13 April 1850 led to the elimination of the very worst slums including the cellars in Lille described in most of the social enquiries of the 1840s, which had become a byword for squalor.[185] The efforts of municipal authorities to improve water supply and sanitation also improved conditions, but within narrow limits. In 1858, the official Comité consultatif d'hygiène publique claimed that the essential obstacle to continued improvement was the reluctance of landlords either to improve their own buildings or to accept increased local taxation. The various municipal commissions lacked the authority to force landlords to carry out repairs and anyway would have been unwilling to question the absolute rights of property owners.[186] Moreover it would take many decades to change popular conceptions of cleanliness and comfort, and as the Paris Commission des logements insalubres pointed out, constant in-migration ensured that even if it took measures to improve sanitation it could do nothing to prevent overcrowding.[187]

The provision of cheap accommodation by speculative builders generally took the form of three-storey blocks, each with 40 to 50 two-room apartments, constructed using the cheapest and poorest quality materials in the

---

[182] AN C963.   [183] 14 Oct. 1852, AN F8/210.

[184] E.g. F. Hordern, *Les crises industrielles en Alsace au 19e siècle et leurs répercussions sur l'emploi des travailleurs* (Aix 1970), p. 380.

[185] Pierrard, 'Habitat ouvrier', p. 38.

[186] Ministre de l'agriculture, du commerce et des travaux publics, circular 27 Dec. 1858, AN F8/210; A.-L. Shapiro, *Housing the Poor of Paris, 1850–1900* (Madison, Wisc. 1985), pp. 25–8.

[187] *Rapport général des travaux de la Commission pendant l'année 1851*, AN F8/210.

popular *quartiers* of the north and east.[188] Few working-class families could afford anything better. To add to the slums caused by the repeated sub-division of older city-centre properties a new *ceinture de misère* developed on its outskirts,[189] offering living conditions which certainly failed to impress English artisans visiting the city for the 1867 Exposition.[190] Most industrial centres saw similar development. In suburban areas and in small towns or villages the impact of overcrowding was at least reduced and workers might even aspire to own their accommodation and eliminate the burden of rent. The ideal was probably to possess a small cottage with its own garden on the edge of town.[191] However, many workers, who had never lived in anything other than squalor, whether in town or countryside, remained essentially apathetic about housing conditions.[192]

The impact of urban population growth on an inadequate housing stock could be measured in terms of misery but also through rising rents, a mat-ter of almost obsessive concern to tenants. Under the pressure of demand, rents rose far more rapidly than the general increase in the cost of liv-ing in most urban areas, and consumed a substantial portion of workers' incomes. Estimates vary, but suggest that the rent paid by the 'average' working-class family rose by somewhere between 50 and 100 per cent dur-ing the life of the imperial regime, with rents in the capital higher than elsewhere, and rising wage levels perceived of as failing to provide adequate compensation.[193]

Frequently, tenants had little choice but to accept high rents and extreme dilapidation. Many of the growing number of people displaced by city-centre demolition, and especially young immigrants, could afford nothing better than furnished rooms in a lodging house (*garnis*). In 1856, 7 per cent of the population of Paris, rising to 18 per cent in the 9th arrondissement, belonged to this group,[194] judged by the hygiene commission to be enduring the most deplorable conditions. Generally landlords spent minimal sums on maintenance and repair. Many – small businessmen or *rentiers* – could hardly afford improvement and saw high rents as necessary compensation for the risk that an impoverished tenant might do a 'moonlight flit'.[195] The situation was much the same as that described by the historian of twentieth-century Detroit:

---

[188] Daumas, *Evolution*, pp. 301–3.   [189] Girard, *Nouvelle histoire de Paris*, p. 165.
[190] *Reports of artisans* . . . , I, pp. 439–41.
[191] E.g. 1848 Enquête, response from Amiens, AN C966.
[192] *Travaux de la Commission pour l'assainissement des logements insalubres* (Nantes 1852), AN F8/210.
[193] Statistique générale de la France. *Salaires et coût de l'existence à diverses époques, jusqu'en 1910* (Paris 1911), p. 89; Shapiro, *Housing*, p. 38.
[194] J. Gaillard, *Paris, la ville*, p. 211.   [195] Pierrard, 'Habitat ouvrier', p. 43.

Landlords who charged high rents often had little stake in their buildings: to maximise profit they minimised repairs. Likewise, tenants who could barely afford to
make rent payments had few resources to maintain their apartments in decent
condition. The high turnover of tenants meant that few had any long-term commitment to the quality of life in their buildings. The result was detrimental to all
concerned.[196]

Certainly, the approach of the moment when rents were due caused
intense anxiety.[197] In October 1856, the Paris Prefect of Police registered his
concern about the rapid increase in rents caused by the shortage of *petits
logements*, and particularly about the political implications – revealed by
placards – of growing worker exasperation.[198] The official analysis of the
reports of the worker delegates to the 1867 Exposition again laid considerable stress on this problem.[199] The roofers' delegates had bitterly contrasted
'buildings resembling palaces, which the rich bourgeoisie can barely fill',
with their own accommodation, 'relegated far from the centre' but still
costing 250 to 300f. a year out of a family income of at most 1,600f., and
this for 'a little room in which one can put two beds, a cupboard, a table,
and a few chairs'.[200] Speakers at public meetings in Paris in 1868/9 were
vehement in their condemnation of landlords. At Belleville on 4 February
1869 a worker was reported to have been greeted with *applaudissements
frénétiques* for pointing out that 'we can never be sure of finding bread and
work, and yet, when the landlord comes and says: you must pay all the
same! He does not ask us: have you worked these past three months? No,
he says, give me the money, or your last crust, your last clothes will remain
in my hands.'[201] The tension between landlord and tenant was probably at
least as great as that prevailing between employer and worker. The words
of one popular song actually suggested that 'if you want to be happy, hang
your landlord'.[202]

In such circumstances, particularly in times of crisis, desperation drove
many workers into petty crime, frequently involving the theft of food, raw
materials, or fuel from employers.[203] Faced with the refusal of shopkeepers
or landlords to renew their credit, there must often have appeared to be

---

[196] T. Sugrue, *The Origins of the Urban Crisis. Race and Inequality in Postwar Detroit* (Princeton, N.J.
    1996), pp. 54–5.
[197] Traugott, *The French Worker*, p. 303.   [198] 26 Oct. 1856, AN BB30/366.
[199] Analysis of 'Rapports des délégations ouvrières à l'Exposition universelle de 1867' by M. Devinck,
    dated 28 Oct. 1868, AN 45 AP 6.
[200] Saveney, 'Délégations', p. 605.   [201] M. Bacot in A. Vitu, *Les réunions publiques*, pp. 31–2.
[202] Quoted R. Guerrand, *Les origines du logement social en France* (Paris 1967), p. 84.
[203] Jacquemet, 'Belleville', ii, pp. 600–1.

little alternative to theft or begging. Misery and crime was concentrated in particular *quartiers* in most towns. The children of paupers were only too likely to follow the example set by their parents. If prostitution was seen by bourgeois critics as certain proof of incorrigible wickedness, for many single or deserted women – typically domestics, washerwomen, and seamstresses unable to find work or earn a living wage in spite of hours of drudgery – it might represent a last resort.[204] Professional or occasional prostitution can hardly have been an attractive prospect. According to a sanitary report from Caen in 1865 the prostitutes, crowded into the old town around the château, the church of St Pierre, and the Palais de Justice, were 'worn out by debauchery and drunkenness; some manage to remain just about healthy at thirty, many succumb, either to tuberculosis or some other organic affection'.[205]

Another potent cause of crime was sheer frustration. Manual workers and miners, men who took great pride in their physical strength and who were likely to drink heavily at the end of an exhausting day's labour, appear to have been particularly susceptible to insults, real or imagined, and to have resorted to violence in response.[206] Families and neighbours, living constantly in close proximity, frequently quarrelled, exchanging insults and blows, and 'hurling faeces'; all minor incidents, which normally went unreported.[207] The general absence of police encouraged 'self defence'. Their presence often provoked even greater resentment. This latent criminality, which, during the authoritarian Empire, provoked a 'paroxysm of penal repression',[208] might well be seen as the expression of popular resentment of impoverishment although, in the case of theft and violence, it was directed largely at other poor people.

Urban pathology

As Louis Chevalier pointed out, 'inequality in death [was] the most certain measure of inequality in life'.[209] Harsh working conditions, lack of adequate nourishment, and poor housing, inevitably had a disastrous impact on the health of working-class families. In spite of generally youthful

---

[204] E.g. PG Lyon, 30 Dec. 1863, AN BB30/379; see also A. Corbin, *Les Filles de noce* (Paris 1978), p. 240.

[205] Désert, *Archives hospitalières*, p. 200.   [206] Chatelard, *Crime et criminalité*, p. 174.

[207] J.-P. Burdy, *Le soleil noir. Un quartier de Saint-Etienne 1840–1940* (Lyon 1989), p. 116.

[208] M. Crubellier and M. Agulhon, 'Les citadins et leurs cultures' in *Histoire de la France urbaine*, vol. IV (Paris 1983), p. 410.

[209] Chevalier, *Labouring Classes*, pp. 425–6.

populations and variations in mortality rates between industrial centres – which suggest considerable differences in working and living conditions – mortality levels were invariably high. In Lille at the end of the Second Empire the mortality rate remained stubbornly at thirty-three per thousand. In the industrial *quartiers* of Wazemmes and St Sauveur 70 per cent of the population would die before the age of forty.[210] Infant mortality was especially high, particularly where bottle rather than breast-feeding was the norm and hygiene poor. As Michael Hanagan has pointed out 'it was far more dangerous to be a child' than to work in a hazardous profession like coal mining.[211]

Although mortality rates were falling gradually, poor health and general debility were basic characteristics of working-class life. Substantial numbers of conscripts were rejected each year because of lack of stature or infirmity.[212] Impoverished workers were reluctant to call upon the services of a doctor, preferring instead herbal remedies and patent medicines. The savings accumulated during a lifetime of hard work could easily disappear as a result of loss of work and the medical bills resulting from an accident or illness.[213] Working-class families could rarely afford the balanced diets or rest, which might have improved their health. Women burdened with gynaecological problems caused by repeated pregnancies or botched abortions had somehow to get on with life. How this situation, together with frequent venereal infections, affected marital relationships is impossible to judge.

Hard and prolonged physical labour, and the effects on the body of repeated gestures, also had negative consequences. The Parisian engineering employer Denis Poulot observed that 'in certain trades, where piece rates are common, after twenty years the worker is deformed, worn-out, if he is not dead'.[214] Work in unhealthy or unsafe conditions was common. Unguarded machinery caused accidents. The use of chemicals in industrial processes resulted in stomach ailments, convulsive coughing and spitting blood.[215] The overheated atmosphere, full of fibres, within which they worked, threatened the health of textile workers.[216] Exposure to extremes of temperature and noxious fumes rendered metalworkers susceptible to rheumatism and respiratory diseases.[217] They also ran constant risks from dangerous machinery and spilling, molten metal. Severe burns and

[210] Noiriel, *Ouvriers*, p. 27.   [211] Hanagan, *Nascent Proletarians*, p. 151.
[212] Husson, *Les consommations de Paris*, p. 63.   [213] See Rapport des fumistes, AN F12/3113.
[214] Quoted Cottereau, 'Vie quotidienne', p. 31.   [215] Lequin, *La formation*, II, pp. 12–14.
[216] E.g. 1848 Enquête, response from canton of Ambert, AN C962.
[217] Hanagan, *Nascent Proletarians*, p. 118.

amputations were common. According to one calculation, miners in the Saint-Etienne basin stood a 33 per cent chance of being killed or seriously injured during twenty years' work.[218] All this added to the workers' sense of insecurity, to immeasurable stress levels and to the emotional cost of poverty. Thus although living conditions were improving slowly and would have a cumulative impact on health from generation to generation, this barely registered on the workers' sense of wellbeing.

Generalisations about the links between poverty and social attitudes are certainly difficult to sustain. So much depends upon perceptions. How many workers were capable of appreciating the development of their purchasing power in historical perspective? The older generations, who had experienced the long period of declining real wages in the first half of the century as well as the dreadful mid-century crisis, might have been more conscious of improvement during the Second Empire than the younger. Many workers, nevertheless, had the contrary impression, as a result of the difficulties faced by particular industries, the impact of cyclical fluctuations in economic activity, and the general tendency for the cost of basic necessities like food and accommodation to rise.[219] Certainly poverty was a frequent subject for discussion in the public meetings held in Paris in 1869. Speakers claimed that it was caused by low wages and unemployment and that these were the result of the unequal division of property, together with the waste of resources on the imperial court, on high salaries for government officials, and on the army. A sense of exploitation and social tension are perhaps central features of a low-wage economy, especially one experiencing rapid technological change.

RELATIONSHIPS

Although, within a structured social system, it was difficult to escape from the sense of belonging to one group rather than another, social identity also incorporated the consciousness of belonging to a wider community. As dependants in a hierarchically ordered society, their day-to-day relations inevitably influenced workers' attitudes towards other social groups. To a substantial degree they responded to the initiatives of others, striving to make the best of their situation. Elite and middle-class attitudes *towards* workers and judgements made on the basis of bourgeois models

---

[218] M. Hanagan, 'Proletarian families and social protest: production and reproduction as issues of social conflict in 19th century France' in Kaplan and Koepp, *Work in France*, p. 446.

[219] E.g. Mayor of Rochefort re arsenal workers, 24 April 1866, AN 45 AP 24; see also Boivin, *Mouvement ouvrier*, I, p. 266.

of success and 'civilised' behaviour thus helped determine the workers' own self-consciousness. These attitudes were informed by three powerful 'myths'.

The first 'myth' was that property owners and employers owed their wealth and superior status to a combination of hard work and thrift. The Lille manufacturer Demesmay asked: 'Who does not know that many of our manufacturers started out as manual labourers? They owe their fortunes, so often envied but accessible to every worker, to a life of sobriety.'[220] It followed that the inferior situation of the worker was the result of intellectual and particularly moral inadequacy, a combination of fatalism with hedonism resulting in a supposed propensity for drunkenness and 'vice'. This encouraged an overwhelmingly negative attitude on the part of the better-off towards the dirty, unkempt, under-nourished, and outwardly deferential and compliant beings they encountered on the streets and in the workplaces. Not untypically, the leading liberal politician Adolphe Thiers expressed contempt for the 'vile multitude', by which he appears to have meant the rootless, 'dangerous part of the working population',[221] although the phrase was frequently taken to apply to workers in general. At a less elevated level, a primary school inspector's report on the population of the working-class Parisian suburb of Belleville in 1856 exemplified the same attitude. He described it as 'almost entirely ignorant and violent', as a collection of 'savages . . . plunged into a frightening mental degradation'.[222] Clearly, those guilty of such gross 'lack of foresight' were in urgent need of direction.

A second, and somewhat contradictory 'myth', however, insisted that workers were free agents, perfectly capable of negotiating the terms and conditions of their employment with their employers, and able to find alternative employment if they were unhappy. As free agents, enjoying equality before the law, they had no need of protection and no right to exert collective pressure on those who employed them.[223] This particular fiction provided a useful argument with which to oppose state intervention to improve workers' conditions and to justify the legislation banning strikes and trades unions. The third 'myth' was that, in a society ordained by God, only the perverted could challenge the eternal values enshrined in a social system based on the family, private property, and religion. Only the wicked could refuse to accept the place in society ordained for them

---

[220] Quoted Pierrard, *La vie ouvrière*, p. 183.   [221] Letter to M. Paultre, 21 May 1869, BN naf 20619.
[222] Quoted Jacquemet, 'Belleville', II, p. 437.
[223] E.g. Demesmay to Lille Chamber of Commerce, quoted Pierrard, *Vie ouvrière*, p. 188.

by God. To question established relationships represented both blasphemy and insubordination and deserved to be punished. It followed that: 'In their own interests, workers needed to appreciate the solidarity which unites capital and labour', and to respect those who provided work and assistance.[224]

'Master–man' relationships

The daily experience of subordination in the workplace must frequently have contributed to the development of a sense of inferiority likely to have been 'deforming and debilitating . . . providing people with a narrow sense of possibility, keeping them in their places'.[225] Historians have generally concentrated on the minority of workers mobilised for protest activity. The study of passivity is probably as important as that of engagement. Thus, within the popular *quartier* social relationships were never based simply on class. Master-artisans, small employers, café proprietors, and shopkeepers were all part of the worker's daily world. They were often bound together by family links and friendship, in spite of tensions over employment practices, rents, and credit. Rather different was the sense of shared interest, which linked the worker to the bourgeois employer. The personality of the *patron* or a paternalistic interest in the labour force might efface some of the harshness of capitalistic relationships and reinforce the tendency of the worker to identify with the employer's interests. Jean-Baptiste Dumay remembered his stepfather, a furnace hand at Le Creusot, as 'an honest worker whose chief concern in life was to be respected by his bosses'. In answer to Dumay's criticisms his habitual response was 'if there were no rich people to give us work, what would become of us?'[226]

This sense of inferiority and dependence was particularly pronounced in such rapidly growing textile centres as Roubaix and Tourcoing in the Nord, where a labour force made up to a large degree of recent migrants from the countryside, uncertain of their futures – including many from Flemish-speaking areas – for some time would continue to lack any sense of collective identity.[227] The least skilled and poorest were always most

---

[224] PG Grenoble, 10 Dec. 1857, AN BB30/378.
[225] N. Dirks, G. Eley, and S. Ortner (eds.), *Culture/Power/History* (Princeton, N.J. 1994), p. 13.
[226] Traugott, *The French Worker*, pp. 311–12.
[227] J.-P. Courtheoux, 'Naissance d'une conscience de classe dans le prolétariat textile du Nord', *Revue économique* 1957, pp. 120–4.

likely to face unemployment. Their need to secure basic family subsistence encouraged submissive behaviour and 'an exemplary resignation'.[228] In periods of depression this docility, especially on the part of Belgian migrants, frequently provoked xenophobic reactions from French workers. It took a generation or two, depending upon the scale of the continuing influx from the countryside, for a sense of working-class community to develop. In the meantime, newcomers were generally resented as competitors in the job market.[229]

At the opposite extreme to the apathetic there were the ambitious, whose energies went into self-improvement. Although substantial upward mobility was extremely unlikely, workers might still hope to improve their status and incomes. Thrift and intense commitment made it possible to accumulate the minimal capital required to set up a small business.[230] Sustained hard work brought the recognition as a 'good' worker which afforded an important means of self-protection. Aspiring contremaîtres might need to sacrifice limited leisure opportunities to attend evening classes. Additionally they would need to be subservient to employers and middle-class managers and engineers. At least vicariously, the ambitious working-class family might also experience social promotion by ensuring that some of its children received the education, at an *école primaire supérieure*, necessary for clerical work.[231] This too required sacrifices.

Success in securing promotion was likely to reinforce aspirations for 'respectability' and to encourage efforts by the ambitious to distinguish themselves from the mass of workers through dress and manners – 'clothing is a language, and above all a symbol of status'.[232] Workers themselves frequently complained about the pretensions of their foremen. The nail makers' delegates at the 1867 International Exposition pointed out that 'forgetting that they have emerged from the great family of workers, [foremen] hide their laziness behind a title which, unfortunately, always draws to them all the sycophants who, willing to commit any mean act in order to please, plunge us further into misery'.[233] This contains so much of the resentment felt for a former worker who had joined the other side and forgotten his roots. The desire for social promotion did not necessarily imply a lack of solidarity with other workers but certainly made it more

---

[228] PG Rouen, 8 Aug. 1856, AN BB30/387.

[229] V. Aelbrecht, 'L'immigration ouvrière belge à Tourcoing durant le Second Empire', *Revue belge d'histoire contemporaine* 1990, pp. 360–2.

[230] E.g. A. Chatelain, 'La main-d'oeuvre dans l'industrie française du bâtiment aux 19e et 20e siècles', *Technique, Art, Science* 1956, p. 36.

[231] E.g. Chatelain, *Migrants temporaires*, II, p. 900; Perrot, *Ouvriers en grève*, I, pp. 301–2.

[232] Burdy, *Le soleil noir*, p. 156.   [233] Quoted Cottereau, 'Vie quotidienne', p. 18.

likely that deference, passive acquiescence and conformity would assume prominence amongst a range of possible survival strategies.

Company paternalism probably reinforced these tendencies, although many workers remained ambivalent, constructing their own understandings of employer motives. Certainly they valued increased personal and family security, and generally struggled to conform to the behavioural norms defined by their 'masters', but the efforts of employers to dominate both the workplace and the home were frequently resented. An official enquiry into a series of strikes in the Saint-Etienne basin in 1869/70 warned that increasingly 'the workers want more than patronage, they want to insist on their rights. Their needs, they say, should be entirely met from their wages; the important thing is to increase their wages to meet these needs.'[234] Even those employers most heavily committed to paternalistic endeavours faced growing resistance from employees who 'refused to provide the deference, compliance, and political support demanded of them'.[235] The wave of strikes in 1869 and 1870 would shatter the confident self-esteem of many employers as well as their habit of taking the gratitude and docility of the workforce for granted.[236]

'Charity' might similarly offend the workers' sense of dignity. Certainly the pre-conditions for assistance were invariably humiliating. Thus the criteria established by the prefect of the Moselle for denying assistance to *indigents* included the lack of a certificate of 'good life and morality' from the mayor; the presence in the household of children over the age of fourteen who had not received their first communion; or members of the family not vaccinated against smallpox; frequenting a *cabaret*; possessing a reputation as a *querelleur*; idleness; refusal of any job offer; ill-treatment of wife or children; keeping dogs; refusal to allow, at any time, entry into one's domicile by a member of a bureau de bienfaisance or by one of the 'Sisters or charitable ladies distributing assistance on behalf of the local Bureau'; and failure to heed their advice on maintaining 'order and cleanliness' in the home.[237] As the delegates of the Paris wood turners insisted, 'it is really painful for the worker to bear the solicitude deployed on his behalf by the charities, the bureaux de bienfaisance and other similar institutions! It is not . . . relief that the workers want; for the future they only ask to help themselves through mutuality.'[238]

---

[234] Mission Desvernay: Rapport sur le bassin houiller de Saint-Etienne, AN F12/2377.
[235] R. Aminzade, 'Breaking the chains of dependency. From patronage to class politics. Toulouse, France, 1830–72', *Journal of Urban History* 1976–7, p. 491.
[236] PG Colmar, 21 July 1870, AN BB30/390.
[237] Circular from Prefect Moselle, 20 Aug. 1853, AN F8/210.   [238] AN F12/3120.

Mutual assistance

The authorities had encouraged self-help throughout the first part of the century but remained suspicious of organisations which often served as fronts for illicit trades union and political organisation. Traditional, pre-revolutionary forms of corporative organisation had survived in many of the skilled trades, in spite of their marginal position in law. Some, such as *compagnonnage*, with its arcane rituals and strict hierarchy, and which offered assistance to geographically mobile craftsmen, particularly in the building trades, were believed to exert a moderating influence on workers and were generally tolerated by the authorities. Sometimes their parades were even accompanied by military bands.[239] Less welcome were attempts to regulate entry into trades and to control working conditions. In a period of tension every form of workers' organisation could appear to officials as potentially threatening. The Société de l'Union which attempted to modernise *compagnonnage*, and to unify the competing groups of artisans, was regarded with growing suspicion and subject to police raids in July 1855.[240] The impact of such repressive measures was magnified because, certain of police support, employers were always likely to seize the opportunity to dismiss and black-list workers suspected of involvement in 'illicit' organisations.[241]

In any case, economic change and urbanisation were breaking up traditional craft communities and reducing their ability to organise collective action.[242] As a result, workers were increasingly attracted to alternative forms of organisation. The mutual aid society (société de secours mutuel) was the most significant of these. The older-established societies were frequently associated with religious fraternities and often retained at least their dedication to a patron saint and an annual mass.[243] Increasingly, however, they became expressions of the workers' desire for security and autonomy.

Typically, in return for weekly payments of between 10 and 25 centimes, members of mutual aid societies were entitled to receive assistance in case of an accident or illness, as well as a decent burial. Some were based on neighbourhoods, others on trades. Many of these societies, meeting in the back rooms of cafés, encouraged social gatherings, and promoted

[239] E. Coornaert, *Les compagnonnages en France* (Paris 1966), p. 107.
[240] Constant, 'Var', III, pp. 742–3.   [241] PG Rouen, 5 July 1853, AN BB30/387.
[242] Gould, *Insurgent Identities*, pp. 116–17 re Paris building trades; Prefect Bouches-du-Rhône, 26 Feb. 1864, AN F12/4651 re reorganisation of Marseille docks and destruction of monopoly of corporation des portefaix.
[243] Constant, 'Var', II, p. 612.

inter-personal relations, as well as serving as insurance societies. Administering them provided invaluable experience of organisation and public speaking. In Paris the bakers' Société de secours mutuels des ouvriers boulangers, the largest single mutual aid society, had 5,361 members in 1869, each paying monthly dues of 2f.50 in return for sick benefits of 2f. per day for the first ninety days and 1f.25 for the following ninety. The society also functioned as an employment service, in effect controlling access to jobs. Generally women gained only indirect protection, through payments to male 'breadwinners'.[244] In Marseille, in 1852, there were already 138 mutual aid societies with 11,000 members. By the end of the decade membership had grown to 39,786.[245] Mutual aid offered a modicum of security to those better-paid workers who could afford to subscribe.[246]

The Emperor had favoured the compulsory establishment of a mutual aid society in every commune. Rouher would take pride in successfully obstructing such proscriptive legislation. According to the social Catholic Armand de Melun, he had realised that 'such a demand would have been absurd and dictatorial'.[247] Instead, the government sought to encourage mutual aid and to control its development by means of the stick and carrot – the requirement for authorisation and the prospect of subsidy. The restrictions previously imposed on the societies were eased by a decree of 26 March 1852, although a circular on 29 May reminded officials that assistance to the unemployed remained illegal. It would only encourage laziness and serve as 'the seed for every strike and the dream of every striker'.[248] In the years that followed, nationally, the number of mutual aid societies increased from 2,438 to 6,139 and membership from 249,000 to 794,000.

The decree also established a national Commission supérieure d'encouragement et de surveillance des sociétés mutuels, dominated by clericals like Melun, to channel subsidies to sociétés approuvées. These were required to accept a president appointed by the administration, and in many cases the initiative for their foundation came from local notables, who were encouraged by the authorities to serve as honorary members, and pay dues without receiving benefits.[249] These financial contributions were certainly important, particularly in a textiles centre, like Rouen, where

[244] A. Cottereau, 'Prévoyance des uns, imprévoyance des autres', *Prévenir* 1984, p. 57; F. Chavot, 'Les sociétés de secours mutuels sous le Second Empire', *Cahiers d'histoire de l'Institut Maurice Thorez* 1977, p. 21.

[245] Gaillard, 'Vie ouvrière', I, p. 129.

[246] See Rapport des maroquiniers portefeuillistes, AN F12/3115.

[247] Quoted B. Ménager, 'Rouher et la politique sociale du Second Empire' in J.-J. Becker (ed.), *Eugène Rouher* (Clermont-Ferrand 1985), p. 42.

[248] Quoted Gaillard, 'Vie ouvrière', II, p. 487.   [249] Gordon, *Merchants*, p. 92.

it was clear that most workers could not afford to pay membership dues and that societies without honorary members would find it difficult to meet their obligations.[250] It also compensated for the small membership of most societies. In Besançon, that established by the printing workers had seventy-five members in 1869, seventeen of whom were honorary.[251] According to Carpentier, a saddler who became President of the Rouen society Emulation chrétienne, the essential objective was to 'reconcile the working class with itself and with the upper classes'.[252]

The paternalistic attitudes of officials and the local worthies who became honorary members and the efforts of some employers to use the funds of mutual aid societies, to which employees were required to contribute, as a means of imposing discipline, were widely resented. As a result, only half of the workers enrolled nationally belonged to approved societies, in spite of the fact that without approval societies were deprived of subsidies and became far more liable to prosecution.[253] In 1855, the President of the Société de secours mutuels des ouvriers de la commune de Pavilly, near Rouen, rejected pressure from the prefect to request approval because contributions by honorary members would represent 'alms . . . and would be considered offensive by many of the society's members who want nothing to do with charity'.[254] The workers' delegations to the 1867 Exposition, as well as speakers in the public meetings in 1869, demanded autonomous workers' control and the right to provide unemployment relief and act as employment agencies.[255] In June 1866, in their determination to escape from company control, and initially encouraged by the local prefect, twenty-five miners at Le Creusot established a Caisse fraternelle de prévoyance des mineurs de la Loire to rival their employer's own *caisse*. Within two years it had 5,000 members and would play a major role in the great strike of 1869.[256]

Whatever their legal status, many mutual aid societies would serve as the organisational base for resistance to pressure from employers and the administration. The Société typographe parisienne de secours mutuels, to which around half of the capital's typographers belonged in 1860, typically created a secret fund to support strikes.[257] In Lyon the hatters

---

[250] PG Rouen, 5 July 1853, AN BB30/387.

[251] M. Cordillot, *La naissance du mouvement ouvrier à Besançon. La Ire Internationale* (Paris 1990), pp. 17–18.

[252] Boivin, *Mouvement ouvrier*, I, p. 77.

[253] E.g. PG Colmar, 2 May 1854, AN BB30/409 – re prosecution of four societies at Wasselonne.

[254] Boivin, *Mouvement ouvrier*, I, pp. 77–8.

[255] J. Gaillard, 'Le VIIe arrondissement' in Girard, *Les élections de 1869*, p. 64.

[256] Lequin, *La formation*, II, pp. 191–5; Hanagan, *Nascent Proletarians*, pp. 185–6.

[257] E.g. *Deuxième procès des ouvriers typographes en Première Instance et en Appel. Juillet 1862* (Paris 1862).

(*chapeliers-approprieurs*) were able to disguise their long-established and illegal trades union as a mutual aid society and organise a strike in 1859 which successfully secured the dismissal of six non-members by their employers.[258] However, it was the silk weavers' societies which particularly concerned the authorities. Early in 1857, J.-B. and F. Martin, silk manufacturers at nearby Tarare, complained that although many employers had become honorary members, all the important decisions were still taken in private by workers notorious for their militancy in 1848, and that this had led to a vote to expel members who had continued to work during a strike in March 1852.[259] On the basis of a host of similar reports the State Prosecutor would conclude that instead of conciliating workers the government's encouragement of mutual aid 'has given greater cohesion and strength to scattered groups'.[260]

Thus, frequently, open, legal, mutual aid activities disguised those more typical of a trades union. At Cette, a wine-marketing centre with a long-established tradition of mutuality amongst coopers, membership flourished in the 1860s, increasing from 800 in 1850 to 2,000 by 1866. There were four societies, each with a president and seven or eight committee members. They closely cooperated and the wine merchants complained that it was impossible to take on workers without the societies' approval and that, furthermore, they were likely to face an *interdit* if they dared reject a wages tariff laid down by the workers. In order to maintain internal discipline those coopers who broke a society's rules faced warnings, fines, and eventual expulsion with loss of all benefits. Workers who refused to join at all were ostracised by their colleagues and treated contemptuously as *Niçards* – Nice having formerly been a haven for French criminals. Those wine merchants who dared employ non-members faced a boycott by the other workers.[261] This pattern of sanctions, intended to ensure unity, appears to have been widespread.[262] Moreover, the lead given by such combative mutual aid societies tended to influence the attitudes of workers outside the circle of those who could afford the cost of membership. Nevertheless, in spite of repeated complaints from its own officials and employers, the government persisted in its efforts to encourage mutuality.[263]

In 1862, the request made to the Emperor by a group of workers, mainly presidents of mutual aid societies encouraged by the Emperor's

[258] Chavot, 'Les sociétés de secours mutuels', p. 23.
[259] Letter included with report from PG Lyon, 8 Feb. 1857, AN BB30/379.
[260] PG Lyon, ? July 1857, AN BB30/379; see also ibid. Prefect Rhône, 21 Nov. 1864.
[261] PG Montpellier, 1 June 1866, AN BB30/380.
[262] E.g. Aminzade, *Ballots and Barricades*, p. 96 re Rouen textile mills.
[263] E.g. PG Paris, 4 May 1868, AN BB30/384 re protest resignation of M. Werlé, mayor of Reims.

cousin Prince Napoleon, for assistance to allow them to visit the London International Exposition, was favourably received. In all, 200 delegates, elected by their trades, were sent.[264] Again, for the Paris Exposition in 1867 around 100 delegates were elected. They were asked to prepare reports on the situation of their industries and on social conditions, and continued to meet for two years. Amongst the issues discussed was the principle of cooperation, so popular in 1848, and still seen by some artisans as offering the means of emancipation from the wages system and of transforming society.[265]

The establishment of producers' cooperatives remained an attractive and seemingly realistic prospect to the skilled craftsmen employed in numerous small workshops.[266] The government even set up a Caisse impériale with 1 million francs to encourage the movement, believing that it would divert workers from more threatening forms of socialism.[267] In practice, however, only thirty-nine producers' associations would be created between 1863 and 1867, involving a derisory number of participants and, in competitive markets, few survived for long.[268] In some areas, there was a more substantial revival of consumer cooperatives. Thus, around Lyon, where cooperative principles appear to have had considerable appeal, there were twenty-five in 1868 with a membership of some 4,000. Some of these had associated study circles which were increasingly politicised.[269] However, neither in Lyon nor in Rouen, where cooperatives were established in most working class *quartiers*, do they appear to have been a great success. Some were controlled by local notables, others by working-class militants with little commercial experience. They were generally too small to be viable.[270] Most workers could ill afford the initial subscriptions and were already tied by credit arrangements to small shopkeepers.[271]

Nevertheless, and in spite of these setbacks, interest in the principle of cooperation survived. According to the manifesto of the Lyon branch of

---

[264] E. Labrousse, *Aspects de l'évolution économique et sociale de la France et du Royaume-Uni de 1815 à 1880* (Paris CDU 1949), p. 106.

[265] E.g. J. Rougerie, '1871' in *La Commune de 1871* (Paris 1972), pp. 71–3.

[266] See *La Mutualité. Journal du travail et des sociétés coopératives*, edited by Jules Vinçard – 10 numbers 1865/66.

[267] G. Bourgin, 'La législation ouvrière du Second Empire', *Revue des études napoléoniennes*, 1913, pp. 230–1.

[268] J. Gaillard, 'Les associations', p. 68.

[269] PG Lyon, 7 Oct. 1864 and 8 Jan. 1866, AN BB30/379. See also G. Sheridan, 'Esprit de quartier et formes de solidarité dans les mouvements sociaux et politiques des ouvriers en soie de Lyon, 1830–88', *Le monde alpin et rhodanien* 1991, pp. 29–35.

[270] PG Paris, 15 Feb. 1868, AN BB30/384.

[271] PG Lyon, 28 Dec. 1864, AN BB30/379; Boivin, *Mouvement ouvrier*, 1, pp. 184–7.

the International Working Men's Association in February 1867, producers' cooperatives would ensure that 'we will be able, on the basis of our own work, to acquire similar riches . . . This will not be through violence, but by means of cooperation, through which, little by little, the workers will themselves create new capital.' At the same time, and given that 'the needs of society are always growing . . . we will need the capital of the old capitalists, who as a result will not find their interests prejudiced'.[272] The hostility shown by many of these advocates of cooperation towards both strikes and political aspirations would prove anathema to many worker militants, however. According to Hins, a delegate at the Brussels congress of the International in 1868, producers' cooperatives were a dead end. They appealed to only a small minority of workers and inevitably would lead to the formation of *castes* within the working class.[273]

Trades unions

Most worker militants appear to have been interested in mutual aid or trades unions (*syndicats*) rather than cooperatives. Their time seemed to have come. The legalisation of strikes in 1864, a feature of the Emperor's opening to the left, was followed by a more tolerant policy towards working-class organisations – openly conceded by the administration in 1868.[274] This spirit of relative tolerance encouraged both the establishment of new organisations and more open activity by existing *syndicats* which had previously disguised themselves as mutual aid societies. The Paris Société de crédit mutuel des ouvriers en bronze which had organised a *société de résistance* since at least 1864 was able to organise, early in 1867, a major strike involving 3,000 workers, half those employed in the industry.[275] On 31 March, at a meeting of some 3,500 workers, the Société philanthropique des maîtres-tailleurs also decided to establish a société mutuelle de résistance. According to the police, at a further gathering, on 4 April, attended by 8,000 workers, a vote was taken to adopt statutes modelled on those of the *bronziers*.[276]

Some seventy *chambres syndicales* were created in Paris between 1867 and 1870, forty in Lyon and another forty in Marseille.[277] By July 1870

[272] In J. Rougerie, 'La première Internationale à Lyon (1865–70): problèmes d'histoire du mouvement ouvrier français', *Annali Istituto Giangiacomo Feltrinelli*, 1961 p. 165.

[273] J. Gaillard, 'Les associations', p. 83.

[274] Report by Forcade, Ministre de l'agriculture et du commerce, 30 March 1868, AN F12/4650.

[275] Paris Prefect of Police, 27 Feb. 1867, AN F12/4652.

[276] Ibid. 4 and 15 April 1867.   [277] Rougerie, 'Second Empire', p. 104.

around 65,000 of the capital's workers, mostly members of skilled trades with long-established traditions of organisation, were unionised. They constituted some 13 per cent of the industrial labour force.[278] The proportion of male workers involved varied considerably between trades, however; according to Willbach's calculations, between 0.56 per cent in the building trades and 87 per cent amongst the bronze workers. In most trades, organisation was limited to small groups of militants. Membership fluctuated, and although the movement was beginning to spread beyond the ranks of habitual militants, in only six or seven skilled, well-paid and literate trades were more than 30 per cent of the labour force involved. These included the *bronziers*, engineering workers, typographers, and hatmakers, and in the Parisian building industry the painters and carpenters, rather than the masons and labourers.[279]

Eugène Tartaret, a cabinet maker and secretary of the Workers' Commission established by the delegates to the 1867 Exposition insisted that 'the first question to resolve . . . is how to organise in defence of wages'.[280] The answer, according to the future communard Dereure lay 'in organising ourselves, by trade first of all, and then by means of federation, in order to resist reductions in our wages'.[281] The delegates of the *tourneurs sur bois* pointed out that in labour relations 'abuses occur, due to the lack of organisation and the isolation of the worker'. In the absence of a negotiating mechanism workers had no alternative but to resort to strikes, which were damaging both to their interests and to those of their employers.[282] In these circumstances, there was an urgent need to secure formal, legal approval of workers' *syndicats*. Certainly official tolerance could not be relied on.[283]

Nevertheless, the trend by 1869/70 was clearly towards more widespread unionisation as skilled workers sought to protect themselves from competition and the threat of de-skilling, and to establish formal negotiating procedures with their employers. Union organisation was also evident in some sectors of modern industry, most notably amongst miners, and engineering and textile workers, and spread by example, as in the case of the workers of Rethel in the Ardennes who were inspired to create a société de

---

[278] Willbach, *Work and its Satisfactions*, p. 10.
[279] Ibid. pp. 119–29; see also PG Aix, 24 Dec. 1869, AN BB30/390 re Marseille.
[280] E. Tartaret (ed.), *Exposition universelle de 1867. Commission ouvrière. Recueil des procès-verbaux des assemblées générales des délégués et des membres des bureaux électoraux*, 1 (Paris 1868), p. 253.
[281] *La Réforme*, 19 Oct. 1869, quoted J. Gaillard, 'Les associations', p. 82.   [282] AN F12/3120.
[283] See views of Tolain, the bronze workers' leader, 24 Feb. 1867 quoted Vanier, *La mode et les métiers*, p. 237 and letter from A. Richard to E. Reclus, 24 Jan. 1870, in Rougerie, 'Première Internationale', p. 182.

résistance in November 1869 by a spokesman for the caisse de résistance already established at Reims.[284]

The growing number of strikes organised by these *syndicats* inevitably aroused rising concern amongst the authorities. The prefect of the Rhône reported in June 1870 that in Lyon the Sociéte civile de prévoyance et de renseignements pour le travail des tisseurs had 25,000 members, tightly organised in subdivisions, and was threatening to organise strikes to secure increased wages.[285] In another major textile centre, Mulhouse in the Haut-Rhin, according to the Prefect, 'there are repeated meetings and new industries . . . have ceased to work and formulated programmes which include mounting demands'. He was particularly concerned about the intimidation by strikers of those who wanted to work.[286]

In Paris, by the end of 1869, a Chambre fédérale des sociétés ouvrières had been established to encourage cooperation between workers belonging to some sixty professional associations.[287] To the authorities, chaos appeared to be spreading. In response, just as the liberal Empire was being inaugurated, the regime launched a new wave of repression. Once more militant trades unionists faced arrest.[288] The Government was also concerned about the development of the International Working Men's Association, founded in London in September 1864, and the dream of solidarity it inspired amongst militants. Estimating the association's influence was, and is, difficult. Officials certainly exaggerated, claiming that its agents were responsible for every instance of unrest, and deliberately seeking to frighten 'respectable' opinion. Worker militants also had an interest in exaggerating the scale of the movement. In contrast with estimates of as many as 200,000 to 300,000 members, the reality was probably a fluctuating total of between 20,000 and 40,000 at its peak, including the collective adherence of some *syndicats*.[289] Initially the French section was made up of a small and dispersed membership found mainly in Paris, Lyon, Vienne, Rouen, and Caen. Its most active members were largely self-taught worker-intellectuals like the bookbinder Varlin and the dyer Malon in Paris, the printing worker Aubry in Rouen, and the clerks Richard in Lyon and Bastelica in Marseille.[290]

The real, and especially the rumoured, role of the International, in promoting solidarity by providing financial assistance to strikers, encouraged

---

[284] Prefect Ardennes, 4 Dec. 1869, AN F12/4652; PG Metz, 11 Jan. 1870, AN BB30/390.

[285] 25 June 1870, AN F12/4652.   [286] Prefect 9 and 11 July 1870, AN F12/4652.

[287] Rougerie, '1871', p. 72.   [288] Boivin, *Mouvement ouvrier*, I, p. 280.

[289] J. Maitron, 'Les effectifs de la Première Internationale en France' in *La Première Internationale, l'institution, l'implantation, le rayonnement* (Paris 1964), pp. 132–9.

[290] J. Maitron, 'La personnalité du militant ouvrier français dans la seconde moitié du 19e siècle', *Le mouvement social* 1960/1, p. 72.

militants.[291] In March 1867, during the Parisian bronze workers' strike, the activities of Fribourg and Tolain, the delegates of the International, and the despatch of representatives to London to seek aid, caused official alarm.[292] During the tailors' strike in April financial assistance was promised by workers in London and Lausanne, whilst two delegates sent by the London tailors promised to blacklist any English employers who attempted to supply orders from France.[293] The police *commissaire* Fontane, responsible for the surveillance of workers' organisations in the capital, claimed, with evident concern, that every working-class organisation in the city was developing links with the International.[294]

The delegates to the first Geneva congress of the International in 1866, influenced mainly by Proudhon, had been opposed to strikes and political engagement, and in favour of the gradual suppression of capitalism through the development of cooperatives.[295] The growing number of strikes and the rise of support for republicanism, as well as the repeated prosecution of members of the International itself stimulated greater militancy, however. Articles in newspapers like *La Marseillaise* (19 December 1869) encouraged the creation of a federal structure to link *chambres syndicales* and *sections* of the International in order to mount a more effective challenge both to capitalism and to the regime. In Paris the federal trades union organisation (Chambre fédérale des sociétés ouvrières) established on 14 November 1869 and that of local groups affiliated to the International (Fédération des sections parisiennes de l'AIT) had substantially overlapping memberships.[296]

This new trend towards organisation and the appeals for solidarity were inspirational. Emile Aubry, the leading Rouen activist, wrote an encouraging letter to Séverin Robert who was attempting to organise watchmakers in the Besançon area: 'Tell your brothers . . . that soon the Rouen Federation hopes to see them enter the lists with it, to lay the foundations for our liberation, making use of the means that universal suffrage and the right to strike have made available to us.'[297] Far less restrained was a letter, published in *La Marseillaise* on 26 April 1870, from a militant called Huart, reporting on a meeting he had addressed in St-Quentin:

[291] E.g. Prefect Seine-Inférieure, 2 Oct. 1869, AN F12/4652.

[292] Prefect of Police, 13 March 1867, ibid.   [293] Ibid. 15 April 1867.

[294] Assemblée nationale, *Enquête parlementaire sur les actes du Gouvernement de la Défense nationale*, v (Paris 1876), p. 393.

[295] J. Rougerie, 'Les sections françaises de l'Association Internationale des travailleurs' in *La Première Internationale*, p. 101.

[296] J. Bruhat, 'Le socialisme français de 1848 à 1871' in J. Droz (ed.), *Histoire générale du socialisme*, 1 (Paris 1972), pp. 521–6.

[297] Quoted Cordillot, *Naissance*, p. 25.

I said to them that it is only through the International that we will be able to . . . secure the complete liberation of humanity. I said that we no longer wish to have bourgeoisie, frontiers, armies, guillotines, and bosses. In their place, associations will exchange their goods. I said that we no longer want to put up with idlers who fatten themselves at our expense, who live in châteaux and ride in carriages, while our children go bare-foot. I said that the worker, through his labour, gives life to the entire world, that in spite of producing everything, he lacks the most essential necessities of life. His wife is obliged to work, whilst his bare-footed children walk the streets. I said that the bourgeoisie which produces nothing save disorder in society, experiences all its joys and material goods, and all the time, in spite of producing nothing it consumes more than the workers. I said that the International will destroy all these abuses, that we will establish a society based on the common good and collectivism throughout the entire world.[298]

In spite of such enthusiasm the foundations of many of these working class organisations remained extremely shaky. Day-to-day workplace issues rather than a determination to change the world probably inspired most workers. Outside the skilled trades they lacked organisational traditions and resources. The unskilled were unable to organise effectively to protect themselves. They were too easily replaced, and too likely to move on, in their constant search for work. The failure of strikes or the intensification of police and employer repression could have a devastating impact. In the woollens centre of Roubaix memories of persecution in 1848 helped ensure the absence of strikes for eighteen years.[299] Even when strikes were legalised, the vast majority of employers firmly rejected any questioning of their authority or interference with the 'freedom to work'.[300] Faced with the threat of a strike by bronze workers in Paris in March 1867 the employers' Association des fabricants de bronzes et d'appareils à gaz, *pour assurer l'indépendence et la liberté du travail* organised a lock-out and agreed to take back only those workers known to be 'independent of the union'.[301] A strike by textile spinners at Darnétal near Rouen in November 1869 was broken when employers brought in workers from other areas. For good measure the strikers were blacklisted throughout the region. The prefect's rather understated conclusion was that 'this decision by the employers is likely to discourage mischievous intentions'.[302]

---

[298] Quoted J. Rougerie, 'Les événements de 1870–1 en province' in *La Commune de 1871* (Paris 1972), p. 42.
[299] Reddy, *The Rise of Market Culture*, p. 218.
[300] E.g. 'Réaction de la Chambre de commerce de Besançon au projet d'Association des graveurs et guillocheurs' in Cordillot, *Naissance*, pp. 69–70.
[301] Paris Prefect of Police, 13 March 1867, AN F12/4652.
[302] Prefect Seine-Inférieure, 2 Dec. 1869, ibid.

The prosecution of leading members of the International in Paris at the end of 1867 further discouraged potential militants and caused dissension over future tactics.[303] Appeals from the International's militants for solidarity between workers in different trades and places could have unexpected consequences. A report on the collapse of membership of the Fédération ouvrière rouennaise, which had been made up largely of hard-pressed textile operatives, following an appeal for contributions to the strike funds of miners and ironworkers at Le Creusot, claimed that 'Norman workers . . . are tired of depositing 40 centimes a fortnight in the corporation's cash box. It seems hard to them to make sacrifices to support the strikes of all the trades, in all the nations, without being consulted on their opportuneness and without really knowing what use will be made of their money.' Membership fell from around 2,600 to 1,100 in 1869.[304]

In May 1870 Ollivier, the new head of a liberal government, ordered the arrest of militant members of the International on the charge of membership of a dangerous secret society, suspected of plotting against the life of the Emperor.[305] In spite of his known concern to respect the law, even Aubry, the organisation's leading figure in Rouen, was sentenced to six months in prison and a fine of 500f. In the suburb of Sotteville the assumption that policemen who were taking names at a workers' meeting would pass these on to their employers caused panic.[306] In these circumstances, agitation and organisation amongst most groups of workers would remain episodic. Although militants increasingly employed the universalistic language of class, a strong sense of craft consciousness and of exclusiveness survived to counteract these calls for solidarity. This seems clear from a review of collective action by workers. Depending on the circumstances, industrial militancy could either reinforce or weaken class-consciousness.

COLLECTIVE ACTION

The strike was the most obviously working-class form of collective action. Strikes were not necessarily more 'modern', nor more rational than other forms of protest, and, although increasingly common, they remained only part of a 'repertoire' of forms of protest and negotiation, influenced, as

---

[303] Boivin, *Mouvement ouvrier*, I, pp. 216–17.
[304] Report of Prefect Seine-Inférieure to Assemblée nationale, *Enquête parlementaire sur l'insurrection du 18 mars 1871* (Versailles 1872), I, p. 592.
[305] *Papiers et correspondance de la famille impériale* (Paris 1871), p. 326.
[306] Boivin, *Mouvement ouvrier*, I, pp. 391, 350.

Charles Tilly has pointed out, by '1. The population's daily routines and internal organisation . . . 2. Prevailing standards of rights and justice . . . 3. The populations accumulated experience with collective action. 4. Current patterns of repression.'[307]

Understanding the motives of those who engaged in collective action thus remains highly problematical. The range and quality of the available evidence is extremely diverse, and as always, information from 'above' is far more plentiful than that from 'below'.[308] In spite of his efforts, the prefect of the Nord felt obliged to admit that 'it is extremely difficult to penetrate . . . into the lower depths of society'.[309] The threat of prosecution ensured, as the prefect of the Isère pointed out, that 'the leaders . . . do not write; they speak and give their orders verbally'.[310] Furthermore, evidence from workers themselves is heavily skewed towards more or less (un)representative militants. Many of the less spectacular confrontations between workers and their employers, and those disputes that did not lead to strikes, were anyway simply not reported,[311] sometimes because workers circumvented legislation against strikes by simply giving two weeks' notice, taking their *livrets* – an internal passport first introduced in 1803 – and collectively moving on to other employers.[312] The likelihood of them adopting this tactic of course depended on conditions within their own portions of a very segmented labour market.

In the light of these problems, the various efforts to compile strike statistics offer only a very approximate insight into the frequency and scale of disputes. Their meaning is further distorted by changes in official policy. According to one calculation, 613 strikes occurred between 1852 and 1858, an average of 87 per year, generally involving between 10 and 50 workers, with the exception of mass strikes by miners.[313] Other research suggests a five-year average for 1850–4 of 73, one for 1855–9 of 81, falling in the next quinquennium to 43 per annum, and then, following the legalisation of strikes in 1864, increasing to reach a maximum of 116 in 1870.[314] Levels of participation also rose sharply in this last phase as greater official tolerance seemed to reduce the risks of taking part. However, the provisions of the

---

[307] C. Tilly, *The Contentious French* (London 1986), p. 10.

[308] See Y. Lequin, 'Sources et méthodes de l'histoire de grèves dans la seconde moitié du 19e siécle: l'exemple de l'Isére (1848–1914)', *Cahiers d'histoire* 1967, pp. 222–3.

[309] 7 April 1866, AN F12/4652.   [310] 26 Sept. 1863, AN F12/4651.

[311] Point made by Prefect Loire-Inférieure, 14 May 1866, AN F12/4652.

[312] E.g. M. Doremieux, fabricant des chaînes at St Amand, letter enclosed with report from Prefect Nord, 14 March 1866; Prefect Eure, 2 Oct. 1869, re fileurs de laine, canton of Montfort – both in AN F12/4652.

[313] A. Dansette, *Du 2 décembre au 4 septembre, le second empire* (Paris 1972), p. 248.

[314] E. Shorter and C. Tilly, *Strikes in France 1830–1968* (Cambridge 1974), Appendix B.

penal code, which criminalised actions in restraint of 'freedom' by either employers or workers, remained on the statute books.

The legal-administrative framework

In the aftermath of 1848 and during the authoritarian Empire efforts were made to reinforce social control. The requirement that workers possess an internal passport, the *livret*, which had gradually been falling into disuse, was revived in June 1854 by a decree which extended the need to carry it to domestic workers and women. Immigrants to Paris were required to have their *livrets* stamped at the Prefecture of Police, and the police were instructed to prosecute workers without a *livret* as vagabonds. Workers found these procedures humiliating. Furthermore, they were legally unable to change jobs unless their employer was prepared to certify that they were free of debts and obligations towards him.[315] Although, as before, this system of control was only partially enforced – rigorously in many large factories, hardly at all in the Paris building trades[316] – this did little to ease the sense of injustice caused by this exceptional legislation.[317] Administrative action was also likely in an effort to prevent strikes, although the character of official intervention varied. Thus, as disputes developed local officials might initially tolerate traditional, but technically illegal, practices which involved workers' delegates entering into negotiations with employers. They might even reveal some sympathy for workers, putting pressure on recalcitrant employers to negotiate or make concessions.[318] However, this preferred image of neutrality was tarnished by repeated interventions to protect 'order' and to preserve the 'freedom to work' of workers not on strike.

At Le Mans in July 1852 the authorities threatened to place striking carpenters under 'preventative' arrest unless they returned to work within forty-eight hours.[319] When, in May 1853, 400 stonemasons went on strike at Saint-Etienne, 103 of them were arrested. Of these, sixty-eight, doubtless severely frightened, were soon released. The others, 'ringleaders' or those suspected of intimidating non-strikers, were likely to be charged with *délit de coalition* or *excitation à la coalition*, and face sentences of

---

[315] T. Zeldin, *France 1848–1945* (Oxford 1982), pp. 198–9.
[316] M. Devinck, Rapports des délégations ouvrières à l'Exposition universelle de 1867, 28 Oct. 1868, AN 45 AP 6.
[317] Boivin, *Mouvement ouvrier*, I, p. 89 note 147.
[318] E.g. Constant, 'Var', III, pp. 741–2; Ménager, 'Vie politique', I, p. 299.
[319] GOC 19e DM, report on 11–15 July 1852, AHG F1/69.

anything between three days' and eighteen months' imprisonment.[320] Troops were deployed whenever disorder or serious economic damage appeared possible. Coalminers were particularly likely to engage in large-scale strikes and possessed a well-earned reputation for violence. Moreover, their action would have negative consequences for other industries. A forceful official response could thus be expected. In February 1855, 200 men of the 92nd infantry were sent from Valenciennes (Nord) to Anzin to support the local police. When they departed they were replaced by thirty heavy cavalry, just in case. Later in the year over 1,200 troops were deployed in a major effort to overawe the population.[321] This was the sort of support employers believed they had a right to expect, and generally the administration complied,[322] although officials sometimes complained that employers took advantage of this support in order to exploit their workers.[323]

In March 1862, faced with another strike at Anzin, and whilst privately recognising the validity of the workers' claims, the Prefect felt that he had no choice but to impose sanctions.[324] The advice given to the miners, in a proclamation by the sous-préfet at Valenciennes was that 'if your wages appear insufficient complain respectfully to those who must naturally understand your needs and who are, I am certain, ready to come to your aid'.[325] Providing strikers returned to work immediately following such official warnings they might expect lenient treatment, at least from the authorities. It is hardly surprising, however, that workers believed in the existence of an alliance between the State and capitalists. Many workers who had believed that the imperial government would be sympathetic towards their interests were rapidly and bitterly disappointed.[326]

Official support considerably reinforced the employers' propensity to reject any sort of challenge to their authority. Employers were invariably convinced that strikes were irrational – 'strikes only have one result: that is to kill the goose which lays the golden eggs', and constituted proof of the ingratitude of those for whom they provided work.[327] Therefore, it might be necessary to bring workers to their senses by the sort of lock-out imposed by ninety Parisian carriage builders in May 1865.[328] Fairly typically,

---

[320] PG Lyon, 4 July 1853, AN BB30/379. On sentencing policy see Ministère . . . des travaux publics to Prefect Pas-de-Calais, 4 Jan. 1859, AN F12/4651.
[321] GOC 3e DM, report on 6–10 Feb. 1855, AHG G8/26; Ménager, 'Vie politique', I, pp. 300–7.
[322] E.g. Perrot, *Ouvriers en grève*, II, pp. 691–700.   [323] PG Rouen, 13 July 1854, AN BB30/387.
[324] 19 March 1862, AN F12/4651.
[325] Proclamation. Le sous-préfet de l'arrondissement de Valenciennes aux Ouvriers de la commune de Fresnes 18 mars 1862 – AN F12/4651.
[326] Observation made by PG Lyon, 5 April 1853, AN BB30 379.
[327] M. Castel, *Les grèves et l'assassinat de M. Watrin* (Saint-Etienne 1866), p. 7.
[328] Paris Prefect of Police, 8 June 1865, AN F12/4651.

M. Wirtz, owner of a textile mill at Cernay (Haut-Rhin) rejected out-of-hand the possibility of discussing his workers' grievances because he did not want them 'laying down the law in his establishment'.[329] The presence of gendarmes or local commissaires de police on the streets, at factory gates, or their visits to *cabarets*, and the 'advice' they proffered, was often enough to prevent or bring a strike to a rapid end.[330] Those who did complain were likely to face the threat of dismissal and blacklisting, measures designed to ensure that protest would be extremely 'costly' for the worker.[331]

Nevertheless, a more tolerant official attitude towards strikes became evident from at least March 1862, when the Emperor pardoned arrested printing workers. This attempt to appeal to the working-class elite continued with the despatch of a delegation of workers to the 1862 London Universal Exposition. On their return, these delegates, inspired by their British colleagues, had demanded the right both to strike and to organise trades unions, and cooperative societies. Once parliamentary discussion of new legislation on strikes commenced, the administration appears to have stopped enforcing the law.[332] This major policy shift was confirmed in 1864 when the Conseil d'Etat reluctantly recommended abrogation of articles 414 and 415 of the Penal Code, and proposed that in future 'no penalties would be imposed on those, workers or employers, who voluntarily form a coalition, without agitation, without trouble, without interfering with the liberty of others: severe penalties against those who by threats, violence or other illicit manoeuvres provoke or compel workers or employers to participate'.[333]

In his Speech from the Throne at the opening of the 1865 parliamentary session, the Emperor expressed his hope that 'As a result of the law on coalitions, those who labour, as well as those who provide work, will learn to settle their differences between themselves.'[334] Apparently Napoleon was determined to engage in liberalisation and social reform, in the face of considerable opposition both from frightened conservatives and wrong-footed republicans. This legislation represented a major breach in the strictly individualistic conception of social relationships, which had inspired the legislators of the Constituent Assembly in 1791. It 'created the conditions for

---

[329] Prefect Haut-Rhin, 13 March 1863, AN F12/4651.
[330] E.g. Prefect Nord, 27 Feb. 1862, AN F12/4651 re textile workers at Tourcoing.
[331] E.g. dismissals of ouvriers terrassiers at Le Creusot, reported by GOC 8e DM, 16–20 March 1853, AHG G8/1; and more general report of Paris Prefect of Police, 26 Jan. 1865, AN 45 AP 6.
[332] E.g. Prefect Rhône, 1 March 1864, AN F12/4651.
[333] Report from Justice Minister to Emperor, ibid.
[334] Quoted Vanier, *La mode et les métiers*, p. 236.

the modern strike'.[335] It was hoped that the legalisation of *coalitions* would promote conciliation. However, it remained to be seen whether it would fundamentally affect workers' attitudes towards the Bonapartist state.

In practice the official response to action by workers would vary according to local circumstances and the general political situation. Dealing with the first important strike following the new legislation, in March 1865, Vallon, the prefect of the Nord, privately expressed his sympathy for miners at Anzin who were threatened with a reduction in their already 'inadequate' wages. He allowed workers to take part in pit-head discussions but despatched troops to prevent the intimidation of non-strikers.[336] Subsequently, in one of a long series of clarifications designed to establish the 'correct' balance between tolerance and repression, the Ministre des Travaux Publics insisted in May 1865 that 'if it is proposed to respect the rights of the workers regarding their employers, care has been taken to avoid disarming the authorities in the face of those abuses to which the employers might find themselves exposed if the free discussion of wages were to be affected by illicit manoeuvres or by intimidation'.[337]

In the aftermath of serious incidents involving textile workers at Roubaix in February 1867, the Interior Minister, the Marquis de La Valette reminded Mouzard-Sencier, Vallon's successor, that 'the law does not permit workers to attempt, by means of gatherings in front of workshops and factories, to intimidate their employers'.[338] Those workers who were anxious to continue or to return to work also had to be protected. According to a prefectoral proclamation posted on the walls of Mulhouse in July 1870, the freedom to work was 'the inviolable right of the citizen'.[339] Thus strikers who threw stones at 'blacklegs' were likely to be sentenced to a week or two in prison, together with fines of 15f. to 25f. They probably also lost their jobs.[340] On occasion troops might even be directly employed as strike breakers. In May 1865 fifty military blacksmiths were employed by the Compagnie impériale des voitures de Paris to end a strike which threatened to cause serious inconvenience. This appeared to be perfectly compatible with the law to the Ministers of both War and Public Works.[341]

It clearly took time for the parties involved to work out fully the practical implications of the changing legal situation. Certainly, employers appear

---

[335] Perrot, *Ouvriers en grève*, I, p. 313.   [336] 11 March 1865, AN F12/4651.

[337] Circular 21 May 1865, AN F12/4651.

[338] 26 March 1867 quoted Ménager, 'Vie politique', II, p. 665.

[339] Included with report of 9 July 1870, AN F12/4652.

[340] E.g. PG Lyon, 2 Oct. and 12 Nov. 1865, AN 45 AP 6 re strike of velvet weavers at Saint-Etienne.

[341] War Minister to Minister of Agriculture, Commerce and Publics Works, 2 May and response 8 May 1865, AN F12/4651.

to have been confused. Officials were made aware rapidly of their 'intense irritation'.[342] Formerly they had felt able to call on the authorities and police for support against their workers, now they felt far more exposed to pressure. The Rouen mill owner Marais found intolerable a situation in which his spinners 'without any warning whatsoever, stop all the machines in the mill, without concerning themselves about the material damage they might cause', and in which 'the authorities will say that this does not concern them'.[343] According to the Prefect of the Loire, textile employers at Saint-Etienne 'do not understand that there is now a law *on* strikes which allows intervention by the authorities only when order is troubled and no longer a law *against* strikes which leads necessarily to this intervention'. He was clearly vexed by their complaints about his 'indolence' and 'partiality'.[344] Employers were frightened and determined to discredit the law.[345]

Workers too were unsure of their position. In a letter to deputies in July 1864, the delegates of the Elbeuf textile workers insisted that 'this new law on strikes will become a dead letter, because workers in general are ignorant of the subtleties of the legislation, and will not dare profit from the means offered to them to defend their injured interests'.[346] The prefect of the Loiret claimed to have loaned a copy of Alphonse Audiganne's *Ouvriers en famille* to two workers who had consulted him and ensured that the local newspaper, the *Journal du Loiret*, reprinted an article on strikes from the *Revue des Deux Mondes*.[347] Many workers were critical of legislation which severely restricted the range of actions possible in support of strikes by banning activities likely to interfere 'with the free exercise of industry and labour', including the formation of strike committees, trades unions, and the use of picket lines to enforce a strike, and reinforcing the penalties for violence and intimidation.[348]

However, it was soon made clear that even if the new legislation did not abrogate the restrictions on the right of association, greater tolerance would be displayed. Meetings might be held provided that previously pre-fectoral authorisation had been obtained.[349] Although initially this appears to have been granted or withheld in fairly arbitrary fashion,[350] gradually

---

[342] Paris Prefect of Police, 26 Jan. 1865, AN 45 AP 6.
[343] Quoted Boivin, *Mouvement ouvrier*, I, p. 161.   [344] 8 Nov. 1865, AN F12/4651.
[345] See e.g. PG Angers, 8 July 1864, AN BB30/371.
[346] A. Darimon, *Le tiers parti sous l'Empire (1863–66)*, 1887, p. 185.
[347] Prefect Loiret, 27 June 1867, AN F12/4652.
[348] Ministre de l'agriculture et des travaux publics to Paris Prefect of Police 4 May and response 9 May 1865, AN F12/4651.
[349] Interior Ministry circular 6 Aug. 1864, AN F12/4651.
[350] Prefect Haute-Vienne, 30 May 1864 and Prefect Haute-Loire, 27 Nov. 1865 – in AN F12/4651.

more liberal trends emerged. Prefects authorised such gatherings as that involving 3,000 weavers at Vienne early in April 1868, which selected delegates to negotiate with employers.[351] The prefect of the Somme appeared quite happy that workers should 'become accustomed' to meeting regularly in local bars to discuss the means of benefiting from the rights conferred on them by this new law.[352] The State Prosecutor at Rouen accepted that it was legitimate for workers to gather outside their factory gates to discuss their options in case of a dispute with employers.[353] Employers were even asked not to victimise strikers.[354] The obligatory presence of police observers at authorised meetings did not inspire confidence amongst workers, however.[355]

Certainly, official tolerance could not be relied on. Warnings were soon being delivered to workers about 'illicit' activity.[356] The State Prosecutor at Angers advised employers that civil action and recourse to the Conseil des Prud'hommes were possible in response to the 'moral violence' of rural weavers who threatened to stop work and return incomplete lengths of cloth.[357] The Paris tailors' delegates who appeared before the Tribunal correctionel de la Seine on 2 August 1867 were accused of organising an unauthorised strike meeting attended by around 2,000 workers. They had previously consulted the local commissaire de police and the Prefect of Police but then simply appear to have assumed that 'since we had the right to strike, we had the right to collect the necessary funds'.[358] Given the restrictions on the right to hold meetings and the fact that unions remained illegal, somehow legal strikes would need to appear to be 'spontaneous'.[359] This enforced reliance on *ad hoc* and temporary committees gravely weakened the ability of workers to engage in prior organisation and marshal support, to negotiate, and subsequently to police whatever agreements might have been reached.

However, if trades unions remained illegal, mutual aid societies might perform their functions. The committee of the Parisian printing workers' mutual aid society habitually negotiated with employers and, in case of disputes, might place them under interdict. Such an obvious act of intimidation was certainly illegal under the terms of the 1864 Law, but harsh experience ensured that printing employers were reluctant to instigate legal

[351] Prefect Isère, 8 April 1868, AN F12/4652.   [352] 3 March 1865, AN F12/4651.
[353] 16 July 1865, AN BB30/387.   [354] PG Lyon, 30 May 1865, AN 45 AP 6.
[355] Response of modeleurs-mécaniciens, AN F12/3117.   [356] PG Lyon, 15 June 1865, AN 45 AP 6.
[357] Letter to Prefect Maine-et-Loire, 27 Sept. 1866, AN F12/4652.
[358] Société fraternelle de solidarité et de crédit mutuel. *Procès des ouvriers tailleurs. Grève de mars–avril 1867. Association de plus de 20 personnes, non autorisée* (Paris 1868), p. 8.
[359] Paris Prefect of Police to Minister of Agriculture and Public Works, 20 Nov. 1864, AN F12/4651.

action, which would result in a further deterioration in labour relations. Thus M. de Mourgues, whose complaint to the police led to the arrest of some of his workers, found himself facing what he described as 'a complete revolt'. Instead of the return to work he had anticipated, he was informed that no-one would work for him until all charges were withdrawn. He rapidly decided that he had little alternative but to comply.[360] The Paris Prefect of Police described similar patterns of strike activity across the city's trades. Typically, he claimed, workers would identify the employer with the largest order book and warn him that unless he made concessions his establishment would be blacklisted. Once he had capitulated the remaining employers could be picked off one by one.[361]

Finally, an official statement in the *Moniteur universel* on 31 March 1868 sought to clarify the government's position by making it clear that providing they avoided discussion of politics, *chambres syndicales* would be tolerated. Nevertheless, the legal framework for renewed repression remained in place. Workers continued to depend on the goodwill of the authorities. The police *commissaire* of the Saint Gervais area of Paris reported that at a meeting held in the Salle Molière in the rue St Martin on 26 November 1868, speakers like Durand, a shoemaker, demanded legalisation of unions rather than 'tolerance, which he compared with a tap which can be turned on or off'. Other speakers insisted that workers should possess the same rights to associate as their employers, with the aim of establishing 'a union for every profession'.[362] This was precisely the recommendation made by Emile Ollivier, when the leading Rouen militant Aubry had consulted him in September 1868. He advised that workers should press for the formal recognition of the right to create permanent organisations, 'instead of losing yourselves in the outdated prescriptions of Jacobinism'.[363]

Occasions for strikes

One of the distinctive features of the Second Empire was to be the virtual disappearance of subsistence disorders, and their replacement by strikes as the most common form of popular protest. This followed a last flare-up in the mid-1850s and some minor incidents in 1861/2 and 1868. It became increasingly likely that workers would protest as employees rather than as consumers, when, as a result of the communications/marketing revolution, wages rather than prices were becoming the main determinant of living

---

[360] PG Paris, 4 Aug. 1865, ibid.   [361] Paris Prefect of Police, 26 Jan. 1865, AN 45 AP 6.
[362] AN 45 AP 6.   [363] Quoted Boivin, *Mouvement ouvrier*, I, pp. 228–9.

standards.[364] Amongst their various causes, the most important appear to have been disputes over wages, followed by those concerning the length of the working day, questions of internal discipline, and, especially in the case of miners, control of mutual aid funds.[365] In practice, however, strikers frequently gave voice to a wide range of inter-related and deeply rooted grievances.

The groups most heavily involved, in terms both of the number of strikes and of participants, belonged to the textiles, mining, and the building trades. Textiles operatives, relatively unskilled and in a weak position in the labour market, were especially likely to engage in defensive strikes, to resist employer efforts to reduce wages or force increases in productivity. In mining, tension and conflict were common over piece rates, working hours, and discipline. In building, where various trades shared a common mentality, difficulties were often caused by subcontracting and the financial problems of small contractors.[366]

Sometimes strikes spread, almost by contagion, throughout a locality or region, through networks of imitation based on residential proximity, the mobility of groups like building workers and the close relations between economic centres and their satellites.[367] Imitation was especially evident in mining regions, particularly in the north where mines were closer together than in the coalfields along the edges of the Massif Central, although even then, localised rivalries ensured that miners in the major pits at Anzin and Denain, owned by the same company, were rarely able to cooperate.[368] On occasion, imitation could occur over quite considerable distances with, for example, striking tailors at Bayonne in the Pyrenees in July 1867 reported to be following the example of their Parisian colleagues.[369] The Prefect of Police in the capital had already complained that the delegates to the London Exposition had returned with exaggerated aspirations to emulate British wage levels.[370] Leap-frogging was another factor, when workers in one establishment or locality realised that other employers were paying higher wages. In May 1870 carpenters in Rouen demanded that their hourly rate be increased from 40 to 50 centimes to match wages at Le Havre.[371] Some trades, in particular places, like the weavers of tulle in Lyon, were particularly prone to strikes, in this case in May 1855, June and

---

[364] Perrot, *Ouvriers en grève*, I, pp. 76–159; II, pp. 490–606; Price, *Rural Modernisation*, ch. 6.
[365] Perrot, I, pp. 262–4.   [366] Perrot, *Ouvriers en grève*, I, p. 354; Lequin, *La formation*, II, p. 117.
[367] E.g. Prefect Ardennes, 17 July 1863, AN F12/4651 re strikes at Sedan; Perrot, *Ouvriers en grève*, vol. I, p. 266.
[368] Perrot, *Ouvriers en grève*, I, pp. 369–70; II, p. 512.   [369] PG Pau, 12 July 1867, AN BB30/384.
[370] 26 Jan. 1865, AN 45 AP 6.   [371] Prefect Seine-Inférieure, 1 June 1870, AN F12/4652.

September–October 1864, April–May 1865 and, partially, in 1866 and 1867, as they tried to defend old-established wage tariffs and negotiating procedures. Observers frequently registered their dismay at the 'greed' of such relatively well-paid workers.[372]

Whilst some trades and particular enterprises experienced repeated strikes, it must be borne in mind that the great majority had none. This was for a variety of reasons, including working conditions, which were, by the standards of the time, acceptable; concessions by employers; repression; and fear of the misery which might ensue. This is far from claiming that workers in these trades were invariably happy with their lot. In general, however, strikes were not entered into lightly. Few succeeded in the face of resolute employer resistance. For the less skilled they were acts of desperation, and even in the case of skilled and well-organised trades, they were actions of last resort, following the break-down of often lengthy negotiations.[373]

According to Michelle Perrot's estimates, during the period 1851 to 1860, 66.7 per cent of those strikes for which information exists were primarily designed to support demands for wage increases and a further 17.6 per cent to resist reductions. In the following decade the proportions were 75.3 and 7.7 per cent.[374] The essential objective was to increase nominal wages, which were still, in so many cases, close to the breadline. Thus the increased cost of living caused by poor harvests and rising prices in the difficult middle 1850s led to a series of strikes, involving, for example, most trades in Lyon in the late spring of 1855.[375] More general, if less dramatic, inflationary pressures in the following decade, almost inevitably promoted demands for higher wages.[376] In Lyon, the silk industry again experienced major strikes during periods of prosperity or of recovery from depression in 1865, and 1869/70.[377] The State Prosecutor had pointed out in 1853 that 'the worker who sees that he is needed becomes demanding. This is a simple fact which should not cause irritation or surprise.'[378] The local gendarmerie commander insisted that 'it is a widely accepted error, that trouble occurs when the worker is miserable. Generally it is the opposite which is the case.'[379]

There was also a widespread desire to gain a more secure income. This was represented by the demand made by the miners of the Loire basin

[372] Lequin, *La formation*, II, pp. 126–7.
[373] *Deuxième procès des ouvriers typographes* . . . evidence of V.-E. Gauthier, Président de la Société de secours mutuels dite typographie parisienne.
[374] Perrot, *Ouvriers en grève*, I, p. 45.   [375] Prefect Rhône, report on May 1855, AN F7/4146.
[376] See e.g. PG Colmar, 21 July 1870, AN BB30/390.   [377] Lequin, *La formation*, II, p. 111.
[378] 15 May 1853, AN BB18/1520.   [379] OC gendarmerie cie. du Rhône, 26 Feb. 1868, AHG G8/151.

for a minimum wage.[380] Paradoxically, given price inflation, in September 1865 velvet weavers in Saint-Etienne wanted their wage rates fixed for the next fifteen years.[381] This establishment of a 'tariff' additionally preserved differentials between groups with differing skills, and was favoured by skilled craftsmen like the Parisian tailors who felt that their status was under threat.[382]

The length of the working day was another potential cause of dispute. Shorter days, arbitrarily imposed by employers during trade depressions, obviously reduced incomes and caused resentment. In the more expansive 1860s demands for a reduction in hours, without reductions in pay, were a feature of many strikes.[383] Typically, workers demanded a ten-hour day and frequently referred back to the ineffective, but precedent-setting legislation which, following the 1848 Revolution, had limited working hours to eleven per day in Paris and twelve in the provinces.[384] In justifying this demand, a petition signed by 400 workers in the Rennes railway workshops pointed out that 'an hour for us, is enormous; it is life, it is liberty, it is study and the development of the intelligence'.[385] Similarly, Parisian bookbinders insisted that a shorter working day would improve both the quality of their family lives and their education.[386] As wages rose, improvements in working conditions assumed a higher priority.

Characteristics of strikes

Strikes were especially likely to occur following weekends when workers had been able to discuss their situation and after they had received their wages.[387] The right to hold meetings was finally recognised in 1868. Previously these might have been held out of town, in the fields or woods.[388] Organisation nevertheless generally remained minimal. Workers normally elected delegates who usually expressed their grievances to their employers in moderate form and deferential tone. The decision taken, the initial sense of freedom from work and from dependence, the affirmation of dignity, was often exhilarating. Thus, in the evening of 4 July 1870, 400 or

---

[380] Hanagan, 'Proletarian families and social protest' in Kaplan and Koepp (eds.), *Work in France*, pp. 448–9.

[381] Prefect Loire, 12 Oct. 1865, AN F12/4651.   [382] Prefect Seine, 15 April 1867, AN F12/4652.

[383] Perrot, *Ouvriers en grève*, I, pp. 75–7.

[384] E.g. Prefect Nord, 22 Jan. 1859, AN F12/4651 re Wallaert frères linen mill in Lille.

[385] Quoted Perrot, *Ouvriers en grève*, I, p. 78.

[386] Circular letter of 26 Aug. 1864, enclosed with report by Prefect of Police, 26 Jan. 1865, AN 45 AP 6.

[387] Prefect Saône-et-Loire, 26 March 1870, AN F7/12657.

[388] E.g. Prefect Seine, report on June 1857, AN F7/4165, especially re strike in dyeworks at Puteaux.

500 striking carpenters gathered in the *cabarets* they habitually patronised, before parading through Mulhouse. Arriving at the *sous-préfecture*, a delegation requested official assistance whilst their colleagues sang and shouted '*Vive l'Empereur!*'[389]

During the course of a strike workers gathered regularly in bars, on the streets and in front of their workshops or factories, shouting and singing and sometimes throwing stones where they wanted to put additional pressure on employers or scare 'blacklegs' creeping back to work under the protection of gendarmes or troops.[390] Those workers whose family needs, anxiety, or sense of loyalty to employers persuaded them to return to work certainly faced verbal abuse with 'traitor' and 'renegade' the favourite epithets.[391] They also risked ostracism or worse. During the Parisian tailors' strike in March 1867, a worker was posted outside every workshop to take the names of those who dared to turn up for work.[392] Typically, building workers went from site to site, calling out fellow workers and threatening the recalcitrant.[393]

Intimidation could be physical as well as verbal, especially where the preservation of solidarity appeared essential to the success of a strike. It might be possible for the police to protect non-strikers at the factory gates but they were never numerous enough to ensure that 'blacklegs' were not abused or beaten up elsewhere, or to prevent the doors of their homes from being smeared with excrement and their windows smashed.[394] When a silent crowd of 500 to 600 people followed two weavers home from the Baboix silk mill in Lyon the menace was obvious but there was little the authorities could do.[395] 'Bosses' men' were always likely to face such reprisals, even in the absence of a strike. The few workers who volunteered to operate two looms simultaneously at the Screpel and Desrousseaux mill in Roubaix in March 1868 were, within days, afraid to go to work at all.[396]

Strikers were especially concerned by the employers' tactic of bringing in strike-breakers from outside the community. This threatened them with permanent exclusion from work. Intransigent employers were thus also likely to suffer reprisals. Windows in their homes and factories might be smashed. *Placards* issued warnings. At Caudry (Nord) in March 1862 a

[389] Prefect Haut Rhin, 5 July 1870, AN F12/4652.
[390] See e.g. Prefect Nord, 9 Jan. 1861, AN F12/4651 re Roubaix.
[391] See e.g. PG Lyon, 1 July 1865, AN BB30/379.
[392] Paris Prefect of Police, 4 April 1867, AN F12/4652.
[393] E.g. PI Saint-Etienne, 7 May 1853, AN F12/4651.
[394] E.g. Prefect Loire, 8 and 27 Nov. 1865, AN F12/4651.   [395] Prefect Rhône, 20 May 1865, ibid.
[396] Prefect Nord, 11 March 1868, AN F12/4652.

crowd estimated at a thousand watched M. Décaudin, a local manufacturer, being burnt in effigy.[397] Where warnings were ignored, employers might be 'punished'. Thus, in a particularly dramatic incident, at Carmaux in 1869 the château of the Marquis de Solages, the mine-owner, was sacked.[398] Luddism, incidents like the burning of the Scamp mill at Roubaix in March 1867, together with the systematic destruction of the contents of the owner's house, and the smashing of machinery in three other mills, was comparatively rare, however. The destruction of the workers' means of earning a living was a sure sign of desperation.[399] Most likely to lead to violence were coalfield strikes during which miners, marching from pit to pit to extinguish steam-engine boilers and cut haulage cables, preventing extraction and bringing the prospect of disastrous flooding, were always likely to clash with troops.[400] In this case a pattern of behaviour, of *violence traditionnel*,[401] had been established. Similar tactics brought the great Le Creusot ironworks to a halt in January 1870.[402]

From the workers' point of view, strikes were costly, carrying the risk of impoverishment, dismissal, and even prosecution. The initial euphoria rapidly diminished. Most strikes were short-lived. The loss of earnings, the threat of hunger, and the prospect of continued unemployment, inevitably bred growing tension amongst people close to penury. However, employer intransigence must often have created the feeling that there was little alternative but to continue. A modicum of organisation, the previous accumulation of money – disguised as a mutual aid fund – and subsequently its careful distribution, might prolong a stoppage. Typically delegates who were responsible for assessing their needs distributed *bons de pain* and small sums of cash to the most desperate families. Bachelors might receive *bons de déjeuner* redeemable at a particular restaurant.[403] Whilst the existence of funds undoubtedly boosted morale, their exhaustion was intensely demoralising.

Starting with limited resources and negotiating strength, the unskilled were in a particularly exposed situation. Their strikes, largely defensive, sudden and angry responses to bad news, generally subsided rapidly. These unplanned movements were likely to collapse within two to three days. As a strike was prolonged, pessimism spread and with it division and conflict

[397] Prefect Nord, 12 March 1862, AN F12/4651.
[398] Prefect, 22 July 1869, AN FI CIII Tarn-et-Garonne 12.
[399] Prefect Nord, 20 March 1867, AN F12/4652.
[400] E.g. Prefect Nord, 19 March 1862, AN F12/4651 re incidents at Anzin; Prefect Loire to GOC Lyon, 12 June 1869, AN AB XIX 174.
[401] Prefect Nord, 6 Nov. 1866, AN F12/4652.   [402] Prefect Saône-et-Loire, 19 Jan. 1870, AN F7/12655.
[403] E.g. Paris Prefect of Police, 15 April 1867; Prefect Gironde, 31 March 1866, AN F12/4652.

between workers. Women, under intense pressure to feed their families, might look for alternative sources of income or food, often in the fields, and press reluctant shopkeepers to extend their credit.[404] Frequently they were opposed to strikes in the first place and, where they occurred, favoured a rapid return to work, although in mining communities the cohesion of the village or *quartier*, as well as the women's own experience of working in the pit, encouraged them to sustain the faint-hearted.[405]

Nevertheless, as initial confidence amongst strikers declined, a drift back to work was always likely. Despair spread rapidly. Once a critical number had returned it became easier, both morally and practically, to join them, lending confirmation to the employers' assumption that only intimidation sustained strike activity.[406] As pessimism grew, minor concessions by employers could well be sufficient to end a strike. Paradoxically, this might involve the dismissal of strikebreakers. M. Bayer, a *fondeur en cuivre* in the rue de Nemours in Paris, was so anxious to reach an agreement with forty-eight strikers, that he gave in to the threat of an *interdit* by craftsmen unless he dismissed two non-strikers.[407] However, employers were more likely to seize the opportunity to re-assert their authority, to press for an unconditional return to work and dismiss 'trouble-makers'.[408] The principal figure in a strike by iron founders in Lille in April 1866, a M. Dupont, was, following its failure, thrown out of his local bar by colleagues aggrieved at their loss of earnings, as well as being blacklisted by employers. When he subsequently moved on to Roubaix in search of work, the mayor of that town was warned of his coming by the prefect, with predictable consequences.[409]

The idealised working-class solidarity so frequently discussed by militants in 1869/70 was in practice relatively rare and limited to 'the most ardent part of the working class'.[410] Workers in the traditional trades might still send financial assistance to comrades on strike in another town. Thus, in June 1864, porcelain workers at Limoges received funds from Bordeaux, Vierzon, and Bourges.[411] More common, however, was the *esprit de clocher*, local loyalties, and, within the workplace, the divisions imposed by age and

---

[404] E.g. Prefect Cher, 19 March 1862, AN F12/4651.
[405] Lequin, *Formation*, II, pp. 138–9; W. Reddy. 'The textile trade and the language of the crowd at Rouen, 1752–1871', *Past and Present* 1977, pp. 82–8.
[406] See Declaration by Mulhouse manufacturers, 11 July 1870, AN F12/4652.
[407] Paris Prefect of Police, 20 Nov. 1864, AN F12/4651.
[408] Prefect Haute-Loire, 2 July 1864, AN F12/4651.
[409] Prefect Nord, 20 April 1866, AN F12/4652.
[410] Paris Prefect of Police, 26 Jan. 1865, AN 45 AP 6.
[411] Prefect Haute Vienne, 9 June 1864, AN F12/4651.

gender, and different skill levels.[412] These divisions inevitably weakened the workers' capacity for self-defence.

The success rate of strikes varied considerably, for this amongst other reasons. These included the economic situation of various sectors of the economy and individual enterprises, the state of the labour market, employers' attitudes, and government policy. If failure had a dampening effect, success encouraged the spread of strikes and promoted solidarity. According to the gendarmerie commander in the department of the Loire, in July 1868, although coal miners were returning to work, 'there blows on the working class a sort of strike wind which appears bound to sweep each of them away in turn'.[413] For the first time, in May and September–October 1869, this 'wind' brought out around 8,000 clerks and shop workers in central Paris in favour of a twelve-hour day and Sunday rest.[414] Even where strikes did not actually occur, there was in the late 1860s evidence of considerable tension, reflecting growing economic difficulties, which encouraged employer efforts to 'rationalise' working conditions and reduce wage costs. It was also a product of a changing political opportunity structure, and a growing assertiveness amongst workers themselves.[415]

Justifying collective action: the 'moral economy'

The traditional precepts of the moral economy combined with socialist ideas to inform and justify the defence of established positions and efforts to enhance security. In the opinion of that well-informed social commentator Alphonse Audiganne, 'one preoccupation torments our workers more than the question of wages: that is the need for a certain consideration, for a certain respect in the exercise of authority, which would increase their own sense of status . . . Indignation concerning anything which appears unjust is the other side of this same sentiment which is rooted in the idea of equality.'[416] The delegates of the wood turners would have agreed, insisting that 'what the worker wants . . . is to be rewarded according to his needs and his merit, not to be considered as an exploitable material but treated instead as a collaborator'.[417]

It was hardly surprising that changes in established practices caused considerable resentment. Invariably wage reductions were seen as 'unjust'.[418]

---

[412] R. Aminzade, *Ballots and Barricades*, p. 94. [413] 28 July 1869, AHG G8/166.
[414] J. Gaillard, *Paris, la ville*, pp. 550–3. [415] Prefect Seine-Inférieure, 30 April 1867, AN F12/4652.
[416] *Les populations ouvrières et les industries de la France dans le mouvement social du 19e siècle*, 1, p. 73.
[417] AN F12/3120.
[418] E.g. Prefect Haut Rhin, 4 April and 5 June 1863, AN F12/4651 re strike at Guebwiller.

Such local customs as the miners' entitlement to free coal were valued greatly. Miners at Le Creusot were enraged when, in March 1870, they suddenly discovered that this privilege had been abolished.[419] The sheer arbitrariness with which wage systems were changed, invariably in a way which favoured the employer, caused intense resentment, with workers simply informed orally or by means of a poster on the factory wall.[420] The introduction of piece rates, or their subsequent modification, was certainly likely to provoke unrest. Thus, at Rive-de-Gier in 1852, the introduction of individual piece rates for payment of miners already competitively organised in *brigades* of 15 to 20 workers was clearly intended to stimulate further competition between workers. In a petition to the Prince-President the miners claimed that they would have to cut 126 hectolitres of coal instead of 105 to earn the same wage. A state mining engineer reported that the increased work rate would increase the likelihood of accidents significantly.[421] In 1864, the sudden imposition of piece rates similarly provoked a series of strikes in the metal-working and leather-working trades in Paris.[422]

The imposition of fines as a means of reinforcing discipline, especially common in industries with large numbers of recent in-migrants like textiles and mining, was another potential cause of strife. Punctuality was certainly a major problem. Typically, in the larger establishments, a bell announced the time of entry into the workshops and foremen or the gatekeeper took the names of latecomers.[423] At the Schlumberger engineering works at Guebwiller (Haut-Rhin) workers went on strike when, on 4 June 1859, the employers decided to end the practice of allowing five minutes' leeway at the beginning of shifts and furthermore, in an attempt to prevent 'time-wasting', ordered workers to remain at their machines during meal breaks.[424] At the Decazeville ironworks in January 1867 workers demanded the demolition of the iron entrance gate whose opening and closure regulated fines for lateness, and in all probability symbolised their subordination.[425] Additionally conflict might be generated by the employers' efforts to reduce absenteeism and to terminate such sacrosanct

---

[419] Letter from miners' strike committee enclosed with report from Prefect Saône-et-Loire, 24 March 1870, AN F7/12657.

[420] E.g. Prefect Seine-Inférieure, 16, 18, 19 April 1867, AN F12/4652; see also sous-préfet St-Die (Vosges), 16 May 1866, AN F12/4652.

[421] Prefect, 10 July 1852, AN F1 CIII Loire 6; R. Gossez, 'Une grève de mineurs à l'avènement de Napoléon III', *Mines* 1955, pp. 505–8.

[422] Paris Prefect of Police, 26 March, 2 July 1864, AN F12/4651.

[423] E.g. Prefect Cher, 12 Sept. 1865, AN F12/4651 re manufacture de porcelaine at Mehun.

[424] Prefect Haut-Rhin, report on June 1859, AN F7/4142.

[425] D. Reid, *The Miners of Decazeville. A Genealogy of De-industrialization* (London 1985), p. 59.

practices as the weekly celebration, by drinking rather than working, of *Saint Lundi*.[426] In Rouen textile workers went on strike in March 1864 and engineering workers in August 1865 when their employers decided to fine workers who absented themselves on Mondays.[427] Other persistent irritants included the fees charged against workers' wages for the provision of light or heating in textile mills,[428] or for the explosives used by quarrymen and miners.[429]

Those directly responsible for the imposition of workplace discipline, and especially foremen, were regarded with considerable hostility, although much depended on individual personality. Arbitrariness and harshness were especially likely to provoke challenges to the sacrosanct *principe d'autorité*.[430] The authors of an 1872 petition from railwaymen, who were subject to an almost military discipline – only partly justified by safety needs – complained about the arbitrariness of fines, suspensions, dismissals, and the blacklisting of those who complained.[431] Favouritism was also resented. At the Ronchamp mines the *maîtres-mineurs* allocated the more easily worked and lucrative coal faces to relatives and friends.[432] A foreman at the Besset foundry in Marseille, who favoured some workers at the expense of others, was violently assaulted as well as causing a strike.[433] In extreme cases strikers demanded the dismissal of supervisory staff.[434]

The threat of a strike was also the means by which some workers sought to protect relatively privileged positions within the labour market. Most such movements involved skilled craftsmen, organised and able to appeal to corporative traditions. Thus glass blowers in the Nord repeatedly took action to protect the custom of recruiting apprentices from within their families.[435] Paris bookbinders in November 1864, and silk dyers in Lyon in June 1865, were determined to enforce the customary practice of limiting the number of apprentices to one per ten craftsmen in order to restrict the

---

[426] Prefect Nord, 26 Feb. 1859, AN F12/4651.   [427] Boivin, *Mouvement ouvrier*, I, pp. 158–9.

[428] Prefect Haut-Rhin, 10 July 1870, AN F12/4652 re strikes at Mulhouse.

[429] Prefect Pas-de-Calais, 11 Aug. 1856, re strike at Bruay; Prefect Tarn-et-Garonne, 7 April 1860, re strike at Carmaux – both in AN F12/4651.

[430] E.g. miners' strike in Jan. 1866 at Ronchamp – see Carel, 'Le département de la Haute-Saône', p. 311.

[431] *Les accidents sur les chemins de fer français dans leurs rapports avec les agents de la traction. Pétition des mécaniciens et chauffeurs à l'Assemblée nationale* (Paris 1872).

[432] PG Besançon, 14 April 1866, AN BB30/373.

[433] Prefect Bouches-du-Rhône, 16 and 19 Sept. 1862, AN F12/4651.

[434] E.g. at Japy ironworks at Beaucourt on 13 Feb. 1860 – reported by Prefect Haut-Rhin, 21 Feb. 1860, AN F12/4651.

[435] Prefect Nord, n.d. but received 25 Nov. 1857, AN F12/4651; see also ibid. 17 Oct. and 12 Nov. 1863; and 29 July 1865, AN F12/4652.

supply of skilled labour.[436] The capital's printing workers were also bitterly opposed to the employment of women, which, no doubt correctly, they saw as a means of undercutting their high wage levels. That the women concerned would have received what were, in gender terms, high rates of payment, did little to counter male objections based on self-interest and an insistent belief that a woman's place was in the home.[437]

Strikes frequently brought a whole range of issues to the fore. Few were as bitter or took place on such a scale as those in Roubaix in February and especially March 1867. They were provoked by the textile employers' insistence that each weaver operate two looms, as was the case in neighbouring Lille and Tourcoing. However, the small increase in wages operatives were offered was not regarded as sufficient compensation for the extra effort and stress to which they would be subjected.[438] Tensions on this issue had been mounting since at least 1860, when violence had been directed against weavers who had agreed to the change in practices.[439] In March 1867, with little explanation, the owners of the town's forty-five mills collectively, and ineptly[440] announced an immediate transition to two-loom working. An estimated 6,000 operatives left work on 16 March and angrily destroyed machinery and spoiled finished cloth. They marched through the town smashing windows, pillaged the house of one mill owner, and set fire to his mill before troops arrived from nearby Lille. Workers saw what employers believed to be an essential means of reducing costs, as degrading their working conditions and a threat to employment. The strength of their feeling was such that, on 22 March, they were able to return to work under the old conditions.[441] Subsequently, ninety-eight suspected participants were arrested and although, as always in such situations, prosecutions were hindered by the ill-will and intimidation of potential witnesses, they must all have received a severe fright. Workers in general were also reminded that, in spite of the improved legal situation, participation in strikes could still involve considerable risk. The widespread dismissals and the gradual imposition of two-loom working which followed, further reinforced worker

[436] Paris Prefect of Police, 20 Nov. 1864, AN F12/4651; PG Lyon, 15 June 1865, AN 45 AP 6.
[437] E.g. *Deuxième procès des ouvriers typographes en 1re Instance et en Appel, juillet 1862* evidence of A. Parmentier, ouvrier typographe; PG Paris 4 Aug. 1865, AN BB30/384.
[438] M. Wallet, *commissaire central de police*, Roubaix to Prefect Nord, 13 April 1867, AN F12/4652; Reddy, *Rise of Market Culture*, pp. 247–8.
[439] Prefect Nord, 9 Jan. and 31 March 1861, AN F12/4651.
[440] View of Prefect Nord, 3 April 1867, AN F12/4652.
[441] Prefect Nord, 1, 30 March, 22 April 1867, 11 March and 20 Oct. 1868, AN F12/4652; and 26, 28 Feb, 18, 19, and 23 March and 8 April 1867, AN F1 CIII Nord 16.

resentment of what they perceived to be the continuing alliance between their employers and the state.[442]

Growing militancy

The May 1864 law legalising strikes, in spite of its limitations, undoubtedly encouraged militancy, particularly in those trades and regions with established activist traditions.[443] Emile Aubry, secretary of the Rouen workers' Cercle d'études économiques, looking back from the perspective of a textile workers' strike at Sotteville in 1868, would see the new law as 'raising the dignity of the worker in allowing him to oppose the demands of monopoly with the numerical strength of his interests'.[444] Workers increasingly appeared to regard the strike as *the* form of action to take against recalcitrant employers. In 1864, 110 strikes were recorded, involving almost 20,000 workers. There were sixty-nine in Paris alone in the eight months which followed the new legislation, with a wave of strikes in the autumn of 1864 and spring of 1865 involving bronze workers, tailors, building workers, and woodworkers. Although the number declined subsequently (fifty-eight in 1865 and fifty-two in 1866),[445] increasingly strikes were seen by the authorities as an indicator of working-class militancy.

Nevertheless, in November 1864, in response to an expression of concern from Pietri, the Paris Prefect of Police, Boudet, Minister of the Interior, sounded quite relaxed. Accepting that 'it was unlikely that this regime which places workers in an entirely new situation *vis-à-vis* their employers, would not result, especially at the beginning, in some of the inconveniences to which you point', he assumed that, in the longer term, 'the more freedom of action is given to the workers, the more one has a right to expect from them respect for the laws and for public order'.[446] Greater official concern would become evident when, from 1867, following a period of relative calm, further waves of strikes developed, each with an essentially regional base. Seventy-six incidents, involving 32,000 workers, were reported.[447] The most serious involved over 7,000 tailors and *bronziers* in Paris in February–March 1867,[448] and 2,000 foundry workers in the Nord, who

---

[442] Prefect Nord, 22 and 30 March, 9 April 1867, AN F12/4652; Ménager, 'Vie politique', II, p. 663.
[443] Report of delegates of outilleurs en bois, AN F12/3118; PG Lyon, 3 July 1864, AN BB30/379.
[444] Document published in Boivin, *Mouvement ouvrier*, II, p. 105.
[445] Perrot, *Ouvriers en grève*, I, pp. 74–5; Magraw, *French Working Class*, I, p. 230.
[446] 23 Nov. 1864, AN F12/4651.   [447] Perrot, *Ouvriers en grève*, I, p. 51.
[448] Paris Prefect of Police, 27 Feb., 13 March, 4 April 1867, AN F12/4652.

stopped work for some forty-four days in the spring. The latter presented a complex of demands, including the ten hour day, overtime payments, the abolition of labour subcontracting and of fines. The employers responded by locking out 6,000–7,000 workers and eventually broke the strike. Nevertheless, it caused considerable concern because of its unusual length, scale, and organisation. The following autumn major strikes occurred in the Anzin coal mines and, as we have seen, at Roubaix. In all around 12,500 workers in the Nord participated in strikes in 1867/8, 5,700 were involved in Aveyron, and 5,000 in Lozère – mainly in mining, textiles, and construction.[449]

In spite of the widespread misgivings such events caused amongst government officials and employers, the analysis of the 'Rapports des délégations ouvrières à l'Exposition Universelle de 1867', prepared for the Emperor by Devinck, optimistically suggested that the new freedoms were encouraging a spirit of negotiation which would gradually reduce social antagonism.[450] The combination of manhood suffrage, the right to strike and, from March 1868, official toleration of trades unions represented, at least potentially, major steps towards the institutionalisation of working-class protest favoured by the Emperor and some of his more enlightened advisors. The State Prosecutor at Rouen, during a strike by *fileurs de laine* in support of a massive 15 per cent wage increase, maintained that 'it is . . . a mark of the improvement in workers' habits that the strikes organised by the cooperative or federal organisations have stopped provoking disorder in the streets'. In place of 'secret and illegal struggles', he welcomed 'the system of routine complaints, the free discussion of interests, and compromise agreements'.[451]

The regime's final two years would see unprecedented militancy. At least seventy-five trades unions (chambres syndicales) were created in Paris, and forty in both Marseille and Lyon. In Lyon metallurgical and engineering workers established a Cercle de l'Union des ouvriers sur métaux which provided a model for other trades. The creation of union federations – in Rouen early in 1869, in Paris in December and Lyon and Marseille early in 1870 – was seen as a means of further strengthening working-class solidarity. In 1869, there were 72 strikes involving 40,600 workers and by August 1870 another 116 with 82,000 participants. The most notable involved 15,000 miners working in the Loire coalfield around Saint-Etienne in June 1869, and 7,000 ironworkers and miners at Le Creusot the following

---

[449] Prefect Nord, 27 March 1867, AN F12/4652; Ménager, 'Vie politique', II, pp. 656–8.
[450] 28 Oct. 1868, AN 45 AP 6.   [451] 9 Oct. 1869, AN BB30/389.

January. Strikes were also common in the textile industry in Normandy and Alsace.[452]

In the Loire coalfield striking bands of miners went from pit to pit stopping the steam engines, which powered the pithead gear and drainage pumps. The authorities were extremely concerned by the prospect of flooding of the mines and the impact on coal supplies, particularly to the local iron industry.[453] The limited size of the police and military force immediately available made it difficult to protect property effectively and to prevent intimidation. A situation developed in which, according to the prefect, 'terror spread everywhere'.[454] He insisted that 'the only means of bringing it to an end would be through a major demonstration of military force'.[455] A violent clash seemed imminent, and was made all the more likely as a result of the Interior Minister's criticism of the prefect's efforts to meet with workers' delegates. He was instructed instead to concentrate on the arrest of 'the principal leaders'. These instructions were transmitted by telegraph at 3.30 p.m. on 14 June. At 6.30 the prefect reported that twenty arrests had been made. At the same time he expressed concern about republican agitators and requested military reinforcements.[456] Tension continued to grow. On the 16th troops escorting miners arrested for intimidating behaviour were suddenly attacked by stone-throwing crowds at Ricamarie, on the outskirts of Saint-Etienne. Frightened soldiers opened fire, without orders, killing thirteen demonstrators.[457] At Aubin in the Aveyron on 8 October another eleven workers, as well as two women and a child of ten, would be shot in similar circumstances.[458]

In spite of the regrettable deaths, from the official point of view intimidation appears to have been regarded as a success.[459] Nevertheless, these developments intensified disquiet amongst employers. Their feelings might be gauged from reactions to an unusually long – three-week – strike by Elbeuf woollen spinners in September 1869. The authorities believed this had been possible because previously the workers had amassed a 30,000f.

[452] Rougerie, 'La Première Internationale', pp. 141–2; Perrot, *Ouvriers en grève*, II, p. 432.

[453] OC Cie. de la Loire, 28 July 1869, AHG G8/166; see also PG Lyon, 10 July 1869, AN BB30/389; Ministre de l'Intérieur to Prefect, 12 June 1869, and official poster dated 13 June 1869, AN F1 CIII Loire 9.

[454] Prefect, 14, 16 June 1869, AN F1 CIII Loire 9.   [455] Prefect Loire, 12 June 1869, AN AB XIX 173.

[456] Prefect to Interior Minister, 12.45p.m. 14 June and Minister's response, 3.30 p.m. Ibid.

[457] Prefect Loire, telegraphed reports 16 and 17 June 1869, AN AB XIX 173 and especially 16 June, AN F1 CIII Loire 9.

[458] F. L'Huillier, *La lutte ouvrière à la fin du Second Empire* (Paris 1957), p. 27; Capitaine Saurel, 'La gendarmerie dans la société de la 2e République et du Second Empire', Doc. d'Etat. Univ. de Paris-Sorbonne, 1956, III, pp. 462–3.

[459] Prefect, 21 and 24 June 1869, AN F1 CIII Loire 9.

strike fund, when in fact the 2,000f. actually collected had been entirely
used during the first week.[460] Jules May, one of the manufacturers involved,
claimed that the workers' motives in prolonging the strike were mixed – 'for
some, it is the sentiment of honour. They feel bound by promises made.
For a small number it is fear; but for all . . . there is a naïve confidence in
certain men, certain counsels, certain ideas, together with a sentiment of
suspicion towards their employers, their natural friends and protectors.'[461]
The role of 'agitators' in leading their fellow workers astray, is invariably
stressed.

In practice little is known about these militants. Workers who enjoyed
personal status in their communities, due to their skills, experience, or verbal
facility, were most likely to have been selected as delegates to represent
their colleagues. However, few can have been as articulate or possessed
such clearly defined objectives as the Parisian bookbinder Varlin who, in
an interview in March 1870, claimed that

> workers' associations . . . offer the immense advantage of accustoming men to social
> relationships and of thus preparing them for a more far-reaching organisation of
> society . . . Many of their members, are initially unaware of the role these associa-
> tions are called upon to fulfil in the future; they think at first only of resisting
> capitalistic exploitation or of obtaining some minor improvement; but the great
> effort they have to make to secure some inadequate palliatives leads them inevitably
> to search for the radical reforms which might free them from capitalist oppression.
> Then they study the social question and seek representation at workers' meetings.[462]

This quasi-Marxist analysis of the development of class-consciousness
reflected the growing optimism of many of the militants taking part in
the evolving political drama of the late Second Empire.

These genuinely 'heroic' figures, so frequently denounced as malign and
corrupting influences by employers and officials obsessed by the urgent
need to separate this 'misguided minority' from the 'honest, hard-working
majority', were especially likely to face dismissal and blacklisting as well
as police harassment.[463] They certainly welcomed the establishment of the
International Working Men's Association which, they believed, as did the
authorities, would be the prelude to the creation of 'a vast strike organisation'.[464] The *Appel aux corporations* made by the Parisian bronze workers
in March 1867 called for 'the solidarity needed to ensure our independence
and our dignity'.[465] Both they and the tailors sent delegates to the General

---

[460] PG Rouen, 7 Jan. 1870, AN BB30/390.   [461] Quoted Boivin, *Mouvement ouvrier*, I, p. 321.
[462] Quoted Rougerie, 'La Première Internationale', p. 156.
[463] 'Déclaration' of Mulhouse manufacturers, 11 July 1870, AN F12/4652.
[464] Prefect Nord, 16 March 1866, AN F12/4652.   [465] Copy in AN F12/4652.

Council of the International in London to request assistance. Affiliation to the International would be sought by sixty-eight of the Parisian *chambres syndicales*.[466] The myth of a powerful, universal organisation was being created, although the reality was more prosaic, amounting to little more than expressions of sympathy between groups of workers and limited transfers of funds to assist strikers. Nevertheless, the chambers of commerce repeatedly claimed that the law legalising *coalitions* threatened to have 'disastrous consequences'.[467]

Increasingly events appeared to confirm their worst fears. There was considerable alarm in Mulhouse in July 1870, when mass meetings of 1,500 to 2,000 workers agreed on a list of demands to present to employers. According to the prefect 'the word solidarité was encountered there for the first time'. The seemingly unstoppable spread of strikes encouraged him to believe in the existence of 'a clandestine leadership'.[468] Alarmed by these, the first significant strikes in Alsace, which had initially involved 15,000 workers in Mulhouse, and by mid-July 30–40,000 throughout the Bas-Rhin,[469] the procureur général at Colmar observed that they were 'the sign and the result of a latent transformation which has taken place, little by little in the spirit of the workers'. He reported that local employers believed that a 'revolution' was under way in which 'their paternal authority was being challenged',[470] and expressed the hope that the politically liberal Alastian business elite would draw the appropriate lessons.

The creation in Lyon of a well-organised Société civile de prévoyance et de renseignements par le travail des tisseurs de la fabrique lyonnaise, with a membership estimated at 24,000 to 30,000, aroused similar alarm.[471] The State Prosecutor in the city explained the growing solidarity amongst silk weavers, which had the immediate effect of reducing the ability of employers to take on workers in the suburbs and countryside as strike-breakers, as a response to the 'doctrines' of the Société Internationale des travailleurs, which 'have penetrated into all the corporations'.[472] At Elbeuf evidence of the machinations of the International seemed even stronger, with one of its affiliates, the Union corporative et fédérative des ouvriers fileurs,

---

[466] Paris Prefect of Police, 15 April 1867, ibid.
[467] E.g. Roubaix, quoted Ménager, 'Vie politique', II, p. 801.
[468] Prefect Haut Rhin, 11 July 1870, AN F12/4652 – word underlined in original.
[469] Prefect Bas-Rhin, 14 July 1870, AN F12/4652; S. Kott, 'Un milieu face à la répression: l'exemple des grèves en Haute Alsace sous le Second Empire' in Société d'histoire de la Révolution de 1848 et des révolutions du 19e siècle, *Répression et prison politique en France et en Europe au 19e siècle* (Paris 1990), p. 294.
[470] 21 July 1870, AN BB30/390.   [471] Prefect Rhône, 25 June 1870, AN F12/4652.
[472] 10 April 1870, AN BB30/390.

promoting a strike involving the best-paid workers in the textile indus-try.[473] A grossly exaggerated conception of the influence of the International turned employer and official concern about unrest amongst workers into fear of social revolution. The authorities' attention was focused increasingly on worker militants with a record of political activity. Certainly it seemed clear to the State Prosecutor at Lyon that, for most of these, 'the strikes and the economic discussions which prepare them are above all a means of encouraging revolution'.[474]

The situation seemed to be getting out of hand. A successful strike only appeared to breed further demands. The concession of a reduction in the working day at the Mieg mill at Mulhouse in July 1870, for example, was immediately followed by a strike at the neighbouring Schlumberger estab-lishment.[475] Bureaucrats and employers professed to be shocked by the 'ingratitude' represented by the demand that workers share in the control of the mutual aid funds established by some large companies. Direct chal-lenges on this issue occurred in a number of mining/metallurgical centres in northern and central France. At Le Creusot in January 1870 an over-confident management actually allowed workers to vote on the issue of whether they should themselves control the mutual aid funds it had previ-ously administered. In spite of a large number of abstentions, 1,843 voted in favour and only 536 against. The furious response of the company, directed by Eugène Schneider, President of the Corps législatif, was to organise a lock-out. The presence of gendarmes supported by two infantry battalions and a squadron of lancers added to the air of intimidation. Together with the elected administrators of their mutual aid society, the workers' leading spokesman, the fitter Assi, was dismissed. A protest strike by metal work-ers, the first since 1848, lasted from 19 to 24 January, and was followed by another brief stoppage by miners at the end of March. However, there was little effective cooperation between these two groups and their strikes were broken quickly.[476]

Subsequently, twenty-five workers were brought to trial. The State Pros-ecutor persuaded the court to impose severe sentences on the grounds that 'the strike is due to the republican party . . . It is not a strike by the pop-ulation, but by those bad workers, the sacred battalion of revolt, who are

[473] PG Rouen, 7 Jan. 1870, AN BB30/390.   [474] PG Lyon, 10 April 1870, ibid.
[475] Prefect, 5 and 7 July 1870, AN F1 CIII Haut-Rhin 14.
[476] Telegram from manager Le Creusot to Directeur-général, Préfecture de Police, 19 Jan. 1870; telegram to editor *Le Figaro* from correspondent in Le Creusot, 20 Jan. 1870, AN F7/12655; letter from miners to Prefect, 4 March 1870, AN F7/12657; P. Ponsot, *Les grèves de 1870 et la Commune de 1871 au Creusot* (Paris 1957), pp. 19–24.

to be found in all the major centres. Accused, I say to you, you do not represent . . . the working class that we love, you are not the children of labour, you have sown disorder, attacked property, you are the soldiers of Revolution . . . No pity for these oppressors'.[477] Certainly Schneider was determined never to re-employ the sixty workers identified as 'militants' by his managers.[478]

In spite of the *relatively* moderate and conciliatory policy followed by the administration in dealing with the many small strikes and even with such mass movements as those in the Mulhouse area in June–July 1870,[479] the growing number of strikes, together with the deteriorating political situation, ensured that the authorities would place increasing emphasis on the need to protect social order. This resulted in large-scale troop deployments and intimidatory action against strikers. Officials saw the hand of the *International* behind every strike.[480] Repression intensified. In May 1870 Emile Ollivier, now Minister of Justice in a liberal administration, ordered the arrest of those suspected to be its 'agents', on a charge of belonging to 'illicit' associations, and this in spite of the doubts expressed by some state prosecutors concerning the legal proprieties.[481]

The widespread gratitude expressed by workers towards a government which had given them the right to strike, turned to bitter disappointment as troops were again deployed against strikers. In many of the public meetings in Paris the repression of the strikes at Le Creusot was indignantly taken to represent clear proof of the alliance between the regime, its police, soldiers, and judges and the 'rich'.[482] The state was seen to have reverted to its habitual role as the defender of capitalistic enterprise. As the republican newspaper *Le Progrès de Rouen* pointed out, 'this was a hard lesson for the workers . . . They have been made to feel that the law on strikes, which some have called the freedom to strike, was only a trap. Almost every strike ends with fines and imprisonment.'[483] Together with the 'massacres' committed by troops, intimidation ensured that many workers continued to believe that equality before the law was a mere fiction. The members of the Rouen Cercle d'études économiques complained that, just as before 1864, they were entirely at the discretion of their employers, invariably

---

[477] *Gazette des Tribunaux*, 29 April 1870.   [478] Ponsot, *Grèves*, p. 24.

[479] Prefect, 11 July 1870, AN F1 CIII Haut-Rhin 14; Ménager, *Les Napoléon*, pp. 194–6.

[480] See Interior Ministry circular to prefects, 22 June 1869, AN AB XIX, 173.

[481] E.g. PG Paris, 30 April and response by Ollivier, 1 May 1870, in *Papiers secrets et correspondance du Second Empire*, ed. P. Poulet-Malassis, 2nd edn 1873.

[482] E.g. Dalotel, Faure, and Freiermuth, *Aux origines*, pp. 267–8.

[483] Quoted Boivin, *Mouvement ouvrier*, I, p. 323.

subject to instant dismissal should they complain about their working conditions.[484]

The law legalising strikes had represented an attempt by an authoritarian regime to find a way out of the political impasse it had created for itself, as well as a step towards the institutionalisation of protest. However, the law had unleashed tensions which the authorities found increasingly difficult to control. Michel Chevalier, the economist, businessman, and advisor to the Emperor, a leading representative of the official view that workers could be won over by rising prosperity, expressed his disappointment in 1868 in an appreciation of the 'Situation morale des classes ouvrières'. He further observed that 'it is clear that the working populations are not content with their situation', and warned that 'it would be supremely imprudent [for the regime] not to take account of this'.[485]

CONCLUSION

The diversity of the working-class experience should be evident. So too should the fact that although many workers experienced an improvement in their working and living conditions during the Second Empire, the degree to which they were aware of this remains in doubt. Their place in the public sphere was also enhanced as authoritarian government gave way to ambitious, but ambiguous, attempts to win worker support, but again with uncertain results. Asked, in repeated elections to judge this regime, which claimed credit for enhancing their position in society, how did workers respond?

---

[484] *Appel . . . aux fédérations ouvrières internationales*, 3 Oct. 1869 – document published in Boivin, *Mouvement ouvrier*, II, pp. 192–3.
[485] *Rapports du jury international* (Paris 1868), pp. cdliv, 363–5.

CHAPTER 7

The working-class challenge: socialisation and political choice

AN EMERGING CLASS-CONSCIOUSNESS?

This chapter and its predecessor are organised around the assumption that working people's politics cannot be explained in isolation from other aspects of their lives. Furthermore, the findings of the previous chapter would appear to suggest that whilst cross-class relationships remained of fundamental importance to the development of a worker's social identity, changes in the workplace and the problems of everyday existence were increasingly given meaning by the development of a partially autonomous working-class culture. The primary focus of the individual worker's loyalties might shift between the family, workplace, trade, neighbourhood, class, or nation, according to the interplay between short-term circumstances and more or less established traditions, animosities, and aspirations. Nevertheless, a sense of class increasingly informed workers' self-perceptions.

In the workplace, resentment of exploitation – generally vague and unformulated – appears to have been widespread. The air of superiority displayed by the employer, the *bourgeoisie*, and the 'rich' in general was especially resented. According to the prefect at Rouen, workers particularly despised bosses who had risen from their ranks, but more generally 'the industrialist, in his view, is no longer a chief who gives him work and a livelihood; he is a master who exploits him'.[1] Wage earning was widely regarded as simply a form of 'servitude'.[2] Thus, M. Bacot, a speaker at a public meeting in Belleville on 4 February 1869 divided society into three 'castes' – 'the bourgeoisie, its valet and the supplicants'. He explained that 'the supplicants, are us, the people, those who are called the vile multitude. The valet is he who, by the use of force oppresses us. The bourgeoisie, a dagger in one hand, a crucifix in the other . . .' The remainder was lost to thunderous

[1] 8 July 1858, AN F1 C111 Seine-Inférieure 9.
[2] R. André, 'De la coopération', *Voix du Peuple*, 10 July 1869.

applause.[3] In a speech at the Salle de La Redoute in Paris in November, a M. Clément also divided society into three – 'the worker, who is exploited by the employer; the employer who is the exploiter; and the aristocrat who lives in idleness at the expense of the worker and the employer'.[4]

In their representations of the *other*, workers frequently portrayed the employer as fat: the result of good living and idleness. They took pride in their own capacity for hard physical labour, the prime symbol of their masculinity. In contrast with an apparent acceptance of subordination, and with the respect normally shown to the employer and his agents in the workplace, behind their backs nicknames, gossip, jokes, and gestures frequently expressed contempt. The exaggerated and often obscene language of café discussion, songs and graffiti presented employers as *fainéants, cochons, bandits,* as *oppresseurs, exploiteurs, tyrans, voleurs, buveurs de sueur, de sang,* as *affameurs* fattening themselves at the workers' expense.[5] Their reward would, hopefully, be 'hanging . . . from the lamp-posts', for behaviour judged to be both immoral and unjust, by workers who believed themselves to be 'the sole artisans of this prosperity which profits especially the master'.[6]

Growing social segregation further enhanced the visible contrasts between wealth and misery. Martin Nadaud was struck by the difference between the ragged, filthy children in the streets around the rue St Victor in Paris and the privileged pupils of the private school directed in the rue de Pontoise by the then Abbé Dupanloup.[7] Whilst taking pride in their skills, artisans often resented their inability to ever purchase the luxuries they produced. Contrasts were constantly drawn between *misère et richesse,* starvation and opulence, between the situation of the worker unable to 'live by his work' and that of the idle, 'parasitic' rich. Such comparisons reinforced awareness of deprivation, caused frustration, and bred resentment. Official reports frequently and anxiously pointed this out.[8]

Typically, the delegates of the 'engineering workers of the department of the Seine' insisted in 1867 that work was the fount of all progress. Work was the essential source of dignity, and both a right and an obligation. It followed that 'those who pass their existence in total idleness, and some of them in the most shameful debauchery, are unworthy of the title of men and of free citizens. These are the unproductive and, by consequence, the useless members

---

[3] Vitu, *Réunions,* pp. 31–2.   [4] Ibid. pp. 35–6.
[5] Perrot, *Ouvriers en grève,* II, pp. 612–14, 622; Price, *Rural Modernisation,* pp. 131–43.
[6] Prefect Nord, 10 Jan. 1859 quoted Pierrard, *Vie ouvrière,* p. 184.
[7] Nadaud, *Mémoires de Léonard,* pp. 159–60.
[8] E.g. PG Rouen, 14 Aug. 1855, AN BB30/387 and PG Agen, 3 July 1865, AN BB30/370.

of society, from whom it is anxious to be delivered.'[9] In their submission to the 1868 Brussels congress of the International Working Men's Association, the representatives of the Rouen Cercle de l'instruction et de l'éducation des classes ouvrières similarly denounced those who avoided *real* work. They demanded that, whether physical or intellectual, work be rewarded with a wage sufficient to support a family. As a form of income, profits were condemned as unjust because they provided an unfair share of wealth to a small minority, which 'commits a theft from society'.[10] On similar, moral grounds, the representatives of the striking Parisian bronze workers in 1867 denounced an economic system responsible 'for this perpetual discord, for freedom without rules, constantly troubled by a restless and boundless cupidity'. The capitalist wholesaler, in particular, was condemned as a use-less 'intermediary', a *parasite manigançant* [underhand, scheming]', 'always at war with his colleagues, never at peace with his suppliers nor with their workers'. Less dramatically, they concluded that those whose labour cre-ated the wealth should be able to 'live less miserably and work with greater dignity'.[11]

Residence was another factor contributing to the formation of a sense of identity. In occupationally specialised localities, neighbourhood links strengthened workplace relationships. This was evident in the case of the cabinetmakers of the faubourg Saint-Antoine in Paris, the ironworkers and miners of Le Creusot, or the railwaymen in the various *quartiers de la gare* developing around stations and marshalling yards.[12] Along with fam-ily, the neighbourhood provided a physical and moral structure for social relationships. Even in occupationally heterogeneous areas a sense of com-mon interest developed. This was the case in Saint-Etienne, for example, and in spite of the survival of significant distinctions between ironworkers, miners, and silk weavers.[13] In Paris the changing spatial location of man-ufacturing weakened traditional occupational solidarities and at the same time reinforced neighbourhood dependencies.[14]

In often hard-pressed communities, living in close proximity, whether in run-down and repeatedly subdivided city centre dwellings in the faubourg St Antoine, or in the rapidly spreading and generally jerry-built accommo-dation of more uniformly working-class suburbs like Belleville, facilitated

---

[9] AN F12/3116.   [10] Document published in Boivin, *Mouvement ouvrier*, II, p. 60.
[11] Circular from the Commission de la Société de Crédit mutuel des ouvriers en bronze, AN F12/4652.
[12] See e.g. P. Guillaume, 'Un quartier cheminot à Bordeaux' in A. Fourcaut (ed.), *La ville divisée. Les ségrégations urbaines en question. France 18e–20e siècles* (Grâne 1991), pp. 191f.
[13] J.-P. Burdy, *Le soleil noir, un quartier de St Etienne, 1840–1940* (Lyon 1989), *passim*.
[14] R. Gould, 'Trade cohesion, class unity, and urban insurrection: artisanal activism in the Paris Commune', *American Journal of Sociology* 1992, pp. 721–2.

the establishment of mutually beneficial relations. However, their survival depended upon reputation and respect for shared behavioural norms. These were defined, and to a considerable degree imposed, through female networks of emotional and material support and by men gathering at the local café. It was important not to be excluded from such groups. Social networks were created through proximity and the existence of a variety of contact points, a shared physical space in courtyards, streets, cafés, churches, bakers' shops, at water sources and laundry places. Overcrowding also promoted frequent quarrels, with abuse shouted from windows and across narrow streets and courtyards, as well as minor brawls caused by all manner of irritants, including noise and drunken behaviour.[15] This was all part of the construction of community.

The café was central to the reinforcement of both neighbourhood and workplace links. Drinking establishments varied in size from the grand *brasseries* of Alsatian towns like Mulhouse offering places to 200 to 300 drinkers, to the small and more intimate wineshops of countless working-class *quartiers* whose proprietors were themselves often former workers.[16] In spite of the decree of 29 December 1851, which authorised prefects to close suspect establishments, their number grew constantly. They provided a place in which to meet after work, during the few hours of leisure, a means of escaping from cold and uncomfortable accommodation, and a location in which to develop male bonding whilst drinking, playing cards or bowls, singing, reading newspapers, and discussing employment opportunities and other matters of common interest. The Lille *cabaret*, 'more cheerful, more fraternal than the family hovel', was *le refuge suprême*.[17] There was of course a downside. If alcohol encouraged sociability, fortified the worker, and cleared the dust from his lungs, its purchase also imposed severe strains on many family budgets. Drunken violence was also all too common.[18] The representatives of the Elbeuf woollen spinners claimed that excessive drinking was 'a constant means of demoralisation . . . and one of the main obstacles to the emancipation of labour'.[19]

Skilled craftsmen with larger incomes and craft traditions of conviviality were nevertheless especially susceptible to the appeal of the café. Those frequented by engineering workers in north-eastern Paris were described locally as the *sénats de la mécanique*.[20] The economist Wolowski found

---

[15] Jacquemet, 'Belleville', IV, pp. 1208–14.
[16] PG Colmar, 6 Feb. 1850, AN BB30/366; W. Haine, *The World of the Paris Café. Sociability among the French Working Class, 1789–1914* (London 1996), pp. 59–60.
[17] Pierrard, *Vie ouvrière*, p. 288.   [18] E.g. Jacquemet, 'Belleville', III, p. 849.
[19] 29 March 1870, quoted Boivin, *Mouvement ouvrier*, I, p. 351.
[20] Stein, *French Engine-Drivers*, p. 149.

workers in Lyon 'distributed amongst gatherings of regulars . . . who assemble in the same cafés, the same halls or reading rooms, for discussions and refreshment'.[21] Strangers immediately felt out of place amongst these little groups of close acquaintances. This increased official suspicion of such *foyers de corruption*, which undoubtedly served as centres for the dissemination of news and views, as meeting places for members of mutual aid societies, and for those contemplating a strike or interested in discussing politics.[22]

Occasional and alarming insights into the sub-culture of the workplace and café were provided by police spies, in reports on characters like Jean Roby, a citizen of Lyon, who insisted to fellow drinkers that 'the people does not need a hoard of thieves who enrich themselves from our efforts or masters who are crooks and rascals'. After fifty years of hard work he remained as poor as ever whilst others were able to make a fortune in 'eight or ten years'.[23] Truquin's memoirs similarly reveal that 'rage and class hatred never lie far below the surface'.[24] The sense of being discriminated against by the State and its agents was another powerful influence. The social discourse of the café or workplace had also been profoundly influenced by the universalistic ideals developed during the first and refined during subsequent revolutions. The intense sense of expectancy in 1848 and resentment of the repression which followed, left 'memories' which continued to influence aspirations. In June 1852, the State Prosecutor at Lyon warned that, in spite of apparent calm, 'political life has not caused so much excitement to then suddenly vanish. The effects are reinforced by class interest.' Furthermore, although 'these interests might well have been stripped of all the paraphernalia of party and renounced the foul pretensions of socialism . . . they nevertheless remain alive [and] the overwhelming hope of satisfying these will end up by leading them, eventually, to join some party or other.' The continued ability to organise collective action was, he felt, symptomatic of the strength of class-consciousness.[25]

This manifested itself through efforts to create workers' organisations, to engage in collective action, and through politicisation. The *process* would, however, be prolonged, intermittent, confused, contradictory, and incomplete. In part this reflected the gradual nature of industrialisation and urbanisation and the semi-rural isolation of much of the labour force. In the major industrial centres the constant influx of migrants hindered the emergence

---

[21] Record of conversation with Walewski in Rémusat, *Mémoires*, IV, pp. 165–6.
[22] PG Douai, 27 Sept. 1855, AN BB30/415.   [23] PG Lyon, 9 June 1859, AN BB30/412.
[24] Traugott, *The French Worker*, p. 251.   [25] PG Lyon, 3 June 1852, 5 Feb. 1853, AN BB30/379.

of new solidarities. Only gradually did developing patterns of social inter-course, through marriage, sociability, and the creation of a network of relationships and a sense of community, establish a *milieu ouvrier*, a sense of common interest and grievance, an invented tradition and shared sense of history, as well as a growing willingness to challenge existing systems of dependency.

In this process the influence of members of the skilled trades was clearly evident. They served as 'core' groups whose systems of representation had much wider influence. Their commitment to autonomous organisation, most notably through mutual aid associations, and willingness to con-test the established social and political order, offered a lead. The issues and grievances raised by the representatives of craftsmen in 1848, and again by the elected delegates to the various expositions in the 1860s, had wide resonance. Indeed, the Paris coachbuilders would remember the despatch of the first delegates to London in 1862 as *une date solennelle*.[26] The survival of distinct and frequently selfish corporate interests, evident in the determination to restrict entry into particular trades and to main-tain wage differentials, should not be allowed to obscure this. Moreover, workers in such trades as tailoring and shoemaking, hard-pressed by tech-nical and commercial change and frequently forced to take on whatever work was available, must have found it difficult to share idealised concep-tions of the craft community. The politicised rhetoric of class solidarity would prove increasingly appealing to such craftsmen, determined to resist 'exploitation'.

The sense of class was thus the outcome of an accumulation of expe-riences. For growing numbers of workers, it would provide the basis for an understanding of the world in which they lived. The working-class autobiographers studied by Mary Jo Maynes 'were uniformly and acutely aware of class as a meaningful category through which to interpret their life experiences'.[27] The same was true of many of the worker delegates to the international expositions.[28] The gendarmerie commander in Lyon understood this. In December 1868, he warned that 'in such difficult cir-cumstances, the instinctive passions of the working class would certainly be successfully exploited by the enemies of order and of the Government'.[29] Furthermore he believed that it was 'material interests rather than political questions [which] divide the classes of Society'.[30]

---

[26] AN F12/3117.   [27] *Taking the Hard Road*, p. 29.
[28] E.g. Rapport des maroquiniers portefeuillistes, AN F12/3115.
[29] 29 Dec. 1868, AHG G8/152.   [30] 28 March 1869, AHG G8/165.

ALTERNATIVES TO CLASS

Nevertheless, a substantial effort was made to counter the development of class-consciousness. As we have seen, the attitudes of workers towards the social systems which structured their lives were influenced, not simply by day-to-day intra-community relationships, but by inter-action with other groups including their employers, landlords, and the representatives of State and Church, all of whom actively sought to promote a sense of inferiority and dependence. A powerful collaborative effort would be made to mould the minds of the young and to build into the popular consciousness an instinctive revulsion of 'subversive' influences.

The Catholic Church had a central role to play. Orthodox theology taught that work was God's punishment for the sins of Adam and poverty an inescapable feature of a God-given society. To criticise His established order was blasphemous. Typically, in 1862, a sermon preached by the parish priest of Saint-Etienne in Lille, warned that 'we must reject this stupid and violent equality, the dream of evil or insane levellers: God does not hate the society He has created, with its ranks, its hierarchy, its precedences'.[31] Every year, after workers belonging to the fraternity of the Oeuvres de St Joseph had processed through the centre of Nantes, with a band at their head, to celebrate the saint's feast day, they listened to an address by their president. In 1853 he told them to take pride in their refusal to listen to those who preached subversion and to appreciate 'the religion [which] consoles you when you are exhausted, when you are suffering, and which helps you to patiently bear this life of labour and misery in the hope of a better life, of a precious reward for all your sorrow'.[32]

The constant criticism by the clergy of Sunday work and attacks on working-class 'immorality' might cause offence, however. In 1862, the chaplain attached to the Nantes tobacco factory condemned the management for its lack of moral rigour in not dismissing a pregnant, unmarried worker on the specious grounds, as he saw it, that unemployment would make it impossible to provide for the child. He also demanded that complete silence be imposed on the largely female labour force to prevent the exercise of bad influences.[33] This kind of unsympathetic moral rigorism, reflecting an obsession with saving souls, ensured that priests were often feared and, sometimes, despised rather than respected. Men frequently appear to have regarded confession with considerable repugnance, especially where priests

---

[31] Pierrard, *Vie ouvrière*, p. 376.   [32] Launay, *Diocèse de Nantes*, II, p. 631.   [33] Ibid. p. 615.

asked searching questions about sexual behaviour in an effort to condemn the spreading practice of family limitation.[34]

Sermons insisting on the need for resignation to one's earthly lot in return for the promise of Divine bliss encouraged quietism on the part of some workers but anticlericalism in others. Thus, in a pamphlet distributed in the Lille area around 1855, the exile Bianchi railed against the clergy and the message they delivered which, 'in promising to the poor, in an unknown heaven, infinite happiness and life eternal, condemns them, whilst they wait, to die of hunger in this real life'.[35] There were very few priests who, like the Abbé Gadenne, parish priest of the industrial suburb of Wazemmes, were prepared to condemn the misery which afflicted the poor. They were disciplined rapidly. The prefect in this case reminded the Archbishop of Cambrai that 'the sole duty of ministers of religion must be to preach resignation and calm to the population'.[36] The representatives of the largely Protestant Mulhouse employers similarly believed that 'moral and religious regeneration' were the only effective antidotes to the class struggle.[37]

Assessing the influence of religion is not easy. The place of the Church in workers' lives varied considerably between regions and milieu. It was most significant in the north, north-east, and west and in small towns in which notables and individual priests were able to exert personal influence. Often deeply religious themselves, the *patronat* in Lille or Mulhouse, supported by their wives and daughters, were committed to the performance of good works, and to assisting the clergy in the provision of spiritual and material comfort to the poor. In such circumstances, church attendance increased the likelihood of obtaining work and *secours* when needed and, for the more ambitious workers, of securing promotion to supervisory functions.[38] In any case, many workers were sincerely religious and the vast majority inspired by at least a latent Christianity, resulting in an almost universal occasional conformity, and respect for the rites of passage. Thus First Communion continued to mark the transition to adulthood. Although Alphonse Audiganne felt disappointed that religious practice in working-class communities involved 'respect for external practices' and suffered from 'ignorance of even the most elementary principles', he concluded, more hopefully,

---

[34] Pierrard, *Vie ouvrière*, p. 403.
[35] 'L'ouvrier manufacturier dans la société religieuse et conservatrice' included in *Almanach de l'exil* (1855).
[36] 14 Aug. 1854, AN F1 CIII Nord 14.
[37] 'Rapport du Comité d'économie sociale', *Bulletin de la Société industrielle de Mulhouse*, 1849, p. 121.
[38] E.g. A. Lanfrey, 'Eglise et morale ouvrier. Les congréganistes et leurs écoles à Montceau-les-Mines', *Cahiers d'histoire* 1978, p. 69.

that at least 'the clergy exercises a powerful influence, due to their character, the instruction they provide, and because of their devotion to the
poor'.[39]

The constant insecurity, which was such a marked feature of workers'
lives, encouraged the search for consolation within an ambient religious
culture. Christianity informed the vocabulary and imagery employed even
by militant socialists.[40] Miners, probably because of the dangerous nature
of their work, celebrated the feast day of Sainte Barbe, their patron, with
enthusiasm. They invariably wore protective medals, and were particularly
concerned to ensure that they would receive a 'proper' burial. However,
there were some signs that religious conformity was turning towards indifference. This was the case in the older-established Nord coalfield, unlike
in the newer Pas-de-Calais, where miners remained closer to their rural
roots.[41]

Similarly, religious practice was more obvious amongst textile workers
in the mushrooming towns of Roubaix and Tourcoing and in the dispersed rural manufacturing communities in the Lys valley, than within
more established communities in Lille.[42] In 1855, the appropriately named
Father Coeurdacier observed that of the 40,000 to 50,000 workers in Lille,
only around 1,500 to 2,000 received Easter communion. Nevertheless, the
fear aroused by cholera inspired huge processions through the streets of the
city's poverty-stricken industrial suburbs. In Wazemmes, on 16 September 1866, the little houses were decorated with flowers and their windows
illuminated with candles in supplication to Saint Roch and the Virgin
Mary.[43] In the southern textile centres of Mazamet and Lodève, encouraged by a dynamic young clergy, workers remained strongly attached to
the Catholic faith of their ancestors, partly in reaction against the Protestantism of their employers.[44] Catholic workers tended to have different
priorities from priests, however. Thus the question of defence of the temporal powers of the Papacy, which appeared so vitally important to the
clergy, hardly stirred the urban masses. In Limoges it was observed that
'the population . . . is superstitious rather than genuinely pious, and the
question of the temporal power of the Papacy affects them much less deeply
than would the least offence to the relics of Saint Martial', the local patron
saint.[45]

[39] Audiganne, *Les populations ouvrières*, I, pp. 79, 99.   [40] Perrot, *Ouvriers en grève*, II, p. 637.
[41] P. Pierrard, *Les diocèses de Cambrai et de Lille* (Paris 1978), p. 248.
[42] G. Cholvy and Y.-M. Hilaire, *Histoire religieuse de la France contemporaine*, I (Toulouse 1985), ch. 8.
[43] Pierrard, *Diocèses*, pp. 242, 247.   [44] Faury, *Cléricalisme et anticléricalisme*, pp. 417–18.
[45] PG Limoges, 5 April 1865, AN BB30/378.

Certainly, in the larger population centres, there was evidence of increasing hostility towards the Church and a concomitant reduction in conservative influence. Rapid population growth frequently resulted in a loss of contact between the clergy and their 'flocks'. In Paris the number of parishioners per priest rose from 1,600 in 1802 to 2,956 by 1861.[46] The clergy and Catholic good works remained concentrated in the city centre. The burgeoning suburbs were neglected.[47] They were populated increasingly by migrants from the Paris basin, an area long notorious for its indifference to religion.[48] Reporting in 1865, the Abbé Meignan observed that although respecting the rites of passage the vast majority of workers were entirely detached from the Church. Religion was increasingly left to a minority of sometimes fervent women and their children.[49] Many priests were isolated further from the masses by their social and financial dependence on a circle of well-off parishioners. The greater respect displayed by the clergy for the 'rich' aroused resentment.[50]

Largely excluded from an active role in parish life, workers often came to associate Church-going with humiliation. The poorest elements of the *prolétariat* felt ill at ease because of their ragged clothes. Fortoul, the Ministre des Cultes, complained to Mgr Sibour the Archbishop of Paris in 1855 that pew rents, which obliged those who could not afford to pay to stand at the back of the church, and ostentatious ceremonies, were driving workers away and that as a result the Church was unable to fulfil its obligations as one of the guarantors of social order.[51] The apparent greed of parish priests was often commented upon. A popular song in Lille, where couples frequently co-habited to avoid the cost of a formal wedding, made much the same point:[52]

> For the poor, as for the rich,
> The Church does nothing for nothing;
> When a priest says a prayer
> He has to be paid, whatever.

In many working-class communities peer pressure increasingly ensured that very few men went to church. In Marseille, a city once famed for the

---

[46] M. Crubellier, *Histoire culturelle de la France, 19e–20e siècles* (Paris 1974), p. 146.
[47] Point made by OC 1er Légion gendarmerie, 28 Jan. 1870, AHG G8/176.
[48] Girard, *Nouvelle histoire de Paris*, p. 279; for similar relationship between Limoges and its hinterland see P. Grandcoing, *La baïonnette et le lancis. Crise urbaine et révolution à Limoges sous la seconde république* (Limoges 2002), pp. 15–16, 38–9, 47–8.
[49] J.-O. Boudon, *Paris, capitale religieuse sous le second empire* (Paris 2001), pp. 215–16.
[50] S. Commissaire, *Mémoires et souvenirs* (Lyon 1888), pp. 36–7.
[51] Boudon, *Paris, capitale religieuse*, p. 316.   [52] Quoted Pierrard, *Vie ouvrière*, p. 363.

intensity of popular religiosity, the imperial years represented an important period of transition as attendance at mass fell from 46 per cent to 31 per cent of the population between 1841 and 1862, and to below 25 per cent in working-class *quartiers*. The interval between birth and baptism, seen by religious sociologists as an indicator of the intensity of faith, widened. In the 1820s 80 per cent of babies had been baptised within three days of birth; by 1860 the proportion had fallen to 40 per cent.[53]

It does not appear that the clergy made much of an effort to understand, much less sympathise with workers' problems. They constantly complained about what they saw as a growing indifference to religion. However, the authoritarian paternalism and missionary spirit of the typical priest seemed more likely to offend the egalitarian sentiments of skilled workers than to re-awaken their piety. The representatives of the Rennes tailors claimed that 'the moral and religious education of workers in the towns . . . is almost non-existent because those charged with this mission fanaticise instead of instructing and reinforcing [the faith]; they substitute the letter which suffocates, for the spirit which revives and the acts which unite'.[54]

The determination of the upper-class social Catholics who became 'honorary' members of mutual aid societies, and members of the Société de Saint Vincent de Paul, to exclude workers from decision-making and restrict them to the role of passive and grateful recipients of charity also caused considerable irritation,[55] whilst the selective way in which assistance was distributed further increased hostility towards the clergy. A police report from Rouen warned that 'the clergy hardly ever gives charity save to those workers who frequent the churches: the impression this gives is deplorable'.[56] The impact of charitable activity was thus mixed, sometimes strengthening religious faith, sometimes reinforcing suspicion of the priests who demanded obedience in return for assistance.[57]

Anti-clericalism varied in significance between localities according to their historical experience and the strength of middle-class republican efforts to associate the Church with tyranny and superstition. It appears to have been most intense in the working-class *quartiers* of Paris and Lyon, and was reinforced in the late 1860s by a widely read anti-clerical press.[58] The vicious attacks frequently made in the public meetings in 1868/9, not

[53] F. Charpin, *Pratique religieuse et formation d'une grande ville . . . Marseille 1806–1958* (Paris 1964), pp. 54–5.
[54] AN C954 II.   [55] E.g. Kale, *Legitimism*, p. 160.
[56] 3 June 1861 quoted Boivin, *Mouvement ouvrier*, I, p. 170, note 113.
[57] E.g. PG Colmar, 10 July 1857, AN BB30/376.
[58] Strumingher, *Women and the Making of the Working Class*, p. 54.

only on the clergy, but on religion itself, attracted vigorous applause, whilst those few speakers who dared defend religion were likely to be howled down. The Church was described by one speaker as 'the strongest of the chains which restrict our liberty'.[59] The future communard Ranvier, speaking in Belleville on 30 January 1869, claimed that workers needed 'to be happy on earth and not in heaven' and to loud cheers affirmed, 'No more masters above or below.'[60] Anti-clerical speakers also condemned religious instruction in the schools and claimed that the teaching orders were intolerably incompetent. The influence of the clergy on women appears to have been a particular matter of concern for these predominantly male gatherings.[61] Nevertheless, it is too easy to exaggerate the intensity of working class anticlericalism. Indeed the efforts of State and Church to influence the poorer classes through the educational system appear to have borne fruit.

Primary instruction was infused with a religious spirit and deliberately shaped to promote both a wider acculturation and the transmission of an overwhelmingly conservative ideology, presenting the Emperor as the symbol of national unity, social order, and a prosperous future.[62] As Claude Lévi-Strauss pointed out, 'the struggle against illiteracy merges . . . with the control of its citizens by those in Power'.[63] Teachers had acquired a radical reputation in 1848 but it seems more likely that their training, place within an authoritarian hierarchy, and career ambitions, served to encourage conservative attitudes and a sense of pride in their role as government agents.[64] Inculcation of the work ethic and the virtues of honesty, discipline, reliability, and respect for property and authority were central features of the message propagated in the schools.

The Falloux Education Law (1850) had been designed as a counter-revolutionary measure.[65] It reinforced the already strong religious ethos in the schools. The regulations which implemented it sought to ensure that every classroom possessed a crucifix and religious pictures, that prayers were said at the beginning and end of every day, and that the teacher should conduct pupils to church at regular intervals. The supervisory powers of the parish clergy over lay teachers were reinforced, and the expansion of the religious orders encouraged. Through its schools, its spiritual and charitable

---

[59] Meeting at Pré aux clercs 17 Nov. – Vitu, *Réunions publiques*, p. 18.
[60] Ibid. p. 19.   [61] Vitu, *Réunions électorales*, pp. 14–15.
[62] M. Gontard, *Les écoles primaires de la France bourgeoise* (Toulouse n.d.), p. 119.
[63] Quoted H.-J. Martin and R. Chartier, *Histoire de l'édition française* (Paris 1985), III, p. 25.
[64] Anderson, *Education in France*, p. 154.
[65] G. Chesseneau (ed.), *La Commission extra-parlementaire de 1849* (Orléans 1937); Price, *Second Republic*, pp. 253–7.

activities and the particular view of the world it diffused, the Church thus frequently impinged upon working-class life. By 1860, associations like the Frères de la doctrine chrétienne were teaching around 20 per cent of boys in primary schools and much higher proportions in the industrial centres on which they tended to concentrate their missionary zeal – 88 per cent in Roubaix, 85 per cent in Elbeuf, 63 per cent in Lyon, Rouen, and Saint-Etienne. The more numerous representatives of the female congregations instructed around 60 per cent of young girls.[66] The selfless devotion of the Petites-Soeurs and the assistance they offered to paupers and the sick earned widespread respect.[67]

Workers' attitudes towards education generally varied according to whether it had obvious practical utility and its cost in terms of fees and the loss of a child's earnings. There appeared to be a close correlation between poverty and non-attendance.[68] By 1872, in the industrial Nord, 60 per cent of the workers in *petite industrie* were classified as able to read and write but only 33 per cent of those in *grande industrie*. Schooling must have seemed irrelevant for the performance of repetitive tasks in the textile mills.[69] However, these figures conceal major generational differences. In Paris 90 per cent of children of school age were inscribed on the rolls, although Octave Gréard, Director of primary education in the Department of the Seine, estimated that 29 per cent of those listed – about 67,500 children – did not really attend.[70] Especially in the suburbs, the situation was heavily influenced by large-scale migration from the countryside and, although most of the newcomers to the capital came from areas in the north with relatively high levels of literacy,[71] Gréard remembered, with horror, visits to schools in the poor 11th, 18th, 19th, and 20th arrondissements. It was not simply the sheer ignorance of the children but 'their physiognomy, their attitudes' which appeared to reveal 'a profound moral misery'.[72]

Of course, all manner of questions need to be asked about the quality of the education working-class children received in classrooms which, in spite of improvement, remained poorly equipped and crowded. In particular the relationship between instruction and functional literacy in later life needs to be considered. Few 'literate' workers appeared to be able to write grammatically correct letters or express themselves with clarity.[73] How, if

[66] Duveau, *Vie ouvrière*, pp. 449–51.

[67] E.g. P. Zind, *L'enseignement religieux dans l'instruction primaire publique en France de 1850 à 1873* (Lyon 1971), p. 21.

[68] Furet and Ozouf, *Lire et écrire*, I, p. 261.   [69] Duveau, *Vie ouvrière*, p. 438.

[70] J. Gaillard, *Paris, la ville*, pp. 274–5.   [71] Girard, *Nouvelle histoire*, pp. 285–6.

[72] *L'Enseignement primaire à Paris et dans le département de la Seine de 1867 à 1877* (Paris 1878), p. 150.

[73] Lequin, *Formation*, II, p. 106.

at all, did their reading habits develop? What was the relationship between regional languages and local slang (*argot*) and the standard French taught at school as part of the process of national integration? For every *bon élève* there were those who attended school only briefly and irregularly. Girls were particularly likely to be kept at home to assist their mothers.[74] Even when children did attend, the potential benefits of education might be lost due to poor teaching, boredom, or an unwillingness to participate in the learning process.

'Literacy' could thus mean anything from fluent reading skills to a stumbling inability to comprehend the meaning of words. A more positive ethos was rapidly developing, nevertheless. In an expansive economic situation, the prospect of social mobility, however limited, encouraged parents to send their children to school. Increasing real incomes and family limitation made it easier to contemplate supporting children for longer. Processes of social imitation were also important, especially within a context of rapid cultural change. Literate parents were likely to encourage their children. Illiterates might develop some notion of opportunities missed. J.-P. Dumay's stepfather, a stoker at Le Creusot, felt that he had done well without being literate and that his son did not need his letters to become a good and honest worker.[75] In contrast, Martin Nadaud's father justified sending his son to school, in spite of the hostility of other family members, by claiming that 'if I'd known how to read and write, you would not be as poor as you are; the opportunities for me to make money have not been lacking; but knowing nothing, I have had to remain a journeyman and keep my nose in the trough'.[76]

Complex and technically innovatory enterprises like the ironworks or railway companies required growing numbers of workers equipped with clerical and professional skills. Engine drivers had to be able to read complicated rulebooks. In modern engineering works like that of Gouin in Paris, new machine tools simplified many tasks. Their operation and maintenance required literacy, however.[77] Paternalistic employers like the Schneiders at Le Creusot insisted that 'improvements to the machinery are in practice only possible with educated workers'.[78] Children there were expected to regularly attend company-funded schools, in which teachers carefully

---

[74] Girard, *Nouvelle histoire*, p. 290.

[75] Traugott, *The French Worker*, pp. 311–12.   [76] Nadaud, *Mémoires*, p. 72.

[77] Ministère de l'agriculture, du commerce . . . Commission de l'enseignement professionnel, *Enquête* (Paris 1864), I, pp. 387–97 evidence of M. Gouin.

[78] Quoted J. Bouvier, 'Le mouvement d'une civilisation nouvelle' in G. Duby (ed.), *Histoire de la France*, III, Paris 1972, p. 57.

maintained notes on their behaviour and ability, with their future employment in mind.[79]

Although promoted by State, Church, and employers, literacy caused them all concern. Certainly efforts were made to provide workers with access to an edifying and useful literature. The government actively promoted the establishment of public libraries in schools and sponsored organisations such as the Société Franklin which assisted in the creation of popular libraries by recommending and subsidising book purchase.[80] The Church similarly encouraged the creation of parish libraries like that established by the Bibliothèque de l'association charitable in Digoin.[81] However, these efforts enjoyed only limited success. The essential problem for the newly established *bibliothèques communales* was 'to address themselves to a public which has not acquired the habit of reading'.[82]

What most workers anyway wanted from reading was 'relaxation of the spirit after a day's work'.[83] The representatives of the Société Franklin in the Haut-Rhin reluctantly concluded that 'The workers . . . lacking instruction, have little taste for reading; those who take books choose entertaining works.'[84] Alongside morally uplifting and self-improving publications, literate workers were also gaining access to novels by the likes of Eugène Suë – a former republican deputy – by Paul de Kock or Alexandre Dumas – available in cheap editions and serialised in the press,[85] as well as to 'bad novels and the often immoral books which the pedlars manage to prevent the censor from seeing',[86] including works like *The Lover's Catechism*; *The Art of Love*; and *Magic Unveiled* published by Le Bailly in Paris.[87] From the late 1860s, those workers, probably the majority, who found reading books too difficult could look forward to popular newspapers such as the *Petit Journal, Journal illustré*, and *Journal pour rire* or the *Petit marseillais*. These, on sale for 5 centimes, published 'human-interest' stories, including lurid accounts of the murders at Pantin in 1869, as well as accounts of the regime's military campaigns and tales of military derring-do in the colonies.[88]

---

[79] Cheysson, *Le Creusot*, p. 113.
[80] *Bulletin de la Société Franklin. Journal des bibliothèques populaires*, 1, 1868/9. See e.g. report p. 229, June 1868, on the popular library of the 3rd arrondissement of Paris with its 1,950 members.
[81] Commissaire de police Digoin, 6 July 1866, ANF17/9146.
[82] *Bulletin de la Société Franklin*, 11, p. 26.
[83] Ibid. 1, p. 230; see also N. Richter, *Les bibliothèques populaires* (Paris 1978), pp. 98–9.
[84] *Bulletin de la Société Franklin*, 11, p. 26.
[85] E.g. Prefect Eure, 20 Aug. 1866, AN F17/9146.   [86] 31 July 1866, ibid.
[87] Prefect Rhône, 28 Aug.; Commissaire de police Châtellerault (Vienne), 2 July 1866, ibid.
[88] E.g. report of police commissaire Condé-sur-Noireau n.d. but 1866 AN F17/9146; C. Bellanger, P. Guiral, and F. Terrou, *Histoire générale de la presse française* (Paris 1972), vol. 11, p. 457.

The development of this mass media increased popular appreciation of the practical value of education.[89] More threateningly, the political press proved to be increasingly attractive to workers, especially as debate developed in the later 1860s. Newspapers, widely available in cafés, like the social Bonapartist *L'Opinion nationale*, the moderate republican *Le Siècle* – one of the very few democratic newspapers tolerated before 1868 – or *L'Avenir national*, frequently printed letters from workers. More attractive again was the radical press re-emerging in 1869 and particularly Rochefort's *La Marseillaise* and Jules Vallès' *Le Peuple*. According to the State Prosecutor at Aix this was because of the sheer novelty of the vicious attacks they launched on the government, and the simple language employed by their journalists.[90]

Distributed by rail,[91] by the mid-1860s these new publications were competing with the traditional literature disseminated by pedlars, which had previously caused the authorities so much concern. Dismissed by the Prefect of Eure-et-Loir as 'without merit, either from the typographical or literary point of view',[92] this older material included almanacs and devotional and moralising works as well as a rich Napoleonic iconography. Although its publication was in rapid decline it nevertheless remained in wide circulation. Song sheets also continued to enjoy considerable popularity. Pierre Pierrard analysed 959 popular songs composed mainly by Lille mill operatives.[93] They generally parodied well-known airs, and expressed traditional sentiments, concerned with love and marriage, and the workers' misery and ways of dealing with deprivation, in a language both 'farcical and ironic'.[94] Religious themes were becoming less common. Instead the song-writers frequently attacked 'superstition'. The use of local dialect was giving way to a more or less standardised, and more prestigious, French. It is worth stressing that politics was overwhelmingly represented by nationalism. The patriotic songs of Béranger as well as the songs and slogans of the Revolution remained a vital part of working-class culture.[95] The democratic and socialist refrains diffused so widely after February 1848 had not been forgotten either.[96] Entertainment was also offered to the masses by theatres,

[89] Conclusion of analysis of 'Rapports des délégations ouvrières à l'Exposition universelle de 1867' prepared for the Emperor by M. Devinck, AN 45 AP 6.

[90] 19 April 1870, AN BB30/390.   [91] J.-Y. Mollier, *Louis Hachette* (Paris 1999), pp. 301f.

[92] 1 Aug. 1866, AN F17/9146.   [93] M. Crubellier, *Histoire culturelle de la France* (Paris 1974), p. 156.

[94] Reddy, *The moral sense of farce*, p. 382.

[95] J. Lorcin, 'Le souvenir de la Révolution française dans la chanson ouvrière stéphanoise' in Société d'histoire de la Révolution de 1848 et des révolutions du 19e siècle, *Le 19e siècle et la Révolution française* (Paris 1992), pp. 192–3.

[96] PG Paris, 3 May 1864, AN BB30/384.

like the *Variétés* in Toulouse, which offered melodramas, operettas, and vaudeville,[97] whilst in Lille the puppet theatre with its repertoire of biblical and historical stories remained popular.[98]

The impact of these diverse sources of ideas is difficult to judge. Formal instruction and the power of those who defined its content, was clearly assuming greater importance. How successful was this process of over-whelmingly conservative indoctrination? How did workers respond to the competing influences of state, church, the media, and traditional popular culture? How were their views of the world affected? The lessons taught in school might simply have been absorbed or else re-interpreted by workers in relation to their own experiences and competing ideologies. In examining the workers' response to education both government officials and subse-quently historians have tended to focus, however, on the political activists who, at least in part, rejected the official message. The degree to which working-class families internalised conservative, conformist, and patriotic discourses is more difficult to assess. The reports of the worker delegates to the 1867 Exposition have surprisingly little to say about education except to declare themselves in favour of obligatory instruction and the abolition of fees in order to eliminate the humiliating formalities involved in securing free education for the children of 'paupers'. The delegates of the Parisian trades, exceptionally, insisted that this was unnecessary 'since belief in the value of education is today in the spirits, in the habits of the workers'.[99] Literacy had become a source of pride, and illiteracy a matter of shame.

However, the cultural capital acquired by workers would not, even in their own eyes, have equipped them for roles in public life. In September 1868, Emile Aubry, delegate of the Rouen workers at the Brussels Congress of the International, blamed the workers' continued 'ignorance' and depen-dence on under-resourced primary schools which offered a very narrow instruction, together with exclusion from secondary education.[100] Martin Nadaud was more positive, claiming that education had made workers less fatalistic, and more aware of opportunities for self-improvement.[101] He appears to have been mindful of labour militants and political activists like himself, prepared to attend evening classes after a long day's work, autodidacts convinced that education was the key to working-class

---

[97] R. Aminzade, *Class, Politics, and Early Industrial Capitalism* (London 1981), pp. 157–8.
[98] Reddy, *Market Culture*, pp. 277–9.
[99] Analysis of Rapports des délégations ouvrières . . . AN 45 AP 6.
[100] Document published in Boivin, *Mouvement ouvrier*, II, pp. 53–6; see similar views of tailleurs de cristaux, AN F12/3120.
[101] Nadaud, *Mémoires*, pp. 109–10.

emancipation.[102] Nevertheless, the enhanced access to ideas which was part and parcel of the transition from an oral to a written culture was to be an important factor in the politicisation process.

POLITICISATION

The 1848 Revolution had revived popular interest in politics. In some areas a challenge had been posed to the quasi-monopoly of decision-making enjoyed by notables and to conservative conceptions of social order. The rhetoric used, and the organisational forms employed, reveal something of the issues which drew (some) workers into politics and the extent to which they were willing, and able, to engage in political activity, as well as the degree to which state-centred politics actually impinged on their lives. The changing political contexts over the succeeding two decades, as 'democracy' was replaced by 'dictatorship' and this was transformed by liberalisation – the successive opening, closing, and re-opening of the opportunities for meaningful political participation – also need to be borne in mind. People became interested in politics and ready to participate in political activity (i.e. politicised) when they were convinced that it was 'relevant' through the experience of 'critical events'[103] such as strikes and when it appeared 'safe'.

During the Second Empire the democratic 'apprenticeship', which had commenced with the introduction of manhood suffrage in 1848, was continued. Regular elections were held, and in spite of repression and official manipulation, they attracted high voter turnouts. Although, by their nature, elections require only intermittent political engagement, nevertheless the cumulative impact was to sensitise people to politics. With the development of mass communications, the arena was also being transformed, although the absence of national parties ensured that local organisational structures, routine social interaction, and the activity of powerful personalities were crucially important. Furthermore, as we have stressed, the 'working class' was subject to a diverse range of influences, promoting a wide range of political options.

Government officials, employers, the clergy, and other local notables certainly made the most of established social relationships to influence political behaviour. According to the State Prosecutor at Douai, 'a very important factor, which must be taken into account in the choice of candidates, is

[102] See G. Duveau, *La pensée ouvrière sur l'éducation pendant la Seconde République et le Second Empire* (Paris 1947), *passim*.
[103] Gould, *Insurgent Identities*, p. 19.

their personal activity, their energy, their wealth. Universal suffrage is hardly qualified to pronounce on nuances and the most active candidate, as long as his personality is pleasant, will stand a great chance of success against a less active competitor.'[104] Exerting the 'legitimate' influence that came with position in society and maintaining a high profile were the means of countering the danger that workers might be led to favour *le candidat du peuple*.[105]

THE POLITICAL OPTIONS

A range of ideologies – Bonapartist, clerico-monarchist, and lib-eral/conservative, as well as republican and socialist – presented workers with alternative frameworks for understanding their situations and acting to protect or improve them. These served to reinforce or counter the ide-als of working-class solidarity promoted by day-to-day experience. They also ensured that the 'political identities of the poor' would remain 'frag-mented'.[106] The problem for the historian is that often there are no obvious links between class and political allegiance. Other analytical difficulties also suggest themselves. How representative were the militants about whom we have most information? To what extent was political participation based on choice or imposed from above? How widespread was the 'indifference' so frequently commented upon? To what extent did it conceal a perceived lack of opportunity or fear of the consequences rather than lack of inter-est? What was the relationship between the small, everyday gesture, and such major political events as an election? To what extent did recourse to alternative means of expression including *placards*, strikes, demonstrations, arson, and even prayer, offer a substitute for a politics judged to be irrel-evant? Whilst the examination of these symbolic expressions depends on awareness of local context, the range of information available is all too often restricted.

Although electoral sociology offers a means of measuring the penetra-tion of political ideas into industrial areas, its results are also problem-atic given the complex appeals of disparate political coalitions, the socially mixed character of many predominantly working class *quartiers*, and the impact of pressure to support both official and opposition candidates. Self-expression was not encouraged. Even when groups like the delegates to the 1867 Exposition were asked to express their views, the printed version

---

[104] 22 July 1857, AN BB30/377.   [105] Ibid. 5 Jan. 1865.
[106] Gouda, *Poverty and Political Culture*, p. 67.

available to the wider public was heavily censored. In the case of the *peintres sur céramique*, for example, the proofs contain marginal instructions to the printers ordering the suppression of twenty-three lines critical of the regime.[107]

Workers would remain divided over a wide range of alternatives. Political opportunity depended very much on local circumstances. The advice proffered to workers by those whose status and education earned respect, the landlords, employers, professionals, priests, and officials who interpreted national events at local level, was overwhelmingly conservative. The imperial regime might be associated with greater prosperity. There was certainly a common concern that renewed political agitation would lead again to economic depression.[108] At Decazeville in 1869 miners supported the mining company's paternalistic manager standing as the official candidate, and sang, in patois, 'Long live bread, Long live wine, Long live Monsieur Deseilligny.' He obtained 85 per cent of the votes in the canton in which the mines were located.[109] Moreover, conservative political patronage was often allied with repressive action directed against those who failed to listen.

The authorities were, however, generally convinced that it was republicanism which shaped working-class politics, and that the regime was 'in danger from the proletariat of the towns'.[110] There were, though, very different forms of republicanism, as the bitter civil war fought in June 1848 between moderate and socialist republicans had already revealed. Moreover, and whatever their politics, the selection of candidates by narrow oligarchies, from amongst those with the 'appropriate' social and cultural qualifications, largely excluded workers from political candidacy, even at the municipal level. Working-class political activists, in spite of their efforts to 'improve' themselves through voracious reading remained heavily dependent on the patronage of the middle-class professionals and businessmen who sought them out or were encountered in cafés and meetings. The procureur général at Lyon took the point and warned the Justice Minister that 'one must never forget that opinion is formed primarily within the middle classes'.[111]

Where they did stand for election, workers could expect little support. In Rouen in 1869, rather than voting for the printing worker Aubry who attacked the 'tyranny of capital', his fellow workers voted either for the textile entrepreneur Pouyer-Quertier, whose programme stressed the shared

[107] AN F12/3119.   [108] PG Grenoble, 10 April 1866, AN BB30/378.
[109] D. Reid, *The Miners of Decazeville*, p. 68.   [110] PG Dijon, 12 July 1864, AN BB30/377.
[111] PG Lyon, 11 Dec. 1864, AN BB30/379.

interests of 'master' and 'man' and condemned the regime's 'free' trade policy, or else for Desseaux, a moderate republican lawyer, who similarly denied the existence of class differences and emphasised the importance of liberty and order in place of equality.[112] In Saint-Etienne, partly through lavish spending and their ability to fund newspapers, paternalistic liberal or moderate republican employers like Fourneyron and Dorian were able to capture the support of miners and steelworkers.[113] In Nantes the saintly reputation of Dr Guépin, a philanthropic moderate republican, long active in the cause of sanitary reform, enabled him to attract large crowds of workers to electoral meetings.[114]

Not surprisingly, class-consciousness ebbed and flowed. Pessimism, resignation, deference, and lack of self-confidence remained significant even as repression grew less intense. Indifference was also widespread. The 1848 Revolution had aroused so much hope but had done nothing to improve workers' lives. The dream of a more egalitarian society had all but vanished. Many, like the worker-poet Bigot at Nîmes, were resigned to accepting the place in society into which they had been born and susceptible to the consolations of religion.[115] Furthermore, individual political sympathies often varied over time and were frequently ambiguous. Thus whilst confirming that the town's workers would welcome a visit by the imperial couple, the State Prosecutor at Limoges warned that in spite of this, at the next election they would once again follow *leurs instincts* and vote contrary to the wishes of *les patrons, les riches, les bourgeois*.[116] Generalisations about political loyalties are thus always dangerous.

It would also be naïve to expect the same degree of commitment from every worker. Political activity was time-consuming and potentially dangerous. It required energy and courage. Writing from Mulhouse to Eugène Varlin in Paris in March 1870, Eugène Weiss complained of the difficulties: 'You cannot imagine what precautions it is necessary to take to win the worker over; they are so timid; everywhere confidence is lacking because they believe that every corner conceals a police spy.'[117] Politicisation processes were more advanced in some areas and amongst some groups of workers than amongst others. In particular, unskilled workers were obsessed with making ends meet and avoiding risk. Norbert Truquin remembered working in a textile mill in Amiens where, in the absence of the foreman, workers told stories and jokes, but never spoke of politics or social

---

[112] Aminzade, *Ballots and Barricades*, p. 8.   [113] Gordon, *Merchants*, pp. 142–6.
[114] PG Nantes, 26 June 1869, AN BB18/1785.   [115] Huard, 'Préhistoire', III, p. 749.
[116] 3 May 1862, AN BB30/378.   [117] Quoted Hordern, *L'évolution*, p. 527.

issues because this would inevitably have resulted in instant dismissal and blacklisting.[118] Representing the Rouen workers at the September 1867 Lausanne congress of the International, Aubry insisted on the difficulty of political organisation and propaganda when 'fear of the authorities and of unemployment is so strong that it prevents every personal initiative'. He felt that workers were rarely able to resist this 'terrible despotism'.[119]

In these circumstances, especially outside the major cities, widespread apathy was likely or else 'indecisive aspirations and vague sympathies'.[120] During economic crises, as crowds formed, individuals might well smash factory windows and hurl insults at the Emperor and his police. However, politics must often have appeared irrelevant or worse to many working-class families. They were not disposed to read political literature or attend meetings. Reports on parliamentary debates left them cold. Doubtless many failed to register as electors. The procedure was complicated and time-consuming. Workers were often nervous in their dealings with clerks. To prove that he was qualified by residence the potential voter had to present the local electoral commission with a *quittance de loyer* – a certificate signed by his landlord, and another signed by the local police *commissaire*. According to an estimate made by the Société de Statistique in 1864, in the Department of the Seine, including Paris, 19.71 per cent of eligible males were not on the lists. Most of these were workers. Many of them were recent migrants. Large numbers of temporary migrants were also excluded. Significantly, and primarily as a result of republican efforts to encourage registration, the number of voters in the department rose from 270,353 in 1863 to 329,437 in 1869.[121]

Even apparent apathy might of course conceal the prudence of the poor. It might represent a genuine sense of respect for and dependence on the better-off or alternatively conceal a bitter hatred born of misery and envy, which could, when it seemed safe to do so, be expressed through the ballot.[122] The authorities were repeatedly surprised when an apparently indifferent labour force turned out, en masse, to support opposition candidates. Moreover, in the agitated conditions of the late Empire politics would again seem relevant to growing numbers of people.[123] It is time to review the options.

[118] In Traugott, *The French Worker*, pp. 273–4.
[119] Congrès de Lausanne, Rapport de la section de Rouen, 3 Sept. 1867, reprinted in Boivin, *Mouvement ouvrier*, II, p. 27.
[120] PG Aix, 2 July 1859, AN BB30/370.   [121] J. Gaillard, *Paris, la ville*, p. 186.
[122] Point made by PG Orléans, 1 July 1858, AN BB30/382.
[123] Point made by PG Paris, 13 Nov. 1865, AN BB30/384.

Bonapartism

In voting overwhelmingly for Louis-Napoleon Bonaparte in the presidential elections in December 1848 workers had seen him as a powerful incarnation of France and had hoped that he would defend their interests. Bonaparte, author of proposals for the 'Extinction of Pauperism', was described as the 'people's friend'.[124] In the plebiscites of December 1851 and November 1852, to approve the *coup d'état* and then the re-establishment of the hereditary empire, it was clear that the Napoleonic legend – such an important feature of popular culture – retained its potency, and provided the basis for a patriotic appeal across the classes.[125] In Paris, in the first plebiscite 132,981 voters approved the *coup d'état*, 80,691 opposed, and 75,102 abstained.[126] In Lyon and the department of the Rhône, 96,513 votes were recorded in November 1852 in favour of imperial restoration and only 9,789 against.[127] In the Nord, 79 per cent of the voters in the Anzin mining community and 84 per cent at nearby Denain had approved the *coup*,[128] whilst in the little textile centres around Le Cateau workers marched, enthusiastically, behind their bands and flags to vote for the Emperor.[129] In the industrial areas of the Nord, and of Normandy and Alsace, support for the new regime increased substantially between the two plebiscites.[130]

Frequently official reports insisted that workers had lost interest in opposition politics.[131] Nevertheless, the persistently high levels of abstention caused some concern.[132] There was also uncertainty concerning the explanation of popular support. To what extent did these votes imply a genuine commitment to the regime? The response to this question in October 1852 from the State Prosecutor at Amiens concerning workers in the departments of Somme, Aisne, and Oise, was not untypical: 'the workers have work and abandon political discussions'. If a small minority of militants remained hostile to the regime, 'their soldiers, more simple and artless men' supported the Emperor, although, he added, they continued to hate the upper classes.[133] Whilst the procureur général at Lyon agreed with officials in other major cities, that the experience of the Second Republic had immeasurably strengthened support for republicanism, he was convinced that everything remained to play for. He conceded that 'the durable effect [of 1848] is that

---

[124] Price, *Second Republic*, pp. 208f.   [125] E.g. PG Lyon, 11 Dec. 1852, AN BB30/379.
[126] AN BB11 1118.   [127] Tulard, *Dictionnaire*, p. 751.
[128] Ménager, 'Vie politique', 1, p. 80.   [129] Ibid. p. 78.
[130] B. Ménager, 'Force et limites du Bonapartisme populaire en milieu ouvrier sous le Second Empire', *Revue historique* 1981, p. 374.
[131] E.g. PG Colmar, 22 Feb. 1852, AN BB30/376.   [132] E.g. PG Rouen, 5 May 1852, AN BB30/387.
[133] 5 Oct. 1852, AN BB30/371.

the working population is linked together by class interests', but was certain that workers' aspirations might just as easily be satisfied by Bonapartism as by republicanism.[134]

To what extent was the popular reaction to the regime's advances a deferential response to pressure from officials and employers? Certainly workers were susceptible to pressure or 'advice' from those who provided them with a livelihood, and officials expected the *patronat* to support the 'conservative' cause. It was made clear to the workers in the great ironworks at Le Creusot in central France and those at Hayange in the east that they were expected to vote in favour of the regime.[135] The exercise of pressure to obtain the 'correct' vote could be seen at its most extreme in the state arsenals in places like Lorient and Toulon, where voting took place at work and under close supervision, in order, it was claimed, to protect the workers from 'disruptive influences'.[136]

But how stable was this support likely to be? In Normandy, workers voted for the establishment of the Empire in the November 1852 plebiscite and then shortly afterwards against official candidates in municipal elections.[137] What should be made of the behaviour of the workers in Saint-Etienne who, after electing the notorious republican Jules Favre to the departmental council in August 1852, had welcomed the visiting Prince-President with notable enthusiasm in September?[138] It seemed, as the State Prosecutor at Dijon warned, that workers were likely to 'succumb, one after the other, just as easily to the enthusiasm aroused by a magical name as to the sentiments of cupidity which the clever representatives of demagogy know so well how to exploit'.[139]

Within a few years of the *coup d'état* officials were providing even less optimistic assessments of workers' loyalties. It seemed clear, to some at least, that a substantial part of the working-class vote in favour of the regime had been induced by fear of repressive government.[140] Efforts were made to retrieve the situation. Official propaganda sought to reinforce the sympathetic image already established by the author of *L'Extinction du paupérisme*, publicising the imperial couple's support for institutions like mutual aid societies, nurseries, orphanages, and for the homes for aged and infirm workers established at Vésinet, Vincennes, Rouen, and Mulhouse, as

---

[134] 3 June 1852, AN BB30/379.　　[135] Ménager, 'Force et limites', p. 386.
[136] Prefect Morbihan, 27 June 1860; see also Ministre de Marine to Interior, 12 Sept. 1855, AN F1 CIII Morbihan 13; and Constant, 'Var', IV, pp. 1106–7.
[137] PG Rouen, 7 Dec. 1852, AN BB30/387 re Seine-Inférieure and Eure.
[138] Duveau, *Vie ouvrière*, p. 102.　　[139] 9 June 1851, AN BB30/377.
[140] E.g. PG Metz, 12 April 1860, AN BB30/380.

well as the efforts, in thirty-six departments, to create free medical services for the poor.[141]

The Emperor was himself determined to demonstrate his concern for his people. Typically, in 1856 he received a delegation of Parisian workers, anxious to express their fears concerning rent increases, and subsequently insisted, in a well publicised speech to the Paris municipal council, that urban renewal would soon lead to reductions, predicting a future with 'the working class enriching itself by labour [and] poverty diminishing through a better organisation of charity'.[142] Visits to the victims of floods in the Rhône and Loire valleys in 1856[143] and to cholera patients in Amiens in 1866 contributed to this image building.

Efforts in the 1850s to alleviate the effects of high food prices, through bread subsidies, and to provide employment by means of public works also appear to have been widely appreciated.[144] Significantly, and in marked contrast with 1847 when Louis-Philippe had frequently been held responsible for 'starving his people', *placards* denouncing greedy speculators and the efforts of the regime's political opponents to discredit it and to oppose the Emperor's desire to reduce prices, appear to have been more common than those blaming the government for the workers' misery.[145] The Emperor's sympathy for the workers was again glorified in a series of cheap brochures published in 1860 and distributed throughout the following decade.[146]

As a result of these efforts, some groups of workers continued to make direct appeals for assistance to the Emperor and his representatives, through petitions and delegations. At Rive-de-Gier, near Saint-Etienne, in July 1852 a delegation of miners went cap-in-hand to local officials to explain their grievances and humbly petitioned the Head of State: 'because they already know the great interest that you take in the class of honest and hard-working workers, and . . . you are just and have a good heart', the signatories 'throw themselves at your feet to call for your great and benevolent protection'. On this occasion the results were encouraging, with concessions being secured from the Compagnie des Mines de la Loire by Interior Minister Persigny.[147]

---

[141] Price, *Second Empire*, pp. 204–9.
[142] Quoted T. Clark, *The Painting of Modern Life* (New York 1985), p. 45.
[143] See Maréchal de Castellane, *Journal*, v (Paris 1897), pp. 138–40.
[144] G. Bourgin, 'La législation ouvrière du Second Empire', *Revue des études napoléonniennes* 1913, p. 224.
[145] E.g. Paris prefect of Police, 26 Oct. 1856, AN BB30/366; Price, *Rural Modernisation*, p. 142.
[146] D. Kulstein, *Napoleon III and the Working Class. A Study of Government Propaganda during the Second Empire* (London 1969), pp. 120–1.
[147] Petition in AN BB18/1506; see also PG Lyon, 5 July 1852, AN BB30/379; Prefect, 10 July 1852, AN F1 CIII Loire 6; R. Gossez, 'Une grève des mineurs', pp. 506–12.

Parisian printing workers, negotiating new wages tariffs with their employers in May 1862, were another group which appealed for imperial arbitration,[148] whilst striking textile workers in Normandy were still expressing their confidence in the Emperor in 1869.[149]

In the early 1860s, as elite support for the regime weakened, it proved tempting to try to balance this with a more direct appeal to the workers. This effort was inaugurated by contacts between Prince Napoleon, together with the political economists Arles-Dufour and Michel Chevalier, and a small circle of Parisian artisans including the printing workers J. J. Blanc and A. Coutant and the tinsmith Chabaud, already alienated from republican politicians by the social conservatism they had displayed in 1848, and by the brutal repression of the June insurrection. The initiative to send delegates to the 1862 London Exposition came from this so-called Palais-Royal group. They assumed that imperial support offered the most realistic possibility of social reform,[150] and in 1861 published a brochure entitled *L'Empereur, le peuple et les anciens partis* which reminded its readers that the monarch's authority was derived from universal suffrage and predicted the repeal of legislation directed against workers.

Indeed, by the end of the decade official propaganda would be able to point, not only to the retention of universal suffrage and the growth of prosperity, but to measures specifically designed to respond to workers' complaints. These included subsidies for mutual aid societies, recognition of the right to strike in 1864, and in 1868 suppression of Article 1781 of the Civil Code which had enshrined the unequal status of employer and employee in law. This had been especially significant for the workings of the Conseils de prud'hommes, locally elected bodies which mediated between employers and workers in disputes over wages, discipline, breaches of contract, etc. The delegates of the Paris masons had previously condemned a provision which 'conferred on the employers the right to be believed when speaking on oath before the conseil . . . , whilst this is refused to the worker', as a 'flagrant injustice'.[151]

Many workers would respond positively to the complex of repressive and liberalising measures introduced by the regime and accept its claims to have brought order and prosperity. In Rouen, it appears that some members of the local section of the International were reluctant to condemn a regime which had proved itself willing to make concessions on such

---

[148] Petition from ouvriers typographes for the establishment of a Commission d'arbitrage pour le révision des tarifs, 2 May 1862, AN F12/2370-4.
[149] L'Huillier, *La lutte ouvrière*, p. 25.   [150] Tulard, *Dictionnaire*, pp. 459–60.   [151] AN F12/3115.

vital matters as the right to strike, as well as on political liberties.[152] Some were encouraged to look to the Emperor for further social reform.[153] Textile workers in Roubaix, Tourcoing, Armentières, and the Lys valley, miners at Valenciennes, and ironworkers in the Sambre valley saw the regime as the defender of their interests against those of their employers and the rich in general.[154]

During the 1869 election campaign, an appeal by the local prefect to miners' leaders in the Saint-Etienne coalfield, to support the official candidate, the Comte de Charpin-Feugerolles, in return for a promise to help them to achieve their objective of sharing control of the mining company's mutual aid society, appears to have been quite successful. However, the subsequent refusal of the employers to make concessions and the bitter miners' strike which followed would win most workers over to the republican cause.[155] Popular Bonapartism was further shaken by massive military deployments against strikers.[156] These were the occasions on which workers encountered the officials, police, and troops who, above all for them, represented the Emperor. Workers were as ambiguous in their attitudes towards the army as they were towards the regime which it represented.

Certainly it was possible to make a patriotic appeal to the masses. At the moment when the last veterans of the first Napoleon's *grande armée* were disappearing, symbols of imperial glory were widely displayed to give new life to the myth. The massive commercial production of plaster statues and lithographed images of the great Emperor and his nephew provided inexpensive decoration for many homes. Even in the major centres of opposition, crowds evidently enjoyed the military parades, music, dancing, and spectacular fireworks displays which celebrated events like the Emperor's marriage, the baptism of the Prince-Imperial, or the highly publicised imperial visits to provincial towns to open new railway stations and boulevards. The 15th of August, which had been established as the national holiday, was celebrated both as the birthday of Napoleon I and the religious feast of the Assumption. It offered occasions for reinforcing the regime's links with the army and Church and for associating the Napoleonic cult with French patriotism. The distribution of decorations and practice of

---

[152] Boivin, *Mouvement ouvrier*, i, p. 403.

[153] E.g. petition from 'Le premier groupe cooperatif des ouvriers maçons et tailleurs de pierre', Paris 26 June 1868, AN F12/2370-4.

[154] Ménager, *Les Napoléon*, p. 224; R. Huard, 'Une géographie politique évolutive. 1848–80' in S. Berstein and M. Winock (eds.), *L'invention de la démocratie* (Paris 2002), pp. 228–9.

[155] Hanagan, *Nascent Proletarians*, pp. 191–3; Gordon, *Merchants*, p. 150.

[156] Justice Minister to PG Douai, 26 Oct. 1866, AN BB18/1731.

amnestying political prisoners were both means of re-affirming national unity.[157]

Many democratically inclined workers supported the wars against reactionary Russia and Austria and in support of Italian unity. The departure of the Emperor to Italy in 1859 was accompanied by the expression of a bellicose popular nationalism by the inhabitants of the popular *quartiers* of Paris and Lyon, which contrasted markedly with the reticence shown by more committed republican militants.[158] The pro-regime press reported these events in considerable detail. Similarly the news of military victories and the return of the army from the Crimea and Italy were celebrated with great enthusiasm by workers. Only a war against the old English enemy might have been more popular.[159]

Such moments of patriotic unanimity were not themselves without ambiguity, however. Whilst welcoming the fact that for the working class 'the Emperor has become a hero', the State Prosecutor at Lyon added, 'but I regret . . . that Garibaldi is placed at his side'.[160] The expression of support for the war also provided an opportunity to express hostility towards the local nobles and clergy who opposed conflict with the conservative powers.[161] In October 1863 the State Prosecutor at Paris concluded that workers' support for another war against Russia in support of the cause of Polish independence made it clear that some still dreamt of a *conflagration générale* leading to revolution.[162]

In any case, fundamental limits were imposed on initiatives intended to win over workers by the opposition of social elites and most government officials to any hint of populism. In effect, the regime was performing a difficult balancing act. There was a desire to do something for the workers, but also a fundamental commitment to protecting the vital interests of the property-owning classes, and to encouraging industrial enterprise. Informed primarily by a liberal non-interventionist ideology, the regime's leading figures hoped that the prosperity engendered by urban renewal and construction of the rail network would win the masses over. Typically, a ministerial circular to the prefects in May 1857 reminded them that 'the condition of the working populations is one of the objects on which the attention of the imperial government is most closely fixed', but warned

[157] R. Dalisson, 'La célébration du *coup d'état* de 1851: symbolique politique et politique des symboles', *Revue d'histoire du 19e siècle* 2001/1, pp. 84–7; R. Sanson, 'Le 15 août: fête nationale du Second Empire' in A. Corbin *et al.*, *Les usages politiques des fêtes au 19e–20e siècles* (Paris 1994), *passim*.

[158] E.g. PG Paris, 8 June 1859, AN BB30/369.　　[159] PG Rouen, 19 June 1859, AN BB30/369.

[160] 10 July 1859, AN BB30/379.　　[161] E.g. PG Besançon, 26 June 1859, AN BB30/373.

[162] 27 Oct. 1863, AN BB30/384.

against any intervention in wage negotiations, the outcome of which should be left entirely to the market.[163]

Over time, there was a tendency for worker support for the regime to weaken. Haussmann remembered the Emperor's inability to comprehend why the building workers, who had benefited so much from urban renewal, remained republicans and the dismay this had provoked.[164] Why, asked the State Prosecutor at Douai in 1859, did the workers of Lille and the other major cities continue to support opposition politicians when 'the mutual aid societies, nurseries for infants, primary schools are multiplying', when bread was subsidised and work plentiful, when they had never been so well treated by any government?[165] Officials could only hope that the trend would be neither unilinear nor irreversible.

They could take some encouragement from events like the gathering of 200,000 to 300,000 spectators at Lille in August 1867, which enthusiastically welcomed the imperial couple and greatly appreciated the gesture they made by keeping the hood of their carriage down, in spite of heavy rain. Similar crowds turned out in Roubaix, where the Emperor pardoned workers involved in the serious riots in March. Even if one should not assume that the collective euphoria of the *fête* was necessarily an expression of enthusiasm for the regime it certainly suggests that workers were not entirely insensible to its appeal. Opposition politicians were indeed extremely worried by these manifestations. They insisted, with only some justice, that the proceedings had been carefully orchestrated, that crowds of peasants had been brought into the city from the surrounding countryside by the authorities, and a *claque* employed to generate popular enthusiasm.[166]

This was certainly not the case, however, when, following the 1869 elections, and during disturbances on the boulevards in Paris, Napoleon on horseback was acclaimed by the crowds. The city's gendarmerie commander concluded from this, perhaps a little optimistically, that workers 'only want the reform of persons and things and not the overthrow of the Empire'.[167] Devinck's analysis, for the Emperor, of the reports of the worker delegates to the 1867 Exposition had already reached similar conclusions. He insisted that these skilled workers, who took a very serious interest in politics, both admired their ruler and recognised his good intentions towards the working class.[168] The procureur impérial at Saint-Etienne went further and claimed

[163] Ministre de l'agriculture, du commerce . . . to Prefect Haut-Rhin, 12 May 1857, AN F12/2370-4.
[164] Haussmann, *Mémoires*, II, p. 200.   [165] 9 April 1859, AN BB30/377.
[166] Pierrard, *Vie ouvrière*, pp. 676-7.   [167] OC cie. de la Seine, 27 June 1869, AHG G8/165.
[168] AN 45 AP 6.

that local workers loved their Emperor but hated their employers and the local notables who stood as official candidates in elections.[169]

Just as approval of the Emperor did not necessarily imply support for his regime in its entirety, so an opposition vote in a contested election did not necessarily imply opposition to the regime *per se*. Even republican candidates in the Nord, 'encountering in the working classes respect for strong government and love for imperial traditions', felt obliged to distinguish between the Emperor and his ministers.[170] Only gradually, in this situation, did workers, 'whilst loving the Emperor, escape from the action of his government'.[171] Even then, considerable variations in political loyalties might still exist, sometimes between different trades within a single town. In Metz, for example, in the 1857 elections, the railway workers voted en masse for the republican candidate Jean Reynaud, whilst more than 500 artisans and ouvriers d'élite enrolled in the Société des secours mutuels et de prévoyance, presided over by the State Prosecutor, decided to support the government's candidate.[172] Workers frequently responded positively to the paternalistic discourse and influence exerted in favour of official candidates like Schneider at Le Creusot, Arnaud Rolle in the Côte-d'Or, Talabot at La Grand' Combe, and Veau de Robiac at Bessèges where, in 1869, miners shouted down the republican candidate Jules Cazot.[173]

Nevertheless, the 1863 and 1869 elections revealed a catastrophic decline in popular Bonapartism, particularly in the Paris and Lyon regions, in eastern France and the Rhône valley. Even then, however, as the results of the 1870 plebiscite would make clear, there remained a substantial number of workers who would have agreed with the sentiments expressed by the Parisian *mécanicien* Duchamp and the thirteen co-signatories to a poster addressed 'Aux ouvriers de Paris et de la banlieue'. This called on fellow workers to support the Emperor who had ended anarchy and restored prosperity. The authors of this poster were anxious, as political tension increased, that the workers might lose out from another period of instability.[174]

In the industrial arrondissement of Béthune, in the Nord, a massive 87 per cent of registered voters returned an affirmative vote in the plebiscite. During the celebratory *fête*, organised by the mining company, miners paraded behind their band and a bust of the Emperor.[175] Workers in

---

[169] 22 Oct. 1866, AN BB30/379.　　[170] PG Douai, 10 Jan. 1862, AN BB30/377.
[171] Ibid. 3 Jan. 1865.　　[172] PG Metz, 25 July 1857, AN BB30/380.
[173] Y. Lequin, 'La classe ouvrière' in J.-F. Sirinelli, *Histoire des droites en France*, vol. III (Paris 1992), p. 488.
[174] BN Lb/55/2632.
[175] Y.-M. Hilaire, 'La vie religieuse des populations du diocèse d'Arras, 1840–1914', Doc., d'Etat, Univ. de Paris IV 1976, III, p. 1060.

Mulhouse and Thann in Alsace, who had formerly supported liberal and republic opponents of the regime, also appear to have largely returned a positive vote. Their motives were mixed, but included a protest by Catholic workers against the Protestant employers who had campaigned hard for a negative vote. Certainly the administration took advantage of the tension between the two. The prefecture published a seven-page brochure addressed 'Aux frères travailleurs de Mulhouse', supposedly written by a peasant called Morand Sondgauer. This reminded workers, that whilst the army had suffered 'for the glory of France, your grand democratic gentlemen in Thann, Munster and Mulhouse peacefully made their millions by keeping their machinery turning'. It further contrasted 'the milliards which the bloody carnival of 1848 cost France' with the prosperity brought by the Empire. One, obviously alarmed, employer complained that his workers had shouted *Vive l'Empereur!* and informed him that 'the Emperor, our father, has promised us a strike if we vote well'.[176]

The procureur général had mixed feelings in this situation. Whilst welcoming the workers' vote as 'an act of political emancipation' from their Orleanist and republican *patrons* he was concerned that this 'new and grave symptom of hostility towards the leaders of industry' might lead workers, in the longer term, towards socialism. His report included the heavily underlined comment '*c'est une révolution*'.[177] Even after the plebiscite, during the massive strikes affecting the Mulhouse area in June and July administrative and military action in support of the employers was sufficiently restrained to allow strike leaders to claim that the authorities were on their side. Workers again paraded to shouts of *Vive l'Empereur!*[178] Although, overall, less whole-hearted than peasants, many workers thus continued to express their support for the imperial regime. This was particularly the case of those living in small towns or dispersed in the countryside, who associated themselves with the peasantry to which they still belonged in many respects.[179] Workers everywhere, however, were not entirely insensible to its populist and patriotic appeal. Nevertheless, Legitimism, liberalism, and especially republicanism offered them alternative social and political visions.

---

[176] L. Strauss, 'Opinion publique et forces politiques en Alsace à la fin du Second Empire. Le plébiscite du 8 mai 1870 dans le Haut-Rhin' in F. L'Huillier (ed.), *L'Alsace en 1870–71* (Gap 1971), pp. 134, 168.

[177] PG Colmar, 21 July 1870, AN BB30/390; see also Prefect, 5 July 1870, AN F1 C111 Haut Rhin 14.

[178] Telegraphed report from Prefect Haut-Rhin, 6 p.m. 7 July 1870, AN F12/4652.

[179] See e.g. PG Douai, 9 April 1859, AN BB30/377.

Legitimism

The influence of local notables might be exercised in favour of a Legitimist and clerical politics. In Toulouse, for example, such views were expressed by the clergy and through the mutual aid and the devotional societies dedicated to Saint-Vincent-de-Paul and Saint Francis Xavier. The latter had 2,000 workers amongst its members in 1858.[180] However, whether they were attracted by, or in spite of the society's political proclivities, is impossible to judge. In any case, the constant influx of migrants from the countryside and the declining relative importance of traditional trades and neighbourhoods threatened to overwhelm the institutional basis for exercising social control. The patron–client relationships built up between noble landowners and workers in the luxury trades producing jewellery, furniture, clothing, and carriages, declined with the economic position of many landowning families.[181] Similarly, in Marseille, the experience of 1848, reconstruction of the docks, in-migration, and the decline of the traditional Provençal culture, combined to weaken the royalist sentiments of the port workers.[182]

Popular Legitimism was more likely to survive in the smaller manufacturing centres, and amongst the stevedores organised in *syndicats* in declining river ports like Beaucaire, in the lower Rhône valley.[183] In nearby Uzès, Alès, and Nîmes confessional loyalties were exploited by Mgr Plantier, the Bishop of Nîmes, who re-directed religious processions through Protestant neighbourhoods from 1855, stimulating hostilities which contributed to the survival of a popular urban Legitimism.[184] The growing insecurity of workers in the southern textile industry could be blamed on the tendency of the largely Protestant merchants to favour members of their own churches as rural outworkers. In a woollens centre like Mazamet combative young priests, supported by landowners, professionals and businessmen typically sought to stem what they perceived to be a growing tide of anticlericalism and republicanism, by means of good works and the *encadrement* of the working-class population in a network of societies and *fêtes*. They carefully cultivated the myth of a previous golden age shattered by the

[180] Aminzade, *Class Struggles*, pp. 218–20.
[181] R. Aminzade, 'Breaking the chains of dependency: from patronage to class politics', *Journal of Urban History* 1977, pp. 486–92.
[182] W. Sewell, 'Social change and the rise of working class politics in 19th century Marseille', *Past and Present* 1974, pp. 76, 99; Musées de Marseille, *Marseille 1860–1914, Photographes et mutation urbaine* (Marseille 1995), pp. 12–35.
[183] Huard, 'Préhistoire', III, p. 851.
[184] Prefect, 6 Oct 1853, AN F1 CIII Gard 13; Huard, 'Préhistoire', III, p. 838.

Revolution.[185] At the Terrenoire steelworks near Saint-Etienne, through close control of their labour force, the directors were able to secure mass support for Legitimism in the 1867 elections in spite of the efforts of local republicans.[186]

The critique of industrial capitalism offered by Legitimists, which expressed a clear preference for paternalistic social relationships in which the 'good' worker was unquestioningly obedient, nevertheless, increasingly lost its appeal.[187] Militant workers resented attacks by Legitimists on trades unions and other forms of autonomous activity, which they insisted only encouraged social disharmony.[188] Republican activists frequently condemned the clear association of the Church, since 1848, with political reaction. The opportunistic rallying by Legitimists to the regime at the time of the *coup*, and again, in 1869, as social unrest increased, appears to have further, and substantially, compromised popular support. The belief in a natural order based upon birth and Divine intercession co-existed badly with notions of popular sovereignty. The same was true of an Orleanist/liberal ideology, which rejected social justice in favour of individual free will and the workings of the market.

Liberalism

'Universal' suffrage certainly encouraged liberal electoral candidates and their supporters to make vigorous efforts to secure the workers' vote. The latter's sense of dependency, and gratitude for work, ensured that they enjoyed considerable success. In comparison with most Legitimists, liberals were more willing to promote issues which were attractive to workers, including greater political freedom. The single question on which employers were most vocal was, however, the regime's tariff policy, an issue of considerable significance in itself, and which could be used to encourage criticism of the Emperor's personal power.

The simple announcement of the commercial treaty with Britain in 1860 had led industrialists in Lille to lay off workers and reduce wages in a deliberate effort to put pressure on the government by increasing discontent.[189] Efforts to mobilise workers there, and in the Rouen area, initially enjoyed little success.[190] According to the police spy Philippon the working class

---

[185] Faury, *Cléricalisme et anticléricalisme*, pp. 417–19.
[186] Aminzade, *Ballots and Barricades*, p. 289, note 82.
[187] E.g. PG Montpellier, 1 June 1866, AN BB30/380 re coopers at Cette.
[188] E.g. Kale, *Legitimism*, p. 182.   [189] Prefect, 26 March 1860, AN F1 CIII Nord 15.
[190] Ménager, *Les Napoléon*, pp. 181–2.

was 'not attached to its employers; it sees in them only exploiters who pay them as little as possible and have not hesitated in time of food shortage to throw them on the street without any resources; the difficulties they are in today are, in their eyes, only what they deserve'.[191] In 1863 the liberal opposition leader Adolphe Thiers, secretary of the apparently all-powerful Anzin company, was defeated in the Valenciennes constituency largely due to the votes of miners and ironworkers hostile to him both as the candidate of the opposition and as the representative of a harsh and exploitative employer.[192] Over time, however, workers would become more concerned. According to an individual overheard in a bar at Noiron (Côte-d'Or), 'the Emperor only protects English trade. French workers are without work. The Emperor really needs to understand that we are 40,000, and that we could tear everything he has to pieces.'[193]

The protectionist campaign against the regime appears to have enjoyed greater success during the recession of 1867/9 when employers blamed their every difficulty on the reduction in tariff protection and organised petitions, meetings and demonstrations in support of their 'crusade'.[194] In Rouen during the 1869 election campaign the liberal textile entrepreneurs Pouyer-Quertier and Brame published addresses specifically directed at workers. They made speeches to captive audiences in their factories, which blamed low wages on the government's tariff policies. As a result, Pouyer-Quertier was only narrowly defeated by the moderate republican Desseaux (11,450 to 11,936). In contrast Aubry standing as the workers' candidate, and accused by Desseaux of splitting the republican vote, obtained a mere 107 votes. An anti-free-trade petition circulating in October attracted 8,614 signatures, whilst in December 8,393 people subscribed 10 centimes each to meet the protectionist campaign's expenses.[195] In 1870 opposition to the commercial treaties would explain the negative vote in the plebiscite in the Norman towns of Vire, Condé, Flers, and La Ferté-Macé.[196]

In many constituencies, in the absence of republican candidates workers, determined to express their opposition to the regime, had little alternative but to vote for conservatives or opposition liberals. However, in spite of the temptations of popular Bonapartism and the pressure to vote for local Legitimist or liberal notables, there can be little doubt that there existed a powerful and growing current of support for republican ideals.

---

[191] Quoted Boivin, *Mouvement ouvrier*, I, p. 113.   [192] Ménager, *Les Napoléon*, p. 129.
[193] PG Paris, 10 July 1865, AN BB18/1707.
[194] PG Rouen, 12 Jan. 1868, AN BB30/387; Fohlen, *Industrie textile*, p. 429.
[195] Boivin, *Mouvement ouvrier*, I, pp. 303, 335–7.   [196] PI Caen, 11 July 1870, AN BB30/390.

Republicanism

Judging by the votes of the major urban and industrial centres, for most of the time, a majority of workers remained alienated from the regime. They continued to be susceptible to a republican discourse, and visions of a just and more egalitarian society. The language of 1792 continued to influence the ways in which people thought about politics, and to impress upon them the sense of continuity between past and present struggles. Parisian artisans were in 1855 described as wanting to 'complete' the Revolution and as 'living in a milieu entirely impregnated with memories of 1848'.[197] Although the outcome had been disappointing, 1848 had revived loyalties and reinforced ideals. In contrast, the *coup d'état* had shattered dreams of democracy and social justice. By so closely identifying Louis-Napoléon with conservative social forces, it had also established, for the first time, a clear distinction between popular Bonapartism and republicanism.

Resistance to the *coup d'état* had been limited. Nevertheless, in the night of 3–4 December 1851, barricades had been constructed in the eastern, working-class districts of Paris, and around 1,200 men had vainly attempted to defend them, at the cost of perhaps 200 lives. In the other major cities and industrial centres, workers had remained quiet, either overwhelmed by preventive arrests and an obvious military presence, or welcoming a Bonapartist *coup* and the restoration of 'universal' suffrage. Only in the rural south-east had large-scale, if short-lived, resistance occurred.[198]

Official reports subsequently stressed the great silence imposed by the *coup*. In the cafés and bars 'politics no longer provides the basis for workers' conversations'.[199] According to the words of a popular song composed in Lille – 'For talking politics/the season has passed.'[200] Whatever political sympathies workers might have had, repression and disillusionment ensured that a substantial de-politicisation occurred, creating at least the appearance of calm. However, there was continued official anxiety that workers appeared less willing to support the new regime than the members of other social groups, particularly in those areas previously disturbed by *démocrate-socialiste* agitation.

The prefect of the Hérault expressed his concern about a gathering of 300 to 400 who attended the funeral of a former insurgent at Florensac near Béziers in May 1852 – 'a gathering of this sort, of workers, who give up a day's pay to honour the memory of a former socialist leader in the

---

[197] PG Paris, 6 April 1855, AN BB30/409. [198] See Price, *Second Republic*, ch. 7.
[199] PG Lyon, 3 June 1852, AN BB30/379. [200] Quoted by Reddy, 'The moral sense of farce', p. 387.

locality, clearly shows that the followers of the secret societies, in spite of the renewed calm and well-being, in spite of the repression directed against them, are far from being disorganised'.[201] In June, whilst riding through the streets of the southern textile town of Bédarieux, on his way to inaugurate a memorial to gendarmes killed the previous December, he was struck by the 'gloomy silence' with which workers greeted him. Recalling 'the insults proffered at several of the witnesses at the military courts, the intimidation so manifestly directed at most of the witnesses', he concluded that 'everything appears to announce that these unfortunates have not returned to better sentiments'.[202]

Nevertheless, during the 1850s, and early years of the following decade, reports constantly concluded that, 'the further we distance ourselves from the crisis of 1848, the more the population becomes a stranger to political questions and preoccupies itself uniquely with its well-being'.[203] Repression promoted a *humble et universelle soumission au régime*, whilst censorship ensured that 'they no longer find in the press the daily theme for their recriminations'.[204] There was also a growing confidence that prosperity would win workers over, particularly once the agitators who had led them astray had been imprisoned or frightened into silence.[205] Even when officials accepted that the generation which had achieved political maturity in 1848, 'is lost forever',[206] they hoped to win over the younger generations through education and a populist politics.[207]

In addition to this general air of optimism, there were, however, also frequent references to 'latent hostility' and an admission that 'much time and effort will be necessary to erase the longstanding influence of revolutionary agitation, of the excitement of 1848'.[208] The pessimism of the procureur général at Lyon in February 1853 was quite striking. He claimed that, 'the working class is generally convinced of the injustice of our social organisation ... The exploitation of man by man, the tyranny of capital, all the language of egalitarian philosophy over the centuries ... is more or less crudely conserved in the thoughts of the working classes', and furthermore that 'hope of triumph is maintained by the memory of past success ... 1831, 1834, 1848 are dates which are not likely to be forgotten.'[209] The regime had no prospect of winning over such groups as the silk weavers of la Croix Rousse.[210] On the anniversary of the founding of the Second Republic in

---

[201] 2 June 1852, AN F1 CIII Hérault 15.　　[202] 20 June 1852, ibid.
[203] PG Orléans, 2 Jan. 1860, AN BB30/382.　　[204] PG Lyon, 7 Jan. 1853, AN BB30/379.
[205] E.g. PG Orléans, 1 April 1859, AN BB30/382.　　[206] Ibid. 20 July 1857.
[207] PG Lyon, 5 Feb. 1853, AN BB30/379.　　[208] PG Angers, 8 Jan. 1856, AN BB30/371.
[209] 5 Feb. 1853, AN BB30/379.　　[210] PG Lyon, 20 Dec. 1853, ibid.

1853 two-thirds of Lyon silk weavers stopped work. A banner seized by the police carried the legend '48, deceived by its good will, demands a 93 to gain vengeance'.[211] Throughout the 1850s, officials in the city would complain about the 'irremediable discontent' of workers who were 'rather submissive than rallied'.[212] Furthermore, the repression of strikes repeatedly placed the administration unambiguously on the side of the capitalist class.[213]

More widely, there was evidence of republican agitation, ranging from shouts and *placards*, to demonstrative attendance at the funerals of militants, and abstention or support for opposition candidates in municipal, as well as general elections.[214] Striking workers were likely to exhibit republican sympathies. Thus *placards* posted on the gates of the iron foundry at Le Creusot on the night of 1–2 March 1858 warned potential blacklegs that they would be 'skewered on the blades of swords like flies', and after insisting that 'it is a republican who speaks', looked forward to the day when 'the red flag will fly and blood will flow in the streets like water in the river'.[215] Domiciliary searches of the homes of suspected subversives continued to turn up something of the legacy of 1848. In 1858, in the case of Bouvier, a craftsman employed in the railway workshops at Metz, this included a statuette of 'La République' wearing a phrygian bonnet and such brochures as *Les Martyrs confesseurs de la Verité démocratique* published by the Ligue des peuples in 1850 and *La législation directe par le peuple ou la véritable démocratie* by Rittinghausen, published in the same year by the Librairie Phalastérienne. The police also found a cavalry pistol and letters from Paris full of political allusions. The local prosecutor expressed his concern that the statuettes were still available from one Détourbet, a founder in the rue du faubourg du Temple in Paris.[216]

The State Prosecutor at Rouen was concerned that with renewed economic difficulties, 'antagonism against the superior classes will manifest itself as powerfully as in 1848, and socialism will quickly recover all the ground it has lost'. The arrests made in December 1851 had removed the upper layer of republican leadership, but now 'subordinate leaders' were taking their turn.[217] Senior officials were critical of what they perceived to be the excessive leniency displayed by the Emperor towards dangerous 'subversives'. The abrasive military commander in Lyon, the Marshal de Castellane, convinced that the regime was engaged in a permanent 'war of

---

[211] Ibid. 4 March 1853. [212] Ibid. ? July 1857; 7 Oct. 1859. [213] Ibid. 7 Jan. and 5 April 1853.
[214] E.g. P. Cousteix, 'L'opposition ouvrière au Second Empire en Haute-Vienne', *Bulletin de la Société archéologique et historique du Limousin* 1955, p. 120.
[215] PG Dijon, 7 March 1858, AN BB30/420. [216] PI Metz, 19 Jan. 1858, AN BB30/441.
[217] PG Rouen, 5 July 1853, AN BB30/387.

the poor against the rich', even took the opportunity presented by a private audience with the Emperor in 1857, to criticise what he regarded as the premature freeing of political detainees.[218] It was widely regretted also that government encouragement of mutual aid societies was likely to provide an organisational basis for worker opposition.[219]

Thus, increasingly, officials in the leading industrial centres came to accept that a 'truce', rather than a lasting peace, had been established between the regime and the working class, and that many workers would again be susceptible to republican propaganda, if ever repression was eased.[220] It seemed evident that, 'the industrial population is . . . burdened by an irreversible discontent'; that, 'in the industrial centres the spirit of opposition is incorrigible'.[221] There was a real concern that workers were simply biding their time. The procureur général at Lyon concluded in 1859 that it was only the continued abstention of most middle-class republicans from political activity that ensured this opposition remained ineffective.[222]

In the meantime, evidence of secret-society activity, together with sporadic disorders, especially during periods of high food prices, sustained official anxiety. Occasional gatherings in private homes were transformed easily by police spies into illicit meetings. Undercover agents had to report something and their superiors were similarly under pressure to update their *fiches*. The historian, just like senior officials, faces difficulties in assessing the accuracy and meaning of these reports. The procureur général at Lyon expressed his gratitude, in June 1856, for the services of a secret agent sent by the Paris prefect of Police. The officer concerned, a M. Lagrange, had conducted investigations leading to fifty-eight arrests. Nevertheless, the prosecutor warned that, 'in general policemen tend to exaggerate rather than diminish apprehension'.[223] The projects apparently discussed in city bars by republican extremists claiming allegiance to the imprisoned revolutionary Blanqui, and which looked forward to a violent *coup* and multiple assassinations in Lyon were dismissed as simply wishful thinking.[224] Similarly, in response to a circular instructing him to update lists of *individus dangereux*, the State Prosecutor at Amiens warned his minister that the criteria for defining such people employed by his subordinates varied enormously.[225]

What significance should be ascribed to the numerous arrests for verbal offences against the imperial family? These typically included descriptions

---

[218] Castellane, *Journal*, v, p. 183, entry of 13 Aug. 1857.
[219] E.g. PG Lyon, 2 July 1857, AN BB30/379.
[220] Ibid. 3 June 1852; PG Paris 18 Feb. 1854, AN BB30/383; Prefect, 21 Feb 1859, AN F1 CIII Nord 15.
[221] PG Rouen, 15 July 1857, AN BB30/387.   [222] PG Lyon, 4 June 1859, AN BB30/379.
[223] 15 Jan. 1856, AN BB30/417.   [224] PI and PG Lyon, 14 June and 11 Aug. 1856, AN BB30/417.
[225] 18 Dec. 1855, AN BB30/414.

of the Emperor as a *brigand, voleur, cochon,* accompanied often by drunken shouts of *Vive la République!* and *à bas Napoléon,* as well as such assertions as, 'If I were in Paris I'd blow out the Emperor's brains, ... slit his throat', etc.[226] Alongside these, the effusions of a factory foreman called Schweighauser in a bar in the Alsatian town of Weiher were quite cogent! He pointed out, in a loud voice, that 'the Bourbons were eaters of bacon! Of pigs! Napoleon Emperor is an ugly bugger! An imbecile! And Christ was a *j ... f ...* , an imbecile who let himself be crucified. What's more there is no God.'[227] It was common too in bar-room discussion to complain that life had been better in 1848 and would be again with the return of Ledru-Rollin and the final establishment of the *République démocratique et sociale.*[228]

Republican sentiment and commitment to the ideals of the 'moral' economy were mutually reinforcing. Between 1853 and 1856 bread prices might have appeared excessively high when compared with those which had resulted from bumper harvests during the Second Republic.[229] In such circumstances, police reports recorded the usual seditious shouts and *placards.* In the working class *quartiers* of the capital, these were likely to demand 'lower rents, bread at 12 sous', generally followed by *Vive la République* or *à bas l'Empereur.* As late as November 1856 the Prefect of Police reported a 'profound discontent', and the arrest, in the 8th arrondissement, of four young men caught in the act of putting up a *placard* on which was written 'Death to the Emperor! Bread at 12 sous! Hang the landlords!'[230] An anonymous letter to the mayor of Metz warned that, threatened as they were with starvation, the workers would revolt and ensure that 'everyone, from the head of state to the most lowly would be burned, shot and guillotined, like dogs'.[231] Crude drawings of guillotines featured on many *placards.*

These expressions of popular political sentiments often caused quite a stir. The *placards* posted on the walls of the textile town of Reims in September 1853 attracted crowds of 60 to 80 at a time, reading and commenting on calls for 'Death to the speculators, Death to the Tyrants, Death to the priests, Death to Napoleon'.[232] However unlikely its realisation might appear, the threat to slit the Emperor's throat clearly alarmed the authorities.[233] Protesters needed to be cautious when even the expression of regret for having voted for Bonaparte in the presidential elections could lead to

[226] See reports collected in AN BB30/411.
[227] Included with report from PG Colmar, 3 Feb. 1857, AN BB30/411.
[228] See e.g. PG Nancy, 26 Aug. 1856, AN BB30/412.   [229] E.g. PG Rouen, 14 Oct. 1855, AN BB30/433.
[230] Paris Prefect of Police, 26 Oct., 2 Nov. 1856, AN BB30/366.
[231] PG Metz, 6 Oct. 1855, AN BB30/433.   [232] PG Paris, 6 Sept. 1853, AN BB30/432.
[233] E.g. PG Nancy, 25 Sept. 1861, AN BB18/1639.

ten days in prison.[234] Beck, an unfortunate wheelwright in Metz, criticised by his neighbours for failing to light a candle in his window to celebrate victory in the Crimea told them that he preferred to buy bread for his family, adding 'you'd have to be crazy to amuse yourself by lighting a candle for a clown, un *j . . . f . . .* , a scoundrel of an emperor . . . who makes us eat such expensive bread'. This tirade was followed by an obscene gesture accompanied by 'This for you and your Emperor, I shit on you . . .'[235] A building labourer on a site at Ancy-le-Franc (Yonne) was imprisoned for eight months for explaining to his son that 'if the government wanted, food would be much less expensive; all that blood shed at Sebastopol, but all that was achieved was to kill the sons of the poor and to defend the rich. The workers of Paris want bread at 3 *sous*; otherwise they will cut the heads off the rich, and the nobles.'[236] Workers also condemned the rural population for its supposed political loyalties. According to Bonnaire, a tailor in Dijon, 'the peasants are all animals, without them he [i.e. Napoleon] would not be where he is'. He received three years in prison and a 500f. fine for this outburst, although in fairness to the court he had previously been convicted for grievous bodily harm on eight occasions.[237]

The more overtly political the comments, the greater the interest shown by the authorities. A *placard* found on New Year's Eve 1853, written by Goujat, a shoemaker at Châtillon-sur-Loire, began by wishing its readers a happy new year and looked forward to 'the overthrow of Bonaparte, the end of the Empire, the ruin of the aristocrats, the triumph of the democratic republic. With that we'll have cheap bread and a low cost of living.'[238] Officials remained concerned that republican secret societies might take advantage of high prices.[239] However, the regime's success in constructing a caring image appears to have ensured that many Parisian workers blamed high prices on the greed of the big grain merchants and farmers of the Beauce.[240] A *placard* found at Nancy expressed similar sentiments. It began with *Vive l'Empereur et son fils* and then attacked 'the monopolisers, speculators and the bad officials' responsible for high prices.[241]

Some official reports pointed at more serious cause for disquiet. In June 1853, investigating a suspected plot to assassinate the Emperor, the Paris Prefect of Police instructed his officers to engage in widespread domiciliary searches. Conducted in the homes of tailors, shoemakers, cabinetmakers,

---

[234] E.g. PG Paris, 27 Dec. 1853, AN BB30/434.   [235] PG Metz, 14 Oct. 1855, AN BB30/433.
[236] PG Paris, 13 Feb. 1857, AN BB30/412.   [237] PG Dijon, 17 Nov. 1855, AN BB30/411.
[238] PG Orléans, 1 Jan. 1854, AN BB30/432.   [239] E.g. PG Rouen, 2 Oct. 1855, AN BB30/433.
[240] PG Paris, 23 Nov. 1853, AN BB30/434; 3 Oct. 1855, AN BB30/435.
[241] GOC 5e DM, 16–20 Aug. 1856, AHG G8/37.

hairdressers, and shop assistants, all men with a revolutionary past, these not surprisingly turned up portraits of such 'heroes' as Robespierre and Barbès, copies of subversive songs, revolutionary emblems, and those pamphlets, previously denounced by the Interior Minister as 'the book of the poor . . . they preserve it carefully, they consult it with a credulous faith',[242] and probably left over from the Second Republic. The discovery of 'incriminating' letters was not enough to provide proof of a plot, but sufficient to justify the arrest of fifty men accused of belonging to a secret society called the Comité révolutionnaire.[243]

Such investigations were given further credibility by the uncovering of flimsy underground networks. The State Prosecutor in Paris reported in April 1855 that efforts were being made to re-establish a secret society known as la fraternité universelle or la Marianne. His informants suggested that those involved were mainly workers who, together with other *gens du peuple*, were committed to violent revolution. They were determined to exclude the *habits noirs*, the bourgeois republicans who were anyway reluctant to risk compromising themselves. Several groups were identified in Paris and its suburbs, especially in Belleville and Batignolles. Those involved, and especially engineering workers, were cautiously creating cells of six to ten members amongst their *camarades d'atelier*, in most *quartiers* of the capital. It was pointed out that 'the framework for secret societies already exists in the affinities of the trade and workplace. They almost always originate amongst workers working side-by-side. The members of these cells, each of whom was required to take a fearsome oath of loyalty and learn the group's passwords, included especially those who live in a milieu impregnated with memories of 1848.' They looked forward to the *triomphe des masses*, following the assassination of the Emperor. Additionally, it was claimed that they had discussed the nationalisation of the railways and canals and the expropriation of property worth over 50,000 francs, and circulated contraband publications imported from London, Brussels, and Jersey.[244]

The authorities were profoundly disturbed by the involvement of members of the younger generations alongside the *vieux révolutionnaires*. Amongst the sixty-one men finally arrested there were twelve engineering workers or locksmiths, seven tailors, and eight carpenters, leading the procureur to observe that 'certain professions have the sad privilege of serving as schools of socialism'. He identified the 'headquarters of socialism',

---

[242] Circular to prefects re colportage, 4 Jan. 1851, AN F18/3.
[243] Prefect of Police to Interior Minister, Préfecture de Police Aa 434.
[244] PG Paris, evidence to Tribunal correctionnel de Paris n.d., ANBB30/413; see also Jacquemet, 'Belleville', II, p. 503.

as 'the foundries, engineering shops, and railways'. They employed men who were well paid and semi-educated, often originating from the departments of central France. It was claimed that other groups like masons were only absent from the secret societies because of the intimidating effect of the habitually close police surveillance of building sites. The Directeur Général de la Sûreté Publique at the Interior Ministry confirmed that links also existed between these Parisian militants and affiliated societies in Bordeaux, Nantes, Rouen, Tours, and Orléans.[245]

As if to confirm the administration's worst fears, in August 1855 a short-lived uprising occurred in the Angers area in the west, involving mostly textile workers and quarrymen belonging to a secret society which also called itself la Marianne. This had first been established in 1850 and some of its members had continued to meet in isolated places in the countryside and in the café Beaudrier in Angers itself. In the night of 26–27 August these groups were instructed to gather in the little town of Trélazé. There they seized weapons, and 600 to 700 men had then marched towards Angers, apparently believing that similar risings were occurring all over France. They were easily dispersed by troops and over 100 were arrested. According to the Minister of the Interior the participants in this affair were inspired not by hunger or even by politics, but by a 'socialism' which taught them arson and murder.[246] The State Prosecutor demanded long sentences for 'ringleaders' like a certain Attibert who, according to four witnesses, had promised that 'we'll hang all the nobles, all the priests, all the landowners with incomes of more than 1,200 to 1,500 francs and we'll slit their throats'.[247] There was considerable concern about what might have happened if the march on Angers had succeeded, leading officials to insist on the need to avoid any future relaxation of the repressive apparatus.[248]

In another incident, in December, apparently in revenge for the beatings she regularly received from her husband, the wife of Nicolas Blaise, a miner and also proprietor of a bar in the important northern mining centre of Anzin, denounced him as the author of subversive *placards* found on the walls of Onnaing and Anzin in October. According to these: 'We demand a reduction in the price of bread; otherwise we'll leave victims. We'll make barricades with their bodies, the priests [*les abis*] . . . , the officials, the grain

[245] PG Paris, 6 April 1855, AN BB30/409; Directeur . . . to Interior Minister, 1 March 1855, AN BB30/410.

[246] Circular, 14 Sept. 1855, printed in F. Simon, *La Marianne, société secrète au pays d'Anjou* (Angers 1939), p. 89; see also PG Angers, telegram 7 a.m. 27 Aug. and reports of 26, 29, 30 Aug. 1855, AN BB30/413.

[247] Réquistoire de M.le Procureur Général Métivier. Affaire de l'attentat d'Angers, 12 Oct. 1855, AN BB30/413.

[248] E.g. Prefect, 20 Oct. 1855, AN F1 CIII Calvados 14.

speculators will be first.' Investigation uncovered a local secret society, la Cocotte. Its most active members appear to have been Jean Charvigne proprietor of another bar – the 'Botte de foin' at St-Vaast – together with a small group of ten miners and metal workers. Letters were also found from sympathisers in Valenciennes, Paris, Brussels and London, and although the police failed to uncover other societies they would remain suspicious. Besides their allegiance to the République démocratique et sociale, under interrogation, and doubtless frightened, those arrested confessed to wanting to nationalise the mines, secure higher wages, and put an end to discrimination by the clergy between rich and poor at funerals.[249] By the beginning of 1859 the prefect of the Nord felt sufficiently confident to report that secret societies no longer existed, whilst warning, however, that 'the community of interests which exists between the workers most certainly renders them accessible to suggestions and to watchwords'.[250]

Thus generally, resistance to the regime during the 1850s, and beyond, was limited to the informal and clandestine. Workers largely remained isolated from the bourgeois republicans who had previously offered leadership.[251] A more substantial political re-awakening would take time. Nevertheless, elections regularly provided an opportunity for workers to express their resentment of the authoritarian regime, offering proof to officials that 'the calm is only on the surface', and causing consternation, particularly in Paris where in 1857 almost 100,000 votes, 'just like in the bad old days', were deposited in favour of opposition candidates.[252] This was a major blow to the regime's prestige and offered encouragement to republicans throughout France. It seemed as if 'wherever there are workers, one can be certain that they will vote for whichever candidate is most hostile to the government'.[253]

Officials were also astounded when, in Lille, Loiset, the 'socialist' candidate, obtained 8,000 votes in spite of a complete lack of press support, of posters or circulars. It was observed that Loiset's supporters 'went to vote in an ordered manner, by street, almost by number, keeping an eye on each other, and of course responding not only to their sympathies but to instructions, the origins of which escape us'. The only answer appeared to be that 'odious remarks are exchanged in the workshops and the *cabarets*', as well as amongst the members of the numerous local singing, bowls, and archery clubs, or the groups formed to support (illegal) cockfighting, or

---

[249] L. Machu, 'Deux aspects de la répression policière dans le Nord à l'époque du Second Empire', *Revue du Nord* 1964, pp. 387f.
[250] 21 Feb. 1859, AN F1 CIII Nord 15.   [251] Point made by PG Rouen, 4 Jan. 1852, AN BB30/387.
[252] PG Paris, 13 Aug. 1857, AN BB30/383.   [253] PG Caen, 15 July 1857, AN BB30/375.

simply play cards and drink. The prefect could only feel grateful that the votes of three rural cantons had 'annihilated' this working-class vote.[254]

In Limoges also, voting had represented a collective act. The State Prosecutor observed that on

the first day of the election, few workers presented themselves to vote, in order not to provoke a reaction to the spectacle of their numbers and also, so they claimed, so as not to leave their ballot papers exposed in the urns overnight. However, the following day, they arrived in large gangs, under the direction of a few leaders, and have deposited their votes in an orderly manner and in silence like well disciplined troops.[255]

High levels of participation and a growing determination to ensure that their names appeared on the electoral register suggest that workers were increasingly committed to the political process.[256]

Historians have stressed the significance of 'democratic patronage' in spreading political ideas within communities, describing a trickling-down process by which ideas spread from middle-class militants to an 'elite' of skilled, and literate craftsmen and then further down the social hierarchy and, less effectively, to other workers. These contacts between members of different social groups were clearly conducive to politicisation. It is also clearly important to consider the development of more autonomous politicisation processes within the web of social relationships which characterised every working-class *quartier*. Individuals were obviously closely associated with family members, with neighbours and the workmates with whom, due to lengthy working days and café sociability, they spent so much time. Each of these networks had political potential. Each of them was part of the wider networks of informal oral communication, which remained so important in a society in which mass communication remained under-developed and formal political organisations did not exist. Alphonse Audiganne also identified networks for the diffusion of ideas amongst Norman textile workers which were based on commercial links – 'the movement begins in Paris, has repercussions in Rouen, agitates Elbeuf, and finally reaches Louviers',[257] whilst officials complained of the ideas spread along the waterways leading to the Loire by boatmen coming from Paris. Railwaymen were another suspect group.[258]

---

[254] PG Douai, 6 and 22 July 1855, AN BB30/377; Prefect, 26 June 1857, AN F1 C𝗂𝗂𝗂 Nord 15; Ménager, 'Vie politique', 1, p. 389.
[255] Quoted A. Garrigou, *Le vote et la vertu. Comment les français sont devenus lecteurs* (Paris 1992), p. 60.
[256] PG Paris, 4 May 1868, AN BB30/384.   [257] Audiganne, *Populations*, 1, p. 92.
[258] PI Tours, ? April 1866, AN BB30/382.

The activities of committed, and largely anonymous, militants were central to these diffusion processes and, in the 1850s, to keeping the republican tradition alive. Who were these activists, willing at the very least to devote time and effort to the cause, and often to risk imprisonment and the impoverishment of their families? Identifying them is never easy. According to the labour historian Jean Maitron, 'the militant is above all . . . a disposition', a self-confident and articulate personality.[259] The Elbeuf Chamber of Commerce represented contemporary conservative opinion in describing working-class militants as degenerate, alcoholic, wife-beating brutes, provoking a bitter response from the skilled craftsmen belonging to the Cercle d'études économiques in Rouen. They too condemned alcoholism, which resulted in 'indifference to beauty and truth, and . . . to the affirmation of human dignity', but insisted that such epithets could not be applied to 'that part of the proletariat which thinks seriously about its emancipation, or that which struggles vainly to bring up its family with dignity'.[260]

It is impossible to generalise, but individuals like the Parisian *ciseleur en bronze* Tolain or the bookbinder Varlin were certainly sober, skilled, and literate, *autodidactes*, fond of reading and attending evening classes. They were personally ambitious and dressed with care as a mark of social status, sharing the dress code as well as the republican culture of the professional men, students, and small businessmen with whom they rubbed shoulders in cafés and at meetings. Many militants were veterans of 1848; some had been arrested during the *coup d'état*, and had earned the status of martyrs. Their sheer combativity earned them respect. François Attibert, a slate quarryman and one of the organisers of the Marianne secret society and its insurrection at Trélazé in August 1855 had been imprisoned on Devil's Island but had escaped in September 1856. On his return to France, following the general amnesty of 1859, he immediately joined a mutual aid society and was arrested in April 1860 for organising a strike. A police report described him as a 'dangerous individual', a 'very good worker, thrifty, sober, a good father, good morality . . . possessing a little education . . . very enterprising, would sacrifice everything for his cause'.[261]

Until well into the 1860s militants needed to be cautious. In Rouen the ubiquitous police spy Philippon observed the gatherings of a group of friends who sang ditties like 'On your knees in front of the worker', discussed politics, and exchanged pamphlets and books left over from 1848 or since smuggled across the easily permeable frontiers. Most of them were,

---

[259] Maitron, 'La personnalité', p. 73.   [260] Quoted Boivin, *Mouvement ouvrier*, I, pp. 265–6.
[261] J. Maitron, *Dictionnaire biographique du mouvement ouvrier français*, I (Paris 1964), pp. 26–7.

he observed, 'miserable tailors, shoemakers, or mill hands'. Intimidated both by the police and their employers, it must have been particularly difficult for such impoverished workers to sustain their opposition. The divisions amongst workers did not help them. In May 1858, another police report from Rouen focused on the 180 engineering workers employed by Buddicom in their railway workshops at Sotteville. These were described as possessing 'a certain science, a more developed education, a lively and earnest character, endowed with a great energy'. They too 'had entered political life through the door opened to them in 1848'. However, the danger they posed was limited by their unwillingness to cooperate with other workers and, indeed by the 'contempt' they displayed towards the impoverished artisans in the shoemaking and tailoring trades and especially for unskilled textile operatives.[262]

Typically, militants were employed in established trades with craft traditions, particularly in the major industrial centres and cities rather than in small towns or scattered rural workshops.[263] They were likely to be employed especially in workshops but also were found increasingly amongst the skilled craftsmen employed in factories and in engineering establishments like the railway repair shops in Paris and such provincial centres as Montigny-lès-Metz and Epernay.[264] These, 'active elements of democracy', were likely to be found amongst the better paid, those who like 'the engineering worker, the fitter, the foreman in a printer's . . . [are] . . . highly skilled, almost artists, to whom their employer owes his fortune'.[265] The State Prosecutor at Limoges regretted that those workers 'who distinguish themselves by their political militancy are generally those who distinguish themselves by their intelligence and professional skill'. Amongst the porcelain workers this was certainly true of 'the most skilful, the painters, the gilders, those initiated by a semi-education into doctrines which they still share because they regret the importance which their brief triumph [in 1848] gave to them'.[266]

In their search for understanding, militants structured their ideas around slogans formulated in newspapers, almanacs, and pamphlets, in treasured publications left over from the heady days of 1848, and newer works smuggled into the country. They discussed articles published in those moderate republican newspapers which were tolerated in the 1850s, and most notably

---

[262] Boivin, *Mouvement ouvrier*, I, p. 107.   [263] See e.g. PG Rouen, 20 Jan. 1861, AN BB30/387.

[264] PG Paris, ? Feb. 1858, AN BB30/383; PG Metz, 25 Jan. 1858, AN BB30/380.

[265] PG Colmar, 24 April 1866, AN BB30/376.

[266] PG, 2 Dec. 1852, AN BB30/378; also J. Merriman, *The Red City. Limoges and the French 19th Century* (Oxford 1985), p. 109.

Le Siècle and its provincial imitators, like *L'Echo du Nord* at Lille or the *Journal de Rouen*.[267] They were often inspired by vaguely progressive concepts of history, which offered a sense of continuity and a legitimacy to political engagement. Historical myth linked the individual, often through the experience of his family, to the past. Whilst younger men were inevitably subject to different formative influences, the role of the veterans of 1848 in the survival of political aspirations and the eventual re-birth of working-class politics was constantly stressed by employers and the police.[268] In Lyon, according to the procureur général, eight of the ten workers elected by their colleagues to the Conseil des Prud'hommes in 1866 were reckoned to be *démagogues* and mostly former members of the revolutionary republican organisation the Voraces in 1848.[269]

Someone like Théodore Six was a living example of the process by which ideas were transmitted between generations. A tapestry weaver (*ouvrier tapissier*) who had fought on the barricades in 1830 and 1848, and been a member of the Luxembourg Commission established by the Provisional Government to discuss working conditions, Six had been deported following the *coup d'état*. After his return to Paris he had helped in 1867 to establish the chambre syndicale des tapissiers.[270] There was little chance of the regime winning over Six, or a man like Cochereau, a building worker living in Blois. He had been arrested on a barricade in Paris in June 1848 and deported to Cayenne. On his return he promised to fight to get rid of 'the workshy, incapable of ruling over us'.[271] Etienne Bacot had first been arrested, aged twenty-four, in 1844, and accused of being the leader of a *société communiste* in Lyon. During the Second Republic he too had been a member of the Voraces, and as a result had been arrested following the *coup d'état* and deported to Algeria, where he remained until 1856. In 1864, his record of commitment and the support of a clandestine *comité central*, secured his election to the Rhône departmental council.[272] It is not difficult to imagine these persecuted militants obsessively discussing politics and dreaming of revenge.

Such emblematic individuals, who had served a hard apprenticeship, and were respected for their willingness to suffer for their beliefs, offered grass-roots leadership. They often faced an uphill struggle. Martin Nadaud, the worker-peasant from the Limousin, remembered how poorly educated

[267] On influence of *Le Siècle* see e.g. PI Gien, April 1866, AN BB30/382.
[268] E.g. letter from J.-B. and F. Martin manufacturers at Tarare (Rhône), forwarded with report of PG Lyon, 2 Feb. 1857, AN BB30/379.
[269] 8 Jan. 1866, AN BB30/379. [270] Rougerie, '1871' in *La Commune de 1871*, pp. 67–9.
[271] GOC 18e DM, 10–15 Sept. 1855, AHG G8/27. [272] Maitron, *Dictionnaire biographique*.

masons on building sites in Paris simply did not understand many of the words and concepts found in newspapers.[273] To a substantial degree their politicisation involved the interiorisation of ritual formulae, which helped keep the faith alive. Workers shared oral traditions, a mechanism for selecting and (re-)interpreting memories, words, and myths. Songs were a popular means of political expression, particularly those of the Revolution – the *Marseillaise* and *Chant du Départ* – and the patriotic refrains of Béranger and Dupont and their many imitators. Frequently, new words were added to old and familiar tunes. In Paris in the autumn of 1856 workers were reported to be singing *Le fou de Biarritz* and *Caligula* both obviously referring to the Emperor. The latter ended with a call for his assassination. The Prefect of Police complained that 'these slogans are introduced through rhymes and songs at every gathering, are repeated by everyone and cause real damage'. He was certain that 'propaganda through the medium of song is very dangerous. By this means the worst doctrines are easily engraved on the memories of the population.'[274]

Strong and often brutal language was frequently employed to condemn those accused of exploitation, who were defined loosely as the 'bourgeois', the 'rich', and 'capitalists', and whose very existence represented a denial of the fundamental truth that labour was the source of all wealth. In August 1856, in a café at Vigneulles (Meuse), a M. Gallant entertained fellow drinkers with a ditty which included a chorus based on the familiar refrain *à genoux devant l'ouvrier* and described the rich as owing everything they had to the labours of the worker. Gallant also looked forward to the return of the exiled Ledru-Rollin when 'we'll make the pot-bellied dance' (i.e. the rich).[275] *Their* Emperor was also roundly denounced, as when a rope maker (*cordier*) called Perrin from Neufchâteau recalled seeing the Emperor pass in his carriage in Paris and went on to describe his Imperial Majesty as 'asleep in his carriage like a fat pig'.[276]

The workers' sense of class identity was often diffuse, and the perceptions and discourse which represented a particular experience and interests were influenced substantially by the ideas and interpretative frameworks offered by the better-educated members of other social groups, who shared a commitment to the ideals of the Revolution.[277] Many militants were in close and daily contact with the professional and businessmen who were likely to act

---

[273] Nadaud, *Mémoires*, p. 110.   [274] 13 Oct. 1856, AN BB30/366.
[275] PG Nancy, 26 Aug. 1856, AN BB30/412.   [276] PG Nancy, 24 April 1866, AN BB18/1728.
[277] E.g. M. Pigenet, 'Les adjectifs de la République. Voies et conditions de la politisation des milieux populaires. L'exemple du Cher au 19e siècle' in M. Vovelle (ed.), *Révolution et république. L'exception française* (Paris 1994), p. 524.

as political 'leaders' at community level, as well as providing contacts with the republican 'movement'. In Saint-Etienne, in 1860, a secret society was uncovered – the Pères de Famille – which included amongst its members 33 silk-ribbon weavers (*passementiers*), 8 gunsmiths (*armuriers*), 1 miner, 3 iron workers, 3 building workers, and 9 from the clothing trades, together with 6 members of the liberal professions, 7 merchants and 7 clerks.[278] Workers generally exhibited a certain degree of deference towards those whose status derived from practical success, education, culture, rhetorical skills, and organisational ability, and whose involvement in politics offered a greater sense of respectability to working-class protest. A republican political culture thus evolved which, as was evident from its linguistic structures, was an amalgam derived from a complex of sources. It frequently combined the language of the streets with the commonplaces of middle-class political discourse, within which, quite significantly, the language of class was generally muted or entirely absent. The more studied and hybrid efforts of many militants, influenced by the imported language and theatricality of middle-class politicians, contrasted with the crude, everyday, pejorative expressions of the grass-roots.

In the major cities the Italian war probably marked the high-point of working-class sympathy for the regime. Certainly, from the 1863 elections, the official outlook became more pessimistic. The Prefect of Seine-Inférieure, commenting on the revival of the republican press, drew a distinction between its moderation, and the alarming tones of oral propaganda in working-class *quartiers*, which had ensured that

the electoral struggle exceeds in terms of intensity of agitation everything one might have feared . . . In Rouen, the misery of the workers and their credulity, are boldly exploited; hatred of those who possess and of the masters who exploit them is being stirred up; they are promised permanent employment, higher wages, the suppression of national and local taxes . . . The principles of 1848 are being resurrected.[279]

The situation would continue to deteriorate. As the political climate changed and repression eased, the expression of working-class discontent became more common. Gendarmerie reports revealed growing tension 'between the working class, the employers and, one might add, the *bourgeoisie*', as well as a growing determination to employ the vote as a means of protesting against a regime which, in spite of its efforts to ingratiate itself with workers, remained closely identified with the 'rich'.[280]

---

[278] Lequin, *Formation*, II, p. 177.   [279] 29 May 1863 quoted Boivin, *Mouvement ouvrier*, I, p. 148.
[280] Ménager, 'La vie politique', p. 719.

Just as prosperity had reinforced the potency of the Bonapartist myth, so economic difficulties intensified criticism of the regime. The serious subsistence crisis of 1853 to 1856, the difficult winter of 1861–2, blamed on the commercial treaty with Britain and prolonged by the cotton famine (1862–5), and then the general recession from 1867, all resulted in political unrest. During the first crisis, official reports generally assume that the government's prestige was not seriously threatened.[281] The crisis associated with the cotton famine was localised, and even in those areas most seriously affected, does not appear to have had substantial political consequences.[282] The cyclical crisis beginning in 1867 was another matter. It occurred at a time when the prestige of the regime had already been weakened considerably.

For many workers, initially attracted by a populist Bonapartism, the regime appeared to have broken its promises. It had dispossessed workers by forcing them out of their lodgings in central Paris, and shown favour instead towards the speculators and the landlords who exploited them.[283] Now even the promise of prosperity had dimmed. As the Marseille commissaire central de police pointed out in July, 'the lack of work and the high cost of food makes life difficult, and provokes complaints from a working class always predisposed to blame the government for everything which is contrary to their interests'.[284] The gendarmerie commander in Lyon was probably correct in assuming that in the immediate future workers were too absorbed with the practical difficulties of making ends meet, but that their sense of grievance would have more substantial political impact once prosperity returned.[285] This was confirmed by the popular response in 1868 to a new conscription law. Thus, in Toulouse, on 9 March, a crowd of around 2,000, mainly workers, gathered in front of the town hall to protest. They then invaded the prefecture, destroyed police records, and marched behind a red flag to the mayor's residence, shouting *Vive la République* and singing the forbidden *Marseillaise*. On the following day most workers stayed away from work and troops had to be deployed to disperse demonstrators.[286]

As we have seen, strikes were a central point of conflict between workers and the agents of the state. In spite of official efforts to create a less repressive environment, experience of policing, and encounters with the law, continued to engender an intense distrust. The intrusion of police

[281] E.g. PG Rouen, 2 Oct. 1855, AN BB30/433.   [282] Boivin, *Mouvement ouvrier*, I, pp. 142–3.
[283] OC gendarmerie de la Seine, 28 Jan. 1870, AHG G8/176.
[284] Quoted L. Gaillard, *Vie ouvrière*, II, p. 482; the same was true in Paris – J. Gaillard, *Paris, la ville*, p. 399.
[285] OC cie. du Rhône, 26 Feb. 1868, AHG G8/151.   [286] Aminzade, *Class Struggles*, II, pp. 384–5.

into working-class space – streets and cafés – was regarded with suspicion and fear; their interference was likely to meet with abuse and occasional violence.[287] The presence of military garrisons with policing responsibilities, in many towns, and the flooding of zones of contention with troops, maintained high levels of hostility towards the army, frequently evident in drunken brawls.[288] After receiving news of Orsini's attempted assassination of the Emperor, Marshal de Castellane, commanding in Lyon, had deliberately, slowly and contemptuously, ridden his horse through a crowd of perhaps 2,000 workers. He confided to his diary that 'they respectfully doffed their caps to me, because they fear me' and then, he was certain, 'after my passage, they expressed the most despicable sentiments'.[289] The regime which slaughtered women and children at La Ricamarie would be perceived to be employing 'the methods of another age', to protect the interests of its capitalist friends.[290]

The politicisation of strikes increased from the early 1860s, as repression eased and republican militants renewed their efforts.[291] The involvement of republican lawyers in the defence of arrested strikers was certainly welcomed. Thus, on his arrival at the railway station at Saint-Etienne for the trial of velvet-ribbon weavers in November 1865, around 1,000 workers greeted Ernest Picard. He used the trial to attack the continued restrictions on the right to strike and on public meetings and to criticise Emile Ollivier for associating himself with the regime's reforms.[292] However, it cannot simply be assumed that the workers on trial shared the political aspirations of the lawyers who spoke in their defence. Indeed, during the 1863 electoral campaign, workers in the traditionally militant Lyon suburb of la Croix Rousse had complained about this *bourgeois* dominance.[293] It cannot even be assumed that the majority of workers shared the views of the militants who assumed the right to speak in their name. Nevertheless, a range of sources combine to confirm the growing resonance of republican ideas. Liberalisation made it less hazardous to diffuse a wide range of republican and socialist publications, which offered workers an explanation of their misery and subordination, and appealed to their dreams of social justice, and workers overwhelmingly favoured the republican press.[294]

[287] E.g. Prefect Marne, report on June 1858, AN F7/4078 re Reims; GOC 9e DM, 25–30 Nov. 1857, AHG G8/45 re disorder in Arles.
[288] E.g. GOC 16e DM, 5–10 Jan. 1853, AHG G8/1 re Laval. [289] Castellane, *Journal*, v, p. 201.
[290] 'Appel de la Fédération rouennaise en faveur des grévistes du Creusot', reprinted in Boivin, *Mouvement ouvrier*, II, pp. 233–4.
[291] E.g. sous-préfet Fougères to Prefect Ille-et-Vilaine, 25 April 1862, AN F12/4651.
[292] Prefect Loire, 17 and 21 Nov. 1865, AN F12/4651. [293] PG Lyon, 3 July, 1864, AN BB30/379.
[294] Ménager, *Les Napoléon*, p. 136.

According to Audiganne, workers in Paris were committed to two basic ideals – equality and nationalism.[295] The reports presented to the government by the worker-delegates elected to attend the 1867 International Exposition offer further insights. These were heavily censored before publication. However, the original drafts survive. They present practical concerns, such as requests for compensation for having been driven out of accommodation in the centre of Paris by demolitions and high rents, as well as expressing egalitarian aspirations, including especially insistence on the need for free and obligatory education, 'to finally procure for their children the means of aspiring to every position in society'.[296] The delegates of the brush makers (*brossiers*) resented being treated as 'living machines' and as children rather than men, and furthermore claimed that it was their duty to 'demand, without cease, the lost Liberties in order to show that we are always ready to affirm the only true principles, those of '89'. The wood turners (*tourneurs sur bois*) pointed out that with these rights there would in future be no need to resort to revolutionary violence.[297] The engineering workers also demanded the free exercise of the vote in order to make popular sovereignty a reality, and to ensure that deputies in the Corps législatif represented the people and not the government. Otherwise, they warned dramatically, blood would flow.[298]

The May 1869 elections revealed a substantial increase in worker support for republican candidates, especially in the Paris region, the textile centres of Lille and Roubaix, and in eastern France – in departments like Aube, Meurthe, Vosges, and Haute-Marne in which hosiery, and small-scale textile and metallurgical production were all in decline, as well as further south in Doubs, Jura, and Côte-d'Or. The authorities had few illusions. Paris and Lyon with their well-established radical traditions had experienced almost constant agitation throughout the 1860s. The election campaign, and the political liberalisation which allowed much greater freedom to publish newspapers, organise public meetings, and conduct door-to-door canvassing, was of particular importance nevertheless in the (re-)politicisation of workers.

Although republican organisation remained fragmented, deputies like Simon, Pelletan, and Favre attempted to provide some coordination through political tours and the establishment of *ad hoc* electoral committees, whilst the candidatures of the radical republicans Gambetta and Rochefort

---

[295] Audiganne, *Populations*, II, p. 163.
[296] Rapports analysed by Devinck for the Emperor, 28 Oct. 1868, AN 45 AP 6.
[297] AN F12/3120.   [298] AN F12/3116.

in Paris certainly attracted widespread publicity.[299] In Marseille the political awakening was linked to the popularity of two newspapers – *Le Peuple* and *L'Ami du Peuple* – whose journalists organised public meetings which inevitably reminded the authorities of the clubs of 1848. Their networks of correspondents helped to create the sense of belonging to a national, and because of the existence of the International, to a universal movement. Involvement conferred a growing sense of power. The procureur général was afraid these meetings might offer the means by which *les soldats de la première heure* would mobilise *les soldats de la seconde*, whether for electoral or revolutionary purposes.[300] He subsequently estimated that around 200 to 300 *démagogues*, not all of them workers, together with 1,000 *partisans secondaires*, were capable of mobilising a further 8,000 to 10,000 sympathisers.[301] In the mining-metallurgical centres of Le Creusot, Epinac, and Montceau-les-Mines the *Progrès de Saône-et-Loire* similarly offered inspiration and a means of coordination.[302]

Participants in public meetings listened attentively to republican and socialist speakers. The Declaration of the Rights of Man of 1789, frequently reinterpreted to offer a solution to the 'social question', continued to offer inspiration. In Paris, at the Vieux-Chêne dance hall in the rue Mouffetard in December 1868, the book-keeper Théophile Ferré reminded his audience that it was 'the Revolution of '93, which was the second revolution, the true one, which gave work to the workers' and had established the price maximum.[303] On 26 January 1869, Ducasse denounced an Empire dependent on '50,000 bayonets' and called on his excited audience to march on the enemy 'full of ardour, equipped with more than sharp swords and guns because we will have, in one hand, the Rights of Man, and in the other the glorious slogan: *Liberté, Egalité, Fraternité*'.[304] For these revolutionaries, the death of the Emperor, whether as a result of assassination or due to natural causes, was to be the signal for a renewal of the struggle. This was the message diffused by such *placards* as that found in March 1868, on the door of the Cercle de la Renaissance in the rue de Noailles in Marseille.[305]

In the public meetings, discordant voices were shouted down. At a gathering in working-class Belleville in January 1869 one speaker who quoted the Emperor's famous pamphlet on *L'Extinction du paupérisme* to the effect that 'the working class owns nothing; we need to endow it with property',

[299] E.g. J. Rougerie, 'Belleville' in L. Girard, *Les élections de 1869, passim*; Boivin, *Mouvement ouvrier*, I, p. 317.
[300] PG Aix, 4 Oct. 1868, AN BB30/389. [301] Ibid., 24 Jan. 1870, AN BB30/390.
[302] PG Dijon, 13 Jan. 1869, AN BB30/389. [303] Vitu, *Réunions publiques*, p. 38.
[304] Ibid. pp. 43–4. [305] PG Aix, 23 March 1868, AN BB18/1766.

was asked the name of the author by an enthusiastic audience. The response 'Louis Bonaparte' met with howls of disapproval and comments like 'I don't know what became of him; perhaps he is dead', together with the response: 'No, but we can hope that he soon will be.'[306] The feminist Paule Minck compared the Emperor's civil list of 30 million francs with the pitiful 14f. 75 per head allocated to paupers by the Paris bureaux de bienfaisance, adding, 'then citizens, they hand out alms, they preach the virtues of philanthropy, and go into raptures on the kindness of a lady of the highest society, I say of the highest society [i.e. the Empress], who brings assistance to you in the hospitals of Amiens'.[307]

The bookbinder Varlin took heart from these meetings. In March 1869, he wrote that 'eight months of political debate has led to the discovery of the strange fact that the majority of politically active workers are communists... The social question has suddenly come into view, troubling the digestion of those who rule, and of those who enjoy the pleasures of life.'[308] The declaration of the election results encouraged riotous celebrations in Paris followed, every evening from 8 June to 11 June, by gatherings in Belleville and the faubourg du Temple, of crowds estimated to number 3,000 to 4,000 which smashed gas lights and windows, looted shops, and constructed small barricades, before dispersing when the police appeared. The Paris gendarmerie commander believed that he was witnessing 'the return of the bad days of 1848'.[309]

The apathy which had characterised previous elections in many places seemed to have been swept away. In Saint-Etienne the crowds, which had gathered in the evening of 24 May to celebrate the election of the republican industrialist Dorian, shouted slogans and sang the *Marseillaise*, before finally setting fire to the Jesuit college.[310] Amongst those subsequently arrested was a certain Guichard, suspected of arson and accused of shouting 'Long live the Reds. Down with the priests. *Vive la République*. We don't want the Jesuits fattening themselves on the sweat of the people any longer. We want the separation of Church and State.' Later, he claimed to have been inspired by Victor Hugo's pamphlet 'Le Christ au Vatican' together with an article in *Le Sentinelle populaire* on 22 May entitled 'Rise up, Sovereign People'.[311] In Toulouse disappointed voters rioted when the

---

[306] Meeting at Belleville, 30 Jan. 1869, reported by Vitu, *Réunions publiques*, p. 59.

[307] Meeting at La Redoute, 21 Jan. 1869, reported ibid. p. 62.

[308] Quoted Cottereau, 'Vie quotidienne', p. 96.

[309] OC gendarmerie de la Seine, 27 Oct. 1869, AHG G8/166; Jacquement, 'Belleville', II, pp. 527–8.

[310] Tribunal correctionnel de Saint-Etienne. Audience 21 June 1869, AN F1 CIII Loire 9; Merley, 'Les élections', pp. 88–9.

[311] PI Saint-Etienne, 25 May 1869, PG Lyon, 23 June 1869, AN BB18/1785.

radical republican Duportal, who had carried the urban districts, lost as a result of the vote in rural communes adjoined to the constituency.[312] In the north the similar impact of gerrymandering provoked riots in Lille and Amiens in the evenings of 24 and 25 May and minor disorders at Calais, Cambrai, and Valenciennes.[313] Workers felt 'humiliated because their votes had been annulled by those of the *Peasants*'.[314]

In the aftermath of the election, the press and public meetings sustained the agitation. M. Fontane, a Parisian police commissaire, expressed concern about the cumulative impetus given to working-class politicisation by first the elections of delegates to the 1867 Exposition, then the numerous strikes in 1867/8, and the activities – real and supposed – of the International. He observed that although formally separate, the mutual aid societies and *syndicats* tended to involve 'the same men, the same principles and the same means of recruitment'.[315] The public meetings brought them together. The future deputy Ducarre, who frequently participated in gatherings in Paris in the winter of 1869 attended by as many as 3,000 to 5,000 people, distinguished between the '25 or 30 leaders who carry the word', the '200 faithful followers', and the 1,500 others who attended on a fairly regular basis; to whom could be added the simply curious, and those who came in out of the cold.[316]

In spite of the obligatory presence of a police commissaire and repeated prosecutions, speakers remained determined to express their contempt for the regime and all its works, often taking up the themes of the new radical newspapers like Delescluze's *Réveil* or Rochefort's *Lanterne*. Ténot's book on the *coup d'état* with its denunciation of the *crime du 2 décembre* also had a considerable impact.[317] The level of interest amongst those attending a meeting varied considerably, of course. Those workers who dared speak in public meetings were often shouted down or exposed to cruel witticisms because of their lack of linguistic facility. Rouyer, one of the slowly increasing number who did pluck up the courage, told his audience that 'what we workers lack, is the words to set out our ideas', adding that 'educated men can do it; but they do not understand the fundamental questions like we do'.[318] Only gradually as some grew in confidence were they listened to. Most workers were too fatigued or insufficiently interested to attend

---

[312] Aminzade, *Ballots and Barricades*, p. 133.   [313] GOC 3e DM, 26 and 31 May 1869, AHG G8/165.
[314] PG Amiens, 18 June 1869, AN BB18/1785.
[315] Assemblée nationale, *Enquête parlementaire. Actes du gouvernement de la défense nationale*, v (Paris 1876), p. 393.
[316] Dalotel, Faure, and Freiermuth, *Aux origines*, pp. 92, 126.
[317] Girard, *Nouvelle histoire*, pp. 389–95.
[318] 3 Aug. 1868, quoted Dalotel, Faure, and Freiermuth, *Aux origines*, p. 127.

at all. Although women were rarely welcome as participants, in the popular *quartiers* a substantial number attended meetings and 'the question of women's work' was a common topic for discussion. Typically, when asked by the feminist Paule Minck: 'Is a woman's life to add up to nothing more than bringing up children?', the militant socialists at a public meeting in Gravilliers responded: 'Yes! Yes!'[319]

Nevertheless, the meetings and press stimulated a much wider debate, carried on in workplaces and cafés. Encouraged by the election results, the employees of the state arsenal at Brest agreed to put 5 or 10 centimes each into a hat in order to purchase a newspaper and pay someone to read aloud as they worked. Those who refused to contribute, or to take an interest in the discussions which followed, were subjected to insults and occasionally to violence.[320] In Lyon a considerable 'effervescence' was reported in the cafés and *café-concerts* of the workers' *quartiers* of la Croix Rousse and Brotteaux-Guillotière, where political debate alternated with popular songs.[321] Administrative reports refer to the development of an *esprit de quartier* and a 'close and powerful solidarity'. Indeed, the federal organisation created by the silk weavers – the Société civile de Prévoyance et de renseignements pour le travail des tisseurs – was able to hold meetings of 7,000 to 8,000 members in 1869/70 and, briefly, to prevent employer victimisation of union members, whilst the delegates elected by the silk workers to visit the 1867 Exposition maintained close contacts with their Parisian colleagues. They were also attracted to the International precisely because its leading figures encouraged these efforts both to organise locally and to establish federal structures in order to reinforce working-class unity.[322] In these circumstances official concern about the growing influence of socialist 'agitators', and especially those associated with the International, was hardly surprising.[323]

In March 1870, a meeting of porcelain workers at Vierzon (Cher), called to discuss the creation of a Crédit mutuel et de solidarité de la céramique, provoked similar concern because all its leading figures were well-known republicans. Meetings attended by around 500 workers listened to speeches on the moral and material situation of *la classe ouvrière*, on the best means of defending themselves against 'despotic employers', and in favour of free and obligatory education. They chose to elect the revolutionary republican Felix Pyat as their honorary president.[324] In the Marseille area the authorities

---

[319] Ibid. p. 173.   [320] Prefect, 18 Jan. 1870, AN F1 CIII Finistère 11.
[321] Sheridan, 'Esprit de quartier', pp. 34–5.   [322] Rougerie, 'La Première Internationale', p. 154.
[323] PG Lyon, 10 April 1870, AN BB30/390.   [324] Prefect, 29 March 1870, AN F1 CIII Cher 9.

were anxious about the rhetoric of newspapers like the *Rappel, Réveil*, and *Marseillaise*, which, with their constant and extreme attacks, threatened to bring the government into disrepute.[325] Even in such relatively placid centres as Bordeaux it was recognised that the commitment of workers to advanced ideas and their advocates was spreading.[326]

Thus, a high level of interest in politics was sustained for the best part of two years, during a period of prolonged crisis for the regime. The workers involved were part of a cross-class and predominantly republican and urban opposition, the leadership of which was mainly composed of local notables – middle-class professionals and businessmen in particular – often with a long record of republican activity, and collectively capable of subsidising organisational activity and in particular the establishment of newspapers. In most areas, only a minority of these local leaders were workers, and these were normally skilled craftsmen. Most politically aware workers, due to the episodic, embryonic character of their interest, their lack of education, and susceptibility to intimidation and repression, were more passively integrated into the wider democratic movement. They were presented with a wide array of ideas by republican politicians representing the different traditions which had emerged after 1789, and the willingness of their advocates to reconstruct their ideological heritage to suit the times.

Those who adhered to the republican 'movement', at least shared a foundation myth, as well as hostility to a corrupt, authoritarian regime, and to the Bonapartes, who in destroying two republics had slowed progress towards liberty. However, they were divided between moderates committed to *progrès sans révolution*, and to harmony between the classes, as well as to social order and economic liberalism, and afraid that strikes and 'extremism' would alienate potential supporters amongst the middle classes and peasants; self-styled 'radicals', who were, in practice, increasingly legalistic in their political tactics, and always afraid of losing control over the masses, but employed a more combative language than moderates, firmly insisting on their commitment to social reform; and revolutionaries, divided themselves between mutualists like Tolain and the increasingly popular collectivists, like the Blanquist Rigault. Within each of these groups there were further divisions between personalities and generations – and particularly those associated with 1848 and younger men – as well as social tensions. This should serve to remind us of 'the complexities of class relations and class identities'[327] and of political choice.

---

[325] PG Aix, 24 Jan. 1870, AN BB30/390.   [326] PG Bordeaux, 12 Jan. 1870, AN BB30/390.
[327] Magraw, *French Working Class*, I, p. 114.

The authorities had tolerated the moderates, and their influential news-paper *Le Siècle*, even during the authoritarian years. They had achieved a degree of 'respectability'. In their concern to exert a moralising and restrain-ing influence on their mass constituency, they differed little from socially conservative liberals. During the difficult 1850s and early 1860s, their rivals on the left had been far more likely to suffer police repression and, as a result, had become less visible. Thus the moderates had made the political run-ning initially but would face growing challenges from other republicans as the regime's second decade moved towards an end. Workers were divided in their responses towards this rivalry between predominantly *bourgeois* republicans. During the years of repression, and in the absence of organ-ised republican activity, worker militants had developed their own social networks and a capacity for independent action.[328] The determination of middle-class republicans to re-assert their leadership, once political activity became safer in the 1860s, together with their denunciations of the divi-sive effects of autonomous worker activity, inevitably provoked resentment amongst working-class militants and led to the development of a current of *ouvriérisme*.

In October 1861 the Parisian bronze worker (*ciseleur*) Tolain had replied to offers of assistance from the Emperor's cousin Prince Napoleon, by pointing out that initiatives from above would inspire little confidence amongst workers – 'we would not feel free, neither in our goals, nor in our decisions'. For him, 'there is only one way, that is to say to us: you are free, organize yourselves, look after your own affairs'.[329] One possi-bility was the selection of worker candidates for election, in the hope of repeating the triumphs of Corbon and Perdiguier in 1848, and in February 1863 Tolain and a small group of artisans nominated their own candidates and in a *Manifeste des Soixante* demanded the abrogation of all 'excep-tional legislation', including that banning strikes and public meet-ings. Its authors insisted that 'equality, written into the law, has not entered into habits and has still to be achieved in practice'. The man-ifesto repudiated revolution and denied any intention of threatening the vital interests of other groups but insisted that workers had the right to be represented in the Corps législatif. If 'universal suffrage has allowed us to come of age politically . . . we still need to emanci-pate ourselves socially', as the *bourgeoisie* had in 1789.[330] Afraid of losing

---

[328] E.g. PG Paris, 30 March 1854, AN BB30/408.
[329] Quoted E. Dolléans and G. Dehove, *Histoire du travail en France* (Paris 1953), p. 298.
[330] Quoted J. Rougerie, 'Le Second Empire' in Duby, *Histoire*, III, p. 92.

electoral support, middle-class republicans denounced them as Bonapartist sympathisers.[331]

Similarly, during the 1869 election campaign some militants condemned a political system which, in spite of liberalisation, ensured that 'the representatives sent by the nation have always been taken from the class whose interests are opposed to ours' with, as a consequence, 'the sacrifice of the interests of the greatest number'. They resented the fact that the Parisian printing worker Raimbaut, a potential candidate in 1869, had felt obliged to desist in favour of Jules Favre, when the republican press, largely opposed to worker candidates, had refused to print his electoral address.[332] Reflecting the widespread distrust of the republican politicians who had betrayed the workers in 1848, another potential candidate, Pailet, insisted on the presentation of a clearly defined programme, as well as the acceptance by every candidate of a *mandat impératif*, and the obligation to resign if they violated this compact.[333]

In Rouen, Aubry, a printing worker well known in the working-class community, turned his back on the abstentionist position he had previously adopted and agreed to stand for election. In a speech to the Cercle d'études économiques, he insisted that it was essential that 'the worker enters into the deliberative bodies'.[334] In his manifesto he warned workers that if they 'again vote for their political patrons, they will delay their emancipation by fifty years'.[335] Aubry condemned both the moderate republicans, 'who aspire only to changes of person'[336] and the radical democrats, who claimed to favour *la République démocratique et sociale*, but were unwilling to present a precise programme of social reform.[337] In spite of an effort to re-assure the electorate by affirming that, 'the difference of epochs requires the difference of means; in 1789 murderous weapons, in 1869 pacific weapons – for the first, powder and shot; for the second, employment of the most important political conquest of the 19th century: . . . universal suffrage',[338] he received only a derisory 826 of the 22,220 votes cast.[339] The majority voted for Desseaux who, as State Prosecutor in 1848, had been associated with the use of the military to repress worker protest.[340]

---

[331] E.g. Girard, *Nouvelle histoire*, p. 377.

[332] Speech at rue Monge, 17 May, recorded Vitu, *Réunions électorales*, p. 124.   [333] Ibid. p. 361.

[334] Boivin, *Mouvement ouvrier*, 1, p. 290; see also PG Rouen, 12 April 1869, AN BB30/389.

[335] Quoted Boivin, *Mouvement ouvrier*, 1, p. 230, note 17.

[336] Article in *Le Mirabeau*, 6 Feb. 1870, quoted ibid. p. 379.

[337] Article in *La Réforme sociale*, 10 April 1870, quoted ibid.   [338] Quoted ibid. 1, p. 275.

[339] M. Boivin, 'La fédération ouvrière rouennaise et les événements de 1870–71', *Revue d'histoire économique et sociale* 1962, pp. 327–8; J. Rougerie, 'Les sections françaises de l'Association Internationale des travailleurs' in Rougerie, *La Ire Internationale*, p. 117.

[340] Boivin, *Mouvement ouvrier*, 1, p. 561.

Paradoxically, whilst many workers still bitterly resented their 'betrayal' by *bourgeois* republicans in 1848, they remained committed to a broad republican alliance. They preferred to support candidates possessing what were taken to be the necessary educational and cultural qualifications, and who had proved themselves to be irreconcilable opponents of the imperial regime, presumably assuming in addition that these stood a better chance of election.[341] The lawyers Jules Favre or Ernest Picard had generated substantial publicity, both for themselves and the republican cause, through their willingness to defend strikers and political activists who had fallen foul of the law. They could pose successfully as defenders of the workers' interests.[342] They insisted on fundamental commitments to equality before the law and equality of opportunity, and to private property as the source of 'individual identity and personal independence' and as part of a gendered, overwhelmingly male-orientated concept of republican citizenship.[343] They favoured education and abstemious behaviour as the essential means of working-class self-improvement. Instruction would free the workers from the tyranny of religion and from their own unfettered instincts. Involvement in such voluntary associations as the Ligue de l'Enseignement provided a means of advancing the cause.[344] These, essentially liberal republicans, remained largely insensitive to the practical difficulties of working-class life and opposed to substantial measures of social reform.[345] Nevertheless, their democratic ideals, together with attacks on militarism and on the regime's bellicose foreign policy, the reconstitution of the 'black' legend of a Bonapartism which wasted lives and resources had considerable popular appeal.

In opposition to Bonapartist authoritarianism and the social dominance of monarchist landlords, 'obscurantist' priests, greedy railway monopolists, and speculative financiers, moderate republicans promised democracy, order, and progress. Furthermore, as they emphasised, their opposition was legal and non-violent. They vigorously denounced the brutal language employed by speakers in the public meetings with their constant references to Robespierre and Marat and the other 'heroes' of the Year II. The calls for a return to the 'terrorism' of 1793 terrified them. Moderate republicans were indeed as susceptible to the *spectre rouge*, as more obvious

---

[341] See e.g. speech by Dumont, 11 May 1869, recorded in Vitu, *Réunions électorales*, pp. 17–18.

[342] See e.g. Prefect Loire, 21 Nov. 1865 AN F12/4651; PG Lyon, 8 Jan. 1866, AN BB30/379.

[343] J. Stone, 'Republican ideology, gender and class: France, 1860s–1914' in L. Frader and S. Rose (eds.), *Gender and Class in Modern Europe* (London 1996), pp. 239–40.

[344] D. Gordon, 'Industrialization and republican politics: the bourgeoisie of Reims and Saint-Etienne under the Second Empire' in J. Merriman (ed.), *French cities in the 19th century*, pp. 136–8.

[345] See e.g. J. Simon, *La politique radicale* (Paris 1868).

conservatives. According to the procureur général at Rouen their programme was essentially liberal and, indeed, increasingly attractive to former
Orleanists as offering 'the best of republics'.[346]

Many workers preferred the combative language of Gambetta and
Rochefort, and their commitment to social reform, however vague. In
the public meetings 'radical' attacks on moderate republicans were warmly
applauded.[347] When republican candidates stood against each other in the
capital, the radical Gambetta would triumph over the moderate Hippolyte
Carnot, Education Minister in 1848, by 21,744 votes to 11,604 in the overwhelmingly working-class Belleville constituency. Tolain had denounced
Carnot's candidature in the Salle des Folies-Belleville on 9 May because
of his association with the repression of the June insurrection. Carnot was
again defeated following Gambetta's decision to opt for a Marseille seat,
by the even more radical aristocratic journalist Rochefort, standing as the
candidat révolutionnaire socialiste (by 17,978 to 13,445). The ageing 'socialist' Raspail also came close to defeating Garnier-Pagès, Finance Minister in
1848, and the symbol to many voters of both *bourgeois* republican reaction
during the Second Republic, and the equivocal attitude of moderate republicans towards the liberal Empire, already revealed by the apostasy of the
former republican deputies Ollivier and Darimon. In Lyon too, the radicals
Bancel and Raspail defeated those stalwarts of the *bourgeois* republic Hénon
and Favre.[348]

Gambetta had responded to the *cahiers des doléances* prepared by local
election committees in his constituency, with the Belleville programme.
In this he demanded greater political liberty, the separation of State and
Church, free, obligatory, and secular education – with access to the highest levels through competitive examinations, tax reform, the election of
officials, and suppression of permanent armies. At the same time, whilst
appealing to Parisian workers, he sought to reassure property owners. The
effective basis of Gambetta's appeal was a resounding call for unity against
the Empire, and for non-violent opposition, a commitment to 'revolution' through the ballot box, which would eventually be achieved as the
inevitable result of 'progress'. The programme contained only a few vague
commitments to further social reform.[349] It was not an attack on capitalism
but only on its 'excesses'.

In spite of such overtures, tension grew between moderate and 'radical'
republicans and working-class militants impatient for change. When the

---

[346] PG Rouen, 12 Jan. 1867, AN BB30/387. [347] E.g. Vitu, *Réunions publiques*, p. 63.
[348] Rougerie, 'Belleville', pp. 3–10, 17–21. [349] Quoted ibid. pp. 12–3.

worker Antide Martin stood for election at Saint-Etienne in competition with the republican ironmaster Dorian, his opponent called for the 'union of capital and labour' and vigorously denounced Martin's 'divisive' tactics.[350] In an indignant response to the result, Martin demanded to know: 'Is Saint-Etienne a village peopled by ignorant serfs? Is it a fief?', and reminded his audience that 'the *bourgeoisie* of the republican Alliance are no different from the conservative *bourgeoisie*, since all live at the expense of the working class, and unite against its emancipation'.[351] Especially in the larger cities it seems clear that a substantial minority of workers were open to the blandishments of a socialist and revolutionary left.

The bitter divisions, which had emerged in 1848, between republicans committed to political reform and those favouring broader social change, were thus replicated during the final years of the Empire. Memories of the 'betrayal' in June 1848 were still fresh, particularly of course in Paris, amongst those who attended the public meetings in the popular *quartiers*. In a meeting in La Chapelle in January 1869 Louis Ulbach, editor of *La Cloche*, was denounced for belonging to 'that obese *bourgeois* democracy, fat and unhealthy, which shot down the people on 15 May, 15 [*sic*] June and during every reaction'.[352] At another gathering at the Vieux-Chêne, denunciation of the moderate republican general Cavaignac as 'the butcher of the people!, the cut-throat who drowned the Revolution in blood!', brought 'thunderous' applause.[353]

Other, living reminders of 1848 like Favre, Marie, and Garnier-Pagès found that working-class audiences received their calls for republican unity with disbelief. Favre was accused of hostility *aux doctrines ouvriers*.[354] Garnier-Pagès, Deputy for the 5th *circonscription* of Paris, which included the faubourg du Temple and that of St-Antoine, having claimed in the Corps législatif that the speakers in the public meetings were paid by the police to discredit the republican cause, was condemned by a meeting in the Salle du jardin de Paris in the rue de la Gaîté.[355] When an unidentified labourer nervously attempted to defend him as a supporter of democracy at a meeting in Belleville on 29 January 1869 the chairman silenced him on the grounds that it was impermissible that 'men who have shot the people' should be defended.[356] The president of a meeting at Ménilmontant similarly demanded to know whether unity was possible between 'the executioners and those they have shot'.[357]

---

[350] Aminzade, *Ballots and Barricades*, p. 139.   [351] Quoted Gordon, *Merchants*, p. 113.
[352] By Ducasse, recorded by Vitu, *Réunions publiques*, p. 66.   [353] Ibid. p. 69.
[354] Vitu, *Réunions électorales*, p. 101.   [355] Vitu, *Réunions publiques*, p. 75.
[356] Ibid. p. 80.   [357] Ibid. p. 7.

Furthermore, there were signs of the development of a virulent hostility towards all middle-class republicans, even the more radical. Many workers expressed suspicion of their motives and clearly resented their condescending attitudes. The liberty they offered was simply a mirage. As Humbert, speaking at Ménilmontant on 27 November 1869 put it: 'Liberty, without equality in political affairs, is the right for some to command the others. In social matters, it is for some the right to speculate on labour, and for the others the right to succumb to the struggle.'[358] Victor Clément, a leading figure in the International, called upon his audience to remember *les journées de juin* and to abstain rather than vote *non* in the 1870 plebiscite, because it was impossible to vote alongside those 'formal republicans, our relentless enemies . . . who refuse to respond when we ask them for the complete abolition of the exploitation of man by man'.[359] There were indications that even Gambetta, who in Marseille had emphasised his devotion to order and even in his Belleville programme had insisted on the primacy of political over social reform, was in danger of losing much of his popular support. Belleville appeared to be a constituency in which much of the electorate habitually preferred the most extreme candidate.

Certainly revolutionary Blanquist groups appear to have attracted some students and young workers, especially in Belleville, La Chapelle, and the faubourg du Temple.[360] Blanquist speakers, as well as less easily definable revolutionaries, were especially in evidence at the Salle des Folies-Belleville.[361] At least initially, their extremism ensured that adherents of the International avoided their meetings.[362] The tension between the two groups can be observed in the worker Héligon's contemptuous dismissal of the violent young Blanquist Rigault in January 1869: 'You have made an awful joke, a student joke. You, and the president [of the meeting] are two scoundrels who want to dominate the meeting.'[363] Rigault's insistence that he was acting in the workers' interests brought an irritated response from the old barricade fighter Napoléon Gaillard: 'I have not entrusted anyone with the defence of my interests', and an even more angry outburst from Héligon, who described Rigault as a 'womaniser; you are a son of the *bourgeoisie* who lives off our sweat, outrages our daughters, steals from our fathers, and who shot them in '48'.[364] The blacksmith Havrez was

---

[358] Quoted Dalotel, Faure, and Freiermuth, *Aux origines*, p. 219. [359] Quoted ibid. pp. 179–80.
[360] R. Wolfe, 'The origins of the Paris commune: the popular organizations of 1868–71', PhD Harvard Univ. 1965, p. 19.
[361] Ibid. pp. 118–19.
[362] E.g. observation of Simonne, commissaire de police, to Assemblée nationale, *Enquête parlementaire*, vol. v, p. 392.
[363] Vitu, *Réunions publiques*, p. 83. [364] Ibid. p. 83.

suspicious of both *bourgeois* republicans and Blanquist activists, insisting on the need for workers to liberate themselves – 'we want to march alone; we are no longer to be wiped out on the morrow by those whom we have carried in triumph the day before'.[365]

However, it became clear following renewed waves of police repression, that members of the International, including such eminent figures as Varlin and Tolain, were drawn increasingly towards the Blanquists, participating in joint meetings at the Salle de La Marseillaise between March and May 1870. Especially in the working-class districts of the capital, there was an increasingly widespread feeling that in a society corrupted by the greed of 'financial feudalism' and subject to repression by police and priests, revolution was the necessary first step in a cleansing process. In the public meetings, mention of the names of such pillars of the regime and symbols of capitalist exploitation as Eugène Schneider, president of the Corps législatif and director of Le Creusot, was likely to lead to a chorus of 'hang him!' Increasingly too the entire *patronat* and property owners in general were associated with these notorious 'parasites'. Proudhon's famous slogan, 'Property is theft', was repeated endlessly.[366] Needless to say, there was little agreement on the form the emerging new society would take.

Working-class militants were torn between the cooperative, Proudhonian programmes, favoured by such influential members of the International as Tolain, and a communistic collectivism based on state ownership of the means of production and distribution. Tolain and the other French delegates to the Congress of the International Working Men's Association in Geneva in 1866 had viewed the basic struggle as economic rather than political. They had claimed that there was nothing to hope for from the State. A revolution would simply lead to the replacement of one ruling group by another. The revival of memories of 1848, together with the posturing of revolutionary extremists, confirmed for many workers the wisdom of autonomous working-class action. Aubry, the Rouen printing worker, warned about 'the practitioners of political Jesuitism who in London, as in Lyon, as in Marseille, as in Paris, employ the same arms: slander and falsehood; in the name of Liberty, they seek to arouse the masses in order to perpetuate their economic slavery'.[367]

In time, Aubry assured Varlin, the Parisian bookbinder, the sheer weight of electoral numbers would give power to the workers.[368] In a brochure on

[365] *Le Pays*, 9 Jan. 1869.
[366] See e.g. Dalotel, Faure, and Freiermuth, *Aux origines*, pp. 231, 317.
[367] *La Réforme sociale*, 27 Feb. 1870, quoted Boivin, *Mouvement ouvrier*, I, p. 403 note 56.
[368] Letter of 26 May 1868, published in Boivin, *Mouvement ouvrier*, vol. II, p. 8.

'Justice et solidarité', published early in 1870, he presented his non-violent conception of social revolution – 'progressive reforms, a succession of rights granted to citizens with the aim of conquering their political, economic, intellectual and moral emancipation . . . The Revolution is nothing other than the progressive march of the human spirit.' He concluded that only their ignorance kept the masses subordinate to the small wealthy minority. Education was thus the key to freedom. It would open the workers' eyes to injustice.[369]

The associationist ideals of 1848 were also revived. A better world could be created through mutuality and the multiplication of producers' and consumers' cooperatives. The retention and re-investment of profits would provide cheap credit and allow the constant expansion of cooperation until entire trades were emancipated from the grasp of capitalism, making possible the establishment of a workers' democracy and the eventual withering away of the state.[370] Even a revolutionary like Varlin could appreciate the potential of cooperation as an alternative to the oppressive hierarchical organisation of capitalist society and to the centralised and authoritarian state favoured by collectivist socialists.[371] He insisted that in the past workers had

been badly led, and mercilessly exploited because we were divided and lacking in strength; . . . soon when we are all united, we will be able to support each other; then, because we are the most numerous and because, after all, production in its entirety is the result of our labour, we will be able to demand, both in practice and as of right, enjoyment of the totality of the product of our work, and that will be just. The parasites will disappear from the face of the earth; they will, if they wish to survive, transform themselves into producers, into useful beings.[372]

Like other militants, Varlin remained nervous. In a letter to Aubry, written in December 1869, he privately revealed his fear that another revolution would only result in a repetition of 1848, 'with corpses in the streets providing a pedestal for the politicians'.[373] He was anxious to avoid a premature movement, and concerned that the current disturbances in Paris, if they got out of hand, might lead 'to the massacre of the finest soldiers of the revolution'.[374] The following March, however, he reiterated his scepticism

---

[369] Cercle de Rouen, 'De l'instruction et de l'éducation des classes ouvrières', Brussels Congress of International, 6–13 September 1868, in Boivin, *Mouvement ouvrier*, II, pp. 53–9.

[370] E.g. PG Lyon, 8 Jan. 1866, AN BB30/379; B. Moss, *The Origins of the French Labor Mouvement. The Socialism of Skilled Workers* (London 1976), pp. 4–5; Gaillard, 'Les associations de production', pp. 80–1.

[371] Rougerie, 'Sections françaises', pp. 126–7.   [372] Printed in annex to ibid. pp. 125–6.

[373] Quoted Boivin, *Mouvement ouvrier*, I, p. 391.

[374] Letter to Aubry, 19 Jan. 1870, quoted ibid. p. 362.

concerning the promises of bourgeois republicans and the prospects held out by parliamentary democracy, insisting that 'we must struggle against our enemies by all possible means and, at this moment, our most serious enemies are the moderate republicans, the liberals in whatever shape'.[375] He concluded that 'we will not be able to achieve social reform if the old political State is not destroyed', and confidently asserted that in one, perhaps two years, the workers would be ready for revolution, and that they would be capable of becoming 'masters of the situation and be assured that the revolution will not escape us for the profit of the non-socialist republicans'.[376]

A substantial amount of support for violent revolution was building up. Blanquists typically denounced both cooperation and electioneering as at best palliatives and at worst as utopian, with the former likely to benefit only a small minority of skilled craftsmen. The authors of the 'Manifeste du comité électoral ouvrier', published in Rouen in August 1870, were concerned that legalism, and engagement in municipal and national politics, carried with it the risk of commitment to a broader republican politics and neglect of distinctive working-class interests.[377] At the public meetings in Paris simple solutions to society's ills were often applauded. Napoléon Gaillard began a speech at La Redoute with a ringing declaration: 'I am a worker, work is the only source of human happiness; those who do not work are the wretched of the earth, they are the idlers who threaten the workers.' He concluded that, 'To raise up the poor, it is necessary to bring down the rich.'[378] The working-class electoral candidate Chamaillard, speaking at the Maison-Dieu in November 1868, had summarised his programme as 'No more landlords, *bourgeois*, taxes, or religion.' At Belleville, the following February, Boyer demanded 'social liquidation', and denounced any suggestion that the *bourgeoisie* be compensated for its lost property.[379]

It was probably more than the drink speaking when the locksmith Garreau, who would become director of the Mazas prison during the Paris Commune, told his audience in March 1870 that 'I want to assassinate the *bourgeoisie*, the capitalists who gorge themselves with everything . . . I want us to take to the streets, weapons in hand, not tomorrow, but now.'[380] Raoul Lafagette, an habitué of public meetings in working-class Belleville, received loud applause when he ended a speech made in his native Gaillac

[375] Ibid. pp. 120–1.   [376] 8 March 1870, quoted Maitron, 'La personnalité', p. 69.
[377] Boivin, *Mouvement ouvrier*, II, pp. 278–81.
[378] Dalotel, Faure, and Freiermuth, *Aux origines*, p. 244.
[379] Vitu, *Réunions publiques*, p. 501.   [380] Dalotel, Faure, and Freiermuth, *Aux origines*, p. 320.

in April 1870, with shouts of 'Down with the priest, war on the priest, death to the priests!'[381] Such vehement expressions of hatred appear to have had considerable appeal, at least in the hothouse atmosphere of the public meetings. Quantitative judgements are impossible. How many workers listened to the socialist feminist Paule Minck on 28 November 1868 at Ménilmontant, regretting the failure of the June Insurrection and telling her audience, to loud applause, that 'only force will give us justice and liberty'?[382] How many amongst her audience, perhaps carried away by a sense of injustice and the heat of the moment, would have agreed in the cold light of day?

A messianic mood nevertheless developed in Paris during the 1869 election campaign. Thousands attended meetings, and subsequently took part in a noisy celebration of the overwhelming republican success in the capital. They also expressed resentment at the defeat of republican electoral candidates in the provinces. These disorders, which involved young workers and the small minority of students willing to translate words into action, spread into the streets. An estimated 20,000 were involved on the night of 10–11 June, smashing street lamps, shouting *A bas l'Empereur*, singing the *Marseillaise*, fighting and throwing stones at the police. Between 7 and 14 June over 1,600 arrests were made, although only 160 were detained.[383] Subsequently posters called for a refusal to pay taxes and a general strike.[384] Pietri, the Paris prefect of Police, was convinced that only the threat of dismissal from their jobs had kept groups like the Cail engineering workers out of these riots.[385]

News of the arrest of Rochefort on 7 February 1870 also resulted in major disturbances, culminating in the construction of barricades in the faubourg du Temple and in Belleville.[386] Again, following the announcement of the results of the plebiscite, there were three successive nights of serious disorder in the faubourg du Temple and around the place du Château d'Eau, resulting in several deaths and over 500 arrests.[387] In some circles, there was a growing belief in the inevitability of a popular revolution, which would lead to the emancipation of the working class. Speakers in public meetings like the cabinet-maker Banneloche, a veteran of the barricades in 1848, and his comrade Serizier, who had first taken up a gun as a fourteen-year old, were certainly ready to fight again.[388] That this commitment to

---

[381] Faury, *Cléricalisme*, p. 83.   [382] Vitu, *Réunions publiques*, p. 41.
[383] OC gendarmerie de la Seine, 27 June 1869, AHG G8/165; Girard, *Nouvelle histoire*, pp. 378–80.
[384] Ibid., 28 April 1870, AHG G8/176.   [385] Dalotel, Faure, and Freiermuth, *Aux origines*, p. 340.
[386] OC gendarmerie de la Seine, 26 Feb. 1870, AHG G8/176.   [387] Ibid., 28 May 1870.
[388] Dalotel, Faure, and Freiermuth, *Aux origines*, p. 318.

violence was not always just verbal, would be confirmed during the Paris Commune.

For most working-class activists there could be no doubt that the regime continued to lack legitimacy, in spite of its liberalisation. During the plebiscite campaign, the panicked efforts of Ollivier to prosecute adherents of the International for membership of a secret society and involvement in a plot against the Emperor provoked the Rouen militant Piéton, whose house had been searched by the police, to comment that, 'if this is the beginning of the liberal Empire, I'll leave to patriots the task of divining the future'.[389] The ban on a workers' congress due to be held in Rouen in June, in spite of the organisers' efforts to respect every legal formality, was taken to be further proof of the liberal regime's fundamental hostility to workers' aspirations.[390] As a speaker at the Folies-Bergère pointed out, to noisy applause, this was the Emperor who had taken the nation 'by theft, by means of an assassination in the night'. He was no better than a brigand.[391] The cabinet-maker Stenson, at the Salle des Folies-Belleville, expressed his utter contempt: 'If the Emperor was in front of me, I would tell him: You are pathetic! You are a scoundrel! You have soiled the honour of France!'[392] At Ribeauvillé in Alsace on 2 May factory workers gathered in force in front of the town hall shouting *Vive la République!* and 'Shit for the Emperor'. Pro-Yes posters were disfigured repeatedly or torn down.[393] The situation was particularly serious in Paris where, every evening, disorderly crowds paraded through the working-class *quartiers*.[394]

The results of the plebiscite revealed that workers were more likely to return a negative vote than members of any other social group, although a not insignificant number must have voted 'Yes'. In Lyon, five out of six arrondissements returned a negative majority with rejection especially significant in working-class districts. Nevertheless, whilst 46,465 voters had supported republican candidates the year before, now only 35,769 voted 'No'.[395] In Lille 51 per cent of the overall electorate voted 'No', a proportion rising to 66 per cent in the working-class *quartier* of St-Sauveur.[396] Influenced by strikes, the vote in Le Creusot resulted in 3,400 negative and 1,500 positive ballot papers, in marked contrast with the 17 per cent voting

[389] Quoted Boivin, *Mouvement ouvrier*, I, p. 388.
[390] See documents published in *La Réforme sociale*, 3 July 1870 and reprinted in Boivin, *Mouvement ouvrier*, II, pp. 263–5.
[391] Quoted Dalotel, Faure, and Freiermuth, *Aux origines*, p. 186.   [392] Ibid. p. 187.
[393] Strauss, 'Opinion publique', pp. 171–2.   [394] Jacquemet, 'Belleville', II, p. 527.
[395] Lequin, *Formation*, II, p. 179; Bayard, Cayez, *Histoire de Lyon*, II, p. 295.
[396] Pierrard, *Diocèses*, p. 247.

'No' in the Department of Saône-et-Loire as a whole.[397] In Saint-Etienne, 77 per cent returned a negative vote, as miners and ribbon weavers combined to express their horror at the shooting of workers at Ricamarie.[398] In Bordeaux, too, workers were reported to have dismissed the liberalisation of the regime as a 'feeble palliative' and begun to hope for the change of regime, which alone might lead to the *révolution sociale* to which they aspired.[399] Further south, the State Prosecutor at Montpellier warned that 'the most general aspirations, amongst the . . . working class population, will certainly not be satisfied by the institutions of the parliamentary Empire, which will be accepted only as a provisional situation, allowing them to prepare for a more radical transformation'.[400]

As a corrective to the emphasis in much of the literature on the activities of the revolutionary socialists, however, it is worth listening to Benoît Malon, who had organised around twenty meetings in the Paris suburb of Puteaux between January and April 1869. He concluded that, in spite of his efforts, most workers would continue to support bourgeois democratic republicans.[401] Norbert Truquin, the much-travelled Lyon silk weaver, insisted that his fellow workers were 'very revolutionary, but only up to the point where it came to taking action'.[402] The turn-out for elections, attendance at public meetings on such subjects as *Salariat et privilège*, *Socialisme et pauvreté* or *Affranchissement du travail* in working-class Belleville were certainly indicators of a widespread, even if intermittent, interest in political questions, intensified from 1868 by the sense of a regime in crisis. However, it took time for republican ideas to spread and for militants to overcome indifference and fear. The extreme left generally lacked the resources necessary to establish newspapers and publicise its cause. As the arrests in May 1870 of members of the International made clear, workers could never be sure that the regime would not revert to repression. The presence of police at public meetings, taking the names of those present, was not exactly reassuring. In spite of the excitement generated in meetings, by appeals to the *buveurs de sang* of 1793 and the heroes of June 1848, the wave of arrests and the determined military response to the construction of barricades in Paris on 10 May in the rue St Maur and around the Château d'Eau, appears to have persuaded many workers and socialist militants of the dangers of taking to the streets.[403]

---

[397] Ponsot, *Grèves*, p. 38.   [398] Hanagan, *Nascent Proletarians*, p. 196.
[399] PG Bordeaux, 12 Jan. 1870, AN BB30/390.   [400] 28 Jan. 1870, AN BB30/390.
[401] Dalotel et al., *Aux origines*, pp. 39–40.   [402] Traugott, *The French Worker*, p. 300.
[403] Price, *Second Empire*, p. 388.

Moreover, respected militants like Malon continued to warn against impatience.[404] Addressing the Lyon section of the International, Albert Richard pointed out that 'the partisans of an immediate revolution tell us that this revolution will carry socialism in its wake. But that of 1848 also carried socialism in its wake, and because it was simply political, when socialism wanted to reveal itself, it was crushed. This was a lesson which should not be forgotten.' It was necessary to organise, propagandise and wait.[405] Richard also took up the suggestion of other speakers at public meetings, that workers should practise electoral abstention, in order to avoid any sort of engagement with the regime. This met with incomprehension, however.[406]

The vast majority of workers preferred to support, or at least vote for, moderate republicans, who clearly enjoyed a much greater chance of electoral success than the candidates of the extreme left. The repressive measures taken by the regime in 1869/70 had shattered dreams of a peaceful transition to socialism, and once again encouraged a tactical alliance with bourgeois republicans.[407] At Aubry's adoption meeting in Elbeuf in May 1869, other workers complained that his candidature was simply divisive.[408] They were influenced by the *Progrès de Rouen*, which denounced the very notion of a worker candidature, asking its readers to remember that

outside the workshop they are above all citizens, they must value and protect this civic dignity which they owe to the two Revolutions of 1789 and 1848 . . . In their eyes there is not a workers' democracy and a *bourgeois* democracy, there is only one democracy, generously pursuing since 1789, in spite of all the reactions, the solution of the social problem, the promotion of the humble through education, and the improvement of the material conditions of the labouring classes.[409]

A petition signed by 350 workers asking Aubry to desist and to stop damaging the democratic cause accompanied this editorial.[410] Most republican candidates paid at least lip-service to the ideals of social reform. For as long as the primary objective was to overthrow the regime, for many workers the logical course of action appeared to be to support these bourgeois republicans. In a letter to the Lyon activist Richard in January 1870, Benoît Malon insisted that abstention by socialists in the face of the 'inevitable' advance of the revolution, would be to 'abandon the movement to the control of those who are purely politicians'. He had decided to throw himself 'without

[404] Dalotel, Faure, and Freiermuth, *Aux origines*, p. 350.
[405] Quoted Boivin, *Mouvement ouvrier*, I, pp. 364–5.   [406] Bayard, Cayez, *Histoire de Lyon*, II, p. 295.
[407] See defence speech written by Benoît Malon and delivered by Varlin, in E. Dolléans and G. Dehove, *Histoire du travail* (Paris 1946), I, pp. 317–18.
[408] Boivin, *Mouvement ouvrier*, I, p. 292.   [409] Quoted ibid. p. 292.   [410] Ibid. p. 307, note 53.

reserve into the republican agitation', and whilst recognising that the impact of 'our feeble support' would be limited, at least hoped to influence the course of the revolution.[411] Once the republic had been established, meaningful social reform would become possible. In the meantime republican unity was essential.

CONCLUSION

In search of mass support and faced with the apparent enthusiasm of the rural population for the regime, inevitably republican politicians had looked to the growing urban working class.[412] Albert Thomas, in his contributions to Jaurès' *Histoire socialiste* and the *Cambridge Modern History* emphasised the role of workers and their growing class-consciousness in the rise of an apparently irresistible opposition to the Second Empire.[413] The reality was much more complicated, the working class far more heterogeneous, and the regime much stronger than Thomas believed. Substantial numbers of workers positively chose to support conservative and particularly Bonapartist electoral candidates. Out of a sense of cultural and social inferiority, in short, of powerlessness, others felt that they had little choice but to follow the lead of those with status and power, aware as they were of their subordination to the State and to their employers.

Nevertheless, workers were more likely than members of other social groups to vote for republican electoral candidates. There was, however, no single republican party, no single political discourse. Republicans disagreed on both ends and the means of achieving them. Furthermore, there was considerable distrust and frequent tension between a republican leadership, which in practice excluded workers, and those they sought to mobilise. Geographical distinctions were also important. Although increasingly influenced by developments in Paris, the issues on which political militants focused their attentions, and the strategies they followed varied according to the social structure, cultural traditions and history of various discrete communities.

The heterogeneity of the workers' experience, the complex nature of social identity, and the alternative forms of political allegiance are clearly evident. Most workers came to share the democratic and egalitarian ideals voiced by bourgeois republicans, particularly those who like Gambetta in Paris or Bianchi in Lille emphasised their Jacobin antecedents. Although

[411] Printed in annex to Rougerie, 'La première Internationale', p. 183.
[412] Point made by e.g. PG Metz, 7 Nov. 1852, AN BB30/380.
[413] See also S. Campbell, *The Second Empire Re-visited* (London 1978), pp. 130–4.

many were probably attracted by the vague, 'sentimental', appeals of social-ism,[414] a substantial proportion accepted the advice of such eminent mod-erate republicans as Simon and Picard to reject socialism as utopian, and avoid wasting their votes. Frequently, in the absence of socialist candi-dates, they would have had no choice anyway but to voice their opposition to the regime by supporting moderate or 'radical' bourgeois republicans. Well-educated politicians, with substantial financial backing and organi-sational experience, and enjoying the support of electoral committees and newspapers, were invariably better able to publicise their candidatures and programmes.

Over time, 'a shifting national political opportunity structure'[415] had increased the scale and intensity of political activity. In these circumstances it seems clear that everyday experience, combined with politics and the demands it encapsulated, stimulated the development of a greater social awareness. By 1870, although regime liberalisation does appear to have had an integrative effect, stimulating a shift towards electoral activity and away from revolutionary objectives, the repressive origins of the regime and its identification with the 'exploiting' classes and a reactionary Church, made it difficult for workers, especially in the excited hot-house atmosphere prevailing in Paris, to continue to credit the Emperor with a genuine desire to improve their welfare. In these circumstances it was republican ideologies which appeared to offer a coherent explanation of current circumstances and the greatest hope for a better future. Thus, and in spite of the efforts of revolutionary militants, working-class political aspirations continued to be influenced by a republican tradition overwhelmingly defined by middle-class politicians. In this respect republicanism remained an obstacle to the development of a 'class-specific identity'.[416]

---

[414] Pierrard, *Vie ouvrière*, p. 503.
[415] Aminzade, *Ballots and Barricades*, p. 53.
[416] D. Harvey, *Constructing Class and Nationality in Alsace, 1830–1945* (DeKalb, Ill. 2001), p. 13; see also Price, *Second Empire*, conclusion to part III.

Conclusion

In the decades after 1815 political competition was largely restricted to a small elite which employed constitutional and legal means to safeguard its particular interests both against the state and the disenfranchised masses. When disorder threatened it was possible to justify the brutal deployment of military force. Subsequently, the rapid emergence of an urban-industrial society, together with renewed revolution in 1830, and particularly 1848, provided reminders of the fragility of the socio-political system and caused intense social fear. With the introduction of manhood suffrage and extension of democratic liberties and aspirations, the Second Republic encouraged a substantial expansion and intensification of political competition. In this situation most members of the social elite, at least temporarily, and irrespective of previous political allegiances, would be prepared to welcome the installation of a dictator capable of safeguarding 'Christian civilisation'.

The development of the political system and evolution of political opportunity structures have previously been considered in my *The French Second Empire: An Anatomy of Political Power*. This book has attempted to chart an alternative course. The primary objective has been to study the emergence of political culture(s), the diverse beliefs and attitudes concerning citizenship and political processes, within a society undergoing rapid institutional and social change. This has required analysis of the values and behaviour of individuals and interest groups. The political scientist Lucien Pye once wrote that 'the notion of political culture assumes that the attitudes, sentiments and cognitions that inform and govern political behaviour in any society are not just random congeries but represent coherent patterns which fit together and are mutually reinforcing'.[1] Perhaps in reaction against the essential neatness of this formulation, and in an effort to avoid causal

---

[1] 'Introduction: Political culture and political development' to L. Pye and S. Verba (eds.), *Political Culture and Political Development* (Princeton, N.J. 1965), p. 7.

determinism, political scientists have also come to insist on the existence, in any society, of diverse political sub-cultures, and on the potential for rapid transformation in response to such factors as institutional change, economic fluctuations, or the international situation.[2] Nevertheless, in their persistent and over-simplistic model building, they have still tended to neglect mass political culture. The analytical difficulties posed by a host of generally neglected causal variables become all the more evident once this omission is rectified.

Political engagement, or indeed indifference, is explicable only once it is contextualised (as fully as possible), that is, when social status; culture – in the widest sense of the word; and social relationships are related to political opportunity. It is also vitally important to identify diversity within, as well as between, social groups, to emphasise the importance of shared, in addition to conflictual interests, and to recognise the degree of consensus imposed upon individuals through membership of discrete communities.

However, incorporating diversity in a meaningful manner depends on the identification of groups which enjoyed some degree of coherence on the basis of everyday experiences, shared problems, and common values. The 'classes' analysed here are much more than categories constructed by historians as a means of imposing order on, and making sense of, the confused evidence left behind by the historical actors. Indeed, they would have been recognised by contemporary observers. Nonetheless, there remains an inescapable risk that the explanatory process has imposed an excessive degree of regularity, coherence, and rationality on social relationships and political behaviour, concerning which we remain, in spite of considerable effort, singularly ill informed.

One response on the part of the social and political elites to the tensions unleashed by democracy in 1848 was to turn towards counter-revolutionary authoritarianism. Severe restrictions on political activity were combined with police repression of the threat from the left. In close alliance with the Roman Catholic Church, considerable efforts were also made to employ the growing network of schools to inculcate a conservative-clerical ideology in the younger generations. Through such traditional means as the public festivities celebrating the end of victorious wars, or celebrations of the birthday of the Emperor, as well as the rapidly developing primary education system and mass media, the regime sought to construct a favourable consensus. Moreover, the Bonapartist State, basing itself on

---

[2] See e.g. H. Eckstein, 'A culturalist theory of political change', *American Political Science Review* 1988, p. 790; G. Almond, *A Divided Discipline: Schools and Sects in Political Science* (New York 1990), p. 153.

popular sovereignty, claimed to be devoted to the interests of the masses. The retention of a manipulative system of controlled democracy as a source of regime legitimacy, however, helped to establish democratic habits and a growing determination on the part of voters to influence the choice of candidates and indirectly of policies. Thus, an alternative process of democratic re-emergence would also develop, particularly once a substantial part of the social elite had begun to recover from its fear of revolution and develop aspirations to restore its own political power and to restrain that of the dictator.

The social and political elite which had played a crucial permissive, but also collaborative role in the emergence of dictatorship, and which provided the key personnel of the authoritarian state would, in changed circumstances, press for liberalisation. This 'critical decision stems initially not from a shift in fundamental values but from strategic decisions – altered perceptions of risk'.[3] Furthermore, it was based on the assumption that a mass electorate could be controlled and used to support elite-defined objectives. Thus political liberalisation developed as an essentially elite-led process, although, in some crucial respects, its course was determined by the willingness of the Emperor and his advisors to adapt the political opportunity structure in ways which made it less risky for political activists to criticise and even challenge authority. This encouraged the (re-)politicisation and involvement of previously largely excluded groups.

The central values of an elite political culture and especially 'liberty' and the rule of law, presented in a universalistic language, had wide appeal. Furthermore, regime liberalisation encouraged the development of political competition and increased participation. It provided an opportunity for the *nouvelles couches sociales* to mount an increasingly effective challenge to established elites. It enhanced the process of political socialisation. By the late 1860s popular commitment to democratic procedures had been reinforced and pressure was accumulating in favour of a further extension of political freedom. A more sustained politicisation was developing partly as a result of habitual participation in elections, partly from a belief that voting involved engagement in meaningful political activity, which might impact on governmental decisions on such matters as taxation, conscription, road and rail construction, or on school and church building, all matters of import within communities or even individual life strategies. In effect, there was a growing determination to assess regime performance and to

[3] L. Diamond, 'Introduction' to *Political Culture and Democracy in Developing Countries* (London 1994), p. 3.

influence the actions of the State-Provider, which had emerged during the Second Empire. Whether this greater involvement entailed militancy, occasional commitment, or general indifference perhaps combined with habitual voting, the active participation of the vast majority of qualified voters strongly suggests the emergence of a political imperative.

However, the renewal of democracy was accompanied by continued efforts to retain control on the part both of representatives of the State and wider social elites. The former continued to represent themselves as serving the 'general interest'. Thus, it was affirmed that the legal and policing systems offered protection to every citizen, whilst the army secured the nation against external threats. The social order blessed by God, together with the Emperor, the symbol of national unity and patriotic endeavour, were glorified in countless churches and schoolrooms throughout France. Additionally, the construction of a shared sense of identity was the result of the vilification of a threatening internal or external *other* – unbelievers, socialists, Jews, and Prussians. More consistently than its predecessors the Second Empire also claimed credit for prosperity.

Outcomes varied. In general terms, and ignoring countless localised differences, satisfaction with the regime was most clearly evident in Normandy, the Centre, and most of the Massif Central where pre-occupation with material and local interests was uppermost; and to a lesser degree in the north and Brittany where conservative elites retained mass support. In contrast in Paris and other major cities, in the east and south east, political pluralism and competition were more evident. The regime was invariably blamed for economic depression. Taxation and conscription were disliked almost universally. Repression, employed to still the voices of critics could easily be counter-productive, particularly where it appeared designed to support the interests of the 'rich' against those of other social groups. The social elite, although increasingly challenged, still possessed the inestimable advantages of wealth and the power derived from a complex of interlocking social roles – landowner, employer, dispenser of 'advice' and charity – and of pre-eminence within a self-centred system of cultural values. Its leading figures continued to affirm their leadership responsibilities within the evolving administrative and political systems. Their objective was to sustain their social dominance, employing tactics which favoured a one-sided process of mutual accommodation with other social groups. This is to stress the importance of conservative as well as democratic patronage in encouraging political participation.

However, the dangers implicit in the process would once again become apparent to the elites in the late 1860s. As mass democratisation gathered pace, social fear once again mounted. The Union libérale turned back towards the Party of Order. With the regime transformed into a constitutional monarchy, and re-legitimised by the 1870 plebiscite, and with widespread popular support it was again possible to effectively marginalise and, if necessary, terrorise those who chose to remain outside the renewed consensus. War, defeat, and revolution would subsequently intensify this social fear and justify, in the closing stages of the Paris Commune, the renewed slaughter of dissidents. The crisis passed; however, there would be every incentive for political activists, supported by most of the population, to construct a political system which, like that of the liberal Empire, held out the promise of 'progress' and prosperity, of 'liberty' and social order. The legitimacy of the Third Republic, just like that of the Second Empire, was to be firmly based on the practice of 'universal suffrage'.

Select bibliography

UNPUBLISHED PRIMARY SOURCES

I. ARCHIVES NATIONALES

Series BB: Justice

BB II 1118 – Results of plebiscite of 21–22 December 1851
BB18: Correspondance générale
BB18: 1460–4 Diverse disorders
    1465 Insurrection de juin 1848: répercussions dans les départements
    1469 Dossier sur les clubs
    1471–3 Dossiers sur les sociétés secrètes
    1475–9 Dossiers concerning strikes and workers' organisations
    Information on popular protest: 1186, 1188–93, 1319–20, 1436, 1438, 1440, 1444,
        1447–8, 1448B, 1449, 1451–2, 1454, 1460–1, 1475–9, 1484, 1517, 1537, 1545, 1553,
        1558, 1563, 1581, 1618, 1633, 1639, 1644, 1707, 1715, 1728, 1754A, 1757, 1765–7,
        1765, 1769, 1772, 1785
    1717 Municipal elections 1865
BB19: 37–42 Procureurs-généraux: reports on subsistence disorders, 1846–7
BB30: Rapports des procureurs généraux
    332–5 Affaires politiques: correspondance 1848–52
    358–61 Troubles postérieurs à la Révolution de février 1848: correspondance et
    rapports
    366 Supplementary reports
    369–90 General reports, 1849–70
    389–402 Commissions mixtes 1851
    391–4 Affaires politiques November 1850–November 1851
    395–7 Evénements de décembre 1851–janvier 1852
    403–4, 409–18 Political situation 1852
    405 Seditious literature
    406–10 Political situation 1852–4
    411–12 Offenses contre l'Empereur
    413–14, 418, 421, 481 Secret societies
    415–17 Political situation 1855–6
    419, 440–1 Orsini affair

420 Political situation 1857–8
422, 442, 444, 450–1 Reactions to war 1859
423 Official response to Ténot's publications on *coup d'état*
426–31 Elections
432–3 Subsistence disorders 1853–6
434–5 False news 1853–6
455 Opposition press 1870

Series C: Assemblée nationale

C930, 934–42 Enquiry into the events of May and June 1848: evidence
C943–69 Enquête sur le travail agricole et industriel. Décret du 25 mai 1848
C1157–61 Agricultural enquiry 1870
C2854 Complaints from chambers of commerce about railway companies
C3078–81 Public assistance

Series F7: Administration

F1a 10: Proclamations et actes publics des préfets à l'occasion des événements de
décembre 1851 et janvier 1852
F1cIII: Correspondance des préfets

Police générale

F7: Rapports et correspondance reçus par le ministère de l'Intérieur
3909–4210: Correspondance des préfets
12654–61 Dépêches des préfets 1870
12710–13 Correspondence concerning individuals condemned following the
events of December 1851

F8: Public hygiene

210–11

F11: Subsistence

2680–4, 2689 Correspondence with cantonal statistical commissions, 1853–65
2694 Subsistence 1867
2734 Enquête agricole 1866
2752 Trade in cereals and flour
2755–6 Subsistences, 1850–1
2758 ibid. 1846–7
2760–6, 2780, 2786, 2790 Bread prices and effects of ending restrictions on bakers,
1863
2801–2 Provisioning of Paris

F12: Commerce and industry

2370–4 Wages, living standards
2337–8, 2446, 7600 Economic effects of 1848 Revolution
2481–2 Commission des douanes, treaty of commerce
2483 Assessments of competitiveness of French industry
2495–6 Economic situation 1849–51
2515 Note sur les effets du Traité de commerce
2522A Price of grain
2533 Economic situation 1853
2715B Chamber of commerce reports
3109–21 Reports of worker delegates to Exposition universelle 1867
4651–2 Strikes: Second Empire
4476C Industrial situation 1849–50
4841 Customs tariffs
4854 Petitions concerning tariffs
6407 Effects of 1860 commercial treaty

F17: Education

2649 Rapports trimestriels de l'état politique, moral et religieux, 1858–9
9109–14 Preparation and implementation of 1833 and 1850 laws
9146 Popular literature
9279–80, 9312–13, 9373–4 Reports of academic rectors and school inspectors
10758–85 Teachers' *mémoires* on needs of primary education in rural communes

F18: Press

294 Situation de la presse départementale 1868
297 Inspection générale de l'imprimerie, de la librairie et du colportage

F20

714 Prix et salaires

F70

422 Voyages de l'Empereur

O

Maison de l'Empereur
297, 305 Presse parisienne

Series AB

AB XIX 173–5 Papers confiscated from the Tuileries Palace in 1870

687–9 Collection Duménil: popular newspapers, almanacs, etc.
1707–8 Telegrams 18–20 June 1870
3321 Diverse, including letters from Blanc, Thiers, Veuillot, etc.

Series AD

AD XIX S 1–7 Paris Prefecture of Police: administration; subsistence 1858–60
AD XIX H 48 Rapport à S. M. l'Empereur sur l'état de l'enseignement primaire . . . 1863

Series AP (Private papers)

44 AP 1 Persigny
43 AP Faucher
45 AP 2–3, 6–11, 23–4 Rouher
116 AP 1 Maurin
271 AP 4–5 Barrot
400 AP 41–4, 54, 67, 69, 93, 129, 139, 144, 150 Bonaparte family
639 AP 1 Crémieux

Series AQ

6 AQ 2, 5, 20 Maurin papers re postal services

2. ARCHIVES DE LA PRÉFECTURE DE POLICE

Aa 427–9 Evénements divers 1848
    432 Workers' associations and secret societies
    433 Events of December 1851
    434 Attentats et complots Second Empire

3. ARCHIVES DU SERVICE HISTORIQUE DE L'ARMÉE DE TERRE

E5 153–9 Correspondance générale, 1846–7
F1: Correspondance militaire générale: République de 1848
    9 Correspondance générale 16–30 juin 1848
    16–17 Rapports des 5 jours (1848–9)
    51–4 Correspondance générale 2 December 1851–January 1852
G8: Justice militaire
    1–176 Correspondance générale, 1852–70
    194–6 Records of the military and mixed commissions established in December 1851
MR 2151 Dispositions à prendre en cas d'émeutes et de troubles en Paris et en provinces
    2259 Reconnaissance. Mémoires topographiques (Paris region)

4. BIBLIOTHÈQUE NATIONALE

n.a.f. 23064–6 Persigny papers
n.a.f. 20617–19 Thiers papers
Vp 9237f Chamber of Commerce requests for improved communications
Vp 9270f ibid. re customs tariffs

5. NATIONAL LIBRARY OF WALES, ABERYSTWYTH

Nassau William Senior papers A36, 39–40; C75, 83–4, 132, 214, 249, 260, 267, 332–3, 256, 367, 445, 450–1, 479, 707, 745, 817

6. UNIVERSITY OF WALES, BANGOR

Nassau William Senior papers

PUBLISHED PRIMARY SOURCES

(Place of publication Paris unless otherwise stated)

I. OFFICIAL PUBLICATIONS, COLLECTIONS OF DOCUMENTS

Assemblée nationale, *Enquête parlementaire sur le régime économique*, 2 vols. 1870
   Enquête parlementaire sur l'insurrection du 18 mars 1871, Versailles 1872
   Enquête parlementaire sur les actes du Gouvernement de la Défense nationale, 7 vols. 1876
   Rapport de la commission d'enquête sur l'insurrection qui a éclaté dans la journée du 23 juin et sur les événements du 15 mai, 2 vols. 1848
Chambre de Commerce de Paris, *Statistique de l'industrie à Paris . . . pour les années 1847–48*, 1851
   Statistique de l'industrie à Paris . . . pour l'année 1860, 1864
Chesseneau, G. (ed.), *La Commission extra-parlementaire de 1849*, Orléans 1937
Conseil d'Etat, *Enquête sur l'application des tarifs des chemins de fer*, 1850
   Enquête sur la boulangerie du département de la Seine . . ., 1859
   Enquête sur la révision de la législation des céréales, 3 vols. 1859
Conseil supérieur de l'agriculture, du commerce et de l'industrie, *Enquête sur le traité de commerce avec l'Angleterre, industrie textile, coton*, vol. I, 1870
Cour impériale de Paris, *Deuxième procès des ouvriers typographes en Première instance et en appel juillet 1862*, 1862
   Affaire du Comité électoral dite des Treize. Réquisitoire et réplique de M. le Procureur Général Marnas, 1864
   Chambre des Appels correctionnels. Audience du 9 mai 1867, 1867
   Les procès de presse depuis la loi du 11 mai 1868 jusqu'à 1 janvier 1869, 1869
Documents pour servir à l'histoire du Second Empire: circulaires, rapports, notes et instructions confidentielles, 1872
Ministère de l'Agriculture, du Commerce et des Travaux Publics, *Enquête. Traité de commerce avec l'Angleterre*. 8 vols. 1860

Documents statistiques et administratifs concernant l'épidémie de choléra de 1854 . . .,
    1862
Enquête sur l'exploitation et la construction des chemins de fer, 1863
Rapport à l'Empereur sur la boulangerie, 1864
Enquête agricole, 37 vols. 1867–72
Ministère de l'agriculture, du commerce et des travaux publics, Bureau des subsis-
    tances, *Récoltes des céréales et des pommes de terre de 1815 à 1876*, 1878
Ministère de l'agriculture, du commerce et des travaux publics, Commission de
    l'enseignement professionnel, *Enquête*, 1, 1864
Ministère de l'Instruction Publique, *État de l'instruction primaire en 1864 après les
    rapports des Inspecteurs d'Académie*, 2 vols. 1866
Procès-verbaux du Gouvernement provisoire et de la Commission du pouvoir exécutif,
    1950
Papiers et correspondance de la famille impériale, 2 vols. 1871
Papiers sauvés des Tuileries, ed. R. Holt, 1871
Papiers secrets et correspondance du Second Empire, ed. A. Poulet-Malassis, 1873 (2nd
    edn)
*Pièces saisies aux archives de la police politique de Lyon. Publiée par ordre du Conseil
    municipal*, Lyon 1870
Préfecture de Police, *Des moyens de prévenir les fluctuations excessives du prix des blés
    en France*, 1853
Commission des subsistances. Taxe du pain. Rapport . . . , 1855
Statistique générale de la France, *Statistique de l'assistance publique de 1842 à 1853*,
    Strasbourg 1858
Salaires et coût de l'existence à diverses époques, jusqu'en 1910, 1911
Ville de Paris, Commission des logements insalubres, *Rapport général . . .*, 1866
Watteville, Baron de, *Rapport à son excellence le Ministre de l'Intérieur sur
    l'administration des bureaux de bienfaisance et sur la situation du paupérisme en
    France*, 1854

2. NEWSPAPERS AND PERIODICALS

*L'Ami du peuple, Annales de l'agriculture française, Annales des ponts et chaussées,
    Bulletin de la Société Franklin, Le Constitutionnel, La Gazette de France, La
    Gazette des Tribunaux, Journal d'agriculture pratique, Journal des chemins de fer,
    Journal des Economistes, La Liberté (Rouen), Moniteur industriel, La Mutualité,
    Le National, Le Peuple, La Presse, La Réforme, Le Représentant du Peuple,
    La Révolution démocratique et sociale, La Revue des Deux Mondes, Le Siècle,
    L'Union, L'Univers, La Voix du Peuple, La Vraie République*

3. CONTEMPORARY BOOKS AND PAMPHLETS

(Place of publication Paris unless otherwise stated)
Albiot, J., *Les campagnes électorales 1851–69*, 1869
Allain-Targé, H., *La république sous l'Empire. Lettres 1867–70*, 1939

Anon., *L'Armée et le socialisme, simples réflexions sur la question du moment, par un paysan qui a été soldat*, 1849

Le Socialisme c'est la famine, Bordeaux 1849

La solution donnée par le Président de la République aux sinistres complications qui pressaient la France avant le 2 décembre 1851, peut-elle être considérée comme définitive?, 1852

Vive l'Empire, 1852

Des moyens de prévenir les fluctuations excessives du prix des blés en France, 1853

De l'enquête agricole par un médecin de campagne, Châteauroux 1866

De la nécessité d'un Nouveau coup d'état avant le couronnement de l'édifice, 1869

Etat de l'ignorance dans le département de la Loire, 1870

Circulaire en faveur du plébiscite, Rive-de-Gier 1870

Appel aux électeurs de la 3e circonscription de l'Ain, Lyon 1870

Apponyi, R., *De la révolution au coup d'état*, Geneva 1948

Arago, E., *Les postes en 1848*, 1867

Arago, E. et al., *Manifeste de la gauche*, 1870

Arnaud, F., *La révolution de 1869*, 1869

Audiganne, A., *Les populations ouvrières et les industries de la France dans le mouvement social du 19e siècle*, 2 vols. 1854

'L'industrie française depuis la révolution de février', *Revue des deux mondes* 2, 1849

'B'., *Notes et réflexions pour M. le Comte de Chambord*, 1870

Barrot, O., *Mémoires posthumes*, II, IV, 1875–6

Bastelica, A., *Avertissement aux travailleurs électeurs de Marseille. Le suffrage universel et la révolution*, Marseille 1869

Baudry, E., *Le paysan aux élections de 1869*, 1869

Benoist, J., *Confessions d'un prolétaire*, 1968

Benoist, M. de, *Utopies d'un paysan*, Clermont-Ferrand 1867

Bergier, J., *Le journal d'un bourgeois de Lyon en 1848*, n.d.

Bersot, E., *La presse dans les départements*, 1867

Blanc, L., *Les prochaines élections en France*, London 1857

Blanc, L. et al., *Lettres et protestations sur l'amnistie du 17 août 1859*, Lausanne 1859

Blanqui, A., 'Les populations rurales de la France en 1850', *Annales provençales d'agriculture* 1851

Bonnet, A., *Enquête sur la situation et les besoins de l'agriculture*, Dijon 1867

Bonsens, M., *Dialogues électoraux. L'ouvrier, le bourgeois, le paysan*, 1869

Boucher de Perthes, J., *Misère, émeute, choléra*, Abbeville 1849

Brame, J., *De l'émigration des campagnes*, Lille 1859

Bugeaud, Marshal, *Veillées d'une chaumière de la Vendée*, Lyon 1849

Camp, M. du, *Souvenirs d'un demi-siècle*, 2 vols. 1949

Carcy, F. de, *Mémoires*, Metz 1979

Castel, M., *Les grèves et l'assassinat de M. Watrin*, Saint-Etienne 1866

Castellane, Maréchal de, *Journal*, IV, V, 1897

Chaline, J.-P. (ed.), *Deux bourgeois en leur temps: documents sur la société rouennaise du 19e siècle*, Rouen 1977

Chaudey, G., *L'Empire parlementaire est-il possible?*, 1870

Chevalier, M., *Des forces alimentaires des états et des devoirs du gouvernement dans la crise actuelle*, 1847

    Examen du système commercial connu sous le nom de régime protecteur, 1852

Cheysson, E., *Le Creusot, conditions matérielles, intellectuelles et morales de la population, institutions et relations sociales*, 1869

Claretie, J., *La volonté du peuple*, 1869

Cochin, A., *Paris, sa population, son industrie*, 1864

Combes, A. and Combes, H., *Les paysans français*, 1855

Comité électoral de la rue de Poitiers, *Simples réflexions morales et politiques*, 1849

Comité des houillères, *Pétitions au Sénat*, Arras 1863

Comité des houillères du Nord et du Pas-de-Calais, *Réponse au questionnaire adressé aux compagnies houillères par la commission d'enquête parlementaire sur le régime économique*, Douai 1870

Commissaire, S., *Mémoires et souvenirs*, 2 vols. Lyon 1888

Commune révolutionnaire . . . , *Lettre au Peuple*, London 1852

Cottin, P., *De l'enseignement primaire dans les campagnes et de son influence sur la vie politique des populations*, 1868

Cyprien de Bellisses, M., *Le SUFFRAGE UNIVERSEL dans le département de l'Ariège*, 1869

Darimon, A., *Histoire du second empire*, 6 vols. 1884–9

Déguignet, J.-M., *Mémoires d'un paysan bas-breton 1834–1905*, Ar Releg-Kerhuon 1999

Deseilligny, J.-P., *De l'influence de l'éducation sur la moralité et le bien-être des classes laborieuses*, 1868

Deslignières, H., *Entretiens politiques du village. Le Second Empire devant l'opinion publique et le suffrage universel*, 1869

Duchêne, G., *L'Empire industriel. Histoire critique des concessions financières et industrielles du Second Empire*, 1869

Dumay, J., *Mémoires d'un militant ouvrier du Creusot (1841–1905)*, Grenoble 1976

Dumon, A., *Révélations sur le plébiscite et le comité central*, 1870

Dupanloup, Mgr, *L'athéisme et le péril social*, 1866

Dupont, P., Sue, E., and Schoelcher, V., *Le républicain des campagnes*, 1849

Duruy, V., *Notes et souvenirs*, 2 vols. 1901

Duvivier, J.-H., *L'Empire en province*, 1861

EDHIS, *Les républicains sous le Second Empire*, n.d. – major collection of pamphlets, manifestos, etc.

Falloux, Comte de, *Memoirs*, 2 vols. London 1888

Faucher, L., *Correspondance*, 2 vols. 1867

Ferry, J., *La lutte électorale en 1863*, 1863

    Discours et opinions, vol. I, 1893

Filippi de Fabj, F., *L'opposition dans la Seine. Aux ouvriers de Paris*, 1869

Flaubert, G., *Correspondance*, IV: *Janvier 1869–décembre 1875*, 1998

Fortoul, H., *Journal*, 2 vols., ed. G. Massa-Gille, Geneva 1989

Franqueville, Comte de, *Souvenirs intimes de la vie de mon père*, 1878

Freycinet, C. de, *Souvenirs 1848–78*, 1912

Gambetta, L. M. and Delescluze, L. C., *Le comité des députés de la Gauche et des délégués de la presse démocratique A L'ARMÉE*, 1870

Garnier, J., *Le droit au travail à l'Assemblée nationale, recueil complet de tous les discours prononcés dans cette mémorable discussion*, 1848

Gastineau, B., *La vie politique et le journalisme en province*, 1869

Gellion-Danglar, E., *Ce qu'on dit au village*, 1869

Goncourt, E. and Goncourt, J., *Journal*, II *1864–78*, 1956

Goulhot de Saint-Germain, M. de, *Etudes sur les campagnes*, 1859

Gréard, O., *L'enseignement primaire à Paris et dans le département de la Seine de 1867 à 1877*, 1878

Guéronnière, Comte A. de la, *Enquête parlementaire. La voix de la France*, 1869

Guichard, V., 'Statistique du morcellement de la propriété dans le département de l'Yonne', *Bulletin de la Société des sciences historiques et naturelles de l'Yonne*, 1862

Guillaumin, E., *La vie d'un simple. Mémoires d'un métayer*, 1904

Guiral, P. and Brunon, R. (eds.), *Aspects de la vie politique et militaire en France au milieu du 19e siècle à travers la correspondance reçue par le Maréchal Pelissier (1828–64)*, 1968

Guizot, F., *Mémoires pour servir à l'histoire de mon temps*, VIII, 1867
  Lettres à sa fille Henriette, 1836–74, 2002

Haussmann, G. E. *Mémoires*, 3 vols. 1890–3

Hugo, V., *Napoleon the Little*, London 1852

Husson, A., *Les consommations de Paris*, 1856

Instruction pastorale de Mgr. l'Evêque d'Amiens sur le Pouvoir à l'occasion du rétablissement de l'Empire, Amiens 1853

Jaegler, E. and Bigaud, N., *Notice biographique. Principaux actes et pensées de SM. l'Empereur Napoléon III*, 1853

Kahan-Rabecq, M.-M., *L'Alsace économique et sociale sous le règne de Louis-Philippe*, 1939

Lacombe, C. de, *Les préfets et les maires*, 1869

Laurent de Villedeuil, P., *Oeuvres de Emile et Isaac Pereire*, 4 vols. 1919–20

Laurier, C., *Simple entretien avec un préfet de l'Empire*, 1867

Lavergne, L. de, *L'agriculture et la population*, 1865

Lavollée, C., 'Statistique industrielle de Paris', *Revue des Deux Mondes* 1865

Lecanu, A., *La révolution par le suffrage universel*, 1869

Lecouteux, E., *L'agriculture et les élections de 1863*, 1863

Lejean, C. and Alexandre, C., *Correspondance (1846–69). Deux républicains bretons dans l'entourage de Lamartine et de Michelet*, 1993

Le Play, F., *La réforme sociale en France*, 1868

Lucas, A., *Les clubs et les clubistes*, 1851

Magen, H., *Histoire de la terreur bonapartiste*, Brussels 1852
  Le Pilori: listes par départements des proscripteurs, Brussels 1854

Magnitot, A. de, *De l'assistance et de l'extinction de la mendicité*, 1855

Malcaze, E., *Les agitateurs*, 1869

Manzut, *Le paysan socialiste*, 1869

Marqfoy, G., *De l'abaissement des tarifs des chemins de fer en France*, 1863

Martinelli, J., *Un mot sur la situation*, Bordeaux 1848

Maupas, M. de, *Mémoires sur le Second Empire*, 2 vols. 1884

Mérimée, P., *Correspondance générale* . . . I, II: *1850–55*, Toulouse 1947, 1953

Michelin, R. (ed.), *Les larmes d'or. La vie rurale en Bresse bourguignonne de Louis-Philippe à Napoléon III*, 2002

Michon, Abbé, *De la crise de l'Empire*, 1860

Mimerel, A., *Du paupérisme dans ses rapports avec l'industrie*, Lille n.d.

Modeste, V., *De la cherté des grains et des préjugés populaires*, 1862

Moilin, T., *La liquidation sociale*, 1869

Montigny, L., *Lettres à un électeur rural*, 1869

Mullois, Abbé, *Confiance! Il y aura du pain pour tous*, 1854

Nadaud, M., *Mémoires de Léonard*, 1948 and 1976

Nolat, C., *Physiologie de l'imprimerie*, 1856

Normanby, Lord, *Journal of the Year of Revolution*, 2 vols. London 1851

Ollivier, E., *L'Empire libéral*, 17 vols., 1895–1918

    Journal 1846–1869, 2 vols. ed. T. Zeldin and A. Troisier de Diaz, 1961

Ordinaire, E., *Des candidatures officielles et de leurs conséquences*, 1869

Persigny, Duc de, *Mémoires du duc de* . . . , 1896

Perdiguier, A., *Mémoires d'un compagnon*, 1964

Petitin, A. (Prefect Haute-Savoie), *Discussion de politique démocratique et mélanges 1834–61*, 1862

Peut, H., *Des chemins de fer et des tarifs différentiels*, 1858

Pichat, O., *L'Empereur devant le peuple*, 1870

Pinet, A., *L'enseignement primaire en présence de l'enquête agricole*, 1873

Pompery, E. de, *La question sociale dans les réunions publiques. Revendication du prolétaire*, 1869

Poulot, D., *Le sublime ou le travailleur comme il est en 1870 et ce qu'il peut être*, 1980 reprint

Prévost-Paradol, L., *Du gouvernement parlementaire. Le décret du 24 novembre*, 1860

    La France nouvelle, 1868

Procès de sociétés secrètes. Etudiants et ouvriers, 1867

Proudhon, P.-J., *La révolution sociale démontrée par le coup d'état*, 1852

    Les confessions d'un révolutionnaire, 1929

Pyat, F. *et al.*, *Lettre à Marianne*, London 1856

Rémusat, C. de, *Mémoires de ma vie*, IV, V, 1962

Renouvier, C., *Manuel républicain de l'homme et du citoyen*, 1848

Réunion démocratique des représentants du Palais national, *Simples avis aux électeurs*, 1849

Réunion des journalistes conservateurs des départements, 7–10 octobre 1869. Hôtel du Louvre, Paris, *Déclaration*, 1869

Reybaud, L., *Le coton*, 1863

    Le fer et la houille, 1874

Rivière, A., *Les petites misères de la vie politique en Touraine*, Tours 1863

Robert, C. (secrétaire-général du Ministère de l'Instruction publique), *De l'igno-rance des populations ouvrières et rurales de la France et des causes qui tendent à la perpétuer*, Montbéliard 1862
  Les améliorations sociales du Second Empire, 1868
  La suppression des grèves par l'association aux bénéfices, 1870
Romieu, M., *Le spectre rouge de 1852*, Berlin 1851
Saint-Léger, V. *et al.*, *Discours prononcé . . . au meeting industriel de Lille. . .* , Lille 1869
Say, H., 'Misère ou charité', *Journal des Economistes*, 1847
Schmit, J., *Aux ouvriers: Du pain, du travail et la vérité*, Bordeaux n.d.
Sempé, J., *Grèves et grévistes*, 1870
Sections parisiens fédérés de l'Internationale et de la Chambre fédérale des sociétés ouvrières, *Manifeste antiplébiscitaire*, 1870
Senior, N. W., *Journals kept in France and Italy from 1848 to 1852*, 2 vols. London 1871
  Conversations with M. Thiers, M. Guizot and other Distinguished Persons during the Second Empire, 2 vols. London 1878
Sibour, Mgr, *Mandements, lettres et instructions pastorales . . .* , 1853
Simon, J., *La politique radicale*, 1868
Société fraternelle de solidarité et de crédit mutuel, *Procès des ouvriers tailleurs. Grève de mars–avril 1867. Association de plus de 20 personnes, non autorisée*, 1868
Society of Arts, *Reports of artisans selected by a committee appointed by the Council of the Society of Arts to visit the Paris Universal Exhibition*, London 1867
Talès, M., *L'Empire, c'est la souveraineté du peuple*, 1852
Tallon, E., *Les intérêts des campagnes*, 1869
Tardif, J.-A., *Le réveil de l'opinion. Antagonisme des idées fusionnistes, césariennes et radicales*, Marseille 1865
Tartaret, E. (ed.), *Exposition universelle de 1867. Commission ouvrière. Recueil des procès-verbaux des assemblées générales des délégués et des membres des bureaux électoraux*, 1868
Ténot, E., *Le suffrage universel et les paysans*, 1865
  Paris en décembre 1851: Etude historique sur le Coup d'Etat, 1868
  La province en décembre 1851, 1868
Thiers, A., *Discours parlementaires*, 1880
Thiers, A. and Dosne, E. S. M., *Correspondance 1841–65*, 1904
Thomas, E., *Histoire des Ateliers nationaux*, 1848
Tocqueville, A. de, *Oeuvres complètes*, VI(1), VII, VIII(2), VIII (3), IX, X, XI, XII, XIII, XIX, 1959f.
Tolain, H., *Quelques vérités sur les élections de Paris (31 mai 1863)*, 1863
Truquin, N., *Mémoires et aventures d'un prolétaire*, 1977
Turgan, V., *Les grandes usines*, VII, 1867
Valori, C. de, *La fusion et les partis*, 1849
Vée, M., *Considérations sur le décroissement graduel du paupérisme à Paris . . . et les causes des progrès moraux et économiques des classes ouvrières*, 1862
Vermorel, A., *Le parti socialiste*, 1870

Véron, L., *Mémoires d'un bourgeois de Paris*, v, 1856
Vitu, A., *Les réunions publiques à Paris, 1868–69*, 1869
  Les réunions électorales à Paris, 1869
Warmington, E., *Qu'est-ce que le Bonapartisme? Le salut de France*, 1852
Wolowski, M., *La liberté commerciale et les résultats du traité de commerce de 1860*, 1869

SECONDARY SOURCES

(Place of publication Paris, unless otherwise stated)
Agulhon, M., *Une ville ouvrière au temps du socialisme utopique. Toulon de 1815 à 1851*, 1970
  La République au village, 1970; *The Republic in the Village*, London 1982
  The Republican Experiment, 1848–52, Cambridge 1983
  (ed.), *Histoire de la France urbaine*, IV, 1983
  Le cercle dans la France bourgeoise, 1977
Agulhon, M. and Bodiguel, M. (eds.), *Les associations au village*, Le Paradou 1981
Agulhon, M., Désert, G., and Specklin, R., *Histoire de la France rurale*, III: *Apogée et crise de la civilisation paysanne 1789–1914*, 1976
Agulhon, M., *et al.*, *La politicisation des campagnes au 19e siècle*, Rome 2000
Amann, P., *Revolution and Mass Democracy; The Paris Club Movement in 1848*, Princeton, N.J. 1975
Aminzade, R., *Class, Politics and Early Industrial Capitalism. A Study of Mid-19th Century Toulouse*, Albany, N.Y. 1981
  Ballots and Barricades. Class Formation and Republican Politics in France, 1830–71, Princeton, N.J. 1993
Anceau, E., *Dictionnaire des députés du Second Empire*, Rennes 1999
  Les députés du Second Empire, 2000
Anderson, R., *Education in France, 1848–70*, Oxford 1975
Ansart, P., 'Des identités de métier à l'identité de classe, un devenir paradoxal?', *L'homme et la société* 1995
Aprile, S., 'Bourgeoise et républicaine: deux termes inconciliables?' in A. Corbin *et al.*, *Femmes dans la cité*
Ardaillou, P., *Les républicains du Havre au 19e siècle*, Rouen 1999
Armengaud, A., *Les populations de l'est-Aquitain au début de l'époque contemporaine (vers 1845–vers 1871)*, 1961
Baker, A., *Fraternity among the French Peasantry. Sociability and Voluntary Associations in the Loire Valley, 1815–1914*, Cambridge 1999
Barbie, T., 'Acculturation et dynamique sociale. L'exemple de la lecture au 19e siècle' in C. Charle (ed.), *Histoire sociale, histoire globale?*
Barbier, F., *Le patronat du Nord sous le Second Empire: une approche prosopographique*, Geneva 1989
  Finance et politique. La dynastie des Fould, 1991
Barral, P., *Les Perier dans l'Isère au 19e siècle d'après leur correspondance familiale*, 1964
  'Depuis quand les paysans se sentent-ils français?', *Ruralia* 1998

Béaur, G., 'Les catégories sociales à la campagne: repenser un instrument d'analyse', *Annales de Bretagne* 1999

Berenson, E., 'Politics and the French peasants', *Social History* 1987

Bergeron, L., *Les capitalistes en France (1780–1914)*, 1978.

Berlanstein, L., *The Working People of Paris, 1871–1914*, Baltimore, Md. 1985

Bernard, M., 'Les populations du Puy-de-Dôme face à la nouvelle république', *Cahiers d'histoire* 1998

Bernard, P., *Economie et sociologie de la Seine-et-Marne, 1850–1950*, 1953

Berstein, S. (ed.), *Les cultures politiques en France*, 1999

Berstein, S. and Winock, M. (eds.), *L'invention de la démocratie*, 1789–1914, 2002

Bianchi, S., 'Le phénomène électoral dans le sud de l'Ile-de-France sous la Seconde République', *Revue d'histoire du 19e siècle* 1998

Bleton-Ruget, A., 'Aux sources de l'agrarisme républicain: la propagande démocrate-socialiste et les campagnes (1848–51)', *Cahiers d'histoire* 1998

'1848 et l'introduction du suffrage universel: enjeux politiques et techniques électorales' in A. Bleton-Ruget and S. Wolikow (eds.), *Voter et élire à l'époque contemporaine*, Dijon 1999

Bluche, F. (ed.), *Le prince, le peuple et le droit. Autour des plébiscites de 1851 et 1852*, 2000

Boivin, M., *Le mouvement ouvrier dans la région de Rouen, 1851–76*, 2 vols. Rouen 1989

Boudon, J.-O., *Paris, capitale religieuse sous le second empire*, 2001

Bourgin, G., 'La législation ouvrière du Second Empire', *Revue des études napoléoniennes* 1913

Bourguinat, N., 'De la question frumentaire à l'idée d'une *économie morale* sous la Seconde République', *Cahiers d'histoire* 1998

Bourillon, F., 'Grands travaux et dynamisme urbain: Paris sous le Second Empire' in A. Faure, A. Plessis, and J.-C. Farcy (eds.), *La terre et la cité*, 1994

'Rénovation haussmannienne et ségrégation urbaine' in A. Fourcaut (ed.), *La ville divisée. Les ségrégations urbaines en question. France 18e–20e siècle*, Grâne 1996

Bouvier, J., 'Lyon la républicaine à la veille de la guerre de 1870', *1848* 1971

Bozon, P., *La vie rurale en Vivarais*, 1963

Brelot, C.-I., *La noblesse réinventée. Nobles de Franche-Comté de 1814 à 1870*, 2 vols. 1992

'Conflits et déclassement: la légitimité de l'histoire des élites en question', *Cahiers d'histoire* 2000

Burdy, J.-P., 'Paternalismes industriels. Les rapports sociaux dans le bassin de la Loire au 19e siècle' in S. Michaud (ed.), *L'Edification. Morales et cultures au 19e siècle*, 1993

Carel, H., 'Le département de la Haute-Saône de 1850 à 1914', Doc. ès lettres, Univ. de Paris-Sorbonne 1970

Caron, F., 'Essai d'analyse historique d'une psychologie du travail. Les mécaniciens et chauffeurs de locomotion du réseau du Nord de 1850 à 1910', *Le mouvement social* 1965

Carrière, B., 'Les premiers mécaniciens, des origines à 1848' in Association pour l'histoire des chemins de fer en France (eds.), *Les chemins de fer, l'espace et la société en France*, 1989

Caty, R., Richard, E., and Echinard, P. (eds.), *Les patrons du Second Empire*, v: *Marseille*, 1999

Cayez, P., *Crises et croissance de l'industrie lyonnaise, 1850–1900*, 1980

Chalaron, F., 'Bonapartisme et paysannerie dans le Puy-de-Dôme', *Revue de l'Auvergne* 1985

Chaline, J.-P., *Les bourgeois de Rouen: une élite urbaine au 19e siècle*, 1982

'Bourgeoisie' in J. Tulard, *Dictionnaire du Second Empire*, 1995

Chanet, J.-F., 'École et politisation dans les campagnes françaises au 19e siècle' in M. Agulhon *et al.*, *Politisation*, 2000

Charle, C., *Les hauts fonctionnaires en France au 19e siècle*, 1980

'Micro-histoire sociale et macro-histoire sociale' in C. Charle (ed.), *Histoire sociale. Histoire globale?*, 1993

Charon-Bordas, J., *Ouvriers et paysans au milieu du 19e siècle. L'enquête de 1848 sur le travail*, 1994

Chassagne, S., 'Une affaire de longue durée. La production d'un grand notable républicain angevin des débuts de la 3e République: Henri Allain-Targé' in J.-L. Mayaud (ed.), *Clio dans les vignes*, 1998

Chatelain, A., 'Les migrants temporaires et la propagation des idées révolutionnaires en France au 19e siècle', *1848* 1951

Les migrants temporaires en France de 1800 à 1914, 2 vols. Lille 1977

Chatelard, C., *Crime et criminalité dans l'arrondissement de Saint-Etienne au 19e siècle*, Saint-Etienne 1981

Chauvaud, F., 'L'usure au 19e siècle: le fléau des campagnes', *Etudes rurales* 1984

Les passions villageoises au 19e siècle. Les émotions rurales dans les pays de Beauce, du Hurepoix et du Mantois, 1995

'La parole captive. L'interrogatoire judiciaire au 19e siècle', *Histoire et archives* 1997

Chauvaud, F. (ed.), *La société agricole de la Vienne au 19e et 20e siècles*, La Crèche 2001

Chavot, F., 'Les sociétés de secours mutuels sous le Second Empire', *Cahiers d'histoire de l'Institut Maurice Thorez* 1977

Chevalier, L., 'Les fondements économiques et sociaux de l'histoire politique de la région parisienne', Doc. ès lettres, Univ. de Paris 1950

Classes laborieuses et classes dangereuses à Paris pendant la première moitié du 19e siècle, 1958; *Labouring Classes and Dangerous Classes*, London, 1973

Chevalier, M., *La vie humaine dans les Pyrénées ariégeoises*, 1956

Cholvy, G., *Religion et société au 19e siècle. Le diocèse de Montpellier*, 2 vols. Lille 1973

'Déchristianisés? Les ouvriers en France (19e–20e siècles)', *Historiens et géographes* 1995

'L'opposition à l'Empire dans l'Hérault (1852–70)' in M. Cadé (ed.), *L'histoire à travers champs*, Perpignan 2002

Claret-Ploquin, N., 'Noblesses en déclassement, noblesses en souffrance', *Cahiers d'histoire* 2000
Cloître, M.-T., 'Aspects de la vie politique dans le département de Finistère de 1848 à 1870', *Bulletin de la Société archéologique du Finistère* 1973
Codaccioni, F.-P., *De l'inégalité sociale dans une grande ville industrielle. Le drame de Lille de 1850 à 1914*, Lille 1976
Constant, E., 'Le département du Var sous le Second Empire et au début de la 3e République', Doc. ès lettres, Univ. de Provence-Aix 1977
Corbin, A., *Archaïsme et modernité en Limousin au 19e siècle*, 2 vols. 1975
    Le village des cannibales, 1991; *The Village of Cannibals: Rage and Murder in France, 1870*, Cambridge 1992
    'La violence rurale dans la France du 19e siècle et son dépérissement: l'évolution de l'interprétation politique' in *La violence politique dans les démocraties européennes occidentales*, 1993
    Le monde retrouvé de Louis-François Pinagot. Sur les traces d'un inconnu 1798–1876, 1998
Corbin, A., Lalouette, J., and Riot-Sarcey, M. (eds.), *Femmes dans la cité*, 1997
Corbin, A. and Mayeur, J.-M. (eds.), *La barricade*, 1997
Cordillot, M., *La naissance du mouvement ouvrier à Besançon. La Ire Internationale*, 1990
Cornu, P., *Une économie rurale dans la débâcle. Cévennes vivaraise, 1852–92*, 1993
Cottereau, A., 'Vie quotidienne et résistance ouvrière à Paris en 1870' in D. Poulot, *Le Sublime ou le travailleur comme il est en 1870 et ce qu'il peut être*, 1980 (reprint)
    'Les règlements d'atelier au cours de la révolution industrielle en France' in A. Biroleau (ed.), *Les règlements d'atelier 1798–1936*, 1984
    'Prévoyance des uns, imprévoyance des autres. Questions sur les cultures ouvrières, face aux principes de l'assurance mutuelle au 19e siècle', *Prévenir* 1984
    'The distinctiveness of working-class cultures, 1848–1900' in I. Katznelson and A. Zolberg (eds.), *Working-Class Formation*, Princeton, N.J. 1996
Courtheoux, J.-P., 'Naissance d'une conscience de classe dans le prolétariat textile du Nord', *Revue économique* 1957
Cousteix, P., 'L'opposition ouvrière au Second Empire en Haute-Vienne', *Bulletin de la Société archéologique et historique du Limousin* 1955
Crebouw, Y., 'Droits et obligations des journaliers et des domestiques, droits et obligations des maîtres' in R. Hubscher and J.-C. Farcy (eds.), *La moisson des autres*, 1996
Crook, M., 'Getting out the vote' in M. Cornick and C. Crossley (eds.), *Problems in French History*, London 2000
Crossick, G. and Haupt, H.-G., 'Shopkeepers, master-artisans and the historian. The petite bourgeoisie in comparative focus' in G. Crossick and H.-G. Haupt (eds.), *Shopkeepers and Artisans in 19th Century Europe*, London 1984
Cubitt, G., 'God, man and Satan: strands in counter-revolutionary thought among 19th century French Catholics' in F. Tallett and N. Atkin (eds.), *Catholicism in Britain and France since 1789*, London 1996

Cuvillier, A., *Un journal d'ouvriers: L'Atelier, 1840–50*, 1954

Dagnan, J., *Le Gers sous la Seconde République*, Auch 1928

Dalisson, 'La célébration du coup d'état de 1851: symbolique politique et politique des symboles', *Revue d'histoire du 19e siècle* 2001/1

Dalotel, A., Faure, A., and Freiermuth, J.-C., *Aux origines de la Commune. Le mouvement des réunions publiques à Paris 1868–70*, 1980

Darmon, J.-J., *Le colportage de librairie en France sous le Second Empire*, 1972

Darriulat, P., *Les patriotes. La gauche républicaine et la nation, 1830–70*, 2001

Daumard, A., *La bourgeoisie parisienne de 1815 à 1848*, 1963

'Les fondements de la société bourgeoise en France au 19e siècle' in D. Roche and E. Labrousse (eds.), *Ordres et classes*, 1967

'Quelques remarques sur le logement des parisiens au 19e siècle', *Annales de démographie historique* 1975

Les bourgeois et la bourgeoisie en France, 1981

'L'oisiveté aristocratique et bourgeoise en France au 19e siècle: privilège ou malédiction?' in A. Daumard (ed.), *Oisiveté et loisirs dans les sociétés occidentales au 19e siècle*, Abbeville 1983

'Noblesse et aristocratie en France au 19e siècle' in G. Delille (ed.), *Les noblesses européennes*

Daumas, M., *Evolution de la géographie industrielle de Paris et sa proche banlieue au 19e siècle*, 1976

Delille, G. (ed.), *Les noblesses européennes au 19e siècle*, Rome 1988

Deloyé, Y. and Ihl, O., 'Le 19e siècle au miroir de la sociologie historique', *Revue d'histoire du 19e siècle* 1999

Delpal, B., *Entre paroisse et commune. Les catholiques de la Drôme au milieu du 19e siècle*, Valence 1989

Démier, F., 'Les ouvriers de Rouen parlent à un économiste en juillet 1848', *Le mouvement social* 1982

Démier, F. and Mayaud, J.-L., 'Un bilan de 50 années de recherches sur 1848 et la Seconde République', *Revue d'histoire du 19e siècle* 1997

Denis, M., 'Les royalistes de la Mayenne et le monde moderne', Doc. d'Etat, Univ. de Paris-Sorbonne 1976

Désert, G., 'Aperçus sur l'industrie française du bâtiment au 19e siècle' in J.-P. Bardet (ed.), *Le bâtiment*, The Hague 1971

Une société rurale au 19e siècle. Les paysans du Calvados, 1815–95, 3 vols. Lille 1975

Les archives hospitalières. Source d'histoire économique et sociale, Caen 1977

'Les éléments structurants de l'espace bas-normands 1re moitié du 19e siècle' in S. Courville and N. Séguin (eds.), *Espace et culture*, St-Foy, Quebec 1995

Desmarest, J., 'L'état économique de la France à la fin du Second Empire', *Revue des travaux de l'Académie des sciences morales et politiques* 1967

Desrosières, A., 'Comment faire des choses qui tiennent. Histoire sociale et statistiques' in C. Charle (ed.), *Histoire sociale. Histoire globale?* 1993

Deyon, P., 'L'industrie amiénoise au 19e siècle et les séductions du protectionnisme', *Revue du Nord* 2000

Dorandeu, R., 'Eléments pour une étude des élites et des organisations politiques' in R. Dorandeu (ed.), *L'Hérault à la fin du Second Empire*, 1989

Dubois, J., *Le vocabulaire politique et social en France de 1869 à 1872*, 1962

Dupeux, G., *Aspects de l'histoire sociale et politique du Loir-et-Cher*, 1962

Dupuy, F., *Le pin de la discorde. Les rapports de métayage dans la Grande Lande*, 1996

Duveau, G., *La vie ouvrière en France sous le Second Empire*, 1946
   La pensée ouvrière sur l'éducation pendant la Seconde République et le Second Empire, 1947

Edelstein, M., 'La place de la Révolution française dans la politisation des paysans', *Annales historiques de la Révolution française* 1990
   'La participation électorale des françaises', *Revue d'histoire moderne et contemporaine* 1993

Estève, C., *A l'ombre du pouvoir. Le Cantal du milieu du 19e siècle à 1914*, Clermont-Ferrand 2002

Farcy, J.-C., *Les paysans beaucerons au 19e siècle*, 2 vols. Chartres 1989
   'Le temps libre au village (1830–50)' in A. Corbin (ed.), *L'avènement des loisirs, 1850–1960*, 2001

Faure, A., 'L'épicerie parisienne au 19e siècle', *Le mouvement social* 1979, no. 108
   'La Révolution ou la mémoire interrompue' in Société d'histoire de la Révolution de 1848, *Le 19e siècle et la Révolution française*, 1992

Faure, A., Plessis, A., and Farcy, J.-C. (eds.), *La terre et la cité. Mélanges offerts à Philippe Vigier*, 1994

Faury, J., *Cléricalisme et anticléricalisme dans le Tarn*, Toulouse 1980

Fel, A., *Les hautes terres du Massif Central. Tradition paysanne et économie agricole*, 1962

Feral, P., *La société d'agriculture du Gers sous le Second Empire*, Auch 1973

Fohlen, C., *L'industrie textile au temps du Second Empire*, 1956

Fortin, A., 'Aspects de la vie sociale du Pas-de-Calais durant le Second Empire', *Revue du Nord* 1970

Frey, J.-P., *La ville industrielle et ses urbanités. La distinction ouvriers/employés. Le Creusot 1870–1930*, Brussels 1987

Fumate, Y., 'La socialisation des filles au 19e siècle', *Revue française de pédagogie* 1980

Furet, F. and Ozouf, J., *Lire et écrire*, 2 vols. 1977

Gaillard, J., 'Notes sur l'opposition au monopole des compagnies de chemins de fer entre 1850 et 1860', *1848* 1950
   'Le VIIe arrondissement' in L. Girard (ed.), *Les élections de 1869*, 1960
   'Les usines Cail et les ouvriers métallurgistes de Grenelle', *Le mouvement social* 1961
   'Les associations de production et la pensée politique en France (1852–70)', *Le mouvement social* 1965
   Paris, la ville, 1977

Gaillard, L., 'La vie ouvrière et les mouvements ouvriers à Marseille de 1848 à 1879', Doc. d'Etat, Univ. d'Aix 1972

Garrier, G., *Paysans du Beaujolais et du Lyonnais*, 2 vols. Grenoble 1973
   'L'apport des récits de vie et des romans paysans' in R. Hubscher and J.-C. Farcy (eds.), *La moisson des autres*, 1996

Garrigou, A., *Le vote et la vertu. Comment les français sont devenus lecteurs*, 1992

Garrigues, J., 'Les images de la Révolution de 1830 à 1848: enjeux politiques d'une mémoire' in Société d'histoire de la Révolution de 1848 (ed.), *Le 19e siècle et la Révolution française*, 1992

    La République des hommes d'affaires, 1870–1900, 1997

Gaudin, O., 'Les élections dans la Sarthe sous le Second Empire', *Province du Maine* 1997

Gaveau, F., 'De la sûreté des campagnes. Police rurale et demandes d'ordre en France dans la première moitié du 19e siècle', *Crime, histoire et société* 2000

George, J., 'Mémoire révolutionnaire et tradition municipale républicaine. Le cas du Var au 19e siècle' in M. Vovelle (ed.), *Révolution et république. L'exception française*, 1994

Gibson, R., *A Social History of French Catholicism 1789–1914*, 1989

Gildea, R., *Education in Provincial France, 1800–1914*, Oxford 1983

Gilon, J.-F., 'Surveillés et condamnés politiques à Bordeaux entre 1850 et 1860', *Revue historique de Bordeaux* 1986–7

Girard, L., *La politique des travaux publics du Second Empire*, 1952

    Nouvelle histoire de Paris. La Deuxième République et le Second Empire, 1981

    Les libéraux français, 1814–75, 1985

    'Jules Ferry et la génération des républicains du Second Empire' in F. Furet (ed.), *Jules Ferry fondateur de la République* 1985

Girard, L. (ed.), *Les élections de 1869*, 1960

Girard, L., Prost, A., and Gossez, R., *Les conseillers généraux en 1870*, 1967

Gonnet, P., 'La société dijonnaise au 19e siècle. Esquisse de l'évolution économique, sociale et politique d'un milieu urbain contemporain (1815–90)', Doc. d'Etat, Univ. de Paris IV 1974

Gordon, D., *Merchants and Capitalists. Industrialization and Provincial Politics in Mid-Nineteenth-Century France*, Tuscaloosa, Ala. 1985

Gosselin, R., *Les almanachs républicains. Traditions révolutionnaires et culture politique des masses populaires de Paris*, 1992

Gossez, R., 'Une grève de mineurs à l'avènement de Napoleon III', *Mines* 1955

    Les ouvriers de Paris, 1967

Gouallou, H., 'Le plébiscite du 8 mai 1870 en Ille-et-Vilaine', *Annales de Bretagne* 1970

Gouda, F., *Poverty and Political Culture. The Rhetoric of Social Welfare in the Netherlands and France, 1815–54*, Lanham, Md. 1995

Goueffon, J., 'Le parti républicain dans le Loiret à la fin du Second Empire' in J. Viard (ed.), *L'esprit républicain*, 1972

Goujon, P., *Le vigneron citoyen. Mâconnais et Châlonnais (1848–1914)*, 1993

    'Les révélations du suffrage *universel*: comportements électoraux et politisation des populations de Saône-et-Loire sous la Seconde République', *Cahiers d'histoire* 1998

Gould, R., 'Trade cohesion, class unity, and urban insurrection: artisanal activism in the Paris Commune', *American Journal of Sociology* 1992

Insurgent Identities. Class, Community, and Protest in Paris from 1848 to the Commune, London 1995

Grandcoing, P., *Les demeures de la distinction. Châteaux et châtelains au 19e siècle en Haute-Vienne*, Limoges 1999
La baïonnette et le lancis. Crise urbaine et révolution à Limoges sous la seconde république, Limoges 2002

Gueslin, A., 'Usure et usuriers dans les campagnes françaises au 19e siècle' in *Recueil d'études offert à Gabriel Désert*, Caen 1992
'Les élites françaises face à la pauvreté au 19e siècle' in R. Rémond (ed.), *Démocratie et pauvreté*, 1996
Gens pauvres, pauvres gens dans la France du 19e siècle, 1998

Guillaume, P., 'Un quartier cheminot à Bordeaux' in A. Fourcaut (ed.), *La ville divisée. Les ségrégations urbaines en question. France 18e–20e siècles*, Grâne 1991

Guillemin, A., 'Le pouvoir de l'innovation. Les notables de la Manche et le développement de l'agriculture (1830–75)', Doc. de 3e cycle, EHESS 1980
'Rente, famille, innovation. Contribution à la sociologie du grand domaine noble au 19e siècle', *Annales* 1985

Guionnet, C., *L'apprentissage de la politique moderne*, 1998
'La politique au village: une révolution silencieuse', *Revue d'histoire moderne et contemporaine* 1998

Guiral, P., 'La bourgeoisie française sous le Second Empire: progrès ou régression' in A. Birke and L. Kettenacke (eds.), *Bürgertum, Adel und Monarchie*, Munich 1989

Haine, W., *The World of the Paris Café. Sociability among the French Working Class, 1789–1914*, Baltimore, Md. 1996

Hamman, P., 'La notabilité dans tous ses états? Alexandre de Geiger à Sarreguemines, un patron en politique sous le Second Empire', *Revue Historique* 2002

Hamon, L. (ed.), *Les républicains sous le Second Empire*, 1993

Hanagan, M., *Nascent Proletarians. Class Formation in Post-revolutionary France*, Oxford 1989

Harrigan, P., *Mobility, Elites and Education in French Society of the Second Empire*, Waterloo, Ont. 1980

Harrison, C., *The Bourgeois Citizen in 19th Century France. Gender, Sociability and the Uses of Emulation*, Oxford 1999

Harvey, D., *Consciousness and the Urban Experience*, London 1985

Harvey, D. A., *Constructing Class and Nationality in Alsace, 1830–1945*, DeKalb, Ill. 2001

Hau, M., *L'industrialisation de l'Alsace (1803–1939)*, Strasbourg 1987

Haupt, H.-G., 'The petite bourgeoisie in France, 1850–1914' in G. Crossick and H.-G. Haupt (eds.), *Shopkeepers and Master Artisans in 19th Century Europe*, 1984

Hazareesingh, S., 'Defining the republican good life: Second Empire municipalism and the emergence of the 3rd Republic', *French History* 1997

From Subject to Citizen. The Second Empire and the Emergence of Modern French Democracy, Princeton 1998

Intellectual Founders of the Republic, Oxford 2001

Hazareesingh, S. and Wright, V., *Francs-maçons sous le Second Empire*, Rennes 2001

Hébrard, J., 'Les nouveaux lecteurs' in H.-J. Martin and R. Chartier (eds.), *Histoire de l'édition française*, III, 1985

Heywood, C., *Childhood in Nineteenth-Century France*, Cambridge 1988

Higgs, D., *Nobles in 19th Century France*, 1987

Hilaire, Y.-M., 'L'Eglise dans le monde rural. Le 19e siècle', *Recherche social* 1971

'La vie religieuse des populations du diocèse d'Arras, 1840–1914', Doc. d'Etat, Univ. de Paris IV 1976

'L'Eglise et les très pauvres dans la 1re moitié du 19e siècle' in R. Rémond (ed.), *Démocratie et pauvreté*, Paris 1991

Hincker, L., 'La politicisation des milieux populaires en France au 19e siècle' in *Revue d'histoire du 19e siècle* 1997

Hordern, F., *Les crises industrielles en Alsace au 19e siècle et leur répercussions sur l'emploi des travailleurs*, Aix 1970

Huard, R., 'La préhistoire des partis. Le parti républicain et l'opinion républicaine dans le Gard de 1848 à 1888', Doc. d'Etat Univ. de Paris IV 1977

'La tradition politique: émergence, contenus, devenir', *Pouvoirs* 1987

La naissance du parti politique en France, 1996

'Le *suffrage universel* sous la Seconde République', *Revue d'histoire du 19e siècle* 1997

'*Rural*. La promotion d'une épithète et sa signification politique et sociale . . .', *Revue d'histoire moderne et contemporaine* 1998

'Les débuts du suffrage universel masculin en France: l'exemple de l'Aude' in S. Caucanas and R. Cazals (eds.), *Armand Barbès et les hommes de 1848*, Carcassonne 1999

'L'affirmation du suffrage universel masculin 1848–80' in S. Berstein and M. Winock (eds.), *L'invention de la démocratie*, 2002

Hubscher, R., 'L'agriculture et la société rurale dans le Pas-de-Calais du milieu du 19e siècle à 1914', Doc. d'Etat, Univ. de Paris 1978

'Réflexions sur l'identité paysanne au 19e siècle: identité réelle ou supposée', *Ruralia* 1997

Hubscher, R. and Farcy, J.-C. (eds.), *La moisson des autres. Les salariés agricoles aux 19e et 20e siècles*, 1996

Igersheim, F., *Politique et administration dans le Bas-Rhin 1848–70*, Strasbourg 1993

Isoart, P. and Bidegaray, C. (eds.), *Des républiques françaises*, 1988

Jacquemet, J., *Belleville au 19e siècle. Du faubourg à la ville*, 1984

Jessenne, J.-P., 'Synergie nationale et dynamique communautaire dans l'évolution politique rurale par-delà la Révolution française' in M. Agulhon *et al.*, *Politisation*, 2000

Johnson, C. 'Patterns of proletarianisation: Parisian tailors and Lodève woollens workers' in J. Merriman (ed.), *Consciousness and Class Experience in Nineteenth-century Europe*, London 1980

Johnson, C., 'Economic change and artisan discontent: the tailors' history (1800–48)' in R. Price (ed.), *Revolution and Reaction*, 1975
  The Life and Death of Industrial Languedoc, 1700–1920. The Politics of Deindustrialization, Oxford 1995
Jones, P. M., *Politics and Rural Society. The Southern Massif Central c. 1750–1880*, Cambridge 1985
  'La République au village dans le sud du Massif Central' in Centre d'histoire moderne et contemporaine de l'Europe méditerranéenne, *De la Révolution au coup d'état: les répercussions des événements parisiens entre Alpes et Pyrénées*, Montpellier 1999
  'Towards a village history of the French Revolution: some problems of method', *French History* 2000
Judt, T., 'The French labour movement in the 19th century' in T. Judt, *Marxism and the French Left*, Oxford 1986
Juillard, E., *La vie rurale dans la plaine de Basse-Alsace: essai de géographie sociale*, 1958
Kaelble, H., *Industrialization and Social Inequality in 19th Century Europe*, Leamington Spa 1986
Kale, S., *Legitimism and the Reconstruction of French Society, 1852–83*, London 1992
Kashuba, W., 'Culture populaire et culture ouvrière, catégories symboliques' in A. Lüdtke (ed.), *Histoire du quotidien*, 1996
Katznelson, I., 'Working-class formation: constructing cases and comparisons' in I. Katznelson and A. Zolberg (eds.), *Working-Class Formation. Nineteenth-Century Patterns in Western Europe and the United States*, Princeton, N.J. 1986
Knibiehler, Y., 'Caractères spécifiques de la pauvreté féminine aux 19e et 20 siècles' in R. Rémond (ed.), *Démocratie et pauvreté*, 1991
Kott, S., 'Un milieu face à la répression: l'exemple des grèves en Haute Alsace sous le Second Empire' in Société d'histoire de la Révolution de 1848 et des révolutions du 19e siècle, *Répression et prison politique en France et en Europe au 19e siècle*, 1990
Krakovitch, O., 'La Révolution à travers le théâtre de 1815 à 1870: à chaque génération sa peur', in Société d'histoire de la Révolution de 1848 et des révolutions du 19e siècle, *Le 19e siècle et la Révolution française*, 1992
Kselman, T., 'The varieties of religious experience in urban France' in H. McLeod, *European Religion in the Age of Great Cities, 1830–1930*, 1995
Kulstein, D., 'The attitude of French workers towards the Second Empire', *French Historical Studies*, 1962
  Napoleon III and the Working Class: A Study of Government Propaganda under the Second Empire, London 1969
Labrousse, E., *Aspects de la crise et de la dépression de l'économie française au milieu du 19e siècle, 1846–51*, 1956
  (ed.), *Colloque d'histoire sur l'artisanat et l'apprentissage*, Aix 1965
Lagoueyte, P., *Candidature officielle et pratique électorale sous le Second Empire*, Doc. Nouveau régime Univ. de Paris I 1990

'Le rôle des femmes dans les élections législatives sous le Second Empire' in A. Corbin *et al.*, *Femmes dans la cité*, 1997

Lagrée, M., *Religion et cultures en Bretagne 1850–1950*, 1992

Lalouette, J., 'Actes, regards et images des femmes' in A. Corbin, J. Lalouette, and M. Riot-Sarcey (eds.), *Femmes dans la cité*, 1997

Lambert-Dansette, J., *Genèse du patronat, 1780–1880*, 1991
La vie des chefs d'entreprise, 1830–80, 1992

Lancelot, A., *L'abstentionnisme électoral en France*, 1968

Langlois, C., *Le catholicisme au féminin. Les congrégations françaises à supérieure générale au 19e siècle*, 1984

Launay, M., *Le diocèse de Nantes sous le Second Empire*, 2 vols. Nantes 1983

Laurent, R., *Les vignerons de la Côte-d'Or au 19e siècle*, 1958

Lavoie, E., 'Les élections municipales sous le Second Empire: un miroir de l'opinion publique en temps paisibles' in *Europe et Etat*, Aix-en-Provence 1993

Le Gall, L., 'Faïences, vitraux et chansons. Expressions républicaines et anti-républicaines en Basse-Bretagne (19e–20e siècles)' in M. Agulhon (ed.), *Cultures et folklores républicains*, 1995
'Motreff (Finistère), la Seconde République et la micro-histoire', *Ruralia* 1999

Lehning, J., *Peasant and French. Cultural Contact in Rural France during the 19th Century*, Cambridge 1995

Lentz, T., 'Le plébiscite du 8 mai 1870 en Moselle', *Les cahiers lorrains* 1988

Léon, P., *La naissance de la grande industrie en Dauphiné (fin du 17e siècle–1869)*, 2 vols. 1954
Géographie de la fortune et structures sociales à Lyon au 19e siècle, Lyon 1975

Léonard, J., 'L'exemple d'une catégorie socio-professionnelle au 19e siècle: les médecins français' in D. Roche and E. Labrousse (eds.), *Ordres et classes*, 1967

Lepetit, B., 'Les formes d'intégration des campagnes à l'économie d'échange dans la France préindustrielle: les semis des foires' in N. Bulst, *et al.*, *Bevölkerung, Wirtschaft und Gesellschaft*, Trier 1983

Lequin, Y., 'Sources et méthodes de l'histoire de grèves dans la seconde moitié du 19e siècle: l'exemple de l'Isère (1848–1914)', *Cahiers d'histoire* 1967
La formation de la classe ouvrière régionale: les ouvriers de la région lyonnaise (1848–1914), 2 vols. Lyon 1977
'L'espace ouvrier: le regard géographique', *Historiens et géographes* 1995

Lequin, Y. (ed.), *Histoire des français 19e–20e siècles*, 3 vols. 1983–4

Lerch, D., 'Imagerie populaire et antisémitisme: le Haut-Rhin en 1848', *Gazette des Beaux-Arts* 1988

Lévêque, P., *Une société en crise. La Bourgogne de la Monarchie de Juillet au Second Empire (1846–52)*, 2 vols. 1983
'Les Français et le pouvoir politique. Institutions et participation (de 1789 à nos jours)' in J. Le Goff (ed.), *L'Etat et les pouvoirs*, 1989
'Conservatisme sans cléricalisme. L'évolution politique du Châtillonnais aux 19e et 20e siècles' in A. Faure *et al.*, *La terre et la cité*, 1994

'Décembre 1851: faibles réactions en pays *rouge*. Le cas de la Saône-et-Loire', *Revue d'histoire du 19e siècle* 2001/1.

Levy, C., 'Les proscrits du 2 décembre' in L. Hamon (ed.), *Les républicains sous le Second Empire*, 1993

Lhomme, J., 'Le pouvoir d'achat de l'ouvrier français au cours d'un siècle, 1840–1940', *Le mouvement social* 1968

L'Huillier, F., *La lutte ouvrière à la fin du Second Empire*, 1957

Livet, R., *Habitat rural et structures agraires en Basse-Provence*, Aix-en-Provence 1962

Locke, R., *French Legitimists and the Politics of Moral Order in the Early Third Republic*, Princeton, N.J. 1974

Lorcin, J., 'Le souvenir de la Révolution française dans la chanson ouvrière stéphanoise' in Société d'histoire de la Révolution de 1848 et des révolutions du 19e siècle, *Le 19e siècle et la Révolution française*, 1992

Luciani, J., 'Logiques du placement ouvrier au 19e siècle et construction du marché du travail', *Sociétés contemporaines* 1990

Lyons, M., 'Oral culture and rural community in 19th century France: the *veillée d'hiver*', *Australian Journal of French Studies* 1986/7

Le triomphe du livre. Une histoire sociologique de la lecture dans la France du 19e siècle, 1987

Machu, L., 'Deux aspects de la répression policière dans le Nord à l'époque du Second Empire', *Revue du Nord* 1964

McMillan, J., *France and Women 1789–1914* 2000

McPhee, P., *The Politics of Rural Life: Political Mobilisation in the French Countryside, 1846–52*, Oxford 1992

'Culture populaire et politique démocratique dans les Pyrénées-orientales' in Centre d'histoire moderne et contemporaine de l'Europe méditerranéenne, *De la Révolution au coup d'etat: les répercussions des événements parisiens entre Alpes et Pyrénées*, Montpellier 1999

Magraw, R., *A History of the French Working Class*, 1, Oxford 1992

Magri, S., 'Les propriétaires, les locataires, la loi. Jalons pour une analyse sociologique des rapports de location, Paris 1850–1920', *Revue française de sociologie* 1996

Maire, C., 'Crise agricole et misère en Lorraine au milieu du 19e siècle', *La Revue lorraine populaire* 1985

Maitron, J., 'La personnalité du militant ouvrier français dans la seconde moitié du 19e siècle', *Le mouvement social* 1960/1

'Les effectifs de la Première Internationale en France' in *La Première Internationale, l'institution, l'implantation, le rayonnement*, 1964

Maneglier, H., *Paris impérial. La vie quotidienne sous le Second Empire*, 1990

Marcilhacy, C., *Le diocèse d'Orléans sous l'épiscopat de Mgr Dupanloup, 1849–79*, 1962

Le diocèse d'Orléans au milieu du 19e siècle, 1964

Marec, Y., *Pauvres et philanthropes à Rouen au 19e siècle*, Rouen 1981

Margadant, T., *French Peasants in Revolt: The Insurrection of 1851*, Princeton, N.J. 1979

Markovitch, T., 'Statistiques industrielles et systèmes politiques' in *Pour une histoire de la statistique*, 1977

Martin, J.-C., 'Emergence et reconnaissance d'une culture paysanne', *Annales de Bretagne* 1993

'Face à la Révolution, quelle politisation des communautés rurales ?' in M. Agulhon *et al.*, *Politisation*, 2000

Mattei, B., *Rebelle! Rebelle! Révoltes et mythes du mineur, 1830–1946*, Seyssel 1987

Maurain, J., *La politique ecclésiastique du Second Empire de 1852 à 1869*, 1930

Mayaud, J.-L., *Les secondes républiques du Doubs*, 1986

'Les paysanneries françaises face à la Seconde République', *1848* 1990

'Ruralité et politique dans la France du 19e siècle', *Histoire et sociétés rurales* 1999

'De la pluri-activité à une re-définition de la petite exploitation rurale', *Annales de Bretagne* 1999

'Pour une communalisation de l'histoire rurale' in M. Agulhon *et al.*, *Politisation*, 2000

Mayeur, F., 'L'Eglise catholique devant l'éducation et l'instruction' in G. Avanzini, P. Dubois *et al.*, *Pédagogie chrétienne, pédagogues chrétiens*, 1996

Maynes, M.-J., *Taking the Hard Road. Life Course in French and German Workers' Autobiographies in the Era of Industrialization*, London 1995

Mazauric, C., 'France révolutionnaire, France révolutionné, France en révolution: pour une clarification des rythmes et des concepts', *Annales historiques de la Révolution française* 1988

Melucci, A., 'Idéologies et pratiques patronales pendant l'industrialisation capitaliste: le cas de la France, 1830–1914', Doc. d'Etat, EHESS, n.d.

Ménager, B., 'La vie politique dans le département du Nord de 1851 à 1877', Doc. d'Etat, Univ. de Paris IV 1979

'La vie politique dans le département du Nord de 1851 à 1877', *Revue du Nord* 1980

'Force et limites du Bonapartisme populaire en milieu ouvrier sous le Second Empire', *Revue Historique* 1981

Les Napoléon du peuple, 1988

'Les plébiscites du Second Empire' in B. Lobricon (ed.), *L'élection du chef de l'Etat en France*, 1988

Merley, J., 'Les élections de 1869 dans le département de la Loire', *Cahiers d'histoire* 1961

La Haute-Loire de la fin de l'Ancien Régime aux débuts de la 3e République, Le Puy 1975

Merlin, P., 'Aux origines du parti républicain dans le Jura. Un aspect de la crise finale de la Seconde République: la sociabilité jurassienne dans la tourmente (mai 1849-déc. 1851)', *Société d'émulation du Jura. Travaux* 1993

Merriman, J., *The Red City. Limoges and the French 19th Century*, Oxford 1985

The Margins of City Life. Explorations on the French Urban Frontier, 1815–51, Oxford 1991

Merriman, J. (ed.), *French Cities in the 19th Century*, London 1982

Mesliand, C., *Paysans du Vaucluse, 1860–1939*, Aix-en-Provence 1989

Moine, J.-M., *Les barons du fer. Les maîtres de forges en Lorraine*, Nancy 1989

Moissonnier, M., 'Les images de la République dans le monde et le mouvement ouvrier lyonnais au 19e siècle' in Société d'histoire . . . , *Le 19e siècle et la Révolution française*, 1990

Mollier, J.-Y., 'Noël Parfait (1813–96): une trajectoire républicaine au 19e siècle' in A. Faure, A. Plessis, and J.-C. Farcy (eds.), *La terre et la cité*, 1994

'Les intellectuels et leur culture en 1848 dans l'espace française' in R. Aldrich, and M. Lyons (eds.), *The Sphinx in the Tuileries*, Sydney 2000

Morabito, M., 'Maintien de l'ordre et intégration politique en Bretagne: l'Ille-et-Vilaine sous le Second Empire', *Revue historique du droit français et étranger* 1998

Moss, B., *The Origins of the French Labor Movement. The Socialism of Skilled Workers*, London 1976

Moulin, A., *Peasantry and Society in France since 1789*, Cambridge 1991

Muckensturm, S., 'L'indigence révélatrice des faiblesses d'une société: l'exemple bas-rhinois au 19e siècle', *Revue d'Alsace* 1998

'La quantification d'un phénomène social: l'indifférence en France dans la 1re moitié du 19e siècle', *Histoire, Economie, Société* 2000

Murard, L. and Zylberman, P., *Le petit travailleur infatigable ou le prolétaire régénéré. Villes-usines, habitat et intimités au 19e siècle*, Fontenay-sous-Bois 1976

Murard, L. and Zylberman, P. (eds.), *L'haleine des faubourgs. Ville, habitat et santé au 19e siècle*, 1978

Musée de Marseille, *Marseille 1860–1914. Photographes et mutation urbaine*, Marseille 1995

Nicolas, J. (ed.), *Mouvements populaires et conscience sociale 16e–19e siècles*, 1985

Nicolet, C., *L'idée républicaine en France*, 1982

Noiriel, G., *Les ouvriers dans la société française, 19e–20e siècles*, 1986

Nord, P., *The Republican Moment. Struggle for Democracy in 19th Century France*, Cambridge, Mass. 1995

Offerlé, M., 'Les Schneider en politique' in *Les Schneider, Le Creusot. Une famille, une entreprise, une ville (1836–1960)*, 1995

'Professions et profession politique' in M. Offerlé (ed.), *La profession politique 19e–20e siècles*, 1999

Palmade, G., 'Le département du Gers à la fin du Second Empire', *Bulletin de la Société archéologique, historique et scientifique du Gers* 1961

Pécout, G., 'La politisation des paysans au 19e siècle', *Histoire et sociétés rurales* 1994

Pellissier, C., 'Les sociabilités patriciennes à Lyon du milieu du 19e siècle à 1914', Doc. de. l'Univ.de Lyon II 1993

Perrot, M., *Les enquêtes sur la condition ouvrière en France au 19e siècle*, 1972

Les ouvriers en grève. France 1871–90, 2 vols. 1974

'Les ouvriers et les machines en France dans la 1re moitié du 19e siècle' in L. Murard and P. Zylberman, *Le soldat du travail*, 1979

'A 19th century work experience as related in a worker's autobiography: Norbert Truquin' in S. Kaplan and C. Koepp (eds.), *Work in France. Representations, Meaning, Organization and Practice*, London 1986

'On the formation of the French working class' in I. Katznelson and A. Zolberg (eds.), *Working-Class Formation*, 1986

Pertué, M., 'L'ordre public comme norme politique et culturelle' in J. Nicolas (ed.), *Mouvements populaires*, 1985

Petit, V., 'Le clergé contre l'ivrognerie. La campagne du Père Ducreux dans les montagnes du Doubs (1864–9)', *Histoire et sociétés rurales* 2000

Petiteau, N., '1848 en Vaucluse ou l'impossible république bourgeoise', *Cahiers d'histoire* 1998

Peyrière, M., 'L'industrie de la machine à coudre en France' in L. Bergeron (ed.), *La révolution des aiguilles*, 1996

Phélippeau, E., 'La fin des notables revisitée' in M. Offerlé (ed.), *La profession politique*, 1999
  L'invention de l'homme politique moderne. Mackau, l'Orne et la République, 2002

Pierrard, P., *Les chansons en patois de Lille sous le Second Empire*, Arras 1965
  La vie ouvrière à Lille sous le Second Empire, 1965
  'Habitat ouvrier et démographie à Lille au 19e siècle', *Annales de démographie historique* 1975

Piette, C., 'Réflexions historiques sur les traditions révolutionnaires à Paris au 19e siècle', *Historical Reflections* 1985
  'La misère à Paris dans la première moitié du 19e siècle: contribution à la critique des statistiques officielles', *Canadian Journal of History* 1992

Pigenet, M., 'Les adjectifs de la République. Voies et conditions de la politisation des milieux populaires. L'exemple du Cher au 19e siècle' in M. Vovelle (ed.), *Révolution et république*, 1994
  'Aux fondements d'une identité. Retour sur deux siècles de travail ouvrier', *Historiens et géographes* 1995

Pilbeam, P., *The Middle Classes in Europe, 1789–1914*, London 1990
  Republicanism in Nineteenth Century France, 1814–71, London 1995

Pinard, L., *Les mentalités religieuses du Morvan au 19e siècle (1830–1914)*, Dijon 1997

Plessis, A., 'La République était-elle dans l'Empire?' in J. Tulard (ed.), *Pourquoi*, 1997
  'La Banque de France sous le Second Empire', 3 vols. Doc. d'Etat, Univ. de Paris I 1980

Ploux, F., *Guerres paysannes en Quercy. Violences, conciliations et répression pénale dans les campagnes du Lot (1810–60)*, 2002
  De bouche à oreille. Naissance et propagation des rumeurs dans la France du 19e siècle, 2003

Ponsot, P., *Les grèves de 1870 et la Commune de 1871 au Creusot*, 1957

Pourcher, Y., 'Les notables en Lozère aux 19e et 20e siècles', *Actes du 110e CNSS* II 1985
  'Parenté et représentation politique en Lozère', *Terrain* 1985

Prévotat, J., 'La culture politique traditionaliste' in S. Berstein (ed.), *Les cultures politiques*, 1999

Price, R., *The French Second Republic. A Social History*, London 1972

'The onset of labour shortage in French agriculture in the 19th century', *Economic History Review* 1975

'Techniques of repression. The control of popular protest in mid-19th-century France', *Historical Journal* 1982

The Modernisation of Rural France: Communications Networks and Agricultural Market Structures in Nineteenth Century France, London 1983

'Poor relief and social crisis in mid-19th-century France', *European Studies Review* 1983

The French Second Empire. An Anatomy of Political Power, Cambridge 2001

Price, R. (ed.), *Revolution and Reaction. 1848 and the Second French Republic*, 1975

Prothero, I., *Radical Artisans in England and France, 1830–70*, Cambridge 1997

Prudhomme, A., 'Les sociétés secrètes républicaines sous le Second Empire (1852–60)', *Mémoires. Société des sciences sociales et des lettres. Loir-et-Cher* 1984

Puech, L., *Essai sur la candidature officielle en France depuis 1851*, Mende 1922

Raison-Jourde, F., *La colonie auvergnate de Paris au 19e siècle*, 1976

Rancière, J., *La nuit des prolétaires*, 1981

'The myth of the artisan: critical reflections on a category of social history' in S. Kaplan and C. Koepp (eds.), *Work in France*, 1986

Ratcliffe, B., 'Classes laborieuses et classes dangereuses à Paris pendant la première moitié du 19e siècle: the Chevalier thesis re-examined', *French Historical Studies* 1991

'Manufacturing in the metropolis: the dynamism and dynamics of Parisian industry in the mid-nineteenth century', *Journal of European Economic History* 1994

Rebérioux, M., 'Les ouvriers du livre' in H.-J. Martin and R. Chartier (eds.), *Histoire de l'édition française*, III, 1985

Reddy, W., *The Rise of Market Culture. The Textile Trade and French Society*, Cambridge 1984

'The moral sense of farce: the patois literature of Lille factory laborers, 1848–70' in S. Kaplan and C. Koepp (eds.), *Work in France*, 1986

Reid, D., *The Miners of Decazeville. A Genealogy of De-industrialization*, Cambridge, Mass. 1985

Reverchon, C. and Gaudin, P., 'Les insurgés de la Drôme: Images héritées, images transmises' in P. Vigier *et al.*, *Répression et prison politique en France et en Europe au 19e siècle*, 1993

Rifkin, A. and Thomas, R. (eds.), *Voices of the People. The Politics and Life of La Sociale at the End of the Second Empire*, 1988

Riot-Sarcey, M., 'Emancipation des femmes, 1848', *Genèses* 1992

Rioux, J.-P. and Sirinelli, J.-F. (eds.), *Pour une histoire culturelle*, 1998

Rivet, D., *La vie politique dans le département de la Haute-Loire*, Le Puy 1979

Rocher, J.-P., 'Les élections dans l'Yonne de 1848 à 1871' in L. Hamon (ed.), *Les républicains*, 1993

Rosanvallon, P., *Le sacre du citoyen. Histoire du suffrage universel en France*, 1992

Rougerie, J., 'La première Internationale à Lyon (1865–70): problèmes d'histoire du mouvement ouvrier français', *Annali Istituto Giangiacomo Feltrinelli* 1961

'Les sections françaises de l'Association Internationale des travailleurs' in J. Rougerie *et al.*, *La Ire Internationale, l'institution, l'implantation, le rayonnement*, 1964

'Remarques sur l'histoire des salaires à Paris au 19e siècle', *Le mouvement social* 1968

'Le peuple de 1870/71' in J.-L.Robert and D. Tartakowsky (eds.), *Paris, le peuple*, 1999

Rudelle, O., 'Le suffrage universel' in J.-F. Sirinelli (ed.), *Histoire des droites*, III, 1992

Sacquin, M., *Entre Bossuet et Maurras. L'antiprotestantisme en France de 1814 à 1870*, 1998

Saint-Martin, M. de, 'Vers une sociologie des aristocrates déclassés', *Cahiers d'histoire* 2000

Salmon, F., 'La gauche avancée en 1849 et en 1870: le pourquoi de la chute' in L. Hamon (ed.), *Les républicains*, 1993

Sanson, R., 'Le 15 Août: fête nationale du Second Empire' in A. Corbin *et al.* (eds.), *Les usages politiques des fêtes au 19e siècle*, 1994

Santucci, M.-R., *Délinquance et répression au 19e siècle. L'exemple de l'Hérault*, 1986

Sawicki, F., 'Classer les hommes politiques. Les usages des indicateurs de position sociale pour la compréhension de la professionalisation politique' in M. Offerlé (ed.), *Professions et profession politique*, 1994

Sceau, R., *Lyon et les campagnes*, Lyon 1995

Schollier, P. and Zamagni, V. (eds.), *Labour's Reward. Real Wages and Economic Change in 19th and 20th Century Europe*, Aldershot 1995

Schwab, R., *De la cellule rurale à la région. L'Alsace 1825–1960*, 1980

Schweitz, A., *La maison tourangelle au quotidien. Façons de bâtir, manières de vivre (1850–1930)*, 1997

Scott, J., *The Glassworkers of Carmaux*, Cambridge, Mass. 1974

'Statistical representations of work: the politics of the Chamber of Commerce's *Statistique de l'industrie à Paris, 1847–48*' in S. Kaplan and C. Koepp (eds.), *Work in France*, 1986

Selig, J.-M., *Malnutrition et développement économique dans l'Alsace du 19e siècle*, Strasbourg 1996

Serman, W., 'Le corps des officiers français sous la Deuxième République et le Second Empire', Doc. d'Etat, Univ. de Paris-Sorbonne 1976

Sewell, W., *Work and Revolution in France. The Language of Labor from the Old Regime to 1848*, Cambridge 1980

Structure and Mobility. The Men and Women of Marseille, 1820–70, Cambridge 1985

'Artisans, factory workers, and the formation of the French working-class, 1789–1848', in I. Katznelson and A. Zolberg (eds.), *Working-class Formation*, Princeton, N.J. 1986

'Collective violence and collective loyalties in France: why the French Revolution made a difference', *Politics and Society* 1990

Shaffer, J., 'Agrarian change and landlord–tenant relations in the French Nivernais', *Research in Economic History* 1989

Shapiro, A.-L., *Housing the Poor of Paris 1850–1900*, Madison, Wis. 1985

Sheridan, G., *The Social and Economic Foundations of Association among the Silk Weavers of Lyon, 1852–70*, 2 vols. New York 1981
  'Esprit de quartier et formes de solidarité dans les mouvements sociaux et politiques des ouvriers en soie de Lyon, 1830–88', *Le monde alpin et rhodanien* 1991

Shorter, E. and Tilly, C., *Strikes in France, 1830–1968*, Cambridge 1974

Simon, F., *La Marianne, société secrète au pays d'Anjou*, Angers 1939

Singer, B., *Village Notables in 19th Century France. Priests, Mayors, Schoolmasters*, Albany, N.Y. 1983

Singer-Kérel, J., *Le coût de la vie à Paris de 1840 à 1954*, 1961

Sirinelli, J.-F., *Histoire des droites en France*, 3 vols. 1992
  'Eloge de la complexité' in J.-P. Rioux and J.-F. Sirinelli (eds.), *Pour une histoire culturelle*, 1997

Skinner, J., 'The revolutionary and royalist traditions in southern village society: the Vaucluse comtadin, 1789–1851' in A. Forrest and P. Jones (eds.), *Reshaping France*, Manchester 1991

Smith, M., *Tariff Reform in France, 1860–1900: The Politics of Economic Interest*, Ithaca, N.Y. 1980

Soulet, J.-F., *Les Pyrénées au 19e siècle*, 2 vols. 1987

Stein, M., *The Social Origins of a Labor Elite. French Engine Drivers, 1837–1917*, New York 1987

Stewart-McDougall, M.-L., *Artisan Kingdom: Revolution, Reaction and Resistance in Lyon, 1848–51*, Gloucester 1984

Stone, J., 'Republican ideology, gender and class: France, 1860s-1914' in L. Frader and S. Rose (eds.), *Gender and Class in Modern Europe*, London 1996

Stoskopf, N., 'L'industrialisation et crises au 19e siècle', *Saisons d'Alsace* 1994
  Les patrons du Second Empire, IV, *Alsace*, 1999
  Les patrons du Second Empire, VII, *Banquiers et financiers parisiens*, 2002

Strauss, L., 'Opinion publique et forces politiques en Alsace à la fin du Second Empire. Le plébiscite du 8 mai 1870 dans le Haut-Rhin' in F. L'Huillier, *L'Alsace en 1870–71*, Gap 1971

Struminger, L., *Women and the Making of the Working Class: Lyon, 1830–70*, St Albans 1979

Taithe, B., *Citizenship and Wars. France in Turmoil 1870–1*, 2001

Tchernoff, I., *Le parti républicain au coup d'état et sous le Second Empire*, 1906

Thibon, C., *Pays de Sault. Les Pyrénées audoises au 19e siècle: les villages et l'Etat*, 1988

Thomas, J., *Le temps des foires. Foires et marchés dans le Midi toulousain de la fin de l'Ancien Régime à 1914*, Toulouse 1993

Thompson, V., *The Virtuous Marketplace. Women and Men, Money and Politics in Paris, 1830–70*, Baltimore, Md. 2000

Thuillier, G., *Pour une histoire du quotidien au 19e siècle en Nivernais*, 1977

Tilly, C., *The Contentious French*, London 1986

Tilly, L., 'Three faces of capitalism: women and work in French cities' in J. Merriman (ed.), *French Cities in the 19th Century*, London 1982

Tollu, P., 'Démocratie et liberté' in A. Troisier de Diaz, *Regards sur Emile Ollivier*, 1985

Traugott, M., 'The mid-19th-century crisis in France and England', *Theory and Society* 1983
  Armies of the Poor. Determinants of Working-Class Participation in the Parisian Insurrection of June 1848, Princeton, N.J. 1985

Traugott, M. (ed.), *The French Worker. Autobiographies from the Early Industrial Era*, Berkeley, Calif. 1993

Trempé, R., *Les mineurs de Carmaux, 1848–1914*, 2 vols. 1971
  'Travail à la mine et vieillissement des mineurs au 19e siècle', *Le mouvement social* 1983

Truesdell, M., *Spectacular Politics. Louis-Napoleon Bonaparte and the Fête Impériale, 1849–70*, Oxford 1997

Tudesq, A. J., *Les grands notables en France (1840–49): Etude historique d'une psychologie sociale*, 2 vols. 1964
  L'Election présidentielle de Louis-Napoléon Bonaparte, 10 décembre 1848, 1965
  'Les survivances de l'Ancien Régime: la noblesse dans la société française dans la première moitié du 19e siècle' in D. Roche and E. Labrousse (eds.), *Ordres et classes*, 1973
  'L'élargissement de la noblesse en France dans la première moitié du 19e siècle' in G. Delille (ed.), *Les noblesses européennes*, 1988

Tulard, J. (ed.), *Dictionnaire du Second Empire*, 1995

Tulard, J. *et al.*, *Pourquoi réhabiliter le Second Empire*, 1997

Vanier, H., *La mode et les métiers: frivolité et lutte des classes*, 1960

Vassort, J., *Une société provinciale face à son devenir: le Vendômois aux 18e et 19e siècles*, 1995

Verjus, A., 'Le suffrage universel, le chef de famille et la question de l'exclusion des femmes en 1848' in A. Corbin *et al.*, *Femmes dans la cité*, 1997

Verley, P., 'L'anticapitalisme quarante-huitard ou l'apprentissage des circuits de la finance' in J.-M. Barrelet and P. Henry (eds.), *1848–1998. Neuchâtel, la Suisse, L'Europe*, Fribourg 2001

Verney-Carron, N., *Le ruban et l'acier. Les élites économiques de la région stéphanoise au 19e siècle*, Saint-Etienne 1999

Vicaire, M., 'Les ouvriers parisiens en face du catholicisme de 1830 à 1970', *Revue suisse d'histoire* 1951

Vigier, P., *La Seconde République dans la région alpin*, 2 vols. 1953
  'Lyon et l'évolution politique de la province française au 19e siècle', *Cahiers d'histoire* 1967
  'Le Bonapartisme et le monde rural' in K. Hanmer and P. Hartmann (eds.), *Der Bonapartismus*, Munich 1977
  'Les troubles forestiers du premier 19e siècle français', *Revue forestière française* 1980
  'Le parti républicain en 1869–70' in L. Hamon (ed.), *Les républicains*, 1993

Vigier, P. *et al.*, *Maintien de l'ordre et police en France et en Europe au 19e siècle, 1987*

Vigreux, M., *Paysans et notables du Morvan au 19e siècle*, Château-Chinon 1987

Vivier, N., 'Salariés agricoles et notables face aux usages collectifs au 19e siècle en Picardie' in J.-C. Farcy (ed.), *La moisson des autres*, 1996

Voillard, O., 'Recherche sur une bourgeoisie urbaine: Nancy au 19e siècle', Doc. d'Etat, Univ. des sciences humaines de Strasbourg 1976

Voss, L. van and Linden, M. van der (eds.), *Class and Other Identities. Gender, Religion and Ethnicity in the Writing of European Labour History*, Oxford 2002

Weber, E., *Peasants into Frenchmen. The Modernisation of Rural France, 1870–1914*, London 1976

'Comment la politique vint aux paysans. A second look at peasant politicisation', *American Historical Review* 1982

Weill, G., 'Le rôle des facteurs structurales dans l'évolution des rémunérations salariales au 19e siècle', *Revue Economique* 1959

Weissbach, L., 'Artisanal responses to artistic decline: the cabinetmakers of Paris in the era of industrialization', *Proceedings of the 9th Annual Meeting of the Western Society for French History* 1982

Willbach, D., 'Work and its Satisfactions: Origins of the French Labor Movement, 1864–70', PhD, Univ. of Michigan 1977

Willemez, L., 'La *République des avocats* 1848: le mythe, le modèle et son endossement' in M. Offerlé (ed.), *Professions et profession politique*, 1994

Williams, R., *Manners and Murders in the World of Louis-Napoleon*, Seattle 1975

Wiscart, J.-M., *La noblesse de la Somme au 19e siècle*, 1994

Wolfe, R., 'The origins of the Paris Commune: the popular organizations of 1868–71', PhD thesis, Harvard Univ. 1965

Wright, G., 'Public opinion and conscription in France, 1866–70', *Journal of Modern History* 1942

Wright, V., 'La loi de sûreté générale de 1858', *Revue d'histoire moderne et contemporaine* 1969

'The coup d'état of December 1851: repression and the limits to repression' in R. Price, *Revolution and Reaction*, 1995

Zeldin, T. (ed.), *Conflicts in French Society: Anti-Clericalism, Education and Morals in the 19th Century*, 1970

Zind, P., *L'enseignement religieux dans l'instruction primaire publique en France de 1850 à 1873*, Lyon 1971

Index

NEW STUDIES IN EUROPEAN HISTORY

Books in the series

Royalty and Diplomacy in Europe, 1890–1914
RODERICK R. MCLEAN

Catholic Revival in the Age of the Baroque
Religious Identity in Southwest Germany, 1550–1750
MARC R. FORSTER

Helmuth von Moltke and the Origins of the First World War
ANNIKA MOMBAUER

Peter the Great
The Struggle for Power, 1671–1725
PAUL BUSHKOVITCH

Fatherlands
State Building and Nationhood in Nineteenth-Century Germany
ABIGAIL GREEN

The French Second Empire
An Anatomy of Political Power
ROGER PRICE

Origins of the French Welfare State
The Struggle for Social Reform in France, 1914–1947
PAUL V. DUTTON

Ordinary Prussians
Brandenburg Junkers and Villagers, 1500–1840
WILLIAM W. HAGEN

Liberty and Locality in Revolutionary France
Six Villages Compared
PETER JONES

Vienna and Versailles
The Courts of Europe's Dynastic Rivals, 1550–1780
JEROEN DUINDAM

Provincial Power and Absolute Monarchy
The Estates General of Burgundy, 1661–1790
JULIAN SWANN

From *Reich* to State
The Rhineland in the Revolutionary Age, 1780–1830
MICHAEL ROWE

Re-writing the French Revolutionary Tradition
Liberal Opposition and the Fall of the Bourbon Monarchy
R. S. ALEXANDER

People and Politics in France, 1848–1870
ROGER PRICE

Lightning Source UK Ltd.
Milton Keynes UK
UKOW02f0842260616

277040UK00001B/112/P